T5-ARZ-433

ABOUT THE PUBLISHER

The New York Institute of Finance

... more than just books.

NYIF offers practical, applied education and training in a wide range of
financial topics:

* *Classroom training:* evenings, mornings, noon-hour

* *Seminars:* one- and two-day professional and introductory programs

* *Customized training:* need-specific, on your site or ours, in New York City,
throughout the United States, anywhere in the world

* *Independent study:* self-paced learning—basic, intermediate, advanced

* *Exam preparation:* NASD licensing (including Series 7), CFA prep, state life and
health insurance licensing

Subjects of books and training programs include the following:

* *Account Executive Training*

* *Brokerage Operations*

* *Futures Trading*

* *International Corporate Finance*

* *Options as a Strategic Investment*

* *Securities Transfer*

* *Technical Analysis*

* *And Much More*

When Wall Street professionals think **training**, *they think* **NYIF**.

Please write or call for our catalog:

New York Institute of Finance
Marketing Dept.
70 Pine Street
New York, NY 10270–0003
212 / 344–2900

Simon & Schuster, Inc.   A Gulf + Western Company
"Where Wall Street Goes to School" ™

■ *FUTURES TRADING*

■ *Concepts and Strategies*

■ **Robert E. Fink**
Independent Floor Trader
Governor, Commodity Exchange, Inc.

■ **Robert B. Feduniak**
Managing Director, Morgan Stanley & Co., Inc.
Director, Options Clearing Corporation

New York Institute of Finance

Library of Congress Cataloging-in-Publication Data

Fink, Robert E.
    Futures trading.

    Bibliography: p.
    Includes index.
    1. Commodity exchanges. 2. Financial futures.
I. Feduniak, Robert B. II. Title.
HG6046.F56 1987   332.64'4   87-24030
ISBN 0-13-345745-1

332.644
F49f

© **1988 by NYIF Corp.**
A division of Simon & Schuster, Inc.
70 Pine Street
New York, New York 10270

All rights reserved. No part of this book may be reproduced, in any part or by any means, without permission in writing from the publisher.

This publication is designed to provide accurate and authoritative information in regard to the subject matter covered. It is sold with the understanding that the publisher is not engaged in rendering legal, accounting, or other professional service. If legal advice or other expert assistance is required, the services of a competent professional person should be sought.

    —From a Declaration of Principles jointly adopted by a Committee of the American Bar Association and a Committee of Publishers and Associations.

Printed in the United States of America
10 9 8 7 6 5 4 3 2

New York Institute of Finance
(NYIF Corp.)
70 Pine Street
New York, NY 10270

■ **To our families**

R.E.F.   **R.B.F.**

University Libraries
Carnegie Mellon University
Pittsburgh Pennsylvania 15213

■ *CONTENTS*

■ FOREWORD

This book evolved from a course that was taught by one of the authors (REF) in the 1970s and early 1980s at the New York Institute of Finance. The course was an introduction to futures markets and the futures business that was designed for those with little or no exposure to either the financial markets in general or to futures in particular. The course used a text that had been written in the early 1970s—before financial futures, before gold trading by U.S. citizens was legalized, before options on futures, and before the Commodity Futures Trading Commission had been formed.

The dramatic changes in the futures business since the early 1970s have been accompanied by a fair number of books on various facets of the futures industry. Most fall into one of two categories. Some cover relatively complex and sophisticated applications of futures and options; others are intended to teach readers how to make their fortunes by trading futures and options. What seems lacking is an up-to-date book that clearly and accurately covers the basics of the futures markets and the futures industry. We hope that this book will be useful to those who have little prior exposure to futures but who want to understand the basics of this fascinating business.

While writing this book we received invaluable help from many colleagues and friends who graciously agreed to assist us with the content, accuracy, and clarity of many of the topics covered. We especially want to acknowledge the assistance of:

George Anagnos of Commodity Exchange, Inc. for his substantial assistance in the research and writing of Part Five; Ira E. Shein for an excellent job of reviewing the manuscript; Dan Amstutz, Jerry Bailey, Martha Brecher, Paul Jones, Barbara Klein, Michel Marks, John Paulus, Wayne Peterson, Vern Pherson, Gary Seevers, and Neal Shear for their expert reviews of portions of the manuscript; Michael Mauro for his friendship and support; John Murphy for permission to reprint the material used in Chapter 17; and, Morgan Stanley & Co., Incorporated and Gelderman, Inc. for material used to illustrate the text. We also thank Corinne Fink Giaccone for her help in gathering data used throughout the book, and mention the special contributions of Heidi, Danny, and Tommy.

We especially want to acknowledge the contributions of Ben Russell, former president of the New York Institute of Finance, who conceived the idea of this book and who gave us continuing encouragement and support throughout its long gestation period.

Finally, we owe special thanks to Nancy Brown, whose dedication and unfailing good humor during the seemingly endless preparation of the manuscript were vital to both the book and the authors' spirits.

Without the contributions of these and others this book never could have been written and published. If readers conclude that it never should have been written and published, the fault lies solely with the authors.

Robert E. Fink   Robert B. Feduniak

PART ONE

■ INTRODUCTION TO CONCEPTS AND TERMS

■ Chapter 1

■ *The Futures Contract*

Whether we mark its beginning with the founding of the Chicago Board of Trade in 1848 or with the advent of bills of exchange in the thirteenth century, futures trading has been a part of the world economic scene for a long time. Its conceptual roots reach back to the beginnings of commercial trade and the efforts of merchants to protect themselves from adversities ranging from declining prices to piracy. It is testimony to the durability of the concept of futures trading that the same basic mechanism used by feudal landowners of eighteenth-century Japan is a routine part of the operations of money-center boardrooms of twentieth-century New York, London, and Tokyo.

THE CONCEPT OF FORWARD PRICING

To lay the groundwork for our understanding of futures markets, let us begin by imagining a world in which they do not exist. Because futures trading originated in the realm of agriculture, we will begin with an agricultural example. We will then go on to explain how and why the same basic concepts are applicable to the capital and financial markets. In this imaginary world, let us place a cotton farmer who in the late summer of one year looks over his fields and estimates that, come October, he will harvest 50,000 pounds of cotton. He also knows from conversations with fellow farmers that local merchants are presently willing to pay 60 cents per pound for the grade of cotton he expects to produce. Because his cost of production based on his expenses for seed, labor, fertilizer, machinery, and so on is 50 cents per pound, the farmer is concerned that a drop in prices from present levels could cut deeply into this year's earnings. A drop of more than 10 cents per pound would actually produce a loss on each pound he harvests.

But what alternatives does he have? In a world that has no form of futures market, the farmer must wait until the harvest is in before selling his cotton at whatever price prevails at that time. His cotton, even in its immature state, represents an inventory of goods whose value will suffer if prices decline.

Wanting to avoid the possibility of a loss, this enterprising farmer calls a textile mill and asks a very important question: "What price would you be willing to guarantee me now for cotton that I will deliver to you two months from now in October?" The manager of the textile mill, meanwhile, is concerned that recent adverse weather in other parts of the Cotton Belt will result in a smaller-than-expected supply and higher prices at harvest time. Because he has already committed to deliver a quantity of cloth to a clothing manufacturer in late fall, he is concerned that a rise in the price of the raw cotton will reduce or eliminate his profit margin. He thinks to himself that he would be pleased to be guaranteed a supply of raw cotton in October at today's price of 60 cents per pound. He makes this known to the farmer, who counters with an offer of 61 cents per pound. After a little friendly haggling, they agree on a price of 60$\frac{1}{2}$ cents per pound. This agreed-on price is known as a *forward price* because it is an expression of the value of something that is to be delivered at a future date.

The forward price of any commodity will fluctuate according to changing expectations of what price the commodity will command at the future date. Reports of a worsening weather outlook might have made the textile mill manager more willing to pay a higher price, or it might have made the farmer less willing to accept a lower one. In our imaginary world there are only two participants so far. As the concept catches on, though, more and more people will want to participate. Information concerning the factors that affect the forward price of cotton will become more abundant and will flow more freely. Sellers will go to the highest bidders among many, and buyers will go to the lowest-priced sellers among many. The market will become more efficient, and a consensus will be formed among a large group of participants as to the value of cotton at some future date or dates. From that day on there will always be multiple prices for cotton: the price for immediate delivery, known as the *spot (or cash) price*, and the prices for delivery at various later dates, known as the *forward prices*. Chapter 9 discusses the factors that influence the relationships between spot and forward prices.

THE FORWARD CONTRACT

Before leaving our imaginary world, let us examine a little more closely the agreement between the farmer and the textile mill. The farmer has agreed to deliver to the textile mill 50,000 pounds of cotton in October. The terms of that agreement are stipulated in a formal contract, known as a *forward contract*. As we will see later, this forward contract is the fundamental building block on which futures markets are based. The terms of the forward contract include the following:

- the quantity to be delivered
- the particular quality of cotton to be delivered
- the month in which the cotton is to be delivered
- the location at which delivery is to be made
- the terms of payment upon delivery

Thus, a forward contract represents a formal agreement between two parties to make and to take delivery of a specific quantity and quality of a commodity at a specific location and future time. The creation of the contract, in this example, allows the farmer to pass on to the textile mill the price risk associated with ownership of the cotton. Likewise, it assures the textile mill a source of supply at a satisfactory price.

Now let us introduce some new elements into the picture. A favorable change in weather brings about a decline in spot cotton prices to 55 cents per pound. The farmer, of course, is pleased by his earlier decision to enter into the forward contract because it will have allowed him an additional profit of $5\frac{1}{2}$ cents per pound. The textile mill manager, however, is regretting his decision because he would have been able to buy his cotton $5\frac{1}{2}$ cents per pound cheaper had he not entered into the contract. What one party to the contract gains, the other loses.

Suppose that the manager of the textile mill becomes convinced that the improved weather outlook will bring about a further deterioration in prices. He wants to cut short his losses and has two ways of doing so. He can ask the farmer to dissolve the contract, but the farmer would be foolish to do so without requiring the textile mill to pay him a penalty equal to the difference between the $60\frac{1}{2}$ cents per pound contract price and the present price of 55 cents per pound. Even with this penalty, the farmer has no assurance that he will find another buyer, so unless he believes that cotton prices have bottomed out, he will hold the textile mill to the contract.

The textile mill manager's second choice is to look for someone else to buy the contract from him. To do this, the manager will have to pay the buyer 5^1/$_2$ cents per pound to compensate him for the difference between the 60^1/$_2$ cents per pound the buyer will have to pay the farmer and the 55 cents per pound at which he would be able to buy cotton in the open market. (We are assuming that this forward contract is a transferable instrument that binds its holders, whoever they may be, to its terms.)* The manager is willing to do this because he feels that prices may be as low as 50 cents per pound in a matter of weeks; he would rather lose the 5^1/$_2$ cents per pound now than risk a possible loss totaling 10 cents per pound or more later in the month. He calls several other textile mills in his area, but all of them also expect prices to drop further and are planning to wait until harvest to buy their cotton.

A local businessman hears about the textile mill's problem. His sense of business conditions tells him that, favorable weather notwithstanding, the strong local economy will result in a heavy demand for cotton goods by fall. He expects prices to be much higher than they are today. He figures that taking ownership of the forward contract now at an effective price of 55 cents per pound (the 60^1/$_2$ cents per pound he would have to pay the farmer minus the 5^1/$_2$ cents per pound the textile mill is willing to pay to transfer the contract) will allow him to sell it to someone else later at a profit. He has no intention of taking delivery of the cotton because he expects to sell the contract to another textile mill prior to the contract's maturity.

Several weeks later, in late September, the businessman's expectations are realized. Cotton rises to 63 cents per pound and he transfers the contract to another textile mill that agrees to pay him 2^1/$_2$ cents per pound (the difference between the 60^1/$_2$ cents per pound he will have to pay the farmer and the going price in the open market of 63 cents per pound).

All along, the farmer has been kept informed about who holds the other side of the contract. During the first week of October he calls the textile mill that now holds the contract and informs them that he intends to make delivery of the cotton on October 15. On that day the cotton is delivered, the farmer receives his 60^1/$_2$ cents per pound from the mill, and the contract—its terms fulfilled—expires.

---

*We are also assuming, for the sake of simplicity, that the spot and forward cotton prices remain equal to each other as the overall price level fluctuates.

Let us summarize the key points of this illustration as follows:

1. The forward contract allowed the farmer to transfer to the textile mill the price risk associated with ownership of his developing crop. It assured the farmer that he would receive 60¹/2 cents per pound for his cotton.

2. The forward contract assured the first textile mill a supply of cotton at 60¹/2 cents per pound, but declining prices and a change in the mill owner's expectations of future prices caused the mill to transfer the contract to a local businessman at a loss of 5¹/2 cents per pound.

3. The local businessman, speculating that the price of cotton would rise, accepted ownership of the contract. His willingness to do so allowed the textile mill to transfer the contract at a time that the farmer was unwilling to cancel or amend it and when no other textile mill was willing to take it off his hands. The speculator's profit was the 5¹/2 cents per pound he received for taking the contract plus the 2¹/2 cents per pound he received from the second mill, or 8 cents per pound.

4. The second textile mill, having accepted the contract from the speculator, was assured a supply of cotton at the then-satisfactory price of 63 cents per pound. It took delivery of the cotton and paid the farmer 60¹/2 cents per pound. Its net cost was 63 cents per pound, which included the 2¹/2 cents that it paid the businessman/speculator for the privilege of buying cotton at 60¹/2 cents per pound when the prevailing market price was 63 cents per pound.

5. If we examine the accounts of each participant, we find that the sum of their receipts and payments equals zero:

The farmer received 60¹/2 cents per pound.	+60¹/2 cents per pound
The first textile mill paid 5¹/2 cents per pound.	−5¹/2 cents per pound
The businessman speculator received 8 cents per pound.	+8 cents per pound
The second mill paid 63 cents per pound.	−63 cents per pound
	0 cents per pound

At each stage of its life, the forward contract provided a benefit to its holders. Changing prices may have negated or enhanced that benefit during a period of time, but the contract's usefulness at the time it was initially and willingly entered into by each participant was never in doubt. To the cotton tradespeople, it provided a means of transferring, or "hedging" risk, whether it was the risk of ownership as in the case of the farmer or the risk of nonownership as in the cases of the textile mills. To the businessman it provided a means of profiting from a correct assessment of the future course of cotton prices.

As the concept of forward trading gained wide acceptance in our imaginary world, a significant problem arose. The problem was that the practical utility of forward contracts was limited by a lack of flexibility. In our example, the first textile mill was fortunate to find a speculator who was willing to buy the forward contract when the mill owner's view of cotton prices changed. Had this not happened, the mill would have been obligated to wait and to buy the cotton at 60$\frac{1}{2}$ cents per pound on October 15.

This is a more serious limitation than it might seem. Suppose that the textile mill's customers wanted earlier delivery of their finished cloth than the mill had anticipated and that the mill would need raw cotton by late September to meet its revised schedule. This would force the owner to find an alternative source of cotton that would be available earlier and might leave him with no use for the cotton to be delivered on October 15. In other words, the textile mill would lack the flexibility to deal with changing delivery requirements as well as with changing price expectations.

Our imaginary farmers and mill operators found that forward contracts were most useful when it was unlikely that changing price outlooks or delivery needs would make it appropriate or necessary to transfer or liquidate the contract on short notice. They also realized that the usefulness of forward contracts would be vastly enhanced if the contracts were more readily transferable. In other words, the success of the forward contract concept depended on greater *liquidity*. Liquidity is a measure of the ease with which any financial instrument or asset can be bought or sold and is a direct function of the number of ready and willing buyers and sellers.

To increase the liquidity of their forward contracts, the cotton tradespeople in our imaginary world devised a plan that consisted of the following:

1. They would provide a central meeting place, known as an *exchange*, where forward trading could be conducted. In this way the holder of a forward contract who was interested in selling it would have a logical place to look for a supply of ready buyers. A farmer who was interested in entering into a forward contract could come to the exchange to find either a textile mill representative who was interested in doing the same or a speculator who was willing to take the opposite side of his contract.

2. The forward contracts that were traded on this exchange would be standardized. To avoid the cumbersome process of negotiating the specific terms of each and every contract, buyers and sellers would deal in standardized contracts that had prespecified quantities, grades, delivery dates, and delivery locations. For instance, standard contracts might call for the delivery of 50,000 pounds (quantity) of middling $1^1/_{16}$-inch white cotton (grade) in Memphis (location) in the months of March, May, July, October, and December (dates). In this market the farmer in the foregoing example would simply come to the exchange and express an interest in being the seller of one October contract. The rest of the terms of the contract would be fixed. However, to avoid a market so rigid as to discourage dealers with other (nonstandard) needs, delivery of other grades and locations would be allowed at price premiums or discounts determined by the exchange.

3. Finally, to instill further confidence in its contracts, the exchange would impose substantial financial requirements on its participants, including the depositing of security with the exchange by each party to a contract. It would also establish rules and regulations to promote fair trading practices among participants and would provide mechanisms to settle disputes.

The exchange would call its contracts *futures contracts* to distinguish them from forward contracts that were created outside the exchange—and it would call itself a *futures exchange*.

THE FUTURES CONTRACT

Although greatly oversimplified, the futures market of our imaginary world shares the same conceptual foundation as futures markets in the real world. A *futures market* is basically an organized forum for the trading of forward contracts that, to promote liquidity, have highly standardized terms. *A futures contract is a formal agreement between two parties to make and to take delivery of a specified quantity and quality of a particular underlying item, at a specified location and time, under the rules of a recognized exchange.* The prices at which these contracts are struck are determined by free competition among participants on the floor of the exchange.

The evolution of futures contracts in the real world proceeded along lines similar to those described in our imaginary world. To protect themselves against seasonal price fluctuations, producers and consumers of agricultural commodities began to buy and sell for forward delivery. These transactions, which became known as *to-arrive contracts,* involved a binding sale by a farmer to a buyer for a designated amount of grain to arrive 10, 20, 30, or 60 days later.

> *Example*: A miller agrees on April 1 to buy 5,000 bushels of corn from a farmer for $2.20 per bushel. The corn is to be delivered on June 1. The buyer and the seller have agreed on a price for a product "to arrive" two months later—hence the term *to arrive.*

Contracts for deferred delivery did not, of course, eliminate the possibility of making incorrect pricing decisions. The producer/seller had estimated sufficient return for a crop before it was even harvested and needed to be concerned only with the production of the crop and its delivery to the buyer. Yet the seller could still incur an *opportunity cost.* He had to contend with the possibility that the price of the commodity would rise before delivery. If the price of corn advanced to, say, $2.40 per bushel by June 1, he would forfeit the additional 20 cents per bushel profit. The buyer, on the other hand, still had to fear a price decrease. Should the price of corn drop to $2.00 per bushel by the time of delivery, the buyer would incur a 20 cents per bushel opportunity cost.

Contracting for deferred delivery did at least enable a merchant, a manufacturer, or a processor to schedule raw-material shipments for arrival at designated intervals. Ensuring their availability for operating needs at all times tended to stabilize the market to a degree because product prices could be projected on the basis of known future costs.

Eventually, these forward contracts were bought and sold many times prior to contract maturity and physical delivery. Many other people who were not in the grain trade were willing to assume the price risks but were *not* usually willing to take the actual delivery. These people were speculators, not merchants; they were interested in a possible gain from any change in value, not in profits on the sale of the physical commodities themselves. The merchant with a contract, who did not want to absorb the risk at all, could transfer ownership of the contract to a third person (such as a dealer or speculator) who was willing to take a chance solely in the hope of making a profit. These people provided the liquidity that our original three-person imaginary world was lacking, and the transformation of forward (or to-arrive) contracts into standardized futures contracts made this possible.

The to-arrive contract, although a step forward, still left much to be desired. Questions often arose about the quality of the delivery; the quantities of the contracts varied among the contracting parties; defaults on contracts were common, and so it was important to know and trust the counterparty on the other side of a contract. These shortcomings eventually led to the formalization of contracts. The market participants organized themselves into an exchange and set up the needed rules to establish strict standards for size, quality, and grade; among themselves, they mutually guaranteed performance on all contracts. Their agreements not only constituted the formation of the first commodity futures exchange but also benefited those associated with the production and the marketing of the commodity itself.

FUTURES MARKETS TODAY

From its early beginnings in the mid-1800s, formalized futures trading has grown to encompass a large family of commodities and financial instruments. The same principles that worked well in the imaginary world of our cotton farmer also work well in the real world of commodities and financial instruments whose price fluctuations put at risk a wide array of producers and consumers, borrowers and lenders. Today's domestic futures industry encompasses eleven major United States exchanges that provide the setting for active trading in futures contracts on more than fifty different commodities and financial instruments. In recent years, trading volume on these exchanges has exceeded 100 million contracts annually, with a total value of more than $10 trillion. Outside the United States, futures trading takes place in exchanges located in a variety of cities including London, Hong Kong, Tokyo, Paris, Singapore, Sydney, São Paulo, and Winnipeg.

Figures 1-1 through 1-5 at the end of this chapter provide some perspective on the growth of futures trading in recent years and on the distribution of this trading among the various products and exchanges. This covers United States futures markets. Information on futures activity in other countries is presented in Chapter 5.

Futures markets today are among the most efficient and liquid trading mechanisms in existence. As noted earlier, the greater the number of participants in any market, the greater is that market's liquidity. Buyers are forced to compete with one another by bidding prices up. Sellers are forced to compete with one another by offering prices down. In highly liquid markets, the spread between the buyers' bid prices and the sellers' asking prices at any time is driven down by this competition. Thus, the size of the bid/ask spread is a good measure of market liquidity.

In today's futures markets, bid/ask spreads can represent as little as 0.1% or less of the price of the commodity or financial instrument. For instance, if gold is trading at about $400.00 per ounce, a typical quote from the futures trading floor might be $400.00 bid, $400.20 asked. This means that buyers are presently willing to pay $400.00 per ounce and that sellers are willing to sell at $400.20 per ounce. With ample volume on both sides of the quote, buyers are reasonably assured that the most they will pay is $400.20 and sellers are reasonably assured that the lowest price at which they will sell is $400.00. Needless to say, quotes will change in time, but at any moment the bid/ask spread is likely to remain at about 20 cents per ounce. This 20 cents equates to less than 0.1% of the price of gold. Compare this with the securities market, where a stock trading at $50.00 per share might have a bid/ask spread of 25 cents. This equates to 0.5% of the price of the stock. Compare it to the real-estate market where the bid/ask spread on a $200,000 house might be as great as $20,000, which equates to 10% of the price. The bid/ask spread in futures markets, and therefore the liquidity of these markets, has few rivals in the trading world. It is this high degree of liquidity that has helped futures trading gain such a prominent role in commerce and finance.

Futures markets today are more active and more economically beneficial than at any other time in their history. Among their most important functions, futures markets provide the following:

1. *A mechanism for shifting price risk from those who do not want this risk to those who do want it:* One important by-product of this

risk shifting is the enhanced creditworthiness of commercial enterprises, which would otherwise be more vulnerable to price fluctuations. Banks and other funding sources are prepared to extend more favorable financing terms to individuals and to organizations that are less exposed to possible changes in the prices of their products or raw materials. This translates into reduced financing costs that, in turn, lead to lower prices for consumers and to a more efficient economy.

2. *Increased price stability:* Critics of futures markets often claim that futures trading leads to abnormal price volatility, but the facts say otherwise. Numerous studies have supported the premise that liquid futures markets increase price stability. Among the most recent and thorough academic looks at this subject is a December 1984 work entitled "A Study of the Effects on the Economy of Trading in Futures and Options," which was prepared jointly by the Board of Governors of the Federal Reserve System, the Commodity Futures Trading Commission, and the Securities and Exchange Commission. This study concluded, among other things, that "financial futures and options markets serve a useful economic purpose, primarily by providing a means by which risks inherent in economic activity (such as market, interest rate, and exchange rate changes) can be shifted from firms and individuals less willing to bear them to those more willing to do so."

3. *A forum for price discovery:* Each day, the prices of contracts that are traded on futures exchanges reflect a broad consensus of what commodities and financial instruments will be worth at various times in the future. This permits more sensible planning by industry participants than would be possible without access to such unbiased consensus forecasts.

4. *Order in the trading practices of diverse market participants:* Futures markets provide a central reference point for prices to all interested parties. The markets provide rules and regulations that promote fair and orderly trading conditions.

5. *A forum for collection and dissemination of information:* This free and open distribution of information that affects prices enables traders to compete on equal terms. Insider information is at a minimum, and prices tend to reflect as accurately as possible all the known forces that act on the supply of and demand for the financial instrument or commodity.

WHAT MAKES A FUTURES CONTRACT SUCCESSFUL?

Since the inception of futures trading, contracts have been devised for a large number of underlying commodities and financial instruments. Many of these contracts have succeeded, but many have failed. Frozen pork belly futures are active while boneless-beef futures are dormant. Silver and copper futures thrive while aluminum futures languish. Eurodollar futures are vastly more successful than Certificate of Deposit futures. It is interesting to consider why one futures contract succeeds and another fails; why one has an average daily trading volume of 100,000 contracts while another has less than 500. The following are the most important characteristics of successful futures contracts:

1. The supply and the demand that relate to the underlying commodity or financial instrument must be large. If they are not, too few people will care about its price to generate the broad interest that is needed to sustain active futures trading. This explains why, for example, corn futures trade far more actively than rye futures and why the enormous success of United States Treasury bond futures would not be replicated if an exchange introduced a futures contract on Peoria general revenue bonds. Large supply is also an important deterrent to price manipulation. Both hedgers and speculators are understandably reluctant to trade contracts that could be easily manipulated by others with greater financial resources.

2. Different units of the underlying item must be interchangeable. This is a prerequisite for the development of standardized, transferable contracts, which are, in turn, a prerequisite for active, liquid markets. One of the great advantages of futures contracts is that traders need not worry about which particular Treasury bill or bar of gold they are trading. Once the contract specifications are agreed upon, all contracts are equivalent. The inability to standardize underlying units is a key reason that certain potentially useful futures contracts (such as real estate futures) have never been developed.

   The items that underlie a successful futures contract need not be strictly homogeneous, as the active live cattle and live hog futures contracts proved. One hog is not identical to another in the same sense that every Swiss franc is identical to every other. What is important is a degree of standardization that is both narrow enough to be consistent with commercial realities and broad enough to include the requisite breadth of supply. A contract that specified delivery of "a hog" would never succeed. Few buyers would, so to speak, purchase a pig in a poke. On the other hand, a futures contract that specified that the hog must weigh exactly 213 pounds and be 266 days old would be too restrictive to permit liquid trading. Striking the correct balance between standardization and breadth of supply is one of the major challenges for designers of futures contracts.

3. Pricing of the underlying item must be determined by free market forces, without monopolistic or government control. No single buyer, seller, or regulator should have undue influence on prices. This is one reason why there is no Moscow Futures Exchange. When prices are fixed by the government there is little incentive to hedge because the price will not change except by government fiat.

This situation may sound appealing from a planning perspective, but problems arise if the price that has been fixed by the planning authorities is too high or too low. Expected future prices not only permit planning; they also *influence* planning. If a government agency sets the price of soybeans too high, farmers will produce a huge surplus; if it sets the price too low, there will be a shortage. The economic advantage of freely traded futures markets is that they are more likely than are centralized planners to react appropriately to changing market conditions and outlooks and are more likely to help keep supply and demand aligned. Few things highlight the difference between free-market economies and planned economies more starkly than the existence of thriving futures markets in the former and their complete absence in the latter.

Monopoly situations also discourage futures trading because monopolists or oligopolists have too great an ability to manipulate prices to their own advantage. This is a key reason why the growth in crude-oil futures trading coincided with OPEC's declining influence in the mid-1980s.

4. Prices must fluctuate. If they are stable or nearly so, then there is no incentive for hedgers to hedge and no incentive for speculators to participate in the market. Interest rate futures would not have

been as successful in the 1950s as they have been in the 1970s and 1980s because the stability of interest rates during the earlier era would have been a disincentive to both hedgers and speculators.

5. The contract should have the support of commercial interests. Hedgers contribute greatly to the volume of trading in any futures contract. Their activities, including the making and the taking of delivery, also provide an important link to the underlying cash market, without which prices might be subject to disruptive speculative forces. Of particular importance here is participation by *dealers*. Dealers are those who trade the underlying commodity or financial instrument for short-term profit and are an important lubricant in the machinery of any market. Once they come to use a futures market as a central pricing point, its success is virtually guaranteed. The pivotal role of dealers in futures markets is discussed in detail in Chapter 12.

6. The futures contract must be supported by a well-capitalized group of traders on the exchange floor. This is particularly important from the perspective of commercial hedgers, who tend to trade in large quantities and expect enough liquidity on the exchange floor to accommodate these quantities. If this liquidity is not present, an exchange will have difficulty attracting the commercial participation necessary for a contract's success.

7. The futures contract must be sufficiently different from other existing contracts to attract speculative participation. "Me-too" contracts are all but doomed to fail, as has been repeatedly demonstrated since the mid-1970s when the success of interest rate and stock index futures contracts spawned a proliferation of unsuccessful financial contracts. The basic problem is that from the perspective of most speculators, one long-term interest rate futures contract is pretty much the same as another. Fixed-income professionals may distinguish between 10-year and 7-year Treasury notes, but few speculators care about the difference. When a particular type of futures contract (e.g., soybeans, long-term United States government interest rates) is established and active, it is extremely difficult to induce speculators to forego existing liquidity and trade another contract which is simply a modest variation on the established theme.

These characteristics are crucial to the success of a futures contract, but they certainly do not ensure success. Futures contracts are products, like automobiles and tickets to baseball games, and products seldom sell themselves. Effective promotion is usually necessary, and some futures exchanges are better than others at promoting their contracts. The timing of a contract's introduction is also important. Futures exchanges must compete with securities exchanges, real estate—indeed, the whole spectrum of trading and investment possibilities. If opportunities abound elsewhere, a new futures contract may have difficulty attracting attention and participation. Weighing all of these factors to develop and maintain a roster of active contracts is one of the key challenges that every exchange must face. Exchanges that adapt existing contracts or that introduce appropriate new contracts as economic conditions change will thrive; those that are less responsive will languish or even disappear from the futures scene.

Figure 1-1.

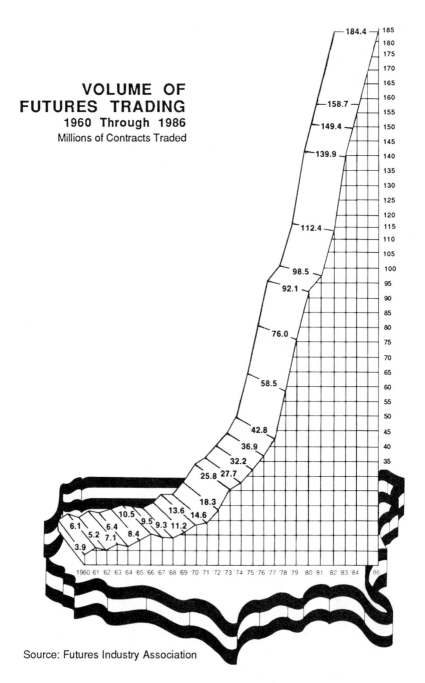

**VOLUME OF
FUTURES TRADING**
1960 Through 1986
Millions of Contracts Traded

Source: Futures Industry Association

18

Figure 1-2. Futures volume highlights—1986 in comparison with 1985.

Rank	Exchange	1986 Contracts	%	1985 Contracts	%	Rank
1.	Chicago Board of Trade	81,135,634	44.01%	70,553,897	44.46%	(1)
2.	Chicago Mercantile Exchange	59,831,171	32.45%	52,115,247	32.84%	(2)
3.	New York Mercantile Exchange	14,644,413	7.94%	7,831,765	4.94%	(4)
4.	Commodity Exchange, Inc.	14,174,698	7.69%	15,116,655	9.53%	(3)
5.	Coffee, Sugar & Cocoa Exchange	5,535,081	3.00%	4,582,878	2.89%	(5)
6.	New York Futures Exchange	3,182,992	1.73%	2,833,614	1.79%	(6)
7.	MidAmerica Commodity Exchange	2,368,547	1.28%	2,485,166	1.57%	(7)
8.	Kansas City Board of Trade	1,716,686	0.93%	1,959,138	1.23%	(8)
9.	New York Cotton & Citrus Exchange	1,477,590	0.80%	915,547	0.58%	(9)
10.	Minneapolis Grain Exchange	284,586	0.15%	300,911	0.19%	(10)
11.	Chicago Rice & Cotton Exchange	3,098	.00%	1,760	0.00%	(11)
	TOTAL	184,354,496	100.00%	158,696,578	100.00%	

Source: Futures Industry Association

Figure 1-3. Futures contracts traded by commodity group.

Rank	Commodity Group	Contracts	Percentage
1986			
(1)	Interest Rate	70,202,183	38.08%
(2)	Ag Commodities	38,276,714	20.76%
(3)	Equity Indices	26,462,813	14.35%
(4)	Foreign Currency	19,352,161	10.50%
(5)	Precious Metals	14,692,890	7.97%
(6)	Petroleum Products	12,869,624	6.98%
(7)	NonPrecious Metals	1,927,481	1.05%
(8)	Other	570,630	0.31%
	TOTAL	184,354,496	100.00%
1984			
(2)	Interest Rate	41,221,424	27.60%
(1)	Ag Commodities	48,860,126	32.71%
(4)	Equity Indices	18,442,464	12.35%
(5)	Foreign Currency	14,000,857	9.37%
(3)	Precious Metals	18,880,269	12.64%
(7)	Petroleum Products	4,619,533	3.09%
(6)	NonPrecious Metals	2,589,518	1.73%
(8)	Other	758,034	0.51%
	TOTAL	149,372,225	100.00%
1982			
(2)	Interest Rate	28,825,112	25.64%
(1)	Ag Commodities	46,310,209	41.20%
(5)	Equity Indices	4,911,121	4.37%
(4)	Foreign Currency	8,690,285	7.73%
(3)	Precious Metals	18,809,458	16.73%
(7)	Petroleum Products	1,875,414	1.67%
(6)	NonPrecious Metals	2,362,625	2.10%
(8)	Other	616,655	0.55%
	TOTAL	112,400,879	100.00%

Source: Futures Industry Association

Figure 1-4. Futures volume highlights—1986 in comparison with 1985.

Rank	Contracts With Volume Over 100,000	1986 Contracts	1986 %	1985 Contracts	1985 %	1985 Rank
1.	T-Bonds, CBT	52,598,811	28.53%	40,448,357	25.49%	(1)
2.	S&P 500 Index, CME	19,505,273	10.58%	15,055,955	9.49%	(2)
3.	Eurodollar, CME	10,824,914	5.87%	8,900,528	5.61%	(3)
4.	Gold, COMEX	8,400,175	4.56%	7,773,834	4.90%	(4)
5.	Crude Oil, NYMEX	8,313,529	4.51%	3,980,867	2.51%	(11)
6.	Deutsche Mark, CME	6,582,145	3.57%	6,449,384	4.06%	(6)
7.	Corn, CBT	6,160,298	3.34%	6,392,812	4.03%	(7)
8.	Soybeans, CBT	6,133,668	3.33%	7,392,128	4.66%	(5)
9.	Swiss Franc, CME	4,998,430	2.71%	4,758,159	3.00%	(9)
10.	Live Cattle, CME	4,690,538	2.54%	4,437,327	2.80%	(10)
11.	T-Notes (6¹/₂-10 yr), CBT	4,426,476	2.40%	2,860,432	1.80%	(15)
12.	Japanese Yen, CME	3,969,777	2.15%	2,415,094	1.52%	(19)
13.	Silver (5,000 oz), COMEX	3,849,687	2.09%	4,821,206	3.04%	(8)
14.	Sugar #11, CSC	3,583,814	1.94%	3,012,929	1.90%	(14)
15.	No. 2 Heating Oil, NY, NYMEX	3,275,044	1.78%	2,207,733	1.39%	(21)
16.	Soybean Oil, CBT	3,182,963	1.73%	3,647,408	2.30%	(12)
17.	NYSE Composite Index, NYFE	3,123,668	1.69%	2,833,614	1.79%	(16)
18.	Soybean Meal, CBT	3,049,005	1.65%	3,339,268	2.10%	(13)
19.	British Pound, CME	2,701,330	1.47%	2,799,024	1.76%	(17)
20.	Wheat, CBT	2,090,316	1.13%	2,127,962	1.34%	(22)
21.	Live Hogs, CME	1,936,864	1.05%	1,719,861	1.08%	(24)
22.	Copper, COMEX	1,872,209	1.02%	2,444,552	1.54%	(18)
23.	T-Bills (90-day), CME	1,815,162	0.98%	2,413,338	1.52%	(20)
24.	MMI Maxi, CBT	1,738,916	0.94%	422,091	0.27%	(39)
25.	Platinum, NYMEX	1,624,635	0.88%	693,256	0.44%	(31)
26.	Pork Bellies (frozen), CME	1,100,339	0.60%	1,457,386	0.92%	(25)
27.	Coffee "C", CSC	1,073,142	0.58%	650,768	0.41%	(33)

Figure 1-4. (Cont.)

Rank	Contracts With Volume Over 100,000	1986 Contracts	1986 %	1985 Contracts	1985 %	1985 Rank
28.	Cotton #2, NYCE	1,015,392	0.55%	636,492	0.40%	(34)
29.	Value Line Index, KCBOT	953,985	0.52%	1,204,659	0.76%	(26)
30.	Municipal Bond Index, CBT	906,980	0.49%	334,691	0.21%	(41)
31.	Leaded Reg. Gasoline, NY, NYMEX	829,733	0.45%	667,172	0.42%	(32)
32.	Cocoa, CSC	777,765	0.42%	800,573	0.50%	(29)
33.	Wheat, KCBOT	744,023	0.40%	735,447	0.46%	(30)
34.	Canadian Dollar, CME	734,071	0.40%	468,996	0.30%	(36)
35.	Soybeans, MIDAM	680,156	0.37%	843,231	0.53%	(28)
36.	Silver (1,000 oz), CBT	511,239	0.28%	1,034,830	0.65%	(27)
37.	Lumber, CME	502,530	0.27%	581,548	0.37%	(35)
38.	T-Bonds, MIDAM	467,639	0.25%	297,033	0.19%	(43)
39.	Unleaded Gasoline, NY, NYMEX	439,352	0.24%	132,611	0.08%	(48)
40.	Feeder Cattle, CME	411,441	0.22%	455,881	0.29%	(38)
41.	Corn, MIDAM	406,694	0.22%	456,661	0.29%	(37)
42.	Wheat, MIDAM	344,749	0.19%	347,355	0.22%	(40)
43.	Wheat, MGE	283,900	0.15%	297,509	0.19%	(42)
44.	Orange Juice (frozen, conc.), NYCE	211,543	0.11%	190,758	0.12%	(44)
45.	Dollar Index, NYCE	166,494	0.09%			
46.	Palladium, NYMEX	145,562	0.08%	133,223	0.08%	(47)
47.	Oats, CBT	140,952	0.08%			
48.	Gold (Kilo), CBT	124,546	0.07%	168,527	0.11%	(45)
49.	Swiss Franc, MIDAM	102,019	0.06%	110,047	0.07%	(49)
	Contracts with Volume Over 100,000 Contracts*			2,201,971	1.38%	
	Contracts with Volume Under 100,000 Contracts	832,603	0.45%	1,142,090	0.72%	
	TOTAL	184,354,496	100.00%	158,696,578	100.00%	

*Contracts over 100,000 traded in 1985 but not over 100,000 in 1986.
Source: Futures Industry Association

Figure 1-5. Commodity futures contracts traded 1982–1986 by exchange.

	Contract Unit	1986	1985	1984	1983	1982
Wheat	5,000 bu	2,090,316	2,127,962	2,974,886	3,886,914	4,031,584
Corn	5,000 bu	6,160,298	6,392,812	9,108,526	11,924,576	7,948,257
Oats	5,000 bu	140,952	99,024	155,110	359,825	424,595
Soybeans	5,000 bu	6,133,668	7,392,128	11,362,691	13,680,324	9,165,520
Soybean Oil	60,000 lb	3,182,963	3,647,408	4,009,548	3,858,558	3,049,313
Soybean Meal	100 tons	3,049,005	3,339,268	3,822,179	3,872,453	2,784,423
Plywood	76,032 sq. ft.			4,466	50,424	100,001
Silver	5,000 oz				21,470	77,682
Silver	1,000 oz	511,239	1,034,830	1,887,257	2,643,166	775,136
Gold	100 oz				4,133	19,515
Gold	Kilo	124,546	168,527	302,717	302,745	
GNMA Mrtges, CDR	$100,000	24,078	84,396	862,450	1,692,017	2,055,648
GNMA II	$100,000			37,615		
Cash Settle GNMA	$100,000	7,351				
T-Bonds	$100,000	52,598,811	40,448,357	29,963,280	19,550,535	16,739,695
T-Notes (2-year)	$100,000				562	
T-Notes (6½-10 yr)	$100,000	4,426,476	2,860,432	1,661,862	814,505	881,325
Domestic CD (90-day)	$1,000,000					145,360
Unleaded Reg. Gasoline	1,000 bbl				51,573	8,736
Crude Oil	1,000 bbl			628	94,591	
Heating Oil	1,000 bbl				3,152	
Municipal Bond Index	$1,000 x Index	906,980	334,691			
Major Market Index	$100 x Index	36,292	2,062,083	1,514,737		
MMI Maxi	$250 x Index	1,738,916	422,091			
NASDAQ-100	$250 x Index	3,743	139,888			
Chicago Board of Trade		81,135,634	70,553,897	67,667,952	62,811,523	48,206,790

23

Figure 1-5. (Cont.)

	Contract Unit	1986	1985	1984	1983	1982
Fresh Eggs	22,500 dz					18
Potatoes	80,000 lb					9
Live Hogs	30,000 #	1,936,864	1,719,861	2,169,030	2,790,746	3,560,974
Pork Bellies, Frozen	38,000 #	1,100,339	1,457,386	1,908,045	2,403,277	2,811,674
Live Cattle	40,000 #	4,690,538	4,437,327	3,553,270	4,248,152	4,440,992
Feeder Cattle	42,000 lb	411,441	455,881	316,985	537,173	603,769
Broilers	30,000 lb					2,118
Lumber	130,000 bd. ft.	502,530	581,548	753,568	731,003	516,619
Plywood	152,064 sq. ft.					35
Gold	100 oz		7	8,841	994,132	1,533,466
Leaded Regular Gas	1,000 barrels			4,045		
No. 2 Fuel Oil	1,000 barrels			4,601		
T-Bills (90-day)	$1,000,000	1,815,162	2,413,338	3,292,817	3,789,864	6,598,848
Domestic CD (90-day)	$1,000,000	3,062	84,106	928,662	1,079,580	1,556,327
Eurodollar (3-month)	$1,000,000	10,824,914	8,900,528	4,192,952	891,066	323,619
European Currency Unit	125,000	43,826				
British Pound	25,000	2,701,330	2,799,024	1,444,492	1,614,993	1,321,701
Canadian Dollar	100,000	734,071	468,996	345,875	558,741	1,078,467
Deutsche Mark	125,000	6,582,145	6,449,384	5,508,308	2,423,508	1,792,901
Japanese Yen	12,500,000	3,969,777	2,415,094	2,334,764	3,442,262	1,762,246
Mexican Peso	1,000,000		12,737	15,364	40,308	65,036
Swiss Franc	125,000	4,998,430	4,758,159	4,129,881	3,766,130	2,653,332
Dutch Guilder	125,000				162	128
U.S. Silver Coins	$5,000					1
French Franc	250,000	2,685	9,335	8,388	26,348	16,474
S&P 500 Index	$500 x Index	19,505,273	15,055,955	12,363,592	8,101,697	2,935,532
S&P 100 Index	$200 x Index	3,514	1,662	166,202	390,902	
S&P OTC 250	$500 x Index	5,270	94,919			
Chicago Mercantile Ex.		59,831,171	52,115,247	43,449,682	37,830,044	33,574,286

Figure 1-5. (Cont.)

	Contract Unit	1986	1985	1984	1983	1982
Rice, Milled	120,000 lb				275	5,262
Rice, Rough Old	200,000 lb		9	2,978	11,964	11,253
Rice, Rough New		3,095				
Cotton	50,000 lb				1,004	8,388
Cotton Short Staple	50,000 lb	3	1,751			
Soybeans	5,000 bu				197	1,998
Corn	5,000 bu				102	971
Chic. Rice & Cotton Ex.		3,098	1,760	2,978	13,542	27,872
Coffee "C"	37,500 lb	1,073,142	650,768	499,133	427,441	556,435
Sugar #11	112,000 lb	3,583,814	3,012,929	2,449,549	3,201,968	2,037,020
Sugar #12	112,000 lb	19,058	99,851	109,448	84,120	51,093
Sugar #14	112,000 lb	72,526	17,433			
Cocoa	10 M tons	777,765	800,573	1,127,752	1,162,540	607,964
CPI-W	$1,000 x Index	8,776	1,324			
Coffee, Sugar & Cocoa		5,535,081	4,582,878	4,185,882	4,876,069	3,252,512
Copper	25,000 lb	1,872,209	2,444,552	2,506,365	3,186,914	2,362,625
Silver	5,000 oz	3,849,687	4,821,206	6,742,508	6,432,982	2,868,639
Gold	100 oz	8,400,175	7,773,834	9,115,504	10,382,805	12,289,448
Aluminum	40,000 lb	52,627	77,063	82,661	11,896	
Commodity Exchange		14,174,698	15,116,655	18,447,038	20,014,597	17,520,712
Wheat (5,000 bu)	5,000 bu	744,023	735,447	956,668	942,971	964,815
Value Line Index	$500 x Index	953,985	1,204,659	910,956	724,979	528,743
Mini Value Line	$100 x Index	18,678	19,032	30,179	25,092	
Kansas City Bd. of Trd.		1,716,686	1,959,138	1,897,803	1,693,042	1,493,558

Figure 1-5. (Cont.)

	Contract Unit	1986	1985	1984	1983	1982
Wheat	1,000 bu	344,749	347,355	404,508	334,413	243,640
Corn	1,000 bu	406,694	456,661	604,992	629,678	274,324
Oats	1,000 bu	2,169	1,746	7,067	11,797	12,981
Soybeans	1,000 bu	680,156	843,231	1,301,916	1,171,294	527,411
Soybean Meal Old	20 tons	3,231	10,981			
Soybean Meal New		2,256				
Live Cattle	20,000 #	58,752	64,510	81,112	88,349	107,329
Live Hogs	15,000 #	80,818	74,388	112,877	108,069	175,624
Refined Sugar	40,000 lb			24	3,306	24,000
Silver	1,000 oz	649	4,510	19,497	96,611	125,409
New York Silver	1,000 oz	9,342	57,886	12,611	30,833	3,810
Gold	33.2 oz	0	76	41,690	349,044	383,499
New York Gold	33.2 oz	21,111	31,467	19,285		
Platinum	25 oz	5,944	1,368	213		
Copper	12,500 lb	892	4,043	492		
Copper High Grade		1,753				
T-Bonds	$50,000	467,639	297,033	251,300	267,259	419,277
T-Bills	$500,000	34,690	36,904	30,486	37,755	100,417
British Pound	12,500	17,270	21,239	8,901	884	
Swiss Franc	62,500	102,019	110,047	99,385	19,632	
Deutsche Mark	62,500	74,662	85,439	67,507	6,607	
Japanese Yen	6,250,000	47,601	32,912	34,677	10,835	
Canadian Dollar	$50,000	6,150	3,370	3,315	171	
MidAmerica Commodity Ex.		2,368,547	2,485,166	3,101,855	3,166,537	2,397,721
Wheat	5,000 bu	283,900	297,509	338,487	379,603	346,226
White Wheat	5,000 bu	686	3,402	2,245		
Sunflower Seeds	100,000 bu				4	38
Minneapolis Grain Ex.		284,586	300,911	340,732	379,607	346,264

Figure 1-5. (Cont.)

	Contract Unit	1986	1985	1984	1983	1982
Cotton #2	50,000 lb	1,015,392	636,492	1,137,141	1,550,117	1,255,792
Orange Juice (frozen, conc.)	15,000 lb	211,543	190,758	317,364	124,267	207,070
Propane	100,000 gal	11,966	13,724	22,005	28,721	16,919
European Currency Unit	100,000	72,195				
Dollar Index	$500 x Index	166,494	74,573			
NY Cotton & Citrus		1,477,590	915,547	1,476,510	1,703,105	1,479,781
T-Bonds	$100,000					4,464
Domestic CD (90-day)	$1,000,000				18	132
NYSE Composite Index	$500 x Index	3,123,668	2,833,614	3,456,798	3,506,439	1,432,913
NYSE Financial Index	$1,000 x Index				3,828	13,933
Cmdty Rsrch Bureau Index	$500 x Index	59,324				
New York Futures Ex.		3,182,992	2,833,614	3,456,798	3,510,285	1,451,442
Palladium	100 oz	145,562	133,223	159,019	241,224	63,829
Platinum	50 oz	1,624,635	693,256	571,127	1,053,282	669,024
Imported Lean Beef	36,000 lb					7
Potatoes	50,000 lb				17,115	67,322
Potatoes (Cash Settlement)	100,000 lb	16,558	16,903	26,595	16,650	
No. 2 Heating Oil, NY	1,000 bbl	3,275,044	2,207,733	2,091,546	1,868,322	1,745,526
No. 2 Heating Oil, Gulf	1,000 bbl					74
Leaded Reg. Gasoline, NY	1,000 bbl	829,733	667,172	653,630	406,843	104,082
Leaded Reg. Gasoline, Gulf	1,000 bbl					77
Unleaded Gasoline, NY	1,000 bbl	439,352	132,611	2,736		
Crude Oil	1,000 bbl	8,313,529	3,980,867	1,840,342	323,153	
New York Mercantile Ex.		14,644,413	7,831,765	5,344,995	3,926,589	2,649,941
Total Futures		184,354,496	158,696,578	149,372,225	139,924,940	112,400,879
Percent Change		16.17%	6.24%	6.75%	24.49%	

Source: Futures Industry Association

■Chapter 2

■The Arithmetic of Futures Trading

Every futures contract is a binding agreement between a seller and a buyer to make and to take delivery of the underlying commodity or financial instrument at a specified future date. By definition, every contract has two principals: a buyer and a seller. The buyer, known as the *long*, agrees to take delivery of the underlying asset. The seller, known as the *short*, agrees to make delivery.

During the life of a futures contract, its price will rise and fall, depending on the prevailing and anticipated balance between supply and demand of the underlying asset. Periods of shortage will generate rising prices, whereas periods of oversupply will precipitate falling prices. Longs profit from rising prices because their earlier purchase of the futures contract means that they are entitled to take delivery of the underlying asset at a lower price than that which prevails today. Shorts profit during periods of falling prices because their earlier sale of the futures contract means that they have agreed to sell the underlying asset at a price higher than today's. To fulfill his obligation, the short would simply buy the asset at the current lower price and deliver it at the higher price agreed on when the contract was first created.

In practice, futures contracts are rarely settled by actual delivery. Most contracts are settled simply by selling an existing long position or by buying back an existing short. These concepts are explained in Chapter 3.

FUTURES CONTRACTS—THE BASIC UNIT

Each futures contract has a standardized unit of trading that is established by the exchange on which trading takes place. For example, a

28

contract of grain (wheat, corn, soybeans, oats, etc.) calls for delivery of 5,000 bushels. In soybean oil, 60,000 pounds constitutes a contract. Futures contracts in three-month Treasury bills call for delivery of a $1 million T-bill. A gold futures contract on the Commodity Exchange, Inc., is 100 ounces. On the International Monetary Market of the Chicago Mercantile Exchange, 125,000 Swiss francs makes up a contract. The units of trading (ounces, pounds, bushels, etc.) and the number of units in a contract are based on the accepted customs and practices of the trade. Figure 2-1 on pages 30 and 31 shows the contract unit and the size of major futures contracts that are listed on exchanges in the United States.

Price Quotations

The manner in which prices are quoted varies from futures contract to futures contract and is also determined by industry convention and the physical properties of the underlying asset. Gold and platinum are quoted in dollars and cents per ounce. Silver is also quoted by the ounce, but because its price has historically been well below that of gold or platinum, further price refinement became the custom. Thus, silver is quoted in dollars, cents, and tenths of a cent per ounce. Grain markets are quoted in dollars, cents, and quarters of a cent per bushel. Many other physical commodities are quoted in cents and hundredths of a cent per pound. These include copper, aluminum, cotton, sugar, soybean oil, livestock, and others.

Still other physical commodities are quoted by such diverse measures as dollars and cents per ton, per hundredweight, and per gallon. Refer to Figure 2-1 for further details.

Quotations in foreign currency futures are the same as those for physical commodities. Currency futures prices on the International Monetary Market (IMM) represent the prevailing ratio between the foreign currency and US $1. A quote of 0.6000 in the Swiss franc means that 1 Swiss franc equals 60 cents ($0.60). A quote of 1.6000 in British pound futures means that 1 British pound equals 160 cents ($1.60). You will realize that this method of quotation is the same as that used for all physical commodities. In physical commodities, just as in currency futures, prices represent a ratio between the physical commodity and $1 US. For example, cotton might be quoted at 60.00 (60.00 cents per pound). Similarly, a quote of 0.6000 in Swiss francs would mean 60.00 cents per Swiss franc.

This is known as the *American system* for quoting currency rates. The interbank market, in which banks trade directly with one another

Figure 2-1. Selected futures contract trading facts.

Commodity	Exch.	Trading Time (Centrl. Time)	Delivery Months	Contract Unit	Price Quoted In	Minimum Fluctuation	$ Value of Minimum Tick	Daily Trading Limit
Corn	CBT	9:30–1:15	Z,H,K,N,U,	5,000 bu.	¢/bu.	$.0025/bu.	12.50	$.10/bu.
Soybeans	CBT	9:30–1:15	F,H,K,N,Q,U,X	5,000 bu.	¢/bu.	$.0025/bu.	12.50	$.30/bu.
Soybean Meal	CBT	9:30–1:15	V,Z,F,H,K,N,Q,U	100 tons	$/ton	10¢/ton	10.00	$10/ton
Soybean Oil	CBT	9:30–1:15	V,Z,F,H,K,N,Q,U	60,000 lbs.	¢/lb.	$.0001/lb.	6.00	1¢/lb.
Wheat	CBT	9:30–1:15	N,U,Z,H,K	5,000 bu.	¢/lb.	$.0025/bu.	12.50	$.20/bu.
U.S. T- Bonds	CBT	8:00–2:00	H,M,V,Z	$100,000 face	% pts.	1/32 pt./100 pts.	31.25	64/32
U.S. T-Notes	CBT	8:00–2:00	H,M,U,Z	$100,000 face	% pts.	1/32 pt.	31.25	64/32
Major Market Index	CBT	8:45–3:15	All Months	100 times index	index pts.	1.25 pt.	12.50	none
Municipal Bond Index	CBT	8:00–2:00	H,M,U,Z	100 times index	index pts.	1/32 pt.	31.25	none
Wheat	KCBT	9:30–1:15	N,U,Z,H,K	5,000 bu.	¢/bu.	$.0025/bu.	12.50	$.25/bu.
KC Value Line Futures	KCBT	9:30–3:15	H,M,U,Z	500 times index	index pts.	.05 pt.	25.00	none
Wheat	MGE	9:30–1:15	N,U,Z,H,K	5,000 bu.	¢/bu.	$.0025/bu.	12.50	$.20/bu.
Live Cattle	CME	9:05–1:00	G,J,M,Q,V,Z	40,000 lbs.	¢/lb.	2.5¢/cwt.	10.00	1.5¢/lb.
Live Hogs	CME	9:10–1:00	G,J,M,N,Q,V,Z	30,000 lbs.	¢/lb.	2.5¢/cwt.	7.50	1.5¢/lb.
Pork Bellies	CME	9:10–1:00	G,H,K,N,Q	38,000 lbs.	¢/lb.	2.5¢/cwt.	9.50	2.0¢/lb.
S&P 500 Futures Index	CME	9:00–3:15	H,M,U,Z	500 times index	index pts.	.05 pt.	25.00	none
Cocoa	CSCE	8:30–2:00	H,K,N,U,Z	10 metric tons	$/ton	$1.00/m.t.	10.00	$88/m.t.
Coffee "C"	CSCE	8:45–1:30	H,K,N,U,Z	37,500 lbs.	¢/lb.	$.0001/lb.	3.75	4¢/lb.
Sugar #11	CSCE	9:00–12:43	F,H,K,N,U,V	112,000 lbs.	¢/lb.	$.0001/lb.	11.20	.5¢/lb.

Figure 2-1. (Cont.)

Commodity	Exch.	Trading Time (Centrl. Time)	Delivery Months	Contract Unit	Price Quoted In	Minimum Fluctuation	$ Value of Minimum Tick	Daily Trading Limit
Cotton #2	NYCE	9:30-2:00	H,K,N,V,Z	50,000 lbs.	¢/lb.	$.0001/lb.	5.00	2¢/lb.
Orange Juice	NYCE	9:15-1:45	F,H,K,N,U,X	15,000 lbs.	¢/lb.	$.0005/lbs.	7.50	5¢/lb.
U.S. Dollar Index	NYCE	8:20-2:40	H,M,U,Z	500 times index	index pts.	.01 pt.	5.00	none
Platinum	NYME	8:00-1:30	F,J,N,V	50 Troy oz.	$/oz.	$.10/oz.	5.00	$25/oz.
No. 2 Heating Oil—New York	NYME	8:50-2:05	All months	42,000 gal.	$/gal.	$.0001/gal.	4.20	2¢/gal.
Crude Oil	NYME	8:45-2:10	All months	1,000 bbl.	$/bbl.	$.01/bbl.	10.00	2¢/gal.
Unleaded Gasoline	NYME	8:30-2:00	All months	42,000 gal.	$/gal.	$.0001/gal	4.20	2¢/gal.
Pound Sterling	IMM	7:30-1:24	H,M,U,Z	25,000 BP	$/BP	.05¢/BP	12.50	none
Canadian Dollar	IMM	7:30-1:26	H,M,U,Z	100,000 CD	$/CD	$.0001/CD	10.00	none
Japanese Yen	IMM	7:30-1:22	H,M,U,Z	12,500,000 JY	$/JY	$.000001/JY	12.50	none
Swiss Franc	IMM	7:30-1:16	H,M,U,Z	125,000 SF	$/SF	$.0001/SF	12.50	none
Deutsche Mark	IMM	7:30-1:20	H,M,U,Z	125,000 DM	$/DM	$.0001/DM	12.50	none
Eurodollars	IMM	7:30-2:00	H,M,U,Z	$1,000,000	% pts.	.01 pt.	25.00	1.0 pt.
U.S. T-Bills (90-day)	IMM	7:30-2:00	H,M,U,Z	$1,000,000	% pts.	.01 pt.	25.00	0.5 pt.
Copper	COMEX	8:50-1:00	F,H,K,N,V,Z	25,000 lb.	¢/lb.	$.0005/lb.	12.50	none
Gold	COMEX	8:00-1:30	G,J,M,Q,V,Z	100 Troy oz.	$/oz.	$.10/oz.	10.00	none
Silver	COMEX	8:05-1:25	F,H,K,N,V,Z	5,000 Troy oz.	¢/oz.	$.001/oz.	5.00	none
NYSE Composite Index	NYFE	9:00-4:10	H,M,U,Z	500 times index	index pts.	.05 pt.	25.00	none

Key to Contract Months

1st Year	Month	2nd Year	1st Year	Month	2nd Year	1st Year	Month	2nd Year
F	January	A	K	May	E	U	September	P
G	February	B	M	June	I	V	October	R
H	March	C	N	July	L	X	November	S
J	April	D	Q	August	O	Z	December	T

Key to Exchange Abbreviations

CBT	Chicago Board of Trade	CSCE	Coffee, Sugar, & Cocoa Exchange
KCBT	Kansas City Board of Trade	NYCE	New York Cotton Exchange
MGE	Minneapolis Grain Exchange	NYME	New York Mercantile Exchange
CME	Chicago Mercantile Exchange	IMM	International Monetary Market (a division of the CME)
		COMEX	Commodity Exchange, Inc.
		NYFE	New York Futures Exchange

and with their corporate customers, uses the *European system*, which is the inverse of the American system. Prices in the interbank market represent the number of foreign currency units per dollar, as opposed to the number of dollars (or cents) per foreign currency unit. The two rates are always reciprocals of one another. For example, if the IMM price for Deutsche marks is 40.00 cents (=$0.40), then the interbank rate will be $1/0.40 = $ DM 2.50. The single exception to this rule is the British pound, which, by custom, is always quoted using the American system.

Price quotations for interest rate futures are slightly more complicated. In the dealer market, Treasury bills are quoted on a discount basis, meaning that quotations are given in terms of yields rather than prices. Buyers in this market are interested in making purchases at the highest possible yield, whereas sellers want to give up the lowest possible yield. Thus, in the dealer market, T-bill bids are actually higher than the offers. For example, a cash 90-day T-bill (as opposed to a futures contract) might be quoted as 6.52 bid/6.50 offered. This means that a buyer is willing to purchase the T-bill if he will receive a yield of 6.52% per annum, whereas a seller is willing to pay a yield of 6.50% per annum. When T-bill futures were being developed in the 1970s, this posed a problem for futures traders who were accustomed to bids being lower than offers. To accommodate this orientation, the International Monetary Market of the Chicago Mercantile Exchange devised a quotation mechanism for its futures contracts called the *IMM index*, which is inversely related to yields. The IMM index is based on the difference between the actual T-bill yield and 100.00. Thus, a T-bill yield of 8% (8.00) would be quoted as 92.00 (=100.00-8.00). A 1% change in the yield of a T-bill would equate to a change of 1.00 in the IMM index. This convention is used for the futures contracts of all instruments that are issued on a discount basis.

For Treasury bonds, Treasury notes, and other coupon instruments, prices are quoted as a percent of par rather than on a discount basis. For example, the Treasury might issue a 7-year note with a 9% coupon at par. The price of this security would be 100 (this is the definition of *par*), which means that the buyer would have to pay $100 for every $100 of face value. In this case, of course, the yield is equal to the coupon rate—no more, no less than 9%. Prices of coupon instruments are quoted in 32nds of a dollar in both cash and futures markets. The *32* is often omitted when quotes are printed, so a price of 97-2 means $97²/₃₂ (=$97.0625) per $100 face value.

Once notes and bonds are issued and find their way into the secondary market, their prices change as interest rates vary. If the rates on comparable securities have risen since the issuance of a particular Treasury note or bond, its price will fall. In our example, if rates had risen to 10% on other T-notes that had approximately 7 years remaining to maturity since our 9% note was first issued, its price might fall to 98-4 ($98⁴/32 per $100 of face value). The reason for the decline in the note price is that holders of the 9% coupon security are inclined to sell it and purchase the higher-yielding 10% notes currently available. This selling pressure drives the price of the note down to a level at which the effective yield on the 9% coupon is in line with the yield on comparable securities. Prices in the futures market follow this convention. No modifications to the dealer market quotation system were necessary because, unlike cash market T-bills, bids were already lower than offers.

The Financial Page

Futures quotations are carried on the financial pages of major newspapers. The contracts are often categorized as (1) grains and oilseeds, (2) livestock and meat, (3) food and fiber, (4) metals and petroleum, (5) wood, (6) financial, and (7) indexes. Figure 2-2 on pages 34 and 35 shows the *Wall Street Journal's* Futures Prices page from March 11, 1987. The prices on this page are those at the close of business on March 10, 1987. To find the daily statistics on May 1987 corn, look under the *GRAINS AND OILSEEDS* section. Next to the word *Corn* is the exchange on which this particular corn contract is traded, the size of the contract, and how it is quoted. The corn on this page is the 5,000 bushel contract that is traded on the Chicago Board of Trade. The first column gives the delivery month: May 1987. The second column indicates where the contract opened: 158¹/2 = ($1.58¹/2 per bushel). The next two columns give the range of trading for the day with the highest price (158³/4) in column three and the lowest price (155¹/2) in column four. Column five is the settlement price: 156. This is a representative price that was recorded during the official closing period that is designated by the exchange. The sixth column represents the change in price from the previous day's settlement price. May 87 corn closed 2³/4 cents lower than where it settled on the previous trading day. Columns seven and eight indicate the highest and the lowest prices for the contract since trading began in this particular delivery month. The highest price at

Figure 2-2. Futures page.

FUTURES PRICES

Figure 2-2. *(Cont.)*

Column 3:
Daily High

Column 4:
Daily Low

Column 5:
Settlement Price

Column 6:
Change

Column 2:
Opening Price

Columns 7 & 8:
Season Highs
& Lows

Column 1:
Delivery Month

Column 9:
Open Interest

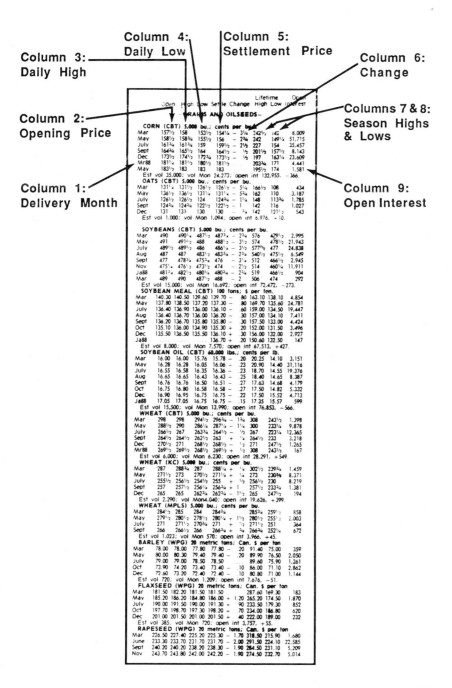

which May 87 corn has traded is 242, and the lowest price is 149¹/4. The last column represents the open interest, or the number of open contracts for each delivery month, as of the close of business two days earlier. There were 51,715 contracts of May 87 corn open on March 9. The bottom line of the section contains cumulative volume and open-interest figures. These statistics are for all delivery months combined. The first number is the estimated volume of trading on March 10: there were 35,000 contracts of Chicago Board of Trade corn traded. Next to that is the actual volume of trading on March 9: there were 24,273 contracts. The open interest figure of 132,955 is also for March 9 and is 366 contracts less than at the close of the previous trading session. This open interest figure can be derived by totaling the open interest figures that are given for each delivery month in column nine.

You should study the price quotations shown in Figure 2-2 while referring to the table of facts in Figure 2-1.

Price Changes

The minimum amount by which a commodity's price can change is established by the exchange on which trading takes place and is known as the *minimum fluctuation*, or *tick*. In grains, for instance, price changes are registered in multiples of ¹/4 cent per bushel. If the last transaction in wheat is at $2.50¹/2, the minimum change would be to either $2.50¹/4 or $2.50³/4. On the trading floors, brokers are prohibited from making bids and offers at levels that are not multiples of this minimum fluctuation.

Many physical commodities are quoted in cents and hundredths of a cent per pound. In these commodities, price changes are registered in ¹/100 cent per pound, which is often called 1 point. Because 1 cent obviously consists of ¹⁰⁰/100, a fluctuation of 1 cent is equal to 100 points.

A word of caution here: 1 point does not necessarily equal a minimum fluctuation, or tick. For example, the minimum fluctuation in copper is ⁵/100 cent, or 5 points. In most livestock markets, a tick is 2¹/2 points. Be cautious about using the terms *point* and *tick* until you are sure what meaning they have for each futures contract.

Figure 2-1 includes the minimum fluctuations for major futures contracts.

CALCULATING CONTRACT VALUE

With the preliminaries of contract sizes and price quotations behind us, the first important step in understanding the arithmetic of futures trading is to be able to calculate the value of any contract, given its price. You should know intuitively that the value of a contract is simply its size multiplied by its prevailing price. A 25,000-pound copper futures contract at 60 cents per pound has a value of $15,000 (=25,000 pounds x $0.60 per pound).

Complications can arise if you are not thoroughly familiar with the meaning of a price quotation. Does a quote of 60.00 in copper mean 60 cents per pound or $60 per ton? The difference has an obvious and significant impact on the calculation of contract value. For this reason and because, in day-to-day practice, units are often omitted from price quotations, we once again urge you to study the contract facts in Figure 2-1. The following examples should help convey the basic idea.

Example 1: What is the value of a contract of cotton when cotton is priced at 48.00?
Answer: 48.00 (cents per pound) x 50,000 pounds equals $24,000.

Example 2: What is the value of a contract of soybean oil, the price of which is 32.08?
Answer: 32.08 (cents/pound) x 60,000 pounds equals $19,248.

Example 3: What is the value of a futures contract in each of the following examples?

Futures Contract	Price (in standard units)
a) Soybeans	5.79¹/₄
b) Live hogs	50.30
c) Cocoa	2072.00
d) Gold	314.00
e) Swiss franc	0.3850
f) Heating oil	70.49
g) Heating oil	69.35

Answers: (a) $28,962.50; (b) $15,090; (c) $20,720; (d) $31,400; (e) $48,125; (f) $29,605.80; (g) $29,127.

Calculating Gains and Losses

As the price of a futures contract rises or falls, its value increases or decreases. For the holder of a long position, profits are generated by rising prices that increase the value of the contract. Declining prices and the resulting drop in the value of a contract represent profits to the holder of a short position. The change in value of any contract for the long or the short is simply the difference between the price when the contract was first entered into and the current price, multiplied by the number of units called for in the specifications of the contract.

If the value of a contract at time t_1 is represented by the symbol V_{t_1}, and the value at time t_2 is represented by V_{t_2}, then the change in value ΔV between time t_2 and time t_1 is as follows:

$$\Delta V = V_{t_2} - V_{t_1} \qquad (1)$$

If ΔV is positive, this represents a profit to the long. If it is negative, this represents a profit to the short.

Now, because the value of a contract at any time is its price multiplied by the contract size, we have:

$$V_{t_2} = P_{t_2} \times C; \; V_{t_1} = P_{t_1} \times C$$

where P = price; C = contract value.

Substituting variables, we get:

$$\Delta V = (P_{t_2} - P_{t_1}) \times C \qquad (2)$$

The change in value of a contract equals its change in price multiplied by its contract size.

As an illustration, let us determine the profit or the loss to the holder of a long position in soybean oil if the price of soybean oil falls from 32.05 to 31.70.

Using equation (1), we get the following:

$V_{t_2} = (60,000 \times 0.3170) = \$19,020$
$V_{t_1} = (60,000 \times 0.3205) = \$19,230$
$\Delta V = \$19,020 - 19,230 = \underline{-\$210}$

Using equation (2) gives the following:

$C = 60,000$ pounds
$P_{t_2} - P_{t_1} = 0.3170 - 0.3205 = -0.0035$
$\Delta V = 60,000 \times (-0.0035) = \underline{-\$210}$

As should be the case, each method produces the same result—a loss of $210 per contract to the long. If more than one contract is involved, the result is simply multiplied by the appropriate number of contracts.

Margin and Leverage

As is explained in greater detail in Chapter 7, every holder of a long or of a short contract must deposit with his or her brokerage house a certain amount of money to guarantee performance on the contract. This deposit is known as *margin*, and its size plays an important role in the explanation of why futures trading can be both very risky and very profitable.

At price levels of about $400 per ounce, the holder of a long (or a short) futures position in gold must typically make a margin deposit of $2,000. At $400 per ounce, the value of a gold futures contract is $40,000. Thus, the margin deposit represents 5% of the value of the contract. Compare this with the equity markets where a margin deposit of 50% of the security's value is currently required. The difference is meaningful. In the case of futures, the trader is controlling an investment with a much smaller amount of money than would be required in securities—or in most other investment arenas, for that matter. *Leverage* is the term that is used to describe the ratio of the investment's full value to the amount of capital that is required to own or to control it. If we buy something worth $100 by putting up a deposit of $50, our leverage is 2:1. If we pay for something in full, the leverage is 1:1. In futures trading, the available leverage is often 10:1 to 20:1, or more.

It is important to realize that the greater the leverage, the smaller the price move that is required to bring about the same percent change in the value of the investment.

Take the following examples:

1. If we buy something that is worth $100 by putting up its full value of $100, then a $10 (= 10%) increase in its price will produce a 10% return on our investment.

> Purchase Value = $100
> Current Value = $110 (+10%)
> Capital Invested = $100
> $$\text{Return} = \frac{\text{change in value}}{\text{capital invested}} = \frac{\$10}{\$100} = \underline{10\%}$$

2. If we buy something that is worth $100 by putting up $50, then a 10% increase in price will produce a 20% return on our investment.

Purchase Value = $100
Current Value = $110
Capital Invested = $ 50
$$\text{Return} = \frac{\$\ 10}{\$\ 50} = \underline{\underline{20\%}}$$

This is the case for the equities market where a 50% margin deposit is required.

3. In futures we can often purchase something that is worth $100 by putting up only $10. A 10% increase in the price of the futures contract will result in a profit of not 10%, not 20%, but 100%.

Purchase Value = $100
Current Value = $110
Capital Invested = $10
$$\text{Return} = \frac{\$10}{\$10} = \underline{\underline{100\%}}$$

To illustrate further, let us compare an investment in futures with one in securities. Suppose that an investor has $10,000 of risk capital and narrows her choice to two possibilities: The common stock of company XYZ that is priced at, say, $5 per share, and silver futures that are priced at, say, $5 per ounce. She expects the prices of both to double.

In the case of Company XYZ, the trader buys $20,000 of the stock (4,000 shares at $5 per share) by making the required 50% margin deposit of $10,000. If the stock doubles to $10 per share, her profit is $20,000 (4,000 shares x $5 per share), a return of 200%.

In the case of futures, the investor might be required to make a deposit of $2,000 for every contract that represents 5,000 ounces of silver. With $10,000, she can buy five contracts that represent 25,000 ounces. If silver rises from $5 per ounce to $10 per ounce, her profit is $125,000 (25,000 ounces x $5 per ounce), a return of 1,250%.

It should be clear that the high leverage available in futures trading can be a source of great profit and great loss. Relatively small changes in price produce very large changes in the value of our investment. If a margin deposit of 5% is required to purchase or to sell short a futures contract, then all that is required to double or to wipe out that investment is a 5% increase or decrease in the price of the commodity or the financial instrument.

Many novice futures traders (and even some professionals) erroneously think that the primary reason that futures trading is notoriously risky is that futures prices are more volatile than are prices in other investment arenas. However, statistical analysis shows that the volatility of futures prices is approximately the same as that of equity prices, for example. What makes futures trading a risky affair is the low margin required and the resulting high leverage. If we were able to trade common stocks on thin margin, they too would be considered very risky investments. In the 1920s, listed equities were traded with margin requirements comparable to those in today's futures markets. Economists and historians still disagree on the extent (if any) to which this leverage contributed to the stock market crash of 1929 and the subsequent Great Depression.

The subjects of margin, leverage, and risk are complex and often misunderstood in connection with futures trading. We return to them in greater detail in Chapter 15.

DAILY TRADING LIMITS

As with many other investment or trading vehicles, futures markets are from time to time jolted by developments that cause dramatic short-run price changes. Weather shifts, outbreaks of war, and unexpected crop or economic reports are among the sparks that set off such price explosions. In an effort to contain the effects of these unexpected and potentially dangerous price changes on both traders and on the entire futures trading system, most United States exchanges have established daily trading limits on prices. These limits are given in Figure 2-1 for some of the more active U.S. futures contracts. Daily trading limits define the amount by which the price of a futures contract can rise above or fall below the previous day's settlement price. These limits tend to take the edge off a price panic by allowing the market to digest developments in an atmosphere that is free of rapidly escalating or declining prices. They also make more orderly the clearing house process of paying and collecting margin funds, because large price changes result in major transfers of funds between customers and clearing houses. These processes are discussed in detail in Chapter 7.

It is very important to understand that daily price limits provide only temporary and artificial restraints on prices. Prices will eventually seek the levels warranted by market forces, regardless of the particular limits imposed by exchanges on their daily movements. Under extreme conditions, prices have risen or dropped to their daily limits for several consecutive days until the full impact of developments has been absorbed. The problems created by strings of "limit-up" or "limit-down" days forced exchanges to make more flexible their rules on daily trading limits. Before we discuss these modifications, let us first take a closer look at how the mechanism works.

The daily price limit for CBT T-bonds is 64/32nds. If the settlement price of June T-bonds on Monday was 95-06, the daily-price-limit rule stipulates that on Tuesday it can advance as high as 97-06 or retreat as far as 93-06. It is important to point out that if either of these daily limits is reached, trading does not necessarily cease. As long as there are willing buyers and sellers at the limit-up or limit-down price, trading will continue. If, however, the market remains at the limit-up price, then sellers may begin to withdraw on the theory that the market's ability to hold its gain is suggestive of further price strength. Eventually sellers will withdraw completely, and only buyers will remain. Then, obviously, trading in the contracts that are limit-up will cease.

When there are no sellers at the limit-up price, a pool of bids is created that reflects the number of contracts that are wanted to be bought and that remain unfilled because of the lack of sellers. Exchanges differ on the ways in which they measure this pool and on the ways in which they choose to allocate any sell orders among the pool of prospective buyers.

In cases of extremely dramatic developments, prices may remain "locked up the limit" for several days. Under previous systems this meant that June T-bonds, using our example, might have risen to 97-06 on Tuesday, 99-06 on Wednesday, and 101-6 on Thursday. On each day the absence of sellers would have resulted in little or no trading. Buyers would helplessly wait until prices rose to levels that attracted some selling. This can be an agonizing ordeal to holders of short positions. To relieve this situation and to promote free trading conditions, most exchanges adopted variable trading limits in the 1970s. To illustrate the mechanics of the variable limits, the Chicago Board of Trade's provision for agricultural commodities states the following:

1. If three or more contracts within a crop year (or all contracts within a crop year if there are less than three open contracts) close on

the limit bid for three successive business days or on the limit offered for three successive business days, then the limit becomes 150% of the current level for all contract months and remains there for three successive business days.

2. If three or more contract months (or all contracts within a crop year if there are less than three open contracts) within a given crop year close on the limit bid for the next three business days or on the limit offered for three successive business days, then the limits will remain at 150% of the original level for another three days.

The limits would remain at 150% for successive periods of three business days until three or more contracts within a crop year (or all contracts within a crop year if there are less than three open contracts) do not close at the limit bid or limit offered. Then the limits would revert to their original level at the end of the three-day period.

The New York Mercantile Exchange's rules are as follows:

1. If the settling price for any month shall move by the maximum permissible variation, the maximum permissible variation for all months during the next business session shall be 50% above the maximum permissible variation that would otherwise be in effect.

2. If the settling price for any month for a business session for which the maximum permissible variation has been established in accordance with (1) shall move by the maximum permissible variation in the same direction, the maximum permissible variation for all months during the next business session shall be twice the maximum permissible variation that would otherwise be in effect.

3. Such increased permissible variation shall remain in effect for all subsequent business sessions of the Exchange until the business session following the first session at which the settling price for NO MONTH shall move by the expanded maximum permissible variation in the same direction, whereupon, the maximum permissible variation for all months shall revert to the original permissible limit.

Although this language sounds formidable, the variable-price-limit system has been helpful in those situations in which a rigid limit can become an artificial and disruptive restraint on a contract whose price is advancing or declining rapidly on the basis of dramatic changes in the supply/demand fundamentals. The variable limits represent a compromise between rigid limits and no limits at all. Price limits are removed on many futures contracts during the delivery month. This facilitates the liquidation of positions as contracts near expiration.

Commissions

One last point that is worth including in this chapter concerns the subject of commissions. Between September 4, 1973, and March 8, 1978, the futures industry, as a result of antitrust and class action suits against various exchanges, phased out its minimum fixed commission rates on futures transactions and adopted a system of negotiated commission rates. During the 4½ year phaseout period, fixed commission rates applied only to a certain number of contracts of a particular delivery that an individual or firm bought or sold on a particular day. Commissions were negotiated on any contracts that were bought or sold above the specified level. As of March 8, 1978, rates of commission became subject to negotiation on all futures transactions.

Although all commissions are now subject to negotiation, most brokerage firms operate on a two-tier system. Less active customers tend to come under *house rates*, a schedule of rates that a brokerage firm feels provides adequate profit for low-volume accounts. Although house rates vary, it is reasonable to assume that a typical roundturn rate of commission under the house schedule will be $40 to $80 per contract. For those accounts where high volume justifies negotiation, commission rates can be as low as $15 to $25 per contract.

■ Chapter 3

■ The Settlement of Futures Contracts

In Chapter 1 we described the evolution of a hypothetical futures market from its relatively crude forward-delivery structure to the highly liquid, standardized market machine in existence today. Figure 2-2, which reproduces the *Wall Street Journal* futures page, illustrates the many commodities and financial instruments that are available for trading on futures exchanges and the many delivery months within each market that can be bought or sold. But where does the process begin, and once begun, how are the thousands of long and short positions settled before the delivery period begins? How does the delivery mechanism work, and what ensures that at its expiration a futures contract will fade smoothly out of existence? These are some of the questions that we seek to answer in this chapter.

THE BIRTH OF A FUTURES CONTRACT

The birth of a futures contract can be a complicated affair. It usually begins when an established futures exchange concludes after extensive research that a particular commodity or financial instrument would be well suited to the futures trading format. Its conclusion is usually based on the existence of an already established forward market, the support of dealers and other industry participants, the likelihood that adequate price volatility will attract speculation, and—most of all—the feeling that this particular market is in need of a formal risk-shifting mechanism.

Once its research is completed and the exchange decides in favor of adding a commodity or a financial instrument to its list of futures contracts, it files an application for approval with the federal regulatory agency, the Commodity Futures Trading Commission (CFTC). Before a contract can be listed for futures trading on any exchange, it must receive the stamp of approval from the CFTC. In reviewing the contract application, the CFTC must begin by questioning whether the establishment of a futures market in the item in question would be in the public interest. Does the proposed futures contract serve a real economic purpose? Does it serve the interests of one group of participants over another? Can the exchange ensure fair and orderly market conditions? Are the proposed delivery locations and procedures suitable for the physical delivery of the underlying item against the proposed contract? These are some of the criteria on which the decision of contract market designation is based. Once approved, the contract may be listed for trading.

THE LIFE OF A FUTURES CONTRACT

Before trading begins, the terms and the specifications of the new contract are made public. These include the size of the contract, delivery grades and locations, and the calendar months in which trading and delivery will be permitted. In cotton, for instance, trading is permitted in the months of March, May, July, October, and December. Most futures contracts do not have trading available in all 12 calendar months because of concern that too many delivery months would dilute participation. Instead, trading usually takes place for delivery in the four to eight months that make sense, based on the characteristics of the particular commodity or financial instrument. Another issue that is decided before trading begins is how far in advance of its expiration a delivery month will be listed for trading. Practices vary from exchange to exchange and from instrument to instrument, but generally contracts are listed one to two years before their expiration. Agricultural futures contracts tend to have shorter lives, whereas industrial contracts and financial instruments tend to have longer ones.

In July 1987, trading was available in the following contract months of corn and United States Treasury bonds, both traded on the Chicago Board of Trade:

Corn	US Treasury Bonds
July 1987	September 1987
September 1987	December 1987
December 1987	March 1988

Corn	US Treasury Bonds
March 1988	June 1988
May 1988	September 1988
July 1988	December 1988
September 1988	March 1989

In the case of corn, the September 1988 contract was made available for trading once the May 1987 contract expired. In other words, it is possible to trade corn for delivery about 1 1/4 years ahead. In bonds, the March 1989 contract was added when the June 1987 contract expired.

The life cycle of futures contracts continues as long as trading activity remains healthy and vital. Year after year, new delivery months are listed as old ones expire in delivery. From time to time a futures market in a particular commodity or financial instrument becomes obsolete and the exchange decides to cease trading in it. It usually does so simply by not adding new delivery months as old ones expire. Eventually, the last delivery month comes to an end and all trading is terminated.

From the time it is first listed for trading (*comes on the board*) to its delivery expiration, a particular futures contract follows a predictable course. After a contract comes on the board from one to two years ahead of expiration, trading activity in it tends to be low. Most volume tends to be concentrated in delivery months that are from one to three months away from expiration, with the more distant (deferred) deliveries receiving little attention. As time progresses, interest builds and reaches a peak from one to three months before maturity. From that peak, volume declines as a contract nears maturity because only those participants who are ready to make and to take delivery are active players. During this period of decay, volume tends to switch to the next available delivery month. Finally, during the delivery month itself, volume tends to dry up, and the few remaining contracts that need to be settled by physical delivery are satisfied in this way. Figure 3-1 on page 48 illustrates the typical pattern of activity for most futures contracts.

The Longs and the Shorts

Throughout the life of the futures contract, market forces are at work changing its price. At any time, the price of the futures contract represents traders' consensus of what the underlying commodity or instrument will be worth when it comes time to make delivery. Holders of

Figure 3-1. Typical trading activity pattern of futures contract.

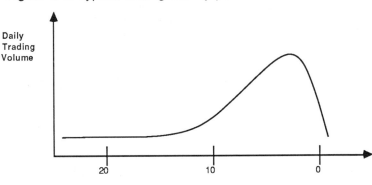

Number of months to expiration

long positions expect prices to rise, and holders of short positions expect prices to drop. As mentioned earlier, the holder of a long position has entered into an agreement to take delivery of the commodity during the delivery period. For example, in September 1987 the holder of a long position in March 1988 T-bond futures has entered into an agreement to take delivery of a specified amount of Treasury bonds six months later in March 1988. The holder of a short position has entered into an agreement to make delivery of that amount. If in September 1987 there were only two participants in the March 1988 contract and they did no subsequent trading, then in September the short would be obliged to deliver to the long in accordance with the terms of the contract.

Obviously, this is not the case. Instead of two participants there are thousands, not all of whom have an interest in going down to the wire by making or taking delivery of the underlying item. This raises a very important issue. In all futures contracts, settlement may be made in one of two ways: by delivery or by offset.

THE SETTLEMENT OF FUTURES CONTRACTS

Settlement by Offset

The vast majority of futures trades are settled by offset. In fact, less than 2% of all futures contracts that are traded actually result in delivery. The remaining contracts are settled long before delivery is even an issue. In settling by offset, a trader simply enters an order to sell a contract he is long or to buy back a contract he is short. The difference in value between the time that the contract was first entered into and its value at liquidation is simply credited to or debited from his account. In the case of a long position that is liquidated by offset, the contract may be sold to a new long. This is analogous to the textile mill manager in Chapter 1 who transferred his contract to the speculator. Otherwise, the contract may be sold to an existing short who is looking to cover his position. This would have been the case in our example had the farmer and the textile mill agreed to cancel the original contract. In either case, the original long is out of his position without having had to take delivery.

This issue provides the basis for a common misunderstanding of futures trading among novice speculators: the mistaken concern that at some point they may receive delivery of 38,000 pounds of frozen pork bellies on the front lawn. Not so. Settlement by offset allows the speculator to participate in futures with no involvement in delivery. It also allows commercial interests to use futures as a temporary non-invasive financial hedge without adding to or drawing down inventory.

The method by which financial settlement is made following offset is described in detail in Chapter 7.

Settlement by Delivery

Those contracts that have not been offset and remain open at the end of the delivery period must be fulfilled by physical delivery. (One exception to this is futures that call for cash settlement, which will be discussed later.)

The precise method by which delivery is made varies from market to market, but a few general comments are in order. Most futures contracts expire in the second half of their delivery month. December corn, for instance, expires about one week before the last day of that month. Two to three weeks before the termination of the contract in question, the delivery period usually begins. It is during the two- to three-week period that most contracts must be settled by delivery. Figures 3-2 and 3-3 on pages 50 to 53 list the last trading days and first notice days (the day on which the delivery process can begin) for major futures markets.

Delivery at the Option of the Seller

It is a feature of all futures markets that, within the parameters of the contract, the time of delivery is at the option of the short. This means

Figure 3-2. *Last trading days for selected futures contracts.*

Chicago Board of Trade

Corn Seven complete business days before the last business day of the month.

Oats Seven complete business days before the last business day of the month.

Soybeans Seven complete business days before the last business day of the month.

Soybean Meal Seven complete business days before the last business day of the month.

Soybean Oil Seven complete business days before the last business day of the month.

T-Bonds Seven complete business days before the last business day of the month.

Wheat Seven complete business days before the last business day of the month.

Chicago Mercantile Exchange

Cattle (live) On the twentieth calendar day of the contract month, or if that is not a business day, on the business day immediately preceding the twentieth calendar day of the contract month. In the event that following the twentieth calendar day of the contract month there remain two or fewer delivery days in the contract month, trading shall terminate two business days preceding the twentieth calendar day.

Hogs (live) On the twentieth calendar day of the contract month, or if the twentieth calendar day is not a business day, on the business day immediately preceding the twentieth calendar day of the contract month. In the event that following the twentieth calendar day of the contract month there remain two or fewer delivery days in the contract month, trading shall terminate two business days preceding the twentieth calendar day.

Pork Bellies On the business day immediately preceding the last five business days of the contract month.

Currencies Two business days before the third Wednesday of the delivery month.

Eurodollars Second London business day before the third Wednesday of the contract month. In the event the third Wednesday of the contract month is a bank holiday in New York City or Chicago, trading shall terminate as of the first London bank business day preceding the third Wednesday of the contract

---

that the short decides *when* during the delivery period he will issue a notice of intention to deliver. Once a delivery notice is received and "stopped" by a long, actual delivery occurs one to two days later. If exchange rules permit, the seller also has some flexibility regarding *what* he will deliver and *where* he will deliver it. Most exchanges allow substitutions of grades that are slightly better or worse than that called for in the par delivery specifications of the contract. This is done to render the contract more flexible to all users and to restrict the possibility of a supply "squeeze" on the specific contract grade. Ex-month. If the termination of trading date that is determined by the preceding two sentences is an Exchange holiday, futures trading shall terminate on the next preceding business day that is common to London banks and the Exchange.

S&P 500 The third Friday of the contract month. If this is not an Exchange business day, then on the preceding business day.

T-bills The business day immediately preceding the first delivery day. Delivery shall be made on three successive business days. The first shall be the first day of the spot month on which a 13-week T-bill is issued and a one-year T-bill has 13 weeks remaining to maturity.

Coffee, Sugar & Cocoa Exchange

Cocoa Ten full business days before the last delivery day, which is the last full business day of the delivery month.

Coffee "C" Seven business days before the last delivery day, which is the last business day of the delivery month.

Sugar #11 The last full business day of the month preceding the delivery month.

Commodity Exchange, Inc.

Copper The third to the last business day of a maturing delivery month.

Gold The third to the last business day of a maturing delivery month.

Silver The third to the last business day of a maturing delivery month.

New York Cotton Exchange

Cotton The tenth business day before the last delivery day of the contract month.

Orange Juice The tenth business day prior to the last business day of the contract month.

New York Mercantile Exchange

Crude Oil The fifth business day before the twenty-fifth calendar day of the month preceding the delivery month.

Heating Oil The last business day of the month preceding the delivery month.

Platinum At the close of business on the fourth business day before the end of the delivery month.

---

changes also provide for multiple delivery points so that delivery can be convenient to more producers, regardless of their business location.

For most commodities, deliveries begin before the last trading day. Anytime on or after the *first notice day*, shorts may notify the exchange clearinghouse through their clearing member firm of their intention to deliver and state the particular grade and location of the product to be delivered. The clearinghouse then allocates delivery notices among the longs as described later. In these commodities all deliveries must be completed by the last trading day.

Figure 3-3. First notice days for selected futures contracts.

Chicago Board of Trade

Corn The last business day of the month preceding the delivery month.
Oats The last business day of the month preceding the delivery month.
Soybeans The last business day of the month preceding the delivery month.
Soybean Meal The last business day of the month preceding the delivery month.
Soybean Oil The last business day of the month preceding the delivery month.
T-Bonds The last business day of the month preceding the delivery month.
Wheat The last business day of the month preceding the delivery month.

Chicago Mercantile Exchange

Cattle (Live) Three business days before the first delivery day of the contract month. Delivery may be made on any day of the contract month.
Hogs (Live) The business day before the first delivery day of the contract month. The first delivery day is the first business day of the contract month. No deliveries on a Friday.
Pork Bellies The business day before the first delivery day of the contract month. Delivery may be made on any business day of the contract month.
Currencies Same as last trading day.
Eurodollars Same as last trading day.
T-Bills Same as last trading day.
S&P 500 Same as last trading day.

Coffee, Sugar & Cocoa Exchange

Cocoa Ten full business days before the first delivery day. Delivery days begin the first business day of the contract month.

In other commodities and financial instruments, the first notice day immediately follows the last trading day. The basic procedures are similar, except that in these markets no new positions or liquidations by offset are permitted during the delivery period.

Delivery notices are of two types: transferable and nontransferable. If a holder of a long position receives a *transferable notice*—even while the contract is still trading, before the end of the delivery month—he or she must accept it. However, all the long has to do is to sell out the long futures position and pass the notice on or "transfer" it to the new buyer. Because the commodity is in the warehouse, certified as to grade and ready for delivery, a time limitation is set on the transfer. Delivery must be made the next day so that anyone who does not wish to accept delivery must sell out the long futures positions within a specified time period (usually a half hour). On the notice itself are lines for the endorsement

---

Coffee "C" Seven business days before the first delivery day. The first day is the first business day of the contract month.

Sugar #11 The first full business day of the delivery month.

Commodity Exchange, Inc.

Copper The second to the last business day of the month before a maturing delivery month.

Gold The second to the last business day of the month before a maturing delivery month.

Silver The second to the last business day of the month before a maturing delivery month.

New York Cotton Exchange

Cotton Five business days before the first trading day of the contract month.

Orange Juice The first business day of the contract month.

New York Mercantile Exchange

Crude Oil* The second business day following the last trading day. This is the same as the third business day preceding the twenty-fifth calendar day of the month before the delivery month.

Heating Oil* The second business day of the delivery month is the only notice day.

Palladium The first business day of the delivery month.

Platinum The first business day of the delivery month.

---

*The last trading day precedes the first notice day.

---

by each long and a box for the time it was received. If the notice remains in the long's hands for more than a half hour or whatever other time is specified, it is considered accepted, or *stopped.* The long must then take delivery.

A *nontransferable notice* is handled differently. The long, upon receiving the notice, can still sell the contract before the last trading day. But the notice cannot be transferred to the buyer immediately. The receiver of the notice, the long, must keep it overnight and absorb one day's carrying charges. However, because he has sold out the long position, he now causes a new notice to be issued and sent to the clearinghouse after the close of the market. In so doing, the long is said to be *retendering* the notice. The following morning, the clearinghouse resumes the procedure. The long has two transactions in his account, one for the futures position and the other for the cash, or actual, position. Most futures contracts call for nontransferable notices.

The Delivery Process

The delivery process begins when the short informs his brokerage firm of his intention to make delivery. If the brokerage firm is a clearing member (see Chapter 7) of the exchange on which the contract is traded, it will handle the delivery procedures directly with the exchange's clearinghouse. If it is not itself a clearing member, it will work through a clearing member firm which will deal directly with the clearinghouse. After verifying that its customer has the available supply, the clearing member firm sends a notice to the clearinghouse of the exchange on which the futures contract trades. Depending on the exchange's system, the clearinghouse then distributes this notice to the holder of an outstanding long position. By one method, the clearinghouse distributes all notices that are received to the clearing member firms with net long positions in proportion to their share of the total outstanding contracts for that particular delivery month. The clearing member firm then distributes the notices that it receives to its customers who are holders of long positions. Until they are depleted, notices are given to the longs with the oldest positions.

A different method, used by some exchanges, involves the polling of member firms to determine the number of long positions that had been established prior to a certain date. The clearinghouse then distributes all the notices that it receives on a given day among the various firms in proportion to the number of such long positions that are held by each firm. In other words, after receiving a certain number of notices in July corn, the Chicago Board of Trade Clearing Corporation might decide that delivery will be made to all holders of the long positions that were established before June 15. It then sends these notices to all clearing member firms that have indicated that they have longs who established positions before that date.

Once a long receives a notice, actual delivery is usually made one to two days later, depending on the exchange and the specific contract. On the delivery day, the long issues payment by certified check to the short and takes delivery of a warehouse receipt that represents the amount and the grade of the commodity in storage at an exchange-approved warehouse. For financial instruments, the long receives documentation that verifies his ownership of the appropriate assets in an exchange-approved bank.

Cash Settlement

A small number of futures markets call for cash settlement rather than actual physical delivery. In these markets, physical delivery of the underlying item is not made. Instead, the long receives the cash value of the commodity or the financial instrument that would have been delivered under ordinary circumstances. The cash value is determined by a precise formula that has been established by the exchange on which the commodity or the financial instrument trades. The subject of cash settlement is discussed further in Chapter 20.

DELIVERY ACCOUNTING

The methods by which deliveries against futures contracts are invoiced and reported on customer statements can be very confusing. One source of this confusion is the expectation that the price at which delivery is taken should be the same price as that of the initial purchase of the futures contract. This would seem to make sense because the purchase of a futures contract entitles the buyer to take delivery at some future date of the underlying commodity at the price that was agreed on when the contract was first struck. How, then, is it possible that the price that the buyer must pay when taking delivery (the invoice price) is something different from that initial price? For example, if a precious-metals dealer buys one contract of June Comex gold on April 1 at $395.00 per ounce, shouldn't he expect to pay $39,500 ($395 per ounce x 100 ounces) if he stands for delivery of this contract?

Not quite. In fact, he will be asked to pay the price that prevails on the day the notice is issued. Well, then, what good was the futures contract? Let's continue with the example to see.

Example:

April 1: A precious-metals dealer buys one contract of June Comex gold at $395.00 with the intention of taking delivery.

June 1: A short issues a delivery notice to the clearinghouse. The current June gold settlement price is $410.30.

June 2: The precious-metals dealer receives a delivery notice and is expected to take delivery of—and make payment for—a warehouse receipt that represents 100 ounces of Comex-approved gold.

June 3: The dealer receives delivery and makes payment of $41,030 ($410.30 per ounce x 100 ounces).

This is what actually happens in practice, but it does not mean that the cost to the dealer was $410.30 instead of $395.00. Realize that the dealer has accrued a profit of $15.30 per ounce in his futures account, which has been marked to the market daily up to the time that the notice was received (see Chapter 7). Thus, although delivery was taken at $410.30, his net price is $395.00 after the $15.30 accrued profit is taken into consideration. This is how his account statements now look:

Futures Account   **Delivery Account**
April 1: Bot 1 June Gold 395.00
June 2: Sold 1 June Gold 410.30   Debit $41,030
Result: Credit $15.30 per ounce x
        100 ounces = $1,530
                   Net Cost = $39,500 ($395 per ounce)

The brokerage firm closes out the dealer's futures position at the invoice price of the delivery notice ($410.30) and properly credits his account with $1,530. It then debits his delivery account for the $41,030 that he will have to pay for the delivery.

Let's take a closer look at the actual bookkeeping involved in the delivery process through the following example, which assumes a non-transferable notice:

Assume that a dealer has established a long position in April gold at $420.00. On Monday, April gold settles at $422.70. On Tuesday morning, which we assume to be the first notice day, the dealer receives a notice of intention to deliver. The invoice price of the notice is $422.70 ($42,270), which is the settlement price of the previous day. On Tuesday, the dealer sells one contract of April gold at $430.00 just before the market drops down to settle at $421.50.

All that has happened here is that the dealer has bought one April gold at $420.00 and sold it at $430.00. One way or another his profit should be $1,000. What muddles the example, however, is that along the way he received a delivery notice. Here's how things work out.

On Tuesday, the clearing member firm receives a delivery notice and immediately informs the clearinghouse of its intention to retender that notice. The actual retendering takes place on Wednesday at an invoice price determined by Tuesday's closing price of $421.50. Summarizing the events, we have the following:

Friday: Dealer buys one April gold at $420.00.

Monday: April gold settles at $422.70.

Tuesday: Dealer receives from clearinghouse a notice of intention to deliver by short at invoice price of $422.70.

Dealer sells one April gold at $430.00 to new buyer.

April gold settles at $421.50.

Dealer instructs the clearinghouse to prepare a notice of intention to deliver at the invoice price of $421.50.

Wednesday: New buyer receives from clearinghouse a delivery notice at invoice price of $421.50.

Dealer receives delivery of gold warehouse receipt and must pay short $42,270.

Thursday: Dealer delivers to new buyer gold warehouse receipt that he received previous day and receives payment of $42,150.

You should note that the settlement period for a gold delivery is one business day from the day that a delivery notice is received by the long. Thus, the dealer receives his delivery notice on Tuesday but does not receive and pay for the actual gold warehouse receipt until Wednesday. This one-day period permits buyers and sellers to prepare their paperwork and to make whatever other arrangements are necessary to effect the delivery. Note also that there is a one-day lag between the time that the dealer notifies the clearinghouse of his intention to make delivery and the time that notice is given to the buyer. This day is needed by the clearinghouse for its paperwork. Finally, note that the invoice price is the settlement price of the day preceding the receipt of the delivery notice by the long, which is two days before actual delivery. This is because that is the most recent settlement price that is available when the clearinghouse is preparing the notices for the longs.

The actual bookkeeping works as follows: On Monday, the brokerage firm puts a sale of one April gold in the dealer's futures account at $422.70 to close out the futures position and debits the dealer's delivery account for $42,270. After issuing the notice the brokerage firm puts a purchase in the dealer's account at $421.50 to offset the sale at $430.00 and credits his delivery account for $42,150, the amount he received from the long who took his delivery. When the dust settles, the bookkeeping is as follows:

Futures Account

Bot 1 April 420.00 (Friday) Sold 1 April 422.70 (Monday)
    Profit = $270
Sold 1 April 430.00 (Tuesday) Bot 1 April 421.50 (Tuesday)
    Profit = $850
Total Profit in Futures Account = $1,120

Delivery Account

Debit $42,270 (Wednesday, after paying for delivery)
Credit $42,150 (Thursday, after receiving payment)
Total Loss in Delivery Account = $120

Net Profit = $1,000

If all this seems a little complicated, it is made so by the need to segregate futures and cash accounts and by the need for same-day settlement in the futures account. Most traders have little reason to be concerned with these details because they are handled capably by the brokerage firms.

OPEN INTEREST AND VOLUME

Now that we have examined the two methods by which futures positions are settled, we will examine the concepts of open interest and volume in more detail. *Open interest* is simply the number of contracts that on any day remain outstanding and await settlement by offset or delivery. To illustrate, we will use the following example that assumes one contract per transaction. Also note that *volume* is the number of purchases or sales that occur on a given day:

	Long	Short
Monday: (first day of trading):		
Transactions: A sells to B.	B	A

Volume: 1
Open Interest: 1

	Long	Short
Tuesday:		
Transactions: C sells to D.	D, E	A, C
B sells to E		
Volume: 2		
Open Interest: 2		

(Notice that B simply transferred his contract to a new long, E, which has no effect on the open interest.)

	Long	Short
Wednesday:		
Transactions: D sells to C.	F	A
E sells to F.		
Volume: 2		
Open Interest: 1		

(Notice that both C and D liquidated their positions, which reduced the open interest by 1, and E transferred his position to F, which has no effect on the open interest.)

Thursday (first delivery day):
 Transaction: A delivers to F.
 Volume: 0
 Open Interest: 0

Figure 3-4 on page 60 summarizes the effect on open interest of each type of transaction.

In reality, open interest and volume for active futures contracts are measured in the thousands of contracts. Also, in real markets, large levels of volume are often associated with relatively small changes in open interest. One reason for this is that many transactions simply involve the transfer of a contract from one participant to another, which has a net zero effect on the open interest. Another, more dominant, reason is that because open interest is measured at the end of a day, it cannot take into account the large volume of transactions that are initiated and liquidated within one trading session. Known as *day trades,* these transactions can account for an extremely large share of a given day's trading volume.

The Importance of Contract Settlement

Whether accomplished by offset or delivery, the orderly settlement of futures positions is an essential element in the health of any futures market. Longs and shorts must feel assured that their purchases and

Figure 3-4.

Transaction	Effect on Open Interest
1. New short sells to new long.	+1
2. New short sells to old short.	0
3. Old long sells to old short.	-1
4. Old long sells to new long.	0

sales are properly matched and that the correct credits and debits are made to their accounts. Persons who are involved in deliveries must have the assurance that deliveries will be made in a fair and orderly way and in keeping with the exact terms of the contract. Any indication to the contrary would undermine traders' faith in a market and set it on the road to extinction.

Equally important is the safeguarding of the system from price manipulation and attempts to corner the supply of deliverable items. All exchanges go to great lengths to monitor traders' positions as the delivery period approaches to ensure that contracts expire on an orderly note. In the long history of futures trading, serious problems have been extremely rare.

PART TWO

THE FUTURES INDUSTRY

■ Chapter 4

■ The Participants

In his classic work *The Wealth of Nations*, published in 1776, Adam Smith introduced the concept of an "invisible hand" that guides a free-market system toward the common good even though each participant in the market is concerned only about his own self-interest. In Adam Smith's words, a participant in a free market system is:

> ...led by this invisible hand to promote an end which was no part of his intention. By pursuing his own interest he frequently promotes that of society more effectually than when he really intends to promote it.

Nowhere are the workings of the invisible hand more apparent than in the futures markets. The many thousands of participants in these markets have a variety of perspectives and motives that underlie their trading. None, however, is personally driven by a desire to enhance economic efficiency or to improve the functioning of the marketplace as a whole. Rather, as Adam Smith suggested, each is motivated by his or her own self-interest, and their interaction yields results that benefit society in ways that are not consciously intended by any of the individual participants.

This chapter covers the major types of participants in the futures markets. We first describe the three important categories of traders and discuss their motives for trading and their roles in the marketplace. We then try to illustrate how this diverse cast of characters interacts to create the remarkable efficiency of the futures markets. We begin with brief definitions of the three major trader categories, which we expand on in the following discussions.

1. *Hedger.* A hedger is a trader who transacts business in the cash markets that underlie a futures contract, and who uses the futures contract to reduce his exposure to price changes.

2. *Floor Trader.* A floor trader is an exchange member who is physically present on the exchange floor and who executes orders in the trading ring.

3. *Speculator.* A speculator is a trader who attempts to profit by correctly anticipating price movements and by trading accordingly.

These categories are not rigidly separate from one another. There are, for example, both hedgers and speculators who operate from the exchange floors. There are also traders who are hedgers in some markets and speculators in others. However, the overwhelming majority of traders fall quite clearly into one specific category. This makes it instructive to discuss each category separately, pointing out instances where the distinctions may be a bit blurred.

HEDGERS

Hedgers are those who use futures and options to reduce exposure to price fluctuations in connection with activities that involve the underlying commodities or financial assets. Both the cash-market presence and the risk-reduction motive must be present for someone to qualify as a hedger. Let us consider several examples:

- *A corn farmer who sells corn futures to protect the value of his crop prior to harvest.* As a corn producer, the farmer is active in the underlying cash market. As an owner of this growing corn, the farmer is vulnerable to a price decline. His sale of corn futures protects against such a decline and therefore reduces the farmer's exposure to price fluctuations.

- *A commercial bank that uses interest rate futures to reduce the maturity mismatch between its assets and its liabilities.* As both a borrower and a lender of funds, the bank is clearly in the interest rate business. Depending on whether its loans have a shorter or a longer average maturity than its deposits, the bank might need either to buy or to sell interest rate futures to reduce its exposure to interest rate fluctuations.

- *A United States importer who buys Deutsche mark futures in connection with a forthcoming payment to his German supplier in the latter's currency.* The importer will be paying for his supplies with Deutsche marks, so if this currency increases in value relative to the U.S. dollar, the importer would have to pay more for his Deutsche marks (and thus for his supplies). Therefore, the purchase of Deutsche mark futures reduces the importer's exposure to currency fluctuations.

The important point to note is that in each case, both criteria for being deemed a hedger are met: a presence in the underlying cash market *and* the use of futures in a manner that reduces risk. If the bank had sold soybean futures, it would not be considered a hedger because it has no involvement in the cash soybean market. If the corn farmer had *bought* corn futures, he would not be a hedger because he would be using futures to *increase* his exposure to price changes. This latter approach, which is essentially the opposite of true hedging, is sometimes called a "Texas Hedge." As the foregoing suggests, it is possible to be a hedger in some transactions and a speculator in others.

Without hedgers there would be no economic justification for futures and options. Hedgers provide actual goods and services to the economy. Futures and options enable them to provide these goods and services more efficiently. Hedging techniques and the benefits to both the hedger and the overall economy will be covered in greater detail in Chapter 10. Let us now discuss in general terms the role that hedgers play in the futures and options markets.

No futures contract can thrive without active participation by hedgers. The reason is that hedgers provide the regular, two-sided order flow that is the lifeblood of a successful contract. The thousands of soybean farmers who are concerned that prices might go down and the various users who fear that prices might go up all have a vested interest in soybean prices. Unlike speculators and floor traders, who enjoy the flexibility of being able to go where the action is, hedgers are much more the captives of their particular markets. Their day-in-and-day-out, year-in-and-year-out attention to price changes generates consistent order flow in successful contracts.

The number of these cash-market participants whose concern about price risk actually leads them to hedge varies with a number of factors. One factor, of course, is the size of the underlying market.

Chief among the other factors are the level of price volatility (i.e., the perceived risk) and the potential hedgers' familiarity with, and access to, the futures and the options markets.

The percent of trading activity that comes from hedgers varies from contract to contract. The data in Figure 4-1 on page 67 is a typical example. The open-interest numbers in this table are taken from the Commodity Futures Trading Commission's "Commitment of Traders" reports, which are published monthly. No comparable statistics exist for trading volume because neither the exchange nor the CFTC requires volume data to be reported.

It is, however, possible to comment in a general sense on hedgers' trading activity. Producers and users often maintain large futures positions, but tend to turn them over infrequently. Referring to our earlier examples, once the corn farmer has sold corn futures and once the importer has bought Deutsche mark futures, they have accomplished their risk-reduction objectives. Barring unexpected changes in their cash-market positions or their anticipated obligations, neither need alter his futures position until closing it out when the related cash-market position is liquidated. Thus, positions such as these often remain unchanged for weeks or months.

Merchants and intermediaries, on the other hand, are often much more active hedgers. Consider our earlier example of the bank—which is, of course, a financial intermediary. As the bank receives new deposits and makes new loans, the mismatch between its asset and liability maturity profiles changes continuously. If the bank chooses to actively manage its futures hedge, it might adjust its futures position daily, hourly, or perhaps even more often as its asset/liability mix varies. The same would be true of intermediaries in other markets—for example, grain merchants who constantly buy from farmers and sell to end users.

Two facts follow from the different perspectives of producers and users on the one hand and of intermediaries on the other. First, producers and users tend to think in terms of, and hedge against, fairly large price changes. A gold producer who mines 100,000 ounces a year is concerned about price changes of $30 or $50 or more per ounce in the value of his output, not about the 50¢ or $1.00 fluctuations that occur constantly. However, the metals merchant who turns over huge inventories for profit margins of 10¢ or 20¢ per ounce must be very attuned to these fluctuations. Second, the more active trading requirements of intermediaries leads them, as a group, to become more involved in the affairs of futures exchanges. They, much more often than producers and

Figure 4-1. Japanese yen—International monetary market commitments of traders in all futures combined and indicated futures, June 30, 1987.

(Contracts of 12,500,000 Japanese Yen)

	Total	Reportable Positions								Nonreportable Positions	
		Noncommercial				Commercial		Total			
	Open Interest	Long or Short Only		Long and Short (Spreading)							
		Long	Short	Long	Short	Long	Short	Long	Short	Long	Short
All	27,969	4,612	5,846	366	366	11,919	5,697	16,897	11,909	11,072	16,060
Old	27,912	4,612	5,846	366	366	11,919	5,697	16,897	11,909	11,015	16,003
Other	57	0	0	0	0	0	0	0	0	57	57

Changes in Commitments from May 29, 1987

		Long	Short	Long	Short	Long	Short	Long	Short	Long	Short
All	-23,712	-11,336	109	-117	-117	-13,931	-20,116	-25,384	-20,124	1,672	-3,588

Percent of Open Interest Represented by Each Category of Traders

		Long	Short	Long	Short	Long	Short	Long	Short	Long	Short
All	100.0%	16.5	20.9	1.3	1.3	42.6	20.4	60.4	42.6	39.6	57.4
Old	100.0%	16.5	20.9	1.3	1.3	42.7	20.4	60.5	42.7	39.5	57.3
Other	100.0%	0.0	0.0	0.0	0.0	0.0	0.0	0.0	0.0	100.0	100.0

Number of Traders in Each Category

	Number of Traders	Long	Short	Long	Short	Long	Short	Long	Short
All	44	7	13	2	2	17	11	25	25
Old	44	7	13	2	2	17	11	25	25
Other	0	0	0	0	0	0	0	0	0

Concentration Ratios
Percent of Open Interest Held by the Indicated Number of Largest Traders

	By Gross Position				By Net Position			
	4 or Less Traders		8 or Less Traders		4 or Less Traders		8 or Less Traders	
	Long	Short	Long	Short	Long	Short	Long	Short
All	21.1	19.3	35.3	28.5	20.3	19.2	33.5	28.4
Old	21.2	19.3	35.3	28.6	20.4	19.2	33.5	28.5
Other	0.0	0.0	0.0	0.0	0.0	0.0	0.0	0.0

end users, become exchange and clearing members (see Chapters 5 and 7), establish a presence on the trading floor and seek representation on exchange committees.

FLOOR TRADERS

Floor traders are those exchange members who are physically present on an exchange floor and who themselves execute contracts in a trading ring. The business that is executed by a floor trader may be either for his own account or for the account of someone else. A floor trader who is trading for his own account is generally known as a *local*. One who is executing transactions on behalf of others is known as a *floor broker*.

Locals can employ any trading approach they like. However, successful locals are usually those who use their physical presence in the trading ring to maximum advantage by providing short-term liquidity to the marketplace. They serve as *market-makers* to the off-floor hedgers and speculators, who are *market-takers*. In other words, locals generally take the opposite side of orders that come from off the trading floor.

A logical question to ask is why this approach makes sense. After all, a large percent of off-floor orders come from hedgers who are usually well versed in the economics of the underlying market or from sophisticated speculators who have a variety of powerful analytic tools at their disposal. The answer is that locals are not in competition with hedgers and speculators. Locals are not in the business of predicting whether prices are going up or down. Rather they profit by having the bid/offer spread work in their favor rather than against them. This favorable bid/offer situation can be considered the compensation that locals receive for providing liquidity. We now examine in a little more detail how it works.

A key point to understand is that there is never a single price for a futures contract (or anything else for that matter). Instead, there is always a two-sided market. The lower price (or *bid*) is the highest price that someone stands ready to pay, while the higher price (or *offer*) is the lowest price at which someone is prepared to sell. The difference between these two prices is called the *bid/offer spread*. If, for example, the highest bid for August crude-oil futures in the trading ring is $15.45 and the lowest offer is $15.47, then the bid/offer spread is $0.02. A trader who is able to buy at the bid price and sell at the offer price will profit even if the price level never changes. Locals are uniquely well positioned to do this because of their position at the focal point of order flow. Let us discuss two reasons why.

Suppose, for example, that a local in the crude-oil ring hears five or six other floor traders bidding $15.44. If he knows that these particular traders often represent futures commission merchants (FCMs), the local will very likely be willing to bid $15.45. Why? Because he will reason that if the price level declines, he will be able to quickly liquidate his position at a minor loss by selling to one of the $15.44 bids. The fact that the bids seem to be on behalf of off-floor customers is important not because they know more or less than the local about the likely course of oil prices, but rather because these customers are at a communications disadvantage that does not permit them to cancel their orders instantaneously if the market's tone changes.

Now consider another situation. Suppose that August crude oil has traded at $15.46 several times in the past few minutes and that there has been no news or activity of note. If a floor broker asks the trading ring for bids, the local might well bid $15.45, reasoning that because nothing appears to have changed since the previous several trades, he likely has a 1¢ cushion in this long position. Furthermore, he will reason that if nothing has changed, the next order that arrives on the floor is as likely to be a buy order as a sell order. If it is a buy order, it might then provide the opportunity for the local to offer at $15.47 and thus liquidate his position at a 2¢ profit.

Locals are able to employ these techniques because their location on the trading floor enables them to act instantaneously. They encounter no delays due to telephones, telexes, or the need to relay their orders through one or more clerks. In this regard, two points deserve mention.

First, a local who bids $15.45, reasoning that nothing has changed since the previous trade at $15.46, is not always correct. In fact, there are times when something important *has* changed and the price level moves dramatically before the local can liquidate his position. The local's hope is that favorable and unfavorable price changes will roughly balance out, leaving a portion of the favorable bid/offer spread as an average profit. However, there is absolutely no guarantee that this will happen. Successful locals are those who develop a sixth sense that tells them whether they are seeing random order flow or an authentic change in market sentiment.

Second, off-floor traders often regard it as unfair that locals enjoy the advantages that are described above. What they tend to overlook is the price of those advantages—namely, the $50,000 to $400,000 cost of an exchange membership; the need to spend five or six hours a day on one's feet in a crowded, noisy trading pit; and the usual absence of sources of income other than their futures trading profits.

Locals who trade in the manner that we have described seldom hold positions for more than a minute or two and often only for a matter of seconds. They rarely, if ever, carry outright positions overnight. Their objective is to earn small trading profits by taking advantage of momentary imbalances between buy and sell orders.

In the process of utilizing their location advantage, locals perform the essential function of providing short-term liquidity to the market as a whole. To understand better what this means, consider the following example:

> *Example*: A gold producer has decided that he would like to sell 5,000 ounces (50 futures contracts). He is more concerned with executing the transaction quickly than with squeezing the last few cents from the market, and therefore he is willing to offer December futures at $345.00 even though they just traded at $345.40. If there were no locals, the floor broker who was handling this producer's order would have to wait until an exactly opposing order arrived on the floor from either a gold consumer or a bullish speculator. It could easily take hours or even days before this happened.
>
> Having locals in the picture makes the process vastly more efficient. Among the dozens of locals who compete for business in the gold ring, at least one would reason along the lines that are described above and pay $345.00 for the December futures. He would then offset his exposure by offering to sell either December itself or any other month in which there was buying interest. The ability to sell any delivery month and to instantaneously lower the price at which he or she is willing to sell gives the local much more flexibility in offsetting his or her 50-contract exposure than the producer's broker had in attempting to execute the original order.

In the scenario described above, both parties benefit. The producer sacrifices a very small amount in price to free himself from having to either wait for or seek out a counterparty for his trade. The local takes on this responsibility, which he or she is far better positioned to implement, in return for the small price concession. In other words, the local has provided short-term liquidity and has been compensated for this service by the opportunity to buy at the bid side of the market.

Now let us turn to floor brokers. Floor brokers are exchange members who, like locals, are physically present in the trading ring. However, unlike locals, they are executing transactions on behalf of others rather than for their own accounts. A floor broker's income comes from brokerage fees rather than trading profits and is directly related to the volume of business he or she executes. These fees are negotiable, but they typically range from $1.00 to $3.00 per contract, depending on the particular futures contract and the nature of a customer's order flow.

The law of supply and demand plays an important role in determining floor-brokerage rates. Some futures trading rings have too few floor brokers to handle the volume of off-floor business, while other rings have a surplus of brokers and not enough order flow. Quite naturally, rates tend to be higher in the former case. Like other businessmen, floor brokers value regular customers and, therefore, often charge lower rates to customers who provide regular order flow day after day.

Floor brokerage is an invisible cost for many futures traders. Floor brokers typically bill FCMs rather than individual customers, and the FCMs usually include floor-brokerage fees in their overall commission rates without specific breakdown. Some large hedgers negotiate floor brokerage directly because their trading volume is so large.

Floor brokers perform the obvious function of enabling nonmembers and off-floor members to trade futures. Because the rules of every futures exchange permit trades to be executed only by members in the trading area, floor brokers are the link to all other sources of futures transactions.

For the sake of clarity, we discussed locals and floor brokers separately. In reality, the categories often overlap. Every futures exchange permits floor traders both to execute orders for others and to trade for their own accounts—that is, to simultaneously act as floor broker and local. This is known as *dual trading* and has been a source of debate within the futures industry on two very different fronts.

Regulators have for years viewed dual trading with some concern. The fear is that floor brokers who also trade for their own accounts are in a position to use their knowledge of customer orders to their own personal advantage at the expense of their customers. The floor-community view is that there are sufficient safeguards to prevent abuses and that the prohibition of dual trading would adversely affect liquidity with no offsetting benefits.

On a very different front, floor traders disagree among themselves on the question of whether dual trading increases or decreases their own personal incomes. Some argue that having two sources of revenue is obviously beneficial. Others take the jack-of-all-trades-master-of-none view and reason that trying to play two very different roles simultaneously results in neither role being played very well, to the detriment of the trader's personal revenue stream.

SPECULATORS

Speculators are those who have no involvement in the underlying cash markets, but who trade futures and hope to profit by correctly anticipating price changes. Unlike hedgers, speculators hope to benefit by *increasing* their exposure to price fluctuations. Unlike floor traders, speculators expect their profits to come from changes in price level rather than from the bid/offer spread or random short-term price vibrations. Their objective is to buy low and sell high. A small number of speculators operate from exchange floors, but the vast majority are nonmember customers of futures brokerage firms. Before we explain why speculators are attracted to futures and options, we briefly discuss why people speculate.

There are two basic reasons to speculate: profit opportunity and enjoyment. Every speculator will admit to the first motive, but the second is often more important. Some people enjoy taking risks, and speculation is risky by definition. The excitement of assuming a well-reasoned risk in the hope of making a large profit can be a powerful lure.

This combination of motives raises the question of whether speculation differs from gambling. Those who don't like speculation often say no. Those who do like it generally claim that gambling involves the creation of risk for risk's sake, while speculation is a mechanism for allocating risks that already exist. For example, nobody has to make or lose money depending on whether or not the dice total seven. The whole world could simply choose not to play. However, somebody must make or lose money, depending on whether cotton prices rise or

fall. The only issue is whether the risk will be borne by the cotton farmer and the textile mill (neither of whom probably welcomes the risk) or
by one or more speculators who do welcome it.

Is this a meaningful distinction or an exercise in splitting hairs?
The answer is both. The psychological motives of futures speculators
do not differ meaningfully from those of gamblers. However, futures
speculation really does reallocate risk from those who do not want it to
those who do. In other words, futures speculation directs appetites for
risk taking into an economically productive channel.

Futures trading holds considerable appeal for someone who is interested in the combination of excitement and the possibility of large,
quick profits. Let us consider a few of the reasons why speculators are
attracted to the futures markets.

- Futures trading offers unusual profit opportunities. The margining
  system that is used in the futures business creates considerable leverage, as we discussed in Chapter 2. This leverage means that it is
  possible to make or lose a large percentage of one's trading capital
  very quickly. It is not particularly unusual for, say, a $25,000 fu-
  tures account to become either $5,000 or $125,000 within a few
  months.

- Futures trading is easy. All that it takes is a telephone call to your
  account executive and within minutes your order can be executed
  on any of the eleven United States futures exchanges, or on various exchanges in other countries. There are thousands of broker-
  age-house branch offices and tens of thousands of account executives who are anxious to be of assistance to futures traders.

- Futures trading is stimulating. It offers both the excitement of making and losing money and the challenge of attempting to analyze and to outsmart the markets.

- Futures markets are interesting and informative. One of the first
  things that futures speculators discover is that very little can happen in the world that does not affect futures prices. So speculators
  start trading futures to make money and often find themselves paying a lot closer attention to developments that affect foreign exchange rates, oil prices, agricultural trade patterns, and so forth.
  Adam Smith's invisible hand takes speculators who are simply trying to make money and makes them more knowledgeable about the
  world in which they live.

Now consider how speculators benefit the futures markets and the overall economy. As we discussed in Chapter 1, futures markets are basically risk-transfer mechanisms that redistribute price risk away from those who are risk-averse to those who welcome risk. Speculators are the participants who welcome risk—without them, there would be no one to whom hedgers could shift their risks—and, as we have seen, these risks cannot be made to disappear. The only issue is who should bear them, and speculators are the volunteers.

In addition to being the only willing bearers of price risk, speculators are also an important source of liquidity. The regular flow of speculative orders into a trading ring combines with the flow of hedging orders to reduce greatly the average time between the arrival of offsetting buy and sell orders, compared with what it would be with hedging orders alone. This makes the locals who provide short-term liquidity more willing to bid and to offer aggressively because the shorter average time period that the locals must hold their positions reduces their risk. Without speculative order flow, locals would be more cautious and liquidity would suffer significantly.

An Illustration. We now present a hypothetical but realistic example of the roles that these various types of participants might play in a sequence of related futures transactions. Let us assume the following cast of characters:

Hedger A: A gold producer who wants to hedge her expected December production at the current $410.00 level of December futures.

Hedger B: A jewelry manufacturer who wants to hedge his expected December gold requirements at the current price.

Speculator C: An off-floor trader who is bullish on gold.

Speculator D: An off-floor trader who is bearish on gold.

Floor Broker A: A floor broker who executes gold futures business for the brokerage firm at which Hedger *A* maintains her futures account.

Floor Broker B: A floor broker who executes gold futures business for the brokerage firm at which Hedger *B* maintains his futures account.

Floor Broker C: A floor broker who executes gold futures business for the brokerage firm at which Speculator *C* maintains his futures account.

Floor Broker D: A floor broker who executes gold futures business for the brokerage firm at which Speculator *D* maintains his futures account.

Local E: A local in the gold ring.

The chronological sequence below illustrates how these various players make it possible for the gold producer and the jeweler to transfer their unwanted price risks. Assume that as we begin, December futures are trading at $410.00 and that October futures are trading at $405.00.

10:00 A.M. The producer, Hedger *A*, gives her brokerage firm an order to sell 10 contracts (1,000 ounces) of December futures at the current market price. Floor Broker *A* executes this order by selling 10 December gold to Local *E* at Local *E*'s bid of $409.80, which is the highest bid in the ring.

10:02 A.M. Speculator *C* decides that gold prices are going higher. He gives his brokerage firm an order to buy 10 contracts of October gold at $405.00 or better. The overall price level has not changed, so Local *E* is willing to sell 10 October gold at $405.00 to Floor Broker *C*, who is acting on behalf of Speculator *C*. This leaves Local *E* short 10 October gold and long 10 December gold at a difference of $4.80. The requirements of Hedger *A* and Speculator *C* have both been satisfied.

11:00 A.M. Gold prices have fallen. October futures are now trading at $403.00, December futures at $408.00.

11:03 A.M. Speculator *D* decides that gold prices are going still lower. He gives his broker an order to sell 10 October futures at the market. This order is executed by Floor Broker *D*, who sells these 10 contracts to Local *E* at $402.90.

11:05 A.M. Hedger *B* gives his broker an order to buy 10 contracts of December gold at the market. Floor Broker *B* executes this order. Local *E* is again on the opposite side, selling the contracts at $408.00.

Now we recap the net result of this sequence of transactions for each of these participants.

Transaction	Net Result
Hedger A sold 10 December futures at $409.80.	Short 10 December futures at $409.80.
Hedger B bought 10 December futures at $408.00.	Long 10 December futures at $408.00.
Speculator C bought 10 October futures at $405.00.	Long 10 October futures at $405.00.
Speculator D sold 10 October futures at $402.90.	Short 10 October futures at $402.90.
Floor Brokers A, B, C, D bought or sold 10 futures contracts each on behalf of their customers.	Each has no market position; each will receive his floor brokerage fee for a 10-contract transaction.
Local E bought 10 December futures at $409.80; sold 10 October futures at $405.00; bought 10 October futures at $402.90; sold 10 December futures at $408.00.	Profit of $2.10 on 10 October futures. Loss of $1.80 on 10 December futures. Net profit of 30¢ on 10 contracts ($300).

The following points are important in this sequence:

- The two hedgers were both able to execute their opposing trades even though their orders were separated by more than an hour and the price moved roughly $2.00 during this interval.

- Had the speculators been absent, the local would have had to carry his position for more than an hour rather than for only two minutes. He would have lost $1.80 per ounce on 10 December contracts ($1,800).

- Had the local been absent, the entire sequence could not have taken place. Speculator *C*'s 10:02 A.M. buy order was for a different month than Hedger *A*'s sell order. Thus, each of these traders would have had to be willing to wait about an hour for their orders to be executed. This would likely stretch their patience too far.

- Had the floor brokers been absent, no trades could have taken place because there would have been nobody in the trading ring to execute the off-floor orders.

Real-life transaction flow tends to be vastly more complex, but this example realistically portrays both the roles played by each type of participant and the relationships and the dependencies among the various participants. Hedgers, speculators, floor brokers, and locals all contribute importantly to the smooth functioning of the futures markets. Without any one of these groups, the markets would be significantly less efficient.

■ Chapter 5

■ *Futures Exchanges*

Futures exchanges are private membership organizations whose purpose is to facilitate the trading of futures contracts. Exchanges provide the organizational framework and the physical facilities that make possible the efficient execution and processing of futures transactions. Futures exchanges exist for two basic and related reasons. One, they perform a variety of important and beneficial economic functions. Two, they enable people to make money.

The economic benefits of futures derive from the intensely competitive environment that successful futures exchanges create. The trading ring of an active futures contract contains dozens of locals who buy and sell for their own accounts, and dozens of brokers who collectively represent thousands of buyers and sellers from all over the world. The participants and their motives were discussed in detail in Chapter 4. However, to understand the economic function that is performed by futures markets, it is necessary only to recognize that competition among so many buyers and sellers enables buyers to buy readily at the lowest available offering price and enables sellers to sell readily at the highest available bidding price.

What this means is that futures exchanges are the purest examples of free, competitive markets. Someone who believes that the future prices of sugar or corn or United States Treasury bonds should be higher or lower than they are can translate his beliefs into action with a simple phone call to his broker. He will be able within seconds to buy or sell large quantities at the most favorable prices available among numerous competing buyers and sellers. Compare this with the situation that is faced by someone who believes that prices should be different for sofa beds or thoroughbred horses or real estate.

BENEFITS OF FUTURES EXCHANGES

Futures exchanges provide four specific benefits to the economy as a whole: risk shifting, price discovery, enhanced liquidity and efficiency, and increased information flow. Let us now discuss each of these in turn.

Risk Shifting

As we saw in Chapter 1, risk shifting was the main reason for the development of futures contracts and exchanges. Futures markets enable price risk to be shifted readily from those who do not want it to those who do. Typically, hedgers use futures to reduce their exposure to price fluctuations, whereas speculators seek out such exposure in the hope of profiting from the accurate anticipation of these fluctuations. For now, the important point is simply that one person's unwanted risk is another person's attractive opportunity. Futures markets facilitate the matching of risk levels with risk preferences.

An important point is that price risk is a fact of life. It exists whether or not one likes it. The only real questions are who should bear the risk and how should it be apportioned. Futures exchanges do a remarkable job of shifting risk to those who welcome it.

Price Discovery

Futures prices are the market's consensus of what the price of the underlying item will be when the futures contract matures. The market includes the thousands of participants who have bought, sold, or done nothing, depending on whether they think prices are too low, too high, or about right. Some people might argue that there are always quite a few thoughtful and well-researched price forecasts for almost any item of interest and that a consensus of these should be more meaningful than a futures price that is influenced in part by floor traders and speculators who may know little or nothing about the actual product that underlies the futures contract. The crucial difference is that every contributor to the consensus that is the futures price has backed his or her view with cash. This suggests a sincerity of belief that need not accompany more theoretical forecasts and analyses. Furthermore, if those who are uninformed move prices away from where they ought to be, those who are well informed can enter the market, remedy the discrepancy, and earn a profit in the process.

The fact that futures prices fluctuate constantly also troubles some people. However, the fluctuations simply reflect the continually changing consensus as various participants receive, analyze, and act on new information. Price fluctuations in fact reflect the remarkable responsiveness of futures markets to this continuous information flow.

Liquidity and Efficiency

Futures exchanges are home to the world's most liquid and efficient markets. A good measure of liquidity is the price difference, or spread, between what one must pay to buy something and what one can receive for selling it. In the most successful futures markets, the bid/offer spread for large quantities is frequently one-tenth of 1% (0.001) or less of the price of the underlying item. This means, for example, that it is often possible either to buy $1 million or more of gold at $430.00 per ounce or to sell it at $429.70. Compare this with the difference between the purchase and the resale prices for automobiles, clothes, listed stocks, or anything else that is traded somewhere other than on a futures exchange.

Efficiency tends to go hand in hand with liquidity and can be measured by the speed and ease with which a transaction can be effected. Futures exchanges are marvels of accessibility. Anyone with a futures brokerage account and a telephone needs no more than a few minutes to obtain current prices, enter an order, and receive a confirmation. This greatly benefits the economy as a whole because it frees producers, consumers, and merchants from having to spend time searching out prices, buyers, and sellers, thus enabling them to concentrate on their basic businesses.

Market Information

An ancillary benefit of futures exchanges is improved information flow. Because exchanges and their members want as much trading activity as possible (because this means more commissions and fees), they work very hard at inducing people to trade. One effective way to do this is to generate and to disperse much information. The more people and institutions know about the Swiss franc, the more likely they will be able to develop an opinion about whether the franc is over- or underpriced. Intense competition among brokers and exchanges ensures an abundance of widely available information on any item that is actively traded on a futures exchange.

We have described several important economic functions that futures exchanges perform. It is important to emphasize one thing that they do *not* do. Futures exchanges *do not* determine the prices of items that trade on their floors. The exchanges merely provide arenas in which market forces can come together to determine prices more efficiently than would be possible in the absence of a central trading facility.

This point is important and often misunderstood. Futures exchanges are sometimes blamed by consumers when prices are too high and by producers when prices are too low. This is a bit like a sports fan who blames Madison Square Garden when his team loses a game that is played there. The point bears repeating: Futures exchanges provide the framework within which market forces can efficiently determine prices.

Futures exchanges are generally organized as corporations that are owned by their members.* Although profitability is not a goal of the exchanges themselves, providing opportunities for members to profit by trading or by executing orders for others is the primary objective of a futures exchange. It is because of the profit opportunities that membership offers that futures exchanges are formed and that individuals and organizations are willing to pay for membership privileges.

RESPONSIBILITIES OF FUTURES EXCHANGES

What, though, do futures exchanges actually do to achieve their twin objectives of the creation of efficient arenas for free market forces and the provision of profit opportunities for members? Among its key responsibilities, a futures exchange must provide the following facilities and services:

- *An adequate physical location for the trading areas in which members execute transactions.* This may sound mundane, but in fact it is extremely important. Even the best-designed futures contract is unlikely to succeed if the physical facility in which it trades is too

---

*The one exception in the United States is the New York Futures Exchange, which is owned by the New York Stock Exchange.

small, is geographically inaccessible to members and their employees, or has acoustical defects that prevent the "open-outcry" trading method from working in practice. As futures trading activity has grown, finding appropriate physical facilities has become a vexing problem for many exchanges. Increasing trading volume requires larger open space for members, their employees, and the exchange staff. High ceilings are needed to permit the proper display of prices and other trading information. The difficulty of finding appropriate physical facilities prompted both the Chicago Board of Trade and the Chicago Mercantile Exchange to construct their own trading floors in buildings in which they hold equity interests. Both Chicago exchanges took occupancy of their buildings in 1983.

The need for an adequate trading facility was a major impetus behind the construction of the Commodity Exchange Center (CEC) in New York. The trading floor, which opened in 1977, currently houses the Commodity Exchange, Inc. (Comex); New York Mercantile Exchange; Coffee, Sugar & Cocoa Exchange; and New York Cotton Exchange.

- *Communications capabilities between the exchange floor and the outside world.* Each exchange must provide the communications infrastructure that connects the trading floor with the rest of the world. Members in the trading areas must be able to efficiently receive buy-and-sell orders from their colleagues and customers and to report back prices, trading volume, and other information that pertains to transactions on the exchange floor. This requires an extensive and intricate network of telephone, telex, and other communications equipment. For example, the Chicago Mercantile Exchange has more than 11,000 miles of telephone wiring and the capacity to install more than 140,000 telephones on its 40,000-square-foot trading floor.

- *Procedures that ensure the swift and accurate processing of transactions that take place on the trading floor.* Successful futures contracts enjoy daily trading volumes of 25,000 to 50,000 or more contracts per day, with individual floor traders often participating in dozens, or even hundreds, of trades daily. At the end of each trading session, reconciliations must be performed to ensure that everyone agrees as to who bought what from whom at what prices. This is a tremendously complex operational challenge that occupies a major portion of a futures exchange's day-to-day attention.

- *Effective margining and clearing systems to guarantee the financial integrity of the exchange's contracts.* Members and nonmember customers must have confidence that any profits that are earned on futures positions will in fact be forthcoming. The ensurance of such confidence is one of the most vital responsibilities of an exchange and is discussed in some detail in Chapter 7.

- *Rules and regulations that meet the requirements of regulatory authorities and that ensure the fair treatment of all market participants.* A futures exchange must have rules that govern a broad array of issues. For example: What are the membership eligibility requirements? How are customer complaints in regard to order executions resolved? What financial resources must floor brokers maintain? The rulebooks of most futures exchanges are hundreds of pages long and are constantly revised to keep abreast of changing market conditions and regulatory requirements.

- *Viable futures contracts.* In Chapter 1, we described how futures exchanges evolved to facilitate the trading of futures contracts. In the modern world, however, the relationship between exchanges and contracts is more complex. Futures contracts need exchanges on which to trade, but exchanges also need successful futures contracts. An exchange cannot thrive without futures contracts that are broadly and actively traded. This means that, as times change, new contracts must be created and introduced, and obsolete contracts must be phased out. Two interesting examples of this process follow:

  Example 1: In 1974, 77% of the trading volume on the New York Mercantile Exchange (NYMEX) was in potatoes. In 1986, 87% of this exchange's volume was in energy-related products.

  Example 2: In 1974, financial futures volume on the International Monetary Market (IMM) accounted for 4% of the overall volume on the parent Chicago Mercantile Exchange (CME). By 1986, the financial contracts on the IMM and Index and Options Market (IOM) subsidiaries had overwhelmed the more traditional agricultural contracts and accounted for 85% of the overall volume on the CME.

STRUCTURE OF FUTURES EXCHANGES

As mentioned earlier, most futures exchanges are structured as corporations that are owned by their members. Management of a futures exchange is a task that is shared by the members and a paid full-time staff. Ultimate responsibility for the management of an exchange rests with the exchange's board of directors. The board is elected by exchange members and is composed of exchange members plus, in most cases, a few outside directors who lend balance and special expertise. Exchange rules, regulations, and policies are set by the board and are implemented by a network of committees that consist of exchange members. These committees are assisted by the exchange's staff. Exchange members who serve on committees receive no compensation, but they serve to further the interests of the exchange.

Every futures exchange has a unique structure. For the purpose of understanding in general terms how an exchange works, however, the similarities are far more important than the differences. We will describe the organizational and administrative structure of the Commodity Exchange, Inc. (Comex), as a typical example.

The Comex Board of Governors numbers 25. The exchange membership is divided into four categories: trade or commercial, exchange floor, commission house, and public. Each of the first three groups is allotted seven seats on the board. Three of the remaining seats are reserved for nonmember public governors. The final seat is that of the Chairman.

The exchange's Board of Governors authorized 13 regular committees for 1987. Among the most important of these are the following:

Committee on Admissions. The Committee on Admissions reviews all applications for membership and interviews all applicants. Its purpose is to determine whether an applicant meets the exchange's financial requirements and has the requisite qualifications that relate to character, integrity, and so forth. The admissions committee's recommendations are presented to the Board of Governors, which then votes to admit or reject the applicant.

Arbitration Committee. The Arbitration Committee appoints panels to resolve disputes that involve claims that are made by one member or member firm against another or by nonmember customers against members or member firms. If, for example, member *A* believes that member *B* delivered against a futures contract gold that failed to meet the required specifications, then member *A* could take this grievance to a panel appointed by the Arbitration Committee. Similarly, if a customer of Comex member firm *XYZ* felt that his gold futures order had been executed improperly, the Arbitration Committee would provide the correct exchange forum in which to present his argument.

Committee on Business Conduct. The Committee on Business Conduct functions as a "grand jury" in connection with the exchange's internal disciplinary proceedings. If the exchange staff believes that there may have been a violation of the exchange's rules or bylaws by a member or member firm, it may bring the matter to the attention of the business conduct committee. The committee then decides whether there is a reasonable basis for the belief that a violation has occurred. If so, the committee will direct the exchange staff to issue a complaint to the member or member firm, and it will refer the matter to the Supervisory Committee (discussed later) for resolution. If, for example, a floor broker is suspected of improperly handling a customer order, the case would first be investigated by the exchange staff and then brought before the Committee on Business Conduct.

Control Committee. The Control Committee is responsible for the monitoring of trade activity, open interest, the expiration of maturing futures contracts, and all other activities in exchange markets. This committee is charged with, among other things, the recognition of undue concentrations of positions and the prevention of squeezes and market manipulation. If an unusually large number of contracts remain open in a contract that is nearing maturity, the Control Committee will investigate to ensure that the shorts and the longs are either prepared to make and to take delivery or planning to liquidate their positions in an orderly manner.

New Products Committee. It is the responsibility of the New Products Committee to study potential new futures contracts that might be introduced on the exchange. The New Products Committee works with the exchange staff to evaluate the potential success of new contracts. It also supervises the preparation of economic-justification studies and other materials that must be submitted to the Commodity Futures Trading Commission before permission can be received to introduce a new contract.

Supervisory Committee. The Supervisory Committee adjudicates any disciplinary matters with respect to which the Committee on Business Conduct (discussed above) has directed that a complaint be issued. The Supervisory Committee functions as judge and jury with respect to charges of violations of the exchange's rules and bylaws. The committee hears evidence from both the exchange's staff and the involved member or member firm, decides whether a violation has occurred, and if so imposes the appropriate sanction.

Floor Committee. The Floor Committee oversees the activities of traders and floor brokers on the trading floor. This committee has the authority to discipline floor members for rule violations that relate to conduct on the exchange floor. For example, a floor trader who makes frivolous bids or offers in the ring could be fined on the spot by a Floor Committee member. Comex Floor Committee members are empowered to impose fines of up to $1,000 per offense on their own authority. The amounts and procedures vary at other exchanges.

These and other committees constitute the framework by which members manage the affairs of their exchange. However, as we mentioned earlier, members receive no compensation for service on committees and naturally cannot devote their full time to such service. Rather, the board and the various committees are assisted by a paid, full-time staff that is largely responsible for running the exchange on a day-to-day basis.

One point that should be emphasized is that exchange-staff personnel are not members of the exchange. Therefore, they do not have trading privileges and do not vote on the issues that come before the various committees and the board. However, members generally give a great deal of weight to the views and the advice of staff personnel. This is logical because the staff is chosen by the members and devotes its full time and energy to furthering the interests of the exchange.

FUTURES EXCHANGE MEMBERSHIP

Membership on United States futures exchanges is available only to individuals. Each exchange has a fixed number of memberships that are available, though the number is occasionally adjusted by the exchange's board. Once all authorized memberships have been sold, prospective new members must purchase a membership from a current member. Every United States exchange maintains a "secondary market" for such memberships, with current bid and offered prices readily available from the exchange. The recent price history of U.S. futures exchange memberships is summarized in Figure 5-1.

Figure 5-1. U.S. futures exchange membership prices.

Exchange	1986 High	1986 Low	1986 Last Sale	1985 High	1985 Low	1984 High	1984 Low	1983 High	1983 Low	1982 High	1982 Low
Chicago Board of Trade	340,000	200,500	315,000	265,000	180,000	325,000	228,000	340,000	200,000	255,000	161,000
Associate Membership	145,000	68,000	126,000	86,500	69,900	92,100	71,000	90,000	66,000	145,000	62,000
Chicago Mercantile Exchange	260,000	149,000	230,000	185,000	155,500	255,000	152,000	255,000	191,000	285,000	242,000
(IMM)	233,000	144,000	209,000	166,500	134,000	195,000	115,000	195,000	145,000	246,000	165,000
(IOM)	122,000	54,500	120,000	62,000	46,500	70,000	38,000	67,000	42,500	—	—
CME Membership Rights	—	—	—	60,000	32,000	60,000	32,000	60,000	50,500	79,000	50,000
IMM Membership Rights	—	—	—	50,000	26,000	50,000	26,000	46,000	37,000	65,000	44,500
Chicago Rice & Cotton Exchange											
Coffee, Sugar & Cocoa Exchange	60,000	38,000	45,000	54,000	32,500	64,000	33,500	80,000	62,000	70,000	51,300
Commodity Exchange	126,000	64,000	86,000	119,000	60,000	200,000	95,000	185,000	140,000	151,000	63,000
Kansas City Board of Trade	59,689	47,500	49,500	52,000	47,500	57,500	49,500	70,000	46,000	69,000	48,000
Class (B)	33,000	21,000	21,000	30,000	27,000	27,000	22,000	27,500	20,000	20,000	20,000
MidAmerica Commodity Exchange	8,000	2,100	68,000	9,500	4,000	13,200	5,600	17,000	8,500	16,300	9,500
Minneapolis Grain Exchange	9,000	3,500	9,000	5,000	2,500	9,600	4,700	10,000	5,125	13,000	6,000
N.Y. Cotton Exchange	35,000	26,000	35,000	55,000	21,000	40,000	23,000	44,000	27,000	40,000	25,000
Citrus Associates	—	—	—	500	250	700	700	700	700	700	700
N.Y. Futures Exchange	3,000	200	300	10,000	600	15,000	5,500	37,000	11,500	38,000	6,000
N.Y. Mercantile Exchange	165,000	63,000	138,500	80,000	53,500	85,000	57,000	75,000	35,000	40,000	22,000
Philadelphia Board of Trade	2,000	1,000	2,000	500	500	—	—	—	—	—	—

Source: Futures Industry Association

The challenge to an exchange in determining the optimum number of memberships is to choose the appropriate balance between liquidity and dilution. If there are too few memberships, then there will be insufficient personnel to develop and handle a large volume of business. However, if there are too many memberships, opportunities will be spread among a larger number of people and the value of an individual membership will decrease. As the figure later in this chapter shows, exchanges can have very different ideas in regard to the appropriate number of memberships. As of March 1987, the authorized number of full memberships ranged from a low of 202 on the Kansas City Board of Trade to a high of 1,680 on the New York Futures Exchange.

Futures exchanges usually focus on character and financial responsibility when they consider applicants for membership. As a general rule, exchanges require that an applicant be sponsored by two current members. Once an applicant's name is submitted, it is circulated to the membership for comment. The applicant then must appear before the Committee on Admissions, which will recommend to the board that he or she be accepted or rejected. Some exchanges permit an applicant to submit a bid for a membership only after the board has approved the application; others require that a membership be bought beforehand by a current member and, in effect, held in escrow until after the applicant has been approved.

Membership on a futures exchange entails both privileges and obligations. The most important privileges are access to the trading area (called *floor privileges*) and reduced transaction costs.

On every futures exchange, only members are permitted to execute transactions in the trading area. Nonmembers must trade by entering orders through members. However, floor privileges are not automatically available to all exchange members. Every exchange requires that a member first demonstrate knowledge of the exchange's trading procedures and an ability to function in a trading ring environment before receiving a *trader's badge*, which permits access to the actual trading ring. This is because it is in the interests of an exchange to ensure that its floor traders have some minimum level of competence. This requirement reduces the likelihood of confusion and errors in the hectic environment of the trading floor. Applicants for trading badges must also meet more stringent financial requirements than those that apply to other members. There are two reasons for this: One, floor traders are liable for errors that they make when they execute orders in the ring. Two, floor traders tend to trade more actively than other members because of their presence at the center of the action.

Exchange members also benefit from lower transaction costs. Every exchange levies an exchange fee on trades that are executed on behalf of nonmembers. These fees vary among the exchanges, but they generally range from 2¢ to 75¢ per contract. They are paid by the executing member or member firm to the exchange and are usually passed on to the nonmember as a portion of the trading commission. Exchange fees are usually lower for members than for nonmembers (in fact, member exchange fees are often zero). This can be a significant benefit for active traders even if they do not personally execute their transactions on the exchange floor. An ancillary benefit of membership on some exchanges is indirect participation in investments that are made by the exchange. For example, as we mentioned earlier, the Chicago Board of Trade and the Chicago Mercantile Exchange each have equity interests in the buildings which house their respective trading floors. Thus, each member has an indirect investment in Chicago real estate.

The most tangible responsibility that accompanies exchange membership is the payment of dues. Annual dues on United States futures exchanges range from several hundred to several thousand dollars. Along with capital that is generated from the initial sale of authorized memberships and the exchange fees that were mentioned earlier, dues provide the revenue that finances the exchange's administration and activities.

Members also assume the responsibility of abiding by an exchange's rules and regulations. Exchanges place particular emphasis on financial and character suitability requirements and on rules that govern the handling of business for nonmembers. Members are subject to the disciplinary apparatus of the exchange, as described earlier in this chapter and in Chapter 6, "Regulation of Futures Trading."

Although only individuals may be members of futures exchanges, every United States exchange permits membership privileges to be conferred on corporations or partnerships by individual members. An organization on which privileges are conferred is entitled to reduced fees on its proprietary transactions, and on some exchanges that organization may maintain nonmember employees on the trading floor to handle clerical tasks that relate to its business. However, only the individual in whose name the membership is held may obtain a trader's badge.

Specific requirements for the conferring of membership privileges on a firm vary from exchange to exchange. Some specify that privileges can be conferred only by two or more individual memberships. Most exchanges require that at least one partner or senior executive be an exchange member in order for privileges to be conferred.

HISTORY OF FUTURES EXCHANGES

The Chicago Board of Trade, which was formed in 1848, is the oldest futures exchange in the world. The exchange began as a spot market and started to trade futures in 1865. During the next century, a varied array of futures exchanges developed. Some disappeared entirely, some merged, and some continue to thrive today. Figure 5-2 on page 91 gives the dates of some of the most important developments in the evolution of United States futures exchanges.

United States Futures Exchanges Today

In mid-1987 there were 11 United States futures exchanges that were recognized as contract markets by the CFTC. A list of these exchanges along with some pertinent facts about them is given in Figure 5-3 on pages 92 to 94. It is important to understand that these exchanges are wholly separate and independent from one another. Although many individuals and organizations are members of more than one exchange, each exchange nonetheless has its own facilities, staff, procedures, history, and traditions.

This independence is a source of pride for some people in the futures business and a source of frustration for others. On the one hand, an individual floor trader might prefer independence and a greater degree of input into the affairs of his or her exchange rather than to join forces with other exchanges. On the other hand, a large brokerage firm might regard it as costly and redundant to maintain the staff that is needed to ensure compliance with the unique rules that govern order execution, trade processing, and supervision on each independent exchange.

FUTURES EXCHANGES OUTSIDE THE UNITED STATES

Futures exchanges have existed in various countries other than the United States since the mid-nineteenth century. However, in the post-World War II era, the United States exchanges have enjoyed overwhelming dominance in terms of trading volume and overall economic significance. Since 1980, for example, the 11 United States futures exchanges that are recognized by the CFTC as contract markets have reg-

Figure 5-2. *Key dates in history of United States futures exchanges.*

1848 Chicago Board of Trade begins operations as a spot market for grain.

1865 Chicago Board of Trade introduces the first contracts that can accurately be described as futures. These contracts were standardized, could be traded only by members, and were secured by margin deposits.

1870 New York Cotton Exchange is formed and begins to trade in cotton futures.

1872 New York Mercantile Exchange is formed to trade spot contracts in butter and cheese.

1882 Coffee Exchange of the City of New York is founded; this organization evolves into the current Coffee, Sugar & Cocoa Exchange.

1919 Chicago Mercantile Exchange is formed through reorganization of the Chicago Butter and Egg Board; introduces futures trading in butter and eggs.

1933 Commodity Exchange, Inc., is formed through a merger of four previous markets: National Metal Exchange, Rubber Exchange of New York, National Raw Silk Exchange, and New York Hide Exchange. Futures trading is conducted in copper, hides, rubber, silk, silver, and tin.

1972 Chicago Mercantile Exchange forms the International Monetary Market (IMM) and inaugurates futures trading in foreign currencies. These were the first financial futures contracts.

1975 Chicago Board of Trade introduces the first interest-rate futures contract—Government National Mortgage Association (GNMA) futures.

1982 The first equity-based futures contract is introduced by the Kansas City Board of Trade, which begins trading in futures on the Value Line Composite Index.

1982 The Commodity Futures Trading Commission approves a pilot program that permits futures exchanges to begin to trade options on futures contracts.

ularly accounted for over 90% of total worldwide futures activity, based on underlying contract value.

The dominance of the futures industry by the United States is the result of a complex combination of circumstances, but three factors warrant particular mention.

Country Risk. The United States is almost universally regarded as the safest country in the world in which to hold assets. This view stems from the combination of political stability, military strength, and an enduring commitment to a free-market economy.

Futures Market Infrastructure. The organization and operation of a futures exchange is a hugely complex undertaking. As the discussions earlier in this chapter have explained, it is necessary to have floor brokers who are capable of executing orders competently, communications specialists who are able to keep the telephones working, administrators who have the knowledge and the experience to develop and to implement both appropriate rules and an effective regulatory apparatus, and a

Figure 5-3. United States futures exchanges.*

Exchange (city)	Date Founded	Number of Full Members**	Active Contracts	Trading Volume 1986	1985
Chicago Board of Trade	1848	1,402	U.S. T-Bonds	52,598,811	40,448,357
			Corn	6,160,298	6,392,812
			Soybeans	6,133,668	7,392,128
			U.S. T-Notes	4,426,476	2,860,432
			Soybean Oil	3,182,963	3,647,408
			Soybean Meal	3,049,005	3,339,268
			Wheat	2,090,316	2,127,962
			MMI Maxi	1,738,916	422,091
			Muni Bond Index	906,980	334,691
			Silver (1,000 oz.)	511,239	1,034,830
			Oats	140,952	99,024
			Gold (1 kilo.)	124,546	168,527
Chicago Mercantile Exchange (Chicago)	1919	625	S&P 500 Index	19,505,273	15,055,955
			Eurodollars (3-month)	10,824,914	8,900,528
			Deutsche Mark	6,582,145	6,449,384
			Swiss Franc	4,998,430	4,758,159
			Live Cattle	4,690,538	4,437,327
			Japanese Yen	3,969,777	2,415,094
			British Pound	2,701,330	2,799,024
			Live Hogs	1,936,864	1,719,861

* Includes all contracts that have trading volumes of 100,000 contracts or more in 1986.
** Most United States futures exchanges also maintain membership categories that relate to subsets of their overall contract listings. Details are available from the membership departments of the exchanges.

Figure 5-3. (Cont.)

Exchange (city)	Date Founded	Number of Full Members**	Active Contracts	Trading Volume 1986	Trading Volume 1985
			T-Bills (90-day)	1,815,162	2,413,338
			Pork Bellies	1,100,339	1,457,386
			Canadian Dollars	734,071	468,996
			Lumber	502,530	581,548
			Feeder Cattle	411,441	455,881
New York Mercantile Exchange	1872	745	Crude Oil	8,313,529	3,980,867
			No. 2 Heating Oil	3,275,044	2,207,733
			Platinum	1,624,635	693,256
			Leaded Gasoline	829,733	667,172
			Unleaded Gasoline	439,352	132,611
			Palladium	145,562	133,223
Commodity Exchange, Inc. (New York)	1933	557	Gold	8,400,175	7,773,834
			Silver	3,849,687	4,821,206
			Copper	1,872,209	2,444,552
Coffee, Sugar & Cocoa Exchange (New York)	1882	527	Sugar #11	3,583,814	3,012,929
			Coffee "C"	1,073,142	650,768
			Cocoa	777,765	800,573
New York Futures Exchange	1980	1,680	NYSE Composite Index	3,182,992	2,833,614

** Most United States futures exchanges also maintain membership categories that relate to subsets of their overall contract listings. Details are available from the membership departments of the exchanges.

Figure 5-3. (Cont.)

Exchange (city)	Date Founded	Number of Full Members**	Active Contracts	Trading Volume 1986	1985
MidAmerica Commodity Exchange (Chicago)	1868	1,205	Soybeans (1,000 bu)	680,156	843,231
			T-Bonds ($50,000)	467,639	297,033
			Corn (1,000 bu)	406,694	456,661
			Wheat (1,000 bu)	344,749	347,355
			Swiss Franc	102,019	110,047
Kansas City Board of Trade	1856	202	Value Line Index	953,985	1,204,659
			Wheat	744,023	733,447
New York Cotton Exchange	1870	450	Cotton #2	1,015,392	636,492
			FCOJ	211,543	190,758
			Dollar Index	166,494	74,573
Minneapolis Grain Exchange	1881	402	Wheat	283,900	297,509

The eleventh U.S. futures exchange is the Chicago Rice & Cotton Exchange, which in recent years has traded fewer than 10,000 contracts annually.

** Most United States futures exchanges also maintain membership categories that relate to subsets of their overall contract listings. Details are available from the membership departments of the exchanges.

host of other very specialized talents. The United States—particularly Chicago and New York—possesses a much better-developed infrastructure and a much deeper pool of experienced futures talent than are found in any other country.

Sales Coverage. A successful futures exchange needs nonmember order flow to complement commercial hedging and market making by floor traders. As in any business, it takes an appropriate sales force to generate this order flow. In the worldwide futures business, the only sales force of real consequence is that of the United States based brokerage firms. The Merrill Lynches, the Shearsons, the E.F. Huttons, the Prudential Baches, and so on, collectively employ tens of thousands of salespeople worldwide. These United States based firms are naturally more familiar and more comfortable with the United States markets. The fact that no other country has institutions that have even remotely comparable sales coverage poses a significant obstacle to the development of truly successful futures exchanges outside the United States.

Despite these barriers to entry, the explosive growth of futures trading activity during the 1970s and the early 1980s led to various attempts outside the United States to revitalize existing exchanges or to develop new exchanges. Before commenting briefly on the more significant futures exchange initiatives outside the United States, we should point out that general statements about futures exchanges in different countries tend to be much less appropriate than general statements about different exchanges in the same country. Margin and clearing procedures, trading rules, regulatory considerations, and a host of other matters are sometimes dealt with very differently than in the United States. Even the distinction between forward and futures contracts can sometimes seem blurred from the perspective of someone used to United States structures, procedures, and terminology.

With this caveat in mind, let us present an overview, by country, of the most prominent futures exchanges outside the United States.

United Kingdom

The United Kingdom is the second-leading futures market center in the world, as Figure 5-4 on page 96 shows. As of early 1987 the United Kingdom was home to 15 organizations that would qualify as futures

Figure 5-4. Selected non-United States contracts.

Country	Exchange	Contracts
United Kingdom	International Petroleum Exchange	Gasoil
	London Commodity Exchange	Cocoa Coffee (robusta) Sugar
	London International Financial Futures Exchange	Financial Times Index 3-month Sterling 20-year Gilts 3-month Eurodollars U.S. T-Bonds
	London Metal Exchange	Aluminum Copper Lead Nickel Silver Tin Zinc
Canada	Winnipeg Commodity Exchange	Wheat Barley Flaxseed Rapeseed
Japan	Tokyo Stock Exchange	Yen Bond
Singapore	Singapore International Monetary Exchange	3-month Eurodollars Deutsche Marks U.S. T-Bonds Japanese Yen
Australia	Sydney Futures Exchange	All Ordinaries Index 90-day Bank Bills Australia T-Bond
France	Paris Commodity Exchange	White Sugar
Bermuda	Intex	Ocean Freight Index

exchanges by most definitions. The most active of these exchanges are listed in Figure 5-4. Two are sufficiently prominent to warrant brief descriptions.

London Metal Exchange (LME). The LME was founded in 1877 and trades aluminum, copper, lead, nickel, silver, tin, and zinc. Strictly speaking, the LME until mid-1987 was not a futures exchange, but rather an organized forward market. Contracts were strictly principal-to-principal, with no clearinghouse system as in the United States. Two important practical issues stemmed from this arrangement: First, counterparty credit exposure had to be considered when transacting LME business because only the particular members who were involved in a contract were obligated to perform. On a United States futures exchange, the clearinghouse stands as counterparty to every transaction, as we have mentioned and will discuss in more detail in Chapter 7. Second, contracts were not settled until maturity, even if they were offset. For example, if a June copper contract was purchased in March and offset in April at a profit, that profit was not paid until June. On United States exchanges positions are continuously marked-to-market, and the clearing mechanism permits immediate and total liquidation by offset.

In late 1985 the LME suffered a massive default. The International Tin Council (ITC), a cartel of tin-producing countries, ran out of cash and was unable to perform on contracts that were valued at about $900 million. Because the LME was a principal-to-principal exchange, the losses, which totaled over $300 million, were absorbed by the LME members who held the opposite side of the ITC's long positions. Many observers and industry participants, which included some important British regulatory authorities, believed that the debacle could have been mitigated if the LME had been subject to the mark-to-market discipline of a clearinghouse system. As a result, the LME made plans to adopt a clearing system in mid-1987 and to end its century-old principal-to-principal approach to settlement.

London International Financial Futures Exchange (LIFFE). This exchange was founded in 1982 in response to the explosive growth of financial futures activity in the United States. It is the only major futures exchange in the world that is devoted solely to financial futures. LIFFE transactions are cleared through the International Commodities

Clearing House (ICCH), which is an independently owned clearing organization that operates much like United States clearing organizations (see Chapter 7).

Of the remaining London futures exchanges, those that trade cocoa, coffee, gasoil, and sugar are approximately comparable in trading volume and global stature to their United States counterparts. All operate more or less along the lines of United States futures exchanges, and all clear their transactions through the ICCH.

Canada

The Winnipeg Commodity Exchange currently trades moderately active futures contracts in barley, flaxseed, oats, rapeseed, rye, and wheat. This exchange was founded in 1887 and operates along the general lines of United States exchanges. Transactions are cleared through the affiliated Winnipeg Commodity Clearing Ltd.

Japan

The Tokyo Stock Exchange (TSE) introduced a futures contract on yen-denominated Japanese government bonds in 1985. The contract has attracted very impressive participation during its relatively short lifetime. Plans are underway for the TSE to offer other financial futures contracts, such as indices on Japanese equities. Japan's economic prominence could provide a solid foundation on which to develop successful futures markets.

Singapore

The Singapore International Monetary Exchange (SIMEX), which opened in 1984, is one of the world's newest futures exchanges. Though its present trading volume is not significant by world standards, this exchange is particularly interesting because of its innovative relationship with the Chicago Mercantile Exchange (CME). The two exchanges developed and implemented a *mutual offset* clearing system. The essence of this system is that a customer may elect to have a transaction in certain contracts *initiated* on one exchange and *offset* on the other. This linkage is viewed by proponents as an important step toward around-the-clock trading. The key question that faces SIMEX is whether there is sufficient natural business flow during Far East daylight hours to support a major futures exchange that offers primarily off-hours trading of contracts listed in another country.

Australia

The Sydney Futures Exchange (SFE), which lists contracts in a variety of agricultural and financial futures, has been in operation since 1960. None of its contracts has ever achieved real success, largely due to Australia's isolation and sparse population (16 million) and also to currency control regulations that severely restricted foreign access to these markets until their repeal in late 1983. In November 1986, the SFE and the Comex in New York initiated a linkage that involves the clearing by Comex of all SFE gold futures transactions. This "common clearing" arrangement carries the Chicago Mercantile Exchange/ Singapore International Monetary Exchange linkage one step further by actually consolidating the clearing process at Comex.

France

The Paris International Futures Market lists futures contracts in refined sugar, cocoa, and coffee. The sugar contract is by far the most active and complements the raw-sugar contracts that are traded in New York and London. An interesting feature of the refined-sugar contract is that nonresidents of France may use United States dollars for original and variation margin even though the contract is quoted in French francs.

Bermuda

The International Futures Exchange Ltd. (INTEX) is certainly the most unusual exchange in the world. It is totally automated and has no trading floor. Instead, members trade via computer terminals which are connected to the exchange's central computer in Bermuda. Transactions are then cleared via the ICCH in London. INTEX became operational in 1984 and presently offers futures contracts in gold and an ocean freight index. Trading volume has been minimal, but the exchange has nonetheless attracted considerable attention. One school of thought holds that automated trading is the wave of the future, owing to techno-logical progress, increasing computer literacy, and the flexibility of hav-ing equal access to the exchange from anywhere in the world. The op-posing view is that, by its very nature, trading requires human contact and that the "black-box" futures exchange will never be more than a novelty.

Hong Kong

The Hong Kong Commodity Exchange opened in 1977 and cur-rently lists futures contracts in cotton, gold, soybeans, and sugar. One unusual feature of the Hong Kong exchange is that full membership is restricted to residents of Hong Kong. Associated memberships are avail-able to nonresidents.

Various other countries are home to one or more futures exchang-es, but none are presently active or prominent enough to be of practical interest except to local professionals. Also, a number of countries are planning to develop and open futures exchanges by the end of the 1980s.

■ Chapter 6

■ *Regulation of Futures Trading*

Successful futures markets require effective regulation. Markets cannot flourish without a large and diverse group of participants, and the group will not remain either large or diverse for very long if some participants are permitted to take systematic advantage of others.

The varied interests and concerns of different market participants make regulation of futures markets a multifaceted challenge. For example, the removal of a particular grain elevator from the list of permissible delivery locations for corn would be of no consequence to retail commission houses and their customers, but would be of great interest to many people in the grain trade. On the other hand, grain-market professionals would be unconcerned about changes in customer margin procedures that might seriously affect commission-house business. Floor brokers would likely pay little attention to either delivery locations or margin procedures for nonmembers, but would take keen interest in regulations that affect record keeping on the exchange floor.

Reconciling the often diverse interests of varied groups to ensure fair and efficient futures markets is a task that is shared in the United States by the federal Commodity Futures Trading Commission (the CFTC, or the Commission) and the futures industry itself. The basic approach can be described as supervised self-regulation. The CFTC has ultimate authority over the entire United States futures industry, but in practice it relies heavily on industry participants to develop and implement effective procedures for the prevention of market abuses. The CFTC continually monitors these self-regulatory efforts to ensure that they are in accord with the Commission's overall guidelines. If not, the Commission has at its disposal various direct-enforcement tools. These tools are discussed later in this chapter.

Both the theory and the practice of modern futures-market regulation in the United States can be better understood with some knowledge of how the regulatory framework evolved to its current state. This evolution has naturally paralleled that of the futures industry itself. It has been motivated by changing business practices and by concerns over the years about various abuses—some actual, some possible, and some imaginary. We will briefly review the historical development of regulation of the United States futures industry and then describe in some detail the current regulatory system.

UNITED STATES FUTURES REGULATION (1848–1974)

Futures markets in the United States were essentially unregulated for more than a half-century after their birth. Each exchange had its own rules and regulations, but there was no governmental oversight of the business. Still, futures hardly went unnoticed in the political arena. The deflation that followed the Civil War brought declining commodity prices, for which producers and their political representatives tended to blame speculators and futures markets. Several states passed laws that prohibited futures trading entirely on the grounds that futures contracts were actually gambling instruments and therefore illegal.

Interestingly, Illinois was among the states that passed such legislation. The Illinois law, which was passed in 1867, essentially prohibited short sales on the premise that selling something you don't own is gambling. For the most part, the law was not enforced. However, on August 10, 1867, a zealous citizen prompted police to arrest seven prominent Chicago Board of Trade members for making illegal short sales. Although all were immediately released, the incident created quite a commotion at the exchange. The law was repealed the next year.

During the half-century between the Civil War and World War I, an uneasy truce existed between futures markets and the government. Various attempts to enact regulatory legislation failed during the late nineteenth and early twentieth centuries. The first to succeed was the Cotton Futures Act of 1916, but this law regulated only the grading of cotton rather than the actual trading of futures.

The first comprehensive regulatory legislation was the ill-fated Futures Trading Act of 1921 (also known as the Capper-Tincher Bill), which was signed into law on August 24, 1921. This law was quickly declared unconstitutional by the United States Supreme Court on the grounds that it was based inappropriately on congressional taxing power.

The law was quickly rewritten and reenacted as the Grain Futures Act of 1922, which became law on September 21, 1922, and took effect on November 1, 1922. The act defined for the first time *contract markets* (the official term for futures exchanges) and provided for the establishment of a Grain Futures Administration within the Department of Agriculture (USDA). The Grain Futures Act regulated trading on the Chicago Board of Trade and nine smaller grain exchanges that then existed. The Grain Futures Administration was given the power to monitor trading, to collect data on market activity, and to examine the books and records of exchange members. However, there were no specific provisions aimed at such issues as the prevention of fraud or the regulation of the sales practices and order-handling procedures of brokerage firms.

In the following decade, Congress considered various modifications to the Grain Futures Act. However, it was not until the wave of New Deal legislation that followed the 1929 stock market crash and the Great Depression of the early 1930s that sweeping changes were enacted. The Commodity Exchange Act of 1936 expanded the regulatory scope of the Grain Futures Act to include more commodities and to strengthen the regulatory mandate. For example, the 1936 Act granted authority to establish trading and position limits on speculative activity. It required the registration of floor brokers and futures commission merchants. It also prohibited the trading of options on commodities, a ban that remained in effect until 1982.

The Commodity Exchange Act of 1936 provided for the formation of the Commodity Exchange Commission, which operated through a new agency of the USDA known as the Commodity Exchange Administration. This agency was given jurisdiction over futures trading in most domestic agricultural products. During the 1940s, the Commodity Exchange Administration underwent several organizational changes. In 1947 it was consolidated into a new entity known as the Commodity Exchange Authority (CEA), which was charged with the administration of the Commodity Exchange Act of 1936.

Over the years, two deficiencies in the CEA's structure became apparent. First, its authority did not encompass the entire range of United

States futures activity. Because its mandate was focused on United States agricultural products, many important futures markets remained unregulated. These included the metals, sugar, cocoa, and the various financial futures that began to develop in the 1970s. Second, the CEA's funding and powers proved inadequate to regulate the explosive growth in futures trading that accompanied the inflationary surge of the early 1970s. Congressional hearings into the adequacy of futures market regulation began on September 25, 1973, and culminated in the enactment of the Commodity Futures Trading Commission Act of 1974 on October 23, 1974. This act amended the Commodity Exchange Act of 1936 and authorized a new and independent regulatory body to replace the CEA. This new agency—the Commodity Futures Trading Commission (CFTC) became operative on April 21, 1975.

The Commodity Futures Trading Commission is an independent regulatory agency authorized by and reporting to Congress. The House Committee on Agriculture and the Senate Committee on Agriculture, Nutrition, and Forestry exercise general oversight and legislative jurisdiction. The CFTC consists of five commissioners (including the chairman), each of whom must be appointed by the President and confirmed by Congress. Each commissioner holds office for a five-year term. In general terms, the Commission's basic responsibilities are to prevent market abuse, protect customers, and ensure that United States futures markets serve the economic purposes of risk shifting and price discovery. In other words, Congress expects the CFTC to keep the markets both honest and efficient.

REGULATION OF PARTICIPANTS

The CFTC has very broad jurisdiction over United States futures market participants. Let us first discuss those regulatory areas of particular importance and then briefly describe how the Commission is organized and how it carries out its responsibilities.

Regulation of Futures Exchanges

By law, futures contracts can be traded only on futures exchanges, and the CFTC has the sole power to designate futures exchanges (or *contract markets*, to use the legal term). This ability to designate contract markets is a potent regulatory tool, especially because a separate designation must be received for each individual futures contract that is listed on an exchange. This requirement is designed to ensure that futures trading takes place within an arena that is clearly and effectively subject to CFTC jurisdiction.

The CFTC has formulated extensive requirements for contract market designation. These range from furnishing detailed economic justification for proposed futures contracts to the establishing of suitable trading rules and rule-enforcement procedures. Designated contract markets are required to obtain CFTC approval in advance for any new rules or rule changes (with certain minor exceptions). They are also required to actually enforce all rules that have received CFTC approval.

This approach is consistent with the philosophy of supervised self-regulation. However, the Commission retains the right to alter or supplement rules if it deems such action appropriate to maintain fair and orderly markets. In the extreme case, the CFTC could revoke contract market designation and halt trading in a particular contract or on an entire exchange. The only recourse an exchange would have in such circumstance would be an appeal to the appropriate U.S. District Court of Appeals. However, revocation of contract market designation is a drastic step that the CFTC has never found it necessary to take.

Registration of Market Professionals

Keeping undesirables out of the business is an obvious and effective regulatory technique. The CFTC attempts to do this by requiring various categories of market professionals to register with the Commission or with the National Futures Association (NFA), which is discussed later in this chapter. The registration process involves fingerprinting and the providing of extensive background information by the applicant.

As of mid-1987, the Commission required market professionals in six different categories to register. Let us now briefly discuss these categories and some of the important regulatory issues relating to each.

Futures Commission Merchants (FCMs). *Futures commission merchant* is the official term for what is more commonly called a *brokerage house.* Any individual or organization that solicits or accepts futures orders from customers and that carries futures accounts for customers must be registered with the CFTC as an FCM. Thus, FCMs range from tiny one- or two-person operations to giant multinational firms such as Merrill Lynch. FCMs are subject to a variety of regulations in regard to record keeping, advertising, supervision of employees, and financial adequacy. Among the CFTC's major concerns in regard to FCMs are the following:

- *Ensuring that the FCM's customers understand the risks inherent in futures trading.* This is accomplished principally by requiring that all customers of FCMs sign certain documents that include a risk disclosure statement, which clearly describes the risks that are involved in futures trading.

- *Preventing false or misleading advertising or excessively high-pressure sales techniques.* The CFTC mandates that FCMs "diligently supervise" the activities of their employees that relate to the futures-brokerage business.

- *Preventing the unauthorized trading of customer accounts.* The CFTC prohibits FCMs or their employees from executing any transaction for a customer unless the customer has either specifically authorized that transaction or given written authorization that grants discretionary authority to his or her account executive or another person. This rule is designed to prevent, among other things, *churning,* which is the overly active trading of an account for the purpose of generating commissions.

- *Safeguarding customer funds.* The CFTC requires that an FCM segregate customer funds from the funds of the FCM itself. The intent of this requirement is to prevent an FCM from using customer funds in connection with the FCM's proprietary activities. An FCM is also prohibited from using the funds of one customer as margin for another customer. The regulations that prevent unauthorized use of customer funds are a particularly important component of the CFTC's customer protection program.

- *Ensuring the FCM's financial soundness.* The CFTC has established minimum capital rules that relate the size of customer futures positions that an FCM is permitted to carry to the net capital of the FCM. Basically, an FCM must have net capital at least equal to the greater of: (1) $100,000 (or $50,000 if a member of a contract market) or (2) 4% of the funds that are required to be segregated by CFTC customer-margin procedures.

Floor Brokers. *Floor brokers* are the individuals who actually execute futures contracts in a trading area on behalf of others. The main regulatory concern in relation to floor brokers is that they not take advantage of customer orders for personal profit. The key enforcement mechanism the CFTC has used in this endeavor is detailed record keeping.

Floor brokers must record the exact times when customer orders are received and reported back to the customer. They must also record the exact times of any alterations to the order made by the customer (e.g., in quantity or price). This record keeping is accomplished with the aid of time-stamping machines that floor brokers must provide for themselves and that are ubiquitous on the floors of futures exchanges. Floor brokers must also record on special trading cards every transaction that they execute. The transactions must be in precise chronological sequence, and the trading card must indicate whether each trade was for a customer or for an account in which the broker himself has a proprietary interest.

The core issue that relates to floor broker regulation is the appropriate balance between efficiency on the one hand and reducing the potential for abuse on the other. Up to a certain point, requiring that floor brokers be able to reconstruct trades and trade sequences is clearly beneficial because it enhances confidence in the marketplace. Beyond that point, however, record keeping can become so burdensome that it prevents floor brokers from effectively performing their basic function of executing orders.

Attempting to define the optimum degree of record keeping precision has kept the CFTC, the exchanges, and floor brokers locked in a lively dialogue for years. Ideally, the CFTC would like to see a trade-reconstruction system that would fix the exact moment when an order was executed. Floor brokers point out that many of their group handle hundreds of orders each day and that unrealistically stringent requirements would paralyze their activities. At present, floor brokers on most futures exchanges are required to maintain records that permit reconstruction of exact trading sequences and that fix the times of specific trades within one-minute intervals. Alternative trade-reconstruction systems have also been approved by the CFTC and are in use on several exchanges.

Associated Persons. The term *associated person (AP)* covers something of a catchall category that includes account executives, sales assistants, branch managers, and anyone else who is associated with an FCM that is involved in the solicitation or the acceptance of customer futures orders. An exception is made for personnel whose involvement is limited to strictly clerical functions.

In practice, the CFTC relies almost exclusively on FCMs to monitor the conduct of their APs. This is the only reasonable approach because APs are so numerous (more than 50,000 as of the end of 1986) and are located in thousands of separate branch offices throughout the world. The CFTC's registration requirements can realistically only assist in keeping individuals who have the most flagrantly unsavory backgrounds out of the futures commission merchant business.

In 1983, the CFTC expanded its registration categories to include APs associated with introducing brokers (discussed later) as well as those associated with FCMs.

Commodity Trading Advisors. A *commodity trading advisor (CTA)* is someone who gives futures trading advice to others in return for direct compensation, a share of any profits, or other considerations. Thus, publishers of trading systems, technical advisory services, and the like must register as CTAs. Certain persons or firms whose provision of advice or market information is incidental to their primary business activities are excluded from CTA registration requirements. Specifically exempt by CFTC regulations are: banks and trust companies; newspapers and general circulation publications, publishers, editors, columnists, and reporters; lawyers; accountants; teachers; floor brokers; FCMs; and designated contract markets.

The regulatory mechanism for CTAs centers on the disclosure of various types of information to prospective subscribers to their services. The CFTC mandates that a CTA's disclosure document contain a variety of detailed information. Among the most important items are the following:

- The name of each principal of the CTA, along with each person's business background for the preceding five years.
- A description of the CTA's trading program. For example, are decisions based on either fundamental or technical considerations alone, or on a combination of the two approaches?
- The CTA's actual trading performance for all accounts that are directed by the CTA and each of its principals during the preceding

three years. The CFTC requires that these data be presented in a specific format that was designed by the CFTC to promote clarity and uniformity and to make it easier for prospective customers to compare the records of different CTAs.

- Information regarding any real or potential conflicts of interest between the trading program and any other activities of the CTA or any of its principals.
- A thorough description of all fees that the CTA plans to charge.
- Information regarding any material legal actions against the CTA or any of its principals within the preceding five years.

The thrust of the CFTC's disclosure policies in regard to CTAs is to ensure that prospective customers have sufficient and accurate information about an advisor and a program to make an informed decision about subscribing to the advisor's services.

Commodity Pool Operators. A *commodity pool operator (CPO)* is similar to a CTA. The crucial difference is that, like a mutual fund, a CPO pools funds from various clients and actually manages these funds rather than simply providing advice that a client may choose either to follow or to ignore. The CFTC is particularly interested in CPOs who manage money for large numbers of clients. Any CPO that operates a pool of less than $200,000 or which has 15 or fewer participants is exempt from registration.

Because CPOs actually control the funds of their clients, they are subject to even stricter rules and disclosure requirements than are CTAs. In addition to the disclosure requirements that relate to CTAs, CPOs must also disclose such information as the following:

- Any beneficial interest or ownership in the pool that is held by the CPO or any of its principals.
- The manner in which the pool will fulfill its original margin requirements.
- Descriptions of the procedures for redeeming an interest in the pool and of any restrictions on the transferability of interests in the pool.
- Any commissions, underwriting fees, or other expenses that are paid by the pool or its principals in connection with the formation of the pool or with the solicitation of funds for the pool.

- A statement that explains the extent to which pool participants might be held liable for amounts in excess of their original contributions to the pool.

Commodity pool operators are also required to furnish each participant in a pool with a certified annual statement of financial condition that contains a variety of detailed information as specified by the CFTC. There are also regulations that relate to record keeping and advertising by CPOs that are basically intended to prevent any attempts to defraud or deceive participants with respect to actual or potential performance and to ensure that the CPO does not misuse the funds in the pool or favor his own proprietary trading over that of the pool.

Introducing Brokers. The registration category of *introducing broker (IB)* was added by the CFTC in 1982. An introducing broker is essentially an independent agent who directs business to one or more FCMs but is himself neither an FCM nor an employee of any FCM and therefore falls outside both registration categories.

Introducing brokers are basically a cross between FCMs and associated persons of FCMs, and they are now regulated as such. Briefly, an introducing broker (call it *XYZ*) might operate as follows. Broker *XYZ* maintains an office that has price quotation equipment, communications and order entry capabilities, and so on. Its business is to solicit customer futures orders, but, unlike an FCM, it does not carry these positions on its own books. Rather, it passes them through to a separate entity, which is an FCM. And unlike an AP of an FCM, the IB is an independent entity rather than an employee or group of employees of the FCM.

The CFTC's regulatory requirements for these hybrid entities can be summarized as follows:

- Completion of registration documents.
- Minimum net capital of at least $20,000, or an agreement with an FCM, approved by the CFTC, in which the FCM agrees to be responsible for the liabilities of the IB.

REGULATION OF TRADING PRACTICES

In the previous two sections, we discussed how the CFTC evolved and how it regulates the organizations and individuals who are involved in the futures business. We now look at the regulation of trading activities themselves. Trading regulations are designed to accomplish the following two key objectives:

1. To ensure that futures transactions actually take place in accordance with competitive, open outcry procedures.
2. To prevent price manipulation, that is, the intentional causing of artificial prices or prices that are not reflective of supply and demand.

Trading regulations are complex and detailed, and vary somewhat from exchange to exchange. However, all must be approved by the CFTC. The best way to understand their general structure and the reasoning behind them is to consider trading regulations from the separate and very different perspectives of floor traders, FCMs, and off-floor traders (including CTAs and CPOs).

Floor Traders

Trading regulations that relate to the activities of floor traders are designed to ensure that customer orders are executed openly and competitively in the trading ring. The CFTC and the exchanges naturally take special care to guard against floor brokers' mishandling of customer orders for personal gain. Among the most important regulations that govern floor trading are the following:

- A floor broker may not execute a trade for his own account while holding an executable customer order in the same future. This rule is designed to prevent *frontrunning* customer orders. An example of frontrunning would be buying 10 contracts for oneself before executing a 100-contract customer buy order on the assumption that the 100-contract order would move the market higher and create a profit on the broker's own trade.

- A floor broker may not directly or indirectly take the other side of a customer order (known as *crossing* the order) except with the customer's consent and in accordance with the exchange's rules. For example, this rule prevents a floor broker from executing a customer buy order by selling to the customer for the broker's own account at an artificially high price. Restrictions on crossing are somewhat controversial because crossing sometimes benefits the customer. In illiquid contracts, a floor broker who also trades for his own account might be willing to take the opposite side of his customer's order at a more favorable price for the customer than is anyone else in the ring. Some exchanges feel, though, that the potential for abuse from unrestricted crossing may outweigh the possible benefits to customers and have established detailed regulations governing crosstrading.

- Floor traders may not prearrange trades. A floor broker is not allowed to agree in advance with a colleague in the trading ring to allow the colleague to take the other side of a customer order. He also may not match the buy and sell orders of his own customers (another form of crossing) outside the trading ring. Rather, he must either execute each order separately and competitively in the trading ring or satisfy the rules governing the crossing of customer orders on the particular exchange. Prohibitions against crossing orders sometimes work against customers. For example, if June crude oil is 15.10 bid/15.14 offered, a floor broker with separate customer orders to buy five lots and sell five lots would likely buy at 15.14 and sell at 15.10. If crossing were permitted, the orders could be matched at 15.12 to the benefit of both customers. On balance, though, noncompetitive customer-to-customer crossing offers sufficient opportunity for abuse that it is prohibited.

- Floor brokers are not permitted to disclose orders that they hold for customers. Thus, if a broker holds a 500-contract customer sell order, he may not tip off others in the ring so that they can front-run the order and later share the profits with him.

- Floor brokers must allocate trades in strict accordance with exchange rules. This means that a broker cannot buy 100 contracts for 6 different accounts and then allocate the lowest prices to his mother, his sister, and his dentist.

One point in regard to floor broker regulation deserves special emphasis. The regulations are designed to ensure *honest* executions, but they cannot ensure *competent* executions. Some brokers are less capable than others and will, on average, obtain inferior executions because of their lack of ability rather than their lack of integrity. The CFTC and an exchange's compliance staff are responsible for monitoring the honesty of floor brokers. Customers and FCMs must monitor the competence of floor brokers for themselves.

Futures Commission Merchants

Trading regulations that pertain to futures commission merchants (FCMs) are, like those that govern floor brokers, designed to ensure that customer orders are executed fairly and competitively. Basically, an FCM is required to transmit all orders to the appropriate trading floor and to establish procedures that ensure that knowledge of customer orders is not used improperly to the advantage of the FCM or any person affiliated with it. Among the most important specific regulations are the following:

- A futures commission merchant that also trades futures for proprietary accounts must maintain appropriate internal controls to ensure that executable customer orders are transmitted to the floor before any proprietary order in the same future is transmitted. An FCM may not frontrun its customers.

  In practice, the prohibition against frontrunning by FCMs is quite complex. For example, consider an FCM that has 100 branch offices and that also uses T-bond futures to hedge its own government securities portfolio. Chance alone guarantees that the FCM's proprietary bond futures orders will occasionally arrive on the floor just ahead of a customer order. Because it is neither practical nor necessary to regulate such purely coincidental sequences of orders, the CFTC requires that customer orders receive priority "to the extent possible" and looks for reasonable safeguards. Such safeguards might include the routing of proprietary and customer orders through different internal paths and the prohibition of traders of proprietary accounts from handling customer futures business.

- An FCM, like a floor broker, may not knowingly take the opposite side of its own customer orders. The *knowingly* is an important qualifier in the case of an FCM. An FCM that uses several different floor brokers will occasionally and unintentionally find itself on the other side of its own customers. As with frontrunning, the regulations instruct FCMs to guard against abuses, not harmless coincidences.

- All FCMs must ensure that their customers' futures orders are executed on the appropriate trading floor in accordance with exchange and CFTC rules. Thus, if the New York order room of an FCM receives simultaneously an order from customer A to buy 10 contracts of June gold at $425.00 and an order from customer B to sell 10 contracts of June gold at $425.00, the FCM may not cross the orders upstairs. Instead, both orders must be sent to the gold ring and executed there in accordance with Comex rules. This is also an example of the CFTC's prohibition of off-exchange futures trading. It may seem unnecessary in this case, but suppose that the price limit on the sell order were $424.00 instead of $425.00. Then there would be a range of $1.00 within which the orders could be crossed, and one or both customers would probably receive a less favorable price than could be obtained through execution by open outcry on the exchange floor.

Proprietary Traders

Regulations that govern proprietary trading are designed to prevent market manipulations, squeezes, corners, and the like. This is accomplished through a combination of position limits and reporting requirements.

The CFTC is empowered to set limits on both the futures trading volume and the futures market positions of all market participants. Limits on intraday trading activity were repealed in 1979 on the grounds that they were not necessary to prevent manipulation but could impair liquidity by forcing large traders to the sidelines in busy markets.

Position limits, however, remain an important cornerstone of regulatory policy. They are the key tool for preventing squeezes or corners. Position limits have been a part of United States futures regulation since the original Commodity Exchange Act was passed in 1936. However, the old CEA was authorized to set such limits only for specified markets—chiefly those of domestically produced agricultural items. As the scope of futures activity widened, many large and important markets were left without position limits (e.g., gold, silver, cocoa, sugar, and all financial futures).

The 1979–1980 silver crisis, during which the Hunt family of Texas and their associates amassed more than 18,000 silver futures contracts at one time (plus a comparable amount of the actual metal), focused the spotlight on this omission and spurred the CFTC to expand the concept of position limits to all United States futures markets. In February 1982 the CFTC passed a rule requiring all contract markets to establish position limits for all their futures contracts. These limits are subject to review by the CFTC. Figure 6-1 on page 117 gives the position limits of the more actively traded United States futures contracts.

Two important points that relate to position limits are the following:

- They do not apply to bonafide hedging transactions. This is because futures hedges are offsets against actual or anticipated positions in the cash market and therefore do not represent net long or short positions that could affect the overall price level as could net speculative positions. Hedgers who wish to obtain an exemption from position limits must file a request with the appropriate exchange, documenting the fact that their transactions are bonafide hedges.

- When it applies position limits, the CFTC looks at all accounts that are controlled by a single person or by several persons who act in concert. This means that a person cannot circumvent position limits by opening several accounts in the names of her father, her husband, and her daughter. It also means that CPOs who manage several futures pools must aggregate the positions of these pools to determine compliance with the limits.

Requirements for position reporting are the other key part of the CFTC's program for trader regulation. Every futures contract has a reporting level, and any trader who controls, or has a financial interest in, an aggregate position equal to or exceeding this limit must file certain reports with the exchange on which the contract is traded and with the CFTC. These limits are also summarized in Figure 6-1 for the most active futures contracts.

The first time a customer position reaches or exceeds the reporting limit for any futures contract, the FCM that carries the account must file

Form 102 (see Figure 6-2 on pages 118–119) with the appropriate exchange and the CFTC. This form requests detailed information that relates to the customer's futures positions and must be updated daily as long as the account remains above the reporting limit.

The CFTC also requires traders who hold reportable positions to file Form 40 (see Figure 6-3 on pages 120–124) annually. This form requires that the trader provide certain background information that includes the trader's identity and the nature of his or her trading activities. The CFTC's intent is to prevent the use of shell organizations or other countries' secrecy laws to conceal manipulative activity or to circumvent position limits.

ENFORCEMENT OF CFTC REGULATIONS

In the preceding sections, we discussed regulations that apply to various facets of the United States futures business. Now we discuss what the CFTC can do to enforce these regulations. The CFTC Act of 1974 significantly strengthened enforcement powers. The Commodity Exchange Authority of the pre-1974 period was widely and accurately viewed as ineffectual when it came to remedying violations of the Commodity Exchange Act and enabling futures market participants to seek redress for grievances. The enforcement powers of the old CEA were, for the most part, confined to limiting speculative futures positions, prohibiting fraudulent activities and fictitious transactions, and registering certain participants in the futures industry. When it came to the promulgation and the enforcement of specific rules and regulations, however, the CEA was a paper tiger.

By contrast, the CFTC Act of 1974 authorized a variety of enforcement actions. Some involve direct action by the CFTC, and others permit private claims against alleged violators of futures regulations. Among the most significant enforcement procedures that are now available to the CFTC are the following:

- The CFTC has the authority to review all disciplinary actions taken by an exchange against members or member firms and to modify decisions if it sees fit. This review procedure effectively prevents exchanges from being either improperly lenient or unfairly harsh with members who are guilty of misconduct.

Figure 6-1. *Position and reporting limits for selected futures contracts.*

	Reporting Limit	Position Limit
Chicago Board of Trade		
Corn	500,000 bushels	3,000,000 bushels
Soybeans	500,000 bushels	3,000,000 bushels
Soybean meal	150 contracts	720 contracts
Soybean oil	150 contracts	540 contracts
T-Bonds	500 contracts	10,000 contracts
T-Notes	200 contracts	5,000 contracts
Wheat	500,000 bushels	3,000,000 bushels
Chicago Mercantile Exchange		
Cattle (feeder)	25 contracts	1,200 contracts in total 600 contracts in any one month
Cattle (live)	100 contracts	450 contracts in any one month
British Pound	200 contracts	4,000 contracts
Deutsche Mark	200 contracts	4,000 contracts
Japanese Yen	200 contracts	4,000 contracts
Swiss Franc	200 contracts	4,000 contracts
Eurodollars	200 contracts	5,000 contracts
Hogs (Live)	50 contracts	1,500 contracts in total 450 contracts in any one month
Pork Bellies	25 contracts	500 contracts in total 400 contracts in May 300 contracts in any other month
S&P	300 contracts	5,000 contracts
T-Bills	100 contracts	5,000 contracts
Commodity Exchange, Inc.		
Copper	200 contracts	4,000 contracts net total 2,000 contracts per month
Gold	200 contacts	none
Silver	150 contracts	2,000 contracts net total
Coffee, Sugar & Cocoa Exchange		
Cocoa	25 contracts	2,000 contracts
Coffee	25 contracts	1,000 contracts
Sugar	200 contracts	6,000 contracts
NY Cotton Exchange		
Cotton	50 contracts	300 contracts
Orange Juice	25 contracts	800 contracts
NY Mercantile Exchange		
Crude Oil	100 contracts	5,000 contracts
Gasoline (unleaded)	25 contracts	5,000 contracts
Heating Oil	25 contracts	5,000 contracts
Platinum	50 contracts	1,500 contracts

Figure 6-2. Form 102: Large trader position report.

OMB No. 3038-0009

COMMODITY FUTURES TRADING COMMISSION Identification of "Special Accounts"	For Administrative Use Only Trader Code:	Firm Code:

NOTICE: Failure to file a report required by the Commodity Exchange Act and the regulations thereunder, or the filing of a false or fraudulent report may be a basis for administrative action under 7 U.S.C. Sec. 9, and may be punishable by fine or imprisonment, or both, under 7 U.S.C. Sec. 13 or 18 U.S.C. Sec. 1001.

INSTRUCTIONS TO FUTURES COMMISSION MERCHANTS, EXCHANGE MEMBERS AND FOREIGN BROKERS

Assign an account number to each special account which is reportable for the first time in futures or options. If an account has been assigned an account number for reporting in futures (options), use the same number for reporting options (futures). (Such account number must not be changed or assigned to any other special account without prior approval of the Commodity Futures Trading Commission.) For futures complete the form CFTC-102 and transmit it in a sealed envelope marked "CONFIDENTIAL" to the Commission accompanying the series 01 report on which the account is reported the first time. For options accounts, transmit the CFTC-102 to the appropriate contract market in accordance with their instructions.

For accounts reportable in futures, if only part of the information requested on this form is available (Items 1 through 7) please insert it and submit the partially completed form to the CFTC. Make a notation that the balance of the information will follow. You are required to follow-up immediately with a revised form CFTC-102 when all the information requested is available. If the information contained in Questions 8, 9, 10 or 11 change, an updated CFTC-102 must be filed within one business day of the change.

Please Type or Print

1. **Is this account being reported for the first time in:**

    (a)   options?   ☐ YES ☐ NO
            If "yes" transmit a copy of CFTC-102 to the appropriate contract market in accordance with their instructions.
    (b)   futures?   ☐ YES ☐ NO *If "yes" transmit a copy to the CFTC.*

    If both (a) and (b) are checked "yes" transmit a copy to both the CFTC and the appropriate contract market.

2. **Name of Account:** *(If Individual, Last, First, Middle Initial)*		3. **Account Number:**
Street:	4. **Business Phone of Account Owner:**	
City:	State/Country:	Zip/Postal Code:

5. **Principal Business and Occupation of the Account Owner:**
    If Kind of Account is Individual, Show the Following:

    Employer _____   Job Title _____

6. **Is this Account:** *(Check one of the following)*

    (a) ☐ An Account Owned or Controlled by the FCM Filing the CFTC-102?
    (b) ☐ A House Omnibus Account of Another FCM, or the House Account of a Non-FCM Member?
    (c) ☐ A Customer Omnibus Account of Another FCM?
    (d) ☐ A House Omnibus Account of a Foreign Broker?
    (e) ☐ A Customer Omnibus Account of a Foreign Broker?
    (f) ☐ Other

7. **If Item 6(a) or 6(f) was checked, show kind of account:** *(Check as many as applicable.)*

    (a) ☐ Individual   (g) ☐ Customer Trading Program of an FCM
    (b) ☐ Corporation   (h) ☐ Commodity Pool
    (c) ☐ Sole Proprietorship   (i) ☐ Other *(Specify)* _____
    (d) ☐ Joint
    (e) ☐ Trust   _____
    (f) ☐ Partnership

8. **Does this account control the trading of any other accounts in any commodity?** ☐ YES ☐ NO
    If "yes" give name and address of such account(s). (Attach a continuation sheet if necessary.)
          NAME(S) *(Last, First, Middle)*   ADDRESS

Continued on Reverse Side

CFTC 102 (Rev. 9-82)

Figure 6-2. *(Cont.)*

9. Does any other person(s) control the trading of this account?   ☐ YES   ☐ NO
    If "yes" complete the following for such person(s). (Attach a continuation sheet if necessary.)

    Name: *(Last, First, Middle)* _____   Business Phone Number: _____

    Street: _____

    City: _____   State/Country: _____   Zip/Postal Code: _____

    Principal Business or Occupation _____

10. Does any other person(s) have a financial interest of 10% or more in this account?   ☐ YES   ☐ NO
    If "yes" give the name(s) and location(s) (city and state or country of such person(s). (Attach a continuation sheet if necessary.)

    _____

    _____

    _____

11. Does this account have a 10% or more financial interest in other futures trading accounts carried on your books?   ☐ YES   ☐ NO
    *If yes, give the name(s) of such account(s) and the principal owners. In addition, show the names and locations
    of offices at which the accounts are carried.   (Attach a continuation sheet if necessary.)*

    Name of Account: _____

    Principal Owners: _____

    Office Name: _____

    City: _____ State/Country: _____ Zip/Postal Code: _____

12 (a). For Futures—Are trades and positions in this account associated with commercial activity of the account owner in related
    cash commoditites (i.e., positions considered as hedging)?   ☐ YES   ☐ NO
    (If "yes", list those commodities traded on futures markets in which the trader hedges.

12 (b). For Options— List the commodity options for which the trader is classified as commercial.

13. Name and business telephone number of the account executive handling the account. *(If account executive is in a
    foreign country, list country and city.)*

    Name: *(Last, First, Middle Initial)* _____

    Business Telephone Number: _____

14. Firm Name and Address:	15. Name *(Print)*	
	16. Signature	
	17. Title	
	18. Date	19. Business Telephone Number

Figure 6-3. Large trader background information.

Complete and return this statement promptly. Print or type. *ALL TRADERS MUST COMPLETE PART A*

PART A

1. **Name of Reporting Trader** *(If Individual—Last, First, Middle Initial)* _____

Street Address _____

City _____ State/Country _____ Zip/Postal Code _____

2a. **Principal Business and Occupation of the Reporting Trader** *(Be specific)* _____
Does the reporting trader's business include the trading of futures or options for customers?
☐ Yes   ☐ No

2.b. Is the reporting trader's futures or option trading for, on behalf of, or in association with, any of the following: *(check at least one and as many more as are applicable.)*

   (1) ☐ A customer trading program of an FCM?
   (2) ☐ A commodity pool?
   (3) ☐ Any speculative activity? *(i.e., futures or option transactions which do not constitute hedging)*
   (4) ☐ Personal use?
   (5) ☐ Other *(Specify)* _____

3. **Type of Trader:** *(Check one only)*

   (a) ☐ Individual
   (b) ☐ Joint Tenant   ➤ *In addition to Part A, complete Part B*
   (c) ☐ Partnership
   (d) ☐ Corporation
   (e) ☐ Association   *In addition to Part A, complete Part C*
   (f) ☐ Trust
   (g) ☐ Other *(Specify)*

4. Is the reporting trader registered under the Commodity Exchange Act as:

	YES	NO
(a) A futures commission merchant?	☐	☐
(b) A floor broker?	☐	☐
(c) An associated person of an FCM?	☐	☐
(d) A commodity trading advisor?	☐	☐
(e) A commodity pool operator?	☐	☐
(f) Introducing broker?	☐	☐

5. **Does the reporting trader control the futures or option trading of any other persons?** Persons include individuals, associations, partnerships, corporations and trusts   ☐ YES   ☐ NO
If yes, give names and addresses of such persons. (Use a continuation sheet if necessary)

NAMES	ADDRESSES
_____	Street Address _____
	City _____ State/Country _____ Zip/Postal Code _____
_____	Street Address _____
	City _____ State/Country _____ Zip/Postal Code _____
	Street Address _____
	City _____ State/Country _____ Zip/Postal Code _____

CFTC FORM 40 (4-80)
Previous Editions Obsolete

120

Figure 6-3. (Cont.)

6. **Do any other persons control the trading of the reporting trader?** *(Do not include brokers who merely execute orders.)*
    ☐ YES ☐ NO *If "yes" give names, addresses and business telephone numbers of such persons. (Use continuation sheets if necessary.)*

LOCATION

Name	Street Address		
Business Phone	City	State/Country	Zip/Postal Code
Name	Street Address		
Business Phone	City	State/Country	Zip/Postal Code

7. **Give names and locations of all firms through whom the reporting trader now carries accounts and the name of the account executive at each firm.** *Use a continuation sheet if necessary. (If U.S. location, give city and state; if foreign country, give city and country.)*

NAMES   **LOCATIONS**

Firm	City	State/Country
Account Executive		

8. **Do any other persons guarantee the futures or option trading accounts of the reporting trader or have a financial interest of 10 percent or more in the reporting trader or the futures or option accounts of the reporting trader?** ☐ YES ☐ NO
    If "yes" give names and locations (city and state) of such persons. Indicate whether they guarantee accounts (G) or have a financial interest in the reporting trader or the accounts (F). Use a continuation sheet if necessary.

NAMES   **LOCATIONS**

        ☐(F) ☐(G)

        ☐(F) ☐(G)

9. **Does the reporting trader guarantee or have a financial interest of 10 percent or more in futures or option accounts not in the trader's name or have a financial interest of 10 percent or more in another futures or option trader?** ☐ YES ☐ NO
    If "yes" give (1) the names of the accounts which the reporting trader guarantees or in which the reporting trader has a financial interest, the names of the principal owners of such accounts and the names and the locations of the brokerage firms through which such accounts are carried; and/or (2) the names of the futures or option traders in which the reporting trader has a financial interest. In addition show whether the reporting trader guarantees the accounts (G) or has a financial interest in the traders or accounts listed (F).

a. _____ ☐ (G) ☐ (F)   b. _____

     Account or Trader Name   Principal owner(s) of the account

c. _____   d. _____

     Brokerage Firm carrying the account   City   State/Country

           (Brokerage Firm Location)

10. **Does the reporting trader represent a foreign government, act as an agent of a foreign government, receive financing from a foreign government either through ownership of capital assets or provision of operating expenses, or is the reporting trader an entity specially acknowledged by a statute or regulation of a foreign jurisdiction?** ☐ YES ☐ NO
    If "yes" give the name of the country which the government represents and complete items (a) through (e) below.

     Name of Country _____

(a) Does the reporting trader act as an agent of the government?
(b) Is the reporting trader acknowledged by a statute or regulation of a foreign jurisdiction?
(c) Does the government directly or indirectly control the trading?
(d) Does the government finance the reporting trader, either through captial ownership of assets or by providing operating capital?
(e) Use a continuation sheet to briefly describe the nature of the relationship(s) with foreign governments indicated in items (a)-(b), above, or any other manner in which the reporting trader represents a foreign government.

This statement should be signed by the reporting trader personally. If the reporting trader is in the name of an organization, a partner, officer or trustee should sign this form. Name and title should be printed on the lines above the signature.

Name: (Print or Type)	Title:
Signature:	Date:

Figure 6-3. (Cont.)

PART B

For Individual, Joint Tenant or Partnership Accounts.
If INDIVIDUAL, JOINT TENANT or PARTNERSHIP is checked as Type of Trader in Part A, Item 3
Complete this part of the form.

NAME of Reporting Trader (as shown on Part A) _____

1. Business Telephone Number of Reporting Trader _____

2. Answer (a) and (b) only if type of trader has been checked "Individual."

(a) Name of Employer _____

(b) Job Title _____

---

3. Is the reporting trader commercially engaged in business activities hedged by use of the futures or option markets? ☐ YES ☐ NO
   This would include production, merchandising or processing of a cash commodity, asset/liability risk management by depository institutions, security portfolio risk management, etc.
   If "yes", complete Schedule 1 listing the futures or option contract used, the marketing occupations associated with hedging uses and the cash commodity(ies) hedged or the risk exposure covered. (For a definition of hedging, see the instructions for completing Schedule 1.)

---

4. Does the reporting trader participate in the management of any organization that holds another futures or option trading account?
   ☐ YES ☐ NO
   If "yes" give names and addresses of organizations and check type. (Use a continuation sheet if necessary.)

   Name of Organization _____

   Street Address _____

   City   State/Country   Zip/Postal Code

   ☐ Corporation

   ☐ Partnership

   ☐ Trust

   ☐ Other *(Specify)*

---

5. For Partnerships and Joint Tenants: List name and address of each partner and/or joint tenant, excluding limited partners in commodity pools, and indicate by an asterisk, which person ordinarily places orders. (Not required if the reporting trader is a Futures Commission Merchant registered under the Commodity Exchange Act.) *(Use a continuation sheet if necessary.)*

   NAMES   **ADDRESSES**

   _____   Street Address _____

                                  City   State/Country   Zip/Postal Code

   _____   Street Address _____

                                  City   State/Country   Zip/Postal Code

   _____   Street Address _____

                                  City   State/Country   Zip/Postal Code

Figure 6-3. (Cont.)

PART C
(For Corporations, Associations, Trusts or "Other" Types of Traders Only)
If corporation, association, trust or "other" is checked as type of trader in Part A, Item 3, complete this part of the form.

NAME of Reporting Trader: (as shown on Part A) _____

---

1. For firms such as Corporations, Associations, Trusts:

   a. Is this firm organized under the laws of any state or other jurisdiction in the United States? ☐ YES ☐ NO

   If "no", give the name of the country under whose jurisdiction the reporting trader is organized. _____

   b. List the names and locations of all parent companies. Indicate whether or not the parents are organized or incorporated under the laws of any state or other jurisdiction in the United States by checking "yes" or "no". If the reporting trader has no parent organization indicate "none".

NAME	LOCATION	YES	NO
		☐	☐

   c. Give names and locations of all subsidiaries, if any, which trade in commodity futures or options. Indicate whether or not each company is organized or incorporated under the laws of any state or other jurisdiction in the United States by checking "yes" or "no." If no subsidiaries, indicate "none."

NAMES	LOCATIONS	YES	NO
		☐	☐
		☐	☐
		☐	☐

2. a. Give name, office address and business telephone number of person(s) controlling the futures or option trading of the reporting trader. *If different persons are responsible for different commodities, use a continuation sheet to list the information below for each controller and indicate the commodities for which they are responsible.*

   Name _____

   Street Address _____

   City   State/Country   Zip/Postal Code

   ( ) _____
   Business Telephone Number

   b. Give name, office address and business telephone number of person to contact regarding the futures or option trading of the reporting trader.

   Name _____

   Street Address _____

   City   State/Country   Zip/Postal Code

   ( ) _____
   Business Telephone Number

3. Is the reporting trader commercially engaged in business activities hedged by use of the futures or option markets? ☐ YES ☐ NO
   This would include production, merchandising or processing of a cash commodity, asset/liability risk management by depository institutions, security portfolio risk management, etc.
   If "yes", complete Schedule I listing the futures or option contract used, the marketing occupations associated with hedging uses and the cash commodity(ies) hedged or the risk exposure covered. (For a definition of hedging, see the instructions for completing Schedule I.)

123

Figure 6-3. (Cont.)

SCHEDULE 1

(See Instructions)

PART A: FOR ALL FUTURES OR OPTION MARKETS OTHER THAN FINANCIAL INSTRUMENTS AND FOREIGN CURRENCIES

Futures or Option Contract Used	Marketing Occupations Associated With Hedging Uses		Cash Commodity(ies) Hedged or Risk Exposure Covered
	(1) ☐ PRODUCER (2) ☐ DEALER OR MERCHANT (3) ☐ PROCESSOR	(4) ☐ LIVESTOCK FEEDER (5) ☐ OTHER *(specify)*	
	(1) ☐ PRODUCER (2) ☐ DEALER OR MERCHANT (3) ☐ PROCESSOR	(4) ☐ LIVESTOCK FEEDER (5) ☐ OTHER *(Specify)*	
	(1) ☐ PRODUCER (2) ☐ DEALER OR MERCHANT (3) ☐ PROCESSOR	(4) ☐ LIVESTOCK FEEDER (5) ☐ OTHER *(specify)*	
	(1) ☐ PRODUCER (2) ☐ DEALER OR MERCHANT (3) ☐ PROCESSOR	(4) ☐ LIVESTOCK FEEDER (5) ☐ OTHER *(specify)*	

PART B: FOR FUTURES OR OPTION MARKETS IN FINANCIAL INSTRUMENTS (e.g. GNMA's and T-Bills)

Futures or Option Contract Used	Marketing Occupations Associated With Hedging Uses	Cash Commodity(ies) Hedged or Risk Exposure Covered
	(1) ☐ DEALER IN FINANCIAL INSTRUMENTS (2) ☐ FINANCIAL INTERMEDIARIES [1] (3) ☐ INVESTMENT GROUPS [2] (4) ☐ OTHER *(specify)*	

PART C: FOR FUTURES OR OPTION MARKETS IN FOREIGN CURRENCIES

Futures or Option Contract Used	Marketing Occupations Associated With Hedging Uses	Cash Commodity(ies) Hedged or Risk Exposure Covered
	(1) ☐ CURRENCY DEALER/BROKER (2) ☐ IMPORTER/EXPORTER (3) ☐ FOREIGN INVESTOR (4) ☐ OTHER *(specify)*	
	(1) ☐ CURRENCY DEALER/BROKER (2) ☐ IMPORTER/EXPORTER (3) ☐ FOREIGN INVESTOR (4) ☐ OTHER *(specify)*	

[1] Includes commercial banks, savings and loans, credit unions, mutual savings banks, mortgage banks.

[2] Includes pension funds, mutual funds, college endowment funds, insurance companies.

- The CFTC is authorized to suspend or revoke the registration of anyone in the futures business for a variety of reasons. The regulations set forth a two-tier approach to the use of this sanction. For certain serious offenses (e.g., a felony conviction), registration can be suspended immediately. For less serious offenses (e.g., failure to reasonably supervise an employee), the person is first entitled to a hearing before a suspension can be imposed.

- The CFTC has injunctive powers that give it the right to request a federal court to issue an order to cease violations of the Commodity Exchange Act and regulations. This is an important power because an injunction can be obtained by the demonstration of reasonable likelihood of a violation, whereas a formal lawsuit (such as a private party might bring) requires a much more stringent standard of proof and involves lengthy litigation.

- Rather than obtain a court injunction, the CFTC can itself issue a cease-and-desist order against someone who is suspected of the violation of a regulation. However, before such a cease-and-desist order can be issued, an alleged violator must be notified of the charges and given a hearing.

- The CFTC's most direct enforcement weapon is the use of its power of administrative action against alleged violators. In an administrative action, an administrative law judge (ALJ) conducts a hearing to determine whether there has been a violation. If a violation has occurred, the ALJ may impose fines of up to $100,000, suspend or revoke registration, and prohibit the violator from trading on any United States futures market. The CFTC, at its discretion, may review the findings of the ALJ.

The foregoing enforcement procedures may be employed by the CFTC against alleged violators. The CFTC Act also provides procedures by which individuals or private organizations can take action against any person or organization who is required to be registered with the CFTC as a futures industry professional. A private party who seeks redress against an alleged violator of the CFTC Act has the following three choices: reparations proceedings, arbitration, or a private lawsuit.

Reparations Proceedings

The CFTC Act of 1974 authorized reparations proceedings that are instituted by private parties. A person or organization who has a complaint against anyone who is required to register with the CFTC as a floor broker, AP, FCM, CTA, CPO, or IB may contact the CFTC and give the particulars of the complaint. If the CFTC believes that a response is warranted, it will either handle the matter internally (if the alleged damages are $5,000 or less) or appoint an administrative law judge to conduct a hearing and render a judgment. Reparations complaints must be filed within two years of the alleged violation, and awards are enforceable through the federal court system for three years after judgment is rendered. Reparations awards may be appealed by either party to the United States Court of Appeals.

When the CFTC Act was passed in 1974, reparations proceedings were intended to be the principal method for handling complaints against futures market professionals. In practice, however, they proved to be extremely time consuming, and a large backlog of cases developed and remained unsettled during the late 1970s and the early 1980s. The CFTC has consequently encouraged the use of arbitration as an alternative to reparations proceedings.

Arbitration

The CFTC Act of 1974 requires all United States contract markets (futures exchanges) to establish arbitration procedures for the settlement of customer grievances against members or employees of the exchange. Thus, a customer who has a complaint about an order execution can initiate arbitration proceedings at the appropriate exchange against either the floor broker who executed the order or the FCM who carried his or her account (assuming that the FCM is an exchange member).

The use of arbitration by a customer is voluntary. Prior to 1983, futures exchanges were required to accept for arbitration only disputes that involved $15,000 or less. In mid-1983, the CFTC eliminated this limitation to help broaden the use of arbitration. Arbitration procedures vary from exchange to exchange, but the CFTC requires that a majority of the arbitrators on a case be nonmembers of the exchange and that a customer who initiates arbitration proceedings be given some specified input into the selection of arbitrators.

Private Lawsuits

The third method for the redress of grievances is to bring a lawsuit into the federal courts. Between 1974 and 1982 the courts were divided over the issue of whether the CFTC Act permitted private lawsuits or whether reparations and arbitration were intended to be the only available means of redress. In 1982, the U.S. Supreme Court ruled on the matter, and upheld the right of complainants to initiate private lawsuits. The ruling gave exclusive jurisdiction over disputes alleging violations of the CEA to the federal courts as opposed to the state courts.

ORGANIZATION OF THE CFTC

Now that we have seen how the CFTC regulates the United States futures industry, we discuss how the Commission is structured and how it actually implements the procedures that we have described.

As mentioned earlier, the Commodity Futures Trading Commission is an independent federal regulatory agency that is authorized by Congress and is overseen by the House Committee on Agriculture and the Senate Committee on Agriculture, Nutrition, and Forestry. The Commission is composed of a chairman and four other commissioners. Each is appointed by the President with the advice and consent of the Senate and holds office for a five-year term. The terms are staggered and, by law, no more than three Commissioners can belong to the same political party. The CFTC is based in Washington, D.C. It has regional offices in New York, Chicago, Kansas City, and Los Angeles, and a regional suboffice of the Chicago office in Minneapolis.

The Commission is supported by a staff that numbered 496 at the end of 1986. The CFTC's budget for fiscal year 1986 was $27.6 million, which is a relatively modest amount by the standards of federal regulatory agencies. For example, the fiscal year 1986 budget for the Securities and Exchange Commission (SEC), which oversees the United States securities industry, was $111.1 million. Ever since the CFTC's formation in 1975, there has been ongoing debate about whether its funding is sufficient to provide effective regulation of the large and complex futures industry.

The CFTC staff, which reports to the Commissioners, is organized into six major units, as depicted in Figure 6-4 on page 128.

Office of the Executive Director

The Office of the Executive Director provides a variety of administrative services to the Commission in relation to budgeting, personnel,

Figure 6-4. Commodity Futures Trading Commission—
Organizational chart.

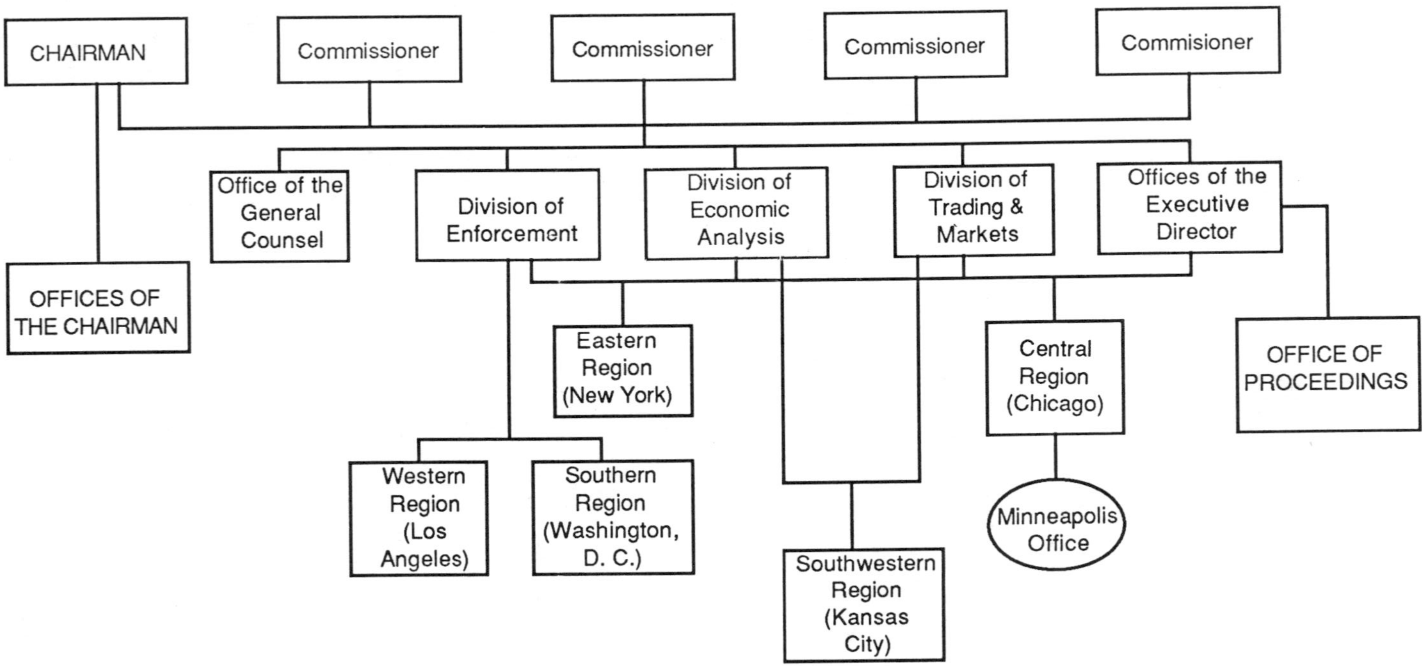

internal audit, and the like. It also manages the administrative law unit, which handles customer complaints against professionals in the futures industry. When a complaint is filed with the CFTC, it goes first to the Complaints Section within the Office of the Executive Director (OED). The Complaints Section either dismisses the complaint or refers it to the Hearings Section of the OED for resolution.

Division of Enforcement

The Division of Enforcement investigates and prosecutes alleged violations of the Commodity Exchange Act and CFTC regulations. Investigations may be initiated on the basis of information that has been referred by other areas within the CFTC or as a result of information that was developed through its own independent investigations. The Division of Enforcement must decide whether it believes that a violation has occurred and, if so, whether to seek authority from the Commission to institute administrative proceedings or to seek an injunction in federal court.

Division of Economic Analysis

The Division of Economic Analysis is responsible for the ongoing monitoring of conditions in the futures markets. The division collects and monitors the large trader position and activity reports that were described earlier in this chapter. It also maintains an ongoing program of surveillance that covers price relationships and supply/demand factors that relate to the various futures markets. The purpose of these activities is to maintain free, competitive markets by the detection and the prevention of price manipulations and other abusive trading practices.

The Division of Economic Analysis is also responsible for the CFTC's ongoing efforts to further public understanding of the futures markets and the Commission's regulatory functions. It accomplishes this through a variety of education programs, newsletters, and publications.

Division of Trading and Markets

The Division of Trading and Markets is responsible for monitoring the various United States futures exchanges to ensure that they meet their responsibilities for market surveillance and enforcement. The Division of Trading and Markets is the section of the CFTC that reviews exchange rules and regulations and that considers applications for new futures contracts and for designation as a contract market.

Office of the General Counsel

The CFTC appoints a general counsel who serves as the chief legal advisor to the Commission in the formulation of policies and administrative practices. The staff of the OGC reviews regulatory, legislative, and administrative matters that are presented to the Commission, and it advises on the application and interpretation of the Commodity Exchange Act. The OGC also represents the CFTC before the United States Court of Appeals when matters involving the Commission are appealed.

Office of the Chairman

The Office of the Chairman provides various support functions to the Commission. These include the coordination of the preparation and distribution of policy documents, as well as the control of the flow of information that goes to the Commissioners. This office also maintains the CFTC library and handles liaison between the CFTC and other governmental bodies, such as the Departments of Agriculture and Treasury, the Board of Governors of the Federal Reserve System, and the Securities and Exchange Commission.

FUTURES TRADING ACTS OF 1978, 1982, 1986

The Commodity Futures Trading Commission Act of 1974, which created the Commodity Futures Trading Commission, provided that Congress must reauthorize the powers of the CFTC every four years. The purpose of this renewal policy is to make the regulatory agency continually responsive to its mandate and to changes that take place in the futures industry. Since 1974, three Congressional reauthorization hearings have been held. Under the Futures Trading Acts of 1978, 1982, and 1986, the CFTC maintained its exclusive jurisdiction over the futures industry. However, state attorneys general and securities commissioners were granted authority to bring civil actions in Federal district courts against individuals or firms who are believed to have violated any provisions of the Commodity Exchange Act. In addition, in response to the proliferation of financial-futures contracts, the CFTC was required under the 1978 Act to maintain communications with the United States Treasury Department and the Federal Reserve. Unlike the 1978 and 1982 reauthorizations, the 1986 Act provided for a reauthorization period of only three years, which will expire on September 30, 1989.

NATIONAL FUTURES ASSOCIATION

The National Futures Association (NFA) is the United States futures industry's self-regulatory organization. It was granted registration by the CFTC in September 1981 and began operation on October 1, 1982. The Commodity Exchange Act permits the formation and registration with the CFTC of futures associations that have explicit self-regulatory obligations with respect to their members. As of mid-1987, the NFA is the only association that has been granted authorization under this provision. The NFA is patterned after the National Association of Securities Dealers (NASD), which is the self-regulatory association for the United States securities business. The NFA is a broad-based organization whose membership is drawn from all segments of the futures industry and also includes a variety of commercial firms, banks, and other users of the futures markets.

The purpose of the NFA—and any new such associations that the CFTC may authorize in the future—is to assume from the Commission various regulatory responsibilities that in the opinion of the Commission can be more effectively or appropriately handled within the futures industry itself. For example, the NFA now has the responsibility for the processing of certain registration applications on behalf of the CFTC and for all NFA member organizations that are not members of any designated contract market (futures exchange).

An interesting and somewhat controversial feature of the NFA is that membership in it is essentially mandatory for a wide spectrum of participants in the futures markets. Since August 8, 1983, the CFTC has required that everyone who is required to register with the CFTC as a futures commission merchant must also be a member of a CFTC-approved registered futures association. The intent is to mandate a minimum level of self-regulation. However, the catch-22 is that the NFA is the only registered futures association in existence. Some industry participants, including some large and extremely reputable FCMs, believe that their own compliance and surveillance efforts are entirely adequate and that NFA membership adds no value for either the FCM or its customers. This tendency to question the benefits of NFA membership is strengthened by the fact that the NFA is financed by fees of 28¢ per roundturn on futures and 16¢ per half turn on options that must be levied on every transaction that is executed for a customer who is not a member of the exchange on which the transaction takes place.

COMMENTARY ON REGULATION OF FUTURES MARKETS OUTSIDE THE UNITED STATES

The CFTC regulates only United States futures business. Exchanges in other countries and the business done on these exchanges are governed by the regulatory framework of their home countries. These regulatory approaches vary substantially from country to country. Most, however, are quite different in both theory and practice from the United States system that this chapter has described.

An interesting contrast is offered by the British futures industry, which has historically been supervised by the Bank of England and the Department of Trade. Unlike the CFTC, which operates by very specific regulations and which has clearly defined powers, the British authorities have traditionally used a more subjective and discretionary approach. For example, if the CFTC suspected that Firm *A*, Inc., might be attempting to manipulate interest rate futures, it would look for violations of a specific rule and choose one of the specific courses of action that was described earlier. In contrast, if the Bank of England harbored similar suspicions regarding Firm *B*, Ltd., it would most likely invite one of the firm's senior people in for an informal chat to convey the bank's concern and to imply discreetly that Firm *B* will likely be better off in the long run if it allays the bank's concern.

This traditional approach to regulation in the United Kingdom is changing as a result of the reregulation of the financial services industry that began in 1986. The Securities and Investments Board (SIB) was formed in 1986 and empowered to oversee Britain's futures markets. The SIB has a very broad mandate which also encompasses the securities industry. In a sense it is comparable to a combination of the SEC and the CFTC. The details of its approach to futures regulation were being developed as of mid-1987.

Other countries employ still other approaches to the regulation of futures markets, but these are not discussed here because of the limited trading activity in most of these markets. However, one point deserves special mention: The advent of cross-border linkages such as those discussed in Chapter 5 has raised interesting and complex regulatory issues that center on the question of whose regulations govern which aspects of these linkages. Suppose, for example, that a futures exchange in country X forms a linkage of some type with an exchange in country Y. Suppose further that a customer of a brokerage firm in country X gives his broker an order to be executed via the linkage in country Y. If the customer believes that his order is mishandled, whose regulations apply: those of country X, where the order was entered, or those of country Y, where it was executed? Questions such as these are likely to receive increasing attention as the futures business becomes more internationalized.

■ Chapter 7

■ *Margin and Clearing Procedures*

Margin is the lifeblood of the futures market system. Each day, as prices rise and fall, many millions of dollars pass back and forth between customers and their clearing firms and between those clearing firms and the central clearinghouses of the exchanges. The smooth circulation of these funds through the system is vital to the health of the futures markets because they represent the ultimate guarantee that all participants in the marketplace will fulfill the financial obligations of their market positions.

In the more familiar margin system of the securities markets, *margin* refers to money that is borrowed from a brokerage firm to purchase securities. The percent of cash that must be deposited with a broker to buy securities on margin is set by the Federal Reserve and, since 1974, has been 50% for common stock. Thus, investors can buy $20,000 worth of stock for $10,000 in cash, borrowing the remainder from and paying interest to their brokerage house by the use of the securities as collateral.

Futures margin differs from securities margin in both concept and mechanics. Because futures contracts do not entail the immediate delivery of their underlying asset as do securities transactions, no immediate payment in full is necessary. Instead of representing the partial payment for something purchased, futures margin is a good faith deposit that is intended to protect the seller against the buyer's default should prices fall and the buyer against the seller's default should prices rise.

Original margin is the deposit that must be made when a futures position (long or short) is initiated. *Variation margin* refers to subsequent cash flows that mark to market the value of the position as prices fluctuate. The concepts and mechanics of both types of margin are explained in detail in the following sections.

Both original and variation margin arise within related, but nonetheless distinct, sectors of the futures industry. These can be summarized as follows:

- Futures exchanges set minimum original and variation margin requirements that exchange members must impose on their customers (regardless of whether these customers are themselves members or nonmembers of the exchange).

- Futures clearinghouses establish margin requirements that clearing members must maintain with the clearinghouse. These margins are usually, but not always, the same or less than the minimum required of members' customers by the related exchange. It is important to note that an exchange member may or may not also be a clearing member. If so, then this member deals in exchange margin requirements for its customers and clearinghouse margin requirements with the clearinghouse. If it is an exchange member but not a clearing member, then it must in turn be a customer of a clearing member. In this case, the member would impose exchange margin requirements on its own customers and would also be subject to exchange margin requirements in its role as customer of the clearing member firm.

- Some futures commission merchants (FCMs) carry futures accounts for customers but are not themselves members of an exchange or a clearinghouse. Such FCMs must themselves be customers of a clearing member (perhaps through one or more FCM intermediaries).

Because futures exchanges are independent of one another, a single firm can simultaneously have different margin procedures with different exchanges. For example, Firm *A* might be both a member and a clearing member of the Chicago Board of Trade (CBOT) but simply a nonclearing member of the Commodity Exchange, Inc. (Comex). In such a case, Firm *A* would collect exchange margin requirements from its own customers, regardless of the exchange on which the customer

Figure 7-1. Typical original margin flows.

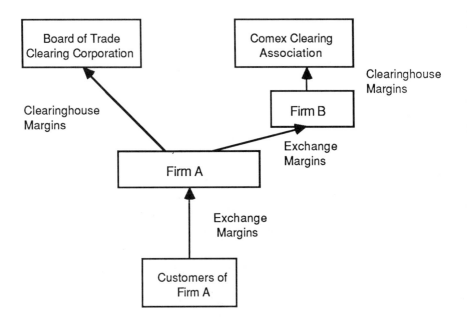

This diagram assumes that Firm A is an FCM which is a clearing
member of the Chicago Board of Trade, but not of the Comex.
Firm A is a customer of Firm B, which is a Comex clearing member.

traded. However, Firm *A* would then post clearinghouse margins with
the Board of Trade Clearing Corporation in connection with CBOT positions, but would itself post exchange margin requirements with some
Firm *B* (which was a Comex clearing member) in connection with Comex positions. Figure 7-1 shows graphically how these margin flows
would work. It is possible, though unusual, to have additional links in
the chain between a nonclearing FCM and the firms that ultimately
handle the clearing. Thus, nonclearing member firm *A* might be a customer of nonclearing FCM *B*, which in turn is a customer of the clearing
member firm *C*.

   With this background in mind, let us now look at how futures
margins work in practice.

ORIGINAL MARGIN

The sum of money that a customer is required to deposit with an FCM when a position is first established is known as *original margin* or *initial margin*. The minimum level of this original margin is determined by the exchange on which the contract is traded and varies according to price level, price volatility, and other factors. Original margins are fixed dollar amounts and generally range from about 2% to 10% of the value of the contract. Margin requirements are usually changed only after fairly substantial moves in the price level of the underlying commodity or financial instrument. Under normal circumstances, minimum original margin requirements for a given item might be adjusted up or down only several times in the course of a year. In periods of extremely rapid price change, margin requirements may be adjusted on a weekly, or even a daily, basis. Besides price level, another factor that determines original margin is price volatility. As noted above, margin requirements of from 2% to 10% of the value of the contract are conventional. In times of high price volatility and greater than usual risk, an exchange may fix margin requirements at the upper end of this conventional range or, in some cases, even higher. During the explosive bull market in silver in the first quarter of 1980, the exchange determined that margin requirements as high as 50% of the value of the contract were necessary to protect customers and clearing members from the prevailing trading hazards. Such measures are taken only in the rarest circumstances.

Futures exchanges and clearinghouses are guided by two opposing considerations when determining the appropriate levels for margin requirements. On the one hand, margins must be low enough to permit the broad participation that provides market liquidity. On the other hand, they must be high enough to ensure the financial integrity of the contracts.

House Margin Requirements

Although the exchanges fix the *minimum* original margins required on each new position, each member firm may impose higher requirements on its customers. *House margin requirements* are the levels of original margin an FCM requires of its *average* client. Generally, for speculative accounts, house requirements are higher than the minimum margins that are established by an exchange, although competition among brokerage firms usually prevents firms from setting requirements at levels that are significantly above the minimum. Obviously, in no case can house requirements be less than the minimum that is established by the exchanges.

House requirements may be increased or decreased by the FCM at any time and by any amount, as long as its requirements do not drop below the exchange minimum. For example, the house margin may increase even though the exchange margin level remains the same. Similarly, if the exchange raises its minimum speculative requirement, the FCM does not have to raise its house requirement unless the house requirement is less than the new exchange minimum. However, brokerage firms often increase their requirements by the same amount as the exchange increase, even when they are already above the minimum.

Other factors may play a role in the establishment of house margin requirements. The most common of these factors involves delivery months that are soon to expire. It is not uncommon for FCMs to raise house margins to the full value of the contract just prior to the notice-of-delivery period of an expiring futures contract. This serves as a powerful deterrent to inadvertent deliveries and limits holders of the spot month to only those participants who stand ready to make or to take delivery.

An FCM may also raise margin requirements if it feels that the overall position of its customers in any particular commodity or delivery month exposes the FCM to excessive risk. This situation tends to occur in commodities that are extremely illiquid and/or subject to large, rapid price moves. Most FCMs seek to avoid having a large share of the open interest in such markets, and the adjustment of house margin requirements is one method of limiting their involvement.

As is evident, brokerage firms can exercise significant freedom in the establishment of house margin requirements. The *Customer Agreement*, which all clients must sign on opening an account, binds the customer to maintain whatever margins the FCM, at its discretion, may require. Failure to maintain required margins can result in the forced liquidation of futures positions or of securities that are held by the FCM in the account of the customer. However, under normal circumstances, house margin requirements are held to levels very close to or equal to the exchange requirements.

Figure 7-2 on pages 140–141 shows the original margin requirements that were set by the exchanges for some of the most actively traded futures contracts. Also shown is the percent of the prevailing contract value that is represented by each original-margin requirement.

Original Margin Calls

An *original margin call* is a demand for additional funds that is made by the FCM to the customer when, for whatever reason, the customer has established a position with insufficient cash or equity (see definitions later in this chapter) in his account. An original margin call may arise for any of the following reasons:

1. A customer initiates a futures position with inadequate funds in his account.

   Example: A speculator who has $50,000 in his account decides to buy 20 contracts of silver, the original margin requirements for which are $3,000 per contract. While most brokerage firms demand that full margin be posted with the firm *before* a trade is initiated, allowances are sometimes made when the client's creditworthiness is known to the FCM. In this case, the FCM permits its customer to buy 20 contracts of silver on the customer's word that he will send the remaining $10,000 immediately. The next morning the margin department of the FCM, noting that a position was established in an account with insufficient capital, will issue an original margin call for $10,000.

2. A customer establishes a futures position on a day when adverse price action in previously established positions devalues the equity in his account to the point that his account had insufficient funds for the new position.

   Example: A textile firm that has $75,000 in its account and a long position of 40 December cotton contracts decides to buy 10 contracts of March cotton. The original margin that is required for cotton is $1,500. When the order is accepted, funds are present in the account to cover the new position. However, that afternoon, cotton prices drop from 54.25 cents per pound to 53.50 cents per pound—a loss of $375 per contract, or $15,000 in total. The next morning, the margin department notes that a new position was established by a client whose account was $15,000 shy of meeting the full original margin that was required. It issues a margin call for that amount.

Figure 7-2. Selected original margins as percentages of contract value (as of October 1986).

Contract	Margin	Approximate Price	Contract Size	Contract Value	Margin as Percent of Contract Value
Chicago Board of Trade					
Wheat	$600	$2.50/bu.	5,000 bu.	$12,500	4.8%
Corn	500	&2,00/bu.	5,000 bu.	10,000	5.0%
Soybeans	1,500	$5.00/bu.	5,000 bu.	25,000	6.0%
Soybean Meal	700	$1.50/ton	100 tons	15,000	4.7%
Soybean Oil	800	15.00¢/lb.	60,000 lb.	9,000	8.9%
US T-Bonds	2,500	$95 per $100 face	95,000	2.6%	
Chicago Mercantile Exchange					
Cattle (live)	600	60.00¢/lb.	40,000 lb.	24,000	2.5%
Hogs (live)	500	50.00¢/lb.	30,000 lb.	15,000	3.3%
Pork Bellies	1,000	66.00¢/lb.	38,000 lb.	25,080	4.0%
British Pound	2,000	$1.40	25,000	35,000	5.7%
Deutsche Mark	2,000	50.00¢	125,000	62,500	3.2%
Swiss Franc	2,000	60.00¢	125,000	75,000	2.7%
Japanese Yen	1,500	0.60¢	12,500,000	75,000	2.0%
S&P 500	6,000	240.00	500 X index	120,000	5.0%
T-Bills	1,000	95.00	$1 million face	950,00	0.1%
Coffee, Sugar & Cocoa Exchange					
Cocoa	1,000	$2,000/ton	10 tons	20,000	5.0%
Sugar	750	6.00¢/lb.	112,000 lb.	6,720	11.0%
Coffee	9,000	$2.00/lb.	37,500 lb.	75,000	12.0%

140

Figure 7-2. (Cont.)

Contract	Margin	Approximate Price	Contract Size	Contract Value	Margin as Percent of Contract Value
Commodity Exchange, Inc.					
Copper	700	65.00¢/lb.	25,000 lb.	16,250	4.3%
Gold	2,000	$400/oz.	100 oz.	40,000	5.0%
Silver	2,500	$6.00/oz.	5,000 oz.	30,000	8.3%
New York Cotton Exchange					
Cotton	1,000	45.00¢/lb.	50,000 lb.	25,000	4.0%
Orange Juice	1,500	$1.20/lb.	15,000 lb.	18,000	8.3%
New York Mercantile Exchange					
Heating Oil	2,000	40.00¢/gal.	42,000	16,800	10.2%
Crude Oil	2,000	$15/bbl.	1,000 bbl.	15,000	13.3%
Platinum	1,250	$600/oz.	50 oz.	30,000	4.0%

141

3. The exchange imposes a retroactive margin increase.

Example: Due to extremely volatile price swings in soybeans, the Chicago Board of Trade raises margin requirements on all positions from $2,500 to $3,500 per contract. While margin increases usually apply only to those accounts that initiate positions after a certain date, in this case the margin change is applied to all positions—both old and new. As a result, any account that has a soybean position and less than $3,500 per contract will receive an original margin call for the deficiency.

The rules of all futures exchanges are clear on one important point concerning original margin: When a customer is called for funds because of a deficiency in original margin, the liquidation by the customer of the position that caused the call does not satisfy the call. An original margin call remains outstanding until cash or suitable securities are received by the FCM, even if the position has been liquidated by the customer in the interim. The reason for this should be obvious. Trading without sufficient original margin is a serious matter. If futures traders were allowed to satisfy an original call by simply liquidating the position, this practice would encourage the establishment of positions without adequate margin. This could easily undermine the financial security of the entire futures market system. Thus, clients must satisfy original-margin calls promptly, regardless of the profit status of the position that generates the call.

Example: A trader who has no funds in his account buys one contract of December silver, the original margin requirements of which are, say, $2,000. The same day, December silver closes 50 cents per ounce above his purchase price—representing a profit of $2,500. The client assumes that the $2,500 equity in his account satisfies the margin call. He is mistaken. Whether the $2,500 profit is realized or unrealized, the client must still deposit the $2,000 to answer the original margin call.

Original margin requirements may be met in one of five ways:

1. *Deposit of cash*. A personal or company check is sufficient for individual or smaller institutional accounts. Wire transfer of funds is

often required for large institutional customers because of the larger amounts that are usually involved.

2. *Deposit of United States government securities.* Most exchanges
limit the use of government securities for original margin purposes
to those with maturities of less than one year. Treasury bills are the
most common form of security that are used as original margin.
Depending on the exchange, certain restrictions may govern the
use of Treasury bills as original margin. For instance, some exchanges do not allow member firms to value T-bills for original
margin at greater than 90% of face value or market value, which-
ever is less.

3. *Transfer of surplus funds or securities from another account.* If
the client maintains another futures or securities account at the
same firm, he may instruct his account executive to transfer surplus assets to the deficient account.

4. *Letters of credit.* Some exchanges permit customers to post letters
of credit (LOCs) as original margin. However, not all FCMs will
accept LOCs because the procedures tend to be operationally burdensome.

5. *Negotiable warehouse receipts.* Some exchanges allow members
to accept warehouse receipts as original margin. Comex, for example, permits the use of metals receipts that are deliverable against
its own futures contracts.

Should a customer fail to meet a call for original margin, the brokerage firm has the authority to liquidate the customer's position after due
notification to the extent the firm deems necessary for its own protection. "Due notification" usually takes the form of a telegram. This subject is discussed in greater detail later in this chapter.

VARIATION MARGIN

Once a position is established and the necessary original margin is
deposited, changes in the price of the futures contract will increase or
decrease the value of the customer's position. Should these price changes be adverse to the customer's position, then his original margin will be
reduced or depleted. All exchanges require that once a client's original

margin is depleted to a certain level, known as the *maintenance margin*, the member firm must call the client for additional funds. This call is known as a *variation margin call* or *maintenance margin call*. It differs from an original margin call in that the request for funds is made because of adverse price variations in the futures contract and not because the customer had insufficient funds in his account to begin with.

Most exchanges set maintenance margin requirements at about 75% of original margin requirements. Thus, if a customer's equity drops to less than 75% of his original requirements, the brokerage firm will ask the client for the amount of money that will restore his equity to the original level.

> *Example*: A client has $4,000 in his trading account and is long two March Eurodollar contracts at a price of 91.50. Original margin requirements are $2,000 per contract (or $4,000 total) and maintenance margin is $1,500 per contract (or $3,000 total). March Eurodollars fall to 91.20, which results in a loss of $750 per contract (or $1,500 total). Thus, the value of the customer's account falls from $4,000 to $2,500. Because this is below the $3,000 maintenance requirement, the customer will receive a variation margin call for $1,500. Notice that the variation call is for the amount of money that will restore the account to the full *original* margin that is required ($4,000) and not to the maintenance level ($3,000).

Figure 7-3 on page 145 shows the original and variation margin requirements for a sample of active futures contracts as of April 1987.

Answering Variation Margin Calls

Variation margin calls may be answered in one of two ways: by depositing the necessary funds, or by liquidating or reducing a position. Remember that once a customer has been placed on variation margin call, he must bring the funds in his account up to his original margin requirements. This can be accomplished either by adding funds to the account or by reducing the original margin that is required. The only way to do the latter is to fully or partially liquidate a position.

> *Example*: Take the previous case of the customer who is long two March Eurodollars and is on call for $1,500. He can answer this margin call in two ways:

Figure 7-3. *Selected initial and variation margins (as of April 1987).*

Contract	Initial	Maintenance
Chicago Board of Trade		
Wheat	$ 600.00	$ 400.00
Corn	500.00	300.00
Soybeans	1,500.00	1,000.00
Soybean Meal	700.00	400.00
Soybean Oil	800.00	600.00
US T-Bonds	1,000.00	750.00
Chicago Mercantile Exchange		
Cattle (live)	600.00	400.00
Hogs (live)	500.00	300.00
Pork Bellies	1,000.00	1,500.00
British Pound	2,000.00	1,500.00
Deutsche Mark	2,000.00	1,500.00
Swiss Franc	2,000.00	1,500.00
Japanese Yen	1,500.00	1,000,00
S&P 500	6,000.00	2,500.00
T-Bills	1,500.00	625.00
Coffee, Sugar & Cocoa Exchange		
Cocoa	1,000.00	750.00
Sugar	750.00	652.50
Coffee	9,000.00	6,750,00
Comex		
Copper	700.00	525.00
Gold	2,000.00	1,500,00
Silver	2,500.00	2,000.00
NY Cotton Exchange		
Cotton	1,000.00	750.00
Orange Juice	1,500.00	750.00
NY Mercantile Exchange		
Heating Oil	2,000.00	1,400,00
Crude Oil	2,000.00	1,400.00
Platinum	1,250.00	875.00

1. Deposit $1,500. In this way the customer brings the value of his account up to $4,000, which is the original margin that is required for two contracts.

2. Liquidate part of the position. The customer may not want to add more funds, in which case the only solution is to liquidate a sufficient number of contracts to reduce his original margin requirements to less than the $2,500 that remains in his account after the $1,500 loss. Because original margin for Eurodollars is $2,000 per contract, the client must bring his position down to one contract.

One point worth remembering: On many exchanges, once a variation margin call has been issued, a subsequent favorable price charge does not eradicate the call. In other words, if in the previous example Eurodollar futures advanced back to 91.50 immediately after the call had been issued, the client would still be required to answer the $1,500 margin call even though his equity was fully in balance with original margin requirements. Of course, he could deposit and then immediately withdraw the $1,500. The degree to which this rule applies varies from exchange to exchange.

An important and often misunderstood point is that variation margin calls can only be met with cash. In this respect, variation margin differs from original margin, which, as we have seen, can be met with Treasury securities and certain other forms of collateral. There is a good reason for the difference. Initial margin is essentially a good-faith deposit that is held by the FCM or the clearinghouse. Variation margin represents changes in the actual value of an account's futures positions. If those positions show a profit, the account is entitled to withdraw the mark-to-market profit. As we shall see, the cash to fund the withdrawal ultimately comes (via the clearinghouse) from a customer on the opposite (and losing) side of the market. If losing positions were permitted to be marked to market with Treasury securities, letters of credit, and so on, then clearinghouses and FCMs would face the impossible task of converting various and sundry types of collateral into the correct amounts of cash for potential withdrawal by customers with margin excesses. This problem is neatly avoided by requiring that variation margin deposits be made in cash only.

COMPUTING ACCOUNT STATUS

Now that you have a basic understanding of original and variation margin, let us take a closer look at how the margin status of a customer is computed each day. Every morning the margin department of an FCM receives a report for each of its customers. Known as the *customer equity and margin status report*, or *equity run*, this report provides the margin clerk and the customer's account executive with the status of the account as of the previous day's close. It is on the basis of this report that the account is determined to be adequately or inadequately margined.

To understand how this computation takes place, we must first define a few terms:

1. *Cash balance (C)*. This is the actual amount of cash in the account. It reflects all deposits and withdrawals of cash from the account as well as the realized results of all closed transactions. As is discussed later, it may be a positive or a negative figure.

2. *Open-trade equity (OTE)*. This figure is the net of unrealized profits and losses on positions that remain open (not yet closed out). For example, if a client's only open position is long one December gold at $410.40 and the previous day's settlement price is $411.50, the open-trade equity is $110. The open-trade equity may be positive or negative, depending on whether the customer's open positions are profitable or unprofitable.

3. *Total Equity (TE)*. This is the sum of cash balance and open-trade equity. It is the key figure in the equity and margin status report.

4. *Securities on deposit (SOD)*. This is the value of all securities (usually Treasury bills) in the account that are to be used for original margin purposes. Notice that the sum of items 3 and 4 represents the total value of the account at any point in time.

5. *Original Margin Requirements (OMR)*. This is the sum of the original margin requirements for all open positions. If the account is long two March cotton (OMR=$3,000) and short one December gold (OMR=$1,300), then the total original margin requirements are $4,300.

6. *Maintenance Margin Requirement (MMR)*. This is the sum of the maintenance margin that is required for all open positions. If the maintenance margin that is required for cotton is $1,200 per contract and for gold $800 per contract, then an account that has a position of two cotton and one gold will have total maintenance margin requirements of $3,200.

7. *Margin Excess (ME)*. The amount by which total equity exceeds original margin requirements. A customer may apply this excess to the purchase or short sale of additional futures contracts, or he may withdraw this amount from his account at any time. Assuming that there are no securities on deposit, a customer is not permitted to withdraw from his or her account funds that exceed this excess because to do so would cause the equity to drop below original margin requirements.

To put these terms into focus, consider these examples.

Example 1—Cash balance: A customer opens an account on March 1 with a deposit of $10,000. During the month her closed-out trades result in a profit of $3,500. Also during the month she withdrew $5,000 from the account. Her cash balance, then, would be $10,000 + $3,500 – $5,000, or $8,500.

Example 2—Open-trade equity: The same customer is long two June Swiss francs at a price of 0.4400. Original margin requirements for Swiss francs are $2,000 per contract, and maintenance requirements are $1,500 per contract. On March 27, June Swiss francs close at 0.4450. Thus, her open-trade equity is $1,250 credit (+ $1,250). If the settlement price of the Swiss franc had been 43.50, the open-trade equity would be $1,250 debit (– $1,250).

Example 3—Total equity: Assuming a settlement price of 0.4450, the total equity on March 27 would be $9,750 ($8,500 cash balance + $1,250 open-trade equity).

Example 4—Securities on deposit: The customer has no securities on deposit.

Example 5—Original margin requirements: Because the customer's only open position is long two June Swiss franc contracts, her OMR is $4,000 ($2,000 x 2).

Example 6—Maintenance margin requirement: Maintenance margin is $3,000 ($1,500 x 2).

Example 7—Margin excess: Margin excess equals total equity minus original margin that is required. Thus ME = $9,750 – $4,000, or $5,750.

Now examine these questions relating to this example:

Question 1: If the customer decided to increase her Swiss franc position, how many additional contracts would she be able to buy without adding additional funds and without incurring an original-margin call?

Question 2: To what price level would Swiss francs have to drop for the customer to be subject to a variation margin call?

Question 3: Assume that the June Swiss franc settles one day at 41.20. What would be the amount of the variation call, and how could the customer satisfy it?

Answers:

1. Because the account has margin excess of $5,750 and OMR for the Swiss franc is $2,000 per contract, the client would be able to purchase two additional contracts. Assuming that there is a settlement price of 0.4450, the purchase of three additional contracts would trigger an original margin call of $250.

2. Because the account's equity is $9,750 and maintenance margin on open positions is $3,000, the equity would have to decline by at least $6,750 to trigger a variation call. Because each point change in the Swiss franc equals $12.50 per contract (or $25 for two contracts), the market would have to drop by at least 270 points. This equates to a price of 0.4180 in the June Swiss franc.

3. At this point the open-trade equity would be $7,000 debit. Because her cash balance is $8,500, the total equity is only $1,500. In order to keep the two-contract position, the customer is required to bring her equity up to the original margin requirement of $4,000 by depositing at least $2,500 in cash. If she chose not to add funds, then to satisfy the call she would have

to reduce her original-margin requirement to less than her equity of $1,500. Because the original margin is $2,000 per contract, she would have to liquidate both contracts voluntarily. If she were able to do so at a price of 0.4120, her account would show a cash balance of $1,500, as the $7,000 realized loss in her position would be subtracted from the previous cash balance of $8,500.

Securities on Deposit

One point that is worth noting in the foregoing example is that the account was assumed to have had no securities on deposit. Would securities have made a difference? The answer is no. Remember that securities on deposit can be used only for original margin purposes and cannot be used to satisfy a variation margin call. Variation margin calls are always based on the difference between total equity and maintenance requirements. If this difference is negative—that is, if equity is less than maintenance requirements—a variation margin call is issued. Securities on deposit would have made a difference only if they were converted to cash by liquidation or collateralized borrowing.

This raises another point. Assume that an account contains $100,000 in Treasury bills, but no cash. If the account is long ten Swiss franc contracts, the securities on deposit more than cover the $20,000 original margin that is required. However, if the Swiss franc closes only *one point* below the purchase price, the account has a negative equity of $125. This is known as a cash deficit, and the procedures of all FCMs require that this deficit be satisfied by the addition of cash to the account.

Problem Margin Situations

As noted earlier, margin problems arise either because an account has insufficient funds at the outset of trading or because adverse price changes on an open position have impaired the customer's original margin. In either case the resulting margin calls must be answered quickly and completely to avoid potentially serious financial loss to the FCM.

In practice, the handling of customer margin varies from situation to situation. Futures exchanges generally require that member FCMs collect original and variation margin from customers within a "reasonable period." The vagueness is intentional because of the wide variations in customer types, the speed with which funds can be delivered in various geographical areas, and so forth. For the most part, though, periods of longer than several days are unlikely to seem "reasonable" in the eyes of exchanges or the CFTC.

Such delays are equally unlikely to seem reasonable in the eyes of the FCM whose customers are slow in meeting margin calls. This is because clearing members must meet all clearinghouse margin obligations regardless of whether their own customers have met the appropriate exchange margin requirements. An example will underscore the potential problems.

> *Example*: Suppose Mr. X is a customer of Firm *A*, which is a clearing member FCM of the Chicago Mercantile Exchange (CME). Assume that on Monday Mr. X establishes a new long position of 50 contracts of June Swiss franc futures through Firm *A*, and that both the exchange and the clearinghouse original margin requirements are $2,000 per contract ($100,000 in total). As a result of this transaction, Mr. X's position at Firm *A* increases by 50 contracts and Firm *A's* gross position at the CME clearinghouse increases by 50 contracts.
>
> On Tuesday morning, Firm *A* must deposit the $100,000 original margin with the CME clearinghouse, *regardless of whether it has received its $100,000 customer margin deposit from Mr. X*. If Mr. X's funds have not arrived, Firm *A* is in the unenviable position of having an unsecured market exposure on 50 Swiss franc contracts *and* a $100,000 drain on its working capital.

Firm *A* would face similar problems if the $100,000 requirement were a variation margin call that resulted from market fluctuations, rather than an original margin call that resulted from the establishment of a new market position. In practice, troublesome margin situations are far more likely to arise in connection with variation margin requirements than with initial margin requirements.

This is because FCMs can (and most do) require either that original margin already be in an account, or that there is an excellent reason to believe its arrival is imminent, before a new position can be established. Because someone who is employed by the FCM is most likely speaking to the customer before a position is initiated, this procedure is realistic and enforceable. Conversely, variation margin requirements can and do arise suddenly. If an FCM cannot contact its customer or if its confidence in the customer's intention or ability to meet the margin call is not high, then the FCM faces a delicate problem. Obviously, it will not want to damage a customer relationship if funds are in fact forthcoming. On the other hand, the excuse that "the check is in the mail" has probably cost every FCM at one time or another.

Whether a customer is given an hour or a week to meet a margin call is a matter that every FCM must decide for itself. In practice, large customers (especially institutional customers) will disburse and receive margin funds daily by wire. If such funds were not forthcoming in the usual manner an FCM might well regard even several hours delay as worrisome. On the other hand, even very wealthy individuals are seldom equipped to make daily wire transfers of funds. Thus, if an FCM found that an established and trusted individual customer incurred a variation margin deficiency during his week-long cruise down the Amazon, it might be very reluctant to take any action.

If an FCM elects to take action against an account that has a margin deficiency, the following procedures are typical. First, ample notification—oral and written—is made to the customer that his or her account is in violation and that failure to deposit funds promptly may result in the liquidation of the position in accordance with the terms of the *Customer Agreement* (see Chapter 8). If funds are still not received and the account's equity is in danger of being completely depleted, the FCM will proceed to liquidate any securities on deposit in the delinquent account. If this is still inadequate, the firm will transfer surplus funds, if any, from other accounts in the customer's name at the FCM in accordance with a Supplemental Customer Agreement. Should all of these actions fail to solve the problem, the firm may liquidate the position. Although this is the customary procedure, the FCM has considerable flexibility to handle delinquent accounts in any manner it sees fit.

Once an account's position has been liquidated, any remaining funds will, of course, be credited to the customer's account. If the situation has been allowed to deteriorate to the point that the customer's account is in deficit, that is if he or she has lost more money than the account had on deposit, the brokerage firm may begin legal proceedings to collect the defaulted amount.

Customer Funds

In accordance with the rules of all United States futures exchanges and the Commodity Futures Trading Commission, all customer funds that are deposited for margin purposes must be maintained in a segregated bank account or deposited in a segregated margin account at an exchange clearinghouse. This means that customer funds are kept separate from the funds of the FCM and cannot be used to defray operating costs or losses that result from any trading that the FCM may engage in for itself. This rule is an important safeguard against the misuse of customer funds.

A large portion of customer funds that are deposited at brokerage firms takes the form of cash in the customer's account and, in most cases, does not earn interest for the customer. On the other hand, the brokerage firms are permitted to invest these segregated funds in approved bank accounts and in certain obligations of the federal government. Thus the brokerage firms can and do earn interest on customer cash deposits, as we will discuss in Chapter 8. For this reason, many customers will choose to deposit Treasury bills rather than cash for original margin. This allows them to earn a return on funds that are posted for original margin.

The Clearing Process

Each day a customer's account reflects changes that occur in the prices of those futures contracts that are held open in the account. If the customer is long and prices rise, his equity will increase because an increase is registered in his open-trade equity. The gain will precisely reflect the change that has taken place in the market value of his open contracts. As discussed earlier, the customer may withdraw these funds or use them as original margin for additional futures contracts. But where does the money come from? The simplest, although not completely accurate, answer is that it comes from another customer who is on the opposite side of the trade and who has lost as much as the winning customer has made. The losing customer's open-trade equity declines and the winning customer's increases, each reflecting the change in the settlement price of the futures contract from one day to the next. This process of direct daily fund transfer from the losing to the winning customer might be possible if the identities of the two participants were easily known or if the two customers maintained their accounts at the same

FCM. However, given the hundreds of thousands of contracts that are traded each day, a simple matchup of this kind is not possible. Instead, each exchange relies on a central clearinghouse to properly process all transactions and to make wholesale transfers of funds each day to and from the various clearing member firms. We will examine the operations of the clearinghouse in greater detail later; for now let us be sure to understand its function and structure.

FUTURES CLEARINGHOUSES

Every exchange in the United States has associated with it an entity whose job is to ensure the operational and the financial integrity of all trades that take place on that exchange. This entity is known as the *clearinghouse*. Membership in a clearinghouse is available only to members of the related exchange and only to those members who meet strict financial requirements. Financial requirements are stringent because it is the collective strength of the clearinghouse members that ultimately guarantees the performance of all contracts that are traded on its affiliated exchange.

The exact structure of clearinghouses varies from exchange to exchange. For example the Board of Trade Clearing Corporation and the Comex Clearing Association are distinct entities with their own staffs and with boards that seldom overlap with their related exchanges. At the Chicago Mercantile Exchange and the New York Mercantile Exchange, the clearing entities are departments within the exchanges. Partisans of the former structure argue that it fosters more objective structuring and implementation of financial procedures and safeguards. Proponents of the latter counter that the integrated approach creates smoother working relationships and greater efficiency. In any event, the differences are invisible to all except clearing members and some other professional market participants.

Anyone who buys a membership on an exchange and obtains a trader's badge is permitted to transact business on the floor of that exchange for himself and for others. However, if that exchange member is not a clearinghouse member, then all transactions must be cleared through a clearing member firm. What this means is that the nonclearing member maintains an account with the clearing member and all trades of the nonclearing member are held in that account. The clearing member firm is responsible for the financial performance of these trades. If the nonclearing member fails to honor these trades, for whatever reason, it is the responsibility of the clearing member firm who carries his account to make good on these trades. Most major brokerage firms are clearing members of the major exchanges and, therefore, take responsibility for their own trades as well as for those of their customers.

Before proceeding further, study the following example to clarify these and other aspects of the clearinghouse. Assume that on Day 1 a doctor in New York who has her account at FCM *A* enters an order with her account executive to buy one contract of December Comex gold. At the same time, a lawyer in Boston sells one contract of December Comex gold through FCM *B*. The orders reach the trading floor at the same time and the floor broker who is acting for FCM *A* buys one contract from the floor broker who is acting for FCM *B* at a price of $410.00.

Because both FCMs are clearing members of the exchange, the trades are taken on their books. At FCM *A*, the doctor's account shows her long one December gold at $410.00, while at FCM *B* the lawyer's account shows him short one December gold at the same price. Both the doctor and the lawyer have deposited $1,500 of original margin at their respective FCMs. In turn, the FCMs have deposited original margin for their customers' positions at the clearinghouse. (*Note:* As we mentioned earlier, the actual amounts of the customer and the clearinghouse margins may differ.)

At the end of Day 1, December gold closes at $411.00. The doctor has an unrealized profit of $100 and the lawyer an unrealized loss of $100. On the morning of Day 2, after all business of the previous day has been settled, the following transfers and entries are made:

1. The clearinghouse transfers $100 from FCM *B*'s account to FCM *A*'s account. This leaves FCM *A* with a balance at the clearinghouse of $1,600 and FCM *B* with a balance of $1,400.

2. FCM *A* credits the $100 to the doctor's account by posting an open-trade equity of $100 to her account. This gives the doctor a total equity of $1,600.

3. FCM *B* debits the $100 from the lawyer's account by posting an open-trade equity of minus $100 to his account. This gives the lawyer a total equity of $1,400.

Figure 7-4. *Typical variation margin flows.*

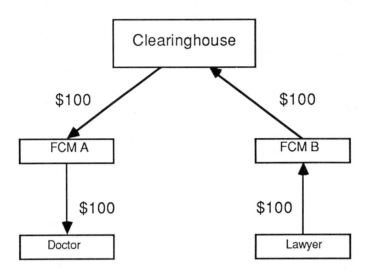

This diagram assumes that the price of gold changes in a manner that generates a $100 profit for the doctor (who is a customer of FCM A) and a $100 loss for the lawyer (who is a customer of FCM B.)

The cash flows are depicted graphically in Figure 7-4.

Several aspects of this hypothetical transaction are important. First, the actual identities of the parties to the transaction are not known by the clearinghouse. The clearinghouse knows only the positions of its clearing member firms. Second, each clearing member firm is responsible for the maintenance of a balance at the clearinghouse that reflects the positions of its customers. Third, each customer is responsible for the maintenance of a balance at the clearing member firm that reflects his position at the firm. Thus, the customer is financially responsible to his clearing member firm, and his clearing member firm is in turn responsible to the clearinghouse.

Still another consideration is that the accounts of all customers and clearing members are brought up to date each day. This process greatly simplifies record keeping and funds transfer. It is not necessary for the clearinghouse to know the original price of any transaction. All it needs to know to properly credit a member firm's account is the member firm's position and the amount that the market moved up or down that day. Likewise, this is all the FCM needs to know to properly credit or debit its customers each day.

In essence, once the transaction is consummated on the exchange floor and the details are confirmed by the clearinghouse staff, the clearinghouse steps in as intermediary. This important concept is known as the *principle of substitution* because the clearinghouse substitutes itself as the buyer from all sellers and the seller to all buyers. As far as the clearinghouse itself is concerned, it always maintains a balanced position. Because every transaction on the exchange floor involves a purchase and a sale, the number of purchases that it accepts must always equal the number of sales that it accepts. As the intermediary to all transactions, the number of contracts it is long must equal the number of contracts it is short.

Clearing Margins

In the example involving the doctor and the lawyer, it was assumed that the original margin that was deposited by these clients at their FCMs was, in turn, transferred by these FCMs to their accounts at the clearinghouse. This assumption is not quite accurate for two reasons. First, as we saw earlier, the actual amount of original margin that is required by the clearinghouse of its clearing member firms may be different from what the exchange requires each member firm to charge its customers. It is possible, for instance, that the customer original margin for one contract of soybeans is $1,200 while the clearing margin (the amount the clearing firm must deposit with the clearinghouse) may be only $1,000.

The second reason our example is not quite accurate is that most clearinghouses require their member firms to deposit original margin on their net position only. Thus, in our example, if FCM *A* had a customer (besides the doctor) who was short one December gold, it would not be required to post any original margin with the clearinghouse. The reasoning is that with one long and one short position, the firm has no exposure to the clearinghouse, assuming that its two accounts are properly margined. This approach is called *net margining*. When a clearinghouse requires its member firms to post original margin on all customer positions even when these positions offset each other, the procedure is termed *gross margining*. The Chicago Mercantile Exchange and the New York Mercantile Exchange both require gross margining. Gross margining is a somewhat more conservative policy because it means that more funds are set aside at the clearinghouse to back the futures positions. However, FCMs often prefer net margining because this approach permits them to retain a greater percentage of their customers' account balances and to earn interest on these balances (see Chapter 8).

Every clearing member firm that trades for its own account must maintain two accounts with the clearinghouse: a customer account and a house account. Each account is margined separately and positions in one cannot be netted against positions in the other. This practice is in keeping with regulations that relate to the segregation of customers' funds.

Variation margin mechanics for clearing member firms are similar in concept to those for customers but are far more precise and rigid. Three facts are especially important. First, there is no maintenance margin level that, once violated, triggers a call for funds. Instead, each clearing member firm must mark its position to market daily, regardless of how small the amount might be. Similarly, a price change that is favorable to the firm's net position will result in a movement of variation margin from the clearinghouse to the clearing member firm.

Second, the regulations in regard to the timing of clearinghouse margin requirements are both precise and strictly enforced. If, for example, the procedures of a clearinghouse require that margin calls be met by 11:00 A.M., then no excuse for late payment is acceptable. A representative of each clearing firm that owes margin must either physically deliver a certified check to the clearinghouse, or make a wire transfer of funds in a manner prescribed by the clearinghouse. If the firm's messenger is caught in traffic and arrives at 11:15 A.M., the firm can expect disciplinary proceedings. Furthermore, unlike the situation with customers of FCMs, neither geographical inconvenience nor vacations on the Amazon count for anything in the case of clearing margins. For example, every Comex clearing firm is required to maintain an office at a location "satisfactory to the Board" and to have an employee who has decision-making authority available at all times during normal business hours. In practice, most clearinghouses require their members to have an office located within several miles of the clearinghouse itself that is equipped to deal with clearinghouse issues.

Third, clearinghouses are empowered to issue intraday margin calls if they conclude that such action is appropriate to protect the exchange's financial integrity. On rare occasions, clearinghouses have issued several margin calls on a single day.

Settlement By Offset

Another important function of the clearinghouse involves the settlement of contracts by offset. We continue with the example of the doctor and the lawyer. Assume that on Day 2 the lawyer decides to cut his losses short by buying back (covering) his short position. Without the clearinghouse, he might have to locate the doctor and arrange to unwind the contract at a loss. With the clearinghouse, he simply enters an order to buy one December gold. When the order reaches the trading ring, a floor broker who has a sell order sells one contract at, say, $411.50 to the broker who is acting for FCM *B*. Thus the lawyer has covered his position, which has been transferred to a different customer who may be establishing a new short or who may be liquidating a previously held long position. The point is, as far as the clearinghouse is concerned, one short position at clearing FCM *B* has been transferred to another clearing FCM. The identity of the customer is not known. All that matters is that the new FCM now has responsibility for the transferred short. This method of liquidating a market position—by simply buying back a short position or selling a long position (settlement by offset)—greatly enhances market liquidity. It would not be possible without the central role played by the clearinghouse.

Clearinghouses and the Delivery Process

The final important function of the clearinghouse involves deliveries. It is the job of the clearinghouse to ensure that all deliveries are carried out smoothly and that no contract defaults occur. Once again, the central position of the clearinghouse makes this possible. The delivery of a commodity or a financial instrument against a futures contract begins when a short notifies his brokerage firm that he intends to make delivery rather than to offset his position by covering the short. Upon verification that the customer has the deliverable supply, it notifies the clearinghouse of its intention to make delivery.

What happens at this point varies from exchange to exchange, but the basic procedures are similar. The clearinghouse prepares delivery notices and distributes them to the clearing member firms who have net

long positions in proportion to their share of the total open interest.* The
firm with the largest net long position will receive the greatest number of
notices. It is then the job of the clearing member firm to distribute these
notices to its customers, usually in accordance with the age of the customers' long positions. Customers who have the oldest long positions
will receive notices first. The receipt of a notice by a customer generally
means that, the next day, the customer will receive delivery of the underlying item and is expected to make appropriate payment. Once delivery
and payment have been made, the corresponding long and short positions
are wiped off the books of the clearinghouse.

A crucial and often misunderstood point is that the principle of substitution (discussed earlier) does not apply to deliveries. A clearing member who receives delivery against a futures contract receives the delivery
from another clearing member, *not* from the clearinghouse. If there is a
problem with the delivery (e.g., if the delivered item appears not to meet
contract specifications), the clearing member firm who is receiving the
delivery does not have direct recourse to the clearinghouse. It must take
action against the delivering clearing member in accordance with either
the rules of the related exchange or those of the CFTC as discussed in
Chapter 6.

This completes the explanation of the general role and the methods
of the clearinghouse. The following is a summary of the three major
functions of the clearinghouse:

1. To guarantee the financial performance of every trade on the exchange.
2. To provide for the easy settlement of contracts by offset.
3. To provide for efficient and fair deliveries against futures contracts.

THE FINANCIAL INTEGRITY OF CLEARINGHOUSES

Because clearinghouses guarantee the financial integrity of futures
contracts, a logical question is: What guarantees the financial integrity of
clearinghouses? Once again, the specifics vary but the structure and procedures of the Comex Clearing Association (CCA) are representative.

---

* The exact method of the distribution of notices, the handling of notices, and the time
and method of deliveries varies significantly by exchange and type of notice. All traders
who anticipate involvement in deliveries should consult the delivery departments of the
brokerage firms that handle their accounts.

The clearinghouse itself, as well as each of its members, has ample protection against default as a result of original and variation margin requirements. Margin deposits, however, form only the foundation for an even more solid financial bulwark that makes it possible for the clearinghouse to guarantee payment for all cleared contracts. As a further safeguard, the CCA maintains a *guarantee fund* to which each member is required to contribute as a condition of clearing membership. The amount required of each clearing member varies according to the clearing member's size and quantity of business. Throughout the period of membership, the deposit stands as a share in the financial stability and integrity of the organization. The guarantee fund is not even lodged with the clearinghouse; it is deposited in the form of cash or government securities in an approved depository. The cash or the securities cannot be withdrawn for payment or delivery either to the clearinghouse or to the clearing member except on an order that bears the signatures of three of the clearinghouse directors. Not only does the deposit of each firm into the guarantee fund guarantee its individual transactions with the clearinghouse, but the aggregate fund also, when necessary, absorbs losses on any one member's account that may exceed all the credits to the member's account. In other words, all the members guarantee the accounts of all other members.

Still another source of funds for the clearinghouse is the *surplus fund* that is accumulated from fees that are charged for clearing each contract and that are billed to each member monthly. In comparison with the services that the clearinghouse renders, these clearing fees are small (usually less than 25¢ per contract), but small fees that are paid on the many contracts that are cleared by all clearing members every business day of the year amount to impressive totals at the end of each year.

The surplus fund also serves as a financial guarantee. The funds are usually invested in United States government securities, and the interest is usually applied to the operating expenses of the clearinghouse. As time passes, the income from the surplus fund may even become sufficient to meet the major part of the operating expenses, which keeps the clearance fee at a nominal figure.

THE CAREFUL PROVISION AGAINST LOSS

Clearinghouse bylaws and rules set forth the procedures in case recourse to the guarantee and the surplus funds should ever be necessary. In the event of a default by a member, the clearinghouse must close out all the member's contracts with the clearinghouse within a reasonable time by purchase or sale on the exchange floor. The closed account must be debited or credited with the resulting losses or profits. If, when the contracts of a failed member are closed out, a deficit is owed to the clearinghouse, then the deficit is made good by recourse first to the member's margin account, next to its contributions to the guarantee fund, and then by the sale of the failed firm's exchange seats.

If these measures prove insufficient to make good the deficit, the surplus fund is applied to an extent that is determined by the Board of Governors. If the loss is so great as to exhaust the surplus fund, the general guarantee fund stands as a second reserve. If the guarantee fund is drawn upon, it must be immediately restored by assessment of all clearing members. This assessment, according to the usual bylaws, would be levied according to the general principle that those who have benefited most from the clearinghouse should contribute most to the replenishment of the guarantee fund. Most clearinghouses base such assessment on some measure of the volume of business that was transacted by each clearing member during a specified period of time (usually six months to one year) prior to the event that caused the deficiency.

If the above measures should prove insufficient, then the clearinghouse is empowered to directly assess members to cover the default. The implementation of a direct assessment has never been necessary in the 140-year history of United States futures trading. Even so, a technical point is worth mentioning. Comex limits its potential assessment to $10 million per default, while most other exchanges retain the right to assess whatever amounts are necessary to completely cover a deficiency. This latter approach is known as "good-to-the-last-drop liability." Though it appears to offer greater security, Comex reasons that in practice, clearing firms would be more likely to initiate legal action or otherwise refuse to pay assessments if faced with unknown and potentially unlimited liabilities.

These elaborate safeguards provide futures clearinghouses with formidable financial strength. Though the financial resources in the guarantee fund and in the surplus fund are strong bulwarks in themselves, and though the right to assess all members is also fully enforceable and effective, the right to call for variation margin deposits— hourly, if necessary—is the most effective practical insurance against losses.

Clearing member failures have occurred on rare occasions, but there has never been a *clearinghouse* failure in the history of United States futures trading. This record testifies to the strength and effectiveness of the financial safeguards that are employed by United States futures clearinghouses.

■ Chapter 8

■ *The Futures Brokerage Industry*

The futures brokerage industry is a far-flung network of some 400 futures commission merchants (FCMs) with more than 50,000 sales representatives who operate out of branch offices throughout the world. These FCMs act as the conduits through which travel all of the transactions executed on the 11 United States futures exchanges. The futures commission merchants, most of whom have membership privileges on one or more major United States futures exchanges, act as member-brokers for nonmember retail and institutional customers. In this capacity an FCM transmits customer orders to the exchange floors, arranges for their execution, and acts as the clearing agent for its customers' transactions. FCMs also act as the clearing agent for many exchange members who execute their own trades (nonclearing members). Some FCMs handle only futures business; others offer a full range of brokerage services that also includes stocks, bonds, and other financial instruments. Although FCMs have become more diversified in recent years, the main line of business for most continues to be providing order execution, bookkeeping, and clearing functions in exchange for commission fees. According to one recent study by the accounting firm of Coopers and Lybrand,* industrywide revenues from these commissions exceeded $1.25 billion in 1984.

---

*"Business Issues Facing the Futures Industry and Their Impact on Operations and Profitability—Results of a Survey of Futures Commission Merchants." Coopers and Lybrand, March 8, 1985.

According to the same study, the futures industry's retail clientele consisted of about 200,000 customers. An estimated 100,000 or more participated in the futures markets through various trading programs that were managed by professional pool operators and trading advisors.

THE ECONOMICS OF FUTURES BROKERAGE

The revenues of the brokerage industry come from two main sources: interest income and commissions. Interest income is generated for the most part by cash on deposit in customer accounts. As noted in Chapter 6, customer cash deposits are held in segregated bank accounts. However, the interest that is paid on these deposits usually accrues not to the individual customers but rather to the FCM in whose name the segregated account is maintained. Although heightened sensitivity to the lost interest has led to greater customer use of Treasury bills for original margin, large sums of cash still remain in the system. A very rough rule of thumb is that interest income accounts for about 10% of FCM revenues.

The remaining 90% of revenues comes from commissions that are charged on customer transactions. Commission charges vary widely from FCM to FCM and from customer to customer, but a few generalities are valid. Retail speculative customers tend to pay the highest commissions, usually $25 to $60 per contract. Institutional hedgers and professional traders are next in line with average commission rates in the $10 to $20 per contract neighborhood. The lowest rates are charged to customers who are exchange members, who execute their own trades on the exchange floor, and who use the FCM strictly for clearing. Rates in this case can be as low as $1.50 or so per contract. All these charges are on a roundturn basis, meaning that the customer pays one fee when he exits from a transaction regardless of whether the initial position was a purchase or a short sale. The 1985 Coopers and Lybrand study indicated that, for a representative sample of firms, average commissions in 1985 were between $14.20 and $14.50 per contract.

It is worth noting that since 1974 when fixed-rate commissions were abolished, all futures commissions have been negotiable between customers and FCMs. Prior to 1974, exchanges established the rates that member firms charged their customers, and discounts from these rates were not permitted. The noncompetitive nature of this system came under attack, as it had in the securities business somewhat earlier, and fixed commission rates were gradually phased out. Since then, the average revenue per contract has dropped markedly, the greatest decline being registered for institutional and trade accounts where large volume has meant greater bargaining power. Average retail commissions have fallen less and, in some cases, have actually risen.

To gain a better understanding of the economics of futures brokerage, examine a hypothetical FCM income statement (Figure 8-1 on page 167) showing sources of revenues and expenses. Although statistics of this kind vary greatly from month to month and from one FCM to another, this hypothetical income statement provides some sense of the sizes and relationships of various income and expense items. This income statement assumes commission income for FCM Inc. of $100.

Transaction-Related Costs

The first major expense category is cost of sales (lines 4–7), which are referred to as *transaction-related costs*. These are costs that are incurred each time a contract is executed for a customer. The largest of these is *commission payout*. As is generally the case in the securities business, futures transactions are generated by salespeople who are known as *account executives (AEs)* or *registered representatives (RRs)*. Working primarily from branch offices, these account executives solicit and handle customer accounts and are paid a portion of the commission that is received by the FCMs. The payouts to account executives generally range from 30% to 40% of gross commissions.

The next component of cost of sales is *floor brokerage* (line 5). This represents the fees that are paid by the FCM to floor brokers who execute orders that are directed to them by the FCM. In some cases these may be independent brokers. In other increasingly common cases, floor brokerage is paid to a broker who is employed by the FCM. Either way, it is an important element of the cost of sales.

The final factor in the cost of sales is clearance and exchange fees (line 6). Every clearinghouse charges its members a fee for clearing a trade. These fees range from a low of 20¢ per roundturn on the Chicago Board of Trade to $1.70 per roundturn on the New York Mercantile Exchange. It is important to note, however, that because clearing associations are not profit-oriented institutions, they periodically rebate excess clearing fees to members. In addition to these clearance fees, most exchanges impose *exchange fees*, which provide the funds to finance such varied items as new construction expenses or promotional costs. These

Figure 8-1. FCM Inc. income statement.

Line		
	Gross Revenues	
1	Commission income	$100.00
2	Interest income	10.00
3	Total income	110.00
	Cost of Sales	
4	Commission payout	34.00
5	Floor brokerage	10.00
6	Clearance and exchange fees	6.00
7	Total cost of sales	50.00
8	**Gross Profit**	60.00
	Operating Expenses	
9	Personnel expense	25.00
10	Communication expense	7.00
11	Rent	4.00
12	Advertising & promotion	3.00
13	Office expense	2.00
14	Legal & accounting	3.00
15	Other expenses	3.00
16	Total operating expenses	47.00
17	Earnings before income taxes	13.00
18	Provision for income taxes	6.00
19	Net earnings	7.00

fees range from zero on the Chicago Mercantile Exchange to $2.00 per roundturn on the New York Cotton Exchange.

Figure 8-2 (page 168) summarizes the approximate transaction-related costs on the major exchanges. Although the figures vary substantially from one exchange to another, it is safe to say that when exchange and clearance fees are added to the commission payout fee to account executives, the total amounts to about 50% of the gross commission that is received from the customer.

Besides these direct, transaction-related expenses, brokerage firms incur a host of other operating expenses. Chief among these are personnel expenses (line 9), which include administrative and office salaries, payroll taxes, employee benefits, and so on. Next in line are communi-

Figure 8-2. Approximate roundturn costs for nonmembers (1987).

	Exchange Fee	Clearance Fee	Floor Brokerage	Total
Chicago Board of Trade	0.04	0.20	2.50	2.74
Chicago Mercantile Exchange	0.00	1.50	3.50	5.00
Commodity Exchange, Inc.	1.50	1.00	5.00	7.50
New York Cotton Exchange	2.00	0.50	5.00	7.50
Coffee, Sugar & Cocoa Exchange	1.50	0.50	5.00	7.00
New York Mercantile Exchange	1.00	1.70	5.00	7.70
Mid-America Commodity Exchange	0.25	1.25	2.00	3.50

cation expenses (line 10)—telephone, telex, and data processing and quotation equipment and services. Add to these such remaining expenses as rent, advertising, printing and postage, bad debt provisions, and so on, and total operating expenses will absorb an additional 45% to 50% of gross profits.

What is left on the bottom line is a pretax profit margin of about 10%–15% of revenues. Although these figures will vary significantly from one year to the next and from one FCM to another, this hypothetical income statement provides a reasonable picture of industry norms for the early to mid-1980s.

ORGANIZATIONAL STRUCTURE OF FCMs

The central processing "plant" of most brokerage firms is a headquarters office that is located in New York or Chicago. While most orders originate from branch offices that are spread across the country and around the world, the processing, bookkeeping, and margin functions are generally housed in the headquarters office. Organizational structure varies among the many FCMs, but the following provides a general description of the major working departments:

New accounts department. Most new accounts are brought into an FCM by account executives who operate from local branch offices. The account executive's job is to be sure that the customer understands the risks that are associated with futures trading and that he or she is financially qualified to bear these risks. The account executive arranges for the full and accurate execution of all new account documents by the customer and forwards these documents to the new accounts department in the headquarters office. The new accounts department reviews the documents and, after performing a credit check on the prospective customer, assigns the new customer an account number. A later section in this chapter describes the requirements and the procedures for opening various types of customer accounts.

Margin department. Once the new account is open and adequate funds are on hand, the margin department sets the account's margin requirements and grants approval for trading. After trading begins, this department both monitors the account to be sure that it is always adequately funded and issues margin calls if and when deficiencies occur. The margin department, in conjunction with senior management, decides what action is to be taken when margin deficiencies go unanswered. It also has responsibility for approving all withdrawals of funds from customer accounts.

Floor-and-order department. The job of the floor-and-order department is to provide for the roundturn communication and execution of all orders that are generated by branch offices and trading departments. Orders reach the trading floors in one of two ways: by wire or by telephone. Many of the large, multiproduct brokerage firms make use of their own wire systems, which are vast electronic communications networks that connect every branch office with the trading floors. Orders are handed by the account executive to an order desk in the branch office where they are typed on a machine that automatically transmits them to a receiving station on the trading floor. On the trading floor, the order is torn off the machine and taken by a runner into the trading pit for execution. Once filled, the order is reported to the branch office by a sending machine on the trading floor. This cycle generally takes a matter of minutes although, in extremely busy markets, account executives have been known to wait hours for reports from the floor. Orders that are more time- or price-sensitive are generally placed by telephone directly to booths on the trading floor.

Data processing department. Once executed and reported back to the customer, all filled orders are sent to the data processing area of the firm. Here, transactions are keypunched and entered into the computer system. From the computer flow a number of reports and statements that confirm the details of the transaction. Confirmations and purchase and sale statements are generated and sent to the customer and his account executive. Equity statements that detail the account's position and margin status are forwarded to the account executive and to the margin department. Transaction statements are compiled and sent to the clearing department, which makes sure that all trades have been properly recorded at the various clearinghouses and that payments to or collections from the clearinghouses are executed. Accurate and timely data processing is vital to the operations of an FCM. It ensures that (1) the customer and his account executive are always aware of the status of the customer's account, (2) the margin department is able to monitor problem situations, (3) senior management is aware of the firm's total customer position and, therefore, its exposure, (4) the FCM is always in proper balance with the various clearinghouses, and (5) all necessary reports are filed with exchanges and regulatory agencies.

Delivery department. This department handles all deliveries and receipts of physical commodities that arise from futures contracts, as well as cash settlements for those futures that do not require physical delivery. It ascertains that exchange-approved inventories are on hand, processes and issues delivery notices, makes payment for and receives delivery of exchange-approved commodities and financial instruments and, in general, keeps all relevant areas of the firm informed of delivery dates and procedures.

The departments that are described in the foregoing paragraphs comprise much of the "operations" area of the FCM. The other major area of the FCM is the sales division, which has responsibility for branch-office management, marketing and sales development, and research. The research department has the responsibility for publishing periodic reports on factors that influence the prices of various futures markets. Other internal departments include personnel, accounting, legal, and compliance.

OPENING CUSTOMER ACCOUNTS

Though the specific procedures and forms that are used to open customer accounts vary from firm to firm, the general methods and goals of the new account process are essentially the same throughout the industry. The legal and financial consequences of failing to abide by prescribed procedures in soliciting customer business can be significant to the FCM, its account executive and the client. Because some of the firms that solicit or accept futures business from customers are also members of the New York Stock Exchange (NYSE) for example, they are required to follow the same rules and regulations as in the opening of a securities account. Firms that handle futures business but that are not members of the NYSE are not necessarily bound by these regulations, but as a general rule they adhere to the same basic procedures.

The first tenet in opening new accounts is "know your customer." Although spelled out differently in the rules of the different exchanges and regulatory agencies, the basic point of the "know your customer" requirement is that FCMs and their representatives learn the essential facts about their customers and their activities and record these facts on a *new account form* (Figure 8-3 on page 174).*

Although the need for such information as the customer's address and telephone number is obvious, other information (such as financial data) is used to help determine the suitability of the customer to trade futures. Along these lines, the CFTC requires that every new account sign a *risk disclosure statement* (Figure 8-4 on page 175) that spells out *some* of the risks associated with futures trading.

All new accounts must sign a *customer agreement* (Figure 8-5 on pages 176–178). This document details the rights and duties of the FCM that carries the customer's account. It covers every aspect of the client-FCM relationship, from margin and delivery procedures to the rights of the FCM in the event of the customer's death.

Joint Accounts. Accounts may be opened in the name of *both* a husband and wife or in the name of two or more other related or unrelated persons, either as *joint tenants with rights of survivorship* or as *tenants in common.*

In the former case, upon the death of either of the joint tenants, the entire interest in the account is vested in the survivor or survivors. In such a case, the estate of the deceased has no claim on the account. In the case of a tenants-in-common account, each participant has a fractional interest in the account. In the event of the death of one of the tenants,

---

*All account forms used as illustrations in this chapter are provided courtesy of Geldermann, Inc.

his or her estate continues to have the same fractional interest in the account and the other tenant or tenants acquire no additional interest. A sample *joint account agreement* is shown in Figure 8-6 on page 179.

Partnership Accounts. A *partnership*, an association formed by two or more people to carry on a business as co-owners, is liable for all acts or representations by each partner in the course of partnership business. Generally, each partner is deemed the agent for all the other partners and, as such, is empowered to contract and bind the partnership under the rules of agency as to actual and apparent authority.

Before accepting any orders from a partner to buy or sell futures, an account executive should obtain a partnership agreement (Figure 8-7 on pages 180–181) that has been signed by all of the partners. This form permits the trader to act on behalf of the partnership—that is, to give orders, receive money, issue notices, and so forth. The form also designates the places where all notices and communications are to be sent. It further authorizes the FCM, in the event of the death or retirement of any of its partners, to take such proceedings, to require such papers, and to retain such portions of the account or to restrict transactions in it as the FCM may think advisable for its protection.

Corporation Accounts. When dealing with corporations as customers, FCMs must assure themselves by adequate investigation that not only the corporation but the individual officer who desires to open a futures account is properly authorized to do so. A corporation is a legal entity that acts through its agents or officers, but these agents and officers have no authority to bind the corporation merely by virtue of their offices. A corporation may act only within the scope of powers that have been conferred on it by its corporate charter or articles of incorporation. Whenever a corporation desires to open a margin account, the provisions of the articles of incorporation should be carefully reviewed to determine whether margin trading is specifically authorized. Because the FCM must have concrete evidence of the authority of the corporation and of its officers, a copy of the corporate charter or articles of incorporation—certified by the appropriate secretary of state—should be obtained.

In addition, a *corporate resolution* (Figure 8-8 on page 182) is required to satisfy the regulations of certain futures exchanges; it is evidence of authorization that is given by the corporation to the particular person(s) named therein to act on behalf of the corporation. A corporate resolution cannot be substituted for a corporate charter or articles of incorporation. Courts of law have held that a resolution reflects only an act of the directors of the corporation and does not constitute the proper authority to bind the corporation to acts that are not approved by the stockholders.

Accounts with Power of Attorney. Any person who has the capacity to contract in his or her own right may appoint another person to perform any act that the principal may legally perform. The same requirements and restrictions that apply directly to an individual also apply to an individual when acting as an agent. Because the law of agency governs transactions of this nature, the account executive must be certain that the agent is carrying out the instructions of the principal and is acting within the scope of his or her authority. The only way to be certain is to require a written original power of attorney that has been properly executed by the principal.

The most common type of power of attorney used in the futures business involves a delegation of authority that is limited to only the purchase and sale of futures (Figure 8-9 on pages 183–184) and which does not permit the withdrawal of funds from the account by the agent. This type of agreement is used frequently by clients who elect to have their account managed and traded by a professional advisor.

Trade or Hedge Accounts. Anyone who handles actual commodities or financial instruments—individuals, proprietorships, partnerships, or corporations—usually maintains trade or hedge accounts.

The CFTC has defined bona-fide hedging and the Commodity Exchange Act has exempted hedgers from the position limits that apply to speculators. However, a hedge account agreement (hedge letter) is required (Figure 8-10 on page 185) before this exemption can be approved by the appropriate futures exchange. Some futures exchanges also require hedge letters to support the customer's treatment as a bona fide hedge account to justify lower-margin requirements.

Omnibus Accounts. An *omnibus account* is a futures account in which the transactions of two or more persons are combined rather than designated separately. Omnibus accounts are usually used by FCMs which are either not clearing members or are not equipped to handle the

Figure 8-3.

CUSTOMER ACCOUNT AGREEMENT

ACCOUNT NUMBER _____

Date _____

Name of Account _____
(Please Print)

Name of individual _____ Soc. Sec. or FED. ID. No. _____ Age _____
(if different)

Mailing Address Street or P.O. Box _____ City _____
(for all notices and statements)

State _____ Zip _____ Home Telephone _____

Home Address _____ Street _____ City _____ State _____ Zip _____
(if different)

Occupation _____ Employer Name _____ Business Telephone _____

Address _____ City _____ State _____ Zip _____

FINANCIAL INFORMATION

Bank References _____(1)_____ _____(2)_____
(Indicate Savings or Checking)

Annual Income ☐ $20,000 or less ☐ $20,000-$30,000 ☐ $30,000-$50,000 ☐ over $50,000

Net Worth $ _____ Risk Capital Available for Trading Commodities $ _____

INDICATE TYPE OF ACCOUNT

☐ Speculative **or** ☐ Hedge (Attach completed Hedge Agreement)
☐ Individual ☐ Sole proprietor
☐ Tenants in Common (Attach completed Joint Account Agreement) ☐ Joint Tenancy (Attach completed Joint Account Agreement)
☐ General Partnership (Attach General Partnership Agreement) ☐ Corporate (Attach Corporate Resolution)
☐ Trust (Attach copy of Trust Agreement) ☐ Limited Partnership, Fund, or Pool (Attach Offering Document)

☐ Managed Account (Attach Geldermann Inc. Managed Account Agreement)

Do you currently or did you in the past have commodity accounts with Geldermann, Inc. or any other commodity brokerage firms? ☐ Yes ☐ No. If yes, please identify _____

Have you ever been involved in any litigation, disputed accounts, or other unresolved matters with Geldermann, Inc. or any other commodity or securities brokerage firm?
☐ Yes ☐ No. If yes, please identify _____

How did you hear about Geldermann, Inc.? _____

REPORTING QUESTIONNAIRE

1. Account number of any other accounts carried by Geldermann, Inc. that the Customer controls or in which he or it has

financial interest: _____

2. Name and address of any person who:
   a. Controls the trading of this account:

   Name: _____ Address: _____ Zip: _____
   b. Has ownership equity of 10% or more in the Account

   Name: _____ Address: _____ Zip: _____

Approved and Accepted:

_____ _____
Date New Accounts Department

Figure 8-4.

RISK DISCLOSURE STATEMENT

Account No._____

This statement is furnished to you because rule 1.55 of the Commodity Futures Trading Commission requires it.

The risk of loss in trading commodity futures contracts can be substantial. You should therefore carefully consider whether such trading is suitable for you in light of your financial condition. In considering whether to trade, you should be aware of the following:

1. You may sustain a total loss of the initial margin funds and any additional funds that you deposit with your broker to establish or maintain a position in the commodity futures market. If the market moves against your position, you may be called upon by your broker to deposit a substantial amount of additional margin funds, on short notice, in order to maintain your position. If you do not provide the required funds within the prescribed time, your position may be liquidated at a loss, and you will be liable for any resulting deficit in your account.

2. Under certain market conditions, you may find it difficult or impossible to liquidate a position. This can occur, for example, when the market makes a "limit move."

3. Placing contingent orders, such as a "stop-loss" or "stop-limit" order, will not necessarily limit your losses to the intended amount, since market conditions may make it impossible to execute such orders.

4. A "spread" position may not be less risky than a simple "long" or "short" position.

5. The high degree of leverage that is often obtainable in futures trading because of the small margin requirements can work against you as well as for you. The use of leverage can lead to large losses as well as gains.

This brief statement cannot, of course, disclose all the risks and other significant aspects of the commodity markets. You should therefore carefully study futures trading before you trade.

I HAVE RECEIVED A COPY OF THIS RISK DISCLOSURE STATEMENT, HAVE READ IT, AND UNDERSTAND IT.

THIS FORM MUST BE SIGNED AND DATED

_____
Customer Signature   Date

_____
                                            Date

Figure 8-5.

CUSTOMER AGREEMENT

In consideration of the acceptance by Geldermann, Inc. ("Broker") of one or more accounts (if more than one account is carried by Broker, all are covered by this Agreement and are referred to collectively as the "account") of the undersigned ("Customer") and Broker's agreement to act as Customer's broker in the purchase and sale of commodity interests, including commodity futures contracts and commodity options, and of securities on margin or otherwise, Customer agrees as follows:

1. **MARGIN AND OTHER PAYMENTS** Customer agrees to (1) deposit with Broker the applicable initial and maintenance margin requirements; (2) pay commission and service charges in effect from time to time, interest at the maximum rate permitted by Illinois law for funds which may be advanced by Broker for Customer's account, and any other costs to Broker occasioned by carrying Customer's account; (3) pay the amount of any debit balance or any other liability that may result from transactions executed for Customer's account, and (4) pay interest at the lesser of (i) the maximum rate permitted by Illinois law or (ii) two percent (2%) over the then prevailing prime rate charged by Continental Illinois National Bank and Trust Company of Chicago, and service charges on any such debit balance or liability together with any reasonable costs and attorney's fees incurred in collecting any such debit balance or liability. Such deposits and payments shall be made immediately following Broker's request for payment to Broker at 440 South La Salle Street, 20th Floor, Chicago, Illinois 60605 or as Broker may specially designate. Customer shall deposit with Broker the full dollar value of commodities to be delivered immediately upon demand thereof if made prior to notice of delivery by Broker. Customer agrees to hold Broker harmless with respect to any and all losses sustained by Broker as a result of any payments made by it for Customer's account and for any debit balances which occur in Customer's account.

2. **DELIVERY ANTICIPATED—STANDARDS THEREFOR** The execution of a Futures contract always anticipates making or accepting delivery. Customer understands that the future market is, however, not the customary or usual means of acquiring or selling cash commodities and that the principal function of the futures market is hedging or risk transference. Customer acknowledges that the making or accepting of delivery may involve a much higher degree of risk than liquidating a position by offset. Broker has no control over and makes no warranty with respect to grade, quality or tolerances of commodity contracts delivered or to be delivered on the several exchanges.

3. **CUSTOMER'S DUTY TO MAINTAIN ADEQUATE MARGIN** Customer shall at all times and without notice or demand from Broker maintain adequate margins in his account so as continually to meet the margin requirements established by Broker for Customer's account. Broker may change the margin requirements for Customer's account from time to time at Broker's sole and absolute discretion and such margin requirements may exceed the margin requirements set by any commodity **exchange or other regulatory authority. Customer agrees, when so requested, immediately to wire transfer margin funds** and to furnish Broker with names of bank officers for immediate verification of such transfers. Failure to demand wire transfer of funds or the acceptance or margin funds by mail shall not constitute a waiver of the right of Broker to demand wire transfer of funds at any time or from time to time.

4. **BROKER'S RIGHT TO LIQUIDATE CUSTOMER POSITIONS** If at any time Customer's account does not contain the amount of margin required by Broker, Broker may, at its sole and absolute discretion, at any time or from time to time, without notice to Customer, close out Customer's open positions in whole or in part, terminate the right of Customer to trade in the account, or take any other action it deems necessary to protect itself or to satisfy such margin requirements. Customer acknowledges his responsibility continuously to keep himself advised of his open positions and of the equity in his account marked to the market. Broker may demand full margin, that is the full value of the contract, at any time, including (but not limited to) any time during or immediately before a delivery month. Failure of Broker so to act in such circumstances, in whole or in part, shall not constitute a waiver of its rights so to do at any time or from time to time thereafter, nor shall Broker be subject to any liability to Customer for its failure so to act.

5. **PLEDGE OF PROPERTIES** All currencies, securities, negotiable instruments, open positions in futures contracts and commodities, or other property now or at any future time held in Customer's account, or held by Broker for Customer, are hereby pledged to Broker and held by it as pledgee. They shall be subject to a security interest in Broker's favor to secure any indebtedness at any time owing to it by Customer. Broker, in its sole and absolute discretion, may liquidate any of the above-mentioned items in order to satisfy any margin or account deficiencies or to transfer said property or assets to the general ledger account of Broker. Customer further agrees that, upon notice, Customer will immediately indemnify and pay any monies to Broker on account of any loss of Broker as a result of a decline in the value of such currencies, securities, negotiable instruments, open positions in futures contracts and commodities, or other property.

6. **INDEMNIFICATION FOR NON-DELIVERY** If at any time Customer shall be unable to deliver any security, commodity or other property previously sold by Broker on Customer's behalf, Customer authorizes Broker, in its discretion, to borrow or to buy and deliver the same, and Customer shall immediately pay and indemnify Broker for any cost, loss or damage (including consequential costs, losses and damages) which it may sustain in making such delivery, and any premiums which it may be required to pay and for any cost, loss and damage (including consequential costs, losses and damages) which it may sustain from its inability to borrow or buy such security, commodity or other property. In the event Broker takes delivery of any security or commodity for Customer's account, Customer agrees to hold harmless and indemnify Broker on account of any loss it may suffer as a result of a decline in value, for whatever reason, of said security or commodity.

7. **BROKER MAY LIMIT POSITIONS HELD** Customer acknowledges Broker's right to limit, without notice to the Customer, the number of open positions which Customer may maintain with or acquire through it, and Customer agrees not to make any trade which would have the effect of exceeding the limitations thus imposed on it.

8. **NOTICES: WHEN DEEMED GIVEN** All communications, monies, securities, negotiable instruments, and other property shall be mailed or otherwise transmitted to Customer at the Customer's account mailing address or to such other address as Customer may hereafter direct in writing and shall be deemed given when so sent regardless of time of delivery thereof.

9. **NO WARRANTY AS TO INFORMATION OR RECOMMENDATION** Customer acknowledges that: (1) any market recommendations and information communicated to Customer by Broker, although based upon information obtained from sources believed by it to be reliable, may be incomplete and not subject to verification; (2) Broker makes no representation, warranty or guarantee as to, and shall not be responsible for, the accuracy or completeness of any information or trading recommendation furnished to Customer; (3) recommendations to Customer as to any particular transaction at any given time may differ among Broker's peronnel due to diversity in analysis of fundamental and technical factors and may vary from any standard recommendation made by Broker in its market letters or otherwise. Customer understands that Broker and its officers, directors, affiliates, stockholders, representatives or associated persons may have positions in and may intend to buy or sell commodities or commodity futures contracts which are the subject of market recommendations furnished to Customer, and that the market positions of Broker or any such officer, director, affiliate, stockholder, representative or associated person, may or may not be consistent with the recommendations furnished to Customer by Broker.

NOTE: NO CHANGES OR ALTERATIONS CAN BE MADE IN THIS CUSTOMER AGREEMENT FORM EXCEPT AS PROVIDED IN PARAGRAPH 15.

Figure 8-5. (Cont.)

10. **DUTIES OF BROKER** Broker assumes no duty to keep Customer apprised of weather, market or national or international political or economic news, or of the value of any commodity futures contracts, collateral or other things pledged, or in any way to advise Customer with respect to the market. The commissions which Broker receives are consideration solely for the faithful execution and reporting of those trades until liquidation by offset or delivery. Broker may process and handle Customer's orders in any manner Broker believes appropriate. Customer's orders may be executed on any exchange Broker selects and Broker shall have absolute discretion over the selection of floor brokers (whether employees of Broker or otherwise) utilized in the execution of such transactions. The price at which a trade is executed on the Mid-America Commodity Exchange may include a changer's fee and the amount of the changing fee if included in a transaction price shall be provided by Broker to Customer upon request. Broker assumes no other duty, fiduciary or otherwise, to Customer. Customer agrees that the agency relationship extends only to the foregoing and that, as to margins, futures contracts and value of commodities bought and sold, and all other sums due to Broker by Customer, the relationship of Customer to Broker is that of debtor-creditor.

11. **TRANSACTIONS SUBJECT TO STATUTE AND RULES** All transactions by Broker on Customer's behalf shall be subject to the applicable constitution, rules, regulations, customs, usages, rulings and interpretations of the exchanges or markets on which such transactions are executed by Broker or its agents for Customer's account. Broker shall not be liable to Customer as a result of any action taken by it or its agents to comply with any such constitution, rule, regulation, custom, usage, ruling, interpretation or with the Commodity Exchange Act or other statutes to which this account is subject.

12. **NO BROKER LIABILITY FOR COMMUNICATION FAILURES** Broker shall not be responsible for delays or inaccuracies in the transmission of orders or other information due to breakdown or failure of transmission or communication facilities, or for any other cause beyond its control.

13. **CONFIRMATION CONCLUSIVE** Confirmation of trades, statements of account, margin calls, and any other notices sent to Customer, whether by mail, telephone, telex or other means, shall be conclusively deemed accurate and complete if not objected to immediately by telephone, telex. Customer shall direct all objections to Geldermann, Inc., 440 South La Salle Street, 20th Floor, Chicago, Illinois 60605, Attention: Director of Compliance. For the reporting of any objections, Broker authorizes and will accept "collect" telephone calls to the Director of Compliance at (312) 663-7500. In addition, if within five business days after Customer has placed an order to buy or sell a futures contract, and has been informed or believes that such order has been or should have been executed, but has not received a written confirmation thereof, Customer shall immediately communicate by telephone such fact to the Director of Compliance and further shall immediately send written notification of such fact, and the details thereof, to Broker, at the above address, by telegram or mailgram. Failing in this regard, Customer shall conclusively be deemed estopped to object and to have waived any such objection to the failure to execute or cause to be executed any transaction for any account of Customer.

14. **BROKER RIGHTS ON DEATH, INCOMPETENCY OR FINANCIAL FAILURE OF CUSTOMER** This Agreement shall inure to the benefit of Broker, its successors and assigns, and shall be binding upon Customer and Customer's personal representatives, executors, trustees, administrators, successors and assigns. In the event a petition in bankruptcy, or any similar state, federal or other insolvency proceeding, is filed by or against Customer, or in the event a receiver of Customer's property or business is appointed in any proceeding whatsoever, or in the event an attachment is levied against Customer's account or a notice of levy with respect to Customer's account is served on Broker by any competent taxing authority, or in the event of Customer's incapacity or death (and whenever the Customer consists of more than one person, then upon the occurrence of any of the aforementioned contingencies to any of them), Broker may, in its sole and absolute discretion, either continue to carry or close and liquidate the account of Customer. Broker shall not be liable to the personal representatives, heirs, successors or assigns of Customer for any act so done absent actual receipt of instructions and formal proof of office or right, from Customer's said personal representatives, heirs, successors or assigns. The receipt of any such instructions shall not affect the rights of Broker with respect to Customer's account under any other section of this Agreement.

15. **MODIFICATION OF AGREEMENT BY BROKER; NON-WAIVER PROVISION** This Agreement may only be altered, modified or amended by mutual written consent of the parties, except that if Broker notifies Customer of changes in this Agreement and Customer continues to retain or thereafter places trades in accounts subject to this Agreement, Customer agrees that such action or inaction by Customer will constitute consent by Customer to such alterations, modifications or amendments even if consent by the Customer is not expressed in writing. No employee of Broker has any authority to alter, modify, or amend in any respect any of the terms of this Agreement and no supplemental or special understanding shall be binding upon Broker unless one of Broker's Vice Presidents shall have consented thereto in writing. The rights and remedies conferred upon Broker shall be cumulative, and its forbearance to take any remedial action available to it under this Agreement shall not waive its right at any time or from time to time thereafter to take such action.

16. **SEVERABILITY CLAUSE** If any term or provision hereof or the application thereof to any persons or circumstances shall to any extent be contrary to any exchange or government regulation or contrary to any federal, state or local law or otherwise be invalid or unenforceable, the remainder of this Agreement or the application of such term or provision to persons or circumstances other than those as to which it is contrary, invalid or unenforceable, shall not be affected thereby.

17. **CUSTOMER WARRANTIES** Customer represents and warrants that information given and representations made to Broker in connection with the opening of Customer's account are true and correct. Customer understands that Broker will rely thereon. Customer agrees promptly to notify Broker in writing of any change in Customer's circumstances which affects the representations and information given or which would in any way affect Customer's ability or right to trade. Customer represents and warrants that funds, securities and other financial instruments deposited to his account belong solely to him.

18. **COMMISSIONS** Customer understands that the Commissions charged to his account may be higher than those charged by other brokerage firms or to other customers of Geldermann, Inc. with equal size accounts and an equal number of monthly trades. Customer further understands that such charges are subject to change without prior notice or approval.

19. **AUTHORIZATION TO SECURE CREDIT INFORMATION** Customer authorizes Broker to contact such banks, financial institutions, credit agencies, employers, brokerage firms and any references it shall deem appropriate, from time to time, for credit purposes and for verification of the matters contained in this Agreement and the continuing accuracy of information

Figure 8-5. (Cont.)

supplied by Customer. Customer understands that an investigation may be made pertaining to his personal and business credit standing and that Customer may make a written request within a reasonable period of time for complete and accurate disclosure of its nature and scope.

20. **TRANSFER OF FUNDS** Broker may at any time, and from time to time, without prior notice to Customer, transfer from one account to another account carried by Broker in which Customer has any interest, such excess funds, equities, securities or other property as in Broker's judgment may be required for margin, or to reduce any debit balance or to reduce or satisfy any deficits in such other accounts. Notices of all transfers of funds made pursuant hereto shall be promptly confirmed in writing to the Customer.

21. **TRANSMITTALS TO BROKER** All monies, securities, negotiable instruments and other property and communications shall be mailed or otherwise transmitted to Broker at 440 South La Salle Street, 20th Floor, Chicago, Illinois 60605, and shall be deemed received only when actually received by Broker.

22. **RISK DISCLOSURE STATEMENT** Customer acknowledges receipt of a "Risk Disclosure Statement" in the form specified by the Commodity Futures Trading Commission.

23. **ACKNOWLEDGEMENT OF INDEPENDENT STATUS** Customer understands that Geldermann, Inc. is an independent operating subsidiary of ConAgra, Inc. The market recommendations of Geldermann, Inc. are based solely on the judgment of its personnel, and Geldermann, Inc. is solely responsible for such recommendations. These market recommendations may or may not be consistent with the market position or intentions of ConAgra, Inc., its other subsidiaries or affiliates.

24. **NO LIABILITY AS CLEARING BROKER** If Customer's account is carried by Broker only as a clearing broker, Customer acknowledges that Broker is not responsible for the conduct, representations and statements of any introducing broker or commodity trading advisor handling the account.

25. **RECORDING OF CONVERSATIONS** Recognizing the protection afforded both Customer and Broker by the recording of telephone conversations, Customer acknowledges, authorizes, and consents to the recording of his telephone conversations with Broker, or any of its agents or solicitors, by means of electronic telephone recording equipment without the use of an automatic tone warning device. Customer understands that such recorded conversations may be used, and Customer hereby authorizes such use, as evidence by either party in any action arising out of this Agreement. Customer acknowledges that Broker, in its absolute discretion, may erase tapes on the seventh business day following the day of recording.

26. **CAPTIONS** All captions used herein are for convenience only, are not a part of this Agreement, and are not to be used in construing or interpreting any aspect of this Agreement.

I have read, understand and agree to all of the provisions of this Agreement.

_____   _____
Date   Customer's Signature

BANKRUPTCY DISCLOSURE STATEMENT

This statement is furnished to you because rule 190.10(c) of the Commodity Future Trading Commission requires it for reasons of fair notice unrelated to this company's current financial condition.

1. **You should know that in the unlikely event of this company's bankruptcy, property, including property specifically traceable to you, will be returned, transferred or distributed to you, or on your behalf, only to the extent of your pro rata share of all property available for distribution to customers.**
2. **Notice concerning the terms for the return of specifically identifiable property will be by publication in a newspaper of general circulation.**
3. **The Commission's regulations concerning bankruptcies of commodity brokers can be found at 17 code of federal regulations Part 190.**

I HAVE READ THIS BANKRUPTCY DISCLOSURE STATEMENT, AND UNDERSTAND IT.

_____   _____
Date   Customer's Signature

LAW GOVERNING—CONSENT TO JURISDICTION IN AND OF COURTS IN ILLINOIS All actions or proceedings arising directly or indirectly in connection with, out of, related to or from this Agreement, or in connection with Customer's account with Broker shall be governed by the law of Illinois, and may, at the discretion and election of Broker, be litigated only in courts whose situs is within the City of Chicago, Illinois. Customer hereby consents and submits to the jurisdiction of any state or federal court located within the City of Chicago, Illinois and appoints C T CORPORATION SYSTEM, whose address is 208 South LaSalle Street, Chicago, Illinois 60604, telephone: (312) 263-1414, his agent for service of process; provided, however, that as a condition of valid service upon him, the agent promptly upon receipt of such process mail same, together with all papers received therewith, to Customer at his current address as then furnished by said Broker. Such mailing shall be by certified mail, return receipt requested. Customer agrees that service on said agent with notice as required herein shall subject him to the jurisdiction of such courts in the City of Chicago, Illinois.

_____   _____
Date   Customer's Signature

NOTE: NO CHANGES OR ALTERATIONS CAN BE MADE IN THIS CUSTOMER AGREEMENT FORM EXCEPT AS PROVIDED IN PARAGRAPH 15.

Figure 8-6.

JOINT ACCOUNT AGREEMENT

ACCOUNT NUMBER _____

Dear Sirs:

1. The undersigned (herinafter referred to as "we") hereby request you to open an account in our behalf on the terms and conditions stated herein, and in your usual form of customers' agreement signed by us or on our behalf, and any one of the undersigned is hereby authorized to sign such agreement on behalf of all of us. We intend to deal through you as brokers, in stocks, bonds and other securities and/or in commodities and futures contracts. You may carry the account under such designation as we may instruct.

2. We hereby state that we are:

IMPORTANT CLAUSE (a) OR (b) MUST BE CROSSED OUT BEFORE SIGNING

(a) joint tenants with right of survivorship and not tenants in common. In the event of the death of either or any of us, the entire interest in the account shall be vested in the survivor, or survivors, on the same terms and conditions as theretofore held and the estate of the decedent shall have no interest in the assets of the account at the date of death or in its operation thereafter. The estate shall, however, remain liable for obligations of the account as provided in paragraph 3 below.

(b) tenants in common, each of us having an undivided interest therein. In the event of the death of either or any of us, you may, in your sole discretion either liquidate the account or accept the instructions of the survivor, or a majority of the survivors, as the case may be, as to its continuance and as to the respective interest of the parties (including the estate) therein, and in either event the decedent's estate shall remain liable for obligations of the account as provided in paragraph 3 below.

3. We hereby state that whether we are joint tenants or tenants in common, our liability hereunder shall be joint and several, and you shall have a lien on the separate property of each of us, as well as on the property in said account, to secure our joint and several liability. We will give you immediate notice in writing of the death of any one of us. You may in the event of the death of any one of us, whether we are joint tenants or tenants in common, take such steps as you may deem necessary or desirable to protect yourselves with respect to taxes and other claims; and you may, before releasing any of the properties in the account, require such proofs of death, tax waivers, other documents, and instruments of guarantee by the survivors as in your judgment may be necessary or desirable in connection with the liquidation or continuation of the account. The estate of any of us who shall have died shall be liable, and the survivor, or survivors, shall continue liable, jointly and severally, for any debit balance or loss in the account resulting from the completion of transactions initiated prior to the receipt by you of written notice of the death of any one of us, or incurred in the liquidation of the account.

4. None of us is under a legal disability and no one other than the undersigned has an interest in this joint account. Each of us shall have authority: (1) to give any instructions with respect to the account, including but not limited to instructions with respect to buying or selling or withdrawals of excess funds, (2) to receive any demands, notices, confirmations, reports, statements, and other communications of any kind; and (3) generally to deal with you in connection herewith as fully and completely as if the other joint tenant or tenants had no interest herein. You shall be under no duty or obligation to inquire into the purpose or propriety of any instruction given and shall be under no obligation to see to the application of any funds so delivered.

5. We agree that if the account shall at any time have no open commitments and no debit or credit balance, you may in your sole discretion treat it as closed, or you may regard it as remaining open subject to further orders or activity, in accordance with the terms of this agreement and the customers agreement signed by or for us. Either, or any of us, however, may terminate the authority of any other of us to reopen the account after it has been closed, upon written notice actually delivered to you.

6. We hereby ratify and confirm all transactions heretofore entered into for said account by any of us. This agreement and your customers' agreement signed by or for us shall be binding upon each of us and our respective heirs, legal representatives and assigns.

NOTE: THIS AGREEMENT IS INEFFECTIVE UNLESS EITHER 2(a) OR 2(b) IS CROSSED OUT. ONE TENANCY MUST BE ELECTED.

_____19

Date

_____

Signatures

Figure 8-7.

PARTNERSHIP ACCOUNT AGREEMENT
PARTNERSHIP CERTIFICATION

Account No. _____

I hereby certify that I am (a) managing partner of _____ ;
a general partnership duly formed under the laws of the State of _____ ;
that as such managing partner, I am authorized on its behalf to execute the within Customer Agreement; that the
following are general partners:

Name	Address

and that the following persons:

Name	Title

are authorized on behalf of the partnership:

    (a) To buy and sell commodities and commodity futures contracts;

    (b) To deposit and withdraw from Geldermann, Inc. money, commodities, futures contracts, securities and
other property;

    (c) To receive all written or oral notices, confirmations, requests, demands and the like sent by Geldermann,
Inc. in connection with maintenance for trading in the account.

Such authorization will continue until notice, in writing, to the contrary is received by Geldermann, Inc.

Dated this _____ day of _____ , 19 _____ .

_____
Managing Partner

ATTEST:

_____
Partner

Figure 8-7. (Cont.)

NOTE: If the managing partner is a corporation, complete the following:

The undersigned, duly authorized by proper resolution of its Board of Directors executes this Agreement on behalf of _____ ,

a corporation duly organized under the laws of _____ ,

said corporation being (a) managing partner of the above-named _____ partnership.

_____
(Vice) President

ATTEST:

_____
(Assistant) Secretary

Representation of General Partners

The undersigned hereby represent that we are all of the partners in a general partnership as identified on the Partnership Customer Fact Sheet, and in consideration of Geldermann, Inc. opening a commodity account for and in the name of the Partnership, we hereby, jointly and severally, represent, agree, and consent to the terms of the basic Customer Agreement and to the following terms:

That person identified on the Partnership Customer Fact Sheet as the Managing Partner is a partner in the Partnership, having a significant interest therein, and is authorized, for its account and risk, to buy, sell, and trade in commodities and commodity futures contracts of every kind whatsoever, and to borrow money for such purposes in said account in accordance with the terms and conditions of the basic Customer Agreement. Geldermann, Inc. may conclusively assume that all actions taken and instructions of the said Managing Partner have been properly taken or given pursuant to authority vested in said Managing Partner by all of the partners in the Partnership. Geldermann, Inc. is authorized to follow the instructions of the said Managing Partner in every respect concerning said account, to make payment of monies as he may order and direct, and to send to him all reports, confirmations, statements, and notices relating to the account. The Managing Partner is authorized to execute and deliver, on behalf of the Partnership and its members, any agreements Geldermann, Inc. may require, to act for the Partnership and its members in every respect concerning said account, and to do all other things necessary or incidental to the conduct of said account, including the designation of an attorney or attorneys-in-fact as fully and completely as if he alone were interested in said account. If new partners are admitted to the Partnership, the undersigned will cause such new members to adopt and be bound by the basic Customer Agreement and related documents. The undersigned further represents that the Articles of Partnership are in writing and provide that the Partnership will not terminate upon the death or incapacity of one of the partners.

_____

_____

_____
(Signatures of All General Partners)

Figure 8-8.

CORPORATE RESOLUTION

ACCOUNT NUMBER _____

ATTESTATION   I hereby certify that I am the Secretary of _____

a corporation organized and existing under the laws of the State of _____;
that as such Secretary I have custody of the records of this corporation, particularly
the records of the minutes of the meetings of the Board of Directors of the

_____ Corporation;

that at a certain meeting of the Board of Directors held on the _____

day of _____, 19_____, at which meeting all of the directors of this
corporation were duly notified in accordance with the by-laws of the corporation, and at
which meeting a quorum of such directors was present, the Board of Directors passed
the following resolutions which are now in force and are not in conflict with the Charter
or by-laws of this corporation.

AUTHORITY TO   RESOLVED, That _____
SIGN CONTRACT   Name
who is _____
                                                    Title
of this corporation, is hereby AUTHORIZED to EXECUTE on behalf of the corporation
ANY AND ALL DOCUMENTATION required of it in order to open and maintain an account in commodities with GELDERMANN, INC. including that certain document
known as "Customer Agreement", an executed copy of which shall be attached to
and made a part of these minutes.

AUTHORITY   FURTHER RESOLVED, that _____
TO TRADE   Name
who is _____
                                                    Title
and_____ who
                                                    Name
is _____
                                                    Title
thereof, or either of them, is hereby AUTHORIZED to BUY AND SELL for and in the name
of this corporation on the Board of Trade of the City of Chicago, as well as on any other
contract market deemed appropriate by either of them.

DESIGNEE TO   FURTHER RESOLVED, that _____
RECEIVE MAIL   Name
_____ who is
                                 Mailing Address
_____ of this corporation, and is not authorized to trade,
is hereby designated as the representative of this corporation TO WHOM WRITTEN
NOTICE OF ACCOUNT ACTIVITY WILL BE MAILED.

NOTE: the representative designated to receive written notices of the transactions must
be someone OTHER than a person(s) authorized to buy and sell for and in the name of
the corporation.

WITNESS, my hand and the corporate seal of this corporation, this _____

day of _____, 19_____.

_____
                              Secretary

_____
                              P.O. Address

(Corporate Seal)

Figure 8-9.

MANAGED ACCOUNT AGREEMENT
LIMITED POWER OF ATTORNEY

ACCOUNT NUMBER: _____

The undersigned, being so authorized and having executed Geldermann, Inc. Customer Agreement for Geldermann, Inc. Account No. _____ standing in the-name of_____ hereby authorizes (Name) _____ (if the attorney-in-fact is a corporation or partnership, indicate the name of the legal entity and the person authorized to act for the entity), who has executed this document signifying his acceptance of the power, as agent and attorney-in-fact for the undersigned, with full power to buy, sell, give orders, and enter into contracts for the purchase and/or sale of commodity futures contracts, options, cash commodities, securities and/or properties in this account with Geldermann, Inc.

In all such purchases, sales, trades, as well as management decisions relating to the account, Geldermann, Inc. is hereby authorized to follow the instructions of the above-mentioned agent and attorney-in-fact in every respect; the agent and attorney-in-fact is authorized to act on behalf of the undersigned in the same manner and with the same force and effect as the undersigned might or could with respect to such purchases, sales or trades and with respect to all other things necessary or incidental to the furtherance, proper maintenance and/or conduct of this account. The undersigned agrees to hold Geldermann, Inc. harmless and to indemnify it as to any liability sustained by it with respect to any and all acts and practices of the agent and attorney-in-fact regarding this account, including all losses arising therefrom and debit balance(s) due thereon.

This authorization is a continuing one and shall remain in full force and effect until revoked by the undersigned, or an authorized person on his behalf, by written notice given to Geldermann, Inc., One Financial Place, 20th Floor, Chicago, Illinois 60605, Attention: Director of Compliance. Such revocation shall become effective only upon actual receipt thereof by Geldermann, Inc., but shall not affect any liability in any way resulting from transactions initiated prior to its receipt. This authorization shall inure to the benefit of Geldermann, Inc., its successors and assigns.

All statements, notices, correspondence and the like generated in this account shall be sent or given to the attorney-in-fact at the address shown for this account and to the undersigned at the address indicated on the Customer Account Agreement, or to such other person or address as the undersigned may hereafter designate in writing.

The acknowledgement of the agent and attorney-in-fact is a certification that he has complied with all applicable registration or other requirements of regulatory bodies and evidences his agreement to be bound by the terms of the Geldermann, Inc. Agreement for the account being managed insofar as the terms thereof may be applicable to him.

_____   _____
Date   Signature of Customer

_____   _____ (Seal)
Date   Signature of Agent and Attorney-in-Fact

Gentlemen:

I have carefully examined the provisions of the document by which I have given trading authority or control over my account to:

_____
(Name)

_____
(Address)

and understand fully the obligations which I have assumed by executing that document including:

(1) I understand that past performance, whether actual or simulated is no guarantee of future results. Any and all representations which have been made to me with respect to past performance or anticipated future results have been made in writing and I have attached copies of any and all such representations to this agreement. Any and all representations which have been made to me with respect to: (a) any trading systems to be used or (b) to the manner

OVER

Figure 8-9. (Cont.)

in which my account will be treated (such as any predetermined trading suspension level) other than as described in the Customer Agreement, have also been made to me in writing and have been attached to this form.

(2) I am aware of the fact that _____ is receiving commissions as part or all of their compensation for managing my account. I am also aware that this creates a potential conflict of interest. I therefore agree to check statements sent to me promptly upon receipt and to immediately contact the Director of Compliance if I should have any complaints about how my account has been handled.

(3) I understand that your firm is in no way responsible for any loss to me occasioned by the actions of the individual or organization named above and that your firm does not, by implication or otherwise, endorse the operating methods of such individual or organization. I further understand that the exchanges of which you are a member have no jurisdiction over a non-member who is not employed by one of its members, and that if I give to such individual or organization authority to exercise any of my rights over my account I do so at my own risk.

_____   _____
Date   Signature of Customer

SPECIAL NOTICE TO CUSTOMERS

We have received a document by which you have granted trading authority or control over your commodity account carried by us to _____

We are required by Exchange rules to bring the following to your attention:

Since the risk factor is high in futures trading, only genuine ''risk'' funds should be used in such trading. A person who does not have extra capital he can afford to lose should not trade in the futures market. No ''safe'' trading system has ever been devised, and no one can guarantee you profits or freedom from loss. In fact, no one can even guarantee to limit the extent of your loss.

Even though you have granted trading authority to another, you should keep posted on what is going on in your account. We shall send you a confirmation of every trade made for your account. In addition, we shall send you monthly statements showing your ledger balance, the exact position in your account, the net profit or loss in all contracts closed since the date of your last previous statement, and the net unrealized profit and loss in all open contracts marked to the market. You should carefully review these statements. If you have any questions, call us.

The preceding paragraph does not apply to bona fide hedging accounts over which a banking institution has trading authority. These bona fide hedge accounts may be carried irrespective of the amount of net equity therein, so long as applicable margin requirements are met and guaranteed by the banking institution. Only the banking institution may make trades in such accounts.

The trading authorization over your account remains in effect until revoked in writing by you.

If, for any reason, you wish to revoke the trading authorization which you have given, please bear in mind that you can do so only by a written revocation directed to Geldermann, Inc.

_____   _____
Date   Signature of Customer

IF THIS ACCOUNT IS CONTROLLED BY A REGISTERED C.T.A., THIS PART MUST BE SIGNED.

I hereby acknowledge that I have received and understood the disclosure document of my account controller.

_____   _____
Date   Signature of Customer

Figure 8-10.

HEDGE ACCOUNT AGREEMENT

ACCOUNT NUMBER_____

You are hereby notified that all transactions affected for this account and all positions taken in this account will be bona fide hedging transactions and positions as described in Section 4(a) of the Commodity Exchange Act as amended and Regulation 1.3(z) promulgated thereunder. Customer agrees that all transactions and positions executed or carried in this account will be consistent with these provisions as presently construed or as amended from time to time. It is agreed that positions carried in the account will be strictly for hedge purposes, and not for speculation, and that a separate account must be used to accommodate non-hedge trades, and further agreed that Broker will rely on the representation that all trades made in this account are bona fide hedges and that it shall have no obligation to inquire into or verify the nature of such trades or incur any liability if, in fact, they may not be such.

This notification is a continuing one and shall remain in force until cancelled in writing by the undersigned.

_____   _____
Date   Authorized Account Signature

CUSTOMER INSTRUCTIONS

Commodity Futures Trading Commission *Regulation 190.06 (d)* requires that a commodity broker must provide an opportunity for each customer to specify when undertaking its first hedging contract whether, in the event of the commodity broker's bankruptcy, such customer prefers that open commodity contracts held in a hedging account be liquidated by the trustee. Accordingly, please indicate below your preference for open contracts in your account if such an event were to occur.

I prefer that, in the event of bankruptcy, the trustee:

☐ liquidate

|check one|

☐ not liquidate

open commodity contracts in my hedge account without seeking my instructions.

_____   _____
Date   Authorized account signature

back-office work that is associated with their customers' futures business. For example, FCM *A*, which is not a clearing member of any exchange, might open an omnibus account with FCM *B*, which clears on all major exchanges. All of FCM *A*'s customer positions would be carried in this single account rather than in separate accounts for each customer. The identities of FCM *A*'s customers may or may not be known to FCM *B*, depending on the type of back-office support needed by FCM *A*. When the identities are not known, the account is termed an *undisclosed omnibus account.*

TRANSFERRING ACCOUNTS

Generally, all purchases and sales of futures contracts must be executed openly and competitively; that is, transactions take place as brokers cry out their bids and offers in the trading pit during the regular trading hours as prescribed by the exchange for the given contract market. Competitive executions are required by both the CFTC and the exchanges themselves.

One exception to this rule is the transfer of futures positions from one FCM to another. Suppose that a customer wants to move his account from FCM *A* to FCM *B*. From the perspectives of both the exchange and the clearinghouse, this transfer is equivalent to the purchase by FCM *B* of the long positions that are held by FCM *A* in the customer's account and the sale by FCM *B* of the short positions that are held by FCM *A* in the customer's account. Such purchases and sales need not be made by open outcry in the trading ring. Rather, they are written up and processed separately after both FCMs involved receive written instructions from the customer involved. These position transfers are known as *ex-pit transactions* because they take place outside the trading pit. Another type of permissible ex-pit transaction is discussed in Chapter 10 on hedging.

When transferring futures contracts from one house to another, the customer may incur extra commission expenses. The FCM that initially carries the open positions must sell all the long contracts and buy in all the short contracts in an ex-pit transaction as described in the preceding paragraph. Also, the firm that takes over the account picks up the contracts that are being transferred. Though they do not have to be transacted competitively, these ex-pit trades are carded and cleared in the usual manner. The FCM that is losing the account gives the customer a confirmation and a statement that shows the closing out of the futures positions. This FCM also charges the regular commission and issues to the receiving FCM a check for the cash balance in the customer's account. The new firm may also charge the regular commission when the contracts are offset. Sometimes, the receiving FCM will waive these commissions in order not to discourage a new customer from opening an account.

MAINTAINING AND SERVICING CUSTOMER ACCOUNTS

Once a customer account has been opened and approved for trading, the responsibilities of the FCM and its account representative are: (1) to make sure that the account is properly margined at all times, (2) to accept and transmit to the trading floor all customer trading instructions (orders) and (3) to keep the customer informed of all trading or other activity in his or her account.

Procedures relating to maintaining proper margin are discussed in Chapter 7.

Handling Orders

An order represents the client's instructions to his FCM's representative to buy or sell a futures contract in a prescribed manner. Normally the order contains information regarding the size of the transaction, its price and the length of time the order is to remain effective. The job of the FCM's account representative is to record the order, assign it proper identification, time-stamp it, and promptly transmit it to the trading floor according to procedures prescribed by the FCM.

All orders executed on the trading floor are to be filled by *open outcry* in the open market during the hours of regular trading. This means that bids and offers must be made openly and audibly by public outcry and in such a manner as to be open to all members in the trading areas at the same time.

The key types of orders used to execute futures transactions are as follows:

Market Order

A *market order* is an order to be executed at the best possible price at the moment the order reaches the trading floor. The price changes, of course, as buyers compete with other buyers and sellers with other sellers. The continuously changing bids and offers persist until a buyer and a seller agree on a price. The best possible "at-the-market" price is therefore the price that results from bids and offers converging to the same level. The advantage of a market order is that it guarantees an execution, since the floor broker is obligated to fill a market order immediately. The disadvantage is that the resulting price may not be very favorable, especially in illiquid markets.

Limit Orders

A customer who wishes either to buy or to sell only at a specified price or at one more favorable must place a limit on the price. A *limit order* is an order that tells the broker to execute a transaction only at a specified price or at one more favorable to the client. A limit order to buy is to be executed at or below the specified limit. A limit order to sell is to be executed at or above the price limit.

The main advantage of a limit order is that the customer determines the least favorable price he or she is willing to pay or to accept. The customer does not have to stay continuously in touch with the broker to get the results if the market does move to the specified limit. In effect, the client is instructing his FCM as follows: "I expect the market to give me the opportunity to buy (or sell) at the level specified in my order. So if the market price hits that level, tell the floor broker to fill this order at that price or at any price that is better. But do not fill the order at any price less favorable than the limit."

No matter what the outcome, though, a limit order never becomes a market order. It is either executed as a limit order or not at all.

Market-If-Touched (MIT) Orders

A *market-if-touched (MIT)* order is an order to execute a transaction at the best available price when the market reaches a price specified by the customer. An MIT order to buy becomes a market order to buy when the futures trade at or below the order price. An MIT order to sell becomes a market order to sell when the futures trade at or above the order price.

The MIT order is therefore like a limit order in some ways but like a market order in others. Like a limit order, the MIT order is not executed until the specified price is reached or "touched." Also like a limit order, the MIT must not be filled if the market never touches the order price. But unlike a limit order, the MIT becomes a market order once the price is touched, and it must be executed at the best possible price. Even if it is impossible to execute the order at the specified price, the MIT must be filled. So the best possible price could be better or worse than the limit.

An MIT order to buy is used by someone who wants to establish a long position or to cover a short position when the market declines to a specific level. That specific level is lower than the current market level.The order does not have to be executed at the MIT price, but it has to be executed when the market trades or is offered at or below the MIT price.

An MIT order to sell is used to establish a short position or to liquidate a long position when the market advances to a certain level. The MIT, of course, assures the trader of getting the order filled. It is appropriate for someone who does not want to take the chance of not being able to sell, as could happen with a limit order when the broker is unable to execute the order at the limit price.

Stop Order

A *stop order*, sometimes called a *stop-loss order* or simply a *stop*, is an order to buy or sell at the market when the market reaches a specified price. A stop order to buy, entered above the prevailing market, becomes a market order when the contract is either traded or bid at or above the stop price. A stop order to sell, entered below the prevailing market, becomes a market order when the contract is either traded or offered at or below the stop price.

Stop orders differ from MITs principally in their relationships to prevailing price levels. Stop orders to buy are entered above the prevailing market price; stops to sell are entered below. MITs are entered in an opposite manner.

As with an MIT order, the client is not guaranteed the specified price. Depending on the action in the market, the price could be at, higher, or lower than the stop price. All the customer is guaranteed, once the limit is hit, is that the order will be filled at the best possible price.

Stop orders are used basically for one of three purposes:

- To automatically cut short the loss on a position if prices reach a predetermined unfavorable level,
- To protect a profit on an existing long or short position, or
- To initiate a new long or short position.

Stop Limit Order

A *stop limit order* is an order that contains both a stop price and a limit price. This type of order, as its name implies, combines the characteristics of a stop order and a limit order. A stop limit order contains two prices: the *stop price*, which is the level at which the order is activated, and the *limit price*, which specifies where the order can be filled. The floor broker is prohibited from paying above or selling below the limit price once the stop price has been touched. In other words, the customer is instructing the floor broker that his or her order should be treated as a stop order, but not to pay more than the specified limit if the order is for a purchase or to take less than the specified limit if for a sale.

This type of order is useful to the customer who wants the automatic activitation of the stop order but also the restrictiveness of a limit order. A customer, anticipating a sharp and rapid change in the market, wants to participate as long as the price seems favorable. But the customer is not willing to enter the market at any price. Once again, the trader is not guaranteed that the order will be filled. He can be assured only that, if executed, the price will be no worse than the limit level.

A stop limit order to buy becomes a straight limit order to buy as soon as the contract either trades or is bid at or above the stop price. It is executed as a limit order only at the limit price or lower. This type of order can either cover a short position or establish a long position. A stop limit order to sell becomes a straight limit sell order as soon as the futures contract is either traded or offered at or below the stop price. It is executed as a limit order only at the limit price or higher.

The limit specified in this type of order does not have to be the same as the stop price. It may be lower in the case of a sell stop limit or higher in the case of a buy stop limit.

Time Orders

Orders may be good for a specified period of time, or they may be *open*, that is, effective until explicitly cancelled by the customer. An order may be entered for a day, a week, a month, or good until cancelled.

Day Orders. A *day order* is an order that expires automatically at the end of the trading session on the day the order is entered, unless it is cancelled or executed before the session closes. All orders are considered to be day orders unless otherwise specified by the customer. They are good for only the day on which they are entered or for that part of the trading session that remains after the order has been entered.

Time-of-the-Day Orders. A *time-of-the-day order* is one that must be executed at a specific time or at specific intervals during the trading session.

Off-at-a-Specific-Time Order. This is a day order with a time contingency. It remains in effect only until the time indicated, whereupon it is cancelled if not executed.

Open Orders. An *open order*, also known as a *GTC order*, is "good till cancelled." However, an open order automatically expires at the end of the trading session on the last trading day when that delivery expires. Open orders remain in effect until the customer explicitly cancels them or until the contract expires. A speculator uses this type of order when he or she feels the market action will eventually bring the desired price, at which time the order will go into effect automatically.

Fill-or-Kill Orders

A fill-or-kill order is one that must either be executed upon receipt by the broker or automatically cancelled. In other words, once the broker receives the order, he or she must try to fill it at the price specified or at a better price. If filling the order is impossible, the broker reports an *unable* to the customer along with the latest quote. If the broker can fill part of the order, he or she will do that and report an unable on the balance. In either case, the broker automatically cancels the order, wholly or partially, and reports the latest quote to the customer.

Scale Orders

A scale order is an order to buy or sell two or more lots of the same future at designated price intervals. If the first part of a scale order is a limit or a stop order at a set price, then all other limits or stop prices are set when the scale order is entered.

Combination Orders

A *combination order* consists of two orders entered at the same time, with one contingent on the other. Sometimes the cancellation of one is contingent upon the execution of the other. Sometimes the purchase or sale of one contract at a limit in one month is dependent on price action in another delivery month. Combination orders can be classed as either *alternative orders* or *contingent orders.*

Alternative Orders. A group of orders may be entered simultaneously with the understanding that the execution of any one of the group automatically cancels those remaining. An alternative order is also referred to as an either/or order or a *one-cancels-the-other order (OCO).*

This type of order might be used by a customer who wants either to take a profit on a short position at a price below the market or to cut short his loss at a certain price above the market. The customer is placing a limit order to buy and a stop order to buy, with the understanding that if one of the orders is executed, the other order is immediately cancelled. For example, the customer might want to buy 5 February pork bellies either on a decline to 50.30 cents or on an advance above 51.30 cents.

Contingent Orders. Contingent orders are grouped orders, each of whose execution depends on the execution of the other. In other words, one order is filled if, and only if, the other is. Since the subsequent order can be filled only when others are done, the contingent order is sometimes referred to as a *when-done* order.

Principally, contingent orders can be executed in two ways:

- the simultaneous purchase of one contract and the sale of another at a stipulated price, or
- the execution of one order before the execution of the other.

On-the-Opening Orders

An *on-the-opening market order* is an order to be executed upon the opening period of the trading session at the best price obtainable at the time. It must be executed within the *opening range* as defined by the exchange where the contract is traded.

On-The-Opening Limit Orders. This type of order is used when the customer wants to buy or sell during the opening call, but only at or below a set limit or at or above a set limit. The order is executed within the limit, if market conditions permit, during the opening call. If it remains unfilled at the end of the opening call, it is cancelled.

On-the-Close Orders

Here the customer desires to buy or sell during the closing period. An *on-the-close order* must be executed within the closing range as defined by the exchange.

Limit or Market On-the-Close Order. Regardless of price, the customer wants an execution that day. The *limit* or *market on-the-close order (MOC)* permits the broker to try for a set limit during the day, but it mandates the broker to get an execution at some price at or before the end of the day. During the day, the order is executed at its limit if the market permits, as a straight limit order. If it remains unfilled at the close of the trading session, it becomes an MOC regardless of the limit that was effective prior to the close.

Spread Orders

A spread order is an order to buy one futures contract and to sell another, either in the same contract or in different contracts and in the same or different markets. A spread order can be either at the market or at a specific difference. For instance, an order may read: buy 5 June gold and sell 5 December gold at the market. Or a client can place an order for a spread when the December delivery is $10 over the June.

Cancellations

Inasmuch as orders are actually instructions from the customer to the broker, changes in these instructions must be handled through the cancellation of prior instructions. The customer may want to cancel the whole order or just part of it. He or she may also want to alter some part of the order. Whether the change involves the whole order or just part of it, it has to be implemented by means of a new order. A *straight cancel* order instructs the broker to cancel the former order in its entirety. A CFO (cancel former order), also known as a *cancel-replace* or an *enter-and-cancel,* instructs the broker to cancel the former order and replace it with new instructions.

Reporting Executed Orders

Once an order has been executed, it is the responsibility of the FCM to report that execution back to the client. The order is to be time-stamped when it is reported to the FCM by the floor broker and time-stamped again when reported by the FCM to the customer.

A customer, upon receiving a report or an execution, may request his or her registered representative to check the *time-and-sales price* on the execution if the report does not seem to coincide with the corresponding prices as reported on the quotation equipment. The discrepancy, as noted by the customer, may be due simply to a lag in reporting as a result of heavy and volatile trading. If such is the case, then the customer will eventually be satisfied that the order was filled according to instructions.

If an error has occurred, however, an employee of the member firm contacts the proper department of the exchange for a record of the transactions at the time of the trade in question, to see if the customer's complaint is justified. If the complaint is legitimate, the FCM may credit or debit the customer's account accordingly. This procedure usually takes a few days.

Otherwise, the prices of all executions are considered binding.

CUSTOMER STATEMENTS

A record of every transaction executed by an FCM for a customer is entered into the account record; these entries are made immediately upon the completion of the transaction and on the same day as the transaction. At the end of the month, the broker sends a copy of the account record to the customer. In addition, the broker reports the outcome of each individual transaction to the client immediately, in writing and/or verbally. Following is a summary of the key documents that are usually received by customers in connection with futures transactions.

Confirmations. When a futures order is executed, the FCM usually reports verbally to the customer. The FCM also mails out a written *confirmation* of the transaction on the same day that it is executed. The written confirmation, or *confirm*, must indicate:

- which futures contract was bought or sold,
- the exchange on which the order was executed,
- the quantity,
- the contract maturity (delivery month), and
- the price.

An FCM must issue a confirm when a client initiates a position and must issue *another* confirm when the customer offsets the position.

Purchase-and-Sale (P&S) Statement. Whenever a client offsets a position, the contract is said to be *closed out*. In other words, whenever a customer either sells a contract to offset (or close out) a long position or buys a contract to offset a short position, the transaction calls for additional documentation. In addition to the other confirmations, a *purchase-and-sale (P&S) statement* must be mailed to the customer. This statement shows:

- the quantities that were bought and sold,
- the prices of the position's acquisition and closeout,
- the gross profit (or loss) on the transaction,
- the commission charges, and
- the resulting net credit (or debit) on the transactions.

Monthly Statement. The monthly statement is a record of all the customer's transactions for the calendar month. It generally includes the quantities of the futures contracts that were bought and sold, realized profit or loss, open positions, and open profit or loss. It also summarizes the financial status of the account as of the last day of the month, and thus would include any deposits or withdrawals of funds from the account.

■ PART THREE
■ COMMERCIAL APPLICATIONS

■ Chapter 9

■ Price Relationships in Cash and Futures Markets

The first and most important step toward understanding the commercial use of the futures markets is to study the relationship between cash prices and futures prices. A knowledge of this relationship is essential to an understanding of the mechanics of hedging and arbitrage.

Because there are significant differences between physical commodities and financial instruments in this subject area, we have divided this chapter along appropriate lines. But whether we are discussing hard, storable commodities such as copper or less tangible instruments such as Treasury bills, an awareness of the link between cash and futures serves as a reminder that futures markets have a solid footing in reality. Prices are not the product of a haphazard mix of speculative forces that operate within the confines of the futures market, but rather are the result of the interplay between the supply of and the demand for the commodity or the financial instrument at the cash market level.

PRICE RELATIONSHIPS FOR PHYSICAL COMMODITIES

Physical commodities can be bought and sold in two separate but related markets—the cash market and the futures market. The *cash market* is the commercial marketplace, the various locations along the line from production to consumption at which the commodity changes ownership for a price. For example, in grains the cash market includes many transactions that are made between farmers and country elevators, between country elevators and manufacturers, between country elevators and terminal elevators, between terminal elevators and exporters, and between exporters and foreign buyers. The cash market is a diverse, far-flung arena of commercial suppliers and buyers whose actions eventually forge prices at the distant futures exchanges.

Cash prices are the prices for which the commodity is sold at the various cash market locations. There are many cash prices, all of which are interrelated by either quality, geography, or state of processing. For instance, the price of a bushel of #2 yellow corn from a farm in central Illinois might be $2.25. The same bushel of corn on the same day in Chicago might be $2.35. Why? Because the Chicago price reflects the cost of transporting the corn from the farm where it is grown to the city where it is consumed. The price premium at a Gulf port would be even greater because of the greater distance that is involved. Prices also vary with quality. Number 3 yellow corn, a grade that is inferior to #2, might have a central Illinois price of only $2.20. State of processing also plays a role in cash price differences. The price of a pound of copper varies significantly, depending on whether and to what extent it has been treated for impurities or whether it has been put into a shape that is more useful to a manufacturer. All these factors go into the determination of price differences in the cash market.

Unlike the cash market where prices vary widely according to quality or location, futures markets have only one set of prices. The futures price represents the current market opinion of what the commodity (par-delivery grade and location) will be worth at some time in the future. A price of $2.45 for December corn futures means that the market expects #2 yellow corn that is delivered in Chicago to be worth $2.45 per bushel in December. That same corn in today's cash market may have a price of only $2.35 per bushel. Time and expectation are the two factors that differentiate the price in the cash market from that in the futures market.

The two markets, cash and futures, tend to parallel one another and to converge as each delivery month expires. The parallel movement occurs because factors that bring about a rise or a fall in cash prices usually affect futures prices in much the same manner. It is this correlation between cash and futures that makes hedging possible.

THE BASIS

Basis is the term that is used to describe the numerical difference between a cash price and a futures price. It is important to remember that,

Figure 9-1. The basis.

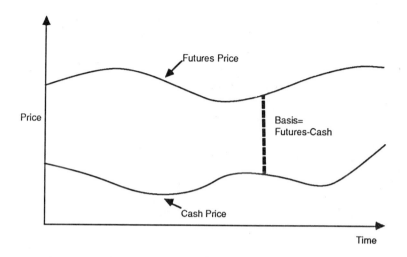

although there may be only one futures price for December delivery of corn, there are many different cash prices for corn, depending on location or quality. As a result, there can be many different bases for the same commodity at the same time. When developing hedging strategies, it is essential that the hedger know "his" basis, that is, the relationship between futures prices and those particular cash prices with which he is involved. In more general terms, however, basis usually refers to the difference between the cash price of the par-delivery* grade at the par-delivery location and that of the nearest active futures contract.

Although there is a high degree of correlation between cash and futures prices, the basis is not constant. As shown in Figure 9-1, cash and futures prices are constantly fluctuating. Hence, unless each changes by exactly the same amount, the basis tends to widen or narrow. During some periods, cash prices advance somewhat faster than futures or they decline faster than futures. In other periods, futures prices outpace cash prices in either direction.

The movement of the basis is brought about by a variety of factors. First and most important is the relationship between supply and demand. Under normal conditions, futures prices of physical commodities are higher than cash prices. As we shall see later, this premium of the

---

*A reminder: *Par-delivery grade* is that grade of the commodity that is called for in the delivery specifications of the futures contract. *Par-delivery location* is that delivery location that is called for in the futures contract.

futures market over cash (known as a *normal market*) usually indicates that supplies are adequate for both present and anticipated levels of demand. Conversely, when the price of futures is lower than the cash price (known as an *inverted market*), it is usually an indication of heavy demand for immediate delivery—demand that is motivated by fears of a possible shortage (see Figures 9-2 and 9-3).

Whether the cash price at the local delivery point is higher or lower than the nearby futures price is largely determined by the amount of the commodity that is available on the market, relative to demand at that time. For example, if the available supply at the delivery point appears to be large enough to take care of prospective requirements until the next futures delivery period, the cash price usually moves to a level that is lower than (*at a discount to*) the price of the nearest futures delivery. If prospective requirements appear to be larger than the supplies that are coming onto that market until the next delivery, the cash price usually moves to a premium above the futures price. In other words, if the immediate demand is in excess of available supplies, the cash price turns out to be higher than (*at a premium to*) the price of the nearest futures, regardless of the cost of carrying (or storing) the commodity from one point in time to another.

In Figure 9-2, futures prices are said to be *at a premium to* cash prices. Cash prices are said to be *at a discount to* futures prices.

In Figure 9-3, futures prices are said to be *at a discount to* cash prices. Cash prices are said to be *at a premium to* futures prices.

The basis is also subject to seasonal influences. The basis for physical commodities tends to widen at certain times during the marketing season and to narrow at other times. The premium of futures over cash prices and the discount of futures under cash prices tend to shift back and forth during the overall season. This widening and narrowing reflects the relative surplus during one part of the season and the relative depletion during another. For example, in a normal market cash grain prices tend to decline faster than grain futures prices during the harvest period because of the abundant supplies coming onto the market over a short period of time. Thus, the basis widens. Once the harvest has been completed and harvest pressures abate, the basis usually begins to narrow. That is, the cash price either rises more quickly or falls more slowly than futures prices. As a season's supplies are used up, the quantity available at some locations may become short, and cash prices at those locations tend to strengthen relative to the futures price. Thus, supply and demand patterns change according to seasonal demands.

Figure 9-2. Normal market (futures prices higher than cash prices).

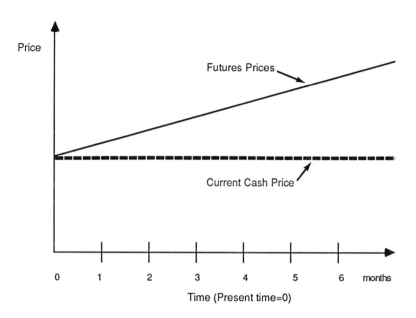

Figure 9-3. Inverted market (futures prices lower than cash prices).

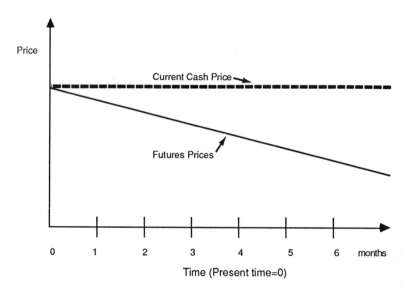

A number of other factors have a bearing on the basis of physical commodities. Transportation problems can cause dislocations in supplies for the cash article, widening the basis in some areas and narrowing it in others. The availability of storage space for the cash commodity is another important factor that influences basis movement. Whatever the particular reason, basis changes do occur. Because the hedger has offsetting long and short positions in the cash market and the futures market, any departure from a constant basis represents a potential profit or loss. Even though the price difference between cash and futures may vary, the risk of an adverse change in the basis is generally much smaller than the risk of a change in the cash price itself. In other words, the risk of going unhedged is greater than the hedger's risk of an unfavorable change in the basis.

Cash and Futures Prices in Time

Under normal circumstances of adequate supply, the price of a physical commodity for future delivery will be approximately equal to the present cash price plus the amount it costs to carry or store the commodity from the present to the month of delivery. These costs, known as *carrying charges*, determine the normal premium of futures over cash and have a profound effect on changes in the basis.

Calculating Carrying Charges

Carrying charges consist of three main components: (1) the cost of storage or warehousing, (2) insurance, and (3) the interest expense that is incurred during storage. To illustrate: A storage facility may charge 5 cents per bushel per month to store corn. Insurance might amount to $1/4$ cent per bushel per month. To calculate the third component, interest, we take the value of the commodity that is being stored and multiply it by an appropriate annual interest rate. Thus, with corn at $2.50 per bushel and interest rates at 10% per annum, the annual interest cost of storing one bushel of corn is 25 cents, or a little more than 2 cents per month. Interest is a key factor in carrying charges and must be included regardless of whether money is actually borrowed (incurring a real interest expense) or is simply tied up in a non-interest-bearing asset such as corn (incurring an opportunity cost).

In our example, we have the following carrying costs:

Storage: 5 cents per bushel per month
Insurance: 1/4 cent per bushel per month
Interest: 2 cents per bushel per month
Total carrying charge: 71/4 cents per bushel per month

To determine the carrying charge for a period of time, multiply the monthly carrying charge by the number of months that the actual commodity is to be stored. If it costs 71/4 cents per bushel per month to carry corn in storage, the full carrying charge between, say, November and March is 29 cents (4 months x 71/4 cents per month). The actual commodity is carried for a maximum of four months: November, December, January, and February. March is not included in the calculations because the actual grain can be delivered against the March contract on March 1. When figuring carrying charges, always assume that delivery will occur at the earliest possible time. As we discussed in Chapter 3, the time of delivery against futures contracts within the delivery period is at the option of the seller. Sellers will generally deliver as early as possible rather than incur the additional carrying costs that are associated with deliveries that are made later than the first possible day.

Carrying charges vary greatly from commodity to commodity, but the procedure for calculating them is the same for all. Storage and insurance rates must be obtained from the providers of these services. Interest costs are then calculated by first figuring the annual rates for loans that were secured by the items being stored and dividing by 12 to arrive at the monthly figure.

In some commodities, such as precious metals, the interest expense is by far the largest component of the carrying charge. This is because the amount of space that is required to store a large value of gold or platinum is relatively small. Thus, interest rates are a key factor in basis changes for the precious metals. For other, bulkier, commodities like potatoes or grains, where large space is required to hold significant value, warehouse charges dominate interest rates in determining changes in the basis.

We noted previously that when supplies are adequate, futures will trade at a premium to the cash price that is equivalent to the cost of carrying the commodity from the present to the first day of the month of future delivery. Put another way, the futures price should approximately equal the cash price plus the cost of carry. Why is this so? Consider two facts: (1) costs are incurred in storing and maintaining the quality of a physical commodity (from our previous discussion we know that these carrying charges consist of storage, insurance, and interest), and (2) the costs that are associated with holding a futures contract are nil. Quite obviously, there are no storage or insurance costs attendant to holding a futures contract. The only interest expense would be that associated with funds that are held as margin, but this is likely to be minuscule. The only real costs are commissions, but these too are usually negligible in comparison with physical commodity carrying costs.

Therefore, we have two methods of owning a commodity. One (the cash market) offers immediate possession but carries with it additional costs. The other (the futures market) entails deferred possession but carries no additional costs. Let us compare these alternatives in an example.

> *Example:* In November, a feed manufacturer knows that he will need to replenish his supply of corn in March. Concerned about rising prices and wanting to lock in his costs now, he has two choices. First, he can buy cash corn now and store it until he needs it in March. This will entail a carrying cost of, say, $7^{1}/4$ cents per bushel per month for four months, or 29 cents per bushel. If the present cash price for corn is $2.25 per bushel, the total cost to the feed manufacturer of buying the corn now and storing it until March is $2.54 per bushel ($2.25 + $0.29 = $2.54). The second option is to buy March futures, hold the position until March, and take delivery. Because there are virtually no costs associated with holding the futures contract, a March futures price of less than $2.54 per bushel would make it the more profitable alternative. Thus, the difference in carrying costs makes the futures contract 29 cents per bushel more valuable than the cash article delivered today. (We have ignored any transportation or quality factors that would alter the arithmetic and obscure the basic point.)

Normal Markets

As we discussed earlier, a normal market is one in which the futures market commands a premium over the cash market that reflects all or some of the relevant carrying charges. Figure 9-4 depicts the price structure of the corn market when carrying charges are $7^{1}/4$ cents per bushel per month. Notice that the price of each succeeding futures delivery

Figure 9-4. *Cash/futures relationship in a full carrying charge market.*

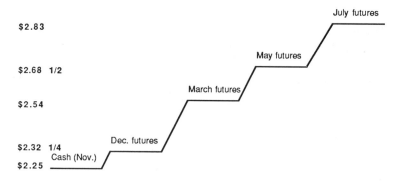

month reflects the full cost of carry. This is known as a *full carrying-charge market.*

The theory of carrying charges states that in a normal market, futures prices will exceed cash prices by an amount that is equal to the cost of carrying the commodity. An important corollary to this theory is that the futures market cannot trade at a premium over the cash market that is greater than the carrying charge. This can best be illustrated with an example.

> *Example:* Using the numbers in the previous example, we know that a price of $2.54 per bushel for March corn futures reflects full carrying costs. Our corollary states that March futures cannot trade at a premium over cash that is greater than the cost of carry (29 cents per bushel). What prevents March futures from trading at a price of, say, $2.60 when cash is $2.25? The answer is that dealers could simply buy cash corn for $2.25 and simultaneously sell March futures at $2.60. They could then carry the corn for four months, incurring the 29 cents carrying charge. Because their total cost is $2.54, they could deliver the corn against the March futures contract at $2.60 and pocket a 6-cents-per-bushel profit. The collective action of dealers who buy cash corn and sell futures would soon narrow the premium to the point where no such profit opportunity existed.

As we shall see later, no market forces can limit the theoretical premium of cash over futures in times of shortage.

The Convergence of Cash and Futures Prices in a Normal Market

It should be obvious that once a futures contract reaches its delivery period, there is little difference between it and the actual cash article. Any premium that futures might have commanded has been erased by the passage of time. Thus, in the actual month of delivery the difference between the price of the cash commodity of par-delivery specifications and that of futures should be approximately zero.

We say "approximately zero" because several technical factors may give futures a slight premium or discount to cash in the delivery month. For instance, because delivery of futures is at the option of the seller, futures are a slightly less desirable way for a buyer to take delivery. This may cause futures to sell at a marginal discount to cash in the delivery period. Other factors such as storage and loading availability may also influence the relationship between cash and futures toward the expiration of the contract. For our present purposes, however, it is safe to assume that futures and cash converge to a negligible price difference at the time and place of delivery.

In a normal market, the convergence of futures and cash prices represents the loss of the time premium (carrying charge) that is attached to the futures contract. Referring to Figure 9-4, we see that in November the July futures contract held a 58 cent premium over cash. This reflects 8 months of carrying the corn at $7\frac{1}{4}$ cents per bushel per month. Obviously, as time passes and the number of months that the commodity must be stored declines, the premium of futures over cash shrinks. Figure 9-5 shows how the premium of July futures over cash decays with time. Beginning at 58 cents per bushel in November, it falls to zero as the futures contract matures. Figure 9-5 is, of course, a chart of the basis because it represents the difference between futures prices and cash prices.

The decay of futures prices from a full carrying-charge premium over cash to parity with cash represents an important force in the economics of most storable commodities. In periods of abundant supply, the decay of the basis encourages users to buy the cash commodity and store it, a desirable goal when supplies are burdensome and prices are falling.

In periods of ample supply, dealers are able to store commodities at little or no net cost by taking advantage of the decay in futures market carrying charges. They simply buy the cash commodity and sell futures

Figure 9-5. Convergence of cash and futures prices in a normal market.

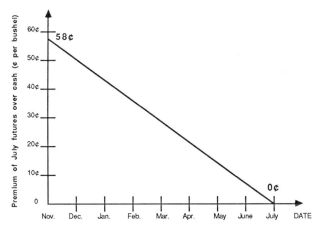

at a full carrying-charge premium. This long-cash/short-futures position is rewarded as the basis gradually declines. The cash-market position gives the dealer an inventory from which the specific needs of his customers can be satisfied.

> *Example:* On November 1 a dealer buys 5,000 bushels of corn from a local farmer at $2.25 per bushel and simultaneously sells March futures at $2.54. On March 1, he sells the cash corn at $2.03 and buys back his March futures at $2.03$1/2$. The result is a profit of 28$1/2$ cents (a loss of 22 cents on the cash position and a profit of 50$1/2$ cents on the futures). This 28$1/2$ cents per bushel covers virtually the entire cost of carrying the cash corn from November 1 to March 1.

In a sense, the futures market has allowed the dealer to buy and maintain an inventory at essentially no cost, and it has done so at a time when burdensome supplies and falling prices would have made prohibitive the risks of carrying an unhedged inventory. The extent to which the relationship between cash and futures reflects carrying charges determines the willingness of dealers to buy and store commodities, and their willingness to do this plays a crucial role in the determination of how excessive supplies are managed by the marketplace.

Inverted Markets

An *inverted market* is one in which cash prices are higher than futures prices. These inversions are a result of supply shortages and the resultant heavy demand for immediate delivery of the commodity. Aggressive buying of immediately available supplies drives cash-market prices to a premium over futures and, as mentioned earlier, there is no theoretical limit to the premium that cash can command over futures. In periods of extreme supply tightness, cash prices can rocket dramatically over those of futures.

An example—perhaps unrealistic, but still instructive—would be to imagine what the price relationship might be between spot water and three-month water futures in the middle of a hot, arid desert. If there were many thirsty people and a shortage of water, nothing would limit the premium that spot water would command over water futures. In more realistic situations, however, large inversions of cash over futures take their toll. Just as normal markets provide an incentive to store commodities, inverted markets provide a disincentive to store and an incentive to bring supplies quickly to market to take advantage of high spot prices.

> *Example:* On November 1 a dealer buys corn from a local farmer at $3.25 and sells March futures against it at $3.00. If he holds the grain until March, when cash and futures will be approximately equal, he will suffer a basis loss of 25 cents per bushel on top of the cost of carrying the grain.

An inverted market punishes dealers who store grain. This means that in times of shortage, stocks are held only by those who need them for immediate consumption or to satisfy commitments. Excess supplies are released to the market where they are needed most.

PRICE RELATIONSHIPS IN INTEREST RATE MARKETS

The first step toward understanding the relationship between cash and futures in interest rate markets involves the *yield curve.* The *yield curve* is a graphical representation of the rates that are associated with instruments of different maturities at a given time. Figure 9-6 is a hypothetical plot of the yields on United States Treasury securities that range from 90 to 360 days maturity.

Another example might depict the yields on government notes and bonds out to the year 2000. In any case, the curve is the net result of all

Figure 9-6. *Normal yield curve.*

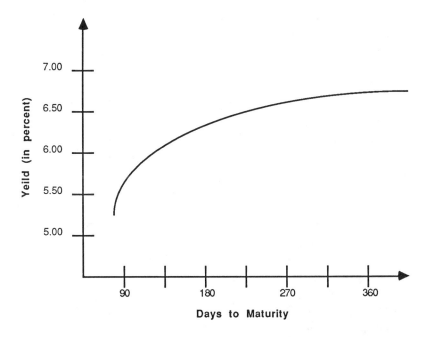

the buying and selling that has taken place. It represents the willingness of investors to hold securities of varying maturities.

The yield curve has two characteristics of particular importance:

- Yields increase with maturity.
- The rate of increase tends to be steepest between the early maturities and flatter between the later ones.

This is the way yield curves are shaped under normal circumstances. It is therefore known as a *normal yield curve.*

The normal yield curve takes its shape largely because of a concept known as *liquidity preference*. The liquidity preference theory argues that shorter-term securities have relatively greater value (lower yields) because they entail less risk. This is true because longer maturity instruments have greater uncertainty associated with them. As an extreme example, take the case of a 20-year Treasury bond versus a 90-day Treasury bill. The bond is subject to greater risks from such factors as inflation or even default than the shorter-term bill. Investors, therefore, will normally require higher yields to compensate for the higher risks that are attendant to owning long-term securities. Another reason that longer-term securities command higher yields is that price volatility tends to increase with term to maturity. An example will help illustrate this point: A 1% increase in the annual yield of a one-year security that has a face value of $1 million would result in a $10,000 decline in the value of the security. The same 1% increase in the yield of a two-year security would produce a decline in value of about $20,000. This is true because yields are expressed on an annual basis. Thus, the $10,000 price decline equates to a 1% increase in yield for the one-year instrument. But for the two-year instrument, a $20,000 decline ($10,000 in each of two years) is necessary to achieve a 1% annual change in yield. For these reasons, the normal yield curve shows rates that increase with maturities.

The normal yield curve also tends to become flatter at the extended maturities. This phenomenon occurs because liquidity preference is a more significant issue for two nearby maturities than for two distant ones. The risks that are associated with owning a two-year versus a one-year security are fairly significant. However, the risk difference between a 30-year instrument and a 29-year one is difficult to imagine. Therefore, investors will ordinarily require a much greater yield premium for the two-year over the one-year instrument than they will for the 30-year over the 29-year instrument.

At times when short-term funds are unusually tight, short-term interest rates can be higher than long-term interest rates. This situation is reflected in an *inverted yield curve*, which is depicted in Figure 9-7. This situation tends to be less common than the normal yield relationship for the reasons described previously.

Implied Forward Yields

The upward slope of the normal yield curve tells us quite clearly that rates increase with maturity. It also reveals something about interest rate expectations. To illustrate, assume that the yield of a one-year instrument is 8% and that of a two-year instrument is 9%. What does this imply about the market's expectation of interest rates during the second year? In other words, interest rates are 8% for year one and 9% for years one and two together. Does this reveal anything about expected rates during year two? Indeed it does. It tells us that rates during year two are expected to be about 10% because 8% in year one and 10% in

Figure 9-7. *Inverted yield curve.*

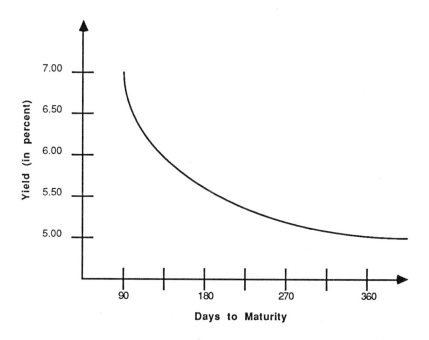

year two average out to 9% for years one and two together. This derivation of the expected interest rate for a future time period from the rates on two existing instruments is known as the *implied forward rate.* The formula for determining the implied forward rate given the rates of two existing instruments is as follows:*

$$IFR = \frac{(L \times I) - (S \times i)}{L - S}$$

where,

IFR = implied forward rate
  I = rate for the longer maturity instrument
  i = rate for the shorter maturity instrument
  L = maturity time of longer instrument
  S = maturity time of shorter instrument

---

*This formula is somewhat oversimplified because it ignores the different rates at which interest income is reinvested as it is received. Interested readers should consult a specialized text on fixed-income instruments.

In our example,

$$IFR = \frac{(2 \times 9\%) - (1 \times \ 8\%)}{2 - 1} = 10\%$$

As we see later, this concept is extremely important in understanding interest rate futures prices.

Interest Rate Futures Prices

All interest rate futures contracts call for delivery of an instrument that will mature at some specified time after the maturity of the futures contract. For example, assume that in March a trader buys a June 90-day T-bill futures contract on the IMM. If the trader were to stand for delivery of this contract, he would receive in June a $1 million T-bill that matures 90 days from the day on which he takes delivery of the futures contract. In other words, the price of the futures contract in March represents the market's expectation of interest rates for the 90-day period from June to September. If you are thinking that this is very similar to the concept of implied forward rates, you are correct.

> *Example:* On March 15, the yield on a 90-day cash T-bill that matures on June 15 is 9.00%, while the yield on a 180-day cash T-bill that matures September 15 is 9.50%. What would you expect the price of June T-bills on the IMM to be, given the above?

> *Answer:* First we must derive the implied forward rate for the period June 15–September 15.

> $$IFR = \frac{180 \times (9.5\%) - 90 \times (9.0\%)}{90} = 10\%$$

Therefore, the price of the June futures should be approximately 90.00. (Remember from Chapter 2 that the IMM index is 100 − yield, or 100.00 −10.00 = 90.00.)

When calculating the *value* of a T-bill or a T-bill futures contract, it is necessary to take into account the lifetime of the T-bill. For example, in the case of a $1 million 90-day T-bill with a discount yield of

10.00%, the dollar discount (D) would be:

$$D = \$1\text{million} \times 0.10 \times \frac{90}{360} = \$25,000$$

This is because the discount yield is always stated as an annualized rate whose actual dollar value depends on the portion of a year (in this case 90 days) that the T-bill is outstanding. More generally:

$$D = F \times d \times \frac{t}{360}$$

where:

D = dollar discount from face value
F = face value of T-bill
d = discount yield (annualized)
t = number of days the T-bill is outstanding

The price of the T-bill is:

$$P = F - D$$

where:

P = price.

We make use of these two formulas in the following example of interest rate arbitrage.

Arbitrage

In the previous example, if the price of June futures were significantly different from the implied forward rate, an arbitrage opportunity would present itself. For example, assume that the futures price was 89.00 (yield = 11%) while the implied forward rate was 10%. An arbitrageur would want to buy the futures (buy the higher yield) and simultaneously sell the implied forward instrument (sell the lower yield). Let's see how this might work:

March 15:

   Futures: Buy June futures @89.00 (yield = 11%)
   Cash: Buy $1 million June 15 cash T-bill (yield = 9.00%)
             and
             Sell $1 million September 15 cash T-bill (yield = 9.50%)

March 15 Accounting:

We must determine the prices of the June 15 and September 15 cash T-bills, given their yields. Bear in mind that the T-bill that matures on September 15 is deliverable against the June futures contract, which calls for delivery of a T-bill that matures 90 days from the June expiration. Recalling the formulas from the previous section, we have:

1. Price of June 15 T-bill = P = Face value (F) – discount (D), where:

$$D = F \times \frac{(d \times t)}{360} = \$1,000,000 \times \frac{0.09 \times 90}{360} = \$22,500$$

which gives:

$$P = \$1,000,000 - \$22,500 = \underline{\$977,500}$$

2. Price of September 15 T-bill = $P = F - D$

$$D = F \times \frac{(d \times t)}{360} = \$1,000,000 \times \frac{(0.095 \times 180)}{360} = \$47,500$$

giving:

$$P = \$1,000,000 - \$47,500 = \underline{\$952,500}$$

Therefore, the arbitrageur has a cash outlay of $977,500 for the June 15 T-bill and a cash receipt from the sale of the September 15 T-bill of $952,500.

June 15:

1. June 15 T-bill matures providing a cash receipt of $1,000,000.
2. Assume that rates have risen and the yields on three-month cash T-bills are now 12%. This means that June futures would have a value of 88.00 (price = $970,000) and that the September 15 T-bill would be priced at $970,000.
3. Take delivery of the June futures to cover the short position in September 15 cash T-bills.

June 15 Accounting:

1. Loss in futures = 89.00 − 88.00 = 1.00 (=$2,500).
2. Cash outlay to take delivery of futures = $970,000.

Summary

Date	Cash Market Transactions	Futures Market Transactions
March 15:	Buy June 15 T-bill: −$977,500 Sell September 15 T-bill: +$952,500	Buy June futures @ 89.00
June 15:	June 15 T-bill matures: +$1,000,000	Take delivery @88.00 Loss: −$2,500 Delivery Cost: −$970,000
Result:	Cash: +$975,000	Futures: −$972,500
	Net Profit: = +$2,500	

Note: The $2,500 profit simply represents the 1% difference between the futures price and the implied forward rate on March 15. The reader can confirm by his or her own calculations that the $2,500 profit would have been achieved regardless of what rates prevailed on June 15. Also note that 90 days was used as the term to maturity. A more precise calculation would require figuring the exact number of days rather than using the 90 day approximation.

The key to any cash/futures arbitrage opportunity is an understanding of equivalent positions in the cash and futures markets. In the above example, on March 15 the purchase of both June 15 cash T-bills and June futures was equivalent to the purchase of September 15 cash T-bills.

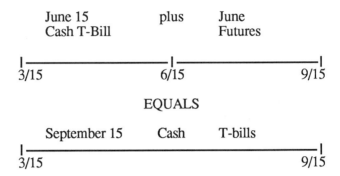

This makes sense because each position represents a six-month investment over the time period that begins on March 15. If an investor wants to invest funds for six months, he can buy a cash T-bill that matures September 15 or he can buy a cash T-bill that matures only three months later on June 15 and "tack on" a futures contract that, if delivery is taken, would provide an investment for the second three-month period from June 15 to September 15.

Consider one more arbitrage situation: We know from the above discussion that the yield of a one-year cash T-bill should approximately equal the combined yields on a three-month cash T-bill, plus 90-day T-bill futures contracts that mature in three months, six months, and nine months.

Because of this equivalency, the cash/futures combination is known as a *synthetic one-year T-bill*. A synthetic bill is created when we combine cash and futures positions such that they are equivalent in the aggregate to another cash T-bill. If the yield on the synthetic bill were, say, 50 basis points lower than that of the one-year cash bill, another arbitrage situation would arise.

Example:
June 15 cash T-bill yield:	9.00%
June futures (90.70)	9.30%
September futures (90.50)	9.50%
December futures (90.20)	9.80%
and	
March 15 (next year) Cash T-bill yield:	9.90%

The yield of the synthetic bill is

$$\frac{9.00 + 9.30 + 9.50 + 9.80}{4} = 9.40$$

or 50 basis points less than that of the equivalent one-year cash bill. Under these circumstances, a dealer could buy the March 15 cash bill and sell June, September, and December futures. He would then finance the one-year cash T-bill for three months. Thus, he would be short the synthetic one-year bill and long the one-year cash bill at a profitable basis difference of 50 points.

The number of arbitrage possibilities in interest rate futures is virtually countless. While the examples above are limited to T-bill futures, opportunities also exist in many combinations that involve T-notes, T-bonds, GNMAs, and so forth. However, it should be remembered that when comparing values of discount and coupon instruments, yields must be expressed in equivalent terms (see Chapter 18).

Price Relationships for Longer-Term Instruments

Given a normal, positively sloped yield curve, interest rate futures trade at a discount to cash. In the case of an inverted yield curve, the opposite is true. As is the case with all physical commodities, the premium or discount at which interest rate futures trade relative to cash generally decays as contract expiration approaches. However, the pattern of this decay and the movement of the basis become a little more complicated when dealing with longer-term coupon instruments. This is true for two reasons. First, prices in the futures market tend to reflect the value of the outstanding cash instrument that is cheapest to deliver against the futures contract. The concept of "cheapness" is explained in the next section, but for now simply note that changes in the underlying instrument on which futures prices are based have an important effect on cash/futures price relationships. The second reason that basis study is more complex for longer-term interest rate instruments relates to the wide range of instruments that can be hedged. The bond futures contract, for instance, is based on the par-delivery 20-year 8% United States T-bond. Basis movements will vary significantly depending on whether we are comparing futures prices to a 10% Treasury bond or a 14% corporate bond because a given change in interest rates will have a markedly different effect on these two instruments. The prices of various coupon instruments must be equated through the use of conversion factors in order for the basis study to have any meaning.

The Concept of Cheapness in Delivery

In general, the price of the futures contract always reflects the price of the par-delivery grade cash commodity called for in the contract. The price of corn futures reflects traders' expectations of the value of #2 yellow corn that is delivered in Chicago. In physical commodities, the number of other grades that can be substituted for the par-delivery grade (#1 or #3 yellow corn, for instance) is rather limited, so the futures price tends to strongly reflect the value of the standard grade. In the case of longer-term coupon instruments, this is not so. At any time, many instruments of different coupon rates and maturities may be eligible for delivery. Because it is in the interest of the short to deliver the instrument that costs him the least, the futures price will tend to reflect whatever that instrument happens to be at a given time.

The long-term Treasury bond contract on the Chicago Board of Trade calls for delivery of a bond with $100,000 principal value and at least 15 years to earliest call or maturity. Using the June 1988 futures contract as an example, any outstanding bonds that have a first call or a maturity date of June 2003 or later would be eligible for delivery against the June 1988 futures contract. A glance at the financial page of any newspaper will show that there are as many as three dozen such issues, although a much smaller number are likely to be delivered.

To determine which bonds are most likely to be delivered, we must make use of mathematical conversion factors that are published periodically by the Chicago Board of Trade. An excerpt from the conversion tables is shown in Figure 9-8 on pages 222–225. These conversion factors, when applied to the price of the futures contract, give the value of a deliverable bond that has a coupon that is different from the 8% coupon called for in the contract. For instance, the conversion factor for a 14% coupon bond that is callable 20 years and 3 months from the futures contract delivery month is 1.5965. This means that the price a short would receive for delivering this bond against a futures contract would be 1.5965 times the price of the futures contract. If the futures price is 88–0, then the delivery value of the 14% bond is 140$16$/32. It might also be possible to deliver a 14$1$/4% bond maturing in 15 years and 6 months. The conversion factor for such a bond is 1.5496. Multiplying the futures price of 88–0 by this factor yields a delivery value for such a 14$1$/4% bond of 136$12$/32. Which of these two bonds is most likely to be delivered depends on their prices in the cash market. If the cash price of the 14% bond is 140^{16}/$_{32}$ and that of the 14^{1}/$_{4}$% bond is 136^{12}/$_{32}$, then neither is preferable for delivery purposes. On the other hand, if the 14% bond has a cash price of 141^{2}/$_{32}$ and the 14^{1}/$_{4}$% bond is priced at 136^{24}/$_{32}$, the choice is obvious. Because the short would receive more than his cost for delivering the 14% bond and less than his cost for delivering the 14^{1}/$_{4}$% bond, he would be apt to deliver the former. If these were the only two bonds available for delivery, the futures price would tend to reflect the value of the 14% bond as long as it remained the cheapest to deliver.

As this reasoning suggests, the futures price tends to reflect changes in the value of the outstanding instrument, among many, that is the cheapest (or most profitable) to deliver.

Convergence of Cash and Futures Prices

As we discussed earlier, futures prices trade at either a premium or a discount to cash prices, depending on whether the prevailing yield curve is negatively or positively sloped. Given a positive yield curve, futures will trade at a discount to cash. To illustrate, suppose three-month financing rates are 8%, long-term bonds rates are 11% for maturities between 19 and 20 years, and futures prices are equal to cash prices. Faced with the choice of buying cash bonds now or buying a futures contract for delivery three months from now, the investor would choose to buy now. He could buy the 11% bonds, borrowing the money to finance his purchase at the 8% three-month rate. The difference between return and borrowing cost makes owning bonds now preferable to buying futures at the same price. This preference would continue to exist until the futures price declined to a level that "compensated" the buyer for the difference between short and long rates during the initial three-month period.

If short-term rates were higher than long-term rates, futures would command an appropriate premium over cash. Otherwise, the purchase of cash bonds would entail an unjustified cost of carry. To illustrate, assume three-month financing rates are 10%, long-term bond rates are 8%, and futures prices are equal to cash prices. Faced with the choice of buying bonds now or buying three-month futures, the investor would prefer buying futures. Otherwise, for this three-month period he would be borrowing money at 10% to receive a return on the bonds of 8%.

Figure 9-8. CBOT conversion factors.

Conversion Factor to Yield 8.000%

Coupon Rate

Yrs-Mos	14%	14¹/₈%	14¹/₄%	14³/₈%	14¹/₂%	14⁵/₈%	14³/₄%	14⁷/₈%
15-0	1.5188	1.5296	1.5404	1.5512	1.5620	1.5728	1.5836	1.5944
15-3	1.5229	1.5338	1.5447	1.5556	1.5665	1.5774	1.5883	1.5992
15-6	1.5277	1.5386	1.5496	1.5606	1.5716	1.5826	1.5936	1.6046
15-9	1.5316	1.5427	1.5538	1.5649	1.5759	1.5870	1.5981	1.6092
16-0	1.5362	1.5474	1.5585	1.5697	1.5809	1.5921	1.6032	1.6144
16-3	1.5400	1.5513	1.5625	1.5738	1.5850	1.5963	1.6075	1.6188
16-6	1.5444	1.5558	1.5671	1.5785	1.5898	1.6011	1.6125	1.6238
16-9	1.5481	1.5595	1.5709	1.5823	1.5938	1.6052	1.6166	1.6280
17-0	1.5523	1.5638	1.5753	1.5869	1.5984	1.6099	1.6214	1.6329
17-3	1.5558	1.5674	1.5790	1.5906	1.6022	1.6138	1.6253	1.6369
17-6	1.5599	1.5716	1.5833	1.5949	1.6066	1.6183	1.6299	1.6416
17-9	1.5633	1.5750	1.5868	1.5985	1.6102	1.6220	1.6337	1.6455
18-0	1.5672	1.5791	1.5909	1.6027	1.6145	1.6263	1.6382	1.6500
18-3	1.5705	1.5823	1.5942	1.6061	1.6180	1.6299	1.6418	1.6537
18-6	1.5743	1.5862	1.5982	1.6102	1.6221	1.6341	1.6461	1.6580
18-9	1.5773	1.5894	1.6014	1.6134	1.6255	1.6375	1.6495	1.6616
19-0	1.5810	1.5931	1.6052	1.6174	1.6295	1.6416	1.6537	1.6658
19-3	1.5840	1.5961	1.6083	1.6205	1.6327	1.6448	1.6570	1.6692
19-6	1.5875	1.5998	1.6120	1.6243	1.6365	1.6487	1.6610	1.6732
19-9	1.5903	1.6026	1.6150	1.6273	1.6396	1.6519	1.6642	1.6765
20-0	1.5938	1.6062	1.6185	1.6309	1.6433	1.6556	1.6680	1.6804
20-3	1.5965	1.6089	1.6213	1.6338	1.6462	1.6586	1.6711	1.6835
20-6	1.5998	1.6123	1.6248	1.6373	1.6498	1.6623	1.6748	1.6873
20-9	1.6024	1.6149	1.6275	1.6400	1.6526	1.6651	1.6777	1.6902
21-0	1.6056	1.6182	1.6308	1.6434	1.6560	1.6686	1.6813	1.6939
21-3	1.6080	1.6207	1.6334	1.6460	1.6587	1.6714	1.6841	1.6967
21-6	1.6111	1.6239	1.6366	1.6493	1.6621	1.6748	1.6875	1.7002
21-9	1.6135	1.6263	1.6390	1.6518	1.6646	1.6774	1.6902	1.7030

Figure 9-8. (cont.)

Conversion Factor to Yield 8.000%

Coupon Rate

Yrs-Mos	14%	14¹/₈%	14¹/₄%	14³/₈%	14¹/₂%	14⁵/₈%	14³/₄%	14⁷/₈%
22-0	1.6165	1.6293	1.6422	1.6550	1.6678	1.6807	1.6935	1.7064
22-3	1.6187	1.6316	1.6445	1.6574	1.6703	1.6832	1.6961	1.7090
22-6	1.6216	1.6346	1.6475	1.6605	1.6734	1.6864	1.6993	1.7123
22-9	1.6238	1.6368	1.6497	1.6627	1.6757	1.6887	1.7017	1.7147
23-0	1.6265	1.6396	1.6526	1.6657	1.6788	1.6918	1.7049	1.7179
23-3	1.6286	1.6417	1.6548	1.6679	1.6810	1.6941	1.7072	1.7203
23-6	1.6313	1.6444	1.6576	1.6707	1.6839	1.6970	1.7102	1.7234
23-9	1.6333	1.6464	1.6596	1.6728	1.6860	1.6992	1.7124	1.7256
24-0	1.6359	1.6491	1.6623	1.6756	1.6888	1.7021	1.7153	1.7286
24-3	1.6377	1.6510	1.6643	1.6776	1.6909	1.7042	1.7175	1.7308
24-6	1.6402	1.6536	1.6669	1.6803	1.6936	1.7069	1.7203	1.7336
24-9	1.6420	1.6554	1.6688	1.6822	1.6956	1.7089	1.7223	1.7357
25-0	1.6445	1.6579	1.6713	1.6847	1.6982	1.7116	1.7250	1.7385
25-3	1.6462	1.6596	1.6731	1.6866	1.7000	1.7135	1.7270	1.7404
25-6	1.6485	1.6620	1.6755	1.6891	1.7026	1.7161	1.7296	1.7431
25-9	1.6502	1.6637	1.6772	1.6908	1.7043	1.7179	1.7314	1.7450
26-0	1.6524	1.6660	1.6796	1.6932	1.7068	1.7204	1.7340	1.7476
26-3	1.6540	1.6676	1.6812	1.6949	1.7085	1.7221	1.7358	1.7494
26-6	1.6562	1.6699	1.6835	1.6972	1.7109	1.7245	1.7382	1.7519
26-9	1.6577	1.6714	1.6851	1.6988	1.7125	1.7262	1.7399	1.7536
27-0	1.6598	1.6735	1.6873	1.7010	1.7148	1.7285	1.7423	1.7560
27-3	1.6612	1.6750	1.6888	1.7025	1.7163	1.7301	1.7439	1.7577
27-6	1.6633	1.6771	1.6909	1.7047	1.7185	1.7323	1.7462	1.7600
27-9	1.6646	1.6784	1.6923	1.7061	1.7200	1.7338	1.7477	1.7615
28-0	1.6666	1.6805	1.6944	1.7083	1.7221	1.7360	1.7499	1.7638
28-3	1.6679	1.6818	1.6957	1.7096	1.7235	1.7375	1.7514	1.7653
28-6	1.6698	1.6838	1.6977	1.7117	1.7256	1.7396	1.7535	1.7675
28-9	1.6710	1.6850	1.6990	1.7130	1.7270	1.7409	1.7549	1.7689
29-0	1.6729	1.6869	1.7009	1.7149	1.7290	1.7430	1.7570	1.7710
29-3	1.6740	1.6881	1.7021	1.7162	1.7302	1.7443	1.7583	1.7724
29-6	1.6759	1.6899	1.7040	1.7181	1.7322	1.7463	1.7603	1.7744
29-9	1.6769	1.6911	1.7052	1.7193	1.7334	1.7475	1.7616	1.7757

Figure 9-8. (cont.)

Conversion Factor to Yield 8.000%

Coupon Rate

Yrs-Mos	14%	14¹/₈%	14¹/₄%	14³/₈%	14¹/₂%	14⁵/₈%	14³/₄%	14⁷/₈%
30-0	1.6787	1.6928	1.7070	1.7211	1.7353	1.7494	1.7635	1.7777
30-3	1.6797	1.6939	1.7081	1.7222	1.7364	1.7506	1.7647	1.7789
30-6	1.6814	1.6956	1.7098	1.7240	1.7382	1.7524	1.7666	1.7808
30-9	1.6824	1.6967	1.7109	1.7251	1.7393	1.7535	1.7678	1.7820
31-0	1.6841	1.6983	1.7126	1.7268	1.7411	1.7553	1.7696	1.7838
31-3	1.6850	1.6993	1.7136	1.7278	1.7421	1.7564	1.7707	1.7849
31-6	1.6866	1.7009	1.7152	1.7295	1.7438	1.7581	1.7724	1.7868
31-9	1.6875	1.7018	1.7162	1.7305	1.7448	1.7591	1.7735	1.7878
32-0	1.6891	1.7034	1.7178	1.7321	1.7465	1.7608	1.7752	1.7895
32-3	1.6899	1.7043	1.7187	1.7330	1.7474	1.7618	1.7762	1.7905
32-6	1.6914	1.7058	1.7202	1.7346	1.7490	1.7634	1.7778	1.7922
32-9	1.6922	1.7066	1.7210	1.7355	1.7499	1.7643	1.7787	1.7932
33-0	1.6937	1.7081	1.7226	1.7370	1.7515	1.7659	1.7804	1.7948
33-3	1.6944	1.7089	1.7233	1.7378	1.7523	1.7668	1.7812	1.7957
33-6	1.6958	1.7103	1.7248	1.7393	1.7538	1.7683	1.7828	1.7973
33-9	1.6965	1.7110	1.7256	1.7401	1.7546	1.7691	1.7836	1.7981
34-0	1.6979	1.7124	1.7270	1.7415	1.7561	1.7706	1.7851	1.7997
34-3	1.6986	1.7131	1.7277	1.7422	1.7568	1.7714	1.7859	1.8005
34-6	1.6999	1.7145	1.7291	1.7437	1.7582	1.7728	1.7874	1.8020
34-9	1.7005	1.7151	1.7297	1.7443	1.7589	1.7735	1.7881	1.8027
35-0	1.7018	1.7165	1.7311	1.7457	1.7603	1.7749	1.7896	1.8042
35-3	1.7024	1.7171	1.7317	1.7463	1.7610	1.7756	1.7903	1.8049
35-6	1.7037	1.7183	1.7330	1.7477	1.7623	1.7770	1.7916	1.8063
35-9	1.7042	1.7189	1.7336	1.7483	1.7629	1.7776	1.7923	1.8070
36-0	1.7055	1.7202	1.7349	1.7496	1.7643	1.7790	1.7937	1.8084
36-3	1.7060	1.7207	1.7354	1.7501	1.7648	1.7796	1.7943	1.8090
36-6	1.7072	1.7219	1.7366	1.7514	1.7661	1.7808	1.7956	1.8103
36-9	1.7077	1.7224	1.7372	1.7519	1.7667	1.7814	1.7962	1.8109

Figure 9-8. (cont.)

Conversion Factor to Yield 8.000%

Coupon Rate

Yrs-Mos	14%	14 1/8%	14 1/4%	14 3/8%	14 1/2%	14 5/8%	14 3/4%	14 7/8%
37-0	1.7088	1.7236	1.7384	1.7531	1.7679	1.7827	1.7974	1.8122
37-3	1.7093	1.7241	1.7388	1.7536	1.7684	1.7832	1.7980	1.8128
37-6	1.7104	1.7252	1.7400	1.7548	1.7696	1.7844	1.7992	1.8140
37-9	1.7108	1.7257	1.7405	1.7553	1.7701	1.7849	1.7997	1.8145
38-0	1.7119	1.7268	1.7416	1.7564	1.7713	1.7861	1.8009	1.8158
38-3	1.7123	1.7272	1.7420	1.7569	1.7717	1.7866	1.8014	1.8162
38-6	1.7134	1.7283	1.7431	1.7580	1.7728	1.7877	1.8026	1.8174
38-9	1.7138	1.7286	1.7435	1.7584	1.7733	1.7881	1.8030	1.8179
39-0	1.7148	1.7297	1.7446	1.7595	1.7744	1.7893	1.8042	1.8190
39-3	1.7151	1.7300	1.7450	1.7599	1.7748	1.7897	1.8046	1.8195
39-6	1.7162	1.7311	1.7460	1.7609	1.7758	1.7908	1.8057	1.8206
39-9	1.7165	1.7314	1.7463	1.7613	1.7762	1.7911	1.8061	1.8210
40-0	1.7175	1.7324	1.7474	1.7623	1.7773	1.7922	1.8071	1.8221

Buying the futures contract would not subject him to this negative 2% annualized cost of carry. Only when futures rise to a level that erases their advantage will market equilibrium exist. The activities of arbitrageurs, taking advantage of short term imbalances in yields of comparable instruments, tend to keep futures prices at appropriate discounts or premiums to cash.

The appropriate premium or discount of futures to cash is determined by the negative or positive cost of carry, as defined previously. However, as time passes and contract expiration approaches, the cost of carry becomes less and less significant. As an example, assume short-term rates of 10% and long-term rates of 11%. In this case futures would trade at a discount to cash, reflecting this 1% annualized difference in rates. For the $100,000 T-bond contract, this 1% difference amounts to $1,000 per year. Six months prior to the expiration of a futures contract, the discount of futures to cash would represent half this amount, or $500. Three months later the difference would be $250. Eventually, when the contract reached expiration, the difference between cash and futures would be zero.

In other words, the same principles that govern the behavior of the basis in physical commodities also govern the behavior of the basis in interest rate instruments. First, a set of market factors determines whether futures trade at a discount or a premium to the cash instrument prior to expiration. In the case of the physical commodities, shortage or surplus of the underlying commodity determines whether the price structure is normal or inverted. In interest rate futures, the dominant force behind futures premiums or discounts is the prevailing shape of the yield curve, which in turn is determined by supply/demand conditions in the underlying credit market. Second, whatever the prevailing relationship of cash to futures, the dominant trend over time is for the basis to decay and finally to vanish entirely at contract maturity. The relationships between cash and futures prices for currencies and stock indexes are discussed in Chapters 19 and 20 respectively.

■ Chapter 10

■ *Hedging Concepts*

If the economic climate of the 1970s and 1980s had one outstanding feature, it was the unprecedented volatility in the prices of just about everything. Commodities from soybeans to gold experienced price swings that were unmatched in any previous period. Sweeping advances and declines in interest rates and foreign exchange rates rocked the foundations of the many businesses and financial institutions that had become accustomed to relatively stable market conditions. No business, regardless of its size, went untouched by the price chaos, and if they were to survive, businesses had to adapt quickly to the new environment.

To minimize the hazards that were posed by wide price fluctuations for either present inventories or transactions for future delivery, businesses turned increasingly to the futures markets. They joined the ranks of the many producers and users of agricultural products who for decades had used futures as a tool for hedging against price adversities. Corn farmers who for many seasons had sold futures contracts ahead of harvest to lock-in a price for their crops were now joined by the presidents of savings and loan associations who sold GNMA futures to lock-in a profit on an inventory of mortgages. The equity portfolio manager who had always considered futures too risky was now found trading S&P futures on the exchange floor where bids and offers in pork-belly futures could be heard in the distance.

While hedging in futures has become an integral part of many businesses, it is not the sole means of protection against hazardous price fluctuations. Obviously, many businesses deal in products or financial instruments that are not traded on futures exchanges. They continue to exist as thriving, profitable enterprises because they have found other ways to deal with short-run price fluctuations or because they and their competitors have become accustomed to cycles of profit and loss that arise from swings in raw material prices, interest rates, or currency values. Even in those industries where futures markets are available, their degree of use depends heavily on the philosophy of the particular business. Those businesses that are risk averse by either temperament or necessity tend to be more active users of futures. Other businesses where risk cycles are a way of life or where the cost of raw materials is an insignificant factor in profit margins tend to be less active users.

The grain industry provides good examples of each approach. Contrary to popular belief, a large number of actively producing farms have never used futures markets. This is due in large part to their ability to transfer risk through the use of forward contracts. Equally important, however, is the fact that many farmers accept the boom-and-bust cycles as a way of life. For generations they have adapted to the years of lean and fat. In the same industry, though, we find the giant international grain trading firms whose successful operations depend on their ability to use futures on a daily basis. In thousands and thousands of transactions, they buy and sell grain around the world. Each transaction may yield a seemingly minuscule profit, but multiplied over and over it provides the foundation for vast trading enterprises. The failure to properly hedge even one transaction can erase the profits from a multitude of other transactions, and it is for this reason that futures trading is indispensable to the large grain trading companies.

TYPES OF RISK

Before deciding whether or how much to hedge, every business must first determine the sources and the sizes of the risks to which it is exposed. Price risks develop in a variety of ways:

1. *Basic Inventory*: This includes present holdings of physical commodities or financial instruments that have not been committed for future sale at a fixed price. These assets, such as copper in a warehouse or an inventory of bonds that are held by a government

securities dealer, are subject to losses in value if prices decline. The assets may conform exactly to the par-delivery specifications of the futures contract or they may not. For instance, copper of a slightly different grade from that called for in the futures contract would fall into this latter category.

2. *Modified Inventory*: This category includes physical commodities that have been transformed by processing or manufacturing, rendering them significantly different from the par-delivery specifications of the futures contract. Examples might include pipeline inventories and work-in-process or finished goods inventories. The extent to which a commodity has been processed and separated from the standard delivery grade makes hedging in the futures market a less certain means of reducing risk.

3. *Anticipated Production*: Future farm or mine output that has not been contracted for forward sale and that will be added to inventories once it is available falls into this category. In this case, the risk is that a price decline will undermine the profitability of the producing facility. In the extreme case, a decline in price to levels below the cost of production would actually result in a loss for every unit produced.

4. *Purchase Agreements at a Fixed Price*: These include all forward contracts that commit the holder to take delivery of a commodity or a financial instrument at a fixed price. Such commitments are as vulnerable to price declines as are actual inventories.

5. *Future Borrowing Requirements*: Most businesses are subject to interest rate risk. This risk might take the form of the expected rollover of a loan or the need to borrow funds for expansion. Here a decline in the value of interest-bearing instruments (an increase in interest rates) would expose the business to risk.

In all the foregoing cases, the potential hazard is a decline in prices. Each represents, in one form or another, a current or anticipated long position in the cash market that can be offset by the sale of futures contracts. Now consider two examples in which the risk is that prices might rise.

6. *Agreements to Sell at a Fixed Price*: These are contracts that bind the holder to make delivery of a commodity, a commodity product,

or a financial instrument at a future date at a predetermined price. For example, an importer of packaging machines from West Germany agrees to pay his supplier 50,000 Deutsche marks when delivery occurs three months in the future. During that time, should the Deutsche mark rise in value relative to the dollar, this cost in dollars will be greater than planned and would cut into whatever profit was expected from the purchase and the sale of the machine. In other words, the importer is short Deutsche marks.

7. *Future Lending Requirements*: This category covers expected cash inflows that will be lent out to cover interest costs. A drop in interest rates (a rise in the price of interest-bearing or discount instruments) results in reduced earnings. An example might be a portfolio manager who plans to roll over a $10 million investment in Treasury bonds that mature three months hence. A decline in interest rates will cause the investment to be rolled over at a lower rate of return.

These are seven basic ways that risks arise in the cash market. Although there are many variations on each of the categories, most forms of risk fall into one or another of these. In the first five categories, the danger is that the prices of financial instruments or raw materials will fall. Each of those situations represents a long position in the cash market because it is a form of ownership, either present or future, to which the business is committed. In the last two categories, price increases are the danger. These categories represent short positions in the cash market because they entail commitments to make delivery of something that is not presently in inventory.

It is extremely important in thinking about these categories of risk that we keep our minds open to the different ways that they appear in actual business. Where hedging once covered only tangible commodities whose inventory or forward sale risks were rather easily identified, it now covers a whole spectrum of financial "commodities." Heightened interest rate and currency volatilities have made holdings of cash or commitments to deliver funds much riskier than was the case prior to the 1970s. Thus, we must think of price risks and the applicability of futures market hedging from four often intertwined perspectives: (a) purchases or sales of physical commodities that are covered by contracts traded on organized futures markets, (b) holdings or commitments to deliver interest-bearing instruments whose value is subject to changes in prevailing interest rate levels, (c) holdings or commitments to deliver foreign currencies that are traded on futures exchanges, and (d) financial commitments whose values are related to various indexes that are traded on organized futures markets (S&P 500 Index futures, Consumer Price Index futures, European Currency Unit futures, and so on).

Before looking into the actual mechanics of hedging, it is worth emphasizing again that not all cash market risks demand the protection of the futures markets. From the foregoing list of seven risk sources, it should be obvious that a commitment in any of the first five categories can be offset, at least theoretically, by a commitment in one of the last two categories, without ever having to resort to the futures market.

For instance, the risk of holding inventory (category 1) in a climate of weakening prices can be offset by (a) actually selling off the inventory or (b) arranging to sell the inventory directly to a user for future delivery at a fixed price. The risk of making forward sales at a fixed price (category 6) can be offset either by acquiring inventory now or by arranging for forward purchases from a producer at a fixed price.

While confining risk-reducing methods to these nonfutures areas is a common practice in most businesses, it is not always practical for several reasons. First, inventories cannot always be readily acquired or liquidated when the manager of the business is concerned about adverse price changes. Those inventories may be a critical part of day-to-day operations. Also, underutilized inventory space can be very expensive. Second, forward contracts to make or to take delivery at fixed prices are usually binding agreements that are not easily voided should conditions change. Third, principal-to-principal forward contracts entail credit exposures that many businesses do not have the resources to evaluate and monitor.

What is needed as an alternative is a method of reducing risk that has four major attributes:

- It is readily available.
- It does not significantly impair management's flexibility.
- It does not simply substitute credit risk for price risk.
- It is not costly.

Futures contracts satisfy these criteria. They are highly liquid instruments that can be entered into or liquidated on short notice at almost all times. They are "paper" transactions that do not interfere with regular business operations. The credit exposure is always to a futures clearinghouse (see Chapter 7). Finally, low margins and commissions make them a relatively inexpensive source of price protection.

The role of the futures market, therefore, is to provide a temporary, flexible means of reducing risks that arise from any combination of the seven categories listed earlier. A dealer may have an inventory of bonds, half of which has been sold at a favorable price. Rather than risk exposure to a price decline on the uncovered half, he or she can sell the appropriate number of futures contracts. If prices deline, the short position in the futures market will "shelter" the inventory. As the dealer arranges to sell more of the inventory, he or she will reduce the futures market position.

HEDGING DEFINED

Hedging is the use of the futures market to reduce the risk of a cash market position. It involves entering into a futures transaction that is a temporary substitute for a similar transaction in the cash market. This futures market position is the opposite of the net position in the cash market and serves to negate or minimize the risk of this position.

Successful hedging is dependent on a close relationship between the price of the cash commodity or financial instrument and the price of a futures contract. The closer the relationship, the more effective the hedge. However, we know that there is never a perfect correlation between cash and futures. There is always the risk that a negative change in cash prices will not be fully matched by an offsetting change in futures prices. The resulting change in the basis exposes the hedger to both risk and opportunity. The essence of hedging is that the hedger substitutes this basis risk for the usually far greater risk of having an unprotected position in the cash market.

Selling Hedge

A *selling hedge* is the use of a short position in the futures market by someone who is long in the cash market. It is used to protect inventories of commodities or financial instruments that are not covered by forward sales. It is also used to protect the value of anticipated production or forward purchase agreements.

A simple example of a selling hedge might involve a country grain elevator that buys corn from a farmer in October for $2.15 per bushel. The grain is brought into inventory and is vulnerable to a price decline should the market weaken. The elevator could simply sell December corn futures and maintain this short position until a buyer for the cash grain is found, at which time the elevator operator would "lift" the hedge by liquidating the futures contract.

Buying Hedge

A *buying hedge* is the purchase of futures by someone who is short in the cash market. It is usually used to protect against exposures that arise from forward sales at a fixed price. Very often the buying hedge is used to protect against price increases in raw materials that are used in manufacturing some stably-priced end product. Purchases in the futures market are made as a temporary substitute for buying the actual raw material.

A simple example of a buying hedge in financial futures might involve a corporation that plans to raise cash by issuing commercial paper in two months, but is concerned that interest rates may rise before the paper comes to market. The corporation could simply sell Eurodollar futures and maintain this short position in futures until the cash is available and the actual commercial paper is issued. This would protect it against a rate increase because both Eurodollar and commercial paper rates will likely move in tandem. The fact that changes in these two different short-term rates will probably not be exactly equal creates both opportunities and risks that are discussed later in this chapter.

ADVANTAGES OF HEDGING

Hedging in the futures market provides businesses with a number of important advantages.

* It substantially reduces the price risks that are involved in dealing with commodities or financial instruments. Although it is not possible to completely eliminate risk, a properly executed hedge in a market that has a relatively stable basis eliminates much of the danger. Along these lines, hedging usually produces much greater sta-

bility in the financial performance of businesses. It tends to minimize the significant swings in profit that can be caused by fluctuating raw material prices, interest rates, or foreign exchange rates.

- Hedging does not interfere with normal business operations. It allows for substantial price protection without the need for change in inventory policy or for engaging in inflexible principal-to-principal forward purchase or sale commitments.

- Hedging allows greater flexibility in planning. Because futures contracts are available for many delivery months in the future, businesses can plan ahead and adjust schedules with greater ease. A soybean crusher (someone in the business of buying soybeans and crushing them into the end products of soybean oil and soybean meal) can buy actual soybeans only when a farmer or a grain merchant is willing and able to sell. He or she might have to hold these beans until someone else is ready to buy one or both of the end products. It is rare that these two events would occur simultaneously. With futures, however, the crusher is able to manage financial exposure by the substitution of transactions in the futures market for opportunities that may not be available in the cash market. This helps make more efficient use of inventory excess or shortage.

- Hedging permits easier and greater financing. In businesses where it is common to collateralize loans with commodity inventory, hedging plays a very important role. For unhedged commodity inventories, banks typically accept about 50% of the present value of the inventory as collateral for financing. In cases where the inventory is hedged in the futures market, financing can exceed 90% of the inventory's present value. This makes a big difference. For example, assume that a company has $1 million for inventory purchases. It could buy $2 million worth of unhedged inventory. The bank would be willing to lend $1 million, with the remainder coming from the company's own funds. If that same company committed itself to a hedging program in futures, the result could be enormously different. It might be able to buy $10 million of inventory—90% financed by the bank and the remaining $1 million coming from its own funds. It should be clear what effect this increased leverage would have on the potential for business expansion. A corollary benefit is, of course, that banks themselves have greater confidence in loans that are made against commitments hedged in futures.

BASIS RISKS IN HEDGING

As noted earlier, hedgers substitute one risk for another. They eliminate the price risks that are entailed in owning the actual commodity or financial instrument and accept the risk that is entailed in "owning" the basis. Hedging is useful if—and only if—the latter risk is meaningfully smaller than the former.

Factors that bring about changes in the basis are discussed in the previous chapter. For now, let us discuss in general terms the effect that basis change has on hedging. The following chapter on hedging applications takes up these issues in greater detail.

A *perfect hedge*, as it is known in the trade, is one that involves no change in basis. For example, a business buys 10 units of a commodity at $2.50 on October 15. It immediately establishes a hedge by selling 10 units of December futures at $2.75. Thus, the basis at the time the hedge is placed is 25 cents. One month later, the business sells all 10 units at $2.00, incurring a loss on the cash market position of 50 cents. If futures also have fallen 50 cents, the cash market loss is offset precisely by the futures market profit. Figure 10-1 on page 236 helps to illustrate.

Because the basis did not change, the futures market provided perfect protection in this selling hedge. Needless to say, the real world provides few such perfect opportunities.

If the futures market had declined more than the cash market, the outcome might look as shown in Figure 10-2 on page 236.

In this case, the $0.05 change in the basis produced a bonus. Not only did the hedge provide protection against the $5.00 loss that would have been incurred in the cash market, but the hedger actually made an additional 50 cents because futures declined faster than cash.

A widening of the basis would have had the opposite effect as shown in Figure 10-3 on page 236.

In the case of Figure 10-3, hedging provided substantial but incomplete protection against the loss in the cash market.

The outcome of any hedge can be determined simply by measuring the change in basis between when the hedge is put on and when it is taken off.* In Figure 10-2, the narrowing of the basis by 5 cents resulted

---

*To avoid confusion we have adopted the convention of using a plus sign (+) to signify that futures are above cash and a minus sign (–) to signify that futures are below cash. We also refer to a market in which futures are over cash as a *normal market*. One in which cash is above futures is referred to as an *inverted market*.

Figure 10-1. No basis change.

Date	Cash Market Transactions	Futures Market Transactions	Basis
October 15	Buy 10 Dec. @$2.50	Sell 10 Dec. @$2.75	+ $0.25
November 15	Sell 10 Dec. @$2.00	Buy 10 Dec. @$2.25	+ $0.25
Result:	− $5.00	+ $5.00	

Net Result: $0

Figure 10-2. Favorable basis change.

Date	Cash Market Transactions	Futures Market Transactions	Basis
October 15	Buy 10 Dec. @$2.50	Sell 10 Dec. @$2.75	+ $0.25
November 15	Sell 10 Dec. @$2.00	Buy 10 Dec. @$2.20	+ $0.20
Result:	− $5.00	+ $5.50	

Net Result: $0.50

Figure 10-3. Unfavorable basis change.

Date	Cash Market Transactions	Futures Market Transactions	Basis
October 15	Buy 10 Dec. @$2.50	Sell 10 Dec. @$2.75	+ $0.25
November 15	Sell 10 Dec. @$2.00	Buy 10 Dec. @$2.30	+ $0.30
Result:	− $5.00	+ $4.50	

Net Result: − $0.50

in that amount of profit to the hedger. To aid the reader in understanding the outcome of hedges in various circumstances, the following is a list of the eight possible combinations of buying and selling hedges in an environment of widening and narrowing bases.

1. *Selling hedge in a normal market followed by a narrowing of the basis*: In this case the hedger establishes a short position in futures at a premium to cash. If prices decline and the basis narrows, the profit on the futures leg exceeds the loss on the cash leg. A net profit results. If prices rise, the narrowing of the basis means that the loss in futures is smaller than the profit in cash. The result is, again, a net profit.

2. *Selling hedge in a normal market followed by a widening of the basis*: In this case the futures leg produces a smaller profit (or a greater loss) than does the cash leg.

3. *Selling hedge in an inverted market followed by a narrowing of the basis*: In this case the futures leg once again produces a smaller profit (or a greater loss) than does the cash leg.

4. *Selling hedge in an inverted market followed by a widening of the basis*: In this case the futures leg yields a greater profit (or a smaller loss) than that of the cash leg.

5. *Buying hedge in a normal market followed by a narrowing of the basis*: In this case the futures leg yields a smaller profit (or a greater loss) than the cash leg.

6. *Buying hedge in a normal market followed by a widening of the basis*: This case will show a greater profit (or a smaller loss) in the futures leg.

7. *Buying hedge in an inverted market followed by a narrowing basis*: In this case the profit (loss) in the futures position is larger (smaller) than that in the cash position.

8. *Buying hedge in an inverted market followed by a widening of the basis*: Here the futures leg will produce a greater loss (or a smaller profit) than that of the cash leg.

BASIS CHARTS

A convenient way of viewing the basis is to construct what is known as a *basis chart*. The basis chart simply plots the difference in price between cash and futures. By setting cash prices equal to zero on a horizontal axis, we can plot the premiums and discounts of futures about this axis. Figure 10-4 on page 239 shows price data on cash and futures for a hypothetical commodity or financial instrument for three years. For each month we calculate the difference between cash and futures and assign a plus sign or a minus sign, depending on whether futures are at a premium (+) or a discount (–). The results are shown in Figure 10-5 on page 240.

In Figure 10-6 on page 240 we construct a basis chart from this data. Cash is set equal to zero on the horizontal axis. The discounts and premiums of futures are plotted against the vertical axis.The construction of an historical basis chart, like the one in Figure 10-6, is a useful tool in establishing and managing a hedging program. First of all, the basis chart helps ascertain typical magnitudes of the premiums and discounts of futures relative to cash. In our hypothetical market, the basis spanned a range of +10 to –6 during the three years under study. Thus, if a hedger were faced with a situation in which the basis were +20 or –20, he would be able to classify it as an aberration and adjust the hedging program accordingly. The historical basis chart also provides some insight into any recurring seasonal patterns that might exist in basis movement. In our hypothetical market, the basis seems to have a tendency to reach a peak in April–May and to drop to a trough in October–November. This, too, influences hedging tactics. As we know from the previous section, selling hedges produce the most profitable results when the basis is narrowing from its widest premium. Therefore, selling hedges that are placed in April or May are likely to yield the best results. Similarly, the best time to establish buying hedges appears to be in the October–November period.

A few words of caution are in order. First, valid conclusions about typical basis patterns come from extensive historical data. Conclusions that are based on short periods of time or on only a few years of statistics can provide hedgers with dangerous conclusions. Typically, five years of history is needed to reach reliable conclusions. Second, the cash prices that are used in an historical basis study should be actual prices that were paid or received by the particular hedger over a period of time or something very close to these prices. Cash prices can vary widely from one market to the next, so, for the sake of accuracy, cash price data should conform as closely as possible to the actual experience of the hedger. Finally, conclusions that arise from basis studies can en-

Figure 10-4. Hypothetical cash futures data.

		1985	1986	1987
January 1	Cash	100	95	110
	Futures	104	97	110
February 1	Cash	105	93	105
	Futures	110	97	109
March 1	Cash	107	90	100
	Futures	115	96	108
April 1	Cash	110	92	95
	Futures	120	100	103
May 1	Cash	108	88	90
	Futures	116	98	100
June 1	Cash	105	85	90
	Futures	111	90	98
July 1	Cash	102	90	85
	Futures	107	92	90
August 1	Cash	100	93	86
	Futures	102	93	87
September 1	Cash	100	95	88
	Futures	98	95	88
October 1	Cash	95	100	90
	Futures	90	97	89
November 1	Cash	100	105	88
	Futures	94	100	88
December 1	Cash	96	110	85
	Futures	96	109	86

Figure 10-5. Hypothetical basis data.

	1985	1986	1987
January 1	+ 4	+ 2	0
February 1	+ 5	+ 4	+ 4
March 1	+ 8	+ 6	+ 8
April 1	+ 10	+ 8	+ 8
May 1	+ 8	+ 10	+ 10
June 1	+ 6	+ 5	+ 8
July 1	+ 5	+ 2	+ 5
August 1	+ 2	0	+ 1
September 1	− 2	0	0
October 1	− 5	− 3	− 1
November 1	− 6	− 5	0
December 1	0	− 1	+ 1

Figure 10-6. Hypothetical basis chart.

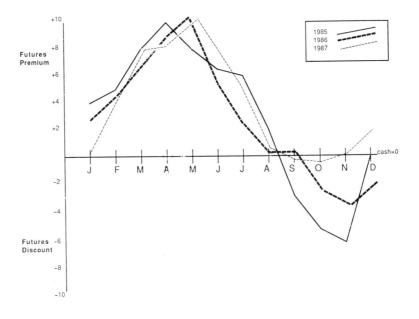

courage unwise speculation. After reviewing an historical basis study, a hedger may decide to defer the establishment of a position in the futures market. This can be a dangerous and costly error. In almost all cases where a reliable correlation of cash and futures can be demonstrated, it is wiser to establish a hedge that produces a net loss than to establish no hedge at all. The net loss simply means that the hedge has failed to provide complete protection against the adverse price change in cash. But partial protection is usually better than none at all.

When hedges are placed, it is essential that the size of the futures position correspond as closely as possible to the size of the net at-risk position in the cash market. If, after netting out all cash market holdings and forward commitments, the hedger has a long position of 100,000 units, then a short position equal to 100,000 units should be established in futures. Hedgers who "lift a leg" by trading their cash and futures positions separately are speculating rather than hedging.

UNDERHEDGING

One exception to the rule of perfectly matching cash and futures positions is related to the margining of positions in futures. To better understand this, imagine a precious metals dealer with a 500-contract inventory of gold (50,000 ounces) and an offsetting position of 500 short futures contracts. If prices rise dramatically, say from $400 per ounce to $500 per ounce, the dealer will be faced with enormous variation margin calls that must be met with cash. No interest is earned on the cash that is used to meet these calls, and the inventory holdings generate no offsetting cash flow even though their value increases as prices rise. In this case, margin calls would approximate $5 million. The real interest or opportunity cost of this cash outflow would be $600,000 annually if the dealer could otherwise earn 12% on his capital. To minimize this cost, sophisticated hedgers make use of a practice known as *variation margin hedging* or *underhedging*. If the short position in futures is slightly smaller than the inventory, then rising prices will generate a net profit on the unhedged portion of the inventory. If this unhedged position is the correct size, this profit will come close to offsetting the variation margin interest loss in a climbing market. In a falling market, the interest gain from variation margin receipts will offset the loss in value of the unhedged portion of inventory.

One method of determining the correct size of an underhedge is as follows:

I = size of inventory
U = unhedged portion of inventory
P = price of commodity; ΔP = change in price
 i = prevailing interest rate
M = number of months position held

The interest loss on the variation margin is approximately equal to:

$$(I - U) \times (\Delta P) \times (i) \times \frac{M}{12}$$

The inventory profit equals

$$U \times \Delta P$$

Equating the two,

$$U \times \Delta P = (I - U) \times (\Delta P) \times (i) \times \frac{M}{12}$$

$$U = \frac{I}{1 + \dfrac{12}{i \times M}}$$

In our example, assuming an annual interest rate of 12%, and a holding period of one month,

$$U = \frac{50,000}{1 + \dfrac{12}{0.12 \times 1}} = 495 \text{ ounces}$$

or approximately 5 contracts.

DISADVANTAGES OF HEDGING

Besides the risks that arise from margining futures in a volatile market, futures markets have a number of other disadvantages that should be understood. We summarize them here:

Basis risk: Because of basis changes, futures may not provide full protection against adverse price changes in the cash market. Basis risk increases the more the cash article departs from the par-delivery specifications of the futures contract. On very rare occasions, in extremely volatile markets or where cash/futures price correlation is small, basis risk can exceed the price risk of a naked long or short position.

Costs: Every futures transaction involves execution and clearing costs. Even when they are small, these fees can add up in time and should be monitored. In addition, we discussed the interest costs that are associated with margining futures contracts. Because underhedging is not always possible (especially when small quantities are involved) or practical (especially when interest rates or prices are extremely volatile), allowances should be made early. Even when the hedger is able to make effective use of underhedging, it is important to have a ready source of cash for margin purposes. A close relationship with a knowledgeable lending institution is essential to avoid having to abort an otherwise successful hedge because cash flow problems prevent meeting margin calls.

Incompatibility of cash and futures: Because futures contracts are standardized, they do not always match precisely the particular terms of a cash market commitment. Quantities may be larger or smaller than what the futures contract calls for. Quality differences exist (as noted earlier). Differences may also exist between the time frame of a cash market forward transaction and that of the predetermined delivery months in futures. The only certain means of precisely offsetting a cash market position is through another tailor made cash market transaction but, as we have seen, this is not always possible or practical.

Limit moves: Because futures trading can be restricted by daily trading limits, it may be impossible to establish or to liquidate hedges on particular days. This occurrence is very rare but can cause considerable unease when it occurs.

THE REGULATORY CLIMATE

In order to qualify as bona-fide hedgers and to benefit from the more liberal position limits and margin requirements, businesses must meet certain requirements that are specified by the Commodity Futures Trading Commission. A *hedger* is defined as someone who enters into futures transactions *where such transactions normally represent a substitute for transactions to be made or positions to be taken at a later time in a physical marketing channel, and where they are economically appropriate to the reduction of risks in the conduct and management of a commercial enterprise.*

The CFTC's hedging definition consists of three main elements:

First, it explains the type of futures transaction and the position assumed that is considered bona-fide hedging. Under appropriate conditions, such transactions arise from potential change in the value of:

1. Assets that a person owns, produces, manufactures, possesses, or merchandises—or of any anticipated assets.
2. Liabilities that a person owes or anticipates owing.
3. Services that a person provides, purchases, or anticipates performing. However, transactions for this purpose must be to offset price risks that are associated with actual commercial operations and such positions are initiated and liquidated so as not to disrupt the orderly marketing process.

Second, purchases and sales of certain items for future delivery are limited to the following conditions:

1. Sales of any commodity for future delivery on a contract market must not exceed in quantity:
   a. the fixed price purchases or ownership of the same cash commodity by the same person; or
   b. the twelve-month unsold anticipated production of the same commodity by the same person, provided that no such position is maintained in any futures contract during the five last trading days of that futures contract.
2. Purchases of any commodity for future delivery on a contract market must not exceed in quantity:
   a. the fixed-price sale of the cash commodity by the same person;
   b. the quantity equivalent of fixed-price sales of one cash product and byproducts of the same commodity by the same person; or
   c. the twelve-month unfilled anticipated requirements of the cash commodity for processing, manufacturing, or feeding by the

same person, provided that such transactions and positions in the last five trading days of any one futures contract do not exceed the person's unfilled anticipated requirements.

The CFTC definition also contains a provision for cross-hedging. This category of hedging consists of purchases and sales of futures that are not the same in quantity or type as the cash item that is being hedged. This qualifies as bona-fide hedging if the fluctuations in value of the cash and the offsetting futures positions are substantially related, and the futures positions are not maintained beyond the last five trading days of the futures contract.

Third, the expanded definition of *bona-fide hedging* exempts from limits certain transactions and positions that were previously fixed by the Commodity Exchange Act.

The introduction of trading in various financial instruments during the 1970s and 1980s has subjected financial hedgers to a new range of regulatory considerations. Most financial institutions in the United States operate under statutory authority that is granted by specific government agencies. Unlike manufacturing businesses and most other corporations, their activities must be approved by these agencies. Before undertaking hedging programs in futures, institutions such as national and state banks, federal savings and loans, insurance companies, and fiduciaries must be certain that they are operating within the guidelines that are laid down by the regulatory agencies that are relevant to their activities. These guidelines tended to be quite restrictive after financial futures were first introduced in the 1970s. However, as regulators have become more familiar with the risk-management flexibilities that are offered by futures, the range of permissible futures trading activities has steadily broadened.

COMPETITIVE CONSIDERATIONS

In some businesses, the reduction of one's exposure to price fluctuations may not be worth the effort and could even be counterproductive. This might sound odd, so let us consider a hypothetical example:

Suppose that you own a chain of butcher shops that, among other things, buy beef at wholesale prices and sell it in retail outlets at a 10 cent per pound markup. If your competitors do much the same thing, then the price risk is effectively borne not by the butchers, but by their customers. Changes in wholesale beef prices are simply passed along to the customers. As long as this situation prevails, there is no reason to hedge because there is no real exposure to changing prices.

Taking this example further, hedging might even be bad business strategy. Suppose that wholesale beef prices are 60 cents per pound, retail prices are 70 cents per pound, and a butcher believes that a sharp price rise is imminent. He reasons that by putting on a long hedge (i.e., by buying cattle futures), he can lock in a 60 cents per pound cost compared with what he expects will be a 70 cents per pound cost to his competitors who are not hedging. This will enable him to choose between two appealing alternatives:

1. Maintaining the same retail price as the competition (80 cents per pound) and having twice the profit margin (20 cents per pound versus 10 cents per pound).

or

2. Maintaining a 10 cents per pound (or even a 15 cents per pound) profit margin and gaining market share by underselling his competitors.

This pleasant scenario is accurate but, unfortunately, is only half the story. Suppose that the butcher is wrong in his forecast and wholesale beef prices fall to 50 cents per pound. The alternatives are then much less pleasant:

3. Maintaining the same retail price as his competition (60 cents per pound) and having zero profit margin.

or

4. Maintaining the customary 10 cents per pound markup and losing market share to the competitors whose prices are lower.

If the hedger's price forecasts are right as often as they are wrong, there will be zero net benefit from the strategy of always matching the competition's prices [in time, the added profits from (1) will be exactly offset by the reduced profits from (3)]. Thus, given this strategy, hedging would be a waste of effort.

What about the constant-profit-margin strategy [(2) and (4)]? If the butcher gains more long-term market share when underselling his competition than he loses when the competition undersells him, then hedging makes sense. If the reverse is true, then hedging is bad business strategy. It is up to the butcher to know his customer base and to make the appropriate business decisions. The choice between hedging and not hedging is simply one of those decisions.

One last point: You may wonder why we assume that the butcher's price forecasts will be correct only half the time. The answer is that we are talking about whether hedging *per se* is an effective strategy and an appropriate business management decision. To do this, we must factor out what amount to speculative profits or losses resulting from price forecasting ability. Clearly, if your price forecasts are right more often than they are wrong, taking futures positions is an appropriate strategy. However, depending on the nature of your business, it may be an appropriate *speculative* strategy rather than an appropriate *hedging* strategy.

■ Chapter 11

■ *Hedging Applications*

This chapter brings into focus the concepts that were discussed in the previous two chapters. It presents a number of representative cases that illustrate the specific ways that hedging strategies are implemented. While basic methodologies are similar for all the cases that are presented, differences in actual applications between the various markets can be significant. For this reason we have selected examples from several of the major market categories. Chapter 26 presents examples of how options on futures can be particularly effective hedges under certain circumstances.

Case 1: Hedging by a Primary Producer with One-Time Seasonal Output

This case covers the broad range of agricultural producers whose output is realized once a year at harvest time. The primary purpose of the hedge in this case is to "fix" the price of a growing crop. Farmers make substantial commitments of labor and capital in the course of the planting and the growing seasons. Whether these expenditures yield an acceptable rate of return depends, in good part, on price conditions at the time that the crops are ready to be harvested. Farmers have two ways of assuring, within a fairly narrow margin, the price that they will receive at harvest. They can contract to sell their crop on a forward basis at a fixed price to a willing merchant, or they can sell an appropriate number of futures contracts.

Figure 11-1.

Date	Cash Market Transactions	Futures Market Transactions
June 1	No transaction. Expects price of $2.26½ in Oct.	Sells 50,000 bushels Dec. @$2.41½
Oct. 15	Sells 50,000 bushels @$2.15	Buys 50,000 bushels Dec. @$2.28½
Result:	$5,750 (opportunity cost)	$6,500 (profit)

Net result: $750 profit relative to June expectations

Assume that on June 1, the price of December corn futures is $2.41½ per bushel. An historical analysis of cash and futures prices by the farmer shows that cash corn prices at his local elevator averaged 15 cents below December futures during the second two weeks of October, which is the period during which he expects to harvest 60,000 bushels. What the futures market is telling him is that it expects corn of par-delivery specifications to be worth $2.41½ per bushel in December. It also implies, assuming that historical cash/futures price relationships hold to the norm, that at harvest his corn will command a price of $2.26½ at the local elevator. Finding this an acceptable price, he sells 50,000 bushels of December corn futures. He chooses 50,000 rather than the full 60,000 bushels because (1) he would like to leave some allowance for loss of crop due to adverse weather, and (2) he would like to leave unhedged a small portion of his crop in the event that prices at harvest are higher than expected. On October 15, with the harvest completed, he sells and delivers 55,000 bushels of cash corn to the local elevator at a price of $2.15 per bushel (5,000 bushels were lost during heavy rains at harvest). Simultaneously, he buys 50,000 bushels of December futures at $2.28½, offsetting his original short position. Actual cash corn prices proved to be 11½ cents less than he had hoped for, but the 13 cent per bushel profit on his short futures position more than offset this. The 1½ cent decline in the basis means that the farmer had an effective selling price for 50,000 bushels of his crop at $2.28, less commissions. Figure 11-1 summarizes what happened.

A whole range of other outcomes were possible. Corn prices might have skyrocketed, leaving the farmer disappointed that he had not waited to sell or to hedge his crop. The basis might have widened, leaving the farmer with a small loss on his hedge but still substantially protected against the price decline. The actual results of hedges that are placed by primary producers depend on a range of often imponderable factors that are at play between the time the crop is planted and the time it is harvested.

Case 2: Hedging a Stream of Production

Not all production operations realize their output at one time of the year. Many, such as livestock farms or mines, produce throughout the year on a regular or an irregular schedule. The basic strategy of fixing the price of production remains the same, but the producer must place his hedges in futures months that correspond to his schedule of output. This requires a knowledge of the production schedule as well as an understanding of the relationships between the various futures months.

Take the case of a gold mine that expects to produce an average of 5,000 ounces every 2 months for the next 12 months. If prices justify a fully hedged position, the mine's futures ledger might show 50 contracts short in each of the available delivery months: February, April, June, August, October, and December. As gold is sold to refiners, the futures position would be lifted and rolled forward one year. In late August of 1988, for instance, the mine would enter a spread order to buy 50 August 1988/sell 50 August 1989 contracts. This process of rolling the hedge forward would be continued until a change occurred either in market conditions or in expected levels of output. Gold futures prices tend to reflect the cost of carrying gold from one period to the next. In other words, April gold will command a premium over February gold that roughly equals the cost of carrying the gold for two months. June gold will command a four-month cost-of-carry premium over February gold, August a six-month premium, and so on. The producer, therefore, has a relatively simple decision to make: Does the present price structure justify hedging the coming year's output? If so, he establishes a hedge portfolio as described above. If not, he may hedge less than the full 50 contracts per delivery month. Or, he may opt for his hedge program to extend only six months rather than a full year.

In other businesses that involve streams of production, decisions can be both more difficult and more speculative. For example, hog futures prices tend to reflect the particular supply/demand forces that are expected to be at work in the delivery month in question. Unlike gold, in which forward deliveries tend to trade at fairly uniform premiums to nearby deliveries, hog futures have no ordered pattern. The price of the February contract may be higher than the June but lower than the December. Next year or next month, relationships may be totally reversed. This poses a problem for the hog farmer, who is geared to a particular level of production. The time period from breeding to slaughter is about ten months, so the producer must look to the futures price ten months ahead to decide whether to increase or to decrease his breeding schedule. He must decide whether to hedge if futures prices imply a loss, or to wait in the hope that higher prices are coming. In general, operations of this kind involve hedge decisions that are sometimes unavoidably based on speculative price forecasting.

Case 3: Hedging Merchant Inventory

On October 1, a cotton merchant buys 100 bales (50,000 pounds) of cotton from a farmer at 50.00 cents per pound, based on prices at a futures delivery point. He sells one contract of December futures at 52.00. In grading the cotton the merchant determines that, in November, it should be worth 75 points (0.75 cents) off (under) the December futures contract. The merchant's buying basis is said to be 200 points (the price of the December sale minus the purchase price in the cash market). By November 1, the merchant finds a buyer at his price of 75 points off December futures, which are now trading at 50.00. The cash transaction is therefore priced at 49.25. He covers his short hedge at the current futures price of 50.00 cents. Calculations are shown in Figure 11-2.

Figure 11-2.

Date	Cash Market Transactions	Futures Market Transactions
Oct. 1	Buys 50,000 pounds cotton @50.00 = $25,000	Sells one contract December futures @52.00
Nov. 1	Sells 50,000 pounds cotton @49.25 = $24,625	Buys one contract December futures @50.00
Result:	− 0.75 or $375 (loss)	+ 200 points or $1,000 (profit)

Net profit: $625

Case 4: Ex-Pit and On-Call Transactions

On October 1, a cotton merchant buys cash cotton from a farmer at 200 points (2 cents per pound) under December futures and hedges with a sale of December futures at that basis. The December futures were sold at 52.00 and the cash cotton was bought at 50.00. A textile mill telephones the merchant to inform him that it needs to buy cotton in 30 days but does not want to fix a price now because it feels that prices are going to be lower. The cotton merchant agrees to sell to the mill 50,000 pounds (one contract) of cotton at 75 points under December—*buyers call*. What this means is that the buyer will fix the price anytime that he wants, prior to first notice day of December futures.

One month later, December futures have fallen to 50.00. The textile mill fixes its price by calling an FCM and directing him to buy one contract of December futures. The broker does so and receives a report back from the floor that indicates that he bought one December at 50.25. The purchase price of the cash cotton to the textile mill, therefore, is 49.50 (75 points under December). The result is that the merchant has made 125 points ($625) on his basis trade, and the textile mill has secured supplies at a price of 49.50 cents per pound. Figure 11-3 summarizes the transactions from the perspective of the merchant.

A *sellers-call transaction* might involve a cotton merchant who agrees to buy cotton from a farmer at a certain number of points above or below futures. In this case the farmer would fix the price by calling the FCM and instructing it to sell a specified number of futures contracts.

Figure 11-3.

Date	Cash Market Transactions	Futures Market Transactions
Oct. 1	Buys 50,000 pounds cotton @50.00	Sells 1 Dec. @52.00
Nov.1	Sells 50,000 pounds cotton @49.50	Buys 1 Dec. @50.25
Result:	– $250 (loss)	$875 (profit)

Net result: $625 (profit)

It is not uncommon in cases like these that the two parties to a cash market transaction have hedged positions in the futures markets. For instance, a merchant may be long cash cotton at 200 points under December, while a textile mill may be short cash cotton at 100 points under December. If the merchant agrees to sell cash cotton to the textile mill, there is no longer any need for their respective hedges. The futures brokers for the merchant and the textile mill execute an *ex-pit transaction* in which the merchant transfers his short December futures to the textile mill at a prearranged price. This erases the hedge positions of both parties simultaneously and without the need for either party to incur unnecessary execution costs. The transaction is called *ex-pit* because it takes place outside the trading pit and is not executed in competitive open outcry. Every futures exchange has rules which permit transactions of this type because they facilitate the efficient use of futures by hedgers.

There are many variations on the themes of ex-pit and on-call transactions. Almost every industry (grains, metals, energy futures, and so on) has some version of these transactions. They represent a kind of harmony between cash market buyers and sellers who commonly use the futures market for price protection.

Case 5: Hedging to Protect Uncovered Forward Sales

Manufacturers and processors often enter into contracts for the forward sale of their products in advance of actual production. For example, a copper fabricator who makes forward sales of rolled sheets finds that he lacks the required inventory for production needed for the forward sale. To ensure a supply of copper at the price estimated in the sale, he hedges by buying futures contracts that are equivalent to the required amount of actual copper.

For example, on June 15 a fabricator obtains an order for a quantity of rolled sheets to be delivered on September 15. Based on the current price of merchant copper and his processing costs, he quotes a fixed price for the copper sheets and signs a contract for their delivery.

However, the actual price of copper on June 15 (the cash price) will not, in all probability, be the same three months later. In the interim, demand may improve, or labor problems may curtail delivery of copper. Any number of events may boost the prices between June 15 and September 15. Enough of a price rise could erase the fabricator's profit margin or even create a substantial loss.

The fabricator could purchase the copper when he first enters into the contract, but he would have to tie up considerable working capital, incur interest expense, and utilize storage space. He would also have to pay insurance for three months. Naturally, these costs would have to be included in the price of the sheets, thereby raising the price of the finished consumer product. As we have discussed in the previous two chapters, there are circumstances in which these costs are not fully reflected in futures prices. In such cases, futures hedges are cheaper as well as more efficient than cash purchases.

The fabricator might also decide to speculate. He may have reason to believe that copper prices will decline before the copper is physically needed. In this case, however, the mill holds only two months' worth of production and the fabricator is not inclined to speculate, so he looks for price protection through the purchase of futures. On June 15 he buys five contracts of September copper at the market, paying a price of 51.50 cents per pound. An experienced hedger, the fabricator knows that the grade of copper he uses is one of the basic grades that is deliverable against the futures contract and that the futures price will fluctuate with the cash. The fabricator also knows that the charges that are associated with the taking of delivery make it an uneconomical option. More important, he cannot be sure that he will receive delivery against the futures contract at a time and location that are suitable for his production because, as we have discussed, delivery is at the seller's option during the delivery period.

On August 4 one of his suppliers offers him an attractive price of 54.00 cents per pound for the quality and the quantity he requires. He accepts the offer and simultaneously sells his five contracts of September futures at 53.75, the going price. His 2.50 cent loss on the forward sale transaction is offset almost entirely by his 2.25 cent gain in futures.

Feed manufacturers, corn and soybean processors, petroleum-product marketers, and other manufacturers and processors of basic commodities may use the futures market to hedge uncovered forward sales of their products in a similar fashion. However, the more the commodity is transformed from its basic state to its manufactured state, the more difficult hedging becomes. An understanding of the conversion factors (if any) that relate the raw material to its finished product are essential. A distiller, for example, who knows that a bushel of corn yields 2.5 to 2.6 gallons of 95% alcohol, that wheat yields 2.4 gallons, and that rye yields 2.2 gallons can readily calculate the number of futures contracts that are needed to cover a forward sale of alcohol.

Case 6: Hedging by an Oil Refinery

In mid-July an oil refinery commits itself to deliver to a customer 2.1 million gallons of No. 2 heating oil in December at the posted cash price as of December 2. If the current cash price of, say, 40 cents per gallon were to prevail in December, the value of the potential sale would be $840,000 (= 2.1 million gallons x 40 cents per gallon). The oil refinery sells 50 contracts of December heating oil futures on the New York Mercantile Exchange (each contract representing 42,000 gallons) at 42 cents per gallon. The value of the sale in the futures market is $882,000.

On December 2, the refinery delivers No. 2 heating oil to a manufacturing company at the prevailing price of 35 cents per gallon. The 5-cents decline in the cash market has resulted in a decline of $105,000 in the value of the products sold compared with the July cash price. However, on December 1 the refiner buys 50 contracts of December futures at a price of 36 cents per gallon, giving him a profit on his short position of $126,000. The final value of the sale is $735,000 (the proceeds of the sale at 35 cents per gallon) plus $126,000 (the profit on the futures position). This total of $861,000 is $21,000 more than the refinery had hoped for back in August. The sequence of events is depicted in Figure 11-4.

Alert readers may have noticed something different in this example. The refinery has compared its actual selling price in December with the cash price that prevailed in July when the hedge was implemented. It

Figure 11-4.

Date	Cash Market Transactions	Futures Market Transactions
July 15	No transaction. Cash price = 40.00	Sells 50 Dec. futures @42.00
Dec. 2	Sells 2.1 million gallons @35.00	Buys 50 Dec. futures @36.00
Result:	$105,000 (apparent opportunity cast)	$126,000 (profit)

Net result: $21,000 profit relative to expectations

would be more appropriate to make the comparison with a *forward* price for December, which is the approach taken by the farmer in Case 1. This is because forward prices are, by definition, a more relevant indicator than are current cash prices of what prices are expected to be in the future. Nevertheless, many hedgers make the mistake of comparing their eventual sale (or purchase) prices with the cash prices that prevailed at the time they established their hedges.

Case 7: Currency Hedging by a Machinery Importer

A New York-based importer of packaging machinery from West Germany enters into a contract to buy 6 machines at a cost of 1.6 million Deutsche marks (DM). In July, when the contract is struck, the value of the Deutsche mark is 0.4503 (one DM = $0.4503). Thus, she estimates her purchase price in dollars to be $720,480. Having lined up a buyer for the equipment who is willing to pay $800,000, she expects to receive a gross profit of $79,520. In September, when it is time to pay the West German manufacturer, the value of the DM has risen to 0.4728. Her actual purchase price, therefore, is $756,480. This leaves her with a gross profit of $43,520, some 45% less than she had expected.

To protect herself against the change in currency values, the importer could have made an advance purchase of Deutsche marks in July in one of two ways. She could have called her bank and arranged to purchase DM 1.6 million to be delivered in September. Assume that the bank quote was 0.4500 bid/0.4508 asked (meaning that the bank would buy Deutsche marks at 0.4500 and sell them at 0.4508). At the same time, the quote for September futures on the IMM was 0.4501 bid/ 0.4505 asked. The importer could buy Deutsche marks in either place and lock in a currency rate in advance. Because the asking price in the futures market was lower than that at the bank, the purchase of futures would seem to be the obvious choice. But this is not necessarily the case. The importer knows that the purchase of futures entails a commission expense of $25 per contract, or $0.0002 per Deutsche mark. In addition, the choice of futures would require her to post original margin of $1,200 per contract. The bank transaction entails neither commission nor margin. A further complicating factor involves the number of contracts that are needed to be purchased in the futures market. Because each contract represents 125,000 Deutsche marks, the importer would have to decide whether to be slightly underhedged with 12 contracts or slightly overhedged with 13 contracts. The bank, on the other hand, would agree to deliver the precise quantity of Deutsche marks needed. For these reasons, she opts to make her forward currency purchase through the bank.

In this example, the rigidity of the futures contract and its transaction costs make the bank a superior hedging source. In highly efficient markets, however, the advantages of bank trading can be offset by significantly narrower bid/ask spreads in futures. For a more detailed discussion of the interbank foreign currency market see Chapter 19.

Case 8: Hedging by a Pension Fund

On April 1 a pension fund manager anticipates receiving $10 million of funds for investment in mid-May. Presently, 20-year 8% U.S. Treasury bonds are priced in the cash market at 95–14 with a yield to maturity of 8.48%, a rate that he decides to lock-in in case yields fall during the next 45 days. To do so, he buys 100 contracts of June T-bond futures (each contract has a face value of $100,000) at the current price of 95–13 (prices are expressed in 32nds, digits to the right of the dash being 32nds). By May 15, yields have declined to 8.26%, and cash bonds are now trading at 97–16. In the futures market, June bonds have risen to 97–13. The decline in yields (0.22%) and the resulting increase in cash bond prices (2–2) have created an opportunity cost to the pension fund manager of $206,250 because he had hoped to pay $9,543,750 for the bonds, but instead had to pay $9,750,000. His futures position, however, shows a profit of 2–0 for each of the 100 long contracts, or $200,000. Thus, the pension fund has offset all but a small part of the opportunity cost.

Case 9: Hedging by a Bond Dealer

Consider a bond dealer who, on March 1, has an inventory of $1 million face value of the 115/8% U.S. Treasury bond that will mature in November 2002. The current value of this bond is 97–29 to yield 8.28%. For whatever reason, the dealer wants to keep these bonds but is concerned that a rise in yields will undermine their value. To protect herself, she sells 10 June T-bond futures at a price of 96–21. Over the next month, rising yields result in a decline in the price of the cash bonds to 94–26, or a loss of $30,937.50 on the cash T-bond position. During that time, June futures have dropped from 96–21 to 93–10, yielding a profit on her 10 shorts of $33,437.50, less commissions.

Case 10: Hedging by an Investment Banking Firm

An investment banking firm is part of a small syndicate that has agreed to underwrite the sale of $30 million of high-grade corporate bonds. Along with two other banking firms, it agrees to buy $10 million of the bonds and distribute them to the public and other dealers at a reasonable profit. The coupon rate of the 10-year bonds has been set at 13%, which the syndicate feels is an adequate rate to move the bonds quickly into investment portfolios. Each syndicate member buys its share of the bonds at 99–16 and hopes to sell them at par and net a profit of $50,000 ($16/32 \times 1\% \times \$10$ million). However, the day after the issue was priced, bond prices plunged in response to an announcement by the Federal Reserve. The price of the corporate bond dropped to 98–31. Let's see how each investment banker made out.

Bank I chose not to hedge its share of the underwriting in the futures market. As a result, it lost $17/32$ on each bond, or a total of $53,125.

Bank II executed a simple hedge by selling 100 ten-year Treasury note futures on the Chicago Board of Trade at a price of 93–16. The results are shown in Figure 11-5.

Figure 11-5.

Date	Cash Market Transactions	Futures Market Transactions
July 1	Buy $10 million ten-year corporate bonds @99–16	Sell 100 ten-year Sept. T-notes @93–16
July 10	Sell $10 million ten-year corporate bonds @98–31	Buy 100 ten-year Sept. T-notes @93–03
Result:	$- 17/32$ or $53,125 (loss)	$+ 13/32$ or $40,625 (profit)

Net loss: – $12,500

Figure 11-6.

Date	Cash Market Transactions	Futures Market Transactions
July 1	Buy $10 million ten-year corporate bonds @99–16	Sell 130 ten-year Sept. T-notes @93–16
July 10	Sell $10 million ten-year corporate bonds @98–31	Buy 130 ten-year Sept. T-notes @93–03
Result:	– 17/32 or $53,125 (loss)	+ 13/32 x 130 contracts or $52,812.50 (profit)

Net loss: – $312.50

In this case the hedge failed to provide complete protection because the banker neglected to realize that a given drop in overall interest rates has a markedly different effect on a 13% instrument than on an 8% instrument (the par-delivery grade of the futures contract).

Bank III , the most sophisticated, knew that the same change in yield would cause a greater price change in the 13% bond than it would in the futures contract that is based on an 8% bond. From his conversion tables the banker knew that the price change of the 13% bond would be about 1.3 times greater than that of the 8%-based futures contract. Therefore, instead of selling 100 futures contracts, he weighted his hedge by selling 130 contracts. The results are shown in Figure 11-6. Chapter 9 contains a more complete discussion of the relationships between cash and futures prices in interest rate markets.

Case 11: Hedging by a Mortgage Banker

In February, a mortgage banker begins to make commitments for a mortgage pool of $5 million. He expects the pool to close on May 15, at which time he intends to sell GNMA certificates to investors (Chapter 18 contains a discussion of GNMAs). If, however, rates rise between the time the mortgage commitments are made and the time the GNMAs are sold, the banker will lose money. In this case, the banker could periodically sell an amount of GNMAs equal to the mortgage commitments made. Figure 11-7 shows how the process would work.

Figure 11-7.

Date	Mortgage Commitments	Cash GNMA 8's	June GNMA Futures Sold	Futures Price
to 2/15	$2 million	85–21	20	85–22
2/15–3/1	$1 million	85–00	10	85–04
3/1–4/1	$1 million	84–26	10	84–30
4/1–5/1	$1 million	84–16	10	84–16
Total	$5 million		50	
Average Price		85–4		85–6

Figure 11-8.

Date	Cash Market Transactions	Futures Market Transactions
2/1–5/1	Acquired $5 million mortgages at average price of 85–4	Sells 50 June GNMAs at average price of 85–6
5/15	Sells $5 million of GNMAs at 84–14	Buys 50 June GNMAs at price of 84–14
Result:	– $34,375 (loss)	= $37,500 (profit)
	Net result: $3,125 (profit)	

Assume that on May 15, when the pool closes and the GNMAs are sold to investors, the equivalent GNMA 8 price is 84–14 and that June futures are also at 84–14. The transaction is then summarized as shown in Figure 11-8.

Case 12: Cross-hedging by a Corporate Borrower

Due to an expected seasonal outflow of cash during the summer months, a corporation plans to raise $10 million by issuing 90-day commercial paper in June. It is now March and prevailing commercial paper rates are 8.50%. The corporation's treasurer figures the cost of this financing to be $212,500 ($10 million x 8.50% x 1/4 year). However, he is concerned about speculation in the financial press that short-

Figure 11-9.

Date	Cash Market Transactions	Futures Market Transactions
March 1	Plans to borrow $10 million through issuance of commercial paper on June 1	Sells 10 June Eurodollar futures @91.65 (8.35%)
	Current 90-day CP rate = 8.50% (Projected interest expense = $212,500)	
June 1	Issues CP at the now higher Eurodollar rate of 9.65% (Actual interest expense = $241,250)	Buys 10 June futures @90.50 (9.50%)
Result:	$28,750 (opportunity cost)	$28,750 profit
	Net result: $0	

term interest rates could rise by 1% or 2% by the beginning of summer and would like to fix his borrowing costs at current levels.

One solution would be for the treasurer to sell 10 contracts of June Eurodollar futures at the current price of, say, 91.65 (in the absence of an active futures market in commercial paper, the treasurer uses the most comparable instrument available–Eurodollar futures). See Figure 11-9.

In this example, the decline in Eurodollar futures precisely offset the opportunity cost of the 1.15% rise in commercial paper rates. In actual practice, hedging rarely succeeds with such perfection, particularly when dealing with cross hedges. *Cross-hedging* is the practice of hedging a cash market risk in one financial instrument with a position in a futures contract of a different but related instrument. Such a hedge is effective only if there is a high degree of correlation between the prices of the two instruments.

Case 13: Hedging a Portfolio of Equities

A corporate treasurer manages a diversified portfolio of blue-chip stocks that is worth $25 million. The treasurer feels that a sharp setback could occur prior to the resumption of a long-term bull market. Because of its greater concentraton of blue-chip issues, S&P 500 futures are a good hedge vehicle for this portfolio. The treasurer sells 200 June S&P futures at the current price of 241.50. With each futures contract worth $500 x 241.50, the value of the short position is $24,150,000.

During the next month, the portfolio's value declines by 5% to $23,750,000. During this time, the S&P 500 index falls 5.3% to 228.70. The paper profit on the short hedge amounts to $1,280,000 (12.80 x $500 x 200), which more than offsets the $1,250,000 decline in the value of the portfolio.

If the portfolio had contained a greater number of speculative, volatile issues, the portfolio manager might have weighted his hedge. The ratio between the volatility of a portfolio and the volatility of the market as a whole is called the *beta* of the portfolio. In this example, a beta of 1.2 instead of 1.0 would have led the portfolio manager to establish a short position of 240 contracts instead of 200. If the S&P index fell by 5%, and his 1.2 beta portfolio fell by 6%, the results would have been as shown in Figure 11-10.

Figure 11-10.

Date	Portfolio Holdings	Futures Market Transactions
March 1	Value = $25,000,000	Sell 240 June S&P @241.50 ($28,980,000)
April 1	Value = $23,500,000 (– 6%)	Buy 240 June S&P @229.40 (– 5%) ($27,528,000)
Result:	$1,500,000 (loss)	$1,452,000 (profit)
	Net loss: – $48,000	

Case 14: Anticipatory Hedging by a Trust Fund

Another form of hedging involves the use of futures as a temporary substitute for a stock market position to be established at a later date. As an illustration, suppose that a trust fund receives contributions that are to be invested on a regular basis. Prior to the actual receipt of quarterly funds, the trust fund manager feels that the recent setback in stock prices provides a buying opportunity that may not be available if he awaits the arrival of the funds. In this case, he could buy stock index futures with an underlying contract value that is equal to the expected funds. Once the funds were available, he would liquidate his futures position and purchase the actual equities.

■ Chapter 12

■ *Dealer Operations and Arbitrage*

Dealers are the intermediaries between producers and consumers. They play key roles in a market economy and are particularly important participants in the futures markets. A dealer is an organization (or person) that stands ready to buy or sell the items in which it deals whenever one of its customers requests. Dealers differ from brokers in that they act as principals in transactions and therefore employ their own capital. Brokers act as intermediaries who match buyers with sellers but do not themselves take market positions. In a futures trading ring, the floor broker who executes an order on behalf of an FCM is acting as a broker. The local who takes the opposite side of the transaction into his own account is, in effect, acting as a dealer. Let us first look at the role that is played by dealers in the cash markets and then examine how and why dealers use the futures markets.

To understand the role that is played by dealers in the cash markets, let us begin by revisiting the imaginary world of Chapter 1 in which there are only a producer and a consumer. For variety, though, let us now move from the realm of agriculture to that of finance. Assume that we have Corporation *A* in California who wants to issue 10-year debt and that we have a pension fund Manager *B* in Houston who is considering buying 10-year corporate debt. If the two are in regular contact, or if they happen fortuitously to stumble across one another at exactly the right moment, then the corporation might place its 10-year paper directly with the investor. In the real world, this is not likely. Corporation *A* probably does not have the staff to monitor the capital markets continuously for prospective investors, and Manager *B* in Houston may have no direct access to information from the California corporate arena.

This is basically a problem of communications and information flow. The two parties simply do not know about each other. If this is the only problem, a broker could provide the solution because a broker's job is to monitor both sides of a market continuously so as to bring together seller and buyer (or, in this case, issuer and investor). In real life, though, communications is often not the only impediment. Corporation *A* may need funding this week, whereas Investor *B* may not have funds that are available until existing investments mature in two weeks. We have seen how Corporation *A* could use the futures markets to hedge against a rise in interest rates prior to the issuance of this debt. But what if its cash flow requirements are such that it needs actual funds, rather than merely protection against rate increases? Neither a cash market broker nor a position in the futures markets can address this problem. This is a job for a cash market dealer.

A dealer would be prepared to use its own capital to purchase Corporation *A*'s debt. In doing so, it would be acting as financial intermediary rather than as end-investor. If Investor *B* had indicated a willingness to pay $1,000 for $1,000 face value of Corporation *A*'s debt, then the dealer might bid $990 as principal in the hope of reselling the paper to Investor *B* in two weeks at a $10 profit. The dealer is, in effect, making a two-sided market in Corporation *A*'s 10-year debt: $990 bid/ $1,000 offered. The dealer differs from an investor in that he is not buying the paper because he perceives it to be an attractive long-term investment. Rather, he believes that he can earn a profit by quickly reselling the debt issue. The dealer differs from a broker because he is committing his own capital rather than simply matching issuer and investor.

The dealer's $10 profit (or dealing spread) represents compensation for the service of providing liquidity by bridging the time gap between the need for funds by the issuer and the availability of funds from the investor. This service is of value, though, only if the dealer is willing to bid for debt when Corporation *A* wants to issue debt. If our dealer bids only when he himself wants to, he will soon find himself going out of business. Issuers either will find another dealer who is more responsive to their timing needs or will turn to the less-costly broker market if dealers are not providing sufficient added value in the form of timing flexibility. If either of these things happened, our original dealer would quickly lose ground among investors as well because he would tend to have a smaller inventory of products from which investors could select at any given time.

This need to be responsive to their customer's timing requirements puts dealers in a position of only limited control over their cash market positions and exposures. Returning to our example above, if the dealer feels that Investor B may change his mind about buying Corporation A's 10-year debt then he, the dealer, might lower his own bid to $985 or $980 because of the perceived additional risk. But if he wants to maintain his relationship with Corporation A, he will not often withdraw his bid entirely or lower it to a level that would seem frivolous or insulting. This means that in the course of servicing his issuing client, our dealer will sometimes find himself owning inventory that he does not really want and is not particularly confident about being able to resell quickly at a profit.

A dealer can find himself in the opposite predicament as well. If Investor B wants to buy a particular bond that a dealer does not currently hold in inventory, the dealer may go short the bond to Investor B rather than risk losing a piece of business and admitting an inability to satisfy a customer request. This would leave the dealer exposed to the possibility of being unable to locate and to purchase the particular securities at a profitable level in time to deliver them to Investor B on schedule.

The basic concept to keep in mind is this: A dealer must be responsive to customers on both sides of his market, and this responsiveness will often force him into long or short positions that he does not really want. We will turn shortly to the subject of how dealers use futures to help manage their positions. First, though, we want to emphasize that what we have discussed here applies to dealers in a wide variety of markets. We have focused our discussion on the specific example of a bond dealer, but the same concepts apply to dealers in any other market. An international bank must be prepared to give its customers bids and offers for the major currencies. A grain merchant must stand ready to buy from farmers and must also maintain sufficient inventory at various locations to meet unexpected export demand. The specifics vary from business to business, but in every case a dealer must develop and maintain relationships with producers and consumers, and at any point in time the dealer's cash market exposure—long, short, or neutral—is determined in good measure by his attempts to service his customer base.

HEDGING REQUIREMENTS OF DEALERS

The nature of a dealer's cash market business flow creates specialized futures requirements. Two of these requirements deserve particular attention. First, a dealer shares with producers and consumers the desire to reduce his exposure to price fluctuations. However, a dealer's exposures are likely to fluctuate much more rapidly as he buys from producers and sells to consumers. An active dealer might make several dozen or more cash market transactions each day. If he wants to keep his futures hedges current, he will need to adjust them at least several times daily and perhaps even after each cash market trade. This contrasts with the hedging requirements of nondealers, whose futures positions tend to change much less frequently. Again, the reason is the more varied cash market activities of dealers relative to other market participants. Dealers are forced to consider far more cash market items and basis relationships than are most producers and consumers. The following examples illustrate the point:

- A fixed-income portfolio manager might typically confine his attention in the corporate bond sector to one or two dozen issues that he either already owns or is considering buying. However, a corporate bond dealer must be prepared to quote markets in any of the hundreds of issues that are followed by one or more of his customers. Both the manager and the dealer will likely use the highly liquid futures on U.S. Treasury securities to hedge their cash market positions, so each cash market corporate security corresponds to a basis relationship that should be understood and monitored.

- A copper mining company need concern itself only with the basis relationships that involve the grades and locations of the ores that it produces. A copper dealer purchases many different grades and locations. Each physical market grade/location combination is another basis relationship that the dealer must follow.

An understanding of basis relationships is important to dealers for another reason as well. Dealers' profit margins are narrow relative to thoses of other hedgers, so basis mishaps can have especially dire consequences. Consider these illustrations:

- Corn farmers typically expect average selling prices to exceed production costs by 50 cents per bushel or more. (This does not always happen, but is a reasonable average over many seasons.) Grain dealers, on the other hand, expect average net profit margins of 1 cent per bushel or less. Consistently leaving $1/2$ cent to $3/4$ cent per bushel on the table through ill-timed basis positions would probably go unnoticed by the farmer but would be devastating for the dealer.

- An investor in over-the-counter securities probably expects to make at least several dollars per share and perhaps much more when he buys a $40- or $50-per-share stock. The over-the-counter dealer who sells him the stock would be delighted to realize a 50¢-per-share margin on the purchase and resale of the security. Clearly, the dealer needs a much keener understanding of the relationship between the stock and the particular equity futures index in which it is hedged.

The unique hedging requirements of dealers create the need for special futures trading capabilities. Dealers need to understand these in order to operate profitably. Let us now discuss those futures-related issues of particular importance to dealers. We will then describe the activities and expense profile of a typical dealer to give a sense of how the concepts work in the real world. Finally, we will address the implicatons of these specialized dealer capabilities for the trading strategies of others who use futures.

FUTURES TRADING REQUIREMENTS OF DEALERS

Three issues are of paramount importance to dealers who hedge in futures:

- Rapid communications with the trading floor
- Low transaction costs
- Careful management of basis risk

Let us now discuss each of these requirements separately.

Rapid Communications With the Trading Floor

The fact that dealers operate on very thin profit margins means that they cannot afford to be even slightly wrong about the price at which they can execute their futures hedges. A speculator who expects December T-bill futures to rise from 91.00 to 94.00 may be content to enter a buy order, knowing only that the last trade that was displayed on his quote screen was at 91.02. A dealer whose typical profit margin is something like 0.02 must be much more demanding: he will almost certainly want to know the prevailing bid and offer prices in the ring or pit and will probably want some idea of how many contracts he could expect to sell at the bid price or buy at the offer price.

A dealer needs this information to preserve his narrow profit margins. If, for example, he is preparing to bid on cash market securities in response to a customer inquiry, he might reason that selling 50 futures contracts at 91.01 would lock in an acceptable margin of 0.03 and that an average sale price of 90.99 would still allow him to eke out a margin of 0.01 that might cover his transaction costs. By this standard of precision, knowing only that the last trade took place a minute or so ago at 91.02 is essentially useless information. The dealer will want to be told something along these lines: "December is 91.01 bid, offered at 91.03. The bidders appear to be collectively good for at least 30 contracts, but there doesn't seem to be much buying interest apart from the 91.01 bids. Also, there are 300 contracts offered at 91.03." Armed with this kind of detail, the dealer will decide whether he thinks that the probability of selling 50 contracts at 91.01 (or better) is high enough to justify bidding aggressively on his customer's securities, or whether he would prefer to reduce his bid and risk losing the cash market business.

Obviously, a dealer must be in extremely close touch with the exchange floor to receive this level of detail whenever he needs it. Typically, this is accomplished by having an open telephone line from the dealer's office to the exchange floor and keeping a clerk on the exchange end of the line to monitor what is happening in the trading ring and relay the information to the dealer's cash market traders as they request it. The phone clerk will probably also relay verbal futures orders from the cash market dealer to floor brokers in the futures pit for execution. In the real-life futures world, the job of phone clerk is quite demanding. It requires paying continuous, careful, and simultaneous attention to what is happening in the hectic futures area and to the requests for specific information that come from the dealer on the other end of the phone. It is seldom possible for a phone clerk to adequately service more than one active dealer. Large cash market dealer operations may need two or more phone clerks (as well as multiple telephone lines) in a single futures contract to provide adequate information-flow and order-handling capabilities.

Low Transaction Costs

The nature of their business makes dealers as a group the most active off-floor futures traders. Some dealers are more active in futures than even the largest locals in the ring, whose transaction costs are, as we have seen, limited to clearing fees and the cost of clerical support to help prepare trading records. It is not at all unusual for a major dealer in an active market such as T-bonds, soybeans, or gold to trade hundreds of thousands of futures contracts per year. Taking this fact together with the narrow profit margins that are typical for dealers makes it clear that controlling transaction costs is of vital importance to the bottom line.

A high level of futures activity provides a dealer with both the motivation and the ability to control costs. Dealers will typically take some or all the following steps to minimize transaction costs:

- Become exchange members to reduce or eliminate per-contract exchange fees that are levied on nonmembers.

- Negotiate low-cost clearing arrangements with a clearing member firm.

or

- Become clearing members to reduce or eliminate both the fees that are paid to the clearinghouse and the commissions that are paid to a clearing member firm. Because clearing entails both financial exposure (via the clearinghouse guarantee of all futures contracts that are cleared) and operational requirements (in the form of trade processing), clearing membership is the most complex of the various cost-control issues that dealers face.

- Unbundle floor brokerage costs from clearing costs and negotiate favorable per-contract brokerage rates with one or more floor brokers.

These cost control measures are, of course, available to any futures market participant who cares to employ them, but typically only floor locals, FCMs, and cash market dealers handle sufficient volume both to justify a comprehensive assault on costs and to provide the leverage to successfully implement such a program. We have previously described how locals provide liquidity and how FCMs act as the liaison between the floor and the rest of the world. Dealers are the largest off-floor traders for their own account and, as we will discuss below, provide the most important link between the futures and the cash markets.

Careful Management of Basis Risk

In our earlier discussion of hedging, we explained how a futures hedge substitutes basis risk for price level risk. When it comes to dealer activities, this is an oversimplification because it assumes that the price level risk already exists. This assumption holds for the large majority of nondealer hedgers, but must be modified for dealers. Dealers basically approach the issue from a different direction. They respond to the fact that a position that is hedged in futures is much less risky than an unhedged position by carrying much larger positions than they would find prudent if they could not hedge. In other words, hedging permits them to substitute a large amount of small basis risk for a small amount of large price-level risk. Combine this with our earlier discussion of why dealers also carry a wide variety of basis exposures, and the importance of monitoring and managing basis risk becomes clear.

Not surprisingly, dealers spend a lot of time, effort, and money monitoring and analyzing basis relationships. A large, sophisticated dealer might have years of proprietary data on various cash market items that can be correlated with the publicly available futures price data to aid in deciding when to try to increase or to decrease cash market holdings of a particular item.

Prudent dealers also focus on measuring the basis risk of their positions. This is not as easy as it may sound. For example, suppose that a grain dealer buys cash wheat in September and hedges by selling December wheat futures. If March wheat futures then rise relative to the December contract and the dealer elects to move his hedge from December to March, how should he measure the change in his basis exposure? On a more mundane level, active dealers may engage in a hundred or more cash market transactions daily (some spot, some forward) and a similar number of futures trades that encompass several different contract months. Simply keeping track of basis exposures can be a daunting task in such cases. Most dealers rely heavily on computer support of one type or another to assist in both the analysis and the position monitoring of basis relationships.

Sometimes a dealer's focus on basis relationships is so intense that he loses track of the absolute price level. A money market dealer may decide that he will pay 20 points under June Eurodollar futures for Bank X's CDs and then forget whether the "42 bid" that he hears from his phone clerk means 91.42 or 92.42. The importance of the basis relationships is such that not remembering price levels usually doesn't matter very much, except to the extent that it can be embarrassing to be a grain trader who doesn't know the price of wheat or a bond dealer who forgets whether 20-year governments are trading at 96-00 or 98-00.

A LOOK AT A DEALER OPERATION

The Dealer Book

We now turn to a discussion of how a dealer actually functions, with particular emphasis on the general use of futures and the specific ideas that were covered earlier in this chapter. We have chosen the example of a gold dealer, but the basic concepts are applicable to any futures-based dealing activity—bonds, grain, etc. A good place to begin is the dealer's "book," which is the record of all cash market positions along with their associated futures hedges. A simplified but realistic gold book might look like Figure 12-1 (see page 273) on February 15.

Several points relating to this "dealing book" are worth making:

- Though cash market quantities and offsetting futures market quantities match closely on each line, there is only one case (the 7,120 ounces on 3/26) in which the specific material being hedged is exactly the same as that which underlies the futures contract. In the last case, for instance, the dealer must figure out how to convert the October Comex futures contract (representing 100 ounce bars) into physical 400 ounce bars that are located in Zurich, Switzerland. Knowing how to do this type of thing by the use of swaps with other holders of gold, physical shipments, and even physical

Figure 12-1. Gold dealer's position book.

Cash Market

February 15

Long or Short	Quantity (ounces)	Settlement Date	Description	Location	Price (per ounce)
L	6,822	Spot	99.5%/400-oz bars	London	$346.30
L	1,130	Spot	Ore equivalent	El Paso	326.85
	.				
	.				
	.				
S	7,120	3/26	Comex receipts	New York	356.20
	.				
	.				
	.				
S	19,512	10/13	99.5%/400-oz bars	Zurich	362.20

Total Net Quantity (physical market): Short 18,680 ounces
Weighted Average Maturities: Longs—February 15
Shorts—August 20

Futures Hedge

Long or Short	Quantity (100 ounce contracts)	Delivery Month	Price (per ounce)
S	68	April	$351.22
S	11	April	332.90
	.		
	.		
	.		
L	71	April	362.10
	.		
	.		
	.		
L	195	October	360.40

Total Net Quantity: Long 187 contracts
Weighted Average Maturities: Shorts—April 1
Longs—August 10
Realized Profit (year-to-date): $96,310

processing of the gold itself is a key ingredient in a successful dealership. It is part of the service that is provided by a dealer to his customers.

- The dates of the related cash and futures positions never match exactly. Cash market obligations settle on a particular day that is chosen to accommodate the dealer's customer, whereas futures settle at the seller's option anytime during the delivery month. Note particularly the third entry. Here the dealer is obligated to deliver warehouse receipts for 7,120 ounces of gold on March 26, but he will not receive the material from his futures hedge until at least April 1. Most probably, our dealer will have to borrow this material for a week or so (perhaps from another dealer), incurring a fee in the process. Presumably, he built such a fee into the price that was quoted to the customer for March 26 delivery.

- Look at the prices for the March 26 sale and its futures hedge. The sale at $356.20 per ounce and the purchase at $362.10 hardly suggest a profitable dealership. The two most likely explanations are these: First, the dealer may have agreed to this transaction months ago when the April contract was distant and illiquid. If so, he would likely have first hedged in the then-active futures contract (say December) and later done a switch (sell December/buy April, to move the hedge to the correct month. If the prices of the purchase and sale of the December futures differed, the dealer's accounting procedures might cause a profit (or loss) to be realized on the last line. The unrealized loss that relates to the prices of the cash contract and its futures hedge is an offset to this realized profit. The second possible explanation is that the dealer may simply have made a poor trade. He may have held his cash market sale unhedged until the market moved more than $5 per ounce away from him. Like the rest of us, dealers do make mistakes.

- The fact that cash and futures maturities seldom match exactly creates for dealers the problem of *gap exposure,* or *implied switch risk.* To see what this means, consider the average maturity information near the bottom of Figure 12-1. Combining cash and futures positions the dealer is, in the aggregate, long 34,552 ounces of gold for settlement July 3, and short 34,532 ounces for settlement July 19.

To illustrate how these numbers are calculated, let us consider the dealer's long positions, both cash and futures. We assume that February 15 is day zero and measure the time to maturity of forwards and futures from that date:

Cash or Futures	Quantity (Q)	Maturity Date	Days to Maturity (D)	(Q x D)
C	6,822	Feb. 15	0	0
C	1,130	Feb. 15	0	0
F	7,100	April 1	45	319,500
F	19,500	Oct.1	228	4,446,000
Total longs	34,552			4,765,500

Weighted average days to maturity = $\dfrac{4,765,500}{34,552}$ = **138**

July 3 is 138 days from February 15, and so is the weighted average maturity date of the long positions.

In terms of concept and risk, this is no different from switch (or spread) positions that traders enter into for profit. The problem is that a dealer typically finds himself with such gap exposures more or less by accident. If, for example, his October 13 Zurich customer had instead wanted September 23 delivery, October futures would still have been the preferred hedge month, but the gap exposure would have been quite different. Often, dealers will try to manage this type of gap exposure by entering into opposing futures switches as a gap hedge. In this example, the dealer might sell June futures and buy August futures in an effort to offset the gap exposure in his basic book.

Dealer Transactions

Let us now consider how a dealer conducts the activities that create and continually modify the type of position book that is shown in Figure12-1. A simple and effective way to do this is to describe what might happen if a customer wanted to make a trade that would modify one of the entries already in the trading book of Figure 12-1. Suppose that a customer wishes to sell 1,000 ounces of Zurich gold for the October 13

Figure 12-2.

April gold futures—$340.30 bid/$340.80 offered

April/October gold futures switch—$16.20 bid/$16.60 offered

---

date already appearing on the dealer's book. Assume that the dealer is prepared to bid 60 cents per ounce less for Zurich gold than the price at which he believes he can hedge by selling Comex futures for the same maturity date. Assume also that the following prices prevail, and that April futures are the active trading month and therefore the month in which the dealer will initially hedge.

The following sequence of events might then occur:

1. The customer phones and requests a bid for October 13 Zurich gold.

2. The dealer knows that his bid will be 60 cents per ounce less than the Comex futures bid for this same date, but he faces two problems. First, October futures are distant and rather inactive, so obtaining a reliable bid is difficult. Second, we have seen that futures contracts usually trade on the assumption that delivery will be made on the first possible day of the delivery month. This is because delivery is at the seller's option, and sellers usually want to receive their money as quickly as possible. This leaves our dealer to face the question of how to relate October futures to the specific October 13 date. Consider these two issues separately.

3. The dealer asks his phone clerk near the Comex gold ring for quotes on April futures and on the April/October switch, and is given the information in Figure 12-2. He realizes that he can sell April futures at $340.30 per ounce and then buy April/sell October at a difference of $16.20, giving him an effective sale price for the October futures of $356.50 per ounce.

4. Because the October futures contract carries a premium of about $16.00 relative to the April contract, and because there are 183 days between April 1 and October 1, the premium is about 9 cents per ounce per day. Therefore, the dealer adds 9 cents x 12 days (= $1.08 per ounce) to the effective October futures bid of $356.50 to arrive at the price of $357.58 per ounce on which he will base his bid for his customer's October 13 Zurich gold.

5. Subtracting the 60 cents-per-ounce discount that the dealer feels is appropriate, he then bids his customer $356.98 per ounce or, more likely, he rounds to $357.00 per ounce.

The foregoing five steps from customer inquiry to receipt of information from the futures exchange floor to analysis of the numbers to a firm bid for the customer's gold would take a competent large-scale dealer no more than a few minutes. Such is the level of efficiency that is needed to be competitive in most dealing businesses. If the customer accepts this bid and agrees to sell his gold to the dealer for $357.00 per ounce, the chain of events might continue as follows:

6. The dealer and the customer verbally agree to the trade with the understanding that the dealer will send a written confirmation covering the details of the cash market transaction.

7. Upon agreeing to purchase the 1,000 ounces from his customer, the dealer must decide whether to hedge his resulting 1,000 ounce long position immediately or to maintain this market exposure. He might choose to maintain the exposure either because he is bullish on gold or because he expects another customer to buy physical gold from him and therefore eliminate the necessity of hedging in futures.

8. Let us assume that the dealer decides to hedge immediately. He will tell his Comex phone clerk to sell 10 contracts of April and to also execute the April/October switch to roll the hedge out to October. The phone clerk will do this and report back the prices in a matter of seconds in most cases.

At this point, the transaction is complete. Before the end of the day, the dealer will need to incorporate this new piece of business into his trading book. Doing so will affect the October 13 entry in the book and also the subsequent aggregate information. The dealer's book would then look like Figure 12-3 on page 278.

Notice that the dealer has accounted for his profit by assuming that the purchase of 1,000 ounces of physical gold at $357.00 covers 1,000 ounces of his 19,512 short position at $362.20 and that the sale of 10 October futures contracts at $356.50 liquidates 10 of his previous 195 long contracts at $360.40. The arithmetic looks like this:

Figure 12-3.

Cash Market

Long or Short	Quantity (ounces)	Settlement Date	Description	Location	Price (per ounce)
L	6,822	Spot	99.5%/400-oz bars	London	$346.30
L	1,130	Spot	Ore equivalent	El Paso	326.85
S	7,120	3/26	Comex receipts	New York	356.20
S	18,512	10/13	99.5%/400-oz bars	Zurich	$362.20

Total Net Quantity (physical market): Short—17,680 ounces
Weighted Average Maturities (physical market): Longs—February 15
Shorts—August 15

Futures Hedge

Long or Short	Quantity (100 ounce contracts)	Delivery Month	Price (per ounce)
S	68	April	$351.22
S	11	April	332.90
L	71	April	362.10
L	185	October	360.40

Total Net Quantity (futures market): Long 177 contracts
Weighted Average Maturity (futures market): Shorts—April 1
Longs—August 5
Realized Profit (year-to-date): $97,610

Realized Cash Market Profit: ($362.20 – $357.00) = $5.20 per ounce
   x 1,000 ounces = $5,200 (profit)
Realized Futures Market Loss: ($356.50 – $360.40) = $3.90 per ounce
   x 1,000 ounces = $3,900 (loss)
Net Realized Profit for Transaction: $1,300

Notice that the *realized* profit of $1,300 exceeds the $600 which the dealer planned to make when he priced the 1,000 ounce purchase at 60 cents per ounce under his hedge price. The difference is due to the accounting methodology that is employed. We omit the details, but point out that the dealer is carrying his inventory and his futures hedges at favorable relative prices. This means that he has *unrealized* profits from previous transactions. A portion of these profits becomes realized each time the dealer offsets a new transaction against these favorable average prices. Other accounting approaches can be used, but this method is relatively common.

Assume that the above steps are all repeated dozens or perhaps hundreds of times each day, and you will have a sense of how a dealer operation works. The necessity of always being prepared to respond to customer inquiries by both quoting cash market prices and then hedging in futures any resulting exposures requires constant monitoring of market information and virtually continuous dialogue between a dealer's cash market traders and his futures phone clerks.

The Economics of a Dealer Operation

In Chapter 8 we examined the costs associated with a hypothetical futures commission merchant (FCM) activity. Let us now do the same for a typical dealer activity. Once again we emphasize that in the real world, expense numbers and relationships vary considerably from dealer to dealer and from year to year. Still, the following discussion will provide some sense of the expense issues which confront a representative dealer who actively hedges in futures. The income statement in Figure 12-4 on page 280 assumes trading revenue of $100.

The key points to notice are these:

- *Compensation-related* expenses are by far the largest expense item. This will be true for almost every dealer activity because the business is so people-intensive. Owners of dealer businesses sometimes comment that their assets walk out the door every evening. This overwhelming dependence on human, rather than fixed, assets is reflected in the dominant position of compensation on the expense breakdown.

- *Floor brokerage* is the next largest expense item. This category, as we have seen, consists of the fees that are paid for physical execution of futures contracts in a trading ring. In some cases it reflects fees that are paid to independent brokers on a per-contract basis. In others, it may represent salaries paid to floor brokers who are employed by the dealer. In any event, if the dealer actively hedges in futures, this will be one of his most important expense items.

- *Communications* is the lifeblood of a dealer and occupies a commensurate position on the income statement. A dealer must maintain continuous telephone contact with futures exchange floors plus sufficient telephone equipment to ensure that he will always be easily reachable by his various customers. This category also includes important data communications costs because a dealer will need news services and price-quotation equipment to supplement the verbal price information that he receives from his futures exchange clerks.

- *Rent/occupancy* are self-explanatory and tend to be significant because many dealers are located in expensive central-city areas where rents command a premium. An interesting ancillary point is

Figure 12-4. *Dealer, Inc., income statement.*

Total Revenue	$100
Operating Expenses	
Compensation & Related Items	$30
Floor Brokerage	10
Communications	7
Rent/Occupancy	4
Futures Clearing	5
Other Operations	6
EDP Expenses	4
General Overhead	14
Other	5
Total Expenses	$85
Net Pre-Tax Income	$15

that dealers often have difficulty finding adequately configured floor space. Information flow that relates to prices, news items, and so on is so crucial to dealers that they prefer unobstructed visual contact among their trading and sales personnel. This means that buildings with pillars, elevator shafts, stairways, and other impediments present problems for the physical arrangement of a large dealing staff.

• *Futures clearing* expenses can take a variety of forms but are always a meaningful expense item on a dealer's P&L. In some cases, this expense consists solely of clearance fees that are paid directly to clearinghouses. In others, it may include commissions that are paid to clear trades through FCMs either because the dealer is a nonclearing member or because he wishes to diversify the location of his futures positions.

• *Other operations* costs cover a variety of functions that range from the movement of physical commodities to the wire transfer of funds through the banking system.

• *EDP expenses* vary widely from dealer to dealer. At one extreme, a dealer might use a personal computer to monitor his positions and to analyze market relationships. At the other extreme, he could use a sophisticated mainframe that has multiple terminals and complex position-tracking and analytic capabilities. The only general point that should be understood is that the increasing complexity of the markets and the growing amounts of information to be sorted and analyzed have forced most dealers to increase both their reliance upon technology and their expenses in this area.

• The final expense category, *general overhead*, includes a wide range of other operating expenses—legal, accounting, personnel, administration, advertising, bad debt allowance, and so forth.

Adding up these various expenses leaves a pre-tax profit margin in the vicinity of 15% of revenues. This number is obviously very sensitive to market conditions and will vary considerably from year to year. Still, the picture that emerges from Figure 12-4 is reasonably representative of what a dealer sees when examining his budget or profit/loss statement.

THE ROLE OF DEALERS IN FUTURES MARKETS

Dealers are the primary link between cash and futures markets. Their businesses are firmly grounded in the cash marketplace, and the need to respond quickly on the futures side keeps them closely attuned to those markets as well. Furthermore, dealers' relatively slim profit margins force them to reduce execution and trade processing costs to the lowest possible levels. These facts when combined mean that dealers are uniquely well positioned to engage in the short-term arbitrage trading that keeps cash and futures markets aligned with each other. They have the information and communications networks to monitor and act on news and/or price discrepancies. They also have the execution and clearing cost structures to justify trading for much slimmer gross profit margins than would be worthwhile for other types of market participants.

A specific example will be illustrative: Suppose that you, a private speculator, read on the newswire that the Fed funds rate has just fallen by 3/8%. Before rushing to buy Eurodollar futures, consider the following:

Money market dealers have already heard the information. They have instantaneous communications with the trading floor, and their futures cost structures are such that they will realize *net* profits at much lower *gross* profit levels than will other off-floor traders. The moral is simply that short-term trading for small profits is best left to the dealers who have information networks and cost structures that are suited to narrow gross profit margins.

ARBITRAGE

Arbitrage occupies a prominent position in the futures world. It is the mechanism that keeps prices of futures contracts aligned properly with prices of the underlying cash items. As we will discuss below, dealers are especially well positioned to arbitrage cash markets against futures markets, and many do so very actively. Before we discuss this type of arbitrage, though, it is worthwhile to pause and define arbitrage in general.

Arbitrage is the simultaneous purchase and sale of the same item in two different markets in an attempt to profit from price discrepancies between the two markets.

This is less straightforward than it might seem because the words *simultaneous* and *same* can be interpreted with varying degrees of precision. Does *simultaneous* mean "within five seconds"? "one hour"? "three weeks"? Must two items be identical to be "the same," or are T-bills that have 13 weeks to maturity sufficiently similar to T-bills that have 14 weeks to maturity? Is Ford common stock sufficiently similar to Chrysler common stock because both manufacture cars? More generally, how do you distinguish between arbitraging two items and speculating on the relative values of two items?

The feature that distinguishes true arbitrage from relative-value trading is the prominence of hard facts rather than opinions in explaining price differences between the two items involved. Let us cite three examples both to clarify this point and to illustrate how typical arbitrage opportunities are analyzed and executed.

Example 1: In the late 1970s and early 1980s, the Comex and the IMM both listed active gold futures contracts that had nearly identical specifications. One of the most conservative arbitrages ever available was trading either of the two common delivery months (June and December) against the same month on the other exchange. Delivery against both futures contracts was by warehouse receipt. Because the underlying items were identical,* any price difference could be treated as both an aberration and an arbitrage opportunity.

This example represents the most straightforward type of arbitrage because the items that are being bought and sold are identical (assuming that the futures contracts are held to delivery). Still, an arbitrageur faces several important issues: First is the question of implementation. How do you actually go about buying one contract more cheaply than you sell the other? The answer is usually simple but inelegant. In the case of the Comex/IMM arbitrage, traders held a telephone to each ear, hearing quotes from and giving orders to an IMM clerk over one phone and a Comex clerk over the other. When the bid price on one exchange exceeded the offer price on the other exchange, an arbitrageur would attempt to sell at the bid and buy at the (lower) offer. Even though the

---

* Actually, a small percentage of the outstanding receipts were deliverable only on Comex, but this was an insignificant issue.

orders were entered within a second or two of each other, the procedure did not always work. If another trader was a split second quicker, a bid or an offer might be gone before an arbitrageur could act on it. This might leave the unpleasant choice of either holding an unwanted net long or short position or establishing the second leg of the arbitrage at a locked-in loss.

The second key issue is cost. Can the expenses that are associated with the arbitrage be kept low enough to ensure a net profit as well as a gross profit? Floor brokerage, clearing expenses, phone-clerk compensation, and telephone expenses mount up quickly. Comex/IMM arbitrageurs would average only about $10 per contract gross profit, which is typical for this type of arbitrage. With such thin gross margins, a low-cost operation is clearly a prerequisite for success.

The third important question is how to handle a position once it is established. Suppose that you succeeded in buying December IMM futures for 50 cents per ounce less than you sold December Comex futures. What next? Do you hold the positions to delivery, or try to trade out of it when the opportunity arises? The answer is that it is almost always preferable to trade out of a position rather than to hold it until maturity. As in any business, turnover means more frequent profit opportunity. Also, deliveries require payment in full, and so they tie up capital or financing capabilities. Finally, deliveries entail paperwork and other operational overhead that simply amount to added costs. Most arbitrageurs view the ability to hold positions to delivery as a safety net that ensures a minimum profit (or loss) if they are unable to trade out of a position prior to maturity.

> *Example 2*: Crude-oil futures call for delivery in the Arco storage facility at Cushing, Oklahoma. Suppose that an oil dealer knows that he can move actual oil through a pipeline system from the West Coast to Cushing at a cost of 30 cents per barrel and that doing so takes four days. If he can buy West Coast crude at a discount to futures of, say, 40 cents per barrel, then buying this oil against a sale of futures represents a profitable arbitrage opportunity. It is an arbitrage rather than a relative-value speculation because the appropriate price differential between the two sides of the transaction depends in a very concrete way on the cost of converting the spot oil into a form that is deliverable against futures. Assuming that the oil is the appropriate grade, all that needs to be

done is to transport it to the Arco tanks in Cushing (at a cost of 30 cents per barrel).

This arbitrage introduces two new dimensions that are shared by most real-life arbitrage opportunities. First, one leg of the transaction is in the cash market and the other is in the futures market. Second, the success of the arbitrage ultimately rests on the ability to transform the cash market item in some way. This is why dealers are often active arbitrageurs. Anybody can recognize that being paid 40 cents to move oil at a cost of 30 cents is a good deal, but actually doing so requires the ability to operate in both the cash and futures markets. As we discussed earlier in this chapter, this is a prime characteristic of dealers.

Example 3: Five currencies enjoy both active futures contracts on the IMM and widespread trading in the interbank market (which is the term that is used to describe principal transactions between banks and their institutional customers. We discuss the interbank market in Chapter 19.)

This creates a variety of arbitrage opportunities. Let us examine how one works.

For the most part, the interbank market deals for spot settlement (which for foreign exchange is two business days from the date of a trade). Foreign exchange futures, by contrast, settle on one specific date in the contract month. The simplest arbitrage would involve these steps, using British pounds (BP) as a typical example:

1. Buy spot British pounds.
2. Sell June British pound futures.
3. Hold the spot pounds in a bank account until the futures contract matures and then deliver them against the short June futures position.

Because one British pound is the same as every other, FX dealers need not be concerned with transforming them from one form into another. They do need to focus carefully on interest rates, though. The dealer will earn interest on his British pound deposit and must take this into account in evaluating a potential arbitrage opportunity. This becomes slightly tricky, but it is worth discussing in some detail as an example of how arbitrageurs analyze markets.

When you compare a spot BP purchase with a sale of BP futures, you must remember to add in the interest that is received on the BP deposit during the time between the spot and futures maturity dates. However, this is not the whole story. If you elected not to buy spot BPs with your dollars, you would receive interest on a dollar deposit during the same interval. As a rule, the dollar interest rate and the BP interest rate will be different. An arbitrageur must accurately calculate and compare the total returns in each case to determine whether a possible arbitrage is worthwhile. Let us use the following specifics to consider an example:

Spot settlement date: May 18

Futures settlement date: June 18

One-month British pound rate: 10% per annum

One-month U.S. dollar rate: 8% per annum

Spot British pound: $1.4100

June British pound futures: $1.4130

The two alternatives look like this, assuming a $141,000 initial position to keep the arithmetic simple:

Alternative 1 (Hold Dollars):

May 18: Make dollar deposit: $141,000
June 18: Collect interest on dollar deposit ($141,000 x 0.08 x $31/_{365}$) = $958.03
Net value on June 18: $141,958.03

Alternative 2 (Establish BP arbitrage):

May 18: Buy British pounds: 100,000 pounds sterling
Sell June BP futures @ $1.4130
June 18: Collect interest on pound deposit (100,000 x 0.10 x $31/_{365}$) = 849.32
Total BP holdings: 100,849.32 pounds
Convert to dollars @ $1.4130
(100,849.32 x $1.4130) = $142,500.09

Comparing the two shows that the arbitrage position would yield a gross profit of $542.06 compared with maintaining a dollar deposit from May 18 to June 18. Because an IMM British pound futures contract is 25,000 pounds, this is a profit of $135.52 per futures contract. Most FX dealers would consider this to be an attractive arbitrage.

WHY DO ARBITRAGE OPPORTUNITIES EXIST?

Arbitrage opportunities arise for one or more of these three reasons:

- Communications imperfections.
- Market inaccessibility.
- Ignorance or apathy.

Communications imperfections can prevent participants in one marketplace from knowing what is happening in another marketplace. The Comex/IMM gold trade of Example 1 was essentially a communications arbitrage. Traders on either exchange did not know of price changes on the other exchange as quickly as did the dealers who continuously monitored both exchanges by telephone. Communications-based arbitrages have become fewer and fewer as global telecommunications have become more efficient and affordable.

Market inaccessibility is an important source of arbitrage opportunities such as the IMM/Interbank British pound trade of Example 3. A small businessman who wants to hedge a $150,000 British pound exposure might not find a bank anxious to accommodate so small a commercial transaction. Similarly, the original owner of the West Coast crude oil in Example 2 might have been unequipped to move the oil through the pipeline system to Oklahoma.

Simple ignorance and apathy have always been major sources of arbitrage opportunities between cash and futures markets. Returning to Example 2, the original owner of the West Coast crude oil may have been perfectly capable of selling oil futures and moving the crude to Oklahoma himself. Perhaps he simply didn't understand futures or didn't want to bother with account forms and margin deposits. As commercial firms become more familiar with futures, this source of arbitrage possibilities may shrink.

Pseudoarbitrage

The examples that we have discussed all rest on the foundation of being able to convert the item you have bought into the item you have sold if you are unable to trade out of the two-sided position profitably. Would-be arbitrageurs sometimes decide that a high degree of similarity between the two sides is enough to justify an apparent arbitrage attempt. We now cite an actual example to show how what may look like an arbitrage can turn out to be a rather risky relative-value speculation.

In May 1986, the February 2016 Treasury bond with a coupon of $9^{1/4}\%$ appeared overpriced relative to June T-bond futures. Many dealers bought futures and went short the $9^{1/4}$'s of February 2016, expecting to trade out of the position for a profit of about $4/32$ after prices realigned. Instead, they ended up trading out at losses of $32/32$ or more. What happened? Japanese institutions had bought a large percentage of the February 2016 bond when it was issued in February 1986. Bond prices then fell steeply, and Japanese accounting rules make it preferable to avoid realizing large losses on investment positions. Thus, even when the price of the $9^{1/4}$'s of February 2016 rose significantly relative to futures and to all other Treasury issues, the Japanese holders were unwilling to sell this particular issue or even to swap it for something more attractively priced. Dealers then had to face the painful reality that you cannot convert a futures contract into a specific Treasury issue regardless of how misaligned their values might appear from a purely economic perspective. What looked like a riskless arbitrage turned out to be a very costly relative-value speculation.

Arbitrage and Basis

As alert readers have undoubtedly noticed, arbitrage is essentially a specialized type of basis trading. Arbitrageurs base their decisions on analyses of the basis between futures and the cash instrument that is being arbitraged, as do hedgers and dealers engaged in other forms of cash versus futures trading. We close by emphasizing again that what distinguishes arbitrage from relative-value speculation is the existence of a clear, objective link between the cash and futures positions.

Chapter 13

■ *Accounting and Taxation of Futures Transactions*

Trading futures adds a variety of new dimensions to one's financial universe. Among them are the specialized accounting and tax considerations that apply to futures contracts. These issues are especially important to hedgers, who obviously have a keen interest in how futures hedging programs will affect their income statements, balance sheets, and tax returns. In all but the simplest cases, issues arise that relate to the interpretation of rules and guidelines that require the advice of accounting and tax experts. However, it is useful for futures traders to have some familiarity with the basic principles that underlie the accounting and tax treatment of futures contracts.

FUTURES ACCOUNTING

The accounting treatment of futures contracts is complicated by the fact that futures are *contingent obligations* from a balance sheet perspective but are *actual obligations* from a profit and loss perspective. The daily mark-to-market feature of futures contracts underscores their immediate profit/loss impact. However, the holder of a long cattle futures contract does not own an asset in the same sense as does the owner of 40 head of maturing steers. For example, the holder of the futures contract need tie up capital only to the extent of his margin requirements, while the owner of actual cattle must somehow finance his inventory. Considerations such as these have led to the adoption by the Financial

Accounting Standards Board (FASB) of certain accounting standards that relate to futures transactions.

Among the most important accounting issues to be addressed in connection with a futures trading program are the following:

- Should hedges and speculative positions be accounted for differently?
- When should gains and losses be taken for hedges and for speculative positions?
- What criteria determine whether or not a futures position qualifies for hedge accounting?
- How are margin requirements accounted for?
- What is the balance sheet impact of futures contracts?
- What disclosure requirements are applicable to futures hedges?

The next several sections provide an overview of the answers to these and other basic questions that relate to futures accounting.

Income Recognition and Hedge Criteria

The general principle that applies to income recognition is that gains and losses must be recognized as they occur on a mark-to-market basis. The rationale is that this appropriately reflects the economic reality of the daily mark-to-market required by United States futures exchanges. However, an important exception to this rule exists for futures positions that qualify as hedges of existing or anticipated exposures. In such cases, gains and losses from futures positions can be treated as adjustments to the value of the item being hedged. In order for a futures position to qualify for hedge accounting treatment, both of the following criteria must be met:

- The item that is being hedged must expose the enterprise to risk. Furthermore, this risk cannot already be offset by other commitments such as fixed-price forward contracts.
- The futures position must be specifically designated as a hedge and must reduce the exposure to the enterprise. This is often termed the principle of *hedge effectiveness*.

One of the crucial issues relating to the assessment of risk to an enterprise is the question of whether "overall" risk must be hedged, or whether futures hedges can be linked to specific, identifiable assets, liabilities, or obligations. For example, can a bank both sell interest rate futures to hedge its overall balance sheet and also permit individual departments to buy interest rate futures as an anticipated hedge against expected loans? The general principle is that hedges should reduce the overall exposure of the enterprise, but in all cases except foreign exchange futures an exception is made when risk is managed on a business unit basis or when the enterprise cannot reasonably be expected to assess risk on an overall basis. Foreign exchange hedging is governed by a different set of FASB guidelines that require that futures hedges be matched with specific risks.

The issue of hedge effectiveness can be highly subjective. The basic principle is that, at the inception of the hedge and throughout the hedge period, there should be a probable high correlation between price changes in the futures hedge and changes in the fair market value of the item being hedged. In real life, hedged items are often not identical to those that qualify for delivery against a futures hedge. The issue is where to draw the line between cross-hedging and outright speculation. The FASB guidelines do not mandate specific levels of price change correlation, but rather imply a concept of reasonableness and intent.

Hedges of Existing Exposures

The guiding principle in accounting for futures positions that hedge actual (as opposed to anticipated) exposures is that the hedge and the item being hedged must be treated symmetrically. In most cases, this means that futures gains or losses are reported as adjustments to the value of the item being hedged. The same principle of symmetry applies to the ultimate recognition of income. For example, if the income or expense that is associated with a hedged item is amortized over some period of time, then the gain or the loss on the associated futures hedge must be treated in the same manner.

An important point is that the notion of symmetry supersedes the concept of adjusting the value of a hedged item by the mark-to-market change in a futures position's value. Thus, if lower-of-cost-or-market accounting is required for a particular hedged asset, the futures hedge must be treated similarly.

Hedges of Anticipated Exposure

Anticipatory hedging presents special accounting challenges because of the uncertainties that surround the question of whether a futures position is actually related to an expected cash market transaction or whether it is simply a speculative transaction. Therefore, the FASB added two conditions that futures positions must meet, in addition to the two hedge criteria cited earlier, in order to qualify for hedge accounting. These two criteria are:

- The significant characteristics and expected terms of the anticipated transaction must be identified. These would include such things as quantity, expected date of transaction, price or interest rate, and so forth.
- It is probable that the anticipated transaction will occur. The assessment of probability is subjective but includes such considerations as the past frequency of similar transactions, the ability of the enterprise to complete the transaction, and the possible loss or disruption that might occur if the transaction were not to occur.

If these two additional criteria are met, anticipatory hedges are accounted for in exactly the same manner as are hedges of existing obligations with one exception. The exception relates to what is often referred to as *breakage*. This term refers to situations in which the size of the anticipated cash market transaction that is being hedged turns out to be smaller than originally expected. In such cases, the appropriate pro-rata portion of the futures gain or loss should be recognized when it becomes apparent that the size of the cash market transaction will be smaller than had been anticipated.

> *Example*: The general considerations that relate to hedge accounting can be illustrated by the following example of an anticipatory hedge by a heating oil wholesaler: On February 1, the wholesaler expects that her customers will require 420,000 gallons of #2 heating oil in mid-May. She has not contracted to sell this oil at a fixed price, but rather plans to sell it at the prevailing market price in May. The wholesaler conducts the following transactions and notes the end-quarter futures price:

- A February 4 purchase of 10 June heating oil futures contracts (= 420,000 gallons) at 50 cents per gallon.

- A May 15 sale of these 10 futures contracts at 52 cents per gallon.

- A May 15 purchase of 420,000 gallons of heating oil through normal commercial channels at 53 cents per gallon.

- In the course of these transactions, June heating oil futures close the first quarter by settling at 48 cents per gallon on March 31.

The accounting would look like that in Figure 13-1.

If the transaction does *not* qualify as a hedge, the wholesaler would report a mark-to-market loss of $8,400 in the first quarter and a profit of $16,800 in the second quarter. On the other hand, if the hedge criteria are met, the wholesaler would not report the $8,400 loss in the first-quarter financials. Instead, the cumulative profit of $8,400 for the two quarters would be recorded as a 2 cents per gallon reduction in the 53 cents per gallon cost of the cash heating oil that was purchased on May 15. Profits or losses would be recognized relative to this cost basis of 51 cents per gallon when the cash heating oil is actually sold.

Margin Accounting

Margin deposits are usually recorded in a margin account that is consolidated into a "Due from broker" or "Due from futures exchange clearinghouse" line item, depending on whether or not the enterprise transacts business through an FCM or whether it is a clearing member who deals directly with an exchange clearinghouse.

Figure 13-1.

	January 1/ March 31	April 1/ June 30
Beginning Futures Price	50.00¢	48.00¢
Ending Futures Price	48.00	52.00
Price Change	(2.00)	4.00
Number of Gallons Hedged	420,000	420,000
Changes in Value	$(8,400)	$16,800

Figure 13-2.

	July	August	September
Initial Balance	$ 0	$137,500	$ 152,500
Initial Margin Deposit	125,000	—	—
Mark-to-Market	62,500	125,000	(62,500)
Cash Deposits (Withdrawals)	(50,000)	(110,000)	35,000
Withdrawal of Original Margin	—	—	(125,000)
Ending Balance	$137,500	$152,500	$ 0

The following example illustrates the procedures. It assumes that the following facts apply to a three-month accounting period:

- On July 15, the enterprise purchases 50 December Eurodollar futures at 92.50 and makes an initial margin deposit of $125,000 ($2,500 per contract).
- Month-end closing prices are as follows: July 31—93.00; August 31—94.00; September 30—93.50.
- All contracts are liquidated on September 30 at 93.50.
- The initial margin deposit is made in cash, and all subsequent mark-to-market profits and losses are dealt with by periodic cash deposits or (withdrawals) from the margin account that total ($50,000) in July, ($110,000) in August, and $35,000 in September. The margin account would be summarized as shown in Figure 13-2.

July and August financial statements would include amounts of $137,500 and $152,500 respectively as "Due from broker" or "Due from exchange clearinghouse." The mark-to-market gains (loss) of $62,500; $125,000; and ($62,500) would be recognized in the months that they occurred in a manner that is consistent with the reporting of other gains and losses.

Readers will recall from Chapter 7 that in certain cases, initial margin requirements can be met with United States government securities or with letters of credit. In such cases, the initial margin requirement would not be classified as "Due from broker" or "Due from exchange clearinghouse," but instead might be subject to disclosure in a footnote depending on the nature of the business and the hedge transaction.

Balance Sheet Implications

Futures contracts are considered contingent assets and liabilities from an accounting perspective. As such, they are off-balance sheet items, as are swaps, interest rate guarantees, and certain other instruments. The off balance-sheet nature of futures positions raises interesting issues relating to risk assessment. For example, a bank that took a large speculative position on long-term interest rates by buying cash T-bonds would be forced to reflect the position on its balance sheet. However, the same risk could be taken by buying T-bond futures without requiring balance sheet disclosure or affecting the various ratios (assets/equity, return on assets, and so forth) that are often used in the analysis of financial statements.

Disclosure Requirements

Speculative futures positions or trading activity require no special disclosure in financial statements. However, FASB requires disclosures of the following in the notes to financial statements for futures positions that have been accounted for as hedges:

• The nature of the items or the anticipated transactions that are being hedged.
• The method of accounting for the futures contracts.

Disclosure of the size or effectiveness of a futures hedging program is not required in financial statements.

FEDERAL TAX TREATMENT OF FUTURES CONTRACTS FOR SPECULATORS

Prior to the Economic Recovery Tax Act of 1981 (ERTA), futures contracts were regarded as capital assets and were treated as such for federal income tax purposes. This meant that all long positions that were liquidated after the required holding period (six or twelve months, depending on prevailing statutes) were long-term assets that were subject to favorable tax treatment. All long positions that were held for less than the required period and all short positions regardless of how long they were held were treated as short-term assets that were subject to the same basic rate as ordinary income. Tax rates for long-term capital gains were generally 60% lower than were tax rates for ordinary income.

The separate treatment of long-term and short-term transactions gave rise to a practice in the futures market that afforded taxpayers the opportunity to defer short-term gains into subsequent years and possibly to convert short-term gains into long-term gains. The practice involved spreads (see Chapter 16) and worked something like this:

> *Example 1*: On August 1, 1977, a taxpayer bought one contract (5,000 ounces) of March 1978 silver at $5.50 and sold one contract of May 1978 silver at $5.60. Suppose that by December 1977, March silver and May silver rose to $6.50 and $6.60, respectively. The taxpayer then bought one May 1978 silver at $6.60 (realizing a short-term loss) and sold one July 1978 silver at, say, $6.70 (establishing a new position). His new straddle position (long March, short July) was held until February 2, 1978 (six months).

The only transaction of tax consequence for 1977 was the realized short-term loss of $5,000, which was offset against the taxpayer's other short-term capital gains for that year. If the prices on February 2 were at least as high as they had been in the previous December, the taxpayer could unwind the straddle and realize a long-term gain on his March 1978 position that was at least equal to the $5,000 short-term loss that was taken in 1977. The net effect was that the taxpayer had converted a short-term gain for 1977 into a long-term gain for 1978. Doing this enabled him both to defer the payment of taxes and to realize the benefits of the more favorable tax treatment of long-term capital gains.

Despite arguments that such spread transactions involved risk and were entered into for legitimate gain, the Internal Revenue Service in 1978 issued a ruling that disallowed the losses that were created by these so-called *tax straddles*. The effect of the 1978 ruling was strengthened with the ERTA of 1981, which provided that all regulated futures contracts (RFCs) were to be marked to the market as of the last day of the tax year. This meant that the net gain (loss) for a given year was, for tax purposes, the sum of both *realized* and *unrealized* gains (losses) as of December 31. It further provided that all positions in RFCs be treated equally, regardless of the length of time that a position is held and regardless of whether it is a short position or a long position.

The futures industry lobbied against these changes on the grounds that the elimination of these straddle transactions would seriously reduce market liquidity and place an unfair burden on futures traders who, because of the short-term nature of most trades, would in most cases be subject to higher tax rates than investors in other areas. A compromise was reached. The ERTA permitted 60% of RFC trading gains to be treated as long-term capital gains. Under the maximum tax rate of 50%, which prevailed until 1987, this had the effect of creating a maximum tax rate on RFCs of 32%, as explained in Example 2.

Example 2: A taxpayer in the 50% bracket had a net futures profit (realized gains plus unrealized gains) of $10,000 in 1986.

The short-term portion of this gain (40%) is $4,000 and was taxed at 50%, or $2,000. The long-term portion (60%) is $6,000 and was taxed at the preferential rate of 20%, or $1,200. The total maximum tax was $3,200 (32%).

The 1986 Tax Reform Act (TRA) made no changes in the mark-to-market 60/40 rule, but the rate at which RFCs are taxed was changed. In 1987, the maximum rate on long-term capital gains was 28% and the maximum rate on short-term capital gains was 38.5%. This works out to a maximum tax rate on RFCs of 32.2%, as explained in Example 3:

Example 3: A taxpayer in the maximum bracket has a net futures profit of $10,000 (realized and unrealized) in 1987. The short-term portion of this (40%) is $4,000 and is taxed at 38.5%, or $1,540. The long-term portion is $6,000 and is taxed at 28%, or $1,680. The total maximum tax is $3,220, or 32.2%.

After 1987, the long-term and short-term distinction disappears and the maximum tax rate on RFCs will be 28% (33% for individuals who have taxable incomes within the phase-out range for the 15% bracket). Figure 13-3 (page 298) illustrates IRS Form 6781, which must be filed in connection with gains and losses from straddles.

Figure 13-3.

Form **6781** Department of the Treasury, Internal Revenue Service	Gains and Losses From Section 1256 Contracts and Straddles ► Attach to your tax return	OMB Nr. 1545-0644 1986 Attachment Sequence No. 82

Name(s) as shown on tax return		Identifying number

A. ☐ Check here if you made the mixed straddle election under section 1256(d) this year or an earlier year.
B. ☐ Check here if you made the straddle-by-straddle identification election under section 1092(b).
C. ☐ Check here to make the mixed straddle account election under section 1092(b).
D. ☐ Check here if you elect to carryback a net section 1256 contracts loss.

Part I Section 1256 Contracts Marked to Market

a. Identification of account	b. LOSS	c. GAIN
1		

2   Add column b and column c, line 1
3   Combine columns b and c of line 2 and enter the net gain or (loss)
4   Form 1099-B adjustments (see instructions, attach schedule)
5   Combine lines 3 and 4
6   If you have a net section 1256 contracts loss and checked box D, enter the amount to be carried back
7   Subtract line 6 from line 5
8   Multiply line 7 by 40%. Enter as a short-term capital gain or (loss) on Schedule D. Identify as Form 6781, Part I
9   Multiply line 7 by 60%. Enter as a long-term capital gain or (loss) on Schedule D. Identify as Form 6781, Part I

Part II Gains and Losses From Straddles (Attach a separate schedule listing each straddle and its components.)

Section A.—Losses From Straddles

a. Description of property	b. Date entered into or acquired	c. Date closed out or sold	d. Gross sales price	e. Cost or other basis plus expense of sale	f. LOSS If column e is more than d, enter difference. Otherwise, enter zero	g. Unrecognized gain on offsetting positions	h. Recognized loss If column f is more than g, enter difference. Otherwise, enter zero
10							

11a   Enter short-term portion of line 10, column h here and on Schedule D. Identify as Form 6781, Part II
  b   Enter long-term portion of line 10, column h here and on Schedule D. Identify as Form 6781, Part II

Section B.—Gains From Straddles

a. Description of property	b. Date entered into or acquired	c. Date closed out or sold	d. Gross sales price	e. Cost or other basis plus expense of sale	f. GAIN If column d is more than e, enter difference. Otherwise, enter zero
12					

13a   Enter short-term portion of line 12, column f here and on Schedule D. Identify as Form 6781, Part II
  b   Enter long-term portion of line 12, column f here and on Schedule D. Identify as Form 6781, Part II

Part III Unrecognized Gains From Positions Held on Last Day of Tax Year (Memo Entry Only—See Instructions)

a. Description of property	b. Date acquired	c. Fair market value on last business day of tax year	d. Cost or other basis as adjusted	e. UNRECOGNIZED GAIN If column c is more than d, enter difference. Otherwise, enter zero
14				

For Paperwork Reduction Act Notice, see back of form.   Form **6781** (1986)

FEDERAL TAXATION OF FUTURES CONTRACTS FOR HEDGERS

RFC transactions that constitute an integral part of the taxpayer's trade or business qualify as hedge transactions for federal income tax purposes. Such transactions are not subject to capital gain or loss treatment and, therefore, are exempt from the mark-to-market 60/40 rule of ERTA. The financial results of such transactions are treated as ordinary income or loss to the taxpayer's business.

To qualify for hedging status, an RFC transaction must be clearly identified in the taxpayer's record as one that is entered into to reduce the cost or risk of assets, the purchase or sale of which are subject to ordinary income treatment as part of the activities of the business.

PART FOUR

MARKET ANALYSIS AND TRADING

■ Chapter 14

■ Fundamental Analysis and Broad Price Influences

The fundamental analysis of futures markets is based on a study of the underlying supply and demand factors that are likely to shape the trend of prices. The pure *technical* analyst is concerned exclusively with the behavior of prices themselves and not with the factors that cause price movement. We discuss technical analysis in Chapter 17. The *fundamental* analyst devotes his or her attention to such influences as the relationship between supply and demand, government programs, international commodity agreements, political developments, inflation, and so forth. The fundamental approach is the subject of this chapter.

The theory behind the fundamental approach to futures trading is that supply and demand interact to determine prices. A supply scarcity results in a higher average price level than a supply surplus, all other factors being equal. As this chapter indicates, however, "all other factors" can have a significant impact on the supply, the demand, and the price of any commodity or financial instrument. The fundamentalist evaluates the existing and probable supply/demand balance, takes into account identifiable exogenous factors that affect it, and then assumes a market position that is based on his price forecast. Fundamentally-based forecasts, as well as their resulting market positions, tend to be more long-term than those that are based on technical considerations.

Fundamental analysis has two broad appeals. First, most traders like to have a "reason" for making a trading decision. Many traders find it psychologically difficult to establish a market position that is based on

the turn of a moving average or the violation of a trend line. A rationale
for a trade that is based on a serious study of supply and demand data
often provides the strength of commitment necessary to stay with a particular trade. Second, a long-term fundamental opinion allows traders to
take positions and to maintain them with a minimum of attention to day-
to-day market action.Without a long-term perspective, short-term price
jolts will often knock a trader out of an otherwise good position.

However, as the sole basis for trading decisions in futures, fundamental analysis has a number of weaknesses:

1. Fundamental analysis is imprecise. The best fundamental forecast
   will predict an "average" high or low or a probable "range" of prices. It is difficult to be more precise than this. Thus, when markets
   are near their fundamental price objectives, it is difficult to know
   how to react. Will prices stagnate, will they shoot beyond all objectives because of speculative excess, or will they reverse? Fundamental analysis provides no easy answers. In addition, the im-
   precision of fundamental analysis makes trade timing difficult. If
   prices are expected to reach a peak six months from now, when
   should we get long? Will prices rise gradually over the next half
   year or will they erode for 5½ months before skyrocketing to new
   highs?

2. Fundamental analysis cannot take into account all the many variables that influence price nor those factors that may not be of influence now but that will be in the future. This, critics say, leaves
   fundamental forecasts vulnerable to the "surprise factor."

3. Modern futures markets tend to be extremely price-efficient. This
   means that their prices tend to reflect, or *discount*, known fundamentals very quickly, even before any formal analysis is conducted. As a result, fundamental analysis may tell us why prices are at
   present levels rather than where they are likely to go.

4. The fundamental approach, in and of itself, does not incorporate
   any risk-control safeguards. It is possible for fundamentals to un-
   dergo no apparent change while prices move against a trader's position and wipe out his entire equity. In fact, one of the strengths
   of fundamental trading—that it gives traders more tenacity in long-
   term price trends—is a major weakness when prices are moving
   adversely for no apparent reason. Sometimes the fundamental rea-

sons for a price move come to light only after a trader's equity has disappeared.

The above weaknesses notwithstanding, fundamental analysis is an important element in good futures trading programs. Used in combination with technical trading signals and money management protection, it provides the basis for trading those major price swings that have made futures markets—and some of their traders—famous.

SUPPLY AND DEMAND THEORY

Because the relationship between supply and demand is the central focus of all fundamental analysis, we begin our discussion by reviewing a few basic principles:

The Nature of Demand

For our purposes, the *demand* for a specific commodity is defined as the quantity of that commodity that consumers are willing to purchase at different prices during a particular time period. It should be obvious that consumers are willing to buy more at lower prices than at higher prices. The quantity that is demanded increases as prices decline, and it declines as prices increase. For this reason, we say that demand is inversely related to price. Figure 14-1 on page 304 graphically depicts the relationship between the quantity demanded and price.

The line in Figure 14-1 is called a *demand curve*. The exact shape and slope of the demand curve will be determined by conditions at a particular time, but the general slope will always be downward to reflect the inverse relationship between quantity demanded and price. Why? First, at a lower price you can afford to buy more of something out of a given amount of income. Second, at a lower price you are likely to want to buy more of something because it becomes more attractive compared with other things on which you might spend your money. Finally, lower prices will encourage the development of alternative uses for a commodity.

Changing conditions (other than price) will alter the shape and slope of the demand curve during a period of time. Either a part or all of the demand curve will steepen or flatten as changes occur in the factors

Figure 14-1. Typical demand curve.

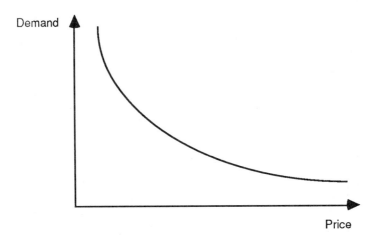

As price increases, demand decreases, and as price decreases, demand increases.

that influence demand. There are four main factors that influence demand and, therefore, the shape of the demand curve. First, consumer income affects demand. An increase in income causes consumers to demand more of some commodities. Beef is a good example. For other commodities an increase in income causes consumers to demand less at each price. Potatoes are often a good example because higher incomes can cause consumers to eat more meat and fewer potatoes.

Second, an increase in the prices of competing commodities will tend to increase the demand for a product. If beef prices increase, demand for pork and chicken will probably increase if their prices remain constant.

Third, changing tastes and values can bring about shifts in demand. Demand for frozen concentrate orange juice (at a given price) increased tremendously during the 1950s as the product gained wide consumer acceptance. Shifts in demand for this product continue to occur as consumer preferences shift between the fresh and the frozen product. Per-capita consumption of beef in the United States declined in recent years due to changing tastes and health considerations.

Finally, consumer expectations affect demand. If consumers expect the price of a particular commodity to rise, their demand for that commodity will also rise. On the other hand, expectations of falling prices will cause some purchases to be postponed. Expectations of coffee shortages and higher prices have led to consumer hoarding a number of times since the 1970s.

The influence of any one of these four components can cause the demand curve to shift left (less quantity demanded at a given price) or right (more quantity demanded at a given price). They may also alter the slope of the curve. A flattening in the slope of the demand curve means that a given increase in price results in a smaller-than-normal decline in the quantity demanded. Conversely, a steepening of the demand curve implies that a given price change results in a larger-than-normal change in the quantity demanded.

The degree to which the quantity demanded responds to a change in price is called the *price elasticity of demand.*. Economists classify demand as elastic or inelastic on the basis of the relative responsiveness of quantity demanded to changes in price. The demand for a commodity is said to be *price inelastic* if a large change in price is required to bring about a relatively small change in the quantity demanded. If a 50% drop in coffee or gasoline prices brings about a 10% increase in the quantity demanded, coffee and gasoline demand are said to be relatively price inelastic.

Demand for a commodity is likely to be inelastic when (1) there are few good substitutes, (2) consumer outlays for the commodity are small, (3) the commodity is a necessity or the demand for it is urgent, and (4) the demand for the commodity derives from the demand for a related product (the demand for tires will be more a function of the demand for cars than of the price of tires).

The elasticity of demand is an important issue for many of the commodities that are traded on futures exchanges. In comparison to such items as televisions, jewelry, or home computers, the demand for most commodities that are traded on futures exchanges is relatively price inelastic. Farm products are a good example. In periods of surplus production, prices must often drop drastically to increase demand and absorb excess supply. Why? Because demand is relatively unresponsive to changes in price. People can eat only so much bread and pork, and animals can consume only so much corn or soybean meal. Very large changes in price are required to bring about very small changes in overall demand. In periods of shortage, very large increases in price are necessary to bring demand down and avert a total depletion of the commodity. In a sense, price elasticity of demand is one of the many factors that account for the excitement of futures trading in certain commodities. Relatively small and seemingly unimportant changes in a market's supply/demand balance produce large and important changes in price and, because of leverage, even larger changes in traders' equities. A 5% change in the supply of corn might produce a 10% or 15% change in its price; a 10% or 15% change in the price of corn can be enough to more than double or wipe out the equity in a corn trader's account.

The Nature of Supply

Supply is defined as the quantity that producers will offer for sale at different prices. Like demand, supply can be plotted on a graph (Figure 14-2) with "Quantity" on the horizontal axis and "Price" on the vertical axis. Unlike the demand curve, the supply curve slopes upward, signifying that suppliers will make more of a product available as the prices they receive increase.

Among the factors that influence the shape and the slope of the supply curve are (1) the cost of the factors of production, (2) the state of relevant production technology, and (3) the prices of competing products.

Equilibrium Price

The price that brings supply and demand into balance is known as the *equilibrium price*. In theory, at least, it is found by combining the supply curve and the demand curve as shown in Figure 14-3.

The essential task of the fundamental analyst is, formally or informally, to construct the expected supply and demand curves for an item and then to estimate the equilibrium prices that will bring market forces into a state of rest. In effect, prices fluctuate in an effort to find their equilibrium. Prices that are too high increase supply, decrease demand, and lead to lower prices. Prices that are too low increase demand, decrease supply, and lead to higher prices. Prices that are "just right" keep supply and demand in balance.

The procedures that are involved in this fundamental quest for price projections vary from market to market. The following sections discuss each market category in general terms. Subsequent chapters in Part Five provide a more detailed view of the supply and demand factors of important commodities, financial instruments, and indexes.

Figure 14-2. Typical supply curve.

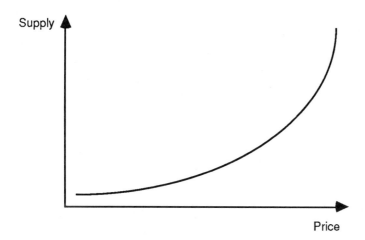

As price increases, supply increases, and as price decreases, supply decreases.

Figure 14-3. Typical supply/demand graph.

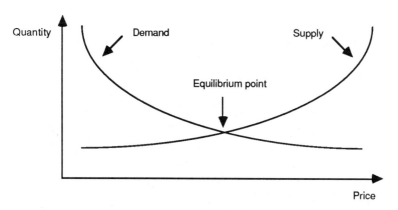

The equilibrium point is the price level at which supply equals demand.

Figure 14-4. *Supply/demand balance sheet for domestic field crop.*

	Last Year	Current Year
Supply		
Carry-in	200	200
New Crop	1,200	1,060
Imports	10	12
Total Supply	1,410	1,272
Demand		
Domestic	810	800
Exports	400	390
Total Demand	1,210	1,190
Carry-out	200	82

Fundamental Analysis of Field Crops

The element that distinguishes field crops from other commodities is that they are produced (harvested) during a brief period of the season and their supply must last until the next year's harvest. The "tone" of any given season is usually set by the size of that season's crop, so much effort goes into accurately forecasting it. Supply is usually the main variable in the price equation of field crops. Demand, as noted earlier, tends to be fairly stable. Fundamentalists, therefore, usually begin their analysis of field crops with an assessment of the supply situation.

For most domestic field crops, the supply for a particular season has three components: (1) the new crop, (2) imports, and (3) the old crop carryover. *Carryover* is the amount of the commodity that is in storage at the end of a season. It is usually made up mostly of the previous season's unused production. For the sake of convenience, we will refer to the supply left over from a previous season as *carry-in* and the supply that is likely to be left over from the present season as *carry-out*.

The new crop, which is usually the bulk of present season supplies, equals harvested acreage times yield. Harvested acreage, in turn, equals planted acreage minus acreage abandonment. For most domestic field crops, imports are small. In certain cases, such as orange concentrate from Brazil, they play a larger role in the supply/demand equation.

On the demand side of the equation, there are usually two broad categories: (1) domestic use and (2) exports.

A typical balance sheet is shown in Figure 14-4.

The balance suggests a rather sharp drawdown in carryover stocks by the end of the current season. With the supply situation basically fixed, it will be necessary for prices to rise and restrict demand. Otherwise a shortage will occur. If a carryover of, say, 150 is considered minimally necessary to fill pipelines, then total demand will have to shrink to 1,122, or 7.3% below last year's level. The job of the fundamentalist is to estimate the increase in price that will prove necessary to bring about a 7.3% decrease in demand for this commodity.

The fundamentalist's job becomes more complicated when he has to take into consideration programs of the federal government that are designed to stabilize farm prices. It may be that overall supplies are ample, but because a significant portion of the crop is committed to the government loan program, an actual scarcity of "free supplies" exists. The workings and the effects on the market of government programs is explained in detail in Chapter 21.

Chapter 21 also contains a more thorough discussion of the factors influencing the prices of domestic agricultural futures.

Imported Crops

The fundamental analysis of commodities that are produced predominantly in other parts of the world (i.e., cocoa, coffee, and sugar) is similar to that of domestic field crops. There are, however, two distinguishing factors. The first involves the availability and reliability of data. The U.S. Department of Agriculture compiles and distributes very comprehensive and accurate statistics on vital United States crops. The same cannot be said for foreign-produced crops. No single organization produces comprehensive statistics on the supply and demand of world commodities in a way that is convenient or useful to the fundamental analyst. Information is drawn from a variety of sources, including the USDA Foreign Agricultural Service, the United Nations, foreign-government reports, and private services. The problem with this is that data is often inconsistent, out-of-date, and sometimes biased.

A second factor that distinguishes foreign-produced commodities from domestically produced ones involves the time lag between changes in price and changes in supply. In the one-year production cycles of most domestic crops, high prices one year usually lead to increased supply the following year as producers increase their planted acreage to take advantage of more profitable prices. For cocoa, coffee, and sugar, the time lag is much greater than one year. There are three key reasons: (1) trees (the source of production for cocoa and coffee) require a long time to reach maturity and contribute to supply. Cocoa trees, for instance, do not usually produce meaningful supplies for two to five years; (2) The production of many imported commodities is concentrated in developing countries which do not have the technological wherewithal to respond quickly to changes in demand or price; (3) Many developing countries market their commodities through government entities that shield individual producers from price changes and make them less responsive to changing world-market conditions.

The net effect of this supply time lag is that price cycles in imported crops tend to be longer than those in domestically produced crops. The inability of supply to increase quickly in times of shortage often results in extensive and extended price advances.

Chapter 24 discusses in more detail the factors that influence supply, demand, and price for cocoa, coffee, sugar, and frozen concentrate orange juice.

Livestock Markets

The fundamental analysis of livestock markets usually begins on the supply side of the balance sheet. An estimate of the total number of cattle or hogs that are available for slaughter in the coming year is made and then, based on the weight breakdown of this inventory of available animals, a schedule is worked out for the likely marketing of animals during specific future time intervals. As noted in Chapter 21, livestock must be marketed within a relatively narrow time frame once they reach mature weight. For this reason the marketing schedule that is derived from the weight breakdown of animals in inventory at the beginning of a period provides the basis for supply analysis for at least the subsequent six to twelve months.

Futures prices for cattle and hogs tend to reflect the most likely marketing schedule based on the initial inventory of animals available for slaughter. Long-term price moves tend to occur in cycles, as described in Chapter 21. Shorter-term price activity is usually a function of the variation of actual marketings from expectations. Producer decisions to market animals at light or heavy weights can have a significant short-run impact on a particular futures contract. Decisions to increase or liquidate breeding stock can have both long- and short-run consequences.

A key characteristic of livestock is that they are not storable. This means that, unlike most other commodities, storage stocks do not play a role in fundamental analysis. Except for frozen pork bellies, prices in the livestock and meat sector are solely determined by the relationship between live marketings and demand in a given period.

Industrial Commodities

In contrast to most other physical commodities, the analysis of industrial markets (copper, aluminum, wood, oil, and oil products) tends to focus more on demand than on supply. The reason for this is that the supply of most of these commodities is determined simply by how much producers want to sell. As natural resources their available supply (for our purposes) is practically unlimited, not bound by a given year's planted acreage or by a defined number of animals in inventory.

The chief measure of demand is usually derived from changes in stock levels. Periods of stock depletion occur when current rates of production are not adequate to meet demand. This results in higher prices and, eventually, greater output. Greater output may come from existing production facilities or from the activation of previously idle, unprofitable sources of production. The most dramatic price rises occur when existing sources of production fail to meet demand because delays are inevitable in bringing forth new supply sources.

Prices of industrial commodities are subject to both seasonal and cyclical influences. Weather has an obviously seasonal effect on the demand for lumber, plywood, oil, and oil products. In the longer run, business and industrial activity cycles are the chief determinants of demand in this sector.

Financial Markets and Precious Metals

Price forecasting in financial markets and precious metals is based on a study of a wide range of factors that broadly influence the state of the United States and world economies. A discussion of these broad influences follows in the next section. Further analysis is presented in the chapters on interest rate futures (Chapter 18), currency futures (Chapter 19), stock index futures (Chapter 20), and metals futures (Chapter 22).

MACROECONOMIC INFLUENCES

Fundamental analysis has two important components. One is the supply/demand balance of the particular item being studied. The other is the macroeconomic background against which these fundamentals must be evaluated. Factors such as inflation, currency fluctuations, and monetary and fiscal policies affect overall price levels and should be incorporated into any fundamental analysis. We now discuss several of the most important of these macroeconomic forces.

Inflation

In 1970 there were 27.2 million futures contracts traded on United States exchanges. In 1986 the number was 184.4 million. This spectacular growth stemmed more from inflation than from any other single factor. Inflation and its mirror image—deflation—can create enormous price instability. This price instability translates directly into enhanced risks and profit opportunities in the futures markets for hedgers and speculators alike. For this reason alone futures traders should develop at least a general understanding of the causes and effects of inflation and the nature of its effects on futures markets.

Inflation refers to an increasing general price level. There is fierce debate among economists regarding both the causes of inflation and the best indicators of probable future inflation rates. However, a few general comments are in order. Most economists agree that dramatic increases in a nation's money supply are likely to produce inflation. This is logical because money can be thought of as a commodity like any other. If more of it is produced, it will be less valuable, which is the definition of inflation. Thus, traders often follow the various money supply numbers that are released by the Federal Reserve as likely indicators of future inflation rates. The level of inflation is crucial because an inflationary environment will cause prices to rise more or to decline less than an analysis of supply/demand balances alone might suggest. This lesson proved exceptionally costly for many futures traders during the inflationary surge of 1972/1974. The United States Wholesale Price Index rose by more than 40% in the 24 months from September 1972 to September 1974. This rising tide of prices in general was superimposed on some very bullish fundamentals in individual markets, and the result was an array of explosive bull markets whose magnitudes could never have been predicted on the basis of production and usage data alone. For example, soybeans had never in history traded above $4.50 per bushel, a fact that attracted many short sellers when futures first rose above $4.00 in December 1972. By the time the July 1973 futures contract hit its peak of $12.90 per bushel even the staunchest bears had long since been vanquished. Sugar was an even more extreme example. The post Civil War peak had been some 23 cents per pound until November 1974 when March 1975 futures touched 66 cents.

In these and other cases the specific fundamentals almost certainly would have lifted prices even in a noninflationary environment. However, the inflationary backdrop provided added impetus for two reasons. One is the simple fact that if the general price level doubles, then a bull market that might otherwise top out around $4.00 per bushel is more likely to reach about $8.00 per bushel. The second reason is more subtle and relates to expectations. Futures prices certainly reflect what *is happening* at any given time but, more importantly, they also reflect what *is expected to happen.* When people see the inflation rate climb from 2% to 5% to 10%, there can be a tendency to extrapolate the trend of inflation and conclude that price advances will become even more extreme. This sometimes leads to precautionary purchases and hoarding, which can further tighten already bullish supply/demand balances. This also can happen in bull markets caused solely by narrow supply/demand imbalances, but an environment of generally rising prices creates a climate that history has shown to be particularly conducive to anticipatory buying.

Deflation, or generally falling prices, quite naturally can be as powerful a bearish influence as inflation can be a bullish influence. This was amply demonstrated in the 1983/1985 period when inflation had ground to a halt and even seemingly bullish supply/demand fundamentals could barely hold many futures prices steady.

The most widely followed indicators of inflation are the *Producer Price Index* (PPI, formerly the *Wholesale Price Index*), the *Consumer Price Index* (CPI), and the Commodity Research Bureau's (CRB) *Futures Price Index.* The PPI and the CPI are released monthly by the United States Department of Commerce. The CRB Index is calculated and published daily by Commodity Research Bureau, Inc. of Jersey City, New Jersey. The New York Futures Exchange (NYFE) lists a futures contract based on the CRB Index.

Monetary Policy

The government exerts a powerful influence on the overall level of economic activity through its control of the nation's money supply. The management of the U.S. money supply is the province of the Federal Reserve and is known as *monetary policy*. In theory, an expansion in the money supply increases the availability of credit and hence should tend to lower interest rates and to raise the level of economic activity. Conversely, a reduction in the money supply should tend to raise interest rates and to restrain aggregate economic activity. This reasoning usually applies in real-life situations, but there can be exceptions. This subject is discussed further in Chapter 18.

In recent years a debate has raged over the appropriate economic tool to control aggregate demand patterns. Monetarists contend that changes in the money supply and its subsequent influence on the availability of credit constitutes the most influential and useful economic tool. Other economists believe that fiscal policy (see the following section) deserves more emphasis. It is beyond the scope of this book to deal with the intricacies of the debate, and in fact the government usually relies on a mixture of fiscal and monetary tools in the creation and implementation of overall economic policy. What is important for our purposes is to note that by altering the supply of money and credit, monetary policy can affect a broad range of futures prices.

A restrictive monetary policy, which raises interest rates, tends to push commodity prices lower. Conversely, an accommodative monetary policy tends to lower interest rates and to support futures prices. The reasoning is straightforward. Higher interest rates raise the opportunity cost of owning commodities, which pay no interest, so the overall demand for commodities will tend to fall. Lower interest rates reduce the opportunity costs of owning non-interest-bearing items and therefore tend to bolster demand.

It is important to stress that the preceding discussion applies primarily to *real* interest rates. Real interest rates are the difference between interest rates themselves and the prevailing inflation rate. In other words, real interest rates represent the return to lenders after allowing for the effects of inflation on the purchasing power of the dollars lent. The periods 1979/1980 and 1980/1982 provide graphic examples.

In 1979/1980, interest rates rose steadily, with 90-day U.S. Treasury bills paying more than 16% at one point. If a trader had focused only on the high level of nominal rates, she would have expected these yields to reduce demand for non-interest-bearing assets such as gold. Instead, gold soared to its all-time high of more than $850 per ounce. The reason was that inflation had climbed even more rapidly than interest rates, which meant that during some periods real interest rates were negative. This in turn meant that holders of high quality interest-bearing assets were actually losing purchasing power despite the interest earned. This provided a disincentive to hold interest-bearing assets and helped boost demand for tangible items such as gold and silver.

In the early to mid-1980s the situation reversed dramatically. Nominal interest rates fell sharply from their 1980 peak to less than 8% for 90-day Treasury bills by late 1982. Despite this plunge in rates, gold prices fell to less than $300 per ounce during the same period. Most other commodity and futures prices also declined. What happened was that inflation fell even faster than nominal interest rates, which pushed real interest rates to unusually high levels of 5% or more. Such attractive rates of return provided a powerful disincentive to buying non-interest-bearing assets.

Most economists consider real interest rates of 2–3% to be normal. Consequently, they tend to expect real rates of less than 2% to discourage purchases of interest-bearing assets and real rates of more than 3% to bolster such purchases. One problem with the concept of real interest rates is that they cannot be known with certainty until after the fact. You can know today what interest rates are available over the next 90 days, but the upcoming inflation rate cannot be known until the 90 days have passed. Most analysts address this difficulty by adjusting the most recent inflation data to estimate the probable inflation rates for the coming period.

Fiscal Policy

Fiscal policy is the term used to describe a nation's taxation and government spending initiatives. Such policies have become much more prominent in economic analysis since the early 1970s because of the large and persistent imbalance between U.S. federal government income (primarily taxes) and federal government expenditures. The excess of spending over revenues is known as the *federal budget deficit* and is considered by most economists to be a key macroeconomic force.

Economists typically reason that if the government persistently spends more money than it receives, one of two things will eventually

happen. One possibility is that the revenue shortfall will be addressed by
increasing taxes. The other possibility is that the government will simply
print more money, which is called *monetizing the debt.* Analysts and
traders spend considerable time and effort on the issue of which approach is the more likely and when and how it might be implemented.
This is appropriate because the two approaches to the deficit issue can
have radically different effects on overall economic activity and on the
general price level. Raising taxes removes money from the private economy and is usually considered bearish for economic activity and prices
in general. On the other hand, increasing the money supply is widely
thought to be inflationary, as discussed previously, and is therefore usually viewed as bullish for the overall price level.

Exchange Rates

The increasing interdependence of the world's major economies
has made currency exchange rates an important factor in price analysis.
All else being equal, a nation whose currency declines in value relative
to the currencies of its trading partners will be able to import less and to
export more. Conversely, a nation whose currency increases in value
will be able to import more but to export less. This is important to remember when analyzing futures markets for items that enjoy significant
international trade. For example, the sharp rise in the value of the United
States dollar during the early 1980s made many U.S. agricultural products such as soybeans more expensive to foreign importers. This contributed to the slump in demand for agricultural products during that
period.

Currency exchange rates are the result of a complex array of economic forces that are described in Chapter 19. All futures traders should
understand these in a general sense. However, it is worth mentioning
that traders sometimes attach too much importance to exchange rate
changes. For one thing, only major changes are likely to affect established demand patterns. Fluctuations of 5% or even 10% seldom have a
meaningful impact. Major realignments of 25% or more are usually
needed to bring about significant changes in demand. For another thing,
traders sometimes forget the extent to which international transactions
are linked to one currency—usually the United States dollar. For example, Chile, Zambia, and Zaire are all major copper producers and exporters. However, changes in the values of these countries' currencies

would have little real impact on copper fundamentals or copper prices. These currencies are not used in international trade because they are not widely viewed as stable and sound. Instead, copper is sold for "hard" currencies, usually U.S. dollars. Similar reasoning applies to some degree to most commodities, since they are often produced in developing countries whose currencies are seldom used in international trade.

Government Commodity Agreements

Government commodity agreements influence many markets. The most obvious example of such an agreement is in oil, where OPEC often plays a dominant role in pricing.

Other commodities are also impacted to varying degrees by international commodity agreements or cartels. Many of the agricultural markets, for example, can react to decisions adopted by the European Community (EC). EC decisions on sugar and feedgrain output and sales sometimes affect futures in these items. The cocoa, coffee, and sugar markets are periodically influenced by cartels or international agreements between producers and consumers. These agreements have seldom proved effective for long periods, but traders should remember that they can have an important short term influence on prices.

Trade Policy

Tariffs, quotas, import restrictions, and bilateral or multilateral trading agreements can significantly affect the flow of internationally traded products. Governments sometimes use trade policy to further political agendas or to protect certain industries within a country from foreign competition. Such policies can radically affect supply/demand fundamentals. Two representative examples warrant mention.

The United States has long subsidized domestic sugar producers whose production costs on the whole far exceed those of most other sugar producers. The government accomplishes this through a combination of subsidies and import restrictions on foreign sugars. The net effect is that sugar prices in the United States are artificially high, which naturally tends to restrict usage.

Another example is the November 1986 imposition of an 8.5% duty on imports of orange juice into the United States from Brazil. Domestic orange juice producers contended that the sharp increase in imports of Brazilian juice since the 1970s was damaging the domestic citrus industry and so sought government aid in the form of a quota or tariff. The levy caused an almost immediate reduction in the flow of juice from Brazil to the United States.

Organizations such as the European Community (EC) are designed to foster political and economic cooperation among their member nations. Thus, steps are often taken to encourage trading activity among members at the expense of trade with nonmember countries.

Macroeconomic considerations, such as those discussed in this chapter, provide the backdrop for fundamental analysis. We turn now to a discussion of speculation and the futures markets. We will return to a discussion of specific supply/demand information beginning with Chapter 18.

■ Chapter 15

■ Speculation and Money Management

Speculators are the most numerous and the least successful participants in the futures markets. No authoritative statistics exist on the number of active futures speculators, but various industry experts estimate that about 150,000 to 200,000 were active in 1986. Though there have been no comprehensive studies of speculative profitability in recent years, few knowledgeable observers would argue that things have changed much since various studies between 1930 and 1970 concluded that only 10% to 30% of all speculators showed net profits in any given year. This chapter will address two facets of this anomaly. First, why are so many people attracted to an endeavor in which so few succeed? Second, what can a speculator do to improve his chances for success? The answers to these questions lie as much in the realms of psychology, statistics, and common sense as in those of market fundamentals and technical analysis.

SPECULATION: ITS MOTIVES AND MERITS

Speculation has always lingered on the fringes of financial respectability. A seemingly perpetual debate rages and subsides about whether futures speculation is gambling (usually considered bad) or investing (usually considered good). This question is irrelevant to one's success or failure as a trader, except to the extent that it affects the legislative and regulatory environment within which the futures industry operates.

However, the speculation/gambling/investing issue deserves some attention because everyone who trades futures periodically hears the matter discussed and debated. Even the definitions are not universally agreed upon, but the following would be pretty widely accepted:

Gambling involves the creation of risk for risk's sake. Gain and loss need not necessarily accompany horse races, card games, or the rolling of dice. Rather, people create financial risks and opportunities that would otherwise not exist.

Speculation involves the assumption of existing risks. Somebody must benefit and somebody else must lose when the price of sugar rises or the price of oil falls. The only issue is whether the winners and the losers are going to be producers and consumers, or whether the price risks can be shifted to noncommercial speculators, to the government, or elsewhere.

Investing is the commitment of capital to an enterprise in the hope of earning a profit. The difference between investment and speculation is largely semantic, but most would agree that commitments with time horizons that are longer than several months qualify as investments regardless of whether the commitment is in securities, real estate, or commodities.

The problem is that the lines that separate investment, speculation, and gambling are very fuzzy, regardless of the particular definitions. Consider these examples:

- If Mr. *A* buys a cattle futures contract from a rancher, and Ms. *B* sells a cattle futures contract to a meat packer, then Mr. *A* and Ms. *B* are both speculating in cattle futures. However, if the rancher sells a futures contract directly to the packer and Mr. *A* and Ms. *B* make a bet with one another on the direction of cattle prices, then they are gambling. Unfortunately for the sake of conceptual precision, the economics of the two situations are identical.

- Mr. *C* provides two entrepreneurs with $100,000 to develop a new type of microcomputer software. He anticipates holding his position in this newly founded company for two or three years. The enterprise succeeds much more quickly than expected. After three months Mr. *C* sells his equity interest for $400,000 to Mr. *D*, who doesn't even know what the company does, but who wants to think of himself as a venture capitalist. Three months later the two entrepreneurs are able to secure debt financing and buy out Mr. *D* for $1 million.

Almost nobody would argue that Mr. *C* is anything other than an investor, but what about Mr. *D*? He sounds like a speculator, but why? He held the same equity position as Mr. *C* for the same length of time. He didn't provide seed capital, but nobody would argue that every secondary market purchaser is a speculator. His cavalier attitude toward the company's fundamentals seems disquieting, but providers of seed capital often understand little about the companies they back. Does this make them speculators, or ill-informed investors?

- Mr. *E* is a boxing enthusiast. He meets a young welterweight and decides that with some expert training the fighter could be another Sugar Ray Leonard. He offers to contribute $50,000 toward one year's training and promotional expenses in return for 30% of the boxer's purses, which he believes could total well over $1 million. Is Mr. *E* a gambler, a speculator, or an investor? What if, instead of this approach, he gave the fighter a $50,000 per year job as a part-time chauffeur and bet on each of his fights? What if the boxer incorporated himself and Mr. *E* bought 30% of the stock for $50,000?

Examples like these can make it tempting to conclude that distinctions among gambling, speculation, and investing are wholly artificial, serving only to facilitate favorable descriptions of activities one happens to like and unfavorable descriptions of those one happens to dislike. To a certain extent this is true, but it is clearly not the whole story. Clever examples do not alter the fact that there are profound economic differences between betting on a boxing match and financing a promising new technology, or between playing roulette and trading soybeans. The fact that precise distinctions are difficult to draw does not mean that distinctions do not exist or do not matter. Distinctions between gambling, speculation, and investing do exist, and the issue is one of legitimate concern to a society that strives to maintain an appropriate balance between entertainment, opportunity, and long-term economic development.

When it comes to futures trading, though, the important point is to distinguish between motives and economic effects because economic effects are what matter. Most futures speculators are motivated by the same basic hope for a quick profit that motivates a casino gambler. Nobody decides to trade soybean futures because of a desire to contribute to the efficiency of the agricultural sector. Yet futures speculation does enhance efficiency and help stabilize prices despite the fact that few motives could be further from the minds of the speculators themselves. This ability to create economic benefits out of a simple desire to make money justifies putting futures trading in the category of free-market competition at its best. It is Adam Smith's "invisible hand" at its most visible.

SUCCESSFUL SPECULATION

Developing a sound approach to futures speculation is a three-step process:

- Define your speculative objectives.
- Decide whether futures trading is appropriate in light of these objectives.
- If futures trading is appropriate, develop capital-management guidelines.

We will discuss each of these steps in turn, looking in particular detail at the subject of money management.

Defining Speculative Objectives

You cannot develop a trading strategy without first deciding what you are trying to accomplish. Goals should be more specific than a vague desire to earn a lot of money. Very different strategies might be appropriate depending on, for example, whether you want to earn 30% annually on your trading capital or whether you are prepared to risk everything on a particularly strong opinion about silver prices. Here are four very different examples of goals that a speculator might have in mind when considering futures trading:

1. Earn a 30% annual return on trading capital during a three- to five-year period.
2. Triple trading capital within six months.
3. Maximize profits given a strongly bullish view of sugar prices for a three-month period.

4. Earn a return on capital equal to the one-year Treasury bill yield during the next year.

Objectives themselves are neither good nor bad. They are simply objectives, and everyone is free to choose his or her own. Some objectives, though, are less likely to be achieved than others. If a trader's goal is to turn $1,000 into $1 million within one year, the objective is understandable but unrealistic. Still, there is nothing necessarily wrong with having unrealistic objectives. The important thing is to select whatever financial program is most likely to achieve the chosen objective. When the objective is as unrealistic as turning $1,000 into $1 million, even the best available approach will not be very likely to succeed, but some will be less unlikely than others. Let us now turn to the question of which financial objectives are well suited to futures speculation.

Why Speculate in Futures?

After you have formulated your objectives it is time to ask whether futures speculation is appropriate for you. Three considerations are important:

1. Is leverage appealing to you?
2. Do you have opinions that can best be acted on by trading futures?
3. Do you enjoy trading futures?

These questions reflect the fact that futures markets offer both leverage and an opportunity to put certain economic opinions to a market test in a way that some people find quite interesting and educational. But it is leverage that futures trading is all about, so let us consider it a bit further.

We discussed in Chapter 7 that futures margins are typically 5% to 10% or less of the underlying contract value. In a few cases the leverage is even more pronounced. The margin requirement on a $1 million T-bill futures contract is generally less than $5,000, or only one-half of 1% of the full contract value. This leverage creates the illusion that futures prices are far more volatile than they actually are. In fact, the typical volatility of futures contracts is comparable to that of common stocks, as the statistics in Figure 15-1 on page 324 show. Futures prices are not themselves particularly volatile. The volatility simply seems greater because

Figure 15-1. Selected volatilities.

Item	Volatility (Calendar Year 1986)
S&P 500 Index	14.9%
Gold Futures	20.2
IBM Common Stock	20.5
General Motors Common Stock	21.5
Corn Futures	21.5
Soybean Oil Futures	29.0

Note: Volatility is quoted as a percent by convention. The important point to note is that the volatilities of the prices of these very different items are fairly similar. Volatility is discussed in more detail in Chapters 25 and 26.

price fluctuations are usually compared with margin requirements rather than with total contract values.

Leverage leads to big percentage fluctuations in trading capital, which is why futures trading is so appealing to speculators who hope for large, quick profits and do not mind the attendant risk of large, quick losses. It is not at all unusual for a futures speculator to triple or lose all of his trading capital within a few weeks. Doing so may not involve the soundest money management procedures, as we will see later in this chapter. Nonetheless, leverage makes it possible, and this is the main appeal of futures trading for those whose objectives include large, rapid gains.

From a speculator's perspective, knowing that leverage exists and recognizing the opportunities and risks that it creates are what matters. Still, it is worth taking a few minutes to understand why this leverage exists in the futures markets to a degree unmatched elsewhere in the financial world. The reason is simple. Futures markets could not exist without leverage. If hedgers were forced to post full contract value (or anything close to it) as original margin, operating capital requirements would be prohibitive. Farmers whose wheat crops generate $1 million in revenue do not usually have $1 million in cash available for futures margins. Furthermore, there is no reason why margin requirements for hedgers need to be comparable to total contract value. As we have seen, prices are not really that volatile, and hedgers by definition have actual or anticipated cash market positions that protect against much of the volatility that does exist.

The importance of leverage in attracting speculators and the liquidity that they provide is even more extreme. Virtually nobody would speculate in futures if margin requirements were large percents of full contract value. The volatility is simply not great enough to create interesting opportunities relative to the yardstick of full contract value. Futures pay no interest or dividends and without leverage would have little appeal relative to other investment alternatives. So leverage is a prerequisite for liquid futures markets. Without leverage, futures trading would not be very interesting and probably would not exist at all.

A second reason to speculate in futures is that futures offer particularly direct opportunities to test certain opinions in the marketplace and hopefully to profit in the process. If you believe that cattle prices are going up or that the dollar will strengthen against the Japanese yen, then buying or selling futures is a straightforward way to profit if you are correct. Absent futures markets, such forecasts could be put to work only indirectly. Someone who is bullish on corn would have few alternatives but to search for a publicly traded company whose stock price might benefit from the expected change in corn prices. But indirect approaches are fraught with potential pitfalls. A copper mining company's gain from rising copper prices could be more than offset by labor difficulties or by increased foreign competition. A firm that imports parts from West Germany might find the benefits of a weakening Deutsche mark less important than the financing problems that are caused by rising United States interest rates. There is only one direct, uncomplicated way to implement opinions on prices of basic raw materials and on many other fundamental economic numbers such as currency exchange rates and Eurodollar interest rates. That is by trading futures.

The fact that futures trading can be interesting and even enjoyable should not be considered irrelevant or inappropriate. If someone enjoys the potential risks and rewards that are attendant to the futures markets, that is a perfectly valid reason for trading futures. It may even be sufficient reason for accepting a lower expected rate of return than is available elsewhere. Consider an example. Suppose that an investor has the following two choices for putting $100,000 to work over the next year:

1. Buy a bank certificate of deposit (CD) paying 6.75% annually.
2. Trade futures knowing that there is a 50% chance of losing half his capital and a 50% chance of increasing the initial capital by 60%.

The expected return from the CD is, naturally, 6.75%. The expected return from futures trading is only 5.00% (0.50 x 60% – 0.50 x 50% =

5.00%). Someone whose sole objective is to maximize expected return would buy the CD. So would someone who had little or no tolerance for risk. But another person might reason that the enjoyment derived from following her position and learning something about corn, oil, or currency rates more than offsets the fact that the expected annual return is 1.75% less in futures. There is nothing wrong with this. In fact, the branch of mathematics known as *game theory* deals specifically with preferences of this sort, using the concept of a *utility function*. Utility functions help explain why so many people speculate in futures even though so few profit consistently. They are worth a brief discussion.

A *utility function* is an attempt to quantify a person's motives and preferences. For example, on a scale of 0 to 100, someone who cares only about maximizing his expected average return would attach a value of 100 to that objective and a value of 0 to everything else. Another person might assign a value of 85 to maximizing expected average return, a value of 10 to finding his investments interesting, and a value of 5 to having significant liquidity. A third person with a high-risk tolerance might value expected average return at 70 and the possibility of an unusually large profit at 30. Game theory does not make value judgments regarding utility functions. It simply assumes that different people have different utility functions and focuses on the question of which endeavors and strategies are most appropriate for given utility functions. If someone's utility function attaches significant values to the possibility of large profits and to learning about the items traded, then futures trading would be quite appealing.

One final point regarding utility functions: Someone whose utility function attaches value only to maximizing expected profit should, in the long run, make more money than someone whose utility function also values such things as excitement or the opportunity to learn about different aspects of the world economy. But this is only a probability rather than a certainty and, as Lord Keynes first pointed out, in the long run we are all dead.

Developing Capital Management Guidelines

Successful trading requires two ingredients: 1) the ability to forecast prices, and 2) knowledge of how to effectively manage the capital that is available for trading. Effective money management cannot turn incorrect trading decisions into profits, but it can contain the impact of the inevitable strings of losing trades that even the most successful speculators must endure. It is a crucial ingredient of every profitable trading program.

The key to money management is correctly balancing three numbers:

- Risk.
- Profit opportunity.
- Available trading capital.

This is true of every financial venture, but is especially difficult to do in futures because the leverage that is involved tends to obscure certain economic and statistical realities.

Let us first consider risk. Almost everyone who buys 1,000 shares of stock for $40 per share will think in terms of having $40,000 committed to the market even if the purchase was made on 50% margin. However, when someone buys one 100-ounce gold futures contract at $400 per ounce, the risk assumptions are usually very different. Most speculators tend to use margin requirements as a measure of risk. Because initial margins will usually be in the $1,000 to $1,500 per contract range when gold is $400 per ounce, they will almost automatically think of their risk as being in the vicinity of $1,000 to $1,500 per contract when gold is $400 per ounce. This is a major mistake because futures risks are only loosely related to initial margin requirements. The risk that is associated with a long position of one 100-ounce gold contract at $400 per ounce is $40,000 (100 ounces x $400 per ounce), exactly as the risk of a 1,000 share long position in a $40-per-share stock is $40,000 (1,000 shares x $40 per share). Few people think of futures risk in this way because the futures industry focuses on margin requirements and price changes rather than on total contract value. But initial margin requirements are merely good faith deposits. Risk is either total contract value (in the case of a long position) or is unlimited (in the case of a short position), just as with stocks, bonds, real estate, or anything else in which traders focus more directly on total value.

Leverage can also cloud the focus on available trading capital, which is the yardstick against which risk should be measured. This is partly because there is seldom a good reason to keep in your futures account all the capital that you are prepared to risk. Margin requirements may not be a good measure of risk, but they are, by definition, the minimum amount needed in a futures account. Furthermore, it is usually prudent to keep little more than the minimum required margin in a futures account. This is because few FCMs pay interest on futures account cash balances, which makes it advisable to transfer into the account only what is needed to meet margin requirements and to maintain a modest cushion to prevent having to continually transfer small amounts as prices fluctuate. Loss of interest is less of an issue for large traders who can more readily post United States Treasury securities as margin (see Chapter 7), but many large traders prefer to keep their idle funds in something other than short-maturity Treasuries. What this means is that few speculators keep their futures trading capital isolated from their other assets, which can obscure the amount against which risks should be measured. From a strictly objective viewpoint, this is a phantom issue because all that is needed is meticulous record keeping or a separate "holding account" for futures capital that is not actually being employed as margin. In the real world, though, few speculators keep their futures trading capital isolated from their other assets, which can make it difficult to keep a clear focus on the amount against which risks should be measured.

How To Measure Risk

Before we move to specific money management guidelines, let us continue with the subject of risk measurement. Total contract value may represent the theoretical risk of a long position, but it is not a very practical measure. Prices do not fall to zero very often. But if neither margin requirements nor total contract value is the correct way to measure risk, what is the correct way? The best answer to this question is a subjective one. The risk on a futures position consists of two parts:

- The amount you are prepared to lose before entering an order to liquidate your position.
- A reasonable "slippage factor" that allows for the possibility that market conditions may cause the actual liquidation price to be significantly different from the planned liquidation price.

The first component is straightforward. If you buy July crude oil at 15.40, you either place a sell stop at, for example, 14.70 or you resolve to enter a sell order as soon as that price level is reached. The second component is much trickier. If you assume that your sell stop will, on the average, be executed at 14.70, you are being unrealistic. The market could close one day at 14.72 and open the next morning at 14.50; a piece of intraday news could cause prices to fall so rapidly that a floor broker can execute a 14.70 sell stop no higher than 14.55 or 14.60. On the other hand, no plausible scenario could cause a 14.70 sell stop to be filled significantly above 14.70. What this means is that you should assume that, on the average, you will exit from a losing position at a less favorable price than you plan. But how much worse? A worst-case scenario would be that prices plunge limit down day after day from 14.71 to zero, but this would be a preposterous assumption. What is needed is some familiarity with market behavior and a degree of common sense. To continue with the same example, if oil futures have had intraday ranges of 20 to 30 points during the past several months and, on the average, open within 10 to 20 points of the previous closing price, then a 10- or 15-point average slippage factor would probably be appropriate. If the market had a history of occasional but unpredictable bursts of volatility, then increasing the average slippage factor to 20 or 25 points might be prudent.

This may sound a little too imprecise for analytically minded readers. It would sound more solid and substantive to say something like: "Calculate the standard deviation of the difference between closing and opening prices over the past 60 trading days, multiply by 2.0 to get a 95% confidence interval, and add 15% of the largest single overnight fluctuation within the past year." Such mathematical approaches to risk measurement can be logical, but they can also contain a good deal of pseudoprecision. Even very successful and sophisticated traders disagree on the question of what combination of intuition and statistics provides the best insight into risk measurement.

MONEY MANAGEMENT GUIDELINES

A successful trader must not only measure risk but also manage it. Some speculators may make only one or two really poor market decisions out of 50 or more trades, but still lose a substantial portion of their futures capital. Others might add up their annual commission costs and discover that they amount to 50% or more of their trading capital. These and other similar experiences result from poor or nonexistent money management techniques and can be eliminated with some planning and self discipline. The following five money management guidelines should help.

1. *Speculate Only with Capital That You Can Afford To Lose.*

Speculation is risky. That is why people speculate. But speculative risks should be taken only with true *risk capital*—that is, money that you could lose without affecting your life-style or your peace of mind. This is just a common sense prerequisite for trading because nobody can made sound decisions knowing that one (or even several) losses would wreak financial or emotional havoc. The specific amount of futures trading capital will obviously vary widely from person to person. So will the appropriate portions of income and net worth that could be reasonably allocated to futures speculation. People have different temperaments, financial objectives, and value systems. One person might be emotionally devastated by a trading loss that equals 3% of his net worth. Another person in the same financial situation might lose 20% of her net worth and shrug it off as a learning experience. It is impossible to give formulas or even guidelines regarding "correct" levels of speculative commitment, but it is essential to recognize that each person must determine the level that is correct for him. If that level is zero, fine. Not everyone is cut out to speculate in futures. If it is 50% of your net worth, fine also, as long as that is a realistic assessment of your risk tolerance.

Speculators should consider the segregation of their futures trading capital from other assets as a simple safeguard against overextending themselves. Two approaches are particularly suitable:

- Traders who have $25,000 or more in speculative funds can keep most of this trading capital in United States Treasury securities. These can be used for original margin and are, of course, earning interest regardless of whether they are actually employed as original margin. Remember, though, that variation margin calls must be met with cash (see Chapter 7). This means that a large trader should consider keeping perhaps 20% to 25% of his speculative capital in his futures account even though few FCMs will pay interest on this cash except to exceptionally large, active accounts. The only alternative would be the transfer of funds into and out of the account with a frequency that would quickly become a nuisance for both the trader and the FCM.

Treasury securities are usually not a viable alternative for traders who have speculative capital of less than $25,000. Treasury bills are sold in minimum lots of $10,000 and many FCMs require futures account balances of $20,000 or even $50,000 before they will accept Treasury bills from a customer as original margin. This reflects the fact that interest income from free credit balances is an important revenue source for FCMs, and no interest is earned by the FCM on customer-owned Treasury bills. Speculators who have less than $25,000 in trading capital should consider keeping the entire amount in their futures account despite the lack of interest income.

The low margin requirements for futures make it possible to trade with modest amounts of capital. Margin requirements for a single contract are often $1,000 or less, but many FCMs require initial deposits of at least $5,000 before opening a futures account for a customer. Still, the fact that something is possible does not necessarily make it advisable. As we will discuss below, it is unwise to risk more than 5% to 10% of one's trading capital on a single trade, and it is unusual to find attractive opportunities that have realistically measured risks of less than $500 per contract. Therefore, speculators who have less than $5,000 in trading capital cannot prudently take advantage of many trading situations and are less likely to succeed in the long run than are better capitalized traders.

2. *Establish Risk Levels and Profit Objectives Prior To Every Trade.*

Planning is vital to speculative success. It is an especially crucial component of risk management because the high leverage in futures can lead to rapidly eroding equity for speculators who do not anticipate and plan for their inevitable losing trades. Countless traders have taken positions expecting to risk $800 or $1,000 per contract and have watched their losses climb to $2,000 or $3,000 per contract before finally cutting short the agony by liquidating. Most traders find it extremely difficult psychologically to take a loss. The reason is an odd combination of hope and fear that is irrational but almost universal. Given an unrealized loss, most speculators reflexively do nothing, hoping that things will somehow improve, rather than accept the unpleasant certainty of a realized loss. This paralysis is usually reinforced by a fear of feeling foolish should the market reverse direction after the position is closed out. Because this same combination of emotions is present whenever there is a loss of any size, the inevitable result is a refusal to liquidate losing positions until forced to do so by margin problems or by losses so large that they have become patently hopeless.

The safeguard against this unhappy but all-too-common scenario is to plan in advance. The best approach is to enter protective stop-loss orders on all positions as soon as the positions are initiated. This ensures that any position will be liquidated automatically if it deteriorates to a predetermined adverse level. Once a protective stop has been established, resist all temptations to cancel it or to move it further away should prices move toward the stop level. The closer the market comes to your stop, the more likely it becomes that you made an error in market judgment in the first place. Do not compound it by increasing your exposure. Learning to accept these errors and losses as an unavoidable part of speculation is an important step toward a successful trading program.

Speculators sometimes hesitate to use protective stop-loss orders because of a concern that knowledge of the stop on the trading floor will work to their disadvantage. This concern is not totally groundless but is much less of a practical issue than most traders imagine. The potential disadvantage of a protective stop is this: If a floor trader holds a sell stop near the market, he will be marginally less likely to bid aggressively either for his own account or on buy orders over which he has some discretion. This would, at the margin, tend to weaken prices, but in active, liquid markets the effect would be imperceptible. The risk that this would lead to being stopped out of a position that would otherwise prove profitable pales in comparison with the advantage of having an automatic ejection mechanism from a deteriorating position.

Profit objectives can be treated more flexibly. The important point is to have a plan that guards against the common tendency to quickly take small profits. As we discuss later, this is a quick route to speculative failure. Two different approaches to the profit side of a trading plan are worth specific mention. One is to set a minimum profit objective and to exit a position before the objective is reached only if the protective stop is hit or if some new development alters your view of the market. The second is to set no limit on profits, but rather to gradually move the protective stop nearer the market until the position is eventually liquidated. Either approach will accomplish the basic goal of preventing too many small profits.

3. Trade for Small Losses and Large Profits.

This is not as obvious as it may seem. Having larger profits than losses sounds appealing, but whether it is a sound trading strategy depends on the probabilities of profits and losses of various sizes. Suppose, for example, that you make $3,000 per contract on every profitable trade, lose $1,000 on every unprofitable trade, and that your profit/loss breakdown is 20% profits and 80% losses. You would be losing an average of $200 per trade despite having average profits three times larger than average losses ($3,000 x 0.20 – $1,000 x 0.80 = –$200). Large profits are worthwhile only if they occur frequently enough to offset the more numerous small losses. Lotteries, casinos, and insurance companies are among the enterprises that thrive by collecting enough revenue in many small pieces to more than offset their occasional, much larger, losses.

Why not trade futures using the same approach that works so well for insurance companies and lotteries—take many small profits and only a few large losses? Why does it make sense to cut losses short and let profits run? The answer lies in the way that futures prices fluctuate. If price fluctuations were completely random, then a $100 per contract move would be exactly twice as likely as a $200 per contract move, 50 times as likely as a $5,000 per contract move, and so forth. Price behavior of this type leads to a *normal distribution* of price fluctuations and is presented graphically in Figure 15-2 on page 335. The horizontal axis represents the size of a price fluctuation. The vertical axis is a measure of the probability that a price change of a given magnitude will occur before a single one unit move occurs in the opposite direction. The choice of units is completely arbitrary. A single unit could be chosen to be $100 per contract, $1,000 per contract, or $833.22 per contract. The important point about a random distribution is this: If price fluctuations are randomly distributed, it makes no difference to your long-term expected profitability (excluding transaction costs) whether you trade for large profits and small losses, small profits and large losses, or anything in between. You could choose to have roughly one $5,000 profit for every five $1,000 losses, five $1,000 profits for every $5,000 loss, or one

$5,000 profit for every $5,000 loss, but in the long run you would approximately break even in each case.

The reason for seeking large profits and small losses in the futures markets is that evidence suggests that futures price changes are *not* randomly distributed. Various analyses have shown that there are more large price fluctuations than chance alone would dictate.*

The graph of typical futures price changes looks something like the solid line in Figure 15-3. We have superimposed the graph of a normal distribution (dashed line) for comparison. Notice that the tails of the actual price change graph are higher than those of the normal distribution, corresponding to the more frequent large price changes. Distributions of this type are called *leptokurtotic*. More colloquially, a leptokurtotic distribution means that prices tend to move in trends. Starting from any given price level, a $1,000 per contract move in a particular direction has more than a random likelihood of being the start of a $5,000 or $10,000 trend. The advantage of trading for large price movements given this type of distribution is that this approach makes the larger than normal number of large price changes work to your advantage. You might, for example, find one $5,000 per contract price movement for every nine $500 movements, rather than for every ten $500 movements as in a normal distribution. Having this imbalance working for you rather than against you is important enough that it is virtually a prerequisite for long-term trading success. Successful speculators have the trending tendency of futures working for them rather than against them.

Astute readers may have noticed that this discussion has not taken into account a trader's ability to predict price movements. Suppose that someone is particularly good at anticipating small or moderate price changes. Would not this ability justify a trading approach that entailed a slight statistical disadvantage? The answer is, probably not, and the reason is the near randomness of futures price changes. Academic researchers have for years debated among themselves and with traders about whether futures price changes are or are not random. As we have pointed out, the evidence suggests that they are not random, but leptokurtotic. However, any deviation from randomness is not great. The markets are efficient enough that regardless of whether a trader bases his decisions on fundamentals, technical signals, or a combination of both,

---

* See "The Distribution of Shortrun Commodity Price Movements," by Jitendar S. Mann and Richard G. Heifner. Economic Research Service, US Department of Agriculture. Technical Bulletin Number 1536.

Figure 15-2. Normal distribution.

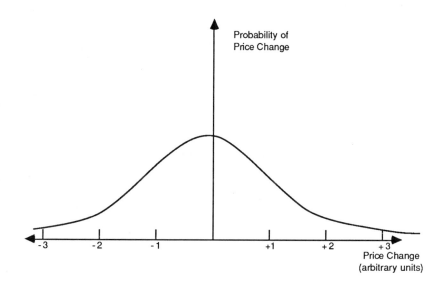

Figure 15-3. Typical distribution of futures price changes.

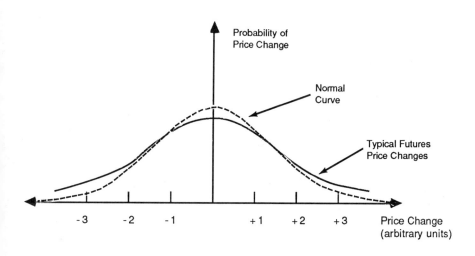

his ratio of the number of profitable trades to the number of losing trades will not deviate drastically from the levels that chance alone would dictate. Thus, a trader who takes equal-sized profits and losses might profit on 52% or 55% of several hundred trades, but it would be almost impossible to profit on 65% or 70% of this many trades if profits and losses are roughly equal in size. Similarly, a trader who takes profits three times larger than his losses might, in the long run, profit on 28% or 30% of his trades rather than the 25% that chance alone would suggest, but he will not profit 40% or 45% of the time. A rough rule of thumb is that a good trader might succeed 10% to 15% more frequently than chance alone would suggest. If chance indicated a 50% success rate, 55% or 58% could be achievable. Given a 20% chance of random success, 22% or 23% could be achieved, and so forth. To expect or plan for much more than this would be wishful thinking. This, of course, assumes a large number of transactions (e.g., several hundred) because small numbers of trades will not give the probabilities enough time to show their effect. You might flip a coin five times and get heads 80% of the time, but you will not get this result after 200 or 300 trials. When it comes to speculating and trends, the point is this: Futures markets are efficient enough that even the most astute market analysis will succeed only modestly more often than would chance alone. Given this somewhat sobering fact, it is best not to forego the statistical advantage that comes from trading for large profits and small losses.

An important point is that the profit/loss ratios of floor traders are not governed by the laws of probability in the same way as are these ratios for other traders. This is not because floor traders are better market analysts or possess unique insights. Rather, we return to a point made in Chapter 4: Floor traders have the bid/offer spread working in their favor. This enables them to make very small profits on a much larger percentage of their transactions than probability alone would suggest. We emphasize again that there is nothing unseemly about this. It is the compensation that floor traders receive for tying up capital in exchange memberships and foregoing other activities to spend each day in the trading ring.

How do we know that the trending tendencies and market efficiencies that futures prices have displayed in the past will also occur in the future? Might not prices behave differently in a way that makes some other trading approach more appropriate? The answer is that this could happen, but the patterns seem pretty well established. Until something occurs to suggest that they may be changing, the best advice is to keep profits large and losses small.

4. Risk No More Than 5% of Your Trading Capital on a Single Position.

Violating this rule has probably caused the demise of more speculators than any other single factor. It sounds so conservative as to be downright stodgy by the standards of someone willing to accept significant risks. But if you trade often and violate this rule regularly, eventual failure is all but guaranteed. To see why, it is necessary to understand something called the *probability of ruin*, which is important enough that we discuss it in some detail.

Suppose that you have a specific amount of capital and risk a certain fixed amount on each trade. For example, you might have $10,000 and risk $1,000 per trade. Your *probability of ruin* is the probability of losing all of your trading capital (in the case of our example, $10,000). This could happen in an infinite number of ways. You could lose on each of your first ten trades; you could make $3,000 on your first two trades and then lose $1,000 thirteen times in a row, and so forth. If you trade indefinitely, the likelihood that some sequence will occur that will completely wipe out your capital base depends on just two things:

- The probability of failure on each individual trade.
- The percentage of initial capital being risked on each trade.

For simplicity, we assume that the same dollar amount is risked on each trade, even though the account will fluctuate in total value.

The formula for computing one's probability of ruin is relatively simple if you assume that profits and losses are always of equal size. Though we have just discussed why this is not an optimum futures trading strategy, it is still a useful starting point for understanding what probability of ruin means to futures speculators. If one trading unit is either made or lost on every transaction, then the probability of ruin is:

$$R = \left(\frac{P}{q}\right)^N$$

where:

R = probability of ruin
P = probability of loss on each trade
q = $1 - P$ = probability of profit on each trade
N = number of units in initial trading capital

As we discussed previously in Rule 3, even the most astute speculators cannot expect to profit on a percentage of their trades that exceeds pure chance by more than about 10%. Thus, a successful trader who aims for equal-sized profits and losses might profit on about 55% of his transactions (55% = 50% + 0.10 x 50%). We use the above formula to see that his probability of ruin depends heavily on the percentage of trading capital that is risked on each trade:

$$R = \left(\frac{P}{q}\right)^N = \left(\frac{0.45}{0.55}\right)^N = (0.82)^N$$

Figure 15-4, which is derived from this formula, summarizes the results for different levels of risk. Note that because N is the number of units in the initial capital base, $100/N$ is the percent of initial capital that is risked on each trade.

In other words, someone who risks 20% of his initial capital per trade has a 40% chance of losing everything, whereas a more conservative trader who risks only 5% of his initial capital has only a 2% chance of ruin.

When profits and losses are not of equal size, the probability of ruin calculations become very complex. We omit the formulas and present in Figure 15-5 the results for three specific approaches in which profits are larger than losses. The assumed probabilities of a profitable trade are realistically optimistic for the targeted profit/loss ratios.

1. Profit/loss ratio = 2:1.
   Probability of profit on single trade = 35%.
2. Profit/loss ratio = 3:1.
   Probability of profit on single trade = 28%.
3. Profit/loss ratio = 5:1.
   Probability of profit on single trade = 20%.

Figure 15-4. *Probability of ruin (Profit/loss ratio = 1:1)*
Probability of profit = 55%.

Percent of Initial Capital Risked Per Trade	Probability of Ruin
50%	67%
40	61
30	51
20	40
10	13
5	2

Figure 15-5. *Probability of ruin (profit/loss ratios = 2:1, 3:1, 5:1).*

Percent of Initial Capital Risked Per Trade	Profit/Loss=2:1 Probability of Profit = 35%	Profit/Loss=3:1 Probability of Profit = 28%	Profit/Loss=5:1 Probability of Profit = 20%
50%	81%	87%	88%
40	78	81	85
30	73	78	76
20	61	69	70
10	38	48	51
5	14	23	26
2	1	3	4

These numbers paint a clear picture. Traders who risk more than 10% of their initial capital per trade will more likely than not lose everything eventually. A 5% rule might remove much of the excitement from futures trading, but it substantially improves the chances of long-term success.

5. Be Sure That Your Average Profit Is At Least 10 to 15 Times Your Costs.

Paying insufficient attention to transaction costs is another common cause of speculative failure. These costs are an ever-present drain on trading capital, and the larger they are as a percentage of trading capital, the smaller will be the chances for long-term success. Transaction costs have two components: 1) commissions, and 2) bid/offer spreads. Each time you complete a roundturn trade, you pay a direct commission charge to your brokerage firm and (unless you are a floor trader) an indirect bid/offer cost to the trading ring as a whole. Your market analysis must overcome the total of these two costs for you to simply break even. Consider an example: Suppose that July crude oil futures are 15.50 bid/15.52 offered and that your FCM charges a roundturn commission of $40 per contract. If you buy July oil at the offer price of 15.52, the market must rally six points, to 15.56 bid/15.58 offered, before you break even. The commission is an explicit cost of $40 (which equals 4 points in crude oil futures), and the two point bid/offer spread is an implicit cost of $20. These are fixed costs that apply to every trade, regardless of whether it is a profit or a loss or whether the amount gained or lost is $100 per contract or $5,000 per contract. Successful speculation depends in large part on minimizing the impact of these fixed costs.

There are two ways to control the effect of these fixed costs. One is to reduce the costs themselves. It obviously makes sense to negotiate the lowest possible commission rates consistent with your service requirements, but the bid/offer spread is simply a fact of life for all except floor traders. The second method of reducing the influence of transaction costs is to trade for larger profits. This can dramatically reduce the impact of transaction costs and is consistent with the philosophy that we discussed previously of staying with trends. A simple example illustrates how advantageous it is to trade for a few large profits rather than numerous small ones.

Suppose that Trader A and Trader B both follow a 3:1 profit/loss rule *before commissions and without considering the bid/offer spread.* Suppose also that both traders pay commissions of $40 per contract and that bid/offer spreads average $20 per contract. Let us assume that Trader A's average profit is $450 per contract and that his average loss is $150 per contract (excluding transaction costs), while Trader B's average profit is $1,800 per contract and that his average loss is $600 per contract. Trader A is effectively taking an average profit of only $390 per contract, but incurring an average loss of $210 per contract net of his $60 costs. He must, therefore, be correct on 35.0% of his trades simply to break even. Trader B, whose net profits and losses are $1,740 and $660 per contract, respectively, will break even if he is correct only 27.5% of the time and would show a profit of $180 per contract should his success percentage reach the 35.0% level that Trader A needs simply to break even. This 7.5-percentage-point difference would be an almost insurmountable obstacle for Trader A to overcome were he in competi-

Figure 15-6. *Percentage of profitable trades that are needed to break even.*

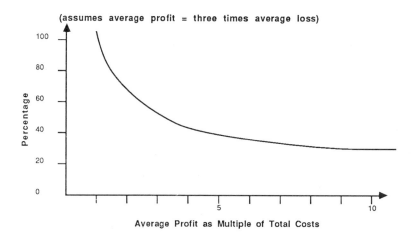

tion with Trader *B* for long-term success. As we mentioned in our discussion of Rule 3, it is very difficult to achieve a long-term success ratio more than 10% better than that expected from pure chance. For a 3:1 profit/loss ratio, chance would yield a success ratio of 25.0%. Thus, a 10% improvement would be 27.5%. This equals the ratio needed by Trader *B* and is an achievable target for a good trader. But the 35.0% rate needed by Trader *A* is a virtually unattainable 40.0% improvement over pure chance.

Figure 15-6 shows how the break-even percentage varies depending on the ratio between average profit and transaction costs. We have chosen a 3:1 profit/loss ratio for this illustration, but the shape of the curve would be similar for other ratios. Notice that the break-even ratio varies widely, approaching the expected 25% for large profits and rising steeply as the ratio falls below 5.0. (The problem with trading for very large multiples of transaction costs, say 60 or 80, is that few such opportunities arise.)

These simple money management guidelines should help speculators to trade more effectively. However, they cannot turn poor market analysis or judgment into profitable positions. Capital allocation is a vital ingredient in a successful futures trading program, but it is not the entire answer. It is a supplement to sound market analysis, not an alternative. A speculator who combines an ability to forecast prices with the use of these money management guidelines will have a very good chance of trading success.

■ Chapter 16

■ *Spreads and Spread Trading*

A *spread* is the simultaneous purchase and sale of different futures contracts in the same market or in related markets. In the parlance of the futures business the terms *spread, straddle,* and *switch* are synonymous. A spread trader establishes a position when he feels that the difference in the prices of the two contracts is out of line and expects that over time the spread relationship (the difference in price between the two) will change. To do this he buys the delivery month that appears underpriced and sells the delivery month that appears overpriced. The trader's profit or loss is determined by the subsequent change in the *relative* prices of the two contracts, not by changes in the *absolute* level of prices.

Spread trading can account for a surprisingly large share of both daily trading volume and open interest. The reasons for this are varied: Dealers often use spreads to shift their futures hedges from one delivery month to another; floor traders use spreads to liquidate positions that are acquired in various delivery months as a result of market-making activities; speculators use spreads to trade futures with less risk than is ordinarily associated with outright long or short positions.

This chapter discusses the reasons for trading spreads and also some reasons for not trading spreads. More importantly, it focuses on the factors that influence the price relationships of different futures contracts and on how these changing relationships can be a source of profit opportunity. Emphasis is on spread trading in traditional commodity futures. Spread trading in financial futures involves certain complexities and is covered in greater detail in the chapters on interest rate futures (Chapter 18), currency futures (Chapter 19), and stock index futures (Chapter 20).

THE BASICS

The spread trader is more concerned with the difference in the prices between the contract he is long (*long leg*) and the contract he is short (*short leg*) and less concerned with the overall direction of prices. Overall market-price movement is of little consequence to the spread trader, except to the extent that it has a predictable effect on spread relationships.

Example: On October 19 the price of March corn futures is 9 cents below that of the July delivery. For instance, suppose that March is $2.26$1/2$ and July is $2.35$1/2$. A trader feels that the March delivery is underpriced in relation to the July and expects the 9 cent difference between the two to narrow. In other words, the trader feels that the March delivery will rise at a more rapid rate than the July or that it will decline at a slower rate than the July.

To initiate his position, the spread trader buys 5,000 bushels of March corn and simultaneously sells 5,000 bushels of July corn.

Assume that after the spread position is established at a 9 cent difference, the price difference between the two contracts narrows to 4 cents by December 9. The trader liquidates both contracts simultaneously (often called *unwinding* the spread) and realizes a profit of 5 cents. Figure 16-1 on page 345 summarizes how the spread might be established and unwound.

Note that it is the *relationship* between the two prices, and not the prices themselves, that counts in spread trading. Although prices increased in the above example, a profit might just as well have been realized if the market had declined. For instance, if on December 9 prices had been $2.15$1/2$ for March and $2.19$1/2$ for July, the result would have been identical to that in the above example. Why? Because the spread difference on the day of unwinding would still have been 4 cents.

For this reason, spread traders pay little or no attention to the prices of the individual legs of their spreads. They are concerned only with

Figure 16-1. *A typical spread from the perspective of individual purchases & sales.*

	Establishing the Spread		
	Long Leg		**Short Leg**
October 19	Buys 5,000 March corn @$2.26½	-and-	Sells 5,000 July corn @$2.35½
	Unwinding the Spread		
December 9	Sells 5,000 March corn @$2.35	-and-	Buys 5,000 July corn @$2.39
	Profit +$.09		Loss –$.04
	Net Profit: +$.05 (=$250 per contract, less commissions)		

Figure 16-2. *A typical spread from the perspective of differentials.*

	Establishing the Spread
October 19	Bought 5,000 bushels of March corn/sold 5,000 bushels of July corn at a differential of 9 cents, July premium.
	Unwinding the Spread
December 9	Sold 5,000 bushels of March corn/bought 5,000 bushels of July corn at a differential of 4 cents, July premium.

price differentials. In the above example, the only relevant information is as shown in Figure 16-2.

Note that we added the expression *July premium* on both dates to the above descriptions to make clear that July was trading above March. In volatile markets it should not be assumed that a particular month is trading at a premium to another or that a market's price structure is *normal* rather than *inverted* (see Chapter 9 for a discussion of these terms). The results of the above spread would be quite different if, on December 9 the differential were 4 cents, *premium March*. Instead of a 5 cent profit, the result would have been a 13 cent profit.

One way of viewing spreads is from the perspective that all spread positions involve either the purchase or the sale of a premium month or contract. If the premium month is purchased (and the discounted month sold), the trader anticipates a widening of the spread between the two. If the premium month is sold (as was the case in the above example), the trader anticipates a narrowing of the spread between the two. This way of thinking about spread positions is especially convenient in markets whose price structures tend to reflect carrying charges. In such markets, (metals, grains, and other storable products) deferred deliveries normally are at a premium to nearby deliveries. Thus, selling the premium almost always entails buying the nearby month and selling the deferred, looking for a narrowing of the spread. Buying the premium tends to entail buying the distant delivery and selling the nearby.

The concept that all spread positions entail being long or short the premium can be helpful in some markets or market conditions but troublesome in others. This is particularly the case when the prices of the legs of a spread are so close to one another that one leg may vacillate between being at a premium to and a discount to the other leg. What does it mean to be long the premium when the role of the premium delivery may shift from one leg to another in a matter of days or even hours? Similar problems arise in markets whose price structure is neither normal nor inverted, but a combination of both. The 1970s and the 1980s are replete with examples of markets whose price structures shifted from inverted in the early deliveries to normal in the later ones. For these and other reasons, readers are cautioned against too casual a use of the conventions and terminology of the spread trade. These conventions can be inconsistent, confusing, and costly. In metals markets, *to buy a spread* means "to sell the nearby delivery and buy the deferred." In almost all other markets, however, *buying the spread* means "buying the nearby and selling the deferred." Extra care needs to be taken to be sure you understand exactly what spread positions you are referring to and what outcomes you expect from these positions.

ENTERING SPREAD ORDERS

Spread orders should be entered as spreads and not as two separate orders to buy and to sell. If the legs of a spread are not executed simultaneously, establishing the spread would create a naked long or short position, depending on which leg was executed first. Even a short time lag between execution of the legs of a spread exposes the trader to risk.

When a spread order is entered on a spread basis rather than as two separate buy and sell orders, it is executed as such on most trading floors. The floor broker who receives the order will not have to fill the two legs separately. In almost all trading pits today there exists a market for spreads as well as for outright orders. Floor traders will provide bids and offers for spreads as quickly as they will for single delivery months. In the gold ring on Comex, for instance, an order to buy five August gold/sell five December gold might encounter a quote of $6.20 bid/$6.30 asked. This means that traders are willing to buy December at $6.20 over August and sell it at $6.30 over August. Exactly how these quotes are arrived at is a function of a mix of market factors that include gold's price and direction, interest rates, and other technical forces. At any rate, the broker who executes the above order could simply hit the bid of $6.20 (that is, establish the spread for his client by selling the December at a $6.20 premium over the August), or he could wait and offer the spread at $6.30 (in the hope that his offer will be taken and the spread established at the more favorable $6.30 differential). The point that is worth emphasizing is that at no time is the client exposed to the costly risk of an outright long or short position. In fact, at no time during the execution of the spread are the prices of the individual long and short legs ever mentioned. Only after the spread is executed at an agreed-upon differential are prices assigned to each leg. In the above situation, the customer might be long five August gold at $342.50 and short five December gold at $348.70, if the order had been executed by simply hitting the $6.20 bid.

Contrast this with a situation where no market for spreads exists. Instead of asking for a quote in the August/December spread, the broker would have to ask for separate quotes in the August and December contracts. In all likelihood these quotes would run something like this: August—$342.30 bid/$342.50 asked, December—$348.50 bid/$348.80 asked. If the broker were to execute the order by buying five August gold at the offer of $342.50 and selling five December gold at the bid of $348.50, the customer would have the spread on at a differential of only $6.00. The spread market that is available in most trading rings provides for greater liquidity and reduced execution costs. Bear in mind that active spread markets exist only for spreads that involve two delivery months of a commodity or financial instrument, where both months are traded in the same pit. Spreads that involve different commodities (*intercommodity spreads*) such as T-bonds/T-bills, gold/silver, or hogs/

pork bellies require separate and usually more costly execution. The same is true for spreads involving the same instrument traded on different exchanges (*intermarket spreads*).

One word of caution: While most spread markets are liquid, some spreads involving distant or otherwise inactive deliveries can be dangerously thin. It is always a good idea either to check the open interest and volume of the months in question or better yet, to check with the floor broker executing the order. Insufficient liquidity can be extremely costly when unwinding a spread.

"Legging" Spreads. Although most spreads are and should be executed as spreads rather than as separate outrights, some traders do place their spread orders one leg at a time in the hope of initiating their position at a more favorable differential than prevailing spread quotes. Anticipating a rally, they may execute the buy leg first, planning to execute the sell leg after the market has moved up. This, of course, is sheer speculation and has little to do with spread trading. Likewise, unwinding a properly established spread by *lifting legs* (liquidating the spread one leg at a time) is equally speculative. Both approaches entail the usual risks of an outright long or short position. Another way that spreads are often *legged* is when a trader uses a spread to protect an outright position that has gone awry. He may be long in the active delivery month, say December, in a declining market. Rather than accept his loss, he sells a different delivery month, say March. This seldom accomplishes anything other than locking in the loss and generating additional transaction costs.

Legging spreads is inadvisable for several reasons:

1. If a trader is really interested in speculating on the relationship between two related futures contracts and not on the outright direction of the market, the spread market is the best way to establish and unwind positions. Spreads can almost always be established at more favorable differentials when executed as spreads rather than separate outrights.

2. When spreads are legged separately, one leg almost always involves the purchase or sale of a relatively illiquid month. The lack of activity in these relatively illiquid deliveries usually means that the opposite side of the trade will be taken by a professional floor trader whose bids and offers reflect his edge of profit and your edge of loss. Let's look further at the previous Comex gold example. Prevailing quotes are

as follows: August $342.30 bid/$342.50 asked; August/December spread $6.20 bid/6.30 asked. Let's assume that you have the long August leg of the spread on at $342.50 and that you now must sell the December leg. You ask for a quote in December. The professional floor trader knows, based on the spread quote, that he would like to buy December at a premium of $6.20 or less over the August. If he has to hit the August bid of $342.30 for himself, he will bid no more than $6.20 over that price for December or $348.50.

If the December delivery lacked competition that day, he might try to bid $348.40 or even $348.30. To establish his selling price for December the professional floor trader uses the prevailing spread quote of $6.20/$6.30 and the quote in August of $342.30 bid/$342.50 asked as follows: He wants to sell December at a premium of at least $6.30 over where he can buy the August ($342.50). Then his asking price might be $348.80 and could go as high as $349.00 depending on ring conditions. All this figuring takes place in a matter of seconds. The professional floor trader turns to your floor broker who has asked for a quote in December and shouts "December 8.30 bid, at 9.00." In other words, he will buy December at $348.30 and sell it at $349.00. If this is the best available quote in the ring your broker may try to offer your December at $348.50, but if the floor trader doesn't budge, your broker will have to hit the bid of $348.30. Let's see what happened. By legging the spread you are long August at $342.50 and short December at $348.30, a difference of $5.80. If instead of legging you had simply entered a spread order to buy August/sell December, the worst premium differential you would have received was $6.20.

3. The third reason that legging spreads is not advisable is that legging entails higher commission costs. Most brokerage firms have a commission rate for spreads that is higher than that for a single outright but much lower than that for two outrights. This commission factor can be extremely important, especially because spread-trading profits tend to be much smaller on a per-contract basis than are profits from outright long or short positions.

4. One last factor worth noting here is that, sometimes, spreads are legged by traders who think they can do better than prevailing spread quotes because the last prices on their quote machine shows the differential between two futures contracts to be much wider or narrower than indicated by the spread quote. Almost always the machine quotes are

misleading. The machine quote for the actively traded leg may be only two seconds old, but that for the less-active leg may be ten minutes old. Differentials that are implied by quotation machines can often be outdated and misleading. They should never be relied on for spread trading.

DEFINITIONS

There are three basic types of spreads:

1. *Intramarket Spread.* Also known as an *interdelivery spread*, it involves the purchase and sale of different delivery months of the same commodity or financial instrument. It is the most actively traded of the three spread types. Examples would be: (a) long October cotton/short December cotton, (b) short September 1988 T-bonds/long September 1989 T-bonds, (c) long December S&P/short March S&P.

2. *Intercommodity Spread.* This spread involves a long position in one commodity or financial instrument and a short position in a related commodity or financial instrument. Examples include: (a) long March corn/short March wheat, (b) short December Eurodollars/long December T-bills, (c) long September S&P/short September NYSE composite. Intercommodity spreads usually involve the purchase and the sale of the same delivery month in the two markets, but this is not always the case. Sometimes, traders will seek to take advantage of whatever delivery months appear over- or underpriced. Another factor that is worth keeping in mind is that the contract sizes of the two legs of an intercommodity spread are frequently unequal. A cattle/hog spread involves a 40,000-pound contract on one leg and a 30,000-pound contract on the other. Spreads of this type must be weighted to ensure that they are properly balanced. The procedures for balancing intercommodity spreads will be discussed later.

3. *Intermarket Spread.* This spread involves a long position in a commodity on one exchange and a short position in the same commodity on a different exchange. An example would be: long Comex silver/short CBOT silver. Other intermarket spreads involve markets in different countries. Examples include New York vs. London silver, or New York vs. Paris sugar. In these cases, currency fluctuations play a major role in the outcome of the spread and are often hedged separately. Other

types of intermarket spreads seek to take advantage of supply/demand considerations for the particular grades of the commodity that are deliverable at each exchange. An example of this type of spread would be long Chicago wheat/short Kansas City wheat. Usually these spreads involve the same delivery month in the two different markets.

Let us now discuss each category of spread in more detail.

INTRAMARKET SPREADS

In Chapter 9 we discussed the theory of carrying charges relating to cash/futures price spreads. The theory is equally applicable to spreads involving different delivery months of the same futures contract. That is, in most cases, near months will tend to rise faster than distant months in a bull market. In bear markets, near months tend to lose ground to distant delivery months.

To understand why this is so, remember from Chapter 9 that, when supplies are ample, the price of a commodity for future delivery will be approximately equal to the present cash price plus the amount it costs to carry the underlying item from the present to the month of future delivery. These costs, known as *carrying charges*, determine the premium of futures over cash. They also determine the normal premium of a distant futures delivery month over a nearby futures delivery month. In periods of ample or rising supply, prices of deferred deliveries will tend to widen out over those of nearby deliveries to reflect the full cost of carry. If distant deliveries were priced at a less-than-carrying-charge premium, buyers would simply buy those contracts and wait to take delivery rather than making purchases in the cash market and paying storage. This would continue until distant deliveries fully reflected the cost to carry the commodity. Thus, as a general rule, as supply/demand balances tip from bullish to bearish, nearby delivery months tend to lose ground to distant delivery months.

As supply/demand fundamentals become more bullish, however, buyers cannot afford to defer purchases to the cheapest futures delivery months. Scarce supplies cause buyers to bid aggressively to fill immediate needs. This tends to exert upward pressure on nearby deliveries relative to deferred ones. Thus, as a general rule, as supply/demand balances tip from bearish to bullish nearby delivery months tend to gain ground relative to distant delivery months.

Among the physical commodities for which this spread price be-havior normally applies are: soybeans, soybean oil, soybean meal, wheat, corn, oats, cotton, heating oil, gasoline, plywood, lumber, sug-ar, coffee, cocoa, orange juice, pork bellies, and copper. This list cov-ers most of the physical commodities. For these commodities, a bullish spread-trading strategy usually involves being long a near delivery and short a distant delivery. A bearish spread stance would normally involve a long position in a deferred delivery and a short position in a near delivery.

A few words of caution are necessary here:

- Interest rates themselves are a major factor in determining carrying charges. Therefore, sharp changes in rates can either exaggerate or mitigate expected spread movements.
- The spread-price behavior that is cited above usually works best during periods of transition in the supply/demand balance of the commodity. This is why we used the phrase "as supply/demand balances tip from bullish (bearish) to bearish (bullish). . . ." If supplies have been burdensome for some time and the market's price structure already reflects the full cost of carry, further price declines will bring about a narrowing rather than a widening of the premium of deferred over nearby deliveries because lower prices translate into lower financing charges. Conversely, in a bull mar-ket the premium of the nearest delivery month may already be enough to choke off demand for this delivery. A general price rise may have little or no effect on the spread.
- Some spreads, particularly those involving the spot month or those involving two different crop years, can be subject to technical, un-predictable, short-term influences.

Exceptions to the Rule

For most physical commodities, nearby deliveries lead the way up and down. Carrying-charge spreads tend to narrow in bull markets as the upward progress of the near month outpaces that of the distant month. In inverted markets (nearby deliveries are above deferred ones), the pace of the advance is also usually set by the nearby rather than the deferred.

There is, however, a small group of physical commodities whose spread-price behavior is precisely opposite that of the norm. In these markets, carrying-charge spreads tend to widen in bull markets and to narrow in bear markets. These markets include gold and silver. When prices rise in these two commodities, distant months usually gain relative to nearby contracts. When prices decline, they ordinarily lose relative to the nearby positions.

Given what we have learned it may seem odd that a bull market would see distant deliveries moving up at a more rapid pace than nearby deliveries. What about the competitive bidding for immediate supplies that tends to exert upward pressure on near deliveries? In gold and silver, a bull market is not usually brought about by a shortage of supply. Unlike soybeans, plywood, or heating oil, demand for the commodity does not result in its disappearance. A shortage of soybeans usually means that the commodity is being consumed at a rate that, if unchecked, will physically deplete the available supply. In gold, and to a lesser extent silver, demand is predominantly for investment and is nonconsumptive in nature. There is rarely a risk of actually depleting supply. Thus spread relationships tend to reflect carrying charges almost all of the time. The rising prices of a bull market have the effect of increasing carrying charges (the interest component of carrying charges rises as prices rise). This, in turn, widens the carrying-charge spreads.

There is another group of commodities that conforms neither to the norm nor to the inverse of the norm. In these commodities there is neither positive nor negative correlation between general-price movement and spread-price movement. These commodities tend to be nonstorable and include such items as hogs and cattle. The main reason for the absence of correlation between spreads and outright prices is that each delivery period has its own unique supply/demand fundamentals. Animals that are due to reach market weight at a certain time cannot be kept off the market for a significantly longer period of time. Animal physiology demands that marketings take place relatively quickly when animals reach optimum weight. For this reason, each time period has a separate supply situation that is determined by breeding and feeding decisions that are made months earlier. Cattle and hog futures often do not behave monolithically. Instead of having a general bull market in hogs, as we would in most storable commodities, we might have a bull market in some deliveries, a flat market in others, and a weak market in still others. The prices for each future delivery period will be a function of that particular month's supply/demand outlook and may only be minimally linked with the price fundamentals of the time periods that precede or follow it. Spread-trading strategies in these markets often are based on the trader's perception of the expected fundamentals for the particular time periods rather than on an overall forecast of bullishness or bearishness.

Strategies in Intramarket Spreads

There are four types of intramarket or interdelivery spreading situations:

- Buying a nearby delivery and selling a distant delivery in a normal market in anticipation of a narrowing of the spread difference. For most physical commodities, this position is taken when the price outlook is bullish and you do not expect a significant rise in interest rates. For gold and silver, this position is taken when the outlook is bearish and you do not expect a significant rise in interest rates. Spreads of this type are known as *limited-risk spreads* when the long nearby/short distant position is put on at levels that are close to full carry. A later example will illustrate this situation.

- Selling a nearby delivery and buying a distant one in a normal market in anticipation of a widening of the spread. This is a bearish trading strategy for most physical commodities and a bullish one for gold and silver.

- Buying a nearby delivery and selling a distant delivery in an inverted market (nearby deliveries are at a premium to deferred deliveries) in the hope of a further widening of the inversion. This strategy is followed when you expect an already bullish situation to become more bullish.

- Selling a nearby and buying a distant contract month in an inverted market in anticipation of either a narrowing of the inversion or possibly a return to a normal market structure. This strategy is usually employed by someone who expects a bearish shift in the supply/demand outlook.

We now consider examples of each of these four types of spreads.

Example 1: Buying the Nearby, Selling the Distant in a Normal Market.

The first example of this chapter, involving corn, illustrates this bullish trading strategy. We would like to take it one step further by describing a situation in which the risk of loss in this type of spread is very limited. Suppose that carrying charges for corn are 7¹/₄ cents per bushel per month. We know, therefore, that full carrying charges between the March and July deliveries are about 29 cents per bushel.

Assume that the prices of March and July are $2.25 and $2.52, respectively. This means that the July delivery is trading at a premium of 27 cents over the March delivery, or just 2 cents less than the full carrying charge. We know from Chapter 9 that the price of the distant contract cannot for long trade over the cash price by an amount that is greater than the cost of carry. Similarly, one futures delivery cannot trade at a premium over a more nearby delivery that is greater than the implied cost of carry between the two contract months. Thus, if carrying costs remain unchanged, July corn will not trade over March corn by more than 29 cents. Because, in our example, the July premium is already 27 cents, the most it could widen by is an additional 2 cents. Theoretically, the risk in a long March/short July position is 2 cents, while the profit potential is unlimited. This extremely favorable reward/risk ratio is the rationale for the limited-risk spread.

Some words of caution are in order regarding these limited-risk spreads:

- Be sure that you have correctly calculated carrying charges. Spreads may appear to be at or above full carry because of a miscalculation in one of the three components of carrying charges: interest, storage, or insurance.

- Remember that carrying charges can change. Limited-risk spreads have the potential to work only if carrying costs do not increase. If they increase, the spread will have a tendency to widen further. Rising interest rates and rising prices are the most common causes of increasing carrying costs.

- Spread relationships usually widen out to full-carry levels for a good reason. Supplies tend to be large relative to demand and seem likely to remain so. The odds are usually slim that the supply/demand balance will tighten enough to significantly narrow the spreads. So, while the profit potential (vis-a-vis the risk) of this spread trade is great, the chances that the potential will be realized are usually small. You must realistically weigh the size of the potential profit against its probability of occurrence.

The rationale underlying limited-risk spreads does not apply to markets that involve nonstorable or perishable commodities. Remember the process that keeps July corn from trading at a premium to March that is greater than carrying charges: Dealers would simply (a) buy March and sell July, (b) take delivery of March and carry the physical corn until July, and (c) deliver the corn against these short July positions in July. An automatic profit would result if July were sold at a premium over March that is greater than what it costs to carry the corn from March to July.

It is this selling of the distant and buying of the nearby by dealers that keeps the spread from widening beyond full carry. But what if we are dealing in a perishable commodity, such as cattle? Then there is no assurance that what we take delivery of in March will meet delivery standards in July. For this reason spreads in perishable commodities are not restrained by carrying charges and, theoretically at least, can widen to unlimited levels.

Example 2: Selling the Nearby, Buying the Distant in a Normal Market.

In the preceding example, the trader purchased the nearby delivery and sold the distant delivery when the nearby was at a discount to the distant. The opposite strategy—buying the distant and selling the nearby—is usually used with a bearish shift in the price forecast. Remember, however, that the profit potential of this spread is limited because the spread can widen no further than implied carrying charges.

Suppose that on October 19 you sell March and buy July soybean oil when the March is at a 48 point ($0.0048 per pound) discount to the July. You expect that supplies will remain burdensome and that spreads will widen out to full carry (assume this is 60 points) by mid-November. You put on a five-contract-spread position as follows:

Establishing the Spread on October 19:

Sell five contracts of March soybean oil ($17.52)/buy five contracts of July soybean oil ($18.00) at a differential of 48 points, premium July.

And if all goes according to plan,

Unwinding the Spread on November 15:

Buy five contracts of March soybean oil ($17.04)/sell five contracts of July soybean oil ($17.62) at a differential of 58 points.

The result is a profit of 10 points per contract, or $300 for the five-contract position.

Example 3: Buying the Nearby, Selling the Distant in an Inverted Market.

Assume that February heating oil is trading at a 2 cents per gallon (200 point) premium over March heating oil. Anticipating a further tightening of supplies due to unseasonably cold temperatures, a trader buys February and sells March. In other words, he expects the inversion of February over March to widen. Unfortunately, a prolonged wave of warm weather takes the pressure off supplies and causes a weakening of the nearby premium.

Establishing the Spread on December 15:

Buy February/sell March at a 200-point differential, premium February.

Unwinding the Spread on January 10:

Sell February/buy March at a 130-point differential, premium February.

Result: A loss of 70 points ($294) per contract.

Example 4: Selling the Nearby, Buying the Distant in an Inverted Market.

Due to a tight supply situation, July cotton is trading at a 150 point (1.50 cent per pound) premium to December. Anticipating a sharp drop in textile mill consumption due to the higher prices, one might sell July and buy December. Any easing of the supply tightness will have the effect of pushing the spreads toward a normal price structure and away from an inverted price structure.

Establishing the Spread on May 15:

Buy 10 December (36.30¢)/sell 10 July (37.80¢) at 150 points, premium July.

Six weeks later, a combination of reduced current demand and a bullish new crop report (which has the effect of bolstering the price of the December delivery) brings about a normalization of spread relationships. The December delivery rises while the July declines.

Unwinding the Spread on June 27:

Sell 10 December (37.05¢)/buy 10 July (36.80¢) at a differential of 25 points, premium December.
Result: A profit of 175 points ($875) per contract, or $8,750.

Intercrop Spreads

Example 4 above illustrates a trade known as an *intercrop spread.* All field crops and some livestock products have statistical crop years that separate one year's production from the next. For field crops such as cotton, the new crop year begins with the first delivery month in which newly harvested supplies are available in size. For cotton this is the October delivery. All delivery months before October are considered *old crop*, and all delivery months from October on are considered *new crop*. Intercrop spreads can be volatile and dangerous. Very often, contract months of different crop years can behave like different commodities. In some cases, like pork bellies, spreads do not even have carrying charge limits because supplies of one crop year cannot be delivered against the contracts of a new crop year. Extra care should always be exercised when trading spreads of this type.

Butterfly Spreads

A *butterfly spread* is really two spreads that involve either three or four delivery months of the same commodity. One spread involves being long nearby/short deferred and the other involves being short nearby/long deferred. An example would be long one August 1988 gold/ short one October 1988 gold, and short one December 1988 gold/long one February 1989 gold. In this case the trader is short the premium in the nearby spread and long the premium in the more distant spread. Butterfly spreads can involve only three contract months if the middle month serves as the short (long) leg of each spread. An example would be long one August 1988 gold/short two October 1988 gold/long one

December 1988 gold (this is the same as long one August 1988/short one October 1988, and short one October 1988/long one December 1988).

Butterflies are really "spreads of spreads"; that is, they are an offsetting combination of two intracommodity spreads. As such they contain less profit potential and less risk than ordinary spreads and much less than outright positions. Because each butterfly involves so many transactions, commission costs are very high relative to the limited profit potential. For this reason, butterflies are mostly an activity of the member or professional trader who enjoys low transaction costs.

Cash-and-Carry Spreads

In the gold and silver markets, deferred months are almost always at a premium to nearby months for the reasons that were outlined earlier. Because the storage and insurance components of carrying charges in these markets are very small, the major factor in the spread premium is interest rates. One can, in effect, lend money to and borrow money from the gold market. For example, suppose that June gold is $360.50 and August gold is $364.00. The $3.50 differential approximately equates to a 6% return on a $360.50 investment for the two month period from June 1 to August 1. A holder of cash could lock in this yield by buying June gold at $360.50 and simultaneously selling August gold at $364.00. He would then take delivery of gold on or about June 1 (paying $360.50 per ounce per contract), carry it for two months, and then redeliver against the short position on August 1 (receiving $364.00 per ounce per contract). This operation is known as a *cash and carry* and is equivalent to lending money to the gold market at 6%.

A dealer who has an inventory of gold could do the opposite by, for example, selling June gold and buying August gold. He would deliver his gold against the short June position and receive $360.50 that he could use for three months. On August 1 he would receive gold back by taking delivery in futures, paying $364.00. This operation is a *reverse cash and carry* and is equivalent to borrowing money from the gold market. Because cash and carries and reverse cash and carries involve making and taking delivery, they are tools of dealers who have the wherewithal to effect such deliveries. Few speculators become involved in these operations.

INTERCOMMODITY SPREADS

The prices of commodities that have similar uses bear a relationship to each other. For instance, because corn and oats are somewhat interchangeable animal feeds, their respective prices should reflect this relationship. When corn prices are higher than oats prices on a feed-value basis, the use of corn in livestock feeding tends to slacken and the use of oats tends to increase. This shift in utilization causes the price of oats to gain on the price of corn until a normal price relationship is reestablished.

> *Example:* A bushel of oats weighs 32 pounds, whereas a bushel of corn weighs 56 pounds. Therefore, on a weight basis, a bushel of oats should be worth approximately 57% of the value of a bushel of corn. However, the feeding value of oats per pound is about 3% better than that of corn. Consequently, the price of oats is normally about 60% of the price of corn on a bushel basis. Therefore, when the price of oats is 60 cents per bushel, the price of corn should be about $1 per bushel.

The spread between oats and corn is usually at its widest during the July–August period as the pressure from the oat harvest causes oat prices to decline, relative to corn prices. Corn prices, on the other hand, need not necessarily decline in conjunction with oats because the corn harvest does not begin until October. Corn prices might actually show a divergent tendency during July–August because bad-weather scares could bolster prices of the growing corn crop. Hence, oat prices during the summer months are usually low relative to the price of corn, sometimes declining to less than 50% of the value of corn, a situation that can offer attractive spreading opportunities. The purchase of December oats and the sale of December corn during the oats-harvest period (July–August) is often a popular spread.

As time passes and autumn approaches, oat prices usually begin to firm up as the pressure from the harvest movement of oats abates. Corn prices usually begin to lose ground to oat prices as the harvest period for corn gets underway (October–December). As the price relationship between oats and corn becomes more normal, you take profits on the spread by selling December oats and buying December corn.

COMMODITY/PRODUCTS SPREADS

Another type of intercommodity spread involves the price relationship between a raw material and its products. For example, soybeans
are not used much in their natural state. Rather, they are crushed into
two products—soybean oil and soybean meal. The oil is an edible vege-
table oil that is used in shortening, margarines, and salad oils. The meal
is a high-protein livestock feed. While soybean prices are closely related
to those of their products, soybean oil and meal prices are each affected
by influences within their own spheres—not necessarily by factors that
affect either of the others. The price movements of soybeans, soybean
meal, and soybean oil all tend to parallel each other. Nonetheless, the
values of the products widen or narrow in relationship to soybeans from
time to time.

The relationship between the price of beans and the value of its oil
and meal is called the *gross processing margin* or the *gross crushing
margin*. When you crush soybeans, you get oil and meal. A bushel of
soybeans weighs 60 pounds and yields approximately 11 pounds of oil
and 48 pounds of meal; about 1 pound is moisture and waste that is lost
in processing. Calculating the gross processing margin is made difficult
because soybean prices are quoted one way and its products are quoted
in other ways. Soybeans are quoted in dollars and cents per bushel,
soybean oil is quoted in cents and fractions of a cent per pound, and
soybean meal is quoted in dollars and cents per ton. All three quotations
must be converted to one common denominator for comparison. The
normal procedure is to convert oil and meal prices to soybean prices on
a per-bushel basis.

To calculate the gross processing margin, determine the dollar value of both the soybean oil and soybean meal that are obtained from a bushel of soybeans; then compare the combined value of the products to
the price of soybeans.

1. *The value of the oil*: Multiply the price of soybean oil by 11; this
   factor is the approximate number of pounds of soybean oil that a
   60 pound bushel of soybeans yields when crushed.

2. *The value of the meal*: Multiply the price of soybean meal by 48,
   which is the approximate number of pounds of meal that a bushel
   of soybeans yields. Then divide the answer by 2,000 (pounds per
   ton) to put it on a comparable basis with soybean oil. Because

meal is quoted on a dollars-and-cents basis per ton and soybean oil is quoted per pound, this step gives you the dollar value of 48 pounds of soybean meal that is obtained from a bushel of soybeans.

A simpler and faster method of calculating the dollar value of soybean meal that is obtained from a bushel of soybeans is to multiply the price of soybean meal by 0.024. This one-step calculation produces the same results as dividing the price of meal by 2,000 and then multiplying the result by 48.

3. *The composite value*: The dollar value of oil is then added to the dollar value of meal, which gives you the combined value of the products that are obtained from a bushel of soybeans.

The combined value of the products is then compared to the price of soybeans. If the combined value of the products is larger than the price of soybeans, the gross processing margin is *plus*, or *positive*. If the combined value of the products is less than the price of soybeans, the gross processing margin is *minus*, or *negative*.

Example: The price of March soybean oil is 21 cents per pound, the price of March soybean meal is $161.00 per ton, and the price of March soybeans is $6.03 per bushel.

To determine the gross crushing margin, multiply the 21 cents by 11, the number of pounds of oil that a bushel of soybeans yields when crushed. This gives you the dollar value of the oil, which is $2.31. Next, multiply the price of soybean meal, $161, by 0.024; this gives you the dollar value of the meal, which is $3.86. Then the dollar values of the oil and meal are added together, giving a combined value of the products of $6.17 per bushel of beans.

This figure is then compared to the price of March soybeans, which is $6.03 per bushel. Because the combined value of the products ($6.17) is higher than the price of soybeans ($6.03), the gross processing margin is a positive 14 cents. If you buy soybeans at $6.03 and you sell the oil that is produced from the beans at 21 cents per pound and the meal at $161 per ton, the gross profit will be 14 cents per bushel. If the total value of the products were less than the price of soybeans, you would lose, not profit.

	Price Per Bushel
1. Oil: 21¢ x 11	$2.31
2. Meal: $161 x 0.024	3.86
3. Combined value of products	6.17
4. Price of soybeans	6.03
5. Gross crushing margin	$0.14

If the gross crushing margin is a positive number, as in this example, and you feel that the value of the products will decline relative to the price of the commodity, buy the soybean futures and sell the product futures. This type of transaction is called a *crush spread.* If the gross crushing margin narrows as you anticipate, and you decide to liquidate the spread, you will realize a profit on the transaction.

Example: The price of soybean oil in the original example advances from 21 to 22 cents per pound, the price of soybean meal advances from $161 to $166 per ton, and the price of soybeans advances from $6.03 to $6.32 per bushel. The relative values are as follows:

	Price Per Bushel
1. Oil: 22¢ x 11	$2.42
2. Meal: $166 x 0.024	3.98
3. Combined value of products	6.40
4. Price of soybeans	6.32
5. Gross crushing margin	+ $.08

Although the prices of all three commodities advance, the price of soybeans advances more than the combined values of the oil and the meal. The price of soybeans advances 29 cents per bushel ($6.32 – $6.03 = $0.29), whereas the equivalent dollar value of oil and meal advances only 23 cents per bushel ($6.40 – $6.17 = $0.23). Thus, you realize a profit of 6 cents per bushel ($0.29 – $0.23 = $0.06). The commodity that you were long (soybeans) gained relative to the products (soybean oil and soybean meal) that you were short, resulting in a narrowing of the spread difference.

If you think that the value of the products will gain relative to the soybeans, buy the product futures and sell the soybean futures. This transaction is referred to as a *reverse crush spread*. Even though the price of the soybeans is already lower than the combined prices of the products, you expect it to decline farther in relation to the products. In other words, you anticipate an improvement in the gross crushing margin.

> *Example:* The gross crushing margin is plus 14 cents, and you believe that the margin will widen. You therefore buy the oil and the meal and sell the beans. Your judgment is correct, and the gross margin widens from 14 to 22 cents. In other words, the combined value of the products gains 8 cents relative to the price of soybeans. So you decide to liquidate the spread and take profits. Even though all three commodities advance in price, the combined value of the products advances 23 cents per bushel, whereas the value of soybeans advances only 15 cents per bushel. Thus, you realize a profit of 8 cents per bushel.

	Price Per Bushel		Profit
1. Oil: 22¢ x 11	$2.42	Increase in products	$ .23
2. Meal: $166.00 x 0.024	3.98	Increase in commodity	.15
3. Combined value of products	6.40	Net gain	$ .08
4. Price of soybeans	6.18		
5. Gross crushing margin	+ $ .22		

The value of the commodities you were long (oil and meal) gained relative to the value of the commodity you were short (soybeans). This results in a widening of the spread difference. If prices had declined, the results would have been the same as long as the soybeans declined more than the combined value of the products.

Figuring the gross crushing margins gives you a rough idea of the profitability or unprofitability of a particular spread transaction, but you should not rely on the calculations alone for precise results. When the spread is done on a one-to-one basis, the dollar gain or loss is somewhat different than the dollar gain or loss that is based on the cents per bushel of actual crushing margin profit or loss. The method that is used in the examples is based on the assumption that when a contract of soybeans (5,000 bushels) is crushed, it yields a contract of soybean oil (60,000 pounds) and a contract of soybean meal (100 tons).

Actual yields, however, are somewhat less. When you crush one contract of soybeans, it does not yield exactly one contract of soybean oil, 60,000 pounds. It yields only 55,000 pounds of oil (5,000 bushels x 11 = 55,000 pounds of oil), which is less than one full contract. Similarly, when you crush one contract of soybeans, it does not yield exactly one contract of soybean meal (100 tons), but rather 120 tons (5,000 bushels x 48 = 240,000 pounds, or 120 tons), which is more than a contract of meal. Consequently, the cents-per-bushel method of figuring a profit or a loss is a little distorted as a result of this imbalance between actual product yields and product contract sizes.

Figure the profit on the preceding example both ways: by the long and correct way and by the cents-per-bushel methods for comparison.

Example: You originally sell soybeans at $6.03 per bushel and buy soybean oil at 21 cents per pound and soybean meal at $161 per ton. You buy the soybean contract back at $6.18 per bushel for a loss of 15 cents per bushel, or $750 per contract. On the other hand, you sell the oil at 22 cents for a 1 cent per pound profit, or the dollar equivalent of $600 per contract. Also, you sell the soybean meal at $166 for a ton profit or the dollar equivalent of $500 per contract.

The profits of $600 on the oil and $500 on the meal combined with the $750 loss on the beans result in an overall profit of $350.

Balancing Intercommodity Spreads

The following are among the most common intercommodity spreads in the nonfinancial markets:

corn vs. oats	hogs vs. cattle
corn vs. wheat	hogs vs. pork bellies
corn vs. soybeans	gold vs. silver
corn vs. hogs	gold vs. platinum
soybeans vs. oil and meal	crude oil vs. gasoline

Before entering into any of these spreads, it is essential that a trader understand his objectives. We may feel that cattle will gain in price relative to hogs, but what exactly do we mean? Will cattle gain on an absolute, 1 cent per pound basis, or will it gain on a percentage basis? Do we simply buy one contract of cattle for every hog contract we sell? These questions must be answered and positions need to be properly balanced in order to take advantage of spreading opportunities between different items.

The first and most obvious step in balancing an intercommodity spread position is to offset the effect of different contract sizes. We do this because the same absolute price move will produce a smaller profit or loss in a commodity that has a small contract size than it will in one that has a larger contract. If we are long one June cattle, short one June hog, and both decline by 5 cents per pound, we will lose more on our long cattle position than we will gain on our short hog position. Why? Because the cattle contract is 40,000 pounds and the hog contract is 30,000 pounds. We can offset this effect simply by selling four contracts of hogs for every three contracts of cattle that we buy. In the hog/pork-belly spread (hog contract = 30,000 lb./pork-belly contract = 38,000 lb.), a reasonably good balance would require five contracts of hogs for every four contracts of bellies.

For commodities that are relatively close in price, this balancing of contract sizes is usually enough. But what about commodities whose prices are significantly different, such as gold vs. silver? Or what about commodities that are not quoted in the same terms, such as corn and hogs? It makes no sense to balance a gold/silver spread by balancing contract sizes. With the gold contract of 100 ounces and the silver contract of 5,000 ounces, this would require 50 gold for every one silver. Instead of a balanced spread, we have a formula for possible financial disaster.

To properly balance intercommodity spreads therefore, we must take into consideration differences in both contract size and price. The best way to do this is to calculate the ratio of the contract *values* of the two commodities, and then to use this ratio to weight the lower valued contract.

Example 1: If December gold is $370.00 per ounce and December silver is $6.20 per ounce, how many contracts of each would a properly balanced spread entail?

Value of gold contract = $370 per ounce x 100 ounces
= $37,000

Value of silver contract = $6.20 per ounce x 5,000 ounces
= $31,000

$$\frac{\$37,000}{\$31,000} = 1.19 \text{ contracts of silver for every contract of gold}$$

Example 2: February pork bellies are 79.00 cents per pound and February hogs are 60.00 cents per pound. How many contracts of hogs would balance a contract of bellies?

Value of pork belly contract = 79.00 cents per pound x 38,000 pounds
= $30,020
Value of hog contract = 60.00 cents per pound x 30,000 pounds
= $18,000

$$\frac{\$30,020}{\$18,000} = 1.67 \text{ contracts}$$

A balanced spread would involve 1.67 hog contracts for every belly contract (or 5 contracts of hogs for every 3 contracts of bellies).

Example 3: The same method can be used for commodities that are quoted in unlike terms, such as hogs and corn. If we feel that the hog/corn ratio is likely to decline, we would sell X contracts of hogs for every contract of corn we buy. To determine X, we use the formula.

$$X = \frac{\text{Contract-value of hogs}}{\text{Contract-value of corn}}$$

It is important to point out that in all these examples the spread positions are calculated to take advantage of *percentage changes in the price of one commodity versus percentage changes in the price of the other commodity.* This is the only way that intercommodity spreads can be properly implemented and effectively managed.

Summary of General Rules of Spread Behavior for Physical Commodities

I. *Storable commodities that are consumed*: (e.g. corn, cotton, heating oil, lumber, plywood, oats, orange juice, soybeans, wheat).

Expectation	*Probable Behavior of Futures*
1. Rising prices	1. Nearby contracts rise relative to distant contracts. No theoretical limit to premium of nearbys over deferreds.
2. Falling prices	2. Nearby contracts fall relative to distant contracts. The premium of a deferred contract over a nearby contract is limited by carrying costs.
3. Rising (falling) interest rates	3. Forward contracts gain on (lose to) nearby contracts.

II. *Storable physical commodities held as investments* (e.g. gold, silver, platinum).

Expectation	*Probable Behavior of Futures*
1. Rising prices	1. Distant contracts rise relative to nearby contracts. The premium of a deferred contract over a nearby contract is limited by carrying costs.
2. Falling prices	2. Distant contracts fall relative to nearby contracts.
3. Rising (falling) interest rates	3. Increase (decrease) in the premium commanded by distant contracts.

III. *Non-storable physical commodities*: (e.g. cattle, hogs).

Expectation	*Probable Behavior of Futures*
1. Rising (falling) prices	1. No predictable relationship between nearby and deferred contracts.
2. Rising (falling) interest rates	2. Distant contracts tend to gain on (lose to) nearby contracts.

Spread trading in financial markets is discussed in Chapter 18 on interest rate futures, Chapter 19 on currency futures, and Chapter 20 on stock index futures.

■ Chapter 17
■ Technical Analysis*

Fundamental analysis, as discussed in Chapter 14, focuses on the supply-and-demand factors that underlie price movements. In farm product futures, for example, the fundamentalist considers the effect of such things as bumper crops and blights. In financial futures, the concern might be for the current level of interest rates or trade deficits. The fundamental approach is therefore said to study the *causes* of price movements.

By contrast, technical analysis studies the *effects* of supply and demand—that is, the price movements themselves. In fact, technical analysis is also called *charting* because it is essentially the charting of actual price changes as they occur. The charting approach reflects the basic assumption of the technician that all influences on market action—from natural catastrophes to trading psychology—are automatically accounted for or *discounted* in price activity.

Given this premise, charting can be used for at least three purposes:

1. *Price Forecasting:* The technician can project price movements either in tandem with a fundamental approach or solely on the basis of charted movements.

---

*This chapter has been drawn almost exclusively from John J. Murphy's *Technical Analysis of the Futures Markets* (New York Institute of Finance, 1986), a comprehensive reference source on the subject.

2. *Market Timing:* Chart analysis is much better suited than the fundamental approach for determining exactly when to enter and exit a position.

3. *Leading Indicator:* If market action discounts all the influences on it, then price movement may be considered as a leading indicator, and it may be used in two ways. First, the chartist may—without regard for why prices are moving in one direction or the other— open or close a position. Second, an unusual price movement can be taken as a signal that some influence or another on the market has not been accounted for in the fundamentalist's analysis and that further study is required.

ELEMENTS OF THE BAR CHART

Most technicians use two working assumptions: (1) markets move in trends, and (2) trends persist. Identifying the trend at an early enough stage enables the trader to take the appropriate positions. The tool used to track price movements and thus to identify trends is the chart.

Two basic types of charts are available to the technician: the bar chart (see Figure 17-1 on page 395) and the point-and-figure chart (see Figure 17-2 on page 395). Note that the point-and-figure (P & F) chart does not indicate time or trading volume. Of the two, the bar chart is the one much more widely used in the futures markets. Although weekly, monthly, and even annual bar charts are used in specialized applications (see Figures 17-3 and 17-4 on page 396), the daily bar chart is by far the one most familiar to the futures trader.

Price Movement

Constructing a bar chart is simple. At the top of the chart enter the name of the contract. To the vertical axis, assign a price scale. On the horizontal axis, mark off the calendar time scale—days, weeks, or months. On a daily bar chart, every five-day period (a trading week) is usually marked by a vertical line that is heavier than the others. For each day, the high, the low, and the closing (or settlement) prices are plotted. (See Figure 17-5 on page 397.) A vertical line, or *bar*, connects the high and the low prices. A horizontal tic to the right of the bar indicates the closing price. (A tic on the left side of the bar marks the opening price for the day.) With so many chart services available, however, plotting one's own charts is often an unnecessary and unprofitable way to spend time.

Volume and Open Interest

The bar chart may also reflect volume and open interest. The *volume* for each day is recorded by a vertical bar under the day's price bar, at the base of the chart. *Open interest* is tracked by means of a straight line, also at the bottom of the chart, that connects each day's open interest. Open interest and volume figures generally include all contracts in the underlying commodity or financial instrument, not just the delivery month being charted. Because exchanges need a day to total and release volume and open interest figures, there is a one-day delay when plotting these figures. As a result, each volume bar on a chart reflects the *previous day's* volume, not the volume on the same day as that of the price bar.

TRENDS AND TRENDLINES

A *trend* is a series of price changes that collectively move in one direction or another. An *uptrend* is a series of peaks and troughs that rises on average (see Figure 17-6 on page 398). A *downtrend* is a series that declines (see Figure 17-7 on page 398). A series of price fluctuations that neither rises nor falls is *trendless,* and the market is said to be moving *sideways* or *horizontally* (see Figure 17-8 on page 398).

Trends are commonly classified according to their duration:

- *Major* trends continue in the same direction for more than six months.
- *Secondary* trends last for one to three months.
- *Minor* trends persist for a few weeks or less.

On a bar chart, a trend is identified by drawing a *trendline,* which is a straight line that connects two or more successive high or low points in a series of price movements. An *uptrendline,* which rises from left to right, connects two or more low points so that all of the price activity is above the line (see Figure 17-9 on page 399). A *downtrendline,* declining from left to right, connects two or more high points so as to keep all the movements below the line (see Figure 17-10 on page 399).

Although either type of trendline can be drawn using only two points, at least one more point is needed to validate the trendline.

Channel Lines

Sometimes prices trend within a clearcut range between the main trendline and another parallel line, called a *channel* or *return* line. In an uptrend, the channel runs above the price activity and parallel to the uptrendline (see Figure 17-11 on page 400). In a declining market, the channel runs below the price activity and parallel to the downtrendline (see Figure 17-10 on page 399).

The identification of both a trendline and channel is a potentially profitable piece of information. With it, the technician has advance notice of turning points in market price. In Figure 17-9, for example, points 1, 3, and 5 would represent good buying prices, while points 2 and 4 are good selling levels. Even when prices move outside the channel, the chartist can profit, because once a breakout occurs, prices typically travel a distance equal to the width of the channel. Once a breakout occurs, the chart user can measure the width of the channel and project that distance from the point of the breakout to calculate a buying or selling point. In Figure 17-12 (see page 400), after a breakout at point 5, prices are likely to move to point 6 before changing direction.

Trendlines and channel lines are two of the technician's simplest tools.

Retracement

In the course of any trend, prices will *countertrend*: that is, they move back against a portion of the current trend before resuming the original direction. These temporary countertrends, called *retracements,* fall into three categories: 33%, 50%, and 66% (see Figure 17-14 on page 401).

What this means to the chartist is that a minimum retracement is *about* 33%, and the maximum is *about* 66%. Faced with a retracement in a strong trend, the analyst may look for a return to the original trend somewhere after 33% and before 50%. Should the countertrend move beyond 66%, the odds shift in favor of a trend reversal.

Key-Reversal Day

Any day on which the market reverses is a potential *key-reversal day*, also known as a *top/bottom reversal day* or *buying-selling climax* (see Figures 17-15 and 17-16 on page 402). When does a reversal day become key? In an uptrend, a *top reversal* is a day on which a new high is established but the market closes lower than on the day before. In a *bottom reversal*, a new low in the downtrend is set but the market closes higher than on the prior day. In either case, volume is usually heavy. Also, if the high and low on the reversal day exceeds the range of the previous day and thereby forms what is known as an outside day, the reversal carries more weight. In many cases, however, a true key-reversal day cannot be positively identified until long after prices have moved significantly past it.

Two-Day Reversal

Sometimes, a reversal takes two days to form and is called, appropriately, a *two-day reversal*. In an uptrend, on day one a new high is set and the close is near the high; on day two, the market opens near day one's high but closes near the bottom of the two-day trading range (see Figure 17-17 on page 403). The reverse formation occurs in a downtrend (see Figure 17-18 on page 403). In both cases, the wider the swings during the two days and the heavier the volume, the more likely a reversal becomes.

Price Gaps

A *gap* is an area on a bar chart where no trading takes place. In an uptrend, the present day's low is higher than the previous day's high. The converse applies in a downtrend (see Figures 17-19 and 17-20 on page 404).

This definition of a gap pertains, of course, to daily (or inter-day) bar charts. Anyone who has access to *intraday* charts, such as a five-minute bar chart, will be able to see gaps that are "hidden" in a daily chart's single bar for the whole day's trading. What follows applies to intraday, as well as to interday, gaps.

There are four general types of gaps:

1. The *common gap*, the least important in charting, occurs in thinly traded markets or in the middle of horizontal trading ranges. Generally ignored by technicians, it reflects merely a lack of trading interest.

2. The *breakaway gap* usually occurs at the completion of an important price pattern on heavy volume and may signal the start of a significant market move. This gap is generally not completely filled by trading on ensuing days. In fact, the upper side of the gap often acts as a support level for subsequent trading. *(Support* is explained in the next section.) (See Figure 17-21 on page 405.)

3. A *runaway gap* occurs on moderate volume, with the market trending effortlessly. It is a sign of strength in an uptrend but one of weakness in a downtrend. A move below a runaway gap in a uptrend is a negative sign. Like the breakaway, this type of gap is usually not filled.

   This formation is also called a *measuring gap* because it commonly occurs about halfway through a trend. The distance from the beginning of the trend to the gap is the probable extent of the trend from the gap to its completion.

4. The *exhaustion gap* appears near the end of a market move, after all objectives have been achieved and after breakaway and runaway gaps have been identified. It is the "last gap," so to speak, of the trend. When prices close under the last gap, the chartist can be quite sure that the exhaustion gap has made its appearance.

Island Reversal

When a trend reverses sharply, with gaps preceding and following the reversal period, the few days' or weeks' worth of price action between the gaps is referred to as an "island." (See Figure 17-21.) The significance of such a formation arises from the two gaps, not from the activity within the island itself. While the exhaustion gap signals that the trend is sputtering, the breakaway gap after the island presages a major move in the opposite direction.

Resistance and Support

Prices change direction for many reasons, not all of which can be identified, much less foreseen. Perhaps the greatest influence on price behavior, however, consists of the expectations and desires of the market participants, who fall into three basis categories:

1. The longs.
2. The shorts.
3. The uncommitted.

Any of these types of participants can affect price movements. For example, with prices in an uptrend, the longs are delighted but wish they had bought more. The shorts are coming to the conclusion that they were wrong and would like to get out without losing too much. Of the uncommitted group, some never opened a position but wish they had, and others liquidated positions and wish they had not. All four of these groups are watching the market for a dip. If prices break downward, they are all liable to become buyers, that is, "buy the dip." As a result, should prices begin to drop for any reason, these would-be buyers respond by buying, thereby creating demand and forcing prices up again.

When declining prices meet with such demand and bounce back, they are said to have hit *support*. The price dip as plotted on the chart is known as a *trough* or *reaction low*. *Support* is therefore a level or area below the market where buying interest is strong enough to overcome selling pressure.

Resistance is the opposite of support. It is a level or area, above the market, at which selling pressure overcomes buying interest. In this case, the market is trending downward. The longs are looking for a chance to sell, while the shorts are waiting for the opportunity to increase the size of their positions. The uncommitted are likely to go short. Should the market turn upward, all these participants are primed to sell, thereby creating supply and eventually causing prices to turn downward again. (The upturn and drop in prices, once charted, are referred to as *peak* or *reaction high*.)

Support and resistance often reverse their roles once they are significantly penetrated by price movements. Penetrated by upward movements, resistance becomes support (see Figure 17-22 on page 406). Support, after being penetrated, becomes resistance (see Figure 17-23 on page 406). What constitutes "significant" penetration, however, is arguable. Some chartists say 10%, others, 3 to 5%. In practice, each technician must set an individual criterion for a "significant" penetration.

PRICE PATTERNS

In addition to trendlines and channel lines, technicians are able to identify a number of *price patterns*. These are price movements that, when charted, describe a predictable pattern. Some price patterns indicate a trend reversal, and they are therefore called *reversal patterns*. Others, called *continuation patterns,* reflect pauses or temporary reverses in an existing trend and usually form more quickly than reversal patterns.

Reversal Patterns

Head and Shoulders. Perhaps the best known of reversal patterns, the head and shoulders has three clear peaks, with the middle peak (or *head*) higher than the ones before and after it (the *shoulders*). (See Figure 17-24 on page 407.) The *neckline* is the trendline drawn to connect the two troughs between the peaks. A close below the neckline signals the completion of the pattern and an important market reversal. A breakaway gap at the point of penetration through the neckline lends weight to the probability that a true reversal has taken place. The minimum extent of the reversal can be estimated. To do so, measure the distance from the head to the neckline and project the same distance from the breakthrough point in the neckline (*F* in the figure). A return move (*F-G*) is likely, but it generally does not penetrate the neckline.

Inverse Head and Shoulders. Picture the head-and-shoulders pattern upside down. Instead of an uptrendline, this pattern occurs during a downtrend. The same principles apply here as to the head-and-shoulders pattern (see Figure 17-25 on page 407).

Complex Head-and-Shoulders Pattern. In this pattern, two heads form on either shoulder. Remember that this pattern tends to be symmetrical: that is, a single left shoulder probably means a single right shoulder, and a double left shoulder increases the likelihood of a double right shoulder.

Failed Head and Shoulders. Sometimes the penetration of the neckline turns out to be a bad signal, that is, prices resume the original trend. When this happens on occasion, the trader usually has to cut losses and get out of the market.

Triple Tops/Bottoms. Picture a head-and-shoulders pattern with "three heads." In this rare pattern, prices repeatedly deflect off resistance and support levels before reversing trend. (See Figures 17-26 and 17-27 on page 408.) The head-and-shoulders measuring principle applies to this pattern also.

Double Tops/Bottoms. Almost as common as the head-and-shoulders pattern, these patterns resemble an *M* (top) or a *W* (bottom). In Figure 17-28 (see page 409), the double top is in the making when prices fail (at point *C*) to penetrate the previous high (point *A*). The reversal is not complete, however, until prices break through point *B's* level (see also Figure 17-29 on page 409.)

There are two ways to measure the minimum extent of the reversal. Once again, the height of the pattern can be used, as in the head-and-shoulders pattern. Alternatively, the downward leg *A-B* can be extended by its own length below the level of point *B*.

Saucers. There are many other names for this pattern. In an uptrend, the pattern may be referred to as an *inverted saucer* or *rounding top*. During a downtrend, it can be a *rounding bottom* or *bowl*. (See Figures 17-30 and 17-31 on page 410.) Regardless of its name, the pattern consists of a gradual turning of the trend on diminishing volume.

No precise measurement can be made of the extent of the reversal by means of a saucer. The duration and size of the prior trend have some bearing on the new trend, as does the time the saucer takes to form. Other criteria are the previous support and resistance levels, gaps, long-term trendlines, and so on.

Spike. Also called a *V formation,* this pattern occurs too abruptly for it to be of use to the chartist. If it can be foreseen at all, the technician needs almost a "sixth sense." Perhaps the only concrete indications of such reversal are:

- A steeply rising or declining market. Such a runaway market tends to "snap back," almost like a rubber band that has been stretched too far. (See Figures 17-32 and 17-33 on page 411.)

- Exhaustion gaps.

- A key-reversal day or island reversal on heavy volume.

Peculiar to some spikes is the formation on declining volume of a platform, slightly against the new trend and to the right of the trend reversal (see points *A-D* in Figure 17-34 on page 412). The platform is considered completed when prices clear its lower range (point *D*). On rare occasions, the platform appears to the left of the spike (see points *A-D* in Figure 17-35 on page 412). There is little value to the chartist in this pattern except that the previous reaction low, once penetrated at point *E*, indicates that the reversal is completed.

Continuation Patterns

As we know, continuation patterns represent not reversals in the making, but rather only pauses in the current trend.

Symmetrical Triangle. Also known as a *coil*, this pattern forms, on diminishing volume, as a triangle that narrows evenly from left to right, with at least four reference points (see Figure 17-36 on page 413). The trend may be expected to resume, with a closing price outside the triangle, sometime after one-half and three-quarters of the triangle's length is developed. Occasionally, there is a return move on light volume, but the penetrated trendline of the triangle acts as support in an uptrend or as resistance in a downtrend. In either direction, volume generally picks up as the trend resumes. The apex itself can also serve as longer-term support or resistance.

A couple of measuring techniques are associated with triangles. To project the minimum extent of the resumed trend, measure the height of the base (distance *A-B* in Figure 17-37 on page 413) and extend a line of the same length from the breakout point (points *C-D*). Alternatively, draw a line from the top of the base (point *A*) that is parallel to the bottom line in the triangle (line *A-E*).

Ascending and Descending Triangles.   These patterns are like the symmetrical triangle, particularly with respect to volume behavior, except that one of the trendlines is parallel or almost parallel to the horizontal axis of the chart (see Figures 17-38 and 17-39 on page 414). In the ascending formation, the top line is parallel; in the descending triangle, it is the bottom line.

There is another important difference. The symmetrical triangle is considered essentially neutral. Yet the ascending triangle is *always* regarded as bullish, and the descending pattern is *always* considered bearish. Thus, the ascending triangle is looked upon as a continuation in an uptrend but as a reversal in a downtrend. Likewise, the descending triangle acts as a continuation pattern in a downtrend but as a reversal formation in an uptrend.

For either type of triangle, the extent of the breakout can be measured by first taking the height of the triangle at its widest point (distance *A-B* in Figure 17-38 or 17-39, and then extending a line of the same length from the breakout point (line *C-D*).

Flags and Pennants.   Whereas triangles may take one to three months to form, flags and pennants develop more quickly, usually on diminishing volume, in one to three weeks. Only rarely do they precede trend reversals (see Figures 17-40 and 17-41 on page 415).

Both formations have a clear measuring feature: They fly at half-mast. Specifically, the distance from the beginning of the existing trend to the start of the formation will be roughly the same as the duration of the trend from the breakout point on the flag or pennant.

Wedge Formation.   Very similar to triangles, this pattern differs from them in that both converging trendlines rise or fall rather steeply. Neither line is parallel to the horizontal axis (see Figures 17-42 and 17-43 on page 416).

Rectangle. Also known as a *trading range* or *congestion area*, this pattern typically reflects a consolidation period before a resumption of the current trend (see Figures 17-44 and 17-45 on page 417).

Because this formation closely resembles a triple top or bottom, the chartist must rely on volume to distinguish the two. If in an uptrend the volume is heavier on the rallies than on the setbacks, then a rectangle is probable. In a downtrend, a rectangle is likely if the dips are accompanied by heavier volume than the rallies. Otherwise, a triple top or bottom could be in the making.

After the breakout, the extent of price movement can be gauged by measuring the height of the trading range and extending a line of the same length up or down from the point of breakout.

Measured Move. Sometimes known as a *swing* measurement, this pattern (as shown in Figure 17-46 on page 418) results from an orderly and well-defined market. When the chartist sees a rally (*A-B*) and then a countertrend (*B-C*), the next leg (*C-D*) is likely to duplicate the first leg (*A-B*) in duration and angle.

Continuation Head and Shoulders. How does the chartist tell whether a head and shoulders is going to be a continuation or reversal pattern? The continuation pattern develops more like a rectangle, but turns into an inverted head and shoulders: that is, in an uptrend the head is lower than the shoulders (Figure 17-47 on page 419), whereas it is higher in a downtrend (Figure 17-48 on page 419). Once this point is recognized, the neckline can be drawn and the pattern interpreted as a continuation once the neckline is broken. In the continuation version of this formation, however, bear in mind that the measuring reliability is diminished and the volume requirement is not so strict.

Two-Way Patterns

Broadening Formations. Referred to by some as an inverted triangle, this relatively rare pattern consists of two diverging trendlines (see Figure 17-49 on page 420). As the price swings become broader (usually three in number: points 1 to 2, 2 to 3, 3 to 4, and 4 to 5), volume increases, reflecting a market that is out of control and unusually "emotional," probably due to a high degree of public participation.

This pattern usually occurs at major market tops and is therefore almost *always* a bearish formation. When it develops in a downtrend, it serves as a continuation pattern; in an uptrend, it is a reversal.

Diamond Formation. This relatively rare pattern usually appears at market tops and, because it is a bearish pattern, generally precedes a reversal. To measure the minimum extent of the downturn, take the greatest height of the pattern (points *A-B* in Figure 17-50 on page 420), and extend a line downward from the point of breakout (*C-D*).

Characterization

Often heard is the statement that "a chart is a chart," meaning that the technician does not need to know the particular item whose price is being plotted. To some extent that observation is valid: Many analytical techniques can be applied universally to charts. Nevertheless, because futures markets represent different industries and financial areas, they can behave surprisingly differently. The experienced futures chartist must become sensitized to the peculiarities of the various markets.

Confirmation and Divergence

Running throughout technical analysis are the two themes of confirmation and divergence. No one pattern, no one indicator can be used in isolation. Instead, the chartist must take into consideration all the elements of the market, always seeking to test the signals given by the price movements. Two basic tests are confirmation and divergence:

- *Confirmation* is the comparision of all technical signals and indicators to ensure that most of them point to the same conclusion and thereby confirm one another.

- *Divergence* is a situation in which the indicators fail to confirm one another. Perhaps other delivery months or related markets are headed in a different direction than that of the one under study. Divergence is not necessarily a negative finding. It can be a valuable concept in market analysis and an early warning signal of an impending trend reversal.

VOLUME AND OPEN INTEREST

By now, it should be obvious that the chartist typically regards price as a primary indicator, with volume and open interest as secondary indicators. To understand the significance of these two elements, let's redefine them.

Volume is the number of contracts traded in a given time period. It is commonly included in daily bar charts, sometimes on weekly charts, but usually not on monthly charts. Every time a trade occurs during the day, volume goes up. It can stay the same as long as no trading takes place, but it cannot decrease.

As a general rule, volume is a gauge of the "pressure" behind a price movement. High volume generally indicates that the current trend had momentum and should persist. A lack of volume might be a sign that the trend is "losing steam."

Open interest is the total number of outstanding or unliquidated contracts at the end of the day. As we discussed in Chapter 3, a transaction can cause open interest to go up, down, or stay the same, according to the following summary:

Buyer	Seller	Change in Open Interest
Buys new long	Sells new short	Increases
Buys new long	Sells old long	No change
Buys old short	Sells new short	No change
Buys old short	Sells old long	Decreases

Open interest therefore measures the flow of money into and out of the market. When it is increasing, money is flowing into the market: New longs are opening positions with new shorts. This enhances the likelihood that the present trend will continue. Decreasing open interest reflects a liquidating market and perhaps a nearing reversal.

When interpreting open interest, the chartist must acknowledge its seasonality. In any futures market, open interest will increase or decline for reasons associated with the nature of the underlying commodity or financial instrument. So all changes in open interest have to be compared against foreseeable seasonal moves before giving them weight as indicators of trend.

Interpretation

Volume and open interest are regarded as strong secondary indicators after price. Following is a chart that summarizes the interpretations of price, volume, and open interest:

Price	Volume	Open Interest	Interpretation of Market
Rising	Up	Up	Strong
Rising	Down	Down	Weakening
Declining	Up	Up	Weak
Declining	Down	Down	Strengthening

This table summarizes a number of useful principles:

• Volume tends to increase when prices are moving in the direction of the trend. In an uptrend, volume will increase on the upswings and taper off on the dips. The opposite is true of a downtrend.

• "Unseasonally" rising open interest in an uptrend is bullish: new longs —with "fresh" money—are entering the market. In a downtrend, increasing open interest is bearish; "short" money is coming into the market.

• In an uptrend, declining open interest is bearish because longs are closing positions and taking money out of the market. Shorts are being forced to cover their positions; when all the shorts are out of the market, the price uptrend will likely turn downward.

• In a downtrend, diminishing open interest is bullish. Losing longs are getting out of the market. Once they are all out, the downtrend should come to a halt.

These are by no means all the possible interpretations of volume and open interest. The intention in this chapter is simply to introduce the most basic ones.

Blowoffs and Selling Climaxes

Sometimes at the end of a long advance or decline, sudden and dramatic market action will lead to a sharp reversal. When this occurs at the end of a prolonged uptrend, it consists of a great deal of buying, which causes prices to rise quickly, and is called a *blowoff*. In the case of a downtrend, it is called a *selling climax*, which is accompanied by much selling and, of course, sharp declines in prices. In either case, as volume picks up, open interest drops off. Under these conditions, be on the lookout for an abrupt reversal.

COMPUTERIZED TRADING METHODS

The 1970s spawned a new methodology in technical analysis that does not depend as heavily on the subjective interpretation of trend that is such a key part of traditional charting techniques. Known broadly as computerized trading methods, these techniques are designed to generate "automatic," nonsubjective trading signals that leave little role for either emotion or interpretation in the trader's decisions to buy or sell.

Moving Averages

The moving average is one of the most versatile and widely used of all computerized technical indicators. Because of its method of construction and its susceptibility to quantification and testing, it is the basis for most "mechanical" trend-following systems in use today.

As its name implies, a moving average is an average of a changing body of data. A ten-day moving average, for instance, is obtained by adding prices for the last ten days and dividing by ten. The term "moving" is used because only the latest ten days' prices are used in the calculation. Therefore, the body of data to be averaged moves forward with each new trading day.

In essence, the moving average is a smoothing device. By averaging the price data, high and low prices are obscured and the basic underlying trend of the market is more easily discerned. By its very nature, however, the moving average line lags the market action. A shorter moving average, such as a five-day, would hug the price action more closely than, say, a forty-day average. Shorter term averages are more sensitive to day-to-day price movements (see Figure 17-51 on page 421).

To illustrate the use of a trading system based on moving averages let us begin with a simple ten-day system. The average of the last ten days' prices is plotted on a bar chart in its appropriate trading day along with that day's price action. When the closing price moves above the moving average, a buy signal is generated. A sell signal is given when the closing price moves below the moving average. For added confirmation, some technicians like to see the moving average line itself turn in the direction of the price crossing.

This simplified method of signal generation gives rise to far more sophisticated ones. When developing a moving average trading system, the trader must make decisions in the following areas:

1. *The length of the average to be used*. If a short-term average is employed (usually less than ten days), the average tracks closing prices very closely and several crossings occur. The use of a sensitive average produces more trades and false signals. On the other hand, a more sensitive average has the advantage of giving trend signals earlier in the price move. Generally, shorter-term averages work better when prices are in a sideways trading pattern because they do a better job of signaling short term swings.

2. *The method of averaging*. Some traders prefer a simple moving average based on the simple arithmetic mean of prices. Others feel that it is more appropriate to attach greater weight in the average to more recent prices. In this case a weighted moving average would be used.

3. *The number of averages to use*. In the simple system described above, one moving average was used, and its relationship to closing prices was the basis for signal generation. In more sophisticated systems, two and even three averages are employed. The interrelationships of these averages to each other and to closing prices are used as the basis for trade decisions.

4. *The use of filters*. In an effort to reduce the number of false signals generated by a moving average trading system, some traders employ the use of statistical filters. These filters require that prices cross through a moving average by a certain minimum amount before a trade signal is generated.

As is evident from the above discussion, the development of a trading system based on statistical indicators is a complicated affair. Many decisions must be made to determine which system works best for different markets and different market conditions. Unless the trader constructs a system that is tested rigorously under different circumstances, he will be dependent on the kind of subjective interpretation that computerized methods aim to avoid.

Oscillators

Unlike moving averages, which are trend-following devices, oscillators are tools that attempt to identify "overbought" or "oversold" market conditions. A market is said to be overbought when its price reaches some upper boundary within a trend and further gains are unlikely.

One example of an oscillator system might be based on the divergence of price from trend as measured by a simple ten day moving average. For example, if a market closes more than, say, two percent above its ten-day moving average trendline, it might be said to be overbought and due for a correction. A close two percent below the moving average would imply an oversold condition. Whether the parameter should be two percent or some other value can only be determined by rigorous testing of historical data.

Another tool used in oscillator systems is that of *momentum*. Momentum measures the rate of change of prices and involves continually calculating price differences for fixed time intervals. To construct a ten-day momentum line, simply subtract the closing price ten days ago from the last closing price. This positive or negative value is then plotted around a zero line (see Figure 17-52 on page 421). In using momentum as a technical tool, traders seek to identify periods in which prices are trending one way but their rate of change is trending the opposite way. For instance, prices may be trending up but the actual rate of change as measured by, say, ten-day momentum, may be trending down. This loss of momentum is often an indication of an overbought state.

Channels

Channels are a technical tool that generate signals when prices rise above the highest price (or fall below the lowest price) of a predetermined time period. Using a twenty-day channel, for example, a buy (sell) signal would be generated when current prices rise above (fall below) the highest (lowest) price of the preceding twenty trading days. Channels are one of the oldest and most reliable mechanical trading techniques. However, as with most computerized methods, the best channel to use under different market conditions can be determined only through rigorous testing.

POINT-AND-FIGURE (P&F) CHARTS

Unlike bar charts, point-and-figure charts record only price move-ments: if no price change occurs, the chart remains the same. Time is not reflected on a P&F chart, although time-reference points, such as a "10:00" for ten o'clock, are sometimes used. Volume is indicated only by the number of recorded price changes, not as a separate entity. Al-though traditionally ignored, gaps may be represented by empty boxes.

Nevertheless, point-and-figure charts have at least two major ad-vantages over bar charts: First, they can be used on an intraday basis to identify support, resistance, and other price-related data—particularly congestion areas—that bar charts can miss completely. Second, P&F charts are more flexible than bar charts in that the analyst can vary the size of the box and the reversal criterion, either of which can drastically change the appearance of the formation.

Box Size

In a P&F chart, a rising price change is represented by an *X*, a de-clining price movement by an *O*. Each *X* or *O* occupies a box on the chart. One of the first decisions in constructing a P&F chart is therefore how great a price change each box should represent. For example, a gold chart might have a box size of $1. On a less sensitive chart, each box might equal $5; a more sensitive scale would be $0.50 a box. Obvi-ously, the smaller the value assigned to a box, the more detailed the price action the chart can convey—and the more tedious it becomes to construct.

Reversal Criterion

On a P&F chart, the analyst moves one row of boxes to the right each time the market reverses. The next question is, what constitutes a reversal? Is a one-box change in direction a reversal? Or is it three boxes worth of movement?

Examples

Perhaps the best way to explain the elements of a P&F chart is to construct one. Following are the actual price changes in an hour or so of cotton trading:

8515	8515	8510
8525	8505	8516
8510	8515	8510
8515	8512	8515
8510	8515	8506

Now let's construct a P&F chart with each box equal to one point and a three-box reversal criterion, that is a "1 x 3" chart (see Figure 17-53 on page 422). Start by placing a dot in the 8515 box in row 1: a dot is used because the chartist does not know whether this is an up or down move. Still in column one, the chartist places Xs in all the boxes up to and including box 8525, representing the upward price change from 8515 to 8525. The next price, 8510, represents a 15-box reversal and certainly qualifies as a reversal on this chart. Shift to the next column to the right and one box down, to reflect the change in direction. Then place Os in column 2 down to and including 8510. You can see how the rest of the price changes are plotted.

The chartist can make the same data plot differently—and make the chart less sensitive—by changing either the size of the box or the reversal criterion. For example, Figure 17-54 (see page 422) is the 1 x 3 cotton chart that was started in Figure 17-53, now plotted out for several hours worth of trading. Compare it with Figure 17-55 (see page 423), which reflects the price changes but in a 2 x 3 format: that is, each box now represents two points, and the reversal criterion is still three days. Also compare the three charts in Figures 17-56, 17-57, 17-58 (see pages 424–425) all of which are based on the same data: One is a 5 x 1 chart, the second is a 5 x 3, and the last is 5 x 5. Notice the compression of the chart and the loss of data.

The Horizontal Count

Whereas price objectives are determined by vertical measurements on a bar chart, they are obtained by what is known as a *horizontal count* on a P&F chart. On intraday, one-box reversal charts, the analyst measures the width of the congestion area and uses that number of boxes to measure the up- or downside target. Usually, the column to count from is the one with the greatest number of Xs and Os.

For example, see Figure 17-59 on page 426. The point of a compass is placed at the extreme right of the area, and an arc is projected up- or downward once the width of the area has been measured.

Price Patterns

Although some patterns, such as gaps, flags, or pennants, are not evident on P&F charts, most formations can be seen. Their appearance, however, is sometimes different from the bar chart variety. (See Figure 17-60 on page 427.)

USING LONG-TERM CHARTS

Technical analysis techniques can be used in any time dimension. They apply not only to daily charts, but also to weekly charts (that contain up to five years of data) and to monthly charts (that can offer up to 20 years of price movements).

In fact, even though this chapter has focused on the daily chart, no analyst could get a broad enough picture of a market without referring first (and often) to longer-term charts.

A reasonable approach is as follows:

• Consult a chart that reflects the general environment of the futures market to be charted. The CRB futures price index and/or group indices are excellent sources in this respect (see Figure 17-61 on page 428). For example, the chartist about to study the silver market might consult the CRB Precious Metals Index.

• Next, turn to long-term charts of the individual market to determine the scope of past price movements. Looking for large-scale patterns in these charts prepares the analyst to properly interpret the day-to-day price action. See, for example, the long-range activity of gold in Figure 17-62 on page 429.

CYCLES AND WAVES

There are many different cycles affecting futures markets. The only ones of real value for forecasting purposes are the *dominant cycles*. Dominant cycles are those that consistently affect futures prices and that can be clearly identified. Most futures markets have at least five dominant cycles. In an earlier section on the use of long-term charts, it was stressed that all technical analysis should begin with the long-term picture, gradually working toward the shorter term. That principle holds true in the study of cycles. The proper procedure is to begin the analysis with a study of long-term dominant cycles, which can span several years; then work toward the intermediate, which can be several weeks to several months; finally, the very-short-term cycles, from several hours to several days, can be used for timing of entry and exit points and to help confirm the turning points of the longer cycles.

Classification of Cycles

Cyclic analysts differ somewhat on the classification of cycle lengths and even in the cycle lengths themselves. Taking this ambiguity into account, we'll attempt here to identify the major cycle categories. The general categories are: *long-term cycles* (two or more years in length), the *seasonal cycle* (one year), the *primary or intermediate cycle* (nine to 26 weeks), and the *trading cycle* (four weeks).

There are even longer-range cycles at work. Perhaps the best known is the approximate 54-year Kondratieff cycle. This controversial long cycle of economic activity, first discovered in the 1920s by a Russian economist by the name of Nikolai D. Kondratieff, appears to exert a major influence on virtually all stock and commodity prices. In particular, a 54-year cycle has been identified in interest rates, copper, cotton, wheat, stocks, and wholesale commodity prices. Kondratieff tracked his "long wave" from 1789 using such factors as commodity prices, pig iron production, and wages of agricultural workers in England (see Figure 17-63 on page 430). The Kondratieff cycle has become a popular subject of discussion in recent years, primarily owing to the fact that its last top occurred in the late 1920s, placing its next major top sometime in the 1980s.

Seasonal Cycles

All commodity futures markets are affected to some extent by an annual seasonal cycle. This seasonal cycle or pattern refers to the tendency of markets to move in a given direction at certain times of the year. The most obvious seasonals involve the grain markets, where seasonal lows usually occur around harvest time when supply is most plentiful. In soybeans, for example, 70% of all seasonal tops occur between April and July with seasonal bottoms taking place 75% of the time between August and November. Once a seasonal top or bottom has been formed, prices usually fall or rise for several months. Therefore, some knowledge of seasonal tendencies can be a valuable adjunct to other trading methods.

Although the reasons for seasonal tops and bottoms are more obvious in the agricultural markets, virtually all markets experience seasonal patterns. *One general seasonal pattern that seems to apply to many markets is that a penetration of the January high is considered bullish.* Examples of some other seasonal patterns can be seen in the metals markets. The copper market shows a strong seasonal uptrend from the January/February period with a tendency to top in March or April. The gold market also shows seasonal strength from January with another bottom in August. Silver has a low in January with higher prices into March.

Seasonal charts can be constructed by studying the frequency of seasonal moves in past years. It can then be determined what the percentage probabilities are for a seasonal move during each month and week of the year, depending on how many times such moves took place in the past during that same time period.

There are a couple of caveats that must be considered when performing seasonal studies. Most cash seasonals are based on the average monthly price and sometimes show different seasonal patterns than the futures markets. Second, futures markets sometimes show two different seasonal patterns. The trader should be aware of both. The question of contra-seasonal moves must be considered. There will be years when prices will not follow the anticipated seasonal tendency. The trader must be on the alert for signs that something has gone wrong. Identifying a contra-seasonal move as soon as possible has obvious benefits and is extremely valuable information. Failure to conform to the normal seasonal pattern often indicates a significant move in the other direction. Knowing when you're wrong early in the game is one of the most useful features of seasonal analysis in particular and of technical analysis in general.

Elliott Wave Theory

Elliott Wave Theory was originally applied to the major stock market averages, particularly the Dow Jones Industrial Average. In its most basic form, the theory says that the stock market follows a repetitive rhythm of a five-wave advance followed by a three-wave decline. Figure 17-64 (see page 431) shows one complete cycle. If you count the waves, you will find that one complete cycle has eight waves—five up and three down. In the advancing portion of the cycle, notice that each of the five waves are numbered. Waves 1, 3, and 5—called *impulse* waves—are rising waves, while waves 2 and 4 move against the uptrend. Waves 2 and 4 are called *corrective* waves because they correct waves 1 and 3. After the five-wave numbered advance has been completed, a three-wave correction begins. The three corrective waves are identified by the letters a, b, and c.

Along with the constant form of the various waves, there is the important consideration of degree. There are many different degrees of trend. Elliott, in fact, categorized nine different degrees of trend (or magnitude) ranging from a *Grand Supercycle* spanning two hundred years to a *subminuette* degree covering only a few hours. The point to remember is that the basic eight-wave cycle remains constant no matter what degree of trend is being studied.

Each wave subdivides into waves of one lesser degree which, in turn, can also be subdivided into waves of even lesser degree. It also follows then that each wave is itself part of the wave of the next higher degree. Figure 17-65 (see page 431) demonstrates these relationships. The largest two waves—(1) and (2)—can be subdivided into eight lesser waves which, in turn, can be subdivided into 34 even lesser waves. The two largest waves—(1) and (2)—are only the first two waves in an even larger five-wave advance. Wave (3) of that next higher degree is about to begin. The 34 waves in Figure 17-65 are subdivided further to the next smaller degree in Figure 17-66 (see page 432), resulting in 144 waves.

The numbers shown so far—1,2,3,5,8,13,21,34,55,89,144—are not just random numbers. They are part of the *Fibonacci number sequence*, which forms the mathematical basis for the Elliott Wave Theory. Each Fibonacci number is the sum of the previous two Fibonacci numbers. Look again at Figures 17-64 through 17-66 and notice a very significant characteristic of the waves. Whether a given wave divides into five waves or three waves is determined by the direction of the next larger wave. For example, in Figure 17-65 waves (1), (3), and (5) subdivide into five waves because the next larger wave of which they are part—wave (1)—is an advancing wave. Because waves (2) and (4) are moving against the trend, they subdivide into only three waves. Look more closely at corrective waves (a), (b), and (c), which comprise the larger corrective wave (2). Notice that the two declining waves—(a) and (c)—each break down into five waves. This is because they are moving in the same direction as the next larger wave (2). Wave (b) by contrast only has three waves, because it is moving against the next larger wave (2).

Being able to determine between threes and fives is obviously of tremendous importance in the application of this approach. That information tells the analyst what to expect next. A completed five-wave move, for example, usually means that only part of a larger wave has been completed and that there's more to come (unless it's a fifth of a fifth). *One of the most important rules to remember is that a correction can never take place in five waves.* In a bull market, for example, if a five-wave decline is seen, this means that it is probably only the first wave of a three-wave (a-b-c) decline and that there's more to come on the downside. In a bear market, a three-wave advance should be followed by resumption of the downtrend. A five-wave rally would warn of a more substantial move to the upside and might possibly even be the first wave of a new bull trend.

Figure 17-1.

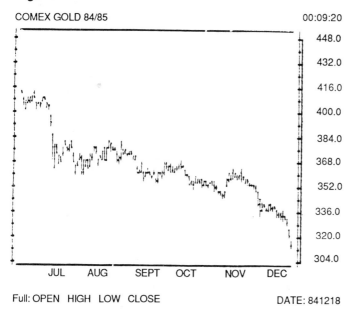

COMEX GOLD 84/85   00:09:20

448.0
432.0
416.0
400.0
384.0
368.0
352.0
336.0
320.0
304.0

JUL   AUG   SEPT   OCT   NOV   DEC

Full: OPEN HIGH LOW CLOSE   DATE: 841218

Figure 17-2.

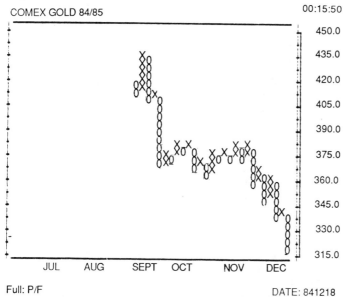

COMEX GOLD 84/85   00:15:50

450.0
435.0
420.0
405.0
390.0
375.0
360.0
345.0
330.0
315.0

JUL   AUG   SEPT   OCT   NOV   DEC

Full: P/F   DATE: 841218

Figure 17-3.

COPPER-MONTHLY RANGE

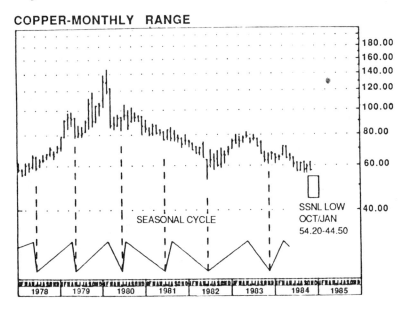

SEASONAL CYCLE

SSNL LOW
OCT/JAN
54.20-44.50

Figure 17-4.

COPPER - WEEKLY CONTINUATION

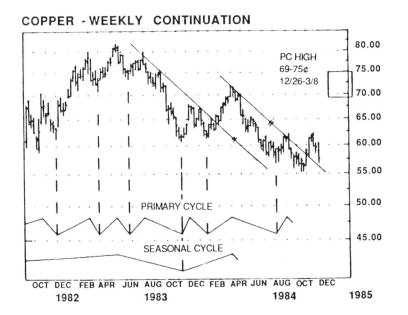

PC HIGH
69-75¢
12/26-3/8

PRIMARY CYCLE

SEASONAL CYCLE

Figure 17-5. Elements of the bar chart.

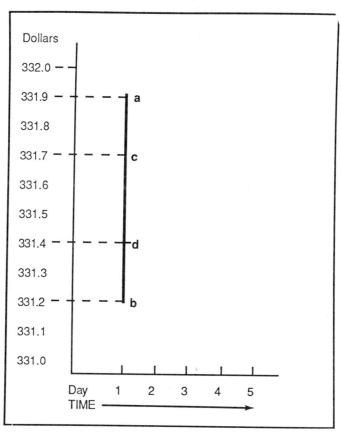

a. The high price for the day, $331.90.
b. The low price for the day, $331.20.
c. The opening price (not always on the bar chart), $331.70.
d. The closing price, $331.40.

Figure 17-6. Uptrend.

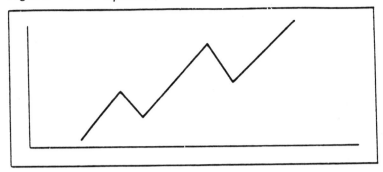

Figure 17-7. Downtrend.

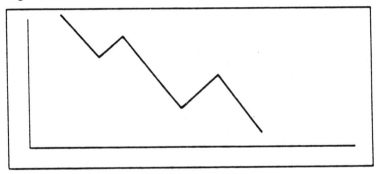

Figure 17-8. Sideways.

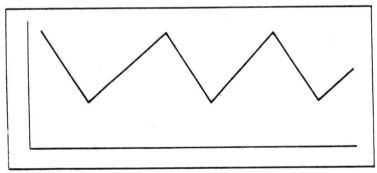

Figure *17-9.* *Uptrend with channel.*

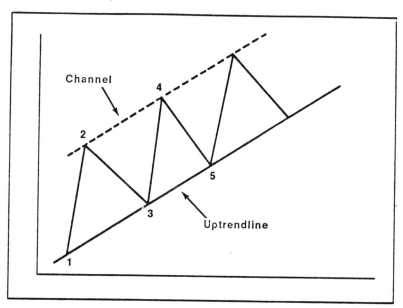

Figure *17-10.* *Downtrend with channel.*

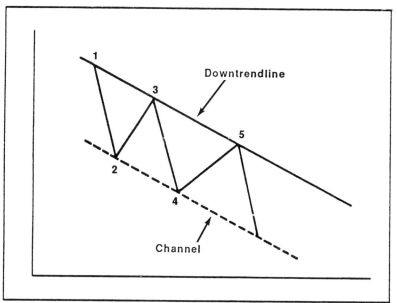

Figure 17-11. Breakout.

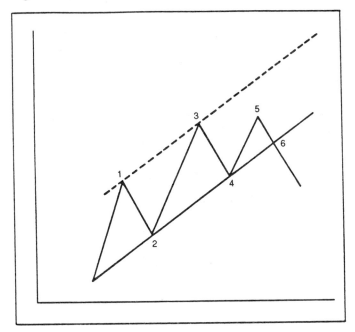

Figure 17-12. Measuring objectives.

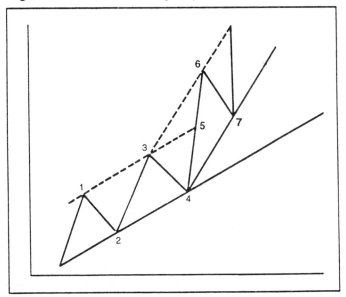

Figure 17-13. Measuring objectives.

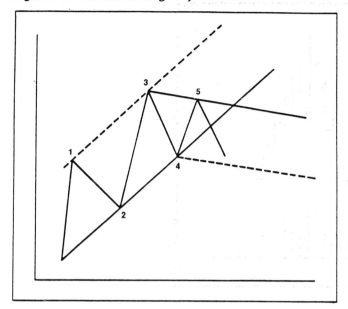

Figure 17-14. Retracement levels.

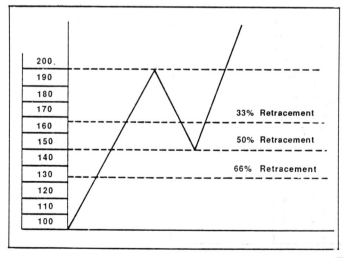

Figure 17-15. Reversal.

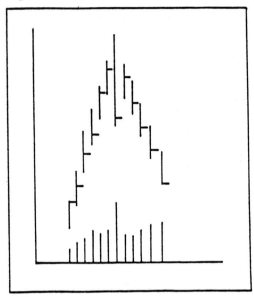

Figure 17-16. Reversal.

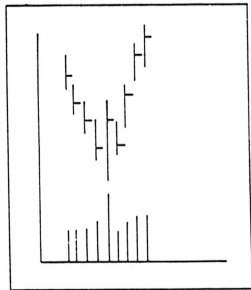

Figure 17-17.
Two-day reversal.

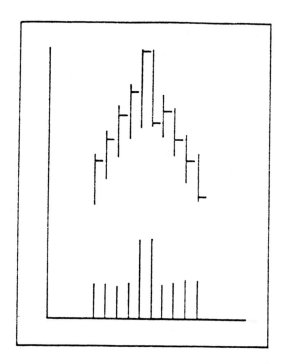

Figure 17-18.
Two-day reversal.

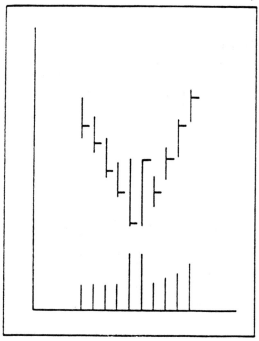

Figure 17-19.

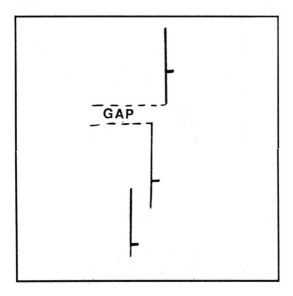

Figure 17-20.

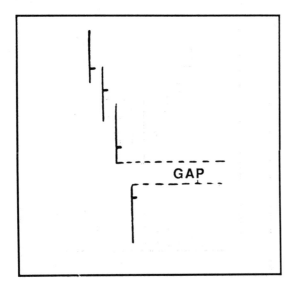

Figure 17-21. Typical gaps.

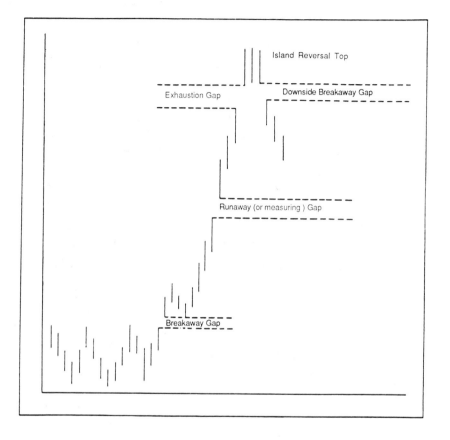

Island Reversal Top

Exhaustion Gap

Downside Breakaway Gap

Runaway (or measuring) Gap

Breakaway Gap

Figure 17-22. Resistance becomes support.

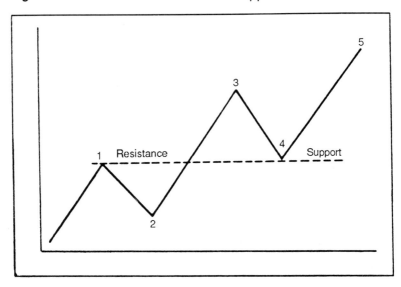

Figure 17-23. Support becomes resistance.

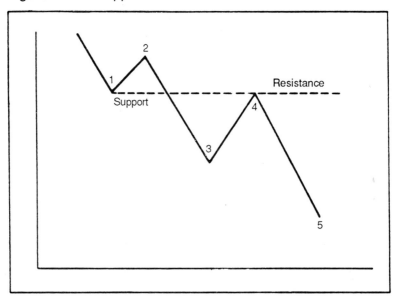

Figure 17-24. *Head and shoulders.*

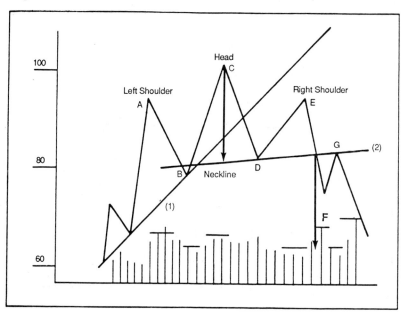

Figure 17-25. *Inverted head and shoulders.*

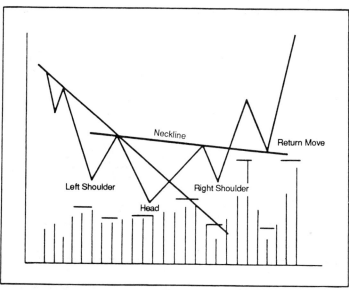

Figure 17-26. Complex top.

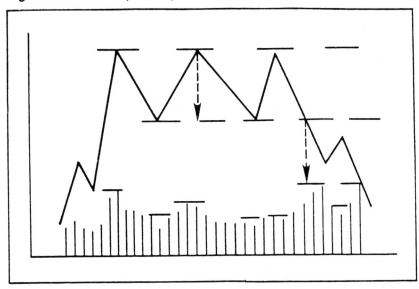

Figure 17-27. Complex bottom.

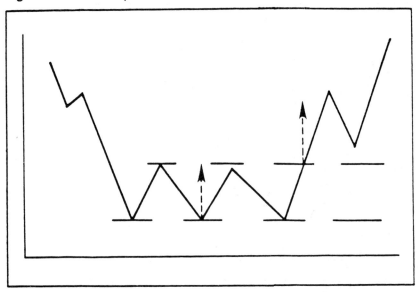

Figure 17-28. Double top.

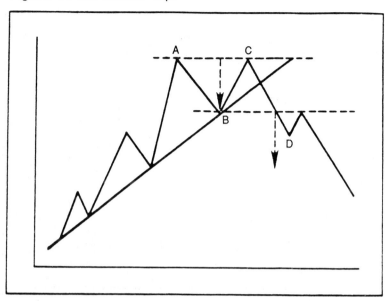

Figure 17-29. Double top.

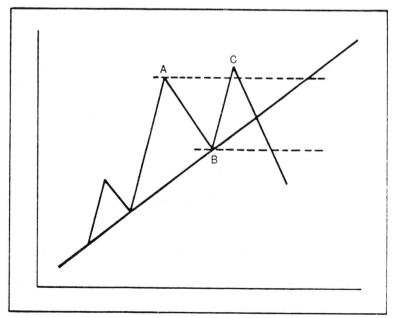

Figure 17-30. *Saucer top.*

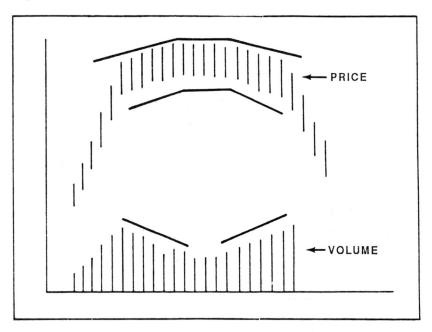

Figure 17-31. *Saucer bottom.*

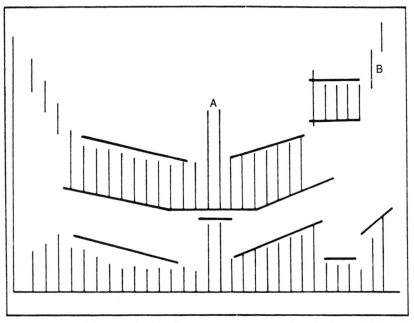

Figure 17-32. *Spike.*

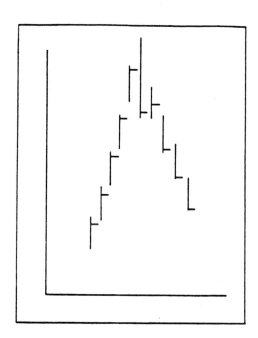

Figure 17-33. *Spike.*

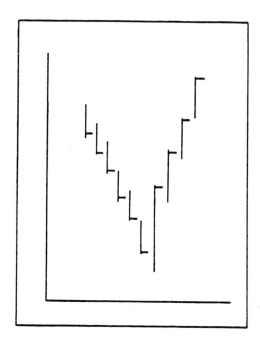

Figure 17-34. Platform after.

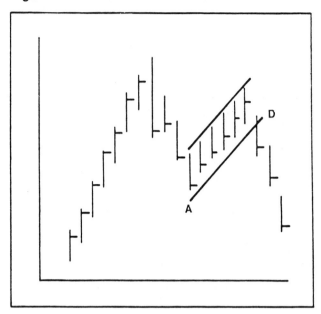

Figure 17-35. Platform before.

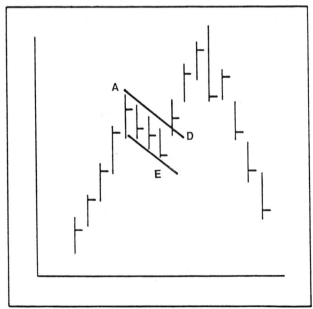

Figure 17-36. Symmetrical triangle.

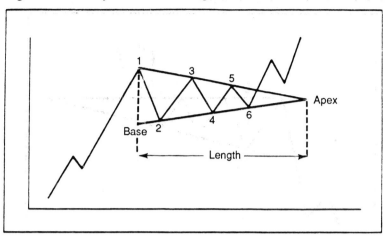

Figure 17-37. Measuring with triangles.

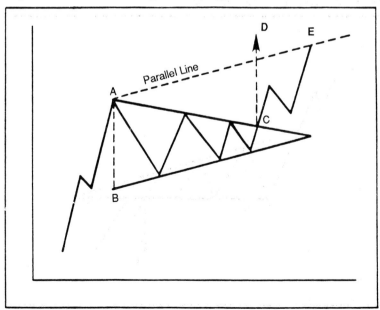

Figure 17-38. Ascending triangle.

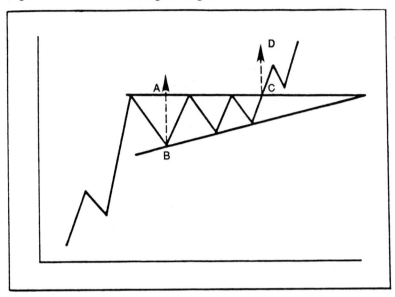

Figure 17-39. Descending triangle.

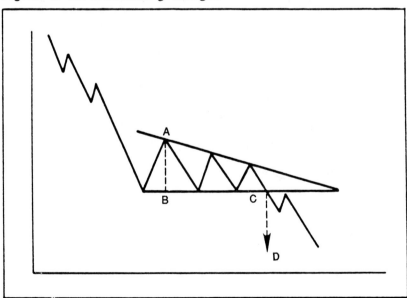

Figure 17-40. Flag.

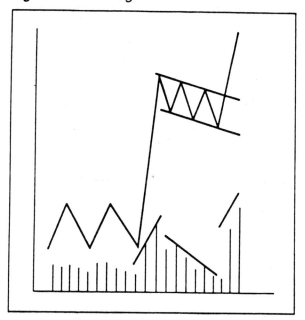

Figure 17-41. Pennant.

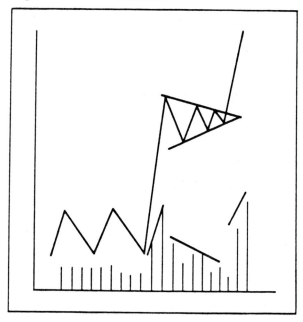

Figure 17-42. Falling wedge.

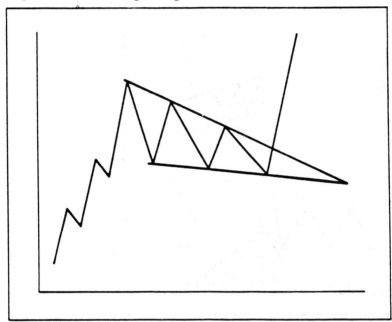

Figure 17-43. Rising wedge.

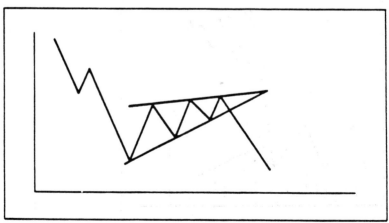

Figure 17-44. Trading range.

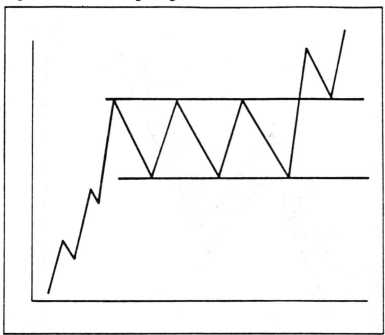

Figure 17-45. Trading range.

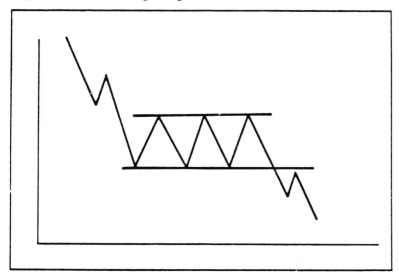

Figure 17-46. *Measured move.*

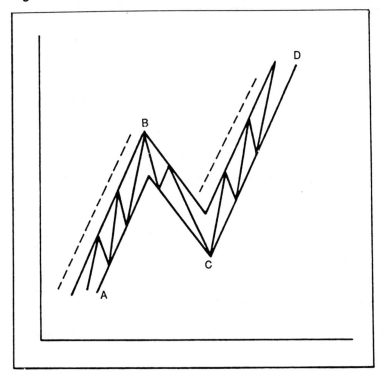

Figure 17-47. *Continuation head & shoulders.*

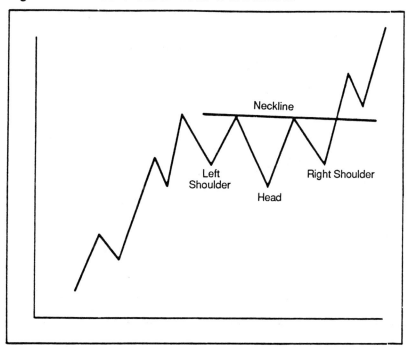

Figure 17-48. *Continuation head & shoulders.*

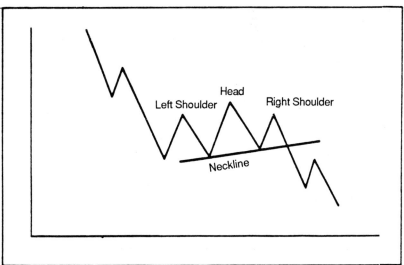

Figure 17-49. Broadening pattern.

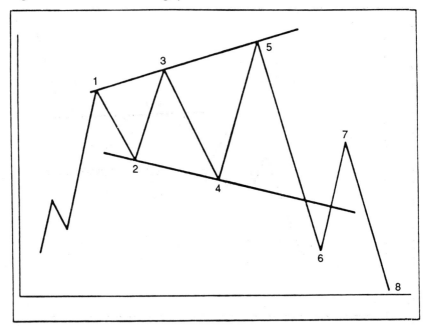

Figure 17-50. Diamond.

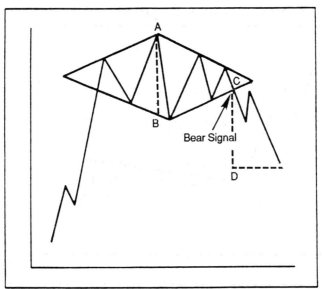

Figure 17-51. *Moving average.*

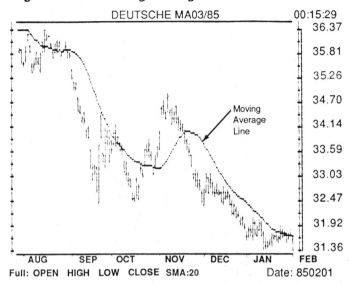

Figure 17-52. *Oscillators & momentum.*

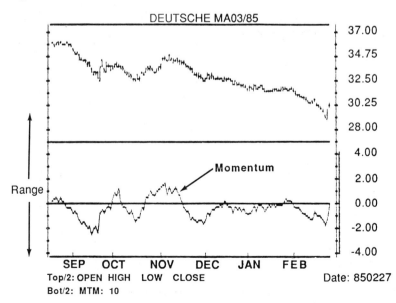

Figure 17-54. Point & figure chart.

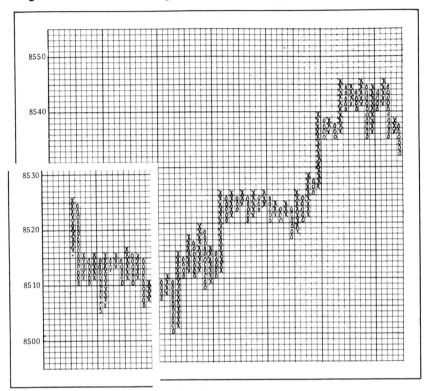

Figure 17-53. Plotting the P&F.

Figure 17-55. P&F in 2 x 3 format.

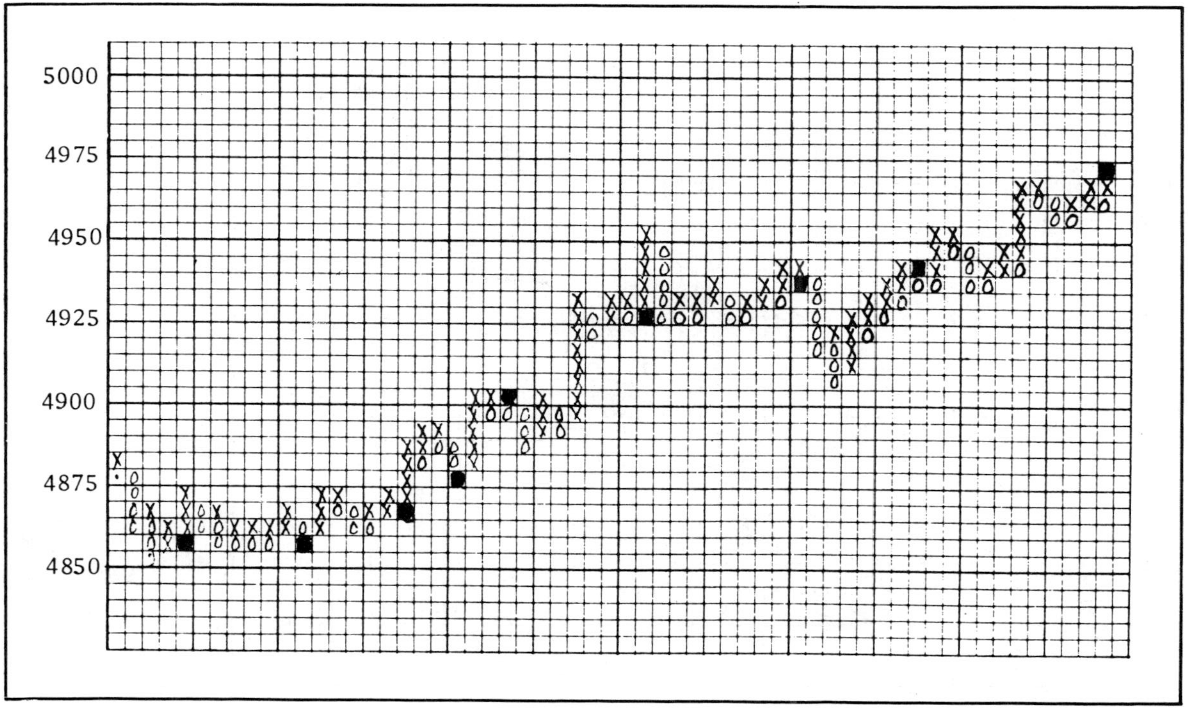

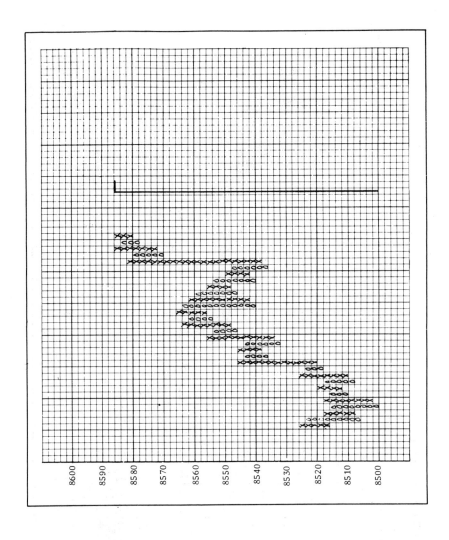

Figure 17-56.
5 x 1 format.

424

Figure 17-57. 5 × 3.　　　　　　**Figure 17-58.** 5 × 5.

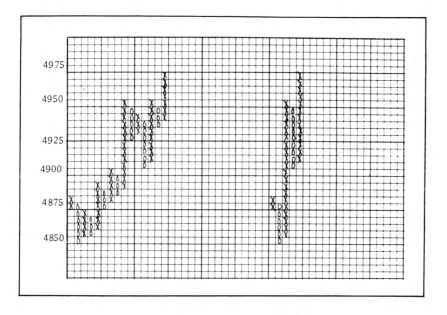

425

Figure 17-59.

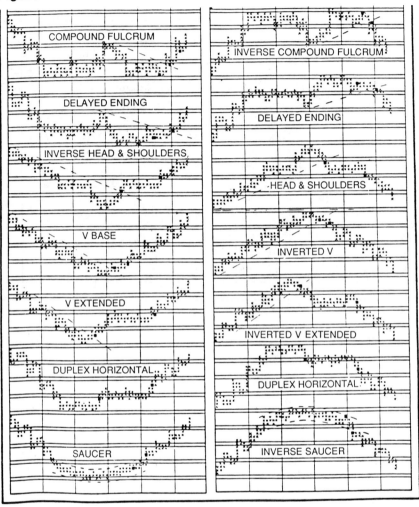

Figure 17-60. Price patterns.

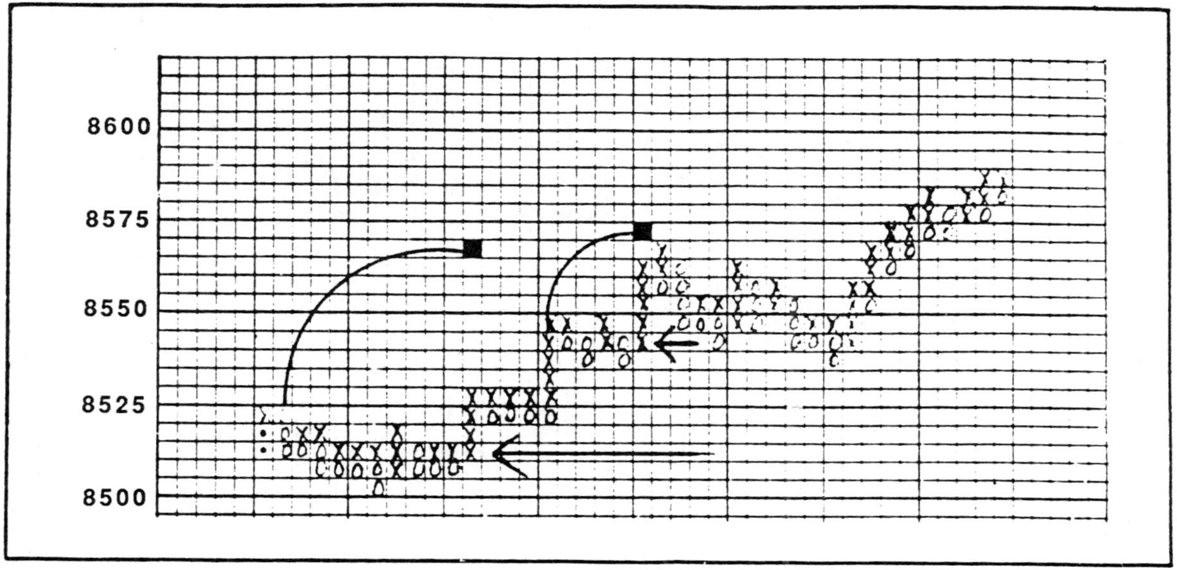

427

Figure 17-61. Long-term index.

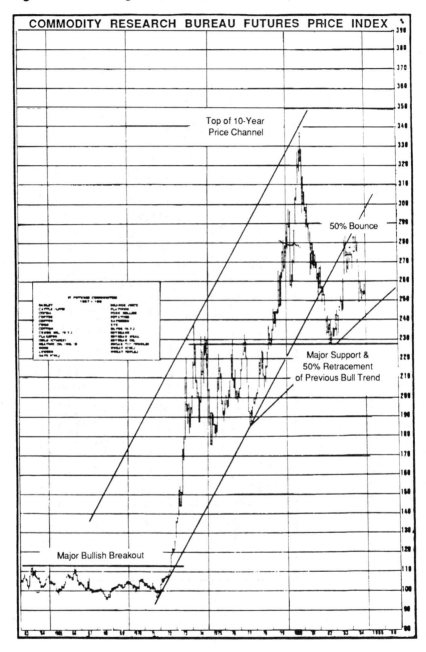

428

Figure 17-62. Monthly chart.

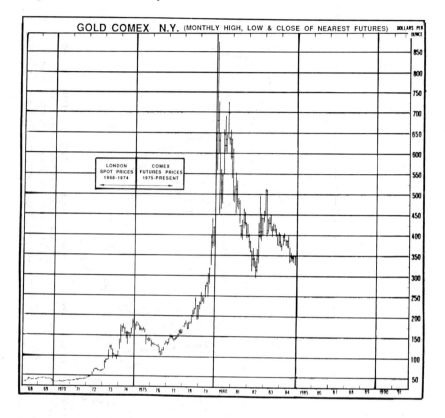

Figure 17-63. Kondratieff cycle.

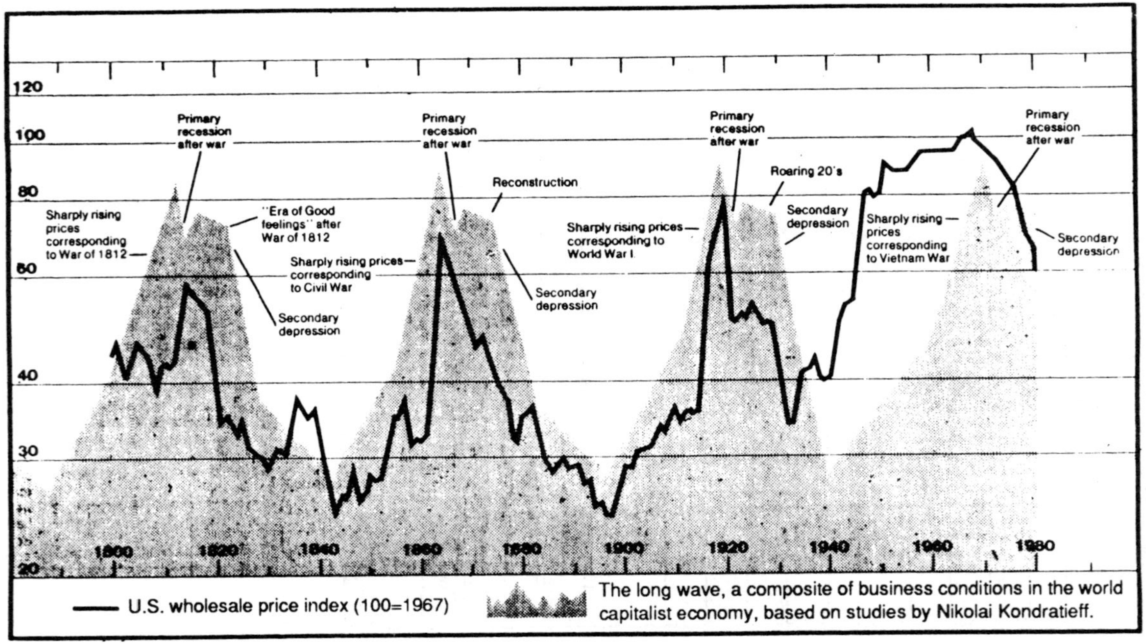

The long wave, a composite of business conditions in the world capitalist economy, based on studies by Nikolai Kondratieff.

— U.S. wholesale price index (100=1967)

Figure 17-64. *The basic Elliott wave pattern.**

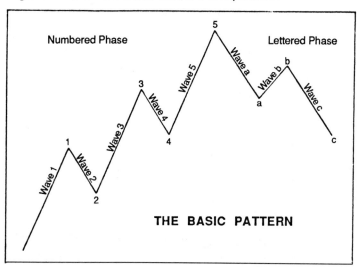

*A.J. Frost & Robert Prechter, *Elliott Wave Principle* [Gainesville, GA: New Classics Library, 1978], p. 20. Copyright © 1978 by Frost & Prechter.

Figure 17-65. *The subdivided wave.*

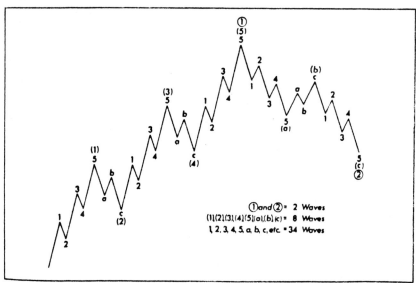

*Figure 17-66.** *The complete cycle.*

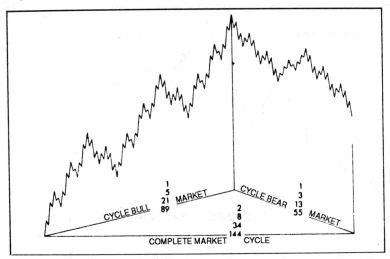

*Frost & Prechter, p. 22. Copyright © 1978 by Frost & Prechter.

■ PART FIVE
■ THE MARKETS

■ Chapter 18

■ *Interest Rate Futures*

INTRODUCTION

Since the introduction of GNMA futures on the Chicago Board of Trade in 1975, the role of interest rate futures in speculation, hedging, and portfolio management has expanded phenomenally. From that uncertain experiment in one market in 1975, the interest rate futures family grew to encompass at one point a dozen different instruments whose combined volume in 1982 approached 30 million contracts. Although in 1987 there were only half as many actively traded interest rate futures contracts, their total volume vastly exceeds that of 1982. In fact, Treasury bond futures alone often trade more than one million contracts per week.

The rapid growth in the volume of these markets stemmed from the increased risk and opportunity that greater interest rate volatility created for both borrowers and lenders since the early 1970s. The significant profit opportunities that are available to speculators played an equally important role in the expansion of these markets.

The rapid growth in volume also brought a maturing of the futures industry for financial markets. Since September 1975 when the Commodity Futures Trading Commission first approved trading in GNMA futures, it has approved some three dozen other applications by various exchanges for contract market designation in more than a dozen different instruments. Most of these have either failed outright or await more favorable market conditions. The active markets as of mid-1987 are listed

Figure 18-1. Active interest rate futures (as of mid-1987).

Instrument	Contract Unit	Maturity	Exchange*
U.S. Treasury Bills	$1,000,000	90 days	IMM
Eurodollars	1,000,000	90 days	IMM
U.S. Treasury Notes	100,000	10 years	CBT
U.S. Treasury Bonds	100,000	20 years	CBT
Municipal Bond Index	1,000 x index	19 years	CBT

*CBT: Chicago Board of Trade.
IMM: International Monetary Market of the Chicago Mercantile Exchange.

in Figure 18-1 and cover a wide range of maturities for both public and private sector debt.

This chapter begins with a discussion of the fundamentals of interest rates and the U. S. money and capital markets. It then provides a description of each cash instrument and its corresponding futures contract, as well as an explanation of the prices of these instruments and how they relate to one another. The chapter also discusses applications in the areas of hedging and arbitrage. It concludes with a discussion of spread trading in interest rate futures.

INTEREST RATE FUNDAMENTALS

Interest is the price paid for the use of money or credit and like any price it is fundamentally determined by the supply and demand forces at work in its marketplace. This section provides an overview of those supply and demand factors and an explanation of issues such as fiscal and monetary policy that determine the level of interest rates. It is important to keep in mind that there are, in fact, many different interest rates. Each reflects the risk and maturity of a type of loan. In this section we will focus on those factors that influence the "general" level of interest rates.

Business Conditions

The most significant demand for private sector credit comes from businesses. When the economy is expanding, demand for funds tends to be strong because businesses expect to make a sufficient return on their borrowings to more than offset the payment of principal and interest. Conversely, a contracting economy is usually characterized by slow business activity and sluggish demand for credit.

Business conditions are rarely stagnant. Economic expansion eventually gives way to recession. Profits, employment, production, and prices decline as demand dwindles. Interest rates weaken. Eventually the bottom is reached and recovery begins. Demand for goods and credit improves, and interest rates tend to rise.

Several areas of economic activity are watched closely by users of the financial futures markets to track business conditions. Among the most important are these:

Inventories. Inventory investment is a major source of business demand for credit. In fact, swings in inventory investment have been such important contributors to the business cycles of the past four decades that many of the cyclical recessions have been called *inventory recessions*. Rising inventories often imply a slowing economy because this suggests that sales may not be keeping up with production. This tends to exert downward pressure on interest rates.

Construction. Some of the most important periods of United States business expansion have coincided with booms in building construction. Likewise, some of the deepest recessions have occurred during downswings in construction cycles. Because of its sheer size in the United States economy, construction activity is an important measure of business activity and a key determinant of interest rates. Key reports issued by the U. S. Department of Commerce include *Housing Starts*, which shows the number of private residential construction starts for a given month and *Construction Activity*, which shows the value of new construction. Generally, rising housing starts indicate growth in the economy and increased credit demand.

Unemployment. Rising unemployment often indicates slowing economic growth. The *unemployment rate*, which is released monthly by the U.S. Department of Commerce, Bureau of Labor Statistics, measures the percent of unemployed people in the civilian labor force. Because unemployment is such a key measure of overall economic health, rising levels may also prompt the Federal Reserve to ease credit, causing rates to drop. Monthly statistics on the average work week of production workers in manufacturing are another important employment measure.

Durable Goods. Each month the Commerce Department publishes data on new orders for durable goods. A rising trend in orders for durable goods is indicative of a pickup in business activity and often leads to increased credit demand and higher interest rates.

Retail Sales. Rising retail sales, as measured by monthly reports from the Bureau of Census, suggest stronger eonomic activity, improved credit demand, and rising interest rates.

Gross National Product (GNP). *GNP* is a measure of the total market value of the nation's output of goods and services. Another important measure of output is the industrial production report issued by the Federal Reserve Board, which measures the physical output of U. S. businesses, services, and utilities. Declining GNP and/or industrial production reflect slowing economic conditions. This may cause the Federal Reserve to be more accommodating in allowing interest rates to fall in order to stimulate the economy. Conversely, increases in GNP are often accompanied by rising interest rates.

Household Conditions

Individual households are another important source of private sector demand. Department store credit sales, automobile loans, and mortgages are just a few examples of the types of borrowings made by households. In addition to these areas of business activity, other areas of interest in this sector are:

Personal Income. Released monthly by the Department of Commerce, personal income statistics are a broad measure of the economic health of households. Generally, higher personal income means increased consumption and higher prices for consumer goods.

Consumer Credit. Consumer credit, as measured by the Federal Reserve Board, is used to finance the purchase of consumer goods and services and includes auto loans, retail credit, and other types of revolving credit.

Fiscal Policy

The taxation and spending policies of both the federal government and local governments can have an extremely important effect on interest rates. When expenses exceed revenues, governments must finance the resulting debt by borrowing in the open market. This tends to exert upward pressure on interest rates. Economic policies that are designed to stimulate growth tend also to stimulate the demand for loans from both individuals and business. Likewise, tax policies that encourage investment tend to reduce interest rates. Some important components of fiscal policy are:

Military Spending. This is the largest single federal government expense category. Therefore, changes in Presidential or congressional attitudes toward military expenditures and changes in the relationships between the superpowers can affect the interest rate outlook.

Interest Rates. Interest rates themselves are important to fiscal policy. Higher rates mean that the government must pay more to borrow, which in turn raises overall expenditures. In recent years, interest costs have become an important part of total federal government expenses.

Public Works. These are government sponsored projects to increase employment. Because most projects of this kind are long term, this form of fiscal stimulus is rarely used as an instrument of short- or medium-term policy.

Welfare Programs. These programs include aid to the poor, unemployed, elderly, and so forth. Since the early 1960s they have become a meaningful portion of total government expenditures.

Tax Rates. Increases or decreases in tax rates can have an important effect on disposable income and on government revenues, thus dampening or exaggerating economic cycles.

Surplus and Deficit Financing. Governments, particularly the federal government, are a major source of demand for credit in times of deficit financing. Policies that are aimed at restoring balance to a deficit budget can have an important impact on interest rates by curtailing the government's need to borrow funds. Conversely, fiscal policy that calls for increased government spending tends to have an inflationary impact that may force interest rates higher.

Monetary Policy

In recent years, U. S. monetary policy, as implemented by the Federal Reserve, has been one of the most important factors influencing all interest rates. The basic objective of monetary policy is to promote stable economic growth. Economic growth can be accelerated or slowed by altering the supply of money and the availability of credit. The Federal Reserve (Fed) uses a number of tools to achieve its broad objective of maintaining a healthy economy through its management of the nation's money supply. Among the most significant are these:

Open Market Operations. The Fed purchases and sells in the open market Treasury bills, notes, bonds, and other U. S. government obligations to dealers who pay for their purchases by transferring money into the Fed or who receive money for their sales from the Fed. Fed purchases of U. S. government or agency securities supply reserves to the banking system, while Fed sales withdraw reserves. When the Fed buys securities in the open market, it creates bank reserves that did not exist before. It pays for the securities by crediting a bank's reserve account.

The dealers who sell securities to the Fed have often borrowed more than 95% of their value from insurance companies, corporations, banks, and investors around the world. When the Fed buys securities and then credits the appropriate bank accounts, loans are immediately repaid and bank reserves spread quickly across the country to a multitude of institutions.

Reserve Requirements. Changes in bank reserve requirements are a less frequently used method of inducing changes in interest rates. Every bank is required to keep a certain percent of its deposits in reserve. When the Fed reduces this requirement, added funds are made available for loans, and interest rates tend to ease. Increases in reserve requirements tend to cause rates to rise because fewer funds are available for loans.

Banks have two important ways of controlling their level of reserves. If a bank loses reserves to other banks through the normal ebb and flow of business transactions, it can borrow reserve balances short term from other banks with excess reserves. These reserve balances are known as *federal funds* or *fed funds*. Banks turn to the fed funds market to borrow when they are short of reserves or to make loans when they have excess reserves. The rate at which these reserves are lent overnight, the *federal funds rate,* is an important indicator of short-term interest rates.

The Discount Rate. Another means of increasing reserves is for the banks to borrow directly from the Fed. The interest rate on such loans is called the *discount rate.* The discount rate of each Federal Reserve Bank is ultimately determined by the Board of Governors of the Federal Reserve System. The Fed may use a reduction in the discount rate to signal its decision to make bank reserves more available. Conversely, it may raise the discount rate to signal a decision to limit the supply of bank reserves.

Margin Limits. To curb the use of excessive credit, the Federal Reserve Board is empowered to set the limit on how much credit broker/dealers can extend to their customers for the purchase of common stock. In the post-World War II period, this limit has ranged between zero and 50% of the securities' value.

Money Supply

Of the Fed statistics that are watched by traders, the *money supply* is by far the most widely followed. As of mid-1987, money supply was defined in three ways: *M1* is the narrowest definition, consisting of currency that is held by the public, travelers' checks, and deposits at banks and other depository institutions. Bank deposits include demand deposits and other checkable deposits. *M2* and *M3,* the more broadly defined aggregates, include *M1* and such other assets as savings deposits, time deposits, and shares in money market mutual funds. The Fed's target growth rates for the various measures of money supply are a matter of public record. When the weekly figures run above or below these targets, the Fed will often intervene to steer the money supply toward its goals.

In theory, it would seem that an increase in the money supply would tend to push interest rates lower because more money is available to borrowers. Higher rates might be expected to follow reductions in the money supply as credit availability tightens. However, the actual relationship between interest rates and changes in the money supply can be both complex and unpredictable. A rapid increase in money supply, for instance, may be regarded as inflationary and therefore lead to higher interest rates. Interest rates are sensitive to both the supply of money itself and also to the effect that any changes in the money supply might have on inflation. Which of these opposing considerations is more important depends on market sentiment and varies significantly over time.

Inflation is one of the most powerful forces affecting interest rates. Interest rates must approximate the rate of inflation to compensate lenders for the fact that they will be paid back with depreciated dollars. Thus, increases in the rate of inflation tend to increase interest rates. Declining inflation tends to have a weakening effect on interest rates.

As we discussed in Chapter 14, the interest rates that are paid by borrowers are referred to as *nominal interest rates*. The difference between the nominal rate and the inflation rate is known as the *real interest rate* because it represents the actual profit to the lender and the actual cost to the borrower after allowing for the reduced value of the principal caused by inflation.

INTEREST RATE MARKETS

The heart of activity for short-term interest rate instruments is a broad, vaguely defined trading arena known as the *money market*. The term generally refers to the market for short-term credit instruments such as Treasury bills, commercial paper, bankers' acceptances, certificates of deposit, and Federal funds. We later define these instruments and others that belong to the market for longer-term debt securities such as Treasury notes, GNMAs, and Treasury bonds. For now, we touch on a few important features of the money market so that the reader is familiar with some basic concepts and terms.

It is a characteristic of business and financial institutions that their cash receipts and disbursements are not usually balanced. For instance, a business may find that on some days its cash holdings accumulate because receipts have exceeded expenditures. At other times, the same business may be short of cash because cash expenses have outpaced cash income. Most businesses prefer to maintain some cash reserve so that expenses can be met with minimal dependence on current cash inflow. Some financial institutions, such as commercial banks, also must maintain cash reserves to comply with statutory reserve requirements. To minimize the cost of these cash reserves, business and financial organizations invest the cash in highly liquid, short-term instruments. During periods of excess cash, they buy these instruments. When in need of cash, they sell them. The money market and the instruments that comprise it help to meet the alternating cash requirements of these enterprises.

Trading in the money market does not occur on specific exchanges as it does in organized futures or securities markets. Instead, participants around the world deal with one another by telephone in a principal-to-principal dealer market. The center of activity is New York and major participants include the Federal Reserve Bank of New York, commercial banks, finance companies, nonfinancial corporations, Government securities dealers, and brokerage firms.

The term *capital market* is used to describe the arena for raising long-term capital. The capital market differs from the money market primarily in the maturity of the instruments. A second distinguishing feature is that the capital markets include both debt and equity instruments, but the money markets deal in only debt securities. The money market is designed for short-term financing, while the capital market finances long-term. Because of these longer maturities, securities in the capital market usually have greater risk than do money market instruments.

The main consumers of funds in the long-term capital market are corporations that borrow long term by selling bonds or raise equity by selling stock, plus governments, banks, and other financial institutions. The main lenders are individuals, banks, savings institutions, governments (federal, local, and foreign), insurance companies, labor unions, and foundations.

Repurchase Agreements (Repos)

Before discussing the specific instruments of the money and capital markets we take a few moments to comment on how these instruments are usually financed. By far the most common financing technique is known as a *repurchase agreement* or a *repo*. Basically, a repo is a short-term loan that is collateralized by securities whose value is approximately the same as the amount of the loan.

For example, suppose Mr. *A* owns a $1 million 90-day T-bill which has a market value of $980,000. A typical repo might involve these components:

- Mr. *A* sells the T-bills to Mr. *B* for settlement tomorrow for a price of $980,000.
- Mr. *A* agrees to repurchase the T-bills from Mr. *B* for settlement one week from tomorrow for a price of $981,507.

The additional $1,507 received by Mr. *B* represents an annualized return of about 8.00% on his $980,000. The T-bill can be viewed as collateral for the loan of $980,000.

Two points regarding repos are worth emphasizing:

- In theory, any instrument could be used as collateral for the related loan. In practice, government securities of various types are the most frequently used instruments in repo transactions.
- Most repos are done for very short periods—often overnight. The *overnight repo rate,* which is the annualized return to overnight lenders of dollars in repo transactions, tends to closely track the *fed funds rate* that we discussed previously.

Traders often use the term *reverse repo.* This is simply a repo as seen from the perspective of the person who lends dollars and receives securities as collateral. The terms *repo* and *reverse repo* describe different sides of the same transaction.

Repos are used by the Fed when it seeks to influence the federal funds rate. As a buyer of repos (lender of cash to dealers) it increases reserves. When we hear that "the Fed is doing repos," this means that it is lending money and increasing bank reserves. Reverse repos by the Fed entail the borrowing of funds or the absorbing of reserves. Thus, repos and reverse repos are an instrument of the Fed's open market operations. Note that the terms *repo* and *reverse repo* have their meanings reversed when applied to Fed activities as seen from the perspective of the Fed. This is simply an established convention.

MONEY MARKET INSTRUMENTS

The United States money markets include a wide array of public and private short-term debt instruments. In this section we focus on four specific instruments on which futures contracts have been based. Two of these contracts (T-bill futures and Eurodollar futures) are thriving in mid-1987. The other two (Commercial Paper futures and Certificate of Deposit futures) are dormant. It is instructive to consider both the specifics of these instruments and the factors that contributed to their success or failure as futures contracts.

Treasury Bills

Treasury bills (T-bills) are obligations of the U. S. government. They are issued with a variety of maturities and denominations to suit the needs of a diverse group of investors. Their high liquidity and strength of credit make them the most widely held of all debt instruments. Their use by the U. S. government in debt management and in the implementation of monetary policy makes them the most important of all monetary instruments.

T-bills with maturities of three, six, and twelve months are offered by the U.S. Treasury through regularly scheduled competitive auctions. The minimum puchase amount is $10,000 (face value), with $5,000 increments available thereafter. At its auctions, the Treasury sells T-bills at a discount from their face (or *par*) value. The return to the investor is the difference between the purchase price and the face value at the time of maturity. Thus, a $10,000, 3-month T-bill bought at $9,750 provides a $250 return when it matures.

Because Treasury bills are issued on a discount basis, their yields are calculated in a manner that is quite different from other instruments that pay interest. To illustrate, suppose an investor buys $100,000 of one-year T-bills at a yield of 10%. This means that the Treasury sells the investor $100,000 of bills that mature in one year at a price approximately 10% below their face value. To calculate the actual discount from face value, we must take into account: (1) that Treasury calculates the discount as if a year had only 360 days, and (2) that the one-year bill has an actual life of 364 days. Thus the portion of the year that the bill exists is 364/360 and the discount is:

$100,000 face value x (0.10 per annum) x (364)/360 = $10,111

The price the investor pays for the bill is:

$$\$100,000 - \$10,111 = \underline{\$89,889}$$

Generalizing from these calculations, we have the formula for figuring the discount from face value for a Treasury bill, or any discount instrument based on a 360-day year that we discussed in Chapter 9:

$$D = F \times d \times t/360$$

where

D = discount from face value ($10,111)
F = face value at maturity ($100,000)
d = rate of discount (10% or 0.10)
t = days to maturity (364)

Using the same notation, the actual price (P) paid for a T-bill is:

$$P = F - D$$

Actual Treasury bills are quoted in *basis points*. A basis point is 1/100 of 1 percentage point or 0.01%. For reasons that will be apparent later, let us calculate the value of a basis point on a 90-day bill with a $1 million face value. First, assuming a discount yield of 10%, we have

$$D = \$1,000,000 \times 0.1000 \times 90/360 = \$25,000$$

and

$$P = \$975,000$$

Next, assuming a discount rate of 10.01% we have

$$D = \$1,000,000 \times 0.1001 \times 90/360 = \$25,025$$

and

$$P = \$974,975$$

Thus, an increase of one basis point lowers the bill's price by $25. Similarly, a decrease of one basis point in yield would increase the bill's price by $25.

It is important to distinguish between the *discount rate(d)* and the more familiar *simple rate of interest (i)*. Simple interest is expressed as follows:

$$i = \frac{(P+I)-P}{P} = \frac{I}{P}$$

where

i = simple rate of interest
P = principal invested
I = interest earned in dollars

If the instrument is held for a period other than a full year, then

$$i = \frac{(P+I)-P}{P} \times \frac{365}{t}$$

where

t = time held

In this case i is the annualized simple interest.

The discount yield that is earned on a discount instrument such as a T-bill understates the rate of return earned on a simple-interest basis. To illustrate, take the case of the 90-day, $1 million T-bill with a discount yield of 10%. On a simple-interest basis, the yield would be:

$$i = \frac{(\$975,000 + \$25,000) - \$975,000}{\$975,000} \times \frac{365}{90} = \underline{10.40\%}$$

This compares with the quoted discount yield of 10.00%.

Readers should be aware that there is one other type of interest rate besides discount and simple that is used frequently in financial futures calculations. It is known as the *equivalent-bond yield*, and will be discussed later in the section on coupon instruments.

Treasury Bill Futures

Futures trading in U.S. Treasury bills began on the International Monetary Market of the Chicago Mercantile Exchange in January 1976. Although several other exchanges have attempted to establish trading in their own T-bill futures contracts, the IMM remains by far the dominant marketplace. T-bills enjoy large supplies and the uniform, unquestioned credit of the U. S. government. These facts have contributed to the success of T-bill futures trading.

The T-bill contract on the IMM calls for delivery of $1 million of 90 day T-bills. Contracts mature in March, June, September, and December for roughly two years into the future. The purchase of the T-bill futures contract obligates the holder to take delivery of and pay for a $1 million T-bill that will mature 90 days from the date of delivery of the futures contract, which is usually in the third week of the delivery month. Of course, as with all futures contracts, delivery can be avoided by liquidating the futures contract prior to its delivery period.

Because cash T-bills are traditionally quoted on a yield basis, the bid is actually higher than the offer. Buyers in the secondary market are interested in making purchases at the highest possible yield, while sellers want to receive the highest possible price for the bills (the lowest possible yield). This posed a problem for futures traders who were accustomed to bids being lower than offers. To accommodate the orientation of futures traders, the IMM devised a pricing system for its futures contracts called the *IMM index*, which is inversely related to yields.

The *IMM index* is based on the difference between the actual T-bill yield and 100.00. Thus, a T-bill yield of 8.00 percent would be quoted on the IMM as 92.00. It is important to note that the IMM index is not the same as the issue price of a 90-day bill because T-bill yields and the IMM index are based on annualized rates.

To illustrate, we will calculate the discounted price of the actual 90-day T-bill that corresponds to an IMM quote of 92.00. If the IMM index is 92.00, the discount yield is 8.00% (100.00 - 92.00 = 8.00). The dollar discount on a 90-day T-bill is therefore:

$$\text{Discount} = \$1{,}000{,}000 \times 0.08 \times 90/360 = \$20{,}000$$

Because the T-bill price equals its face value minus its discount, the price of the T-bill that corresponds to an IMM index of 92.00 is as follows:

$$\text{Price} = \text{Face Value} - \text{Discount} = \$1{,}000{,}000 - \$20{,}000 = \$980{,}000$$

The minimum price fluctuation of the T-bill futures contract is one basis point, or 1/100 of 1%. To calculate the value of this minimum fluctuation, we must multiply the size of the contract ($1 million) by 0.01% and then by 1/4, which equals $25. The reason we multiply by 1/4 is to account for the fact that we are dealing with 3-month bills (one-quarter of a year). Thus, a 1% change in the yield of a $1 million, 3-month T-bill is equivalent to a 1% change in that of a $250,000 one-year T-bill.

Take the case of a trader who buys one contract of March 90-day T-bill futures at 92.00 and later sells it at 94.00.

Example.

Purchase: IMM index = 92.00
           Yield = 8%
           T-bill price = $980,000
Sale: IMM index = 94.00
           Yield = 6%
           T-bill price = $985,000
Gain: $5,000 (Each basis point change equals $25)

Now we will take the same example using a $250,000 one-year T-bill:

Purchase: Yield = 8%
           T-bill price = $230,000
Sale: Yield = 6%
           T-bill price = $235,000
Gain: $5,000 (For the one year T-bill each basis point change also equals $25)

By now it should be apparent that because the IMM index is inversely related to yields, a trader who expects interest rates to rise would sell T-bill futures. A trader who expects rates to fall would buy futures.

In later sections we will discuss some of the trading and hedging opportunities that are provided by these futures contracts.

Commercial Paper

Commercial paper is an unsecured promissory note that is issued by large firms to raise short-term funds. For many corporations, the issuance of commercial paper has become a popular alternative to bank loans when they are in need of cash. Commercial paper is classified as unsecured because the instrument is not backed by specific assets of the issuing firm. It derives its creditworthiness strictly from the general creditworthiness of the issuer. Most commercial paper is rated by private rating services such as Moody's or Standard and Poor's. Maturities are limited to less than 270 days, although most paper is issued for 30-day maturity. As such, commercial paper is an important barometer of very short-term interest rates in the private sector.

Most commercial paper is quoted on a discount basis, regardless of whether it is initially sold as a discount instrument or as an interest-bearing one. Hence, yield calculations are based on the same principles and formulas that are used for Treasury bills.

Commercial Paper Futures

The Chicago Board of Trade (CBT) listed futures contracts in commercial paper for both 90-day maturity (1977) and 30-day maturity (1979). In both cases the contract called for delivery of paper rated A-1 by Standard and Poor's and P-1 by Moody's and approved as deliverable by the CBT. The basic trading unit was $3 million for 30-day commercial paper and $1 million for 90-day paper.

Both contracts failed to generate sustained trading volume and came to a virtual standstill. One reason for the failure is instructive. The CBT was unable to devise specifications that permitted the delivery of paper for a broad range of issuers who were viewed as equally creditworthy. This inability to ensure the integrity and fungibility of deliverable items led to the demise of these futures contracts.

Certificates of Deposit

Certificates of deposit (CDs) are negotiable receipts for funds that are deposited in a bank for a specified period of time at a specified rate of interest. Negotiable CDs were first issued in the early 1960s when interest rates had risen above the rates that banks were allowed by the Federal Reserve Bank to pay under Regulation Q. Earlier, large bank deposits had to be held to maturity, a feature that offered limited appeal to businesses and individuals who were concerned about liquidity. The negotiable CD, by virtue of its saleability before maturity, attracted greater corporate deposits and allowed banks to compete more effective-ly for short-term funds. It now accounts for an important share of trad-ing in money market instruments.

CDs are usually issued with maturities of one to three months, at which time the holder of the certificate receives both principal and inter-est. They are issued in denominations ranging from $100,000 to $10 million. CDs pay interest on a 360-day basis at maturity. The rate of in-terest is known as the *coupon rate*. This means that an investor buys a CD of face value (*F*) and receives this face value plus a dollar amount of interest (*I*) at maturity. The CD's value at maturity is equal to *F* plus *I*.

The amount of interest received (in dollars) is expressed as follows:

$$I = F \times i \times t/360$$

where

I = interest received (in dollars)
F = face value
i = CD coupon rate (simple interest)
t = time to maturity

For a 90 day, $1 million CD at a rate of 10%, interest earned is:

$$I = \$1,000,000 \times 0.10 \times 90/360 = \$25,000$$

This CD's value at maturity *(F + I)* would be $1,025,000.

CD Futures

Futures trading in certificates of deposit began on three different exchanges (CBT, IMM, and New York Futures Exchange) in July 1981. The IMM contract was the only one to enjoy much success, but its popularity peaked in 1984 and declined rapidly thereafter. By 1987, it had became dormant. The demise resulted from the combination of the near failure of Continental Illinois National Bank and Trust Company (discussed below) and the growing popularity of the IMM's own Euro-dollar futures contract (see the following section).

To be deliverable against the IMM contract, a CD must be issued by a so-called top-tier bank, one with high credit rating and one whose

CDs are interchangeable in the secondary market with banks of equally high rating. However, in 1984 Continental Illinois was withdrawn from the approved list as problems with its loan portfolio brought it near failure. This incident focused traders' attention on the uncertainties surrounding the credit qualities underlying CD futures. After the Continental Illinois incident, CD futures steadily lost popularity.

Eurodollars

Eurodollars are deposits of U.S. dollars in banks outside the United States, including deposits at foreign branches of U.S. banks. The term *Eurodollar* is something of a misnomer because the market now encompasses U.S. dollar deposits in any country other than the United States. At any rate, because these deposits are held outside of the United States, they are not subject to many of the banking regulations that govern domestic deposits. This fact, along with others, has promoted the growth of the Eurodollar market to such an extent that it now is a major arena for the borrowing and lending of dollars at the international level.

Eurodollar deposits usually have a fixed term of less than six months and are made by corporations, central banks, U. S. banks, dealers, and wealthy individuals. Banks that receive Eurodollar deposits make dollar loans to the business, governmental, and banking sectors.

A significant amount of Eurodollar activity is between the Eurobanks themselves. Because domestic banks with reserve surpluses may use the Euromarket as an alternative to the fed funds market, Euro rates for overnight delivery are closely tied to the fed funds rate.

Eurodollar Futures

Eurodollar futures trading began in late 1981 on the IMM. The contract calls for trading in 90-day Eurodollar time deposits with prime London banks. Unlike most other futures contracts that require delivery of a particular instrument, the Eurodollar contract calls for *cash settlement* at time of delivery. The final settlement price of the contract is determined by a polling method described in Chapter 39 of the *Rules of the Chicago Mercantile Exchange*. Like CDs, Eurodollars are quoted on a simple interest basis and are based on a 360-day year. Delivery months are March, June, September, and December. Contract size is $1 million. Quotes are based on an index such that 100 minus the index equates to the Eurodollar yield. Eurodollar futures grew explosively in popularity after the Continental Illinois problem in 1984 shifted activity away from CD futures. By 1987, Eurodollar futures had become the most active of all short-term interest rate futures contracts by a wide margin.

LONG-TERM COUPON INSTRUMENTS

The three instruments discussed next (GNMAs, Treasury notes, and Treasury bonds) have two features that distinguish them from the money market instruments discussed previously. First, their maturities are much longer. Second, they pay interest through semiannual coupon redemptions. Following our discussions of these coupon instruments and their futures contracts, we touch briefly on municipal bonds and the CBT's Municipal bond index futures contract.

A $100,000 bond that has a coupon rate of 8% would yield two $4,000 coupon payments per year. Coupon instruments are quoted on the basis of *yield to maturity*. If a bond that has an 8% coupon were trading at par, its yield to maturity would be 8%. It should be noted that, all other factors constant, yield-to-maturity quotes tend to understate true yield because they do not take into consideration the rate at which the semiannual coupon payments must be reinvested. Another consideration is that yield to maturity assumes a single (rather than double) annual payment that is reinvested at the same coupon rate. In other words, all future income from an 8% coupon bond is assumed to be reinvested annually at 8%. However divorced from reality this may be at times, it is a convention that allows traders to make comparisons between yields of different instruments.

To compare yields of different types (simple, discount, bond yield to maturity), the standard practice of the industry is to convert all rates to their *equivalent-bond yield*. For instruments with maturities of less than six months, this simply involves multiplying the discount rate by the fraction 365/360 to offset the effect of the difference in the assumed length of a year. For instruments with maturities of more than six months, the arithmetic becomes much more complicated.

Coupon instruments are quoted in the cash market as a percentage of par, with minimum price gradations usually in 32nds of a point. For example, the Treasury might issue a 6-year note with a 9% coupon at par. The price of this security would be 100, which means that the investor would have to pay $100 for every $100 of face value. In this case, of course, the yield is equal to the coupon rate—no more, no less.

However, once notes and bonds are issued and find their way into the secondary market, their prices will change as general interest rates vary. If the rates on comparable securities have risen since the issuance of a particular Treasury note or bond, its value and price will be diminished. In our example, if rates on other 6-year T-notes rose to 10% since our 9% note was first issued, its price might fall to 98–4 ($98^4/32 per $100 of face value). The reason for the decline in the note's price is that holders of the 9% coupon security are inclined to sell it and purchase the higher yielding 10% notes currently available. The selling pressure drives the price of the note down to a level where the effective yield on the 9% coupon note is in line with the yield on comparable securities.

How does the decline in price of a note or bond bring its effective yield into line with that of other higher yielding securities? Because the note will mature at full face value, the investor who buys the note at a discounted price receives a capital gain that is equal to the difference between his purchase price and the value at maturity. This capital gain must be added to the coupon's interest payments to determine the total effective yield. When the note's price has been driven down to a level where its effective yield equals the yield on notes of similar risk and maturity, investors will once again be willing to purchase it.

It should be clear that this process also occurs when interest rates on comparable notes increase. When this happens, the price of the higher coupon security will be driven above par by an amount that makes the capital loss entailed in its ownership equal (in yield) to the difference between its coupon and others. We now turn to four specific coupon instruments which are important in the futures markets.

GNMAs

The Government National Mortgage Association (*GNMA* or *Ginnie Mae*) is an agency within the Department of Housing and Urban Development that guarantees the timely payment of home mortgages that are insured by the Federal Housing Administration or by the Veterans Administration. It then allows approved financial institutions to issue certificates backed by these mortgages. These certificates are standardized, very liquid instruments with interest payments comparable to those of government guaranteed securities.

The holder of a GNMA certificate is essentially investing in a pool of mortgages for which the interest and principal payments are guaranteed by an agency of the Federal government. While most certificates represent single family mortgages of a 30-year maximum maturity, the average life of the mortgage pool is less than 12 years, due to prepayments by homeowners. All mortgages in a pool have the same interest rate and approximately the same maturity date. Like notes and bonds, GNMA certificates are issued with a coupon and trade in the secondary market at a percentage of par.

GNMA Futures

GNMA futures trading began in October 1975 on the Chicago Board of Trade. GNMAs were the first contracts based on an interest rate instrument ever to trade on a futures exchange. Their success ushered in a new era in futures trading. The basic trading unit is a $100,000 principal balance GNMA with an 8% or equivalent coupon. Delivery months are March, June, September, and December. Prices are quoted as a percent of par with a minimum fluctuation of 1/32 of a point ($31.25 per contract). By early 1987, trading in GNMA futures had all but evaporated as traders flocked to T-bond futures to hedge and to speculate in long-term interest rates.

Treasury Notes

Treasury notes (or *T-notes*) are interest-bearing securities that are issued by the U. S. Treasury at or near face value and that are redeemed at face value. When issued, T-notes have maturities ranging from one to ten years. Like T-bills, notes are typically sold at Federal Reserve auctions. As noted earlier, interest on Treasury notes is paid semiannually through the redemption of coupons.

Treasury notes are sold to public investors to raise funds for government programs and to refund maturing debt. Like T-bills, they are backed by the full faith and credit of the U. S. government and are almost universally viewed as one of the safest types of investments.

Treasury Note Futures

Between 1979 and 1982 several attempts were made to establish futures trading in T-notes. In mid-1979, the Chicago Board of Trade initiated trading in 4 to 6 year notes, while at the same time the IMM started its 3 to 4 year note contract. In 1980, Comex made an attempt at a two-year note contract. All of these efforts met with little success, but in 1982 the Chicago Board of Trade (CBT) began trading in 10-year notes, which captured significant trading volume.

The CBT's 10-year T-note contract is based on a security with a face value of $100,000, maturing in 6½ to 10 years. An 8% coupon is the par grade used for pricing all notes delivered against the futures contract. The 8% rate was chosen by the CBT to correspond with the standards used in T-bond and GNMA futures. Prices are quoted as a percentage of par, with minimum fluctuations that are equal to 1/32 of a point ($31.25 per contract). Delivery months are March, June, September, and December.

Treasury Bonds

Like Treasury notes, *Treasury bonds (T-bonds)* are sold to investors to help meet long-term government obligations. The only difference between Treasury notes and Treasury bonds is that bonds are issued in longer maturities. T-bonds are issued in two separate cycles. Since early 1981, 20-year bonds have been auctioned quarterly and 30-year bonds at less regular intervals averaging about three times per year. A typical T-bond auction offers several billion dollars in bonds to domestic and foreign investors.

Treasury Bond Futures

The CBT's Treasury bond contract was started in 1977 and has risen to be the most successful contract in the history of futures trading. The basic trading unit is a $100,000 bond with an 8% standard coupon, maturing at least 15 years from the date of delivery of the futures contract. Like notes, bond futures are priced as a percent of par, with minimum fluctuation equal to 1/32 of a point (31.25 per contract). Delivery months are March, June, September, and December.

Municipal Bonds

Municipal bonds are long-term debt instruments that are issued by states and municipalities to raise funds for a variety of purposes. Some municipal bonds relate to specific public projects such as hospitals, power, pollution control, or transportation. Others represent general obligations of the state or municipality that issued the bond.

Municipal bonds are unique among debt instruments because the interest that the holders of these securities receive is usually exempt from federal taxation and sometimes from state and local taxation as well. Furthermore, the credit qualities of municipal bonds can and do vary significantly from issuer to issuer, as is also true of corporate bonds. These two features combined can cause changes in municipal bond yields to correlate only loosely with changes in U. S. Treasury bond yields. This situation makes it difficult to cross hedge municipal bonds in T-bond futures and led the Chicago Board of Trade to introduce a municipal bond futures contract in 1985.

Municipal Bond Futures

The development of a municipal bond futures contract was made difficult by the fact that there are literally thousands of separate municipal bonds. No one of these enjoys such liquidity or such prominence that it can serve as an accepted benchmark for long-term municipal interest rates in the way that T-bonds serve as the benchmark for long-term federal government rates.

The CBT addressed this problem by creating a futures contract that is based on *The Bond Buyer Municipal Bond Index*. This is an index of 50 select long-term municipal bonds that is computed daily by *The Bond Buyer*, which is a trade publication. The prices of the bonds in the index are obtained by excluding the highest and lowest quotes provided by five bond dealers and averaging the remaining three quotes for each issue. The contract calls for cash settlement, rather than for delivery of the underlying bonds. Cash settlement is discussed in Chapter 20. As of mid-1987, the municipal bond futures contract appeared to be gaining acceptance among both hedgers and speculators.

TRADING AND HEDGING APPLICATIONS IN INTEREST RATE FUTURES

The use of futures by financial institutions and other businesses to hedge interest rate risk has grown dramatically. So has participation both by dealers who seek low-risk, arbitrage-type opportunities and by speculators who seek trading profits. The following examples illustrate how a variety of market participants make use of interest rate futures for protection and/or profit.

Example 1: Speculating on a rise in short-term interest rates. After a severe drop, 3-month Treasury bill rates have begun to stabilize. Fundamental data suggests that the economy is moving out of its recent recession. Recent moves by the Federal Reserve Board suggest a more accommodative stance. The prices of most commodities have begun to strengthen in a possible early signal of renewed inflation.

To profit from a possible upswing in rates, you might sell one December T-bill futures contract at 93.50 (6.50% discount yield) based on the expectation that bill prices will fall to 92.00 (8.00% discount yield). If your analysis proves correct, you will make a profit of 150 points that, at $25 per point per contract, represents a gain of $3,750.

To protect yourself from a prolonged adverse price move, you might enter a buy stop to close out the position if prices rise to 94.00. This would represent a loss of $1,250, and a reward/risk ratio of 3:1, neglecting commissions and order-execution slippage.

Example 2: Hedging borrowing costs. A corporation intends to borrow $5 million during the last quarter of the year on a loan that is tied to the prime rate. As the corporate treasurer, you are concerned that an increase in interest rates could make this loan prohibitively expensive. The prime rate is now $7^1/2\%$, which seems attractive given your expectations of a rise to $8^1/2\%$ or 9%. How can the corporation lock in present rates?

Because there is no futures market in prime rates, you must select the hedging vehicle whose price behavior most closely resembles that of the prime rate. Your basis studies suggest that T-bill futures are the best match. On March 1 you sell five September T-bill futures at a price of 93.55. By late August the prime has risen to 9% and September T-bills are now trading at 92.20. Your borrowing costs have increased by $18,750 ($5 million x 1.5% x 1/4 year). Your short hedge in T-bill futures, while not providing perfect protection, produced a profit of $16,875.

Example 3: Hedging the cost of issuing certificates of deposit. In early June, a bank anticipates having to reprice $10 million of CDs in September. Current 90-day CD rates are 8.50%. On June 15, to protect itself against rising interest rates, the bank sells 10 September CD futures at 91.00. On September 1, the bank reprices the $10 million of 90-day CDs at 8.90%. September CD futures are trading at 90.60.

At the June 15 rate of 8.50%, the bank's interest expense would be as follows:

$$I = \$10 \text{ million} \times 0.0850 \times 90/360 = \underline{\$212,500}$$

At the September 1 rate of 8.90%, the bank's interest expense will be:

$$I = \$10 \text{ million} \times 0.0890 \times 90/360 = \underline{\$222,500}$$

The increased interest cost due to the rise in rates is $10,000.
Meanwhile, the September CD futures contract declined by 40 points, yielding a profit of precisely $10,000.

Example 4: Hedging a floating-rate LIBOR loan. LIBOR, the London Interbank Offered Rate, is the rate at which banks offer to lend dollars in the Euromarket. Eurodollar loans are often tied to the LIBOR rate.

Assume that on March 15 a borrower negotiates a three-month loan at a 90-day LIBOR rate of 8.38%. Because she plans to roll the loan at maturity for another three months, she also sells short June Eurodollar futures at a yield of 9.07% to fix a 9.07% borrowing rate for the three-month period beginning in June. The hedger accepts this 9.07% rate as attractive in view of the prospects for even higher rates in June when the loan will be repriced. For instance, if 90-day LIBOR were to increase to 10.00%, the effective borrowing cost for the full 180-day period would be 9.19%. The hedge created on March 15 would result in a six-month borrowing cost of 8.73%, for a savings of 46 basis points.

Example 5: Hedging gold spreads with Eurodollar futures. Assume the following prices on September 1:

Comex Gold		IMM Eurodollar Futures	
December	$400.00	December	92.00
February	405.00	March	93.00
April	410.00	(Implied 6-month forward rate	
June	415.00	equals 7.50%)	

A floor trader on Comex establishes a position of short 25 December gold/long 25 June gold because he expects much higher gold prices over the next two months. However, he is concerned that a decline in interest rates may exert pressure on the spread and could offset any widening that would occur from the higher gold prices. To hedge this risk he buys one contract each of December and March Eurodollars at 92.00 and 93.00, respectively. The $1 million Eurodollar contract is equal in value to the 25 gold contracts. Two successive three-month contracts are needed to cover the six-month period of the gold spread.

By November 15, December gold has risen to $460.00. Had forward interest rates remained at 7.50%, the six-month interest cost of carry would suggest a June price of $477.20. Because the spread was established at $15.00 and would be trading at $17.20, the trader would enjoy a profit of $5,500 ($220 per contract x 25 contracts).

Instead, the six-month forward rate drops to 6.38%. The six-month interest cost would now be $14.70 ($460 x 6.38% x $1/2$), and June futures would be $474.70. The spread has actually narrowed by 30 cents because declining interest rates more than offset the higher gold price in the cost of carry.

Fortunately, the Eurodollar futures reflected the drop in rates. On November 15, December Euros traded at 93.10 and March Euros at 94.00. The results are summarized in Figure 18-2.

Figure 18-2.

Gold Position	

September 1	November 15
Bought 25 June @$415.00	Sold 25 June @$474.70
Sold 25 December @$400.00	Bought 25 December @$460.00

Net Loss: $750

Eurodollar Position

September 1	November 15
Bought 1 December @92.00	Sold 1 December @93.10
Bought 1 March @93.00	Sold 1 March @94.00

Net Profit: $5,250

Had interest rates remained unchanged, the gold spread would have yielded an approximate profit of $5,500. Unhedged, it would have produced a loss of $750.

The combined gold/Eurodollar position produced a profit of $4,500.

Example 6: Hedging the Gap. All banks, financial institutions, and many corporations have unavoidable mismatches in their interest-sensitive assets and liabilities. A bank, for instance, might be using six-month money market certificates to fund 30-day loans. Gap analysis involves putting interest-sensitive assets and liabilities into time categories and then netting the assets and liabilities in each category. A positive gap (assets mature before liabilities) in any category means that the institution will benefit from a rise in relevant interest rates because it will roll-over the maturing asset at a higher rate.

Suppose that a bank's analysis of its gap revealed the following as of February 10:

Maturity Range	Gap
0–90 days	+ $3 million
91–180 days	+ $2 million
181–270 days	– $2 million
271–360 days	–$6 million

If we look at each maturity range separately we see that the bank needs to hedge against falling interest rates for its 0 to 90 day and its 91 to 180 day portfolios and against rising interest rates for the 181 to 270 day and the 271 to 360 day intervals. If we assume for the sake of simplicity that the *average* maturity mismatch between assets and liabilities within each interval equals 90 days, then the appropriate hedges for the individual intervals would be:

Maturity Range	Gap	Hedge
0–90 days	+ $3 million	Buy 3 March Eurodollars
91–180 days	+ $2 million	Buy 2 June Eurodollars
181–270 days	– $2 million	Sell 2 Sept. Eurodollars
271–360 days	– $3 million	Sell 6 Dec. Eurodollars
Net Futures hedge:		Buy 3 March, Buy 2 June, Sell 2 Sept., Sell 6 Dec. Eurodollars

The correct hedge for the position as a whole is obtained by combining the hedges for the separate maturity ranges. Within each time interval the long futures contracts lengthen the average maturity of the liabilities. The overall result is a better match between asset and liability maturity profiles.

It is extremely important to be aware of the difficulties involved in hedging gaps. There is a considerable debate over the relative merits of *macrohedging* and *microhedging*. Macrohedging involves adopting a futures position that reduces the overall net portfolio risk of an organization. Microhedging is based on hedging the risks of individual assets or liabilities. To determine which hedge method to use, a statistical relationship that involves individual assets and liabilities, overall portfolio risk, gap risk, and relevant futures contract behavior should be studied. Only then can the most effective hedge mechanism be determined.

Example 7: Hedging a Treasury Note Auction. The following example that is provided by the Chicago Board of Trade shows how a government securities dealer might limit his exposure when bidding for T-notes at a Federal Reserve auction.

On June 30 a primary government dealer is preparing to bid on a new 7-year Treasury note with a coupon of 14% that is to be auctioned during the quarterly financing. Economic uncertainty and a growing supply of new debt have depressed note prices. The dealer is concerned that between the time he makes his bid (committing to a purchase price) and the time he sells the 7-year note to other dealers or to retail customers, prices will fall further.

To protect the price at which he will sell his 7-year notes, the dealer puts on a short hedge. If note prices decline, the hedge should allow him to sell his position at a break-even price or to wait for prices to return to a profitable level. If prices begin to rise, he may close out his futures position and profit in his cash position.

In order to fully cover his cash position, the dealer weights his hedge as explained previously:

$$\frac{\$10,000,000}{\$100,000} \times 1.3169 = \underline{132 \text{ contracts}}$$

The factor 1.3169 enters the picture because the maturity of the note that is being hedged (7 years) differs from the par maturity of the futures contract (10 years). It comes from the CBOT booklet entitled "Chicago Board of Trade Conversion Factors," pages 36 and 37 of which are shown in Figure 18-3 (see pages 465–468) and which we discussed previously in Chapter 9.

On each successive day that he is selling out his cash position, the dealer uses this same formula to calculate the correct number of contracts he must buy back. We omit the calculations and give only the resulting actions and results:

Cash	Futures
June 30	*June 30*
A bid of 14.125% on $10 million of 7-year notes is accepted. Coupon: 14%, Current price: 99-14	Sell 132 September contracts at 75-20

July 1	*July 1*
Sell $3 million at 98-28	Buy 39 September contracts at 75-06
Loss: $16,875	Profit: $17,062
July 2	*July 2*
Sell $2 million at 99-2	Buy 26 September contracts at 75-11
Loss: $7,500	Profit: $7,312
July 6	*July 3*
Treasury note prices begin to rally	Buy 67 September contracts at 75-24
Current price: 99-20	Loss: $8,375
Sell $5 million notes at 100-12	
Profit: $46,875	
Profit: $22,500	Profit: $15,999

Net Gain: $38,499

As prices moved in favor of his cash position, the dealer lifted the remainder of his hedge so that he could profit from rising note prices. If he had kept the hedge on for the duration of his note-selling activities, the protection afforded by hedging would actually have dampened profits. The success of this strategy of lifting or "managing" a hedge is obviously dependent on the dealer's ability to judge price movements and is therefore subject to market risk.

Example 8: Pure Hedge by a Bond Dealer. On March 1 a bond dealer has an inventory of $5 million of long-term U.S. Treasury bonds that have an 8% coupon. Concerned about rising rates, he sells 50 contracts of T-bond futures.
    The results are as follows:

Cash Market

March 1:	Owns $5 million 8% U.S. T-bonds at 99-08 to yield 8.07%
March 15:	Sells $5 million 8% U.S. T-bonds at 94-08 to yield 8.56%

Loss = $250,000

Futures Market

March 1:	Sells 50 March futures at 98-16 (yield 8.15%)
March 15:	Buys 50 March futures at 93-16 (yield 8.69%)

Profit = $250,000

Net Result: $0

Figure 18-3. CBOT conversion factors (excerpt).

Conversion Factor to Yield 8.000%

Coupon Rate

Yrs-Mos	14%	14¹/₈%	14¹/₄%	14³/₈%	14¹/₂%	14⁵/₈%	14³/₄%	14⁷/₈%
15-0	1.5188	1.5296	1.5404	1.5512	1.5620	1.5728	1.5836	1.5944
15-3	1.5229	1.5338	1.5447	1.5556	1.5665	1.5774	1.5883	1.5992
15-6	1.5277	1.5386	1.5496	1.5606	1.5716	1.5826	1.5936	1.6046
15-9	1.5316	1.5427	1.5538	1.5649	1.5759	1.5870	1.5981	1.6092
16-0	1.5362	1.5474	1.5585	1.5697	1.5809	1.5921	1.6032	1.6144
16-3	1.5400	1.5513	1.5625	1.5738	1.5850	1.5963	1.6075	1.6188
16-6	1.5444	1.5558	1.5671	1.5785	1.5898	1.6011	1.6125	1.6238
16-9	1.5481	1.5595	1.5709	1.5823	1.5938	1.6052	1.6166	1.6280
17-0	1.5523	1.5638	1.5753	1.5869	1.5984	1.6099	1.6214	1.6329
17-3	1.5558	1.5674	1.5790	1.5906	1.6022	1.6138	1.6253	1.6369
17-6	1.5599	1.5716	1.5833	1.5949	1.6066	1.6183	1.6299	1.6416
17-9	1.5633	1.5750	1.5868	1.5985	1.6102	1.6220	1.6337	1.6455
18-0	1.5672	1.5791	1.5909	1.6027	1.6145	1.6263	1.6382	1.6500
18-3	1.5705	1.5823	1.5942	1.6061	1.6180	1.6299	1.6418	1.6537
18-6	1.5743	1.5862	1.5982	1.6102	1.6221	1.6341	1.6461	1.6580
18-9	1.5773	1.5894	1.6014	1.6134	1.6255	1.6375	1.6495	1.6616
19-0	1.5810	1.5931	1.6052	1.6174	1.6295	1.6416	1.6537	1.6658
19-3	1.5840	1.5961	1.6083	1.6205	1.6327	1.6448	1.6570	1.6692
19-6	1.5875	1.5998	1.6120	1.6243	1.6365	1.6487	1.6610	1.6732
19-9	1.5903	1.6026	1.6150	1.6273	1.6396	1.6519	1.6642	1.6765
20-0	1.5938	1.6062	1.6185	1.6309	1.6433	1.6556	1.6680	1.6804
20-3	1.5965	1.6089	1.6213	1.6338	1.6462	1.6586	1.6711	1.6835
20-6	1.5998	1.6123	1.6248	1.6373	1.6498	1.6623	1.6748	1.6873
20-9	1.6024	1.6149	1.6275	1.6400	1.6526	1.6651	1.6777	1.6902
21-0	1.6056	1.6182	1.6308	1.6434	1.6560	1.6686	1.6813	1.6939
21-3	1.6080	1.6207	1.6334	1.6460	1.6587	1.6714	1.6841	1.6967
21-6	1.6111	1.6239	1.6366	1.6493	1.6621	1.6748	1.6875	1.7002
21-9	1.6135	1.6263	1.6390	1.6518	1.6646	1.6774	1.6902	1.7030

Figure 18-3. (Cont.)

Coupon Rate

Yrs-Mos	14%	14¹/₈%	14¹/₄%	14³/₈%	14¹/₂%	14⁵/₈%	14³/₄%	14⁷/₈%
22-0	1.6165	1.6293	1.6422	1.6550	1.6678	1.6807	1.6935	1.7064
22-3	1.6187	1.6316	1.6445	1.6574	1.6703	1.6832	1.6961	1.7090
22-6	1.6216	1.6346	1.6475	1.6605	1.6734	1.6864	1.6993	1.7123
22-9	1.6238	1.6368	1.6497	1.6627	1.6757	1.6887	1.7017	1.7147
23-0	1.6265	1.6396	1.6526	1.6657	1.6788	1.6918	1.7049	1.7179
23-3	1.6286	1.6417	1.6548	1.6679	1.6810	1.6941	1.7072	1.7203
23-6	1.6313	1.6444	1.6576	1.6707	1.6839	1.6970	1.7102	1.7234
23-9	1.6333	1.6464	1.6596	1.6728	1.6860	1.6992	1.7124	1.7256
24-0	1.6359	1.6491	1.6623	1.6756	1.6888	1.7021	1.7153	1.7286
24-3	1.6377	1.6510	1.6643	1.6776	1.6909	1.7042	1.7175	1.7308
24-6	1.6402	1.6536	1.6669	1.6803	1.6936	1.7069	1.7203	1.7336
24-9	1.6420	1.6554	1.6688	1.6822	1.6956	1.7089	1.7223	1.7357
25-0	1.6445	1.6579	1.6713	1.6847	1.6982	1.7116	1.7250	1.7385
25-3	1.6462	1.6596	1.6731	1.6866	1.7000	1.7135	1.7270	1.7404
25-6	1.6485	1.6620	1.6755	1.6891	1.7026	1.7161	1.7296	1.7431
25-9	1.6502	1.6637	1.6772	1.6908	1.7043	1.7179	1.7314	1.7450
26-0	1.6524	1.6660	1.6796	1.6932	1.7068	1.7204	1.7340	1.7476
26-3	1.6540	1.6676	1.6812	1.6949	1.7085	1.7221	1.7358	1.7494
26-6	1.6562	1.6699	1.6835	1.6972	1.7109	1.7245	1.7382	1.7519
26-9	1.6577	1.6714	1.6851	1.6988	1.7125	1.7262	1.7399	1.7536
27-0	1.6598	1.6735	1.6873	1.7010	1.7148	1.7285	1.7423	1.7560
27-3	1.6612	1.6750	1.6888	1.7025	1.7163	1.7301	1.7439	1.7577
27-6	1.6633	1.6771	1.6909	1.7047	1.7185	1.7323	1.7462	1.7600
27-9	1.6646	1.6784	1.6923	1.7061	1.7200	1.7338	1.7477	1.7615
28-0	1.6666	1.6805	1.6944	1.7083	1.7221	1.7360	1.7499	1.7638
28-3	1.6679	1.6818	1.6957	1.7096	1.7235	1.7375	1.7514	1.7653
28-6	1.6698	1.6838	1.6977	1.7117	1.7256	1.7396	1.7535	1.7675
28-9	1.6710	1.6850	1.6990	1.7130	1.7270	1.7409	1.7549	1.7689
29-0	1.6729	1.6869	1.7009	1.7149	1.7290	1.7430	1.7570	1.7710
29-3	1.6740	1.6881	1.7021	1.7162	1.7302	1.7443	1.7583	1.7724
29-6	1.6759	1.6899	1.7040	1.7181	1.7322	1.7463	1.7603	1.7744
29-9	1.6769	1.6911	1.7052	1.7193	1.7334	1.7475	1.7616	1.7757

Figure 18-3. (Cont.)

Conversion Factor to Yield 8.000%

Coupon Rate

Yrs-Mos	14%	14¹/₈%	14¹/₄%	14³/₈%	14¹/₂%	14⁵/₈%	14³/₄%	14⁷/₈%
30-0	1.6787	1.6928	1.7070	1.7211	1.7353	1.7494	1.7635	1.7777
30-3	1.6797	1.6939	1.7081	1.7222	1.7364	1.7506	1.7647	1.7789
30-6	1.6814	1.6956	1.7098	1.7240	1.7382	1.7524	1.7666	1.7808
30-9	1.6824	1.6967	1.7109	1.7251	1.7393	1.7535	-1.7678	1.7820
31-0	1.6841	1.6983	1.7126	1.7268	1.7411	1.7553	1.7696	1.7838
31-3	1.6850	1.6993	1.7136	1.7278	1.7421	1.7564	1.7707	1.7849
31-6	1.6866	1.7009	1.7152	1.7295	1.7438	1.7581	1.7724	1.7868
31-9	1.6875	1.7018	1.7162	1.7305	1.7448	1.7591	1.7735	1.7878
32-0	1.6891	1.7034	1.7178	1.7321	1.7465	1.7608	1.7752	1.7895
32-3	1.6899	1.7043	1.7187	1.7330	1.7474	1.7618	1.7762	1.7905
32-6	1.6914	1.7058	1.7202	1.7346	1.7490	1.7634	1.7778	1.7922
32-9	1.6922	1.7066	1.7210	1.7355	1.7499	1.7643	1.7787	1.7932
33-0	1.6937	1.7081	1.7226	1.7370	1.7515	1.7659	1.7804	1.7948
33-3	1.6944	1.7089	1.7233	1.7378	1.7523	1.7668	1.7812	1.7957
33-6	1.6958	1.7103	1.7248	1.7393	1.7538	1.7683	1.7828	1.7973
33-9	1.6965	1.7110	1.7256	1.7401	1.7546	1.7691	1.7836	1.7981
34-0	1.6979	1.7124	1.7270	1.7415	1.7561	1.7706	1.7851	1.7997
34-3	1.6986	1.7131	1.7277	1.7422	1.7568	1.7714	1.7859	1.8005
34-6	1.6999	1.7145	1.7291	1.7437	1.7582	1.7728	1.7874	1.8020
34-9	1.7005	1.7151	1.7297	1.7443	1.7589	1.7735	1.7881	1.8027
35-0	1.7018	1.7165	1.7311	1.7457	1.7603	1.7749	1.7896	1.8042
35-3	1.7024	1.7171	1.7317	1.7463	1.7610	1.7756	1.7903	1.8049
35-6	1.7037	1.7183	1.7330	1.7477	1.7623	1.7770	1.7916	1.8063
35-9	1.7042	1.7189	1.7336	1.7483	1.7629	1.7776	1.7923	1.8070
36-0	1.7055	1.7202	1.7349	1.7496	1.7643	1.7790	1.7937	1.8084
36-3	1.7060	1.7207	1.7354	1.7501	1.7648	1.7796	1.7943	1.8090
36-6	1.7072	1.7219	1.7366	1.7514	1.7661	1.7808	1.7956	1.8103
36-9	1.7077	1.7224	1.7372	1.7519	1.7667	1.7814	1.7962	1.8109

Figure 18-3. (Cont.)

Conversion Factor to Yield 8.000%

Coupon Rate

Yrs-Mos	14%	14¹/₈%	14¹/₄%	14³/₈%	14¹/₂%	14⁵/₈%	14³/₄%	14⁷/₈%
37-0	1.7088	1.7236	1.7384	1.7531	1.7679	1.7827	1.7974	1.8122
37-3	1.7093	1.7241	1.7388	1.7536	1.7684	1.7832	1.7980	1.8128
37-6	1.7104	1.7252	1.7400	1.7548	1.7696	1.7844	1.7992	1.8140
37-9	1.7108	1.7257	1.7405	1.7553	1.7701	1.7849	1.7997	1.8145
38-0	1.7119	1.7268	1.7416	1.7564	1.7713	1.7861	1.8009	1.8158
38-3	1.7123	1.7272	1.7420	1.7569	1.7717	1.7866	1.8014	1.8162
38-6	1.7134	1.7283	1.7431	1.7580	1.7728	1.7877	1.8026	1.8174
38-9	1.7138	1.7286	1.7435	1.7584	1.7733	1.7881	1.8030	1.8179
39-0	1.7148	1.7297	1.7446	1.7595	1.7744	1.7893	1.8042	1.8190
39-3	1.7151	1.7300	1.7450	1.7599	1.7748	1.7897	1.8046	1.8195
39-6	1.7162	1.7311	1.7460	1.7609	1.7758	1.7908	1.8057	1.8206
39-9	1.7165	1.7314	1.7463	1.7613	1.7762	1.7911	1.8061	1.8210
40-0	1.7175	1.7324	1.7474	1.7623	1.7773	1.7922	1.8071	1.8221

The preceding illustrations depict only a handful of the many ways that interest rate futures are used by individuals and institutions. Further examples and discussions are contained in the interest rate sections of Chapters 9, 10, 11, 12, and 16.

Interest rate futures allow institutions better control over the risks of interest rate fluctuations. As noted in Chapter 10, futures are very effective in reducing risk but do not eliminate it altogether. Even the best hedging programs do not screen out all the risk. Every organization must be able to identify the size and nature of the risks to which it is exposed. This includes being able to monitor changes in that risk. Once the risk has been determined, the appropriate futures instrument must be selected. This involves studying the basis to establish which futures prices correlate most closely with the cash market exposure in question. Finally, it is important to have in place a system to monitor the results of the hedging program. Changing conditions can easily undermine the most well-planned hedging strategy.

For those organizations that are willing to devote the time to developing and monitoring a hedge program, the rewards can often spell the difference between success and failure. Figure 18-4 (see page 470), published by the Chicago Mercantile Exchange, shows many of the ways that organizations can use futures for risk management.

OTHER IMPORTANT INTEREST RATE HEDGING CONSIDERATIONS

1. When using 90-day instruments to hedge for any period other than 90 days, the size of the hedge must be adjusted for the desired maturity. For example, to hedge a one-year liability or asset, the size of the hedge in a 90-day futures contract must be four times the principal amount hedged. A 30-day hedge would require a futures position one-third the size of the principal amount. The reason for this, of course, is that the value (in dollars) of most 90-day instruments is determined in part by the factor $t/360$, where t is the holding period. A given change in rates will have a larger effect on a longer term instrument than on a shorter term one.

The question arises: what is the most effective way of combining 90-day futures to hedge maturities longer than 90 days? The choices are two, and they are called *stacking* and *stripping*. A *stack* involves putting the total number of required contacts in one delivery month (usually the nearest). At the end of each period the stack is reduced and rolled into the next delivery month. A *strip* involves the initial sale or purchase of the required number of contract months for each period hedged. At the end of each period the nearest hedge position is lifted. Stacks tend to entail greater basis risk than strips. On the other hand, strips may require establishing positions in contract months that are distant and illiquid.

2. As described in Chapter 10, there are two important risks involved in interest rate hedging. The first concerns proper matching of securities and futures. This occurs in cases of *cross-hedging*, where the security that is hedged is something other than that underlying the futures contract. Cross-hedges are used when hedging assets or liabilities for which active futures do not exist. Examples include prime rate loans, commercial paper, or two-year corporate notes. Cross-hedges are based upon an assumed relationship between the cash and futures markets that is founded on a study of the basis. Changes in the actual relationship relative to the assumed relationship will result in unplanned profits or losses.

Figure 18-4. *Primary risk management uses.*

Fixed Income Dealer

1.   Sell futures to hedge securities inventory
2.   Buy futures to lock-in cost of future securities
3.   Increase trading flexibility; spreads; arbitrage; intramarket spreads

Investor

1.   Lock yields on future cash flows
2.   Protect the value of purchased instrument
3.   Reduce or lengthen the "interest rate maturity" of a fixed security
4.   Create synthetic money-market instruments

Banks

1.   Uses of a fixed income dealer and investor (above)
2.   Adjust the interest rate maturity GAP between assets and liabilities
3.   Lock-in cost of funds or returns on future loans

Savings and Loans

1.   Uses of banks (rates on money market certificates, a key funding vehicle, are tied to T-bill rates)
2.   Hedge value of mortgage portfolio
3.   Hedge value of mortgages to be sold

Fixed Income Security Underwriters
(Investment Banks)

1.   Protect value of issue until sold
2.   Provide information about expected future rates

Insurance Companies

1.   Uses of investors (above)
2.   Hedge the outflow of policy loans from rising interest rates

Pension Funds

1.   Uses of investors(above)
2.   Use futures to lock-in yields on projected cash inflows
3.   Short-term protection of long-term investments

Corporate Treasurer

1.   Hedge borrowing cost
2.   Lock-in returns on excess cash
3.   If using "shelf registration," same uses as underwriters

---

Source: "Trading and Hedging with Short-Term Interest Rate Futures." Chicago Mercantile Exchange, 1984.

Another risk relates to the matching of maturities. The issue of stacking vs. stripping was discussed previously. Very often the rigid, standardized form of the futures contract makes it impossible to match maturities with the less rigid cash market commitments.

3. As described in Chapter 9, the serial rate that is created by combining a number of different futures contracts is a function of the implied forward rate. The cost of creating a hedge for each quarter can be determined by subtracting the current cash price from the stated futures price for the related delivery month. For example, if the implied forward yield on a futures contract is 8.50% when the current cash yield is 8.20%, the hedger is locking in an 8.50% cost of funds for the period covered by the futures contract. Thus, the hedge costs 30 basis points relative to current levels. If interest rates remain constant, the futures yield (8.50%) will creep, or converge, to the cash level (8.20%) as the delivery date approaches. This behavior, known as *creep to cash*, represents a real cost to the hedger.

4. Except for the underhedging technique discussed in Chapter 10, hedging in most physical commodities involves a one-for-one relationship between the size of the futures position and the size of the cash-market position being hedged. A pork belly inventory of 76,000 pounds will usually be hedged with two futures contracts of 38,000 pounds each. In interest rate markets, however, it is often necessary to establish a *hedge ratio*. A hedge ratio is the number of units of futures that are required to effectively hedge one unit of the underlying maturity. The need for a hedge ratio stems from disparities in the price volatilities of the futures and the cash. Sometimes these disparities arise from security mismatch. For example, commercial paper may tend to be 10% more volatile than cross-hedged T-bill futures. In this case it would be necessary to use 1.1 T-bill futures for every $1 million of paper to be hedged. In the case of longer-term coupon securities, the disparity can arise for somewhat different reasons. For a given change in yield, the dollar value of higher coupon bonds or notes changes by a larger dollar amount than does the dollar value of lower coupon instruments. Because the CBT note and bond contracts are based on an 8% coupon, hedging $100,000 of higher coupon bonds or notes with one futures contract that represents $100,000 of 8% bonds or notes will not provide adequate protection. Using the conversion factor tables provided by the various exchanges, hedgers must weight their hedges to compensate for this coupon-related volatility disparity.

SPREAD TRADING IN INTEREST RATE FUTURES

Spread trading is somewhat more complicated in interest rate futures than in traditional commodity futures. One reason for this is that quotes in one interest rate market are not always comparable to quotes in other interest rate markets. Some instruments are quoted on a simple interest basis (CDs and Eurodollars) while others are quoted on a discount basis (T-bills). Still others are quoted on a yield to maturity basis (GNMAs, T-notes, and T-bonds). Traders of interest rate futures spreads should be aware of discrepancies caused by differences in quotation conventions and, where appropriate, weight the legs of spreads to neutralize the effects of these differences.

Another complicating factor is the yield curve. The outcome of interest rate spreads is often determined by changes in the shape of the yield curve. Physical commodity spreads tend to correlate more closely with the general movement of prices than do interest rate spreads. Rising or falling prices in most physical commodities tend to have predictable effects on spreads, as we discussed in Chapter 16. However, in interest rate markets such generalizations are less reliable.

Another important point is that longer maturity instruments tend to be more volatile than shorter maturity instruments. A given change in yield will produce a greater price change in T-bonds than in T-notes or T-bills. Thus a spread of one T-bond vs. one T-note can go awry even if the trader's prediction about interest rate differentials proves correct.

Intramarket Spreads in Interest Rate Futures

The behavior of intramarket spreads in interest rate futures is determined by the relative changes occurring between shorter and longer maturities. More specifically, the price of a nearby futures contract will rise relative to the price of a distant delivery when longer term interest rates rise relative to shorter term rates. Conversely, short nearby/long deferred spreads tend to be profitable when the rates for longer maturities fall relative to those for shorter maturities.

To illustrate the reason for this behavior, let us take an example (which for the sake of simplicity is not very realistic):

Example: On September 1, yields on cash T-bills are as follows:

3 month yield = 7%
6 month yield = 8%
9 month yield = 9%

We know from our discussion of implied forward rates earlier in this chapter that December futures will have a value of about 91.00. Why? Because the rate that is projected by December futures should approximately equal the implied rate for the 3-month period beginning three months hence. The following formula for determining the implied forward rate was given in Chapter 9:

$$\text{IFR} = \frac{(L \times I) - (S \times i)}{L - S}$$

where

IFR = implied forward rate
I = yield for the longer period
i = yield for the shorter period
L = length of the longer period
S = length of the shorter period

On September 1 the implied forward rate for the 3-month period corresponding to December futures is

$$\frac{(8.00 \times 6) - (7.00 \times 3)}{6 - 3} = 9.00$$

Thus, December T-bill futures should have a value of about 91.00.

The same process yields a value for March T-bill futures of 89.00. Therefore, the spread between December and March futures on September 1 should be around 2.00, premium December.

Assume that one day later (September 2) the yield configuration is as follows:

$$3 \text{ month yield} = 7\%$$
$$6 \text{ month yield} = 7.5\%$$
$$9 \text{ month yield} = 8.0\%$$

The new futures market configuration would reflect the change as follows:

December futures yield = 8.00% (price = 92.00)
March futures yield = 9.00% (price = 91.00)
December T-bill/March T-bill spread = 1.00, premium December

The decline in the longer maturity cash T-bill rate relative to that of the shorter maturity bill rate resulted in a weakening in the price of the nearby delivery relative to that of the deferred. The general behavior can be summarized as follows:

- When rates on longer maturities gain on rates of shorter maturities, the prices of nearby deliveries will gain on the prices of forward deliveries.
- When rates on longer maturities lose to rates of shorter maturities, the prices of nearby deliveries will lose on the prices of forward deliveries.

The above rules are useful if you have an opinion on what changes are likely to take place in the shape of the yield curve. They can be implemented if you expect long rates to rise or to fall relative to short rates. Does this mean that spread trading is appropriate only when you expect major changes in the shape of the yield curve? Not really. It is also possible to trade spreads based on an opinion of general rate movements. In periods of declining interest rates, the rates on longer maturing instruments tend to decline more slowly than their shorter maturing counterparts. Conversely, in periods of rising rates, short rates usually gain on long rates and the yield curve tends toward inversion. Recognizing that there can be exceptions to this behavior, these generalizations still can be useful when trading intramarket spreads:

- In periods of generally declining interest rates, the best intramarket spread position is long nearby/short deferred.
- In periods of generally rising interest rates, the best intramarket spread position is short nearby/long deferred.

Interproduct Spreads in Interest Rate Futures

Another common type of interest rate futures spread involves the simultaneous purchase and sale of two different instruments such as June T-notes and June T-bonds. The outcomes of such spread positions are determined by a combination of two factors: (1) changes in the shape of the yield curve, and (2) changes in perceptions of creditworthiness. Let us discuss each of these factors separately.

Generally, traders execute bull spreads in interest rate futures when they expect the yields on the longer term instruments to decline relative to those of the shorter term instruments. If the yield curve is positively (upwardly) sloped, the bull spreader buys the longer term instrument and sells the shorter term instrument, expecting the slope to become flatter. If the yield curve is negatively sloped (inverted), the bull spreader is anticipating that the downward slope will become even steeper. Bear spreads in a normal yield curve situation are held by traders who expect the slope of the curve to remain the same or to become steeper.

Credit quality is the second key element in interproduct interest rate futures spreads. Better quality credits always pay lower interest rates than do lesser quality credits. However, the difference in rates varies, depending on a variety of factors. The most important of these for spread traders to understand is known as *flight to quality*. This refers to the tendency of interest rate differences between higher and lower quality credits to widen when the overall level of rates rises. This is because higher interest rates can increase the likelihood of defaults, which makes lenders more likely to favor the most creditworthy borrowers. Because the U.S. government is almost universally perceived as the best of all credit risks, the tendency is for prices of government securities (such as T-bills) to decline less than the prices of private sector securities (such as Eurodollars) when the overall level of interest rates is rising (prices are falling).

The risk associated with any spread position is generally a function of the "dissimilarity" of the two legs of the spread and the amount of time that separates their maturities. The diversity of interest rate futures makes it possible to adopt spread positions, the risks of which range from negligible to very large. The following are some examples of interproduct spreads in interest rate markets:

- *T-notes vs. T-bonds* — This is strictly a maturity play since there are no "quality" differences between T-notes and T-bonds. This spread seeks to take advantage of changes in the longer portion of the yield curve (10-25 years). Traders anticipating that yields on the 20-year instrument will decline relative to those of the 10-year instrument should establish the spread of short T-notes/long T-bonds.

- *T-bills vs. T-bonds* — This spread entails significant risk because its legs straddle almost the entire yield curve.

- *T-bills vs. Eurodollars* — This is a credit-quality spread. Because T-bills represent U.S. government credit, traders expecting sharply higher rates would tend to buy T-bills and sell Eurodollars, expecting that flight to quality will cause the rate difference to widen.

It is important to note that interproduct spreads often require balancing the legs of the spread. Remember that a given yield change will produce a greater change in the price of an instrument with a long maturity than in one with a short maturity. The reason for this is that a given price change spread over a large number of years has a smaller impact on annual yield than the same price change spread over a small number of years. Thus, a given yield change requires a much larger price increase or decrease in the longer security. A spread involving one T-note and one T-bond is likely to produce a profit or loss even if the yield spread between the two is constant as long as the overall level of rates fluctuates. The most precise way to balance spreads is to use the conversion factors from published tables available through futures exchanges or FCMs. An alternative solution is to estimate the dollar profit (loss) resulting from a given yield change in each instrument and weight one leg accordingly. For instance, a trader might estimate that a given yield change would produce a $500 profit in T-bills and a $1,000 profit in T-notes. Therefore, to neutralize the effect of maturity on yield each spread might have two T-bills for each T-note.

The following table summarizes typical spread behavior in interest rate futures.

Summary of General Rules of Spread Behavior for Interest Rate Futures

Expectation	Probable Behavior of Futures
1. Rates on longer maturities will rise relative to rates on shorter maturities (steepening yield curve)	1. (a) Prices of nearby deliveries will rise relative to prices of distant deliveries. (b) Prices of longer term instruments will fall relative to prices of shorter term instruments.
2. Rates on longer maturities will decline relative to rates of shorter maturities (flattening yield curve)	2. (a) Prices of nearby deliveries will fall relative to prices of forward deliveries. (b) Prices of longer term instruments will rise relative to prices of shorter term instruments.
3. Yield curve will not change	3. Prices of nearby contracts will gain on prices of distant contracts.
4. Generally rising (falling) rates	4. Prices of nearby contracts will decline (rise) relative to prices of distant contracts.

■ Chapter 19

■ Currency Futures

THE FOREIGN EXCHANGE MARKET

The foreign exchange (FX) market is a vast, global activity encompassing all transactions in which the currency of one country is exchanged for that of another. An American tourist exchanging dollar bills for local currency at a hotel or a store is a small participant in a market whose players include exporters and importers, multinational corporations, central banks, and all financial and non-financial institutions who in the course of their activities receive or disburse a variety of currencies. Each day more than $300 billion flow between the major bank and non-bank dealers of Europe, the Far East, and the United States (see Figures 19-1 and 19-2 on pages 479 and 481).

London is the world's largest foreign exchange trading center, representing some 30% of overall volume. The United States and continental European dealing centers account for about 25% each, with the Far East accounting for most of what remains. However, the nature and size of foreign exchange transactions is changing constantly. Historically, most foreign exchange transactions were trade-related. For example, if a Swiss exporter sells a machine to an American buyer, the American's dollars must be changed into Swiss francs, because this is the currency sought by the supplier of the machine. Traditionally, therefore, the growth of foreign exchange activity was tied to the growth of international trade.

Figure 19-1. The global foreign exchange market.

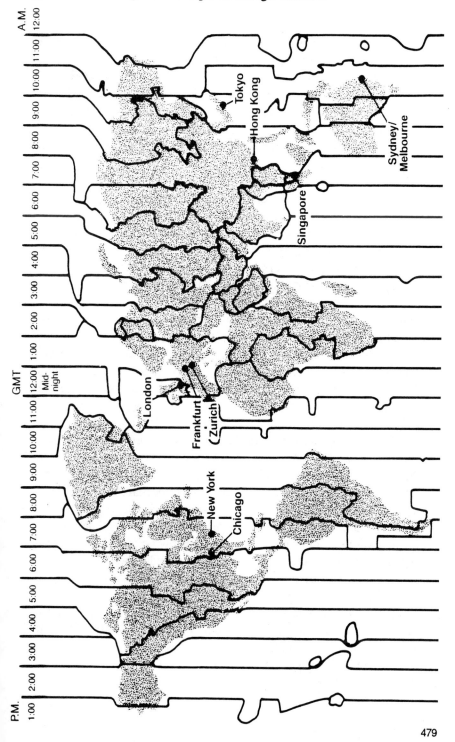

Since the late 1970s, however, the major source of growth in foreign exchange volume has been the flow of capital rather than the flow of merchandise. The liberalization and deregulation of capital flows initiated by most major governments in the late 1970s and early 1980s created a tremendous increase in flows of investment and funds among countries. From 1979 to 1984, trade flows grew by 4% annually while foreign exchange trading volume is estimated to have increased 20% annually. Trading volume is believed to have doubled again between 1984 and 1987.

Commercial and investment banks, the primary dealers, are the leading participants in the foreign exchange marketplace. These banks are equipped to buy or to sell foreign currencies for their commercial customers and correspondent banks, as well as for the international banking activities of their own institutions. In addition, many of the major banks act as market makers in most of the actively traded currencies. As such, each is prepared at any time to make a two-way market to customers and to other market making banks and dealers. The activities of these major dealers help even out the temporary excesses of supply and demand that inevitably emerge from thousands upon thousands of individual transactions each day. These activities comprise the vast foreign exchange trading arena known as the *interbank market*. It is in this market that overall supply and demand interact and free market foreign exchange rates are determined.

The next most important participants in the foreign exchange market are the central banks. Central bank operations encompass government transactions, transactions with other central banks and various international organizations, and intervention that is intended to influence exchange rates. The latter is one of the most important factors in determining both short-term and long-term currency exchange rates. Before March 1973, the intervention tactics of central banks were designed to limit fluctuations of currency values to a narrow band on either side of an official rate vis-a-vis the dollar. Since the abandonment of fixed rates in 1973, central bank activity usually has been aimed at influencing market conditions rather than at maintaining specific rates.

Intervention techniques vary from country to country. In most cases the central banks will deal directly with major banks or brokers, buying or selling currencies to bring about the desired degree of stabilization. To finance the purchase of dollars against their own currencies, foreign central banks must create domestic currency. To finance the sale

Figure 19-2. *Foreign exchange market volume by trading center—* *Approximate daily trading volume: $300 billion.*

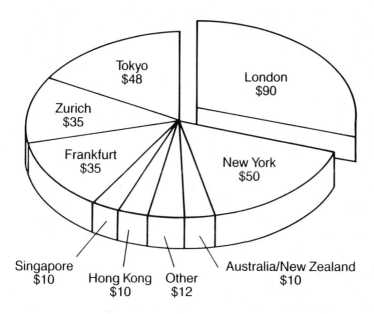

of dollars, foreign central banks must either use international reserves or borrow dollars from financial institutions, the International Monetary Fund (IMF), or the Federal Reserve.

Borrowings by and from the Federal Reserve are usually done through the Fed's swap network. The *swap network* consists of reciprocal short-term credit arrangements between major central banks and the Bank for International Settlements (BIS), which is essentially a central bank for central banks. A swap involves the purchase (sale) of dollars for spot delivery and the simultaneous sale (purchase) of dollars for forward delivery approximately three months later. Swaps may be rolled over for additional three month periods by mutual agreement.

The third major participant group in the foreign exchange market is the trade sector. Transactions in this category are usually made in connection with the purchase or sale of a product, service, or financial asset across country lines. In *spot* transactions, delivery of the currency is usually made two business days following the date the trade was made. This allows time for the two parties to make arrangements for the appropriate debiting and crediting of bank accounts. However, not all transactions are for spot delivery. It is a common feature of international commercial transactions that a business knows it will be paying or receiving some amount of foreign currency at some future date. For example, a U.S. importer of televisions from Japan may arrange in July for a shipment to arrive in December. The contract with the Japanese manufacturer may call for payment in yen on December 1. Between July and December, however, the yen might rise against the dollar. If the importer waits until December to buy the yen needed to cover the payment for the televisions, it could cost him more dollars than anticipated. One method of avoiding this problem would be for the importer to buy spot yen in July, invest them in Japan for about four months, and use the proceeds to pay the manufacturer in December.

Another method would involve buying the yen from a bank in July for forward delivery. In this case, the yen are bought in July, but are not actually delivered until they are needed on December 1. The exchange rate is fixed at the time the transaction is struck, but no money changes hands until the maturity date. The relationships between the spot exchange rate and those of each forward maturity are determined by factors that are discussed later in this chapter.

The last major participant group is known as the *capital sector* and includes investors and speculators. Activity in this sector has grown dramatically since the mid-1970s. Capital sector transactions differ from these of the trade sector in one major respect: they relate to investment rather than to the purchase or sale of a product or service.

Figure 19-3 depicts the structure and transaction flow of the foreign exchange market. The branch on the right side of the chart shows the role played by futures and options exchanges in the market. Until the early 1970s the interbank market was the only channel through which foreign exchange transactions took place. Since then, there have been major innovations in foreign exchange trading. On May 16, 1972, the International Monetary Market (IMM) opened as a division of the Chicago Mercantile Exchange. The IMM has expanded greatly since its inception and currently provides an active market for futures and options in six major foreign currencies (Australian dollar, British pound, Canadian dollar, Japanese yen, Swiss franc, and West German mark).

As we know from Part One of this book, there is an important distinction between forward contracts and futures contracts. The former are individual agreements between the two parties. The latter are standardized contracts traded on an organized futures exchange.

Figure 19-3. *Structure of foreign exchange markets.*

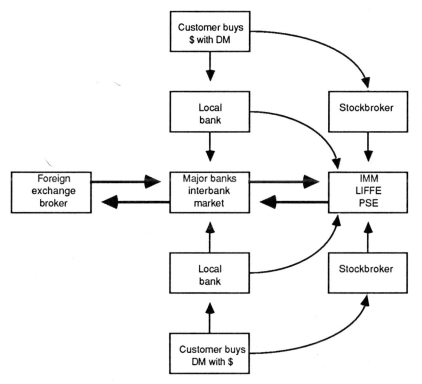

NOTE: The International Monetary Market (IMM) in Chicago trades foreign exchange futures and futures options.
The London International Financial Futures Exchange (LIFFE) trades foreign exchange futures.
The Philadelphia Stock Exchange (PSE) trades foreign currency options.

Source: The Federal Reserve Bank of St. Louis, *Review*, Vol. 66, No. 3, March 1984.

The major disadvantage of currency futures compared to the interbank market is that existing actively traded contracts cover only six currencies (plus the European Currency Unit and a U.S. dollar index, both of which are listed on the N.Y. Cotton Exchange) and are offered in standard sizes with relatively inflexible delivery dates. It is unlikely that the particular cash market commitment of, say, an exporter or an importer will conform precisely to the terms of the futures market. A second disadvantage of futures is that transactions entail margin deposits and commission costs, although the latter are small relative to the total contract value. The exact costs of doing business in the interbank market are difficult to measure but, except for the frequent requirement that bank customers maintain compensating balances, explicit transaction costs are negligible. Instead, interbank dealers make their profits from their bid/offer spreads, in the same manner as do futures market floor traders (see Chapter 4).

The futures market has two compelling advantages, however. First, and most important, prices are determined in an open, competitive environment. Bid/ask spreads are determined by an open auction involving many buyers and sellers who compete very directly with each other. The second advantage is that the IMM provides a market for currency trading that is readily accessible to a broad spectrum of participants.

Another recent innovation in foreign exchange markets is options. The Philadelphia Stock Exchange was the first to trade foreign exchange options. The IMM began options trading in January 1984. The IMM offers options on futures contracts whereas the Philadelphia Exchange offers options on spot currencies. (See Chapters 25 and 26 for a detailed discussion of futures options.) There is also a growing over-the-counter market for currency options in which primary dealers provide principal-to-principal options quotes for their institutional customers.

FUNDAMENTALS OF FOREIGN EXCHANGE PRICE DETERMINATION

Like other prices, exchange rates between currencies of different countries are determined by the interaction of supply and demand. Increase the supply of a currency and its price will drop; decrease the supply and its price will rise. This section discusses the major factors that determine the supply and demand of currencies in the foreign exchange market.

Balance of Payments

Fundamental to a country's exchange rate are all the commercial and financial transactions between it, its people and the rest of the world. The sum of these transactions is the country's *balance of payments*. These transactions include such things as exports and imports of goods and services, foreign investments, and foreign aid transactions. It is important to define some terms relating to the balance of payments concept. A country's balance of payments includes *all* payments made to or received from other countries. Another term, *balance of trade*, refers to just the purchases and sales of goods and services between individuals and businesses in different countries—imports and exports. Included in the balance of trade are such items as agricultural commodities, computers, and tourist spending. Besides these goods- or service-related transactions, there are private and public transfers that include remittances to foreign-based friends or relatives or government transfers of military goods or money. Based on the back-and-forth flow of transfers, a net figure for transfers for a given period is derived in much the same way that the netting out of the imports and exports results in the balance of trade. The sum of the net exports of goods and services and the net transfer payments to foreigners is known as the *balance on current account* (see Figure 19-4 on page 486).

In addition to the balance on current account, there is a second important group of transactions. These include foreign payments made to acquire such items as land, housing, plant and equipment, and stocks, notes, and bonds issued by foreign governments or corporations. The net of these transactions is known as the *balance on capital account*. Figure 19-5 (see page 487) shows one component of the U.S. balance on capital account—foreign purchases and sales of U.S. government securities.

The sum of the current account and the capital account is the balance of payments. The main determinants of balance of payments are:

1. *Economic Conditions*. This refers primarily to income in the private sector. Individuals and businesses with money to spend are a source of demand for foreign products and foreign investment. This demand creates a flow of money out of the country and can weaken the currency by stimulating demand for other currencies. This weakening influence is often offset by incoming investment flows that are attracted by the strong economy.

2. *Prices and Inflation*. A nation's price level is an important determinant of its export/import balance. Countries whose products and services are highly priced will export less of them than will countries that have similar products and services that are priced lower. In addition, the country that has higher prices will be a good market for less expensive foreign imports. The more that imports exceed exports, the weaker a

Figure 19-4.

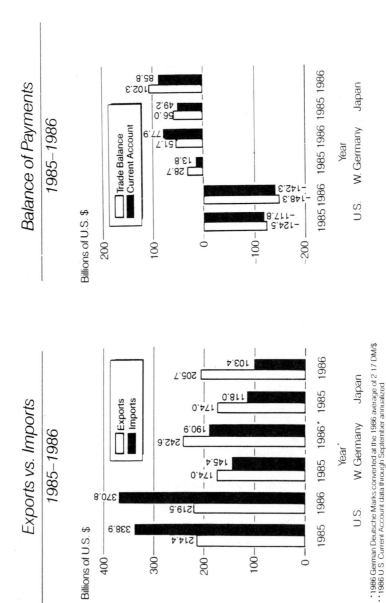

486

Figure 19-5. *Foreign purchases and sales of U.S. government securities as reported by U.S. dealers.*

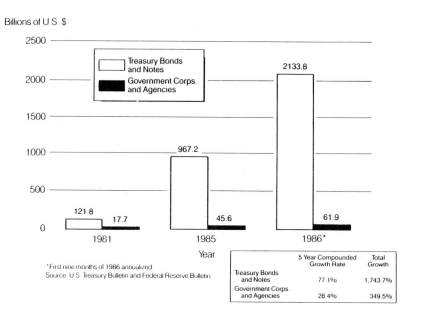

Billions of U.S. $

	5 Year Compounded Growth Rate	Total Growth
Treasury Bonds and Notes	77.1%	1,743.7%
Government Corps. and Agencies	28.4%	349.5%

*First nine months of 1986 annualized
Source: U.S. Treasury Bulletin and Federal Reserve Bulletin

country's currency becomes because there is less foreign demand for its currency to pay for products that it exports.

A country's prices may be relatively high because its national income is high or because its labor and raw material costs are high. Or prices may be high due to general inflation that is brought on by stimuli such as government spending or rapid money supply growth. Either factor ordinarily has a negative effect on balance of payments.

Most economists believe that, in the long run, exchange rates change to bring about purchasing power parity among countries. *Purchasing power parity* means that a dollar's worth of the foreign currency will buy the same amount of goods in the foreign country as a dollar will buy in the United States. In a simple and stable world, this would imply that the ratio of two countries' price levels would equal their exchange rate. However, real world issues such as interest rate changes, labor and productivity inequality between countries, and trade restraints can result in substantial departures from the theory. Nonetheless, it is fair to say that changes in the ratio of U.S. to foreign price levels have an important impact on the value of the dollar.

3. *Interest Rates.* These are an equally important element in balance of payments swings. If a country's interest rates are high, foreigners will be more inclined to invest money there than if interest rates are low. This results in an inflow of capital and has a positive effect on balance of payments and on that country's currency. Eventually, the inflow of funds tends to bring down interest rates and stems foreign-driven investment.

It is important to bear in mind that it is changes in *real*, not *nominal*, interest rates that produce shifts in the international movement of capital and that induce changes in currency values. We discussed the differences between real and nominal interest rates in Chapter 14. It is changes in the relationship of real interest rates between countries that produce changes in the ratio of their currencies.

Like purchasing power parity, interest rate parity plays an important role in exchange rate determination. Explained in more detail in this chapter's section on spot and forward price relationships, interest rate parity essentially means that the real yield obtained by investing in securities in one currency will be roughly equal to the real yield obtained from securities in any other currency.

Government and Central Bank Influence

Government influence on foreign exchange can be significant. Fiscal and monetary policy shape the course of interest rates. Trade policies—including treaties, quotas, tariffs, and embargoes—can produce important changes in the export/import balance.

A government's attitude toward the value of its own currency is also very important. A central bank will often buy or sell large quantities of its own currency on foreign exchange markets in an attempt to raise or to lower the currency's value. This type of intervention can have both short run and long run effects on currency relationships. Since 1973, when major currencies were allowed to float under free market conditions, most intervention has been made to counter what central bankers perceive to be disorderly market conditions. Needless to say, whether a currency's price behavior is disorderly or whether it simply reflects shifting views of fundamental supply/demand influences is largely a matter of perception and opinion.

Expectations

Decisions to buy or sell a foreign currency in the FX market are basically financial decisions. As such, these decisions are largely dependent on expectations about future exchange rate movements. These, in turn, are influenced by an imponderable array of economic, political, social, and psychological factors.

Figure 19-6 (see page 490) shows the effect that political and economic changes can have on currency values. The election of President Reagan in November 1980 reversed years of currency outflows experienced during the Carter Administration. In April 1981, France's election of Francois Mitterand and the introduction of socialist policies resulted in a weakening of the French franc, when both French and foreign investors concluded that profit opportunities in France would be limited.

International political events can have a powerful short-term effect on currency values. When President Anwar Sadat of Egypt was assassinated on October 6, 1981, the U.S. dollar rallied sharply against European currencies as investors felt that political and military instability in the Middle East could make Europe a riskier place for investment than the United States. Throughout the 1980s, political and military developments in the Middle East, Afghanistan, Central America, and many other locations were major factors in the currency markets.

Seasonal Factors

Exchange rates are also influenced by seasonal considerations. Demand for a country's currency will be high during a season of heavy exports as foreigners need the currency to pay for goods. Likewise, periods of peak imports are negative for a country's exchange rate. Countries that have important tourist industries often have weather-related currency flows.

Spot and Forward Price Relationships

As explained earlier, foreign exchange transactions are of two types, spot and forward. Spot transactions are used to meet immediate demand and are for two-day settlement among major banks. They include everything from tourist purchases of currency to the purchase of a foreign currency by a multinational corporation to pay for imported machinery.

Figure 19-6. *Major factors: Political.*

Deutsche Marks per U.S. Dollar

Jan. 3, 1977 to Dec. 31, 1981

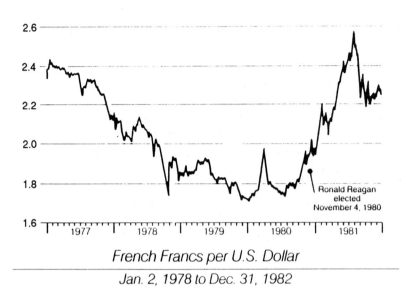

French Francs per U.S. Dollar

Jan. 2, 1978 to Dec. 31, 1982

Major political changes often precipitate a dramatic shift in international capital flows.
— Ronald Reagan's election in 1980 produced a reversal of capital outflows evident during the Carter years.
— Francois Mitterand's election to the French presidency in 1981 resulted in capital outflows due to investor unease with a radical change in governmental policy.

Forward transactions are for deferred delivery. Most banks that deal in foreign exchange will enter into a contract with an established customer to buy or sell any amount of a currency at any date in the future that suits the customer. This forward market is a part of the interbank market, which also includes spot transactions among banks and their large customers. Forward transactions in the exchange market are similar to those of most physical commodities. They are tailor-made transactions that call for the delivery of a specific amount of a currency, at a specific exchange rate on a specific date.

As we mentioned earlier, the relationship between spot and forward rates is determined in good part by a concept known as *interest rate parity*. Simply put, interest rate parity means that the forward premium or discount of a currency relative to the dollar will approximate the differential between interest rates that are available in that currency and dollar interest rates. Otherwise, currency arbitrageurs would have the opportunity to lock-in profits by moving funds between currencies.

As an example, take the case of a U.S. company that must make a payment of one million British pounds one year from today. To hedge this obligation the corporation can either buy one year forward pounds in the interbank market, or it can buy spot pounds and place them in a pound-denominated investment. In the former case the company would earn one year's interest on dollars; in the latter case it would earn one year's interest on pounds. Suppose that the one-year British pound interest rate is 8%, the one-year Eurodollar rate 4%, and the dollar price of one-year British pounds is just 3% below the spot dollar/pound rate. A trader would buy pounds with dollars, invest the pounds at 8%, and sell the pounds forward at a discount of 3%. The trader would therefore earn 5% on his dollars by temporarily converting them to pounds, rather than 4% by investing them in dollars. Traders would obviously do this until the 1% advantage disappeared. This is the gist of interest rate parity.

THE FOREIGN CURRENCY FUTURES MARKET

Trading in currency futures at the International Monetary Market of the Chicago Mercantile Exchange began in May 1972. It was developed as an adjunct to the established forward market in much the same way that grain futures developed as an adjunct to their forward markets. Oth-

Figure 19-7. Currency futures contract sizes (May 1987).

Currency	Contract Size	Exchange Where Traded
Australian Dollar	100,000	IMM
British Pound	25,000	IMM
Canadian Dollar	100,000	IMM
Deutsche Mark	125,000	IMM
Swiss Franc	125,000	IMM
Japanese Yen	12,500,000	IMM
U.S. Dollar Index	500 x index	N.Y. Cotton
European Currency Unit	100,000	N.Y. Cotton

er exchanges have since attempted to develop currency futures contracts, but as of mid-1987 only the IMM and the New York Cotton Exchange contracts had trading activity, with the IMM contracts accounting for more than 90% of the total volume. Figure 19-7 provides contract sizes for actively traded currency futures.

Spread Trading in Foreign Currency Futures

Intramarket Spreads. We know from Chapter 16 that intramarket spreads involve the simultaneous purchase and sale of different delivery months of the same commodity—or, in this case, the same currency. We also know from our discussion of interest rate parity in this chapter that the price spread between spot and forward currency rates is a function of the interest rate differential between dollar-based accounts and accounts that are based in the given currency. An important corollary of this concept is that the price spread between two different forward rates of the same currency will be a function of the differential between the *implied forward interest rates* for dollars and for the currency in question.

To illustrate:

1. F is the one year Deutsche mark (DM) rate. To buy one DM a year from now costs F x 1 DM.

2. S is the spot exchange rate for DM.

3. R is the dollar interest rate.

4. r is the DM interest rate.

5. If we invest one DM for one year at r, at the end of that year we will have $1 + r$ DM. Therefore $1 \text{ DM}/(1 + r)$ invested for a year will equal 1 DM. In dollars it costs $S \times 1 \text{ DM}/(1 + r)$.

6. The foregone dollar interest is: $S \times 1 \text{ DM} \times R/(1 + r)$.

7. If we add together the two costs in (5) and (6) we have the total dollar cost of buying one Deutsche mark and investing it for a year. Reducing terms significantly we arrive at a cost for this transaction of

$$S \times 1 \text{ DM} \times (1 + R)/(1 + r)$$

8. Now because the cost of buying one DM and investing it for a year should be equivalent to buying one DM one year forward, then

$$F \times 1 \text{ DM} = S \times 1 \text{ DM} \times (1 + R)/(1 + r)$$

9. Dividing both expressions by $(S \times 1 \text{ DM})$ yields

$$\frac{F}{S} = \frac{1 + R}{1 + r}$$

10. $(F/S) - 1$ is the percentage forward premium or discount. So, when the interest rate parity condition is satisfied

$$\frac{F}{S} - 1 = \left(\frac{1 + R}{1 + r}\right) - 1 = \frac{R - r}{1 + r}$$

11. In other words, the percentage premium or discount on forward Deutsche marks is approximately equal to the difference between dollar and Deutsche mark interest rates.

So far we have dealt with the premium or discount of spot to forward. It is a simple matter to adapt for forward-to-forward spreads.

12. Let F_1 equal the nearest forward exchange rate.

13. Let F_2 equal the most distant forward exchange rate.

14. Let I be the implied forward rate for dollar investments.

15. Let i be the implied forward rate for Deutsche mark investments. (Both (14) and (15) are the rates covered by the time period F_1 to F_2.)

16. Substituting the new symbols with (10), we get:

$$\frac{F_2}{F_1} - 1 = \frac{I - i}{1 + i} \tag{16}$$

Because futures contracts are simply formalized forward contracts, we can summarize as follows:

The percentage premium or discount of one futures month relative to another futures month of the same currency is approximately equal to the difference between the implied forward interest rate of that currency and the implied forward interest rate of dollars.

Example: On March 1, June Deutsche mark futures are trading at 0.4550. Forward interest rates for the period June through December are 6% per annum for dollar denominated investments and 5% per annum for Deutsche mark denominated investments. Theoretically, what should be the price of December Deutsche marks?

In substituting known values into equation (16), we must use $I = 0.03$ and $i = 0.025$ because the interest rates of 6% and 5% are annualized and we are concerned with only the six-month period. So

$$\frac{I - i}{1 + i} = \frac{0.03 - 0.025}{1 + 0.025} = \frac{0.005}{1.025} = 0.0049$$

or about 1/2%. Thus December futures should command about a 1/2% premium over June futures. If June futures are 0.4550, interest rate parity considerations suggest that December futures will be approximately 0.4572 (0.0049 x 0.4550 = 0.0022).

United States and foreign interest rate differentials are the main determinants of intracurrency spreads. A rise in U.S. interest rates (or, more precisely, forward interest rates) that is not matched by a rise in the interest rates of a foreign country will cause nearby deliveries of that country's currency to gain on distant deliveries. Lagging U.S. interest rates will cause distant contracts to gain on nearby contracts.

Intercurrency Spreads. These spreads involve the simultaneous purchase and sale of the same delivery month in two different currencies. It should be realized that intercurrency spreads are really two outright currency trades that have another currency substituted for the implied long or short in the U.S. dollar. A long position in Swiss francs means that we are short dollars against Swiss francs. A short position in Deutsche marks means that we are long dollars against Deutsche marks. In a long Swiss franc/short Deutsche mark spread, the dollar positions are negated and the new position is simply an outright long Swiss franc position that happens to be against Deutsche marks instead of dollars. Such positions can be as risky as outright long or short positions against the dollar and should not be viewed as anything less than that simply because they appear to be spreads.

One other consideration in intercurrency spreads relates to the balancing of the long and short legs. Suppose, for example, that June Swiss francs are trading at 0.5500 while June Deutsche marks are trading at 0.4200. Therefore, the June *crossrate* (the rate of exchange between two foreign currencies) is 1 SF = 1.31 DM (= 0.55/0.42). Let's say we expect the relationship to drop to 1 SF = 1.20 DM.

If we buy 10 June Deutsche marks and sell 10 June Swiss francs we are exposed to the following hazard: June Deutsche marks rise to 0.5000 while June Swiss francs rise to 0.6555. The crossrate relationship is still 1:1.31, yet the net result of the spread is a loss of $31,875!

The only way to protect against this hazard is to weight the spread according to the dollar value of each contract. In this case, because the contract sizes of the Swiss franc and the Deutsche mark are the same, the relationship of their contract values is the same—1:1.31. For currencies with different contract sizes it is necessary to compute the actual contract values. In any event, a properly balanced spread in this case would be about 1.3 Deutsche mark contracts long for every Swiss franc contract short. A spread position of long 13 June Deutsche marks/short 10 June Swiss francs in the above case would have produced a loss of only $1,875 instead of $31,875.

The following table summarizes the typical behavior of FX spreads under different sets of circumstances.

SUMMARY OF GENERAL RULES OF SPREAD BEHAVIOR FOR CURRENCY FUTURES

Expectation	Probable Behavior of Futures
1. The U.S. dollar will lose ground to Currency 1 faster than to Currency 2.	1. Currency 1 will gain on Currency 2.
2. The U.S. dollar will rise relative to Currency 1 but will remain unchanged relative to Currency 2.	2. Currency 1 will decline relative to Currency 2.
3. U.S. interest rates will gain on those of a foreign country.	3. Forward contracts of that country's currency will gain on nearby contracts.

A BRIEF HISTORY OF INTERNATIONAL MONETARY AGREEMENTS

The roots of the present-day international monetary system reach back to the *Gold Standard*, a system of fixed exchange rates that gained acceptance in the late 1800s and lasted until World War I. Under this system, each participating country pegged its currency to gold at an established parity, and the exchange rate between any two currencies was determined by the ratio of their established parities. For example, if the parity for the U.S. dollar were $20 per ounce of gold and that of the British pound were 4 pounds per ounce of gold, the dollar-sterling exchange rate would be $5 per pound sterling.

In addition, the central bank of each participating country agreed to exchange its domestic currency for gold at the prevailing parity. This meant that when exporters within a country received gold for goods sold abroad, they were able to exchange this gold at their own central bank for domestic currency. Thus, countries with balance of payments surpluses were compelled to create more domestic currency to pay for gold. This, in turn, led to inflation and an eventual reduction in the balance of payments surplus. Countries that imported more than they exported experienced declines in their gold reserves and contractions in their domestic money supply, which led to deflation and an improvement in their balance of payments deficits.

The major appeal of the Gold Standard was its automatic nature. The flow of trade automatically determined the growth of money supply in each country. And the steady flow of gold from new production meant that gold reserves of all countries would increase at a stable rate.

In practice, however, the Gold Standard had weaknesses. New gold discoveries generated periods of unexpected instability. More importantly, countries periodically went off the gold standard in order to direct their monetary policies toward domestic objectives. This was especially true during and after World War I when wartime financing needs, inflation and, in general, the pursuit of nationalistic military and economic goals undermined the system.

The period between the wars gave rise to international interest in creating a monetary system that would allow for stable exchange rates and enable countries to pursue domestic economic objectives. In July 1944, the United States and Great Britain took the initiative in developing a multinational agreement to achieve these goals. The new arrangement, known as the *Bretton Woods Agreement*, had as its major features, first, a system of rules governing exchange rates that was based in good part on the Gold Standard and, second, the creation of the *International Monetary Fund*, which would lend money from a multinational pool to nations in need of financing for payments deficits.

The Bretton Woods Agreement prevailed with mixed success for more than 25 years. However, several factors, such as the pursuit of national policy objectives, inflation, the Vietnam War, and the growing dependence on the U.S. dollar for world financing, eventually led to a breakdown of the system. In 1971, the United States officially abandoned *dollar-gold convertibility*. Later that year, after a realignment of the major currencies, the *Smithsonian Agreement* established new guidelines for exchange rates. But without dollar-gold convertibility the system was doomed to failure. By 1973, the system of fixed exchange rates was abandoned and the currencies of the major industrialized nations were allowed to "float" according to market forces.

Since 1973, the international monetary scene has been characterized by a mix of fixed and floating systems. The major industrialized countries allow their currencies to be determined by market forces, but practice various forms of intervention during periods of instability. A group of European countries participate in the *European Monetary System* (EMS), which provides for relatively fixed rates between members but floating rates relative to the currencies of non-member countries. An important feature of the EMS is the *European Currency Unit* (ECU), which is, in effect, a basket made up of nine European currencies. The rules of the EMS provide that member countries take intervention measures when their currencies diverge from the ECU value by more than a specified amount.

There can be little doubt that in the years ahead efforts will be made to reform the existing system of "managed" floating rates. The success of such reforms will, as always, be dependent on their ability to promote global currency stability while enabling nations to pursue independent economic objectives.

■ Chapter 20

■ Stock Index Futures

INTRODUCTION

Stock index futures began to trade in February 1982 when the Kansas City Board of Trade introduced a contract based on the Value Line Average (VLA). Soon thereafter, trading in two other stock indexes was introduced. In April 1982, the Index and Options Market of the Chicago Mercantile Exchange began to trade a stock index contract based on the Standard and Poor's (S&P) 500 stock index. In May 1982, the New York Futures Exchange received CFTC approval to begin to trade in a stock index future based on the New York Stock Exchange Composite Index (NYSE). Other stock index futures contracts have since been introduced, but of these only the CBOT's Major Market Index (MMI) has enjoyed much success. This index is comprised of 20 leading blue-chip stocks and is used by some traders as a proxy for the popular Dow Jones Industrial Average.

A *stock index futures contract* is an obligation to deliver at a future date an amount in cash that is some dollar multiple of the value of the underlying index at expiration of the contract. The profit or the loss from a futures contract that is settled by "delivery" is the difference between the value of the index at delivery and the value when originally purchased or sold. It is important to emphasize that delivery at settlement cannot be in the underlying stocks of the index, but must be in cash as described later.

Figure 20-1.

-INDEXES-

MUNI BOND INDEX(CBT)$1,000; times Bond Buyer MBI

	Open	High	Low	Settle	Chg	High	Low	Open Interest
June	88-10	88-31	88-10	88-24	+ 37	101-22	83-28	11,023
Sept	87-00	87-20	87-00	87-14	+ 38	100-12	82-13	12,036

Est vol 8,000; vol Thur 10,375; open int 23,090, -847.
The index: Close 88-11; Yield 8.84.

S&P 500 INDEX (CME) 500 times index

June	294.00	294.50	289.30	289.45	− 2.70	306.10	228.90	84,406
Sept	296.50	296.60	291.30	291.50	− 2.80	307.95	229.90	40,297
Dec	298.05	298.70	293.75	293.75	− 2.75	310.00	243.20	4,751

Est vol 73,934; vol Thur 84,057; open int 129,475, −525.
Index (pre.) High 292.87; Low 289.70; Close 290.10−.66

NYSE COMPOSITE INDEX (NYFE) 500 times index

June	165.80	165.95	162.80	162.90	− 1.70	173.35	131.05	8,169
Sept	166.90	166.90	163.75	163.85	− 1.75	174.50	133.55	2,728
Dec	167.80	167.80	167.20	164.80	− 1.85	175.45	140.30	446

Est vol 10,747; vol Thurs 13,583; open int 11,417, −266.
The index: High 164.70; Low 163.29; Close 163.48 −.13

KC VALUE LINE INDEX (KC) 500 times index

June	260.00	260.50	257.30	257.45	− 1.75	275.15	219.50	5,647
Sept	259.25	259.40	256.00	256.10	− 1.90	274.40	221.70	701
Dec	257.90	257.90	254.80	255.30	− .90	272.40	240.00	173

Est vol 2,200; vol Thur 2,092; open int 6,521, −14.
The index: High 260.10; Low 258.73; Close 259.77 +1.06

MAJOR MKT INDEX (CBT) $250 times index

June	460.00	460.00	450.00	450.35	− 4.70	479.00	381.00	6,290
July	458.50	460.70	452.00	452.20	− 4.80	471.00	435.30	180
Sept	463.00	463.00	453.50	453.60	− 4.50	477.50	436.50	169

Est vol n.a; vol Thur 9,789; open int 6,655, +832.
The index: High n.a; Low n.a; Close n.a

THE UNDERLYING INDEXES

S&P 500. The S&P 500 index is a value-weighted arithmetic mean of the market value of the component stocks. It consists of 500 stocks, with the price of each stock weighted according to its market value. The index reflects the aggregate value of the underlying securities and can be viewed as hypothetical portfolios that consist of the entire market value of each security that is included in the index. Each day the index is recalculated so that the previous day's index has no bearing on the current day's value.

The base value for the S&P 500 is the average market value of the 500 stocks during the period 1941 to 1943, with that base-value set equal to 10. Thus an index price of 298.00 today means that the average market value of the basket of stocks is 29.8 times the base level.

NYSE Index. The NYSE index is computed in the same way as the S&P 500. The major difference is that the NYSE Index includes all of the more than 1500 stocks listed for trading on the New York Stock Exchange. The base value of the NYSE index is the total worth of all New York Stock Exchange issues as of December 31, 1965, and that value was set equal to 50. Thus, a current NYSE index price of 150 means that the index is now valued at three times its base amount.

VLA Index. The Value Line Average has a different and somewhat more complicated method of calculation than the previous two indexes. It is derived by computing the percentage change of every stock in the index and adding their geometric mean to the previous day's average. The VLA is an equally weighted index in terms of the percentage change of each stock. Thus, a given percent increase in the price of a small company has the same effect as the same percent change of a giant company. In all, there are about 1700 stocks contained in this index. The base date of the VLA is June 30, 1961, which was set equal to 100. Thus a current-index price of 270.00 means the index is worth some 2.70 times its base value.

MMI Index. The Major Market Index is a broad-based stock index that measures the performance of 20 leading blue-chip securities on the New York Stock Exchange. These issues represent well-known corporations in industries that include merchandising, computers, oil and gas, chemicals, drugs, and consumer products. The MMI is a price-weighted index, computed by adding together the prices of the individual stocks and dividing by a factor that changes from time to time to account for splits and dividends.

Index Characteristics

The S&P 500 attempts to capture the overall price movements of a broad range of industry groupings. Each stock that is included in the index is intended as a good representative within its particular industry group. Although the component issues are not necessarily the largest, their combined market value is more than three-fourths of the total capitalization of all stocks traded on the Big Board.

Both the S&P 500 and the NYSE indexes, because they are capitalization-weighted, are dominated by the more heavily capitalized corporations. For this reason and because the two indexes share a large number of stocks, their price movements are very highly correlated. This means that a percent move in the price of one index will be accompanied by a similar percent change in the price of the other index. What little differences exist in overall price behavior between the two stem from the roughly 1,000 stocks that are in the NYSE index but not in the S&P 500 index. Most of these issues are smaller, so the NYSE tends to reflect these smaller corporations somewhat more than does the S&P 500.

Smaller stocks tend to be more volatile than larger, well-capitalized ones. This fact is particularly meaningful when considering the relative characteristics of the VLA. Because of its computation method, the VLA attaches equal weight to small and large companies. In the S&P 500 and NYSE indexes, capitalization weighting tends to minimize the importance of small-stock price changes. The VLA, on the other hand, does not. Consequently the VLA tends to be more volatile than the other two indexes. To the extent that small stocks are leading indicators of major price moves in the market, as some believe, the VLA may be somewhat ahead of the other indexes at important market tops and bottoms.

As its name implies, the Major Market Index tends to reflect the performance of the top-tier, highly-capitalized industry leaders. Although it is not weighted by capitalization, its very makeup creates price movements that are similar to those of the S&P 500.

Figure 20-2. Futures contract specifications.

S&P 500 INDEX

Exchange:	Index and Options Market of the Chicago Mercantile Exchange.
Components:	Market capitalization weighted index of 500 NYSE, AMEX, and OTC stocks. This value is expressed as an index, with the 1941-1943 market value of these stocks as the base value.
Contract Size:	$500 times the value of the S&P 500 index, i.e., at 200.00 the value of the futures contract is $100,000 ($500 x 200.00).
Minimum Price Fluctuation:	The minimum price fluctuation is 0.05, or $25.00 per tick.
Trading Hours:	10:00 AM to 4:15 PM (Eastern Time).
Contract Months:	March, June, September, and December cycle.
Last Trading Day:	The third Thursday of the contract month.

Figure 20-2. (Cont.)

NEW YORK STOCK EXCHANGE COMPOSITE INDEX

Exchange:	New York Futures Exchange.
Components:	Capitalization weighted index based on the more than 1,500 stocks listed on the NYSE.
Contract Size:	$500 times the value of the New York Stock Exchange Composite Index, i.e., at 95.00 the value of the futures contract is $47,500.00 ($500 x 95.00).
Minimum Price Fluctuation:	The minimum price fluctuation is 0.05 or $25.00 per tick.
Trading Hours:	10:00 AM to 4:15 PM (Eastern Time).
Contract Months:	March, June, September, and December cycle.
Last Trading Day:	The third Friday of the contract month.

VALUE LINE INDEX

Exchange:	Kansas City Board of Trade.
Components:	Equally weighted geometric average of 1,700 NYSE, AMEX, regional and OTC stocks, expressed in index form.
Contract Size:	$500 times the value of the Value Line Average (VLA) index, i.e., at 250.00 the value of the VLA futures contract is $125,000 ($500 x 250.00).
Minimum Price Fluctuation:	The minimum price fluctuation is 0.05 or $25.00 per tick.
Trading Hours:	10:00 AM to 4:15 PM (Eastern Time).
Contract Months:	March, June, September, and December cycle.
Last Trading Day:	The last business day of the contract month.

MAJOR MARKET INDEX

Exchange:	Chicago Board of Trade.
Components:	20 leading blue-chip stocks, including 15 of those listed on the Dow Jones Industrial Average.
Contract Size:	$100 times the value of the Major Market Index (MMI), i.e., at 335.00 the value of the MMI futures contract is $33,500.00 ($100 x 335.00).
Minimum Price Fluctuation:	The minimum price fluctuation is one-eighth of one point, or $12.50 per tick.
Trading Hours:	9:45 AM to 4:15 PM (Eastern Time).
Contract Months:	The first three consecutive months and the next month in the March, June, September, and December cycle.
Last Trading Day:	The third Friday of the contract month.

CASH SETTLEMENT AT DELIVERY

Unlike most other commodity or financial futures, deliveries against maturing stock index contracts are made by cash settlement. The primary reason for this is that the physical delivery of securities is not practical. The costs and the difficulties of delivering all the component securities of any broad-based index are too great. In addition, the potential for manipulation at delivery time by those holding large blocks of the component stocks makes cash settlement a more viable method than that of traditional physical delivery.

Until early 1987, all stock index futures contracts called for cash settlement based on the *closing* prices of the underlying securities at contract maturity. In early 1987, the IMM amended the S&P 500 index contract so that cash settlement is based on the *opening* prices of the underlying securities on the day following the last trading day. This change was made in response to concerns voiced by regulatory authorities regarding market volatility at the so-called *triple witching hours*. These are the four Fridays each year when stock options, stock index options, and stock index futures all expire simultaneously. Some authorities believed that by splitting the expirations between opening and closing prices there would be less activity and less volatility upon these expirations.

Cash settlement at maturity is based on the closing (or opening) value of the underlying index, not on the closing (or opening) value of the futures contract. On the last day of trading in the contract month, settlement is based on the difference between the previous day's futures contract settlement price and the closing (or opening) value of the actual underlying index. Prior to the last day the trader's account has been credited and debited daily, based on the closing price of the futures contract.

To illustrate, assume that a trader takes a long position in the December S&P 500 on the Tuesday prior to the last day of trading on Thursday. The index is purchased at a level of 225.00. The original margin in his account is $5,000.00.

Tuesday
- December S&P 500 closes at 227.50.
- The difference between the purchase price of 225.00 and the closing price of 227.50 is 250 points, or $1,250 per contract.

- This $1,250 is credited to the customer's account making his total equity $6,250 ($5,000 original margin plus $1,250 profit).

Wednesday
- December S&P 500 closes at 224.50.
- The difference between yesterday's closing price of 227.50 and today's 224.50 represents a 300-point decline, or $1,500.
- The customer's total equity is now $4,750.

Thursday
- Last trading day.

Friday
- The opening value of the underlying index is 225.00.
- At 225.00 the value of the futures contract is $112,500.
- To "take delivery," the customer would *in theory* have his futures position marked up to the invoice price of the delivery (225.00), giving him a credit of $250 and raising his equity back up to $5,000. At this point the long would put up $112,500 in order to receive $112,500 in cash settlement from the short. Obviously, this last step is of no economic consequence and can be eliminated.
- Thus, the "making or taking of delivery" in stock index futures simply means adjusting the customer's account to reflect the difference between the closing (or opening) value of the underlying index and the previous day's settlement price in futures.

It is worth pointing out that many of the complications that might arise from physical delivery are avoided in cash settlement. Such issues as delivery-supply squeezes, defaults, and distorting effects caused by the cheapest-to-deliver concept are avoided by cash settlement. However, cash settlement is not without its problems. Because cash and futures prices are not inextricably linked via the delivery mechanism, convergence of cash and futures is not assured. This opens the door, at least theoretically, to a new type of manipulation. For example, suppose that a trader had a very large long position in one of the stock index futures. The trader might consider buying a moderate amount of actual stock just before the futures contract expires. This would make sense if there were reasons to believe that these purchases would move the index higher by an amount such that the incremental profit on the large long index futures position would outweigh the loss that resulted from paying artificially high prices for a moderate amount of actual stock. Stock index futures contracts are carefully designed with sufficient breadth of issues and capitalization to make such approaches impractical in real life.

THE NATURE OF STOCK MARKET RISK

Stock investors face two types of risk: unsystematic and systematic. *Unsystematic risk* is sometimes called *stock-specific risk*. This is essentially the risk that a particular security (or industry group) will perform much worse than the stock market as a whole. Unhappily, numerous investors have discovered that their particular holdings can decline even though the stock market as a whole is rising. The investor who purchases one issue may maximize profits if correct in his stock selection, but he could suffer severe losses if incorrect on the particular investment, while being "right" on the market. One remedy for this type of risk is *diversification*, or purchasing a number of different issues. As the number of issues is increased, unsystematic risk decreases quickly. Some studies show that as few as 12 to 18 different stock issues can reduce unsystematic risk to a point where further diversification has small effect.

In practical terms, suppose that an investor held 1,000 shares of a silicon chip manufacturer. The unsystematic, or firm-specific, risk is very great. The share price could be depressed by any of a number of factors: product recall, foreign competition, sudden obsolescence through a competitor's new development, and so forth. This could even happen during a bull market when other share prices were generally rising. If the investor sold 400 shares and used the proceeds to purchase 100 shares each of an auto maker, an oil driller, a supermarket chain, and an airline, his non-systematic risk is sharply reduced. The eggs, as it were, are no longer in one basket.

Diversification addresses unsystematic risk but is not very useful as a defense against the more general *systematic (broad-market) risk*. When the market goes into a general decline, most stocks—blue chip or lesser quality—suffer, although not necessarily to the same extent. This may be illustrated by observing the performance of well-diversified mutual funds during bear markets. Those with high quality blue-chip portfolios usually go down by less than those that hold more speculative, lower-quality issues. Nevertheless, they both decline, and it is apparent that the decline is not so much influenced by the number of different issues as by their exposure to the market as a whole.

Futures contracts, based on major indicators of stock market performance, allow stock market participants to trade with minimal company-specific risk (selecting the wrong issue) and also to reduce greatly the systematic risk that is associated with owning a diversified portfolio of equity securities. For example, suppose that a mutual-fund portfolio manager controls $500 million in stock values and foresees a sharp near-term drop in the market. Trying to sell $500 million worth of equities quickly at reasonable prices would be technically very difficult, and is probably an undesirable course of action anyway if his long-term view is bullish. Selling listed call options against the portfolio securities offers some protection but has two major drawbacks:

- If the market drop is sharper than anticipated, the premium income from the options will not fully offset the losses on the portfolio.
- If the market rises rather than falls, a number of the options may be exercised and some of the portfolio thereby sold prematurely.

A stock index futures contract, on the other hand, offers greater downside protection without exposing the portfolio to sale if prices rise rather than fall. This is called *noninvasive hedging*. In essence, the portfolio manager becomes a farmer who has a silo jammed full of stock certificates rather than ears of corn. A short futures position may be used by each as a hedge against the loss of inventory value. Speculators and others likewise attempt to profit by taking outright long or short positions, thus providing the same type of risk transfer mechanism that has worked so well previously with farm products, industrial goods, and other financial instruments.

HEDGING IN STOCK INDEX FUTURES

The first step in constructing a hedge in stock index futures is to determine the total value (V) of the portfolio that is at risk. The second step is to create a position in the futures market whose value is comparable to that of the portfolio. Assume that the hedge will be in S&P 500 futures. Because the contract unit of S&P 500 futures is $500 times the price of the index *(P)*, the following formula gives the necessary number of futures contracts *(N)* for a perfectly balanced hedge.

$$N = \frac{V}{\$500 \times P}$$

If the portfolio value is $1 million and S&P futures are trading at 200.00, then we have:

$$N = \frac{\$1,000,000}{\$500 \times 200.00} = \underline{10.0}$$

The success of this hedge depends on there being high correlation between the value of the portfolio and the value of the futures contract. If a 10% drop in the value of the stock portfolio is matched by a 10% drop in the S&P 500 futures, then the hedge will have performed its job perfectly.

Unfortunately, this is rarely the case. Depending on their composition, stock portfolio values will rise or fall at rates greater or less than that of the overall index. The extent to which a stock or a portfolio of stocks moves faster or slower than the average is known as its *beta*. If a stock has a tendency to rise or fall by the same percent as the overall index, it is said to have a beta equal to 1.0. More speculative issues with volatility greater than the average have betas greater than 1.0. More conservative issues have betas of less than 1.0.

To calculate a stock's beta we simply divide its percent change in value by that of the relevant index. If a 10% change in the index is usually accompanied by a 12% change in the stock, then the stock has a beta of 1.2. Therefore, to construct a more effective futures hedge we must multiply the number of contracts derived from the above formula by the appropriate beta (β).

$$N = \frac{V}{500 \times P} \times \beta$$

If the beta of a $1 million portfolio were 1.2, and S&P 500 futures were trading at 200, the appropriate number of futures contracts would be derived as follows.

$$N = \frac{\$1,000,000}{\$500 \times 200.00} \times 1.2 = \underline{12.0}$$

Beta is, at best, an imprecise measure of a stock's relative volatility. It becomes even less precise when applied to a portfolio. For this reason, no hedge provides perfect protection against value declines. A more realistic and attainable objective is significant protection against major market setbacks.

HEDGING EXAMPLES

Example 1: Hedge involving low systematic risk. The most extreme case of hedging a stock market position with low systematic risk involves a "portfolio" containing only one or two stocks. Suppose that an individual owns 2,000 shares of Company *A* valued at $22 per share and 2,000 shares of Company *B* priced at $38 per share. His total portfolio, then, has a value of $120,000. Concerned about a possible decline in the overall market, he decides to sell one S&P 500 futures contract at the current price of 227.50. The futures contract has a value of $113,750. Stock prices decline, but his own holdings do not decline as much as the average. The S&P 500 index falls by 8%, to 209.30, but his own holdings fall by only 3% to $116,400. His loss of $3,600 on his portfolio is more than offset by the profit of $9,100 on his futures position.

But is this really a hedge? What reason is there to believe that there is anything but the most limited correlation between this two-stock portfolio and the S&P 500 index? This hedge leaves the investor exposed to considerable stock-specific, unsystematic risk. Suppose that the index had *risen* by 10% and the stock by only 3%. In fact, with just two stocks it is quite possible that a decline in the market could be accompanied by a rise in the stock prices or vice-versa. In a sense, hedges that involve portfolios of very low systematic risk are not really hedges but rather two loosely related but separate investments.

Example 2: Hedge involving high systematic risk. Now take the case of a large, well-diversified portfolio containing, say, 50 stocks, the total value of which is $10 million. Based on a study of past performance, the portfolio manager estimates the portfolio's beta at 0.90.

The first step in this hedge is to create a futures position, the value of which is comparable to the value of the portfolio. If S&P 500 futures are trading at 245.10, the value of the futures contract would be $122,550. Dividing this into the $10 million portfolio value, the manager concludes that it is necessary to sell 81 futures contracts to hedge the full value of the portfolio against a systematic market decline. However, because the portfolio has an estimated beta of only 0.90, it is appropriate to sell only 90% of that amount, or 73 contracts.

What would happen if the S&P 500 index fell by 10% and the portfolio had a decline of 9%, as would be expected from the beta of 0.90? This would put the S&P futures at 220.60, and the portfolio would have a new value of $9,100,000.

- The loss on the portfolio would be $900,000.
- The profit on the futures hedge would be $894,250.

In this hypothetical case of high systematic risk, the hedge would provide ample protection against the market decline.

These are just two examples of the many ways that stock index futures are applied to securities positions. Chapter 11 contains other examples. Other uses include hedging stock-option positions, hedging by underwriters to minimize risk during the distribution period, and hedging by specialists or market makers. These cases involve short hedges. Long hedges are used to protect a position in puts on a group of securities, by institutions that anticipate receiving cash and that want to lock-in present securities values, or by dealers who are committed to make future delivery of securities to institutions.

PORTFOLIO INSURANCE

Thus far we have discussed static, one-time hedging situations. These have been cases in which the hedger sought to protect himself against unusual market adversities of limited duration. Hedges were lifted once the adversity was perceived to have passed. The growing financial futures marketplace has also developed a new style of risk management that is an ongoing, dynamic part of portfolio strategy. It is known as *portfolio insurance.*

As the name implies, portfolio insurance seeks to provide protection against loss without simultaneously negating profit opportunities. The basic method used in portfolio insurance is to shift the portfolio out of stocks and into risk-free assets as stock prices decline, and into stocks and out of risk-free assets as stock prices increase. The methodology has the effect of reducing risk during periods of adversity and increasing risk and opportunity during periods of price appreciation.

The movement of the portfolio into and out of securities could be accomplished by simply buying and selling the actual securites. If the hedge program called for a reduction from being 80% stock invested to being 75% stock invested, the portfolio manager could obviously sell stock worth 5% of the portfolio. Besides having to deal with the issue of which securities to sell, the portfolio manager would have to contend with the difficulties and costs associated with moving into and out of blocks of stock. It would be preferable to keep the basic portfolio intact but somehow to shelter changing portions of it from risk. An increasingly popular tactic among portfolio managers is the use of purchases and sales of stock index futures as substitutes for purchases and sales of the securities in a portfolio. In the above example, the portfolio manager would sell stock index futures in an amount equal to 5% of the total portfolio. This is equivalent to selling off that part of the portfolio and putting it into cash. As the portfolio value declines, requiring a lower equity position, the short futures position is increased. As it rises, the short position is reduced.

The two major decisions involved in designing portfolio insurance are: (1) what portion of the portfolio should be insured, and (2) at what level beneath the portfolio's current value should the protection come into play? Strategies can be designed to substantially reduce all exposure if the portfolio's value drops below, say, 85% of its present level, but to participate fully in any appreciation if its value is above it. Other strategies can provide the portfolio with a beta of, say, 0.85 if the portfolio's worth is above a certain level, but reduce its beta to, say, 0.50 if it drops below that level. The combinations are both numerous and complicated.

A precautionary word: portfolio insurance sounds all well and good in theory, but in practice it can be fraught with problems. Quite obviously, selling futures contracts as prices drop and buying them back when prices rise can become very expensive in terms of transaction costs. This is particularly true in markets with high short-term volatility but low long-term volatility. A good example might be a wide-swinging trading range in which the strategy produces considerable short-term losses from the changing size of the hedge, but realizes no insurance benefit because the portfolio value never remains much below its initial level.

PRICE RELATIONSHIPS IN STOCK INDEX FUTURES

A good starting point for studying the relationship between two delivery months of the same index is to explore the theoretical relationship between spot and forward prices. We used this method in Chapter 9 for storable physical commodities and in Chapter 19 for currencies.

Given an efficient arbitrage environment, we know that the following two transactions should be roughly equivalent:

1. Buying a stock index future for delivery in one year.
2. Buying the component stocks now and holding them for one year.

There are no costs or revenues associated with alternative 1 except for negligible commission expenses. Alternative 2 entails interest expense and dividend income. Let us now equate these two alternatives.

Let:

S = the present value of the component stocks
F = the value of one year futures
I = interest rates per annum
D = dividend yield annualized

From the foregoing we have

$$F = S + (S \times I) - (S \times D)$$

or

$$F - S = S \times (I - D).$$

In words, the difference between the spot value and the one-year forward value is equal to the difference between the interest expense and the dividend income. This should sound familiar. In physical commodities the spot to forward difference is also determined in good part by interest expense (storage and insurance make up the rest). The only difference with stock indexes is that stocks pay a dividend, which must be subtracted from the interest expense to arrive at the net carrying cost.

Thus far we have concerned ourselves only with the one-year spread. To calculate the theoretical spread for shorter periods or for periods between two futures delivery months, we need make only these additions.

Let:

S = either the present value of the component stocks or the value of the nearby future
F = the value of the more distant future
I = either short-term interest rates or the relevant implied forward rate
D = the expected annualized dividend yield for the relevant time period
t = number of days between the two dates

The more general equation would then be:

$$F - S = S \times (t/365) \times (I - D)$$

which also says that the difference in value between the two delivery months equals the difference between the interest expense and the dividend income during the period between the two deliveries.

The foregoing assumes that it is possible for arbitrageurs to take advantage of money-making disparities to keep stock prices aligned with stock index futures prices. This is not easy in the case of stock indexes. Buying or selling all the stocks that comprise an index can be done neither quickly nor easily. *Program trading,* as this type of arbitrage is known, is the province of a few large securities firms that have the infrastructure to execute and process large numbers of nearly simultaneous stock transactions.

Intramarket Spreads

Because stock index futures call for cash settlement, arbitrage between two different futures delivery months is not possible in the strictest sense of the word "arbitrage." This is because the cash delivery feature makes it impossible to take delivery against a futures contract and to redeliver against a later-maturing delivery, as is possible with most contracts that call for delivery of the item underlying the futures contract. But the reasoning of the previous section can be applied to such intramarket spreads to get a "ballpark" idea of what various intramarket spreads should be worth. Such an analysis also helps understand what effect a change in any variable ought to have on the spread.

A few generalizations are possible:

1. Increasing (declining) stock index prices should cause forward months to gain on (lose to) nearbys, *when interest rates are above dividend yields.*
2. Dividend yields on large portfolios do not usually change much, so changes in interest rates and in the index price are the main variables in intramarket spread behavior. With index prices held constant, rising (falling) interest rates have a tendency to cause distant deliveries to outpace (lag) nearby deliveries.

Intermarket Spreads

The relationships between different indexes are fundamentally determined by the index characteristics discussed earlier in this chapter. In general, the VLA tends to be the most volatile of the available indexes. In rising or falling markets, it will tend to outpace the other indexes. For this reason a long VLA/short other-index spread can be used as a substitute for an outright long position. A short VLA/long other-index spread can be a proxy for an outright short position. The high degree of correlation between price movements of the S&P 500 and NYSE indexes limits the potential for spreading these indexes against each other. It is important that intermarket spreads be weighted so that the dollar values of the long and short legs are balanced. The intentional or unintentional failure to do so will increase both the risk and the profit potential of the spread.

The following table summarizes some information regarding typical behavior of stock index futures spreads.

Summary of General Rules of Spread Behavior for Stock Index Futures

Expectation	*Probable Behavior of Futures*
1. Smaller companies will outperform (underperform) the larger ones.	1. NYSE index will gain on (lose to) S&P 500 index.
2. Generally rising (falling) stock prices.	2. Value line index will gain on (lose to) NYSE index and S&P index.
3. Dividend yields will rise (fall) relative to interest rates.	3. Deferred contracts will tend to decline (advance) relative to nearby contracts.

■ *Chapter 21*

■ *Domestic Agricultural Commodities and Government Programs*

- Corn
- Cotton
- Soybeans
- Soybean Meal
- Soybean Oil

- Wheat
- Hogs
- Pork Bellies
- Cattle
- Government Agricultural Programs

CORN

The United States is by far the world's largest corn producer, accounting for about 40% of total world output. China ranks second with some 15% of the global total. With annual production in recent years of more than 8 billion bushels, corn is easily the largest crop grown in the United States. Some 80% of U.S. production is concentrated in the Corn Belt states of Iowa, Illinois, Minnesota, Indiana, Missouri, Ohio, and South Dakota. About 60% of this production is used as domestic animal feed. Cattle, hogs, and poultry are the primary consumers. Roughly 25% of the rest is exported, with Japan, West Germany, and Mexico almost always among the largest importers. The U.S.S.R. sometimes purchases large amounts of U.S. corn, depending largely on the size of its own grain crop. The quantity of Soviet purchases varies widely from season to season and is often a key influence on prices.

Figure 21-1. U.S. corn supply and disappearance (millions of bushels).

Crop Year Beginning Oct. 1	Beginning Stocks	Production	Total Supply[1]	Domestic Use	Exports	Ending Stocks
1978/1979	1,111	7,268	8,381	4,944	2,133	1,304
1979/1980	1,304	7,939	9,244	5,194	2,433	1,618
1980/1981	1,618	6,645	8,264	4,874	2,355	1,034
1981/1982	1,034	8,119	9,154	5,013	1,967	2,174
1982/1983	2,174	8,235	10,410	5,420	1,870	3,120
1983/1984	3,120	4,175	7,297	4,793	1,902	723
1984/1985	723	7,674	8,684	5,170	1,865	1,648
1985/1986	1,648	8,877	10,536	5,255	1,241	4,040
1986/1987[2]	4,040	8,253	12,295	5,450	1,125	5,720

[1] Includes imports
[2] Preliminary
Source: USDA

The corn planting season runs from mid-April to mid-June. Weather is critical at this early stage because heavy rains can delay plantings, which in turn delays crop maturity and exposes the crop to frost during harvesting. During the growing season (June-September) the crop is subject to the dual hazards of summer drought and autumn rains. Dry and hot conditions during August can cut yields, while rains during September and October can adversely affect quality.

Because corn competes primarily with soybeans for acreage in the United States, price relationships between these two commodities are very important around planting time. The *Preliminary Planting Intentions* survey, issued by the U.S. Department of Agriculture (USDA) in January, provides the first indication of the probable size of the upcoming crop. A *Prospective Plantings* report is issued in March, by which time farmers have firmer plans for their plantings. The first estimate of actual acreage comes in the July crop report from the USDA. Yield per acre and production are estimated monthly beginning with the August crop report.

Domestic use of corn is divided into two major categories: (1) livestock feed, and (2) food, industry, and seed. Livestock feed is easily the most important, accounting for more than 80% of all United States consumption. Factors that influence the amount of corn that is consumed in this category are: (1) the price of corn, (2) the price of livestock, and (3) the number of animals on feed. Although no official estimates of corn use (*disappearance*) are issued during the season, good approximations can be derived by factoring exports out of the USDA's *Stocks-in-all-Positions* reports issued in January, April, July, and October.

About one-quarter of the U.S. corn crop is sold for export. Statistics on exports are released by the USDA each week and can have an important short-term impact on prices. Foreign demand depends largely on foreign livestock inventories and the general worldwide availability of competing feed grains such as oats, sorghum, and barley.

Government programs are a major influence on supply/demand fundamentals in the corn market. The last section of this chapter describes in detail government programs and their effect on agricultural prices.

COTTON

Domestic production of cotton is concentrated in the range of Southern states known at the *Cotton Belt.* The largest producing area is the Delta region, made up of Mississippi, Arkansas, Tennessee, Louisiana, and Missouri. This area accounts for a little less than one-third of U.S. output. The Southwest region (predominantly Texas and Oklahoma) accounts for about an equal share. California, Arizona, and New Mexico (the key states of the Western region) account for one-fifth of all U.S. cotton. Remaining production comes from a handful of states in the Southeastern region.

Early spring marks the beginning of the planting season in southernmost Texas, with virtually all plantings for the rest of the country completed by late May. The growing season lasts approximately 180 days, with the first two months being the most critical for plant development. Most harvesting is completed by late October, although picking operations can continue into late November and December in the hotter zones. The final output in any season is a function of the land planted and the yield per acre. Planted acreage depends on the relative profitability of cotton versus other crops such as soybeans and corn. A favorably high price during the winter and early spring will tend to expand cotton acreage at the expense of these other crops. Yield, of course, is dependent primarily on weather conditions during the approximately six months between planting and harvesting.

Cotton consumption is divided into two major categories: (1) domestic mill consumption and (2) exports. As for domestic consumption, the most important end-user of cotton is the U.S. apparel industry, which accounts for about 50% of domestic usage. The household market (sheets, pillowcases, towels, and so on) is the second largest consumer. Cotton's share in these and other markets varies according to the prices of competing synthetic fibers. More generally, demand for cotton products depends on price level, per capita income, and overall economic conditions.

Exports have always played an important role in the cotton market, representing about one-third of annual U.S. production. Japan is the world's leading importer of cotton. Other major foreign buyers include Korea, China, Canada, Italy, and Indonesia. The basic factors that influence U.S. cotton exports are the rate of cotton consumption abroad, available foreign supplies, and the value of the U.S. dollar versus the currencies of consuming countries. Besides the United States, other major producers of cotton are China, the Soviet Union, India, Brazil, Pakistan, and Turkey. The United States, China, and the Soviet Union each usually produce about 15% of the world's total cotton output.

Figure 21-2. U.S. cotton supply and distribution (thousands of 480 lb. bales).

Crop Year Beginning Aug. 1	Beginning Stocks	Production	Total Supply	Mill Consumption	Exports	Ending Stocks
1978/1979	5,326	10,405	15,807	6,352	6,180	3,782
1979/1980	3,782	14,190	18,177	6,506	9,229	3,027
1980/1981	3,027	10,627	13,897	5,891	5,926	2,595
1981/1982	2,595	15,106	17,767	5,043	6,567	6,399
1982/1983	6,399	11,486	17,907	5,259	5,207	7,561
1983/1984	7,561	7,502	15,235	5,926	6,786	2,906
1984/1985	2,906	12,382	15,379	5,540	6,215	4,088
1985/1986	4,088	13,432	17,520	6,205	2,000	9,352
1986/1987[1]	9,352	9,790	19,142	7,010	6,760	5,492

[1] Preliminary
Source: USDA

Analysis of a given season's supply/demand outlook usually begins with an estimate of total supplies (carryover plus current year's production). USDA production estimates are released monthly, beginning in July. Estimates of total supply are compared to projections for demand to arrive at a forecast of the end-of-season carryover. Should these calculations suggest that stocks are low in relation to expected consumption, prices will likely rise to levels that will reduce consumption and encourage future production. A high ratio of stocks to expected consumption would likely result in weakening prices.

SOYBEAN COMPLEX

Soybeans

Soybeans compete with corn as the nation's number one cash crop. Soybean products represent a major source of protein for poultry and livestock as well as key ingredients in the manufacture of shortening, margarine, and cooking and salad oils.

Most U.S. production is concentrated in the Corn Belt states of Illinois, Iowa, Indiana, Ohio, Missouri, and Minnesota. Plantings usually take place between late April and mid-June. The most active plant growth occurs during July when normal or above-normal rainfall is essential if yields are not to be adversely affected. Most harvesting is completed by the end of October. Major crop hazards include excessive moisture during planting and drought during the late summer.

Soybeans are grown for their two major products, soybean meal and soybean oil. When a 60-pound bushel of soybeans is processed it will yield approximately 47 pounds of meal and 11 pounds of oil, with 2 pounds as waste after crushing. The value of soybeans, therefore, is determined by the value of the meal and oil. The difference between the value of the soybeans and the value of its end-products is known as the *crushing margin* and represents a yardstick of profit to the soybean processor. A large crushing margin represents profit for soybean processing, thereby strengthening the demand for soybeans and increasing the supplies of oil and meal. Conversely, a low or negative crushing margin will discourage demand for beans and reduce the production of products.

Figure 21-3. U.S. soybean supply and distribution (millions of bushels).

Crop Year Beginning Sept. 1	Beginning Stocks	Production	Total Supply	Domestic Crushings	Exports	Feed, Seed & Residual	Ending Stocks
1978/1979	161	1,869	2,030	1,018	739	99	174
1979/1980	174	2,261	2,437	1,123	875	81	359
1980/1981	359	1,798	2,156	1,020	724	99	313
1981/1982	313	1,989	2,302	1,030	929	89	255
1982/1983	255	2,190	2,444	1,108	905	86	345
1983/1984	345	1,636	1,981	983	743	79	176
1984/1985	176	1,861	2,037	1,030	598	93	316
1985/1986	316	2,099	2,415	1,060	750	85	536
1986/1987[1]	536	2,007	2,543	1,080	760	90	615

[1] Preliminary
Source: USDA

About two-thirds of the total U.S. crop is crushed domestically, and the remaining one-third is exported. Japan and Western Europe are the dominant foreign buyers. Most exports are shipped out of Gulf ports and the Great Lakes. Brazil has become an important competitor of the U.S. on the export front since the mid-1970's.

Important USDA reports begin with the January release of the Preliminary Planting Intentions report, which gives the acreage that farmers intend to plant to soybeans, corn, and other crops. Because soybeans compete with corn and cotton for acreage, price relationships between these commodities can be an important determinant of planting intentions. A final planted acreage figure is available in July, and production estimates are released by the USDA monthly from August to December. Also of importance are quarterly stocks-on-hand reports, which detail total domestic soybean supplies in on-farm and off-farm locations.

Government programs have an important impact on soybean prices. The USDA attempts to maintain alignment between supplies and usage through acreage allotments, loan programs, and target prices. These programs and their effect on prices are described in the last section of this chapter.

Soybean Oil

Soybean oil accounts for more than half of all food fats and oils consumed in the United States. In turn, food product usage accounts for almost all of the domestic consumption of soybean oil. The major sources of demand are salad and cooking oils, shortening, and margarine.

Because of the fairly high degree of interchangeability among fats and oils in the domestic market, the availability and price of competing edible oils can be a major factor in the price of soybean oil. Lard, cotton oil, and butter are the major competitors in the domestic market. Shifts in the availability of any of these products can significantly affect the use of soybean oil.

The issue of substitution becomes even more complex when viewed from a world perspective. The United States accounts for about 90% of all soybean oil exports, but a number of other oils provide stiff competition in different parts of the world. Chief among these other oils are palm oil, coconut oil, sunflower seed oil, groundnut oil, cottonseed oil, and rapeseed oil.

Palm oil enters the United States from Malaysia and Indonesia, and the main product for which it competes with soybean oil is shorten-

Figure 21-4. U.S. soybean oil supply and disappearance (millions of pounds).

Crop Year Beginning Oct. 1	Beginning Stocks	Production	Total Supply	Domestic Use	Exports	Ending Stocks
1978/1979	729	11,323	12,052	8,942	2,411	776
1979/1980	776	12,105	12,881	8,981	2,690	1,210
1980/1981	1,210	11,270	12,480	9,113	1,631	1,736
1981/1982	1,736	10,979	11,715	9,536	2,077	1,103
1982/1983	1,103	12,040	13,143	9,857	2,025	1,261
1983/1984	1,261	10,872	12,133	9,588	1,824	721
1984/1985	721	11,468	12,185	9,917	1,660	632
1985/1986	632	11,617	12,257	10,053	1,257	947
1986/1987[1]	947	11,878	12,825	10,400	1,200	1,225

[1] Preliminary
Source: USDA

ing. Coconut oil is used primarily in confectionary and baked products and to a smaller extent in shortening and margarine. Its major source is the Philippines. Both of these oils compete with soybean oil in the United States and abroad. Sunflower seed oil originates in the Soviet Union and neighboring Eastern European countries, and is a uniquely important competitor of soybean oil in Europe. Another major competitor on the European continent is groundnut oil. Major producers of this oil are India, Nigeria, Senegal, and neighboring African nations. Cottonseed oil competes with soybean oil in the cooking and salad oil market, both in the United States and overseas. Rapeseed oil is produced mainly in Canada, India, and China.

The most important factor in the soybean oil price outlook for any season is usually the size of the U.S. soybean crop. Once this crop size is determined, the available supply of soybean oil in the United States can be estimated by using the normal percentage of the crop crushed in a season (55%-65%). The rate of crush, as measured by the Census Bureau's monthly statistics, is an important price-making factor in soybean oil. It is worth noting that the rate of crush tends to be a function more of soybean meal demand than of soybean oil demand. This is because meal is usually the more valuable of the two products and is somewhat less storable.

Soybean Meal

Soybean meal is a major source of high-protein supplementary animal feed. Soybeans contain about 38% to 45% protein, and it is this protein content that has become a key ingredient in the raising of cattle, hogs, and poultry in the United States.

The supply of soybean meal in any season is a function of the quantity of soybeans available for processing. Most meal is processed in one of about 100 U.S. processing plants that convert the raw soybeans into crude soybean oil and soybean meal that contains approximately 44% protein. Higher-protein-content soybean meal is obtainable through additional processing. While the maximum amount of meal that can be produced is limited by the amount of available soybeans, the actual supply of meal is determined by the rate of crushings. This, in turn, is influenced by the profitability of processing. As noted earlier, the meal value of soybeans generally exceeds the oil value, so crushing rates depend largely on demand for meal. Because meal cannot be stored for

Figure 21-5. U.S. soybean meal supply and disappearance (thousands of short tons).

Crop Year Beginning Oct. 1	Beginning Stocks	Production	Total Supply	Domestic Use	Exports	Ending Stocks
1978/1979	243	24,354	24,597	17,720	6,610	267
1979/1980	267	27,105	27,372	19,214	7,932	226
1980/1981	226	24,312	24,538	17,591	6,784	163
1981/1982	163	24,634	24,797	17,714	6,908	175
1982/1983	175	26,714	26,889	19,306	7,109	474
1983/1984	474	22,756	23,230	17,615	5,360	255
1984/1985	255	24,520	24,774	19,480	4,917	387
1985/1986	387	24,951	25,338	19,118	6,008	212
1986/1987[1]	212	25,488	25,700	19,500	5,900	300

[1] Preliminary
Source: USDA

long periods, sudden and unanticipated changes in demand or production can spark dramatic price moves.

Soybean meal produced in this country is used primarily for two purposes—exports and animal feed. Exports go principally to Western Europe, Canada, and Japan, and account for about 20% of total production. The large remaining amount is used as a feed supplement for poultry, cattle, and hogs. Animal numbers, particularly when measured by the USDA's *protein-consuming animal unit,* are an obviously important factor in the demand outlook for meal in any given season.

On the international front, soybean meal competes with a variety of other protein feeds, of which fishmeal and peanut meal are among the most important. Peru is the largest shipper of fishmeal, and India is the largest exporter of peanut meal.

WHEAT

Wheat is harvested somewhere around the world in every month of the year. In the United States, harvesting begins in the south end of the wheat belt (Texas) in early summer and progresses northward. Kansas, Washington, Nebraska, Oklahoma, and North Dakota are major producing states. Worldwide, the Soviet Union is the largest producing nation, followed by the United States, India, and the People's Republic of China. France, Canada, Australia, and Argentina are also key producers.

Wheat is classified in two ways: by planting or growing time, and by physical trait. Winter wheat is planted in the early fall and is harvested in the early summer. Spring wheat is planted in the spring and harvested in the late summer. Most wheat is classed as either hard or soft, with the former used primarily in bread and the latter in crackers and pastries. A third category, durum, is especially suited for the manufacture of pasta. Hard winter wheat constitutes about 80% of the U.S. crop. Soft red wheat is the par grade deliverable against the Chicago Board of Trade contract, while Kansas City Board of Trade futures are based on hard red winter wheat. Minneapolis Grain Exchange wheat futures call for delivery of spring wheat.

Domestic consumption of wheat is concentrated in the food sector and tends to be more stable than export usage. Wheat is the main ingredient in flour. It takes roughly $2^{1}/_{2}$ bushels of the grain to produce 100

Figure 21-6. U.S. wheat supply and disappearance (millions of bushels).

Crop Year Beginning June 1	Beginning Stocks	Production	Total[1] Stocks	Domestic Use	Exports	Ending Stocks
1978/1979	1,178	1,776	2,955	837	1,194	924
1979/1980	924	2,134	3,060	783	1,375	902
1980/1981	902	2,374	3,279	776	1,514	989
1981/1982	989	2,785	3,777	847	1,771	1,159
1982/1983	1,159	2,765	3,932	908	1,509	1,515
1983/1984	1,515	2,420	3,939	1,112	1,429	1,398
1984/1985	1,398	2,596	4,004	1,155	1,424	1,425
1985/1986	1,425	2,425	3,865	1,045	915	1,905
1986/1987[2]	1,905	2,087	4,002	1,105	975	1,922

[1] Includes imports
[2] Forecast
Source: USDA

pounds of flour. Wheat may also be used as an animal feed, especially during periods of relatively high corn prices.

Exports are a major influence on wheat prices and are heavily dependent on world crop conditions. The United States sells approximately half of its crop abroad and is traditionally the world's largest exporter. Conditions in the U.S.S.R., both a major producer and a major consumer of wheat, play an important role in determining wheat prices. This was dramatically illustrated by the price upheaval that accompanied massive Soviet wheat purchases in 1972. Major importers of wheat include China, Japan, Korea, the Netherlands, and Brazil. Foreign supplies of wheat are an important determinant of U.S. exports, but these supplies are not easy to measure. Southern-hemisphere producers harvest their crops about six months after the U.S. harvest, and this ongoing addition of wheat to the global supply makes this market especially difficult to analyze fundamentally.

Total U.S. disappearance of wheat is reflected in the USDA's quarterly Stocks-in-all-Position reports that are released in January, April, July, and October. Export shipments and commitments are reported weekly. U.S. production estimates are provided by the USDA in its series of monthly crop reports beginning in May. The USDA also estimates foreign production, but these estimates tend to be less reliable than those of the U.S. crop because information-gathering networks and procedures are less well developed outside the United States.

LIVE HOGS AND PORK BELLIES

Live Hogs

The Corn Belt states of Iowa, Illinois, Indiana, and Missouri account for more than half the hogs raised in the United States. From the farms where they are raised, hogs are brought to terminal markets where they are bought by meat packers, slaughtered, and processed into pork products such as ham and bacon.

The supply cycle for hogs begins when they are born (farrowed) and raised on feed consisting mostly of corn with soybean meal and other supplements. Gaining more than a pound per day, hogs reach a market weight of some 220 pounds after about six months. Because birth occurs about four months after breeding, the full period from breeding

Figure 21-7. U.S. live hog statistics as of Dec. 1
(thousands of head).

Year	All Hogs & Pigs on U.S. Farms	Sows Farrowed*	Pig Crop*	Value of Hogs on Farms ($ per Head)
1978	60,100	12,432	88,512	
1979	67,318	14,498	102,792	56.00
1980	64,462	14,084	101,720	74.70
1981	58,698	12,708	93,853	70.10
1982	54,534	11,548	85,189	89.90
1983	56,694	12,477	93,155	58.80
1984	54,073	11,551	86,586	75.00
1985	52,313	11,239	86,029	69.60
1986	50,960	10,656	82,283	NA

*12 months beginning December 1 of previous year
Source: USDA

to market readiness takes about ten months. This long delay is the
source of a dominant influence on the price of hogs—the *hog cycle*. Hog
farmers are required to make breeding decisions some ten months before
the effect of these decisions will be realized in the form of market-ready
hogs. Because such decisions often tend to be made on the basis of current market conditions, they frequently tend to lag behind the market. A
high price for hogs one year usually stimulates overproduction during
the next year or two. This high level of production then depresses the
price of hogs which, in turn, causes a contraction in farmer breeding intentions. With supplies cut back, prices rise once again and the cycle begins anew. This cycle, from production high to production high, has
historically had an average length of about four years.

The demand for hogs is determined by consumer purchases of
fresh pork and pork products. Consumer purchases are a reflection of
pork prices, prices of competing meats, disposable income, and diet

Another factor that influences the supply of hogs is the hog:corn
ratio, which is the number of bushels of corn that it takes to buy 100
pounds of live hog. Published regularly by the USDA, this statistic is a
measure of the profitability of feeding hogs. When the hog:corn ratio is
favorable (high) farmers generally respond by breeding more animals
and feeding them to heavier weights. The opposite is true when the ratio
is low. Fewer hogs are bred, and those tend to be marketed at lighter
weights.

preferences. Pork demand tends to reach its peak during the summer and early fall and drops to a seasonal low during the winter and early spring. Hog production has a definite seasonal pattern. The spring pig crop (born in the December–May period) constitutes more than half of annual production. Most of these animals are slaughtered in the fall period of peak demand. Marketings rise to their peak between October and January.

Pork Bellies

Pork bellies are the part of the hog that is used to produce bacon. One hog yields two bellies with an average weight of 12 to 14 pounds each. The seasonal nature of hog slaughter dictates that during the period from October to May, pork belly supplies tend to accumulate in cold storage. The seasonal decline in storage stocks lasts from June to September. The USDA issues data on frozen supplies in cold storage on a monthly basis throughout the year. Other data on stored bellies is available daily. An estimate of total pork belly supplies is derived by combining cold-storage supplies with fresh supplies that are made available from slaughter. The latter figure can be approximated by using farrowings reported six months earlier, estimating the number of hogs to be slaughtered, and multiplying this by the 24 to 28 pounds of bellies in the average hog.

The demand for bacon tends to be fairly stable, responding significantly only to the most extreme price moves. This inelasticity of demand means that small changes in supply can produce magnified changes in price. The best statistical measure of demand for pork bellies is the *bacon slice,* published by the USDA.

An important source of information on hogs and pork bellies is the *USDA Hogs and Pigs* report, which is issued quarterly in March, June, September, and December. The USDA also issues a monthly *Cold Storage* report that gives the quantity of frozen belly inventories. This data is closely followed by pork-complex traders.

LIVE CATTLE

The cattle business is one of the largest components of the U.S. agricultural sector. In a typical year more than 20 million head of cattle are marketed with a total wholesale value of more than $10 billion. Only corn and soybeans are comparable to the beef industry in terms of market value produced. Cattle are almost exclusively consumed in the countries where they are produced, so futures traders need focus only on the fundamentals in the United States beef industry. The reason, of course, is that the bulk and perishability of live cattle preclude meaningful exports.

Calves are usually born in the early spring and weaned after about six months when they weigh approximately 400 pounds. At this point, some are moved directly to feedlots while the majority are sent to rangeland, where they are grass-fed for about six months. By the age of one year, most animals are on feedlots where they gain roughly 2¹/₂ pounds per day until they reach an average market weight of a little over 1,000 pounds after more than six months on feed. Including the gestation period of nine months, the total time from breeding to market readiness is about 2¹/₂ years.

The long delay from the decision to breed to the time a steer is ready for slaughter gives rise to a supply cycle similar to, but much longer than, that prevailing in the hog market. High prices generally cause producers to expand their breeding stocks. When the larger number of new calves from the expanded herds reach maturity, slaughter begins to increase. Prices come under pressure, causing producers to liquidate breeding stock. Ultimately the low breeding stock leads to reduced slaughter, higher prices, and the beginning of a new upswing in the supply cycle.

During this long cycle (as much as ten years), cattle prices respond to a number of factors, chief among which is the variable movement of cattle off feedlots to market. Although mature animals must be moved to market within a relatively narrow time span, short-term marketing decisions by feedlot operators can have a significant impact on prices. For instance, a temporary surplus of heavy, market-ready animals can put pressure on cash and futures prices even when the longer-term outlook suggests reduced supplies. As noted in Chapter 16, these short-run influences can cause disparate price movements in the various contract months of the cattle futures market.

The major source of information on feedlot conditions is the monthly USDA *Cattle-on-Feed* report. The more comprehensive quarterly Cattle-on-Feed report divides the number of animals on feed into weight groups, from which it is possible to estimate beef supplies several months in advance. Cattle demand is a direct function of consumer beef purchases and, as such, is influenced predominantly by beef prices, competing meat prices, disposable income, and dietary preferences.

Figure 21-8. U.S. cattle supply and distribution (thousands of head).

Year	Cattle & Calves on Farms Jan. 1	Imports	Calves Born	Total Supply	Total Slaughter	Deaths on Farms	Exports
1978	116,375	1,253	43,818	161,446	44,272	5,680	122
1979	110,864	732	42,603	154,199	36,932	5,600	66
1980	111,192	681	44,998	156,871	36,795	5,413	66
1981	114,351	680	44,666	159,676	38,151	4,897	88
1982	115,444	1,005	44,200	160,649	39,264	5,440	58
1983	115,001	921	43,925	159,847	40,136	5,501	56
1984	113,700	753	42,500	156,955	41,290	5,475	71
1985	109,749	836	40,045	151,030		5,030	125
1986	105,468						
1987	102,031						

Source: USDA

GOVERNMENT AGRICULTURAL PROGRAMS

Government programs designed to influence the supply or price of farm commodities have an enormous impact on prices in the futures markets. This section discusses in detail the methods by which the government influences agricultural prices, the effects of these methods, and the meaning of the Food Security Act of 1985 (which we refer to as the *1985 Farm Bill*), which will have an important influence on agricultural markets for many years.

Loans

The most widely known elements of modern-day agriculture programs are the loans that the government offers to farmers. The USDA's Commodity Credit Corporation (CCC) makes loans available to farmers who pledge a portion of their crop as collateral. The amount of the loan is determined by the specified loan rate for a crop multiplied by the amount of the crop being pledged as collateral. Eligible farmers must then repay the loan plus interest (which is usually no more than the rate which the CCC must pay to the U.S. Treasury for borrowed funds) within a period of usually less than one year. If the farmer fails to repay the loan, his pledged crop is then forfeited to the CCC. The farmer can, of course, redeem the loan at any point prior to the expiration date.

Farmers will usually choose to forfeit their crop to the CCC if the prevailing price for their grain is below the loan rate plus the appropriate interest obligations. Conversely, if a bull market develops for a crop eligible for CCC loans, farmers will repay the principal plus the interest charges in order to redeem their crops and sell them at the higher free market prices.

The CCC loan program essentially provides a floor for grain prices and, under certain conditions, will mitigate otherwise bearish fundamentals. In essence, CCC loans allow participating farmers the option of enjoying a minimum price for their crop (the loan rate) while at the same time preserving the option to repay the loan plus interest if prices rise sufficiently. The CCC, which may find itself the owner of a substantial amount of a crop purchased at prices exceeding free market levels, assumes all the risk.

Farmer-Owned Grain Reserve

In contrast to the nonrecourse loans described above, the Farmer-Owned Grain Reserve program (FOR) extends long-term loans to farmers. The loans, which have a traditional maturity of three to five years, are given to eligible farmers who agree to store their crop (which is once again pledged as collateral) for such a lengthy period of time. The interest obligations of participating farmers generally do not exceed the rate for funds paid by the CCC to the U.S. Treasury.

The FOR program contains a number of provisions that are designed to encourage participation and, thereby, ensure that a substantial amount of a crop is taken off the market for an extended period. For example, the CCC reimburses the farmer a specified amount each year for his costs of storing the collateralized crop. Additionally, FOR often provides for a loan rate that exceeds the level existing on the more conventional CCC loans. Finally, the USDA has the option of waiving the interest charges to farmers. In practice, this has been done for loans with one to two years left to maturity. The storage repayments, interest rate concessions, and potential for a higher loan level are designed to encourage potentially eligible farmers to hold a portion of their crop off the market for an extended period of time.

The USDA also endeavors to keep this grain off the market by providing for penalties that are designed to deter the repayment of loans before maturity unless free market prices achieve a certain minimum level (the so-called *release* or *trigger* price). If a farmer attempts to pay off his loan when prices are below the release level, FOR legislation provides for the mandatory repayment to the government of storage reimbursements that the farmer had received plus interest penalties.

The 1985 Act does permit the government to release grain for both domestic use and for export when farmers redeem certificates that they have received as deficiency payments (discussed later in this chapter). These releases are at market prices and can play an important role in determining available supply. They were a key feature of the 1986/1987 crop year.

Theoretically, FOR provisions also mandate the repayment of loans if the release price, which is set higher than the conventional wheat and corn loan rate, is reached. The Secretary of Agriculture has the authority to call outstanding loans, demand the redemption of storage reimbursements, and the immediate payout of interest obligations. In practice, however, the USDA is generally reluctant to assume such an aggressive stance.

The advantage of FOR to the government is that the reserves potentially provide for removal of a substantial amount of a crop from free supplies for an extended period of time. The incentives that are designed to encourage farm participation are, however, more expensive than conventional loan provisions. The farmer who is willing to forfeit the use of his crop for a period of a few years benefits from relatively generous FOR provisions.

Both the USDA loan and the FOR programs have, at times, impacted the futures markets. For example, the conventional loan rate often constitutes a floor for agricultural products because when open-market prices are below CCC loan levels, farmers benefit by pledging their crops to the CCC. Similarly, at low price levels, most farmers will probably forego loan repayment and forfeit their crop to the CCC. In both cases, the crop would remain in storage and be unavailable to the marketplace.

At times, however, the loan rate has not provided a firm floor to the market. If a substantial number of farmers choose not to fulfill loan-eligibility requirements, the supportive effects of the loan rate are diluted. Similarly, a farmer who expects higher prices may decide to redeem his CCC-pledged crop even if prevailing prices are below the loan rate. Traders should note that a grain futures price that falls to loan plus carry does not necessarily represent a buying opportunity. Theoretically, if the bearish fundamental environment remains intact, spot levels will stabilize while the maturing futures price will gradually decline because of the erosion of carrying charge premiums.

The FOR program has also affected the futures markets. The grain embargo against the Soviet Union in early 1980 was a case in point. After the embargo was instituted, the USDA, in an attempt to buttress prices, increased incentives to participate in FOR and succeeded in reducing free supplies of wheat. Free supplies remained tight until the market adjusted.

The Soviet grain embargo represented a dramatic example of how the government, through CCC and FOR loans, can influence the agricultural markets. The point is that an aggressive government campaign to entice farmers either to place grain into FOR or to participate in CCC loan programs may alter an otherwise abundant supply situation. At a certain level, supplies will become sufficiently tight to generate a price rise that will encourage farmers to repay CCC loans or to trigger the automatic release provisions of FOR. Unless such a price adjustment occurs, free supplies would remain tight. Therefore, it is important when developing a trading strategy in agricultural futures to consider the level of free supplies and the participation in government loan programs in addition to overall supply/usage statistics.

The USDA influences the markets in other ways besides the conventional loan programs and FOR. A review of these other programs is essential for an appreciation of the government's effects on the agricultural markets.

Target-Price Program

With the exception of the loan programs described above, target prices are perhaps the best known of all USDA efforts to aid farmers. Under this program, the USDA endeavors to guarantee that eligible farmers receive at least certain minimum prices for their crops. These prices are based on a number of considerations that include the costs of producing various crops, parity considerations, and a general evaluation of farm income levels. The program provides for deficiency payments when the average market price of a crop is less than the specific target price for a specified period of time. If free-market prices exceed target levels, then no deficiency payments are made.

In most instances, the target-price program does not impact the futures markets. The deficiency payments represent a transfer from the government to farmers and have no direct effect on the agricultural markets. One can argue, however, that if deficiency payments are particularly generous, farmers may attempt to meet eligibility requirements by participating in acreage-reduction programs such as the set-aside (discussed later in this chapter). Thus, to the extent that target-price deficiency payments provide an incentive for farmers to participate in acreage-reduction plans, the program may prove mildly supportive to prices.

Commodity Credit Corporation (CCC) Activity

The CCC, because of the huge amount of grain it collects from loan forfeitures by farmers, potentially represents a major force in the

agricultural markets. Currently, the USDA prohibits the CCC from selling its inventory of farm products until free-market prices for a specific
crop exceed FOR trigger levels by a specified amount. For agricultural
products where FOR is not relevant, the CCC is prohibited from selling
inventory unless conventional loan levels are exceeded by an established
amount.

In practice, therefore, the CCC generally does not constitute a market force unless prices rise to FOR trigger levels or to conventional loan
levels. Even in these instances, however, it is not necessarily clear that
CCC sales provide a ceiling for the market. Although aggressive CCC
sales will almost certainly temper a rally in the grains, one must remember that the overall fundamental situation of the market is usually quite
positive if such sales are possible. Thus, CCC sales may temper price
advances but not necessarily alter the fundamental situation that allowed
farm prices to exceed FOR trigger price and loan levels in the first place.

Acreage Reduction Programs

The USDA has also established acreage reduction programs that
are designed to mitigate the effects of crop surpluses. Potentially, these
programs can impact the agricultural markets. A review of major
acreage-reduction plans follows:

1. *Set Aside.* This program was established under provisions of
the 1977 Farm Bill. The set-aside plan requires producers to idle farm
acreage in order to qualify for cash payments and target-price support
programs. The program is not crop specific. Therefore, in order to comply with set-aside regulations, a farmer need only divert a certain amount
of acreage.

2. *Reduced Acreage Program.* A farmer is also required to comply
with the provision of this act in order to fulfill eligibility guidelines of
CCC loan, FOR, and target-price programs. In contrast to the set aside,
the reduced acreage plan is crop specific. The USDA, based on an involved analysis, instructs the participating farmer to limit his plantings of
each particular crop to a specified number of acres.

3. *Payment in Kind (PIK).* The genesis of this program was a decision by the government during the early 1960s to reduce and divert
acreage from certain crops. Under provisions of the program, the farmer

is granted grain equal to a percentage of his estimated yield lost because of participation in other acreage-reduction plans. Initially, USDA officials envisioned giving eligible producers the grain they stored to fulfill CCC and FOR loan provisions. When the program was resurrected in 1983, however, farmers were also given the option of submitting a plan to divert their entire acreage from production. PIK payments were a large influence in many agricultural markets during the 1983 crop year, particularly in the case of cotton.

4. *Paid Diversion.* When active, this program provides for cash payments to farmers who fulfill the acreage reduction requirements of other programs.

The acreage reduction programs just described are intended to bolster crop prices. As participation levels increase, more land is diverted from production and harvest supplies are reduced. The effects of these programs on the markets, however, are very dependent on participation rates. In recent years, for example, farmers have occasionally chosen not to meet the guidelines established by the programs. As a result, the supportive implications of the acreage reduction plans were diluted. Also, farmers who decide to follow the dictates of the program will invariably attempt to idle their least productive land. Thus, even if participation rates are relatively high, the amount of grain that is ultimately not produced may well be far less than expected on the basis of the number of acres set aside. On a more subtle level, one should also consider that the implementation of PIK provisions may actually mitigate the supportive effects of acreage reduction programs. This is because PIK essentially transfers marketing control of a commodity from the government to the farmer. As a result, active participation in PIK programs should theoretically boost free supplies to levels higher than would ordinarily be possible.

A BRIEF HISTORY OF GOVERNMENT AGRICULTURAL PROGRAMS

We have discussed in general terms the various methods utilized by the USDA to influence the agricultural markets and the implications of these programs on prices. However, USDA farm programs should not be viewed in isolation but rather as tools used by policymakers to achieve their agricultural goals. An appreciation of these broad policies is helpful for those who are interested in trading agricultural futures and for an understanding of the 1985 Farm Bill, which establishes the general direction of farm policy for at least the remainder of the 1980s.

Government farm programs have been a fixture in the domestic farm economy for years. Modern-day agricultural policy, which has attempted to adjust production to demand and to maintain a certain level of farm income, was conceived as part of the New Deal programs of the early 1930s. It was during this period that the goverment first offered nonrecourse loans, developed the CCC, and conceived the notion of a grain reserve.

Aside from the CCC and the concept of offering farmers nonrecourse loans, the two most important agricultural policy developments during this period were price support and soil conservation programs. These programs laid the foundation upon which modern day agricultural policy was established.

The soil-conservation program is important because farmers were offered cash payments for diverting acreage from crops that were deemed to be in surplus to plants that have a regenerative effect on the land. Although the USDA still seeks to promote the conservation of soil, the keys to the program were the diversion of acreage and the establishment of direct transfer payments to the farmer. These notions have been refined through the years and are of crucial importance to modern day agricultural policy.

It was also during these years that government price support and loan programs evolved. The government decided to design farm programs in such a way that both price and parity would be assured. The concept of *parity* attempts to assure that prices of farm products in any given year will roughly approximate the real purchasing power of crops during a base period of 1910 through 1914. The design of the index and the assumptions in regard to the base years and unit values of farm goods have been questioned. Nevertheless, the index survives and is used in the determination of loan values. Similarly, experts have challenged government computations of farm income and production costs that underlie calculations of support prices. A full discussion of parity and measures of farm income and costs are beyond the scope of this book. Nevertheless, it is worth pointing out that these computations form the basis of loan, target, and support prices, and also influence other aspects of agricultural policy.

Agricultural policy during the 1940s was, of course, heavily influenced by the wartime economy. During this time, the concepts of parity and of acreage diversion programs were assimilated even further into the mainstream of agricultural policy. Perhaps the most important policy development of the 1940s and 1950s was Public Law 480, which was enacted in 1954 to facilitate the export of surplus farm goods. PL 480 remained an important part of agricultural policy during the next 20 years.

Acreage diversion and price support programs evolved further during the 1960s. In 1970, the government designed set-aside programs that were not crop specific and that supported prices through a broad spectrum of loans, transfer payments, and acreage diversion methodologies. Agricultural policy then changed abruptly. The 1973 Farm Bill emphasized the full production of agricultural goods in response to global grain shortages. The most lasting legacy of the 1973 Farm Bill was not its emphasis on restricted production but rather the advent of *target prices*. The bill provided for a deficiency payment to farmers when market prices of a crop fell below the target-price level set by the USDA. Target prices were developed from an analysis of relevant production costs. Like the computation of parity levels, these calculations are sometimes disputed.

The target-price concept was developed further in the 1977 Farm Bill. This bill required farmers to divert a minimum amount of acreage in order to qualify for the deficiency payments of the target-price program. Additionally, the USDA was empowered to offer cash payments to those farmers who chose to divert more than the required amount of acreage from production.

The Agriculture and Food Act of 1981 established the direction of farm policy through 1985. By maintaining crop prices at relatively high levels, the bill resulted in burdensome supplies in government inventory. For example, wheat prices were maintained at such artificially high levels by government price support programs that only once between 1981 and 1985 did annual demand exceed annual output. As a result, the average annual wheat crop of 2.6 billion bushels swelled government inventories to levels that approached 90% of yearly utilization. Although the 1981 bill succeeded in maintaining farm prices, the cost of such active government involvement in the agricultural markets was high. Farm price and income-support programs averaged less than $4 billion annually prior to 1981. Under the 1981 Farm Bill the annual cost rose to over $10 billion and in some years approached $20 billion.

The major goal of the latest farm bill, the Food Security Act of 1985, was to alleviate this imbalance between the supply and demand of many crops. The bill, which is the foundation of U.S. policy for the crop years 1986/1987 through 1990/1991, represents a drastic departure from the previous emphasis on sustained loan levels and target prices. The intent is that the flexibility of new farm programs will increase the export potential of domestic crops, lead to reduced government spending on agriculture, and establish a greater consistency between farm programs and national trade objectives.

The 1985 Farm Bill is innovative in that loan rates are tied to free-market prices and, therefore, fluctuate in line with supply and demand. In the previous farm bill, only cotton and soybean loan rates were tied to actual market values. Additionally, the Secretary of Agriculture can allow for the repayment of loans even if free-market prices are below established loan rates. Essentially, the government endeavored to reduce agricultural price and income support levels through an immediate and dramatic cut in the loan rate and a more gradual decline in target prices. Finally, the 1985 bill provides for the establishment of a conservation reserve of up to 45 million acres. Farmers wishing to participate in this conservation program will receive government rental payments. The 1985 Farm Bill will influence agricultural markets for years to come. Additionally, the near-term impact of the bill was such that it serves as an excellent example of how government policies influence prices. Therefore, a quick review of some specifics of the bill is warranted.

The key change in the bill relative to previous legislation was the dramatic reduction of loan rates. The loan rate for 1986/1987 (September through August) corn, for example, was lowered from $2.55 per bushel to $1.92 per bushel. Similarly, the 1986/1987 wheat (June through May) loan rate fell from $3.30 per bushel to $2.40 per bushel.

The 1985 Farm Bill mandated that loan rates for 1987 through 1990 crop wheat and corn will be at 75% to 80% of the average farm price during the five years immediately preceding a given year, but excluding the highest and lowest years. Additionally, the Secretary of Agriculture is forbidden from reducing the loan rates by more than 5% unless the farm price in the previous year is more than 110% of that year's loan level, or if it is determined that, in the interest of facilitating the export competitiveness of domestic agricultural markets, a lower loan rate is desirable. In such cases, the Secretary of Agriculture is empowered to reduce loan rates by an additional 20%.

The 1988 through 1990 loan rates for soybeans are set at 75% of the five-year average farm price, excluding the highest and lowest years. In no year may the rate drop by more than 5% from the previous year's level, or below a floor of $4.50 per bushel.

The 1985 Farm Bill established a minimum loan rate of 55 cents per pound for 1986 upland cotton. In future years, the rate was mandated to be the lower of: (1) 85% of a five-year weighted average price, with the exclusion of the highest and lowest annual prices, or (2) 90% of an adjusted average of the five lowest-priced grades of cotton during a period specified by the USDA.

For many feed grains the target levels under the 1985 Farm Bill were left essentially unchanged. This contrasted with the dramatic reductions in loan levels specified by the bill. Target prices for wheat and corn were left unchanged at $4.38 and $3.03 per bushel for two years. During the years through 1990, wheat target prices were legislated to fall to $4.29, then to $4.16, and finally to $4.00 per bushel. The rates established for corn were $2.97, $2.88, and $2.75 per bushel. By contrast, the target level of 81 cents per pound for cotton was left unchanged for only one year. During the four years from 1987 through 1990, target prices for cotton were legislated to be 79.4 cents, 77.0 cents, 74.5 cents, and 72.9 cents per pound, respectively. Conforming with previous policy, the 1985 Farm Bill did not establish target prices for soybeans. The Secretary of Agriculture is not permitted to alter these legislated levels.

Deficiency payments under the 1985 Farm Bill were set equal to the target price minus the higher of: (1) a national average price for a crop during the calendar year, or (2) the specified loan rate for that particular product. Therefore, total deficiency payments equal the payment rate times the farm program yield times planted acreage. The impact of deficiency payments on farmers will vary if an acreage reduction program is in effect. The so-called *50/92 program,* for example, is designed to limit the impact of target prices on production. If a farmer plants between 50% and 92% of his permitted acreage, deficiency payments were set to be made on 92% of the plantings. For example, a grower mandated to reduce plantings on a 100-acre farm by 25% can collect deficiency payments on 69 acres (0.92 x 75 acres) if only 37.5 acres (0.50 x 75 acres) are actually utilized. The unplanted acreage is to be devoted to conservation uses, plantings of nonprogram crops, or to fulfill other requirements of the USDA crop-reduction program. The 1985 Farm Bill also authorized in-kind partial payment of deficiency requirements. Payment in-kind varies from 5.0% of total deficiency payments for cotton to 2.5% for wheat.

Provisions limit annual payments to farmers under deficiency and diversion provisions on all crops to $50,000 per person. However, the bill exempts loan-deficiency payments (the difference between the loan rate and loan repayment rate) from the $50,000 per person limit.

The Secretary of Agriculture was mandated to advance deficiency payments to 1986 program participants. The advance payment was permitted to be made in cash, in-kind, or in negotiable certificates redeemable for CCC-owned commodities. Advance payment was not permitted to exceed 50% of total estimated payments. Up to half of the advance could be in-kind or certificates for CCC-owned crops.

The 1985 Farm Bill also mandated an acreage reduction program if the anticipated carryout at the end of a crop year exceeds 1 billion bushels of wheat *and* 2 billion bushels of corn. The program stipulates that participating corn producers are mandated to divert their base acreage by a minimum of 12.5% to a maximum of 20%, with a maximum in-kind paid diversion of 2.5%. Similarly, the maximum acreage reduction allowable for cotton is 25% of anticipated base plantings. The Secretary of Agriculture is allowed to alter these land reduction provisions by 5.0%.

Similarly, a wheat producer must reduce his base acreage by a minimum of 15% and a maximum of 25%. As under the corn provisions, a maximum 2.5% in-kind diversion was specified. The Secretary of Agriculture also has the authority to alter the acreage-reduction plan by 7.5%. Additionally, the Secretary of Agriculture was required in 1986 only to offer farmers who planted prior to the enactment of the 1985 Farm Bill an opportunity to idle an additional 10% of their acreage in return for a paid diversion of $2.00 per bushel based on previous actual yields.

The 1985 Farm Bill applies to crop years through 1990/1991. As its expiration nears, the government will begin to focus on legislation that will succeed this bill and provide the foundation for agricultural policy in the 1990s. Traders of agricultural futures should monitor discussions that relate to new farm legislation as the 1980s draw to a close.

■ Chapter 22

■ *The Metals Markets*

- Gold
- Platinum
- Palladium

- Silver
- Copper

GOLD

Supply

South Africa is by far the largest producer of gold in the world. During the last century it has produced more than 40% of the gold in existence today and still boasts substantial reserves of relatively rich ore. These reserves guarantee that South Africa will remain the world's dominant producer of gold well into the twenty-first century, assuming a stable political situation.

Gold production in South Africa has stagnated a bit in recent years. For example, in 1975 South Africa produced approximately 22.9 million troy ounces of gold, representing 75% of free-world output. In 1980, South African production fell to 21.7 million troy ounces, or 71% of free-world output. In 1986, South Africa produced about 20.5 million troy ounces of gold, or 61% of free-world production.

A number of factors are responsible for stagnant levels of gold production in South Africa. First, the sharp devaluation of the rand (South

Figure 22-1. Free-world gold production (millions of troy ounces) *

Nation	1980	1981	1982	1983	1984	1985
South Africa	21.7	21.1	21.4	21.9	22.0	21.6
Canada	1.6	1.7	2.1	2.4	2.7	2.8
United States	1.0	1.4	1.4	2.0	2.2	2.5
Brazil	1.1	1.1	1.1	1.9	1.8	2.0
Australia	0.5	0.6	0.9	1.0	1.3	1.8
Philippines	0.7	0.8	1.0	1.1	1.1	1.2
Papua New Guinea	0.5	0.6	0.6	0.6	0.6	1.1
Total (Free World)	27.1	27.3	28.5	30.9	31.7	33.0

*A number of other sources also add modestly to the free world's production of gold.
Source: Consolidated Gold Fields.

Africa's currency) against the U.S. dollar in the world's currency markets lowered effective mine costs (in rands) and encouraged the mining of low-grade ore. As a result, absolute levels of gold output have declined. Second, the depletion of very high-grade ore reserves, particularly in the Orange Free State and Far West Rand gold fields, has taken its toll on production. Finally, South African laws that require the prolonging of mine reserves have also moderated output in recent years.

Communist Bloc Sales: In 1985 and 1986, the communist bloc sold an average of 6.7 million troy ounces of gold a year to the free world. The Soviet Union is by far the largest seller, although North Korea, the People's Republic of China, and a few East European nations also engage in bullion sales. It is difficult to predict accurately the availability of gold from centrally planned economies, although there appears to be a correlation between Soviet hard currency needs and gold sales. A poor Soviet grain harvest or reduced revenues from oil exports are often associated with enhanced gold sales.

Official Sector Activity: Official sector activity, which consists of central bank and government agency purchases and sales, has also been rather volatile in recent years. The official sector was a net buyer of gold in 1985, but in recent years has generally been a net seller. Many Latin American and African central banks have been net buyers of gold, both to support their local mining industries and to ensure that bullion remains in the country. The United States remains a net seller of gold, although in recent years the intensity of U.S. dishoarding has moderated.

Secondary Gold: It is very difficult to gauge accurately the supply of gold from secondary sources. Scrap gold is generally available from two sources. The first, *new scrap*, consists of gold generated from manufacturing processes. Because this gold is simply recirculated, it creates no change in net supplies. *Old scrap* gold is recovered from the dishoarding of old jewelry and the breakdown of old industrial supplies. This gold does change overall supply because it is reentering the market after a period of unavailability. The difficulty in obtaining accurate data on the activity of refiners and the recycling of jewelry muddles these figures. It is estimated that, in recent years, between 8 and 10 million ounces of gold has become available to the market annually from old scrap, down from more than 20 million ounces during the late 1970s and early 1980s when gold prices were at all-time highs. As these numbers suggest, secondary availability of gold is very price elastic.

Demand

The demand for gold is also very price elastic. This is particularly true because demand by the jewelry industry, the largest single consumer of gold, is extremely sensitive to the prevailing price of bullion. Industrial demand for gold has remained relatively steady during the mid-1980s. In contrast, coinage demand has fluctuated widely, but is rather price inelastic. Rather, it tends to be a function of governmental and private interest in commemorative coins.

An examination of recent demand trends for gold highlights its sensitivity to changes in price. For example, Consolidated Gold Fields estimated free-world gold demand at only 20 million troy ounces in 1980, the year prices peaked at more than $800. As prices moderated, gold demand gradually increased. In 1981, free-world demand for gold improved to over 34.5 million ounces, and by 1984 it totaled approximately 38.7 million troy ounces. Clearly, the moderation of gold prices during that period led to a sharp increase in demand for the metal.

We now briefly examine the major components of gold demand.

Jewelry: The jewelry industry is by far the largest consumer of gold. Using Consolidated Gold Fields' numbers, the jewelry industry accounted for 49.6% of the total free-world fabricated gold demand of 243.2 million troy ounces between 1980 and 1985. In recent years, the jewelry industry has assumed an even more important role in gold's fundamental equation, accounting for 67.9% of usage in 1984 and 72.9% in 1985.

Jewelry demand, as we previously noted, is highly price elastic. In 1980, for example, the jewelry industry consumed less than 4.1 million troy ounces of gold. According to Consolidated Gold Fields, jewelry usage improved to 19.1 million troy ounces in 1983 and totaled almost 29 million troy ounces in 1985, when prices reached a nadir of approximately $280. In 1980 in India and in other developing nations, the jewelry industry was a net supplier of gold because recycling and dishoarding exceeded gross consumption levels.

The jewelry industry in Italy, which is the largest in the world, consumed almost 6.2 million troy ounces of gold in 1984, up 120% from 1980. Among other large users, the Indian jewelry industry consumed just over 3 million troy ounces of gold in 1984 after being a net *supplier* of 290,000 troy ounces during 1980. Similarly, Indonesian jewelry usage totaled more than 1.4 million troy ounces in 1984 after supplying the market with almost 1.8 million troy ounces in 1980. The U.S. jewelry industry consumed 2.7 million troy ounces in 1984, up 41.9% from 1980. Western European jewelry demand totaled 9.6 million troy ounces in 1984, 66.7% higher than in 1980. Japanese jewelry demand grew from 700,870 troy ounces in 1980 to over 1.2 million troy ounces in 1984.

In recent years, a growing movement by United States and European consumers away from carat jewelry and toward less expensive items made of wood, plastic, and other metals has hurt gold demand. On the whole, however, the jewelry industry remains a robust consumer of gold.

Electronics: Although gold consumption by the electronics industry is dwarfed by jewelry demand, usage by this sector has grown substantially in recent years. Consolidated Gold Fields estimates that the electronics industry consumed 3.95 million troy ounces of gold in 1984, up 86% from 1975 levels.

Gold is used in a variety of ways in the electronics industry. The computer industry has become a particularly large consumer of gold. Gold is also considered an indispensable material for the defense and commercial aerospace industries. Although the miniaturization of many electronic components has moderated electronics demand for gold in recent years, this reduction in unit usage appears to have ceased. Similarly, gold remains unthreatened by substitutes in many sensitive electronics processes.

Japan and the United States, which boast vibrant computer and electronics industries, are the largest consumers of gold in this sector. Prior to 1984, the U.S. electronics industry was the largest consumer of gold. Japan, which utilized 1.37 million troy ounces of gold for electronics purposes in 1985, currently has this distinction. Together, Japan and the United States accounted for 72% of electronics consumption of gold during 1985, according to Consolidated Gold Fields figures.

The consensus among analysts is that electronics demand for gold will continue to grow. The expanding importance of computers and electronic processes in our increasingly industrialized world supports such positive demand prospects. Additionally, gold's conductivity and anticorrosion properties are necessary in many sensitive electronics applications.

In contrast to the electronics sector, the demand for gold for other industrial processes has moderated in recent years, totaling only 1.71 million troy ounces in 1985. This sector includes a wide range of uses, including gold plating and demand by the porcelain industry. Many of these uses are price elastic and were adversely affected by the 1979/1980 rise in gold values. In 1979, for example, gold demand in other industrial applications totaled 2.53 million troy ounces.

The dental industry used 1.66 million ounces of gold in 1984, only slightly less than was used by other industrial applications. The high point for dental demand for gold occurred in 1978, at 2.99 million ounces. Since then, however, consumer preference for dental composites that have a more natural look has limited gold usage. This preference is expected to constitute a long-term threat to gold demand. Even the West Germans, the largest consumers of gold for dental purposes, have moderated usage in recent years. Finally, the introduction of preventive dental techniques in the Third World has lessened the amount of repair work that was once necessary.

Gold demand for the fabrication of medals, medallions, and fake coins has also declined in recent years. This is because Saudi Arabia, Yemen, Kuwait, and other Gulf Arab nations, which accounted for 73% of free-world demand in this sector during 1985, experienced a sharp drop in demand related to the rapid erosion of oil prices. Demand for gold by this sector is also in a long-term downtrend, totaling only 447,000 ounces in 1985 versus 1.67 million ounces in 1977.

Gold usage in official coins also suffered in the mid-1980s. Consolidated Gold Fields estimated official monetary usage of gold at 7.7 million ounces in 1980 and at less than 3.5 million ounces in 1985. This decline in usage reflects the general environment, which between 1980 and 1985 was hardly conducive to investments in gold. The most important development in the coin market in recent years is the demise of the South African Krugerrand. Investor demand for Krugerrands has suffered largely because of political considerations. The coin, which once dominated both the United States and international gold coin markets, has been displaced by the Canadian Maple Leaf and other, newer, coins.

The outlook for gold coinage improved dramatically in 1986. Japan, for example, imported over 6.5 million troy ounces of gold in 1986 to mint a coin commemorating the sixtieth anniversary of the reign of Emperor Hirohito. The introduction of the coin made Japan the largest consumer of gold in 1986 and boosted gold coin demand to more than 8 million troy ounces. Similar levels of gold coin demand may well be achieved in subsequent years because of the introduction of new U.S. gold coins and enhanced efforts by countries including Australia, Brazil, China, Mexico, and Luxembourg.

Figure 22-2 summarizes gold supply/demand data for recent years.

Investment demand: Commercial usage is only part of the demand picture for gold. Investors constitute the swing component of bullion fundamentals. Investor demand is usually the primary factor behind a major rally or decline in the price of gold. This fact is important to recognize when evaluating price outlooks for gold. Within broad parameters established by supply and fabricator demand fundamentals, investment demand determines the course of gold prices.

Many investors regard gold as a store of value and a safe haven for funds during times of political or monetary turmoil. Periods of heightened tension between the superpowers, armed conflicts in strategically important areas, and economic instability often generate at least short-term strength in gold. The tendency to turn to gold during periods of political or economic uncertainty is particularly evident among investors outside the United States. This reflects the history of much greater political and monetary turmoil in other countries and the consequent memories of disastrous losses in the values of currencies, stocks, bonds, and other intangible assets.

Figure 22-2. Free-world gold supply/demand (millions of troy ounces).

	Mine Production	Net Exports from Communist Bloc	Net Central Bank Sales	Supply[1]	Fabrication[2] Demand	Surplus[3]
1980	30.7	2.9	-7.4	26.2	17.4	8.8
1981	31.4	9.0	-8.9	31.5	33.4	-1.9
1982	32.9	6.5	-2.7	36.7	34.4	2.3
1983	35.7	3.0	4.6	43.3	32.2	11.1
1984	36.9	6.6	2.7	46.2	39.6	6.6
1985	39.0	8.0	-4.3	42.7	39.6	3.1
1986(E)	40.0	10.0	-1.0	49.0	47.2	1.8

Source: Shearson Lehman Brothers Inc.
[1] Does not include secondary supplies of gold.
[2] Includes jewelry, electronics, other industrial, dentistry, decorative and official coins.
[3] Includes net investment accumulation although gold coin demand is also a reflection of investor demand for gold.

Because gold is viewed as a safe haven for funds in times of uncertainty, bullion prices often fluctuate inversely to the United States dollar. During times of confidence in dollar-denominated investments, the demand for gold generally suffers. For example, the early 1986 rally in stocks and bonds reduced the flow of investor funds into gold. Later, when these markets receded, an influx of funds into gold enhanced a previously existing rally. Similarly, gold prices dropped from $600 per ounce to below $300 between 1981 and early 1985, as the value of the dollar soared. Subsequent depreciation of the dollar in 1986 and 1987 pushed gold prices well above $400 per ounce.

Similarly, gold is recognized by investors as an inflation hedge that is likely to retain its value during periods of widespread price increases. Thus, gold soared above $800 per ounce in early 1980 in reaction to oil price rises and other manifestations of inflation. The deflationary economic environment of later years, of course, precipitated a sustained decline in the price of gold.

It is often difficult to sort out conflicting influences on gold prices. For example, in 1985 and early 1986 the sharp decline in oil prices was deflationary and, therefore, ordinarily bearish for gold. Instead, gold prices rallied slightly as investors focused on banking difficulties and a deteriorating international debt situation. It is conflicting signals such as these that present investors with the greatest challenge in attempting to project gold prices. Another example: civil unrest and labor difficulties in South Africa boosted gold prices during the summers of 1985 and 1986. The 1985 rally was short lived. However, macroeconomic conditions in 1986 were sufficiently bullish to support a more sustained rally in gold. Predicting how investors will react to political and economic de-

Figure 22-3.

Category	World Stocks of Gold (millions of troy ounces)
Official reserves (held by the IMF, other world agencies and central banks)	1,204
Jewelry	879
Gold in fabricated products	454
Gold coins and private bullion holdings	318
Total:	2,857

Source: Intergold

velopments is not easy but is the essential element in an accurate forecast of gold prices.

Finally, we mention that the very qualities that attract investors to gold also lead to hoarding. In fact, a substantial amount of gold produced each year is held either in inventory (official or otherwise) by individual investors, in cash, or as jewelry. In 1980, world stocks were as listed in Figure 22-3.

PLATINUM

South Africa dominates free world production of platinum. Its dominance over the platinum market is so complete that it is the only nation that is a primary producer of the metal. In other countries, platinum is produced as a by-product of nickel and, occasionally, copper.

Supply

South African platinum resources come from the abundant Bushveld Igneous Complex (BIC), an area of approximately 15,000 square miles that includes the city of Pretoria. The BIC contains 80% of world reserves of platinum group metals, and a large proportion of other metals such as chromium and manganese.

South Africa's platinum production is dominated by three companies. Rustenburg Platinum Holdings Limited is the largest platinum producer in the world and its mines (Rustenburg Platinum Mines Ltd., Atok, and Maandugshoek among others throughout the BIC) are responsible for almost half of all South African output. Impala Platinum Ltd., another large platinum producer, is also active throughout the BIC and is responsible for about 37% of South African output. Western Platinum Ltd. has mines east of Rustenburg in the BIC and accounts for less than 10% of South African production.

South African platinum production, which averaged 1.5 million troy ounces during the 1970s, jumped to over 2.1 million troy ounces as prices soared above $1,000 per ounce in 1980. Production then fluctuated between approximately 1.8 million and 2.0 million troy ounces during the next three years before jumping back to 2.1 million troy ounces in 1984 as Rustenburg, Impala, and Western commenced tapping other reserves.

Figure 22-4. Platinum supply (thousands of troy ounces).

New Mine Output	1980	1981	1982	1983	1984	1985	1986
South Africa	2,180	1,940	1,795	1,865	2,145	2,270	2,200
Canada	155	145	110	75	150	150	150
Others	30	30	30	35	35	35	40
Total (free world)	2,365	2,115	1,935	1,975	2,330	2,455	2,390
Centrally Planned Economies	320	345	340	285	240	200	235
Secondary	225	275	275	190	180	140	165
Total Supply	2,910	2,735	2,550	2,450	2,750	2,795	2,790

Source: Drexel Burnham Lambert, Inc.

Canada, the free world's second-largest producer of platinum, is dwarfed by South Africa. Canadian output of platinum is dependent on nickel and copper prices and has not exceeded 200,000 troy ounces annually. Another factor that limits Canadian output is the relatively poor concentration of the ore. South African ores are approximately six to ten times richer in platinum than Canadian ore. The vast majority of Canadian platinum production stems from the abundant nickel and copper-sulphide deposits of Sudbury, Ontario. A small amount of by-product platinum is also produced in Manitoba. Although new mining operations have started around Sudbury and in other regions in the 1980s, Canadian output will continue to pale in comparison to South African platinum production.

A variety of other countries account for the balance of free-world production of platinum. However, the combined output of the metal by these nations is dwarfed by Canada and is minuscule in comparison to South Africa.

A small and declining amount of platinum is also exported to the free world from centrally planned economies—primarily the Soviet Union, China, and Yugoslavia. For the Soviet Union, nickel/copper deposits in northern Siberia account for approximately 90% of the nation's platinum output. Information on Chinese platinum output is sketchy, but nickel-sulphide deposits around Jinchang are almost certainly an important part of production. A relatively small amount of platinum is also recovered from scrap or secondary sources.

Demand

Platinum demand was relatively stable in the first half of the twentieth century, staying below 500,000 ounces annually through 1950. Three events since 1950 combined to boost free-world demand for platinum to well over 2 million troy ounces annually. The first was the success of the Japanese economy in the years after World War II. The sharp rise in Japanese disposable income was a boost to platinum demand from the Japanese jewelry industry, which historically prefers platinum over gold. The growth of the oil refinery business also increased platinum demand because the metal is used as a catalyst in the refining process. Finally, the development of auto emission standards in the United States, Japan, and Western Europe provided a tremendous boost to demand because platinum is used in catalytic converters.

The jewelry industry is the largest single user of platinum. In 1984, the jewelry industry consumed about 775,000 troy ounces of platinum, or 30% of platinum usage. Japanese jewelry demand for platinum totaled some 626,000 troy ounces, or approximately 81% of total industry usage. Japanese women continue to prefer platinum over gold for wedding and engagement rings. Japan favors platinum necklaces as well, although gold jewelry has made inroads in recent years. There is no reason to suspect that Japanese jewelry demand for platinum will drop dramatically. Overall, however, jewelry demand is quite price elastic and falls off rapidly during periods of high platinum prices.

Platinum demand by the automobile industry, which totaled 725,000 ounces in 1984, is centered on catalytic converters. Virtually all gasoline fueled cars and light trucks in the United States are fitted with such converters. U.S. use of platinum in catalytic converters currently accounts for close to 70% of free-world industry usage. However, enhanced emission regulations in Japan and West Europe have boosted platinum's use in catalytic converters outside the United States. The outlook for this industry remains bright. The Environmental Protection Agency (EPA) has shelved plans to relax emission standards, and palladium has not proved to be an effective substitute for platinum in catalytic converters. Clearly, however, demand for this purpose is tied to the future of the automobile industries.

Platinum is also used by the petroleum and chemical industries as a catalyst for certain chemical reactions. In 1984, the free world used over 377,000 ounces of platinum in this field. Platinum facilitates the production of nitric acid, which is used as a domestic fertilizer. Poor agricultural demand or acreage reduction programs can reduce platinum usage by as much as 100,000 troy ounces.

Total free-world platinum demand has ranged from 2.20 million to 2.85 million troy ounces between 1983 and 1985. As a result, a market that was in balance during the 1970s, and in a surplus situation in the years immediately following the 1980 price advance, has fallen into a deficit situation.

Platinum prices, like gold prices, generally rise during periods of dollar depreciation, international tension, inflation, or economic uncertainty. As with gold, investors often constitute the swing component of platinum demand and can play a large role in the determination of prices.

Platinum fundamentals, however, differ from those of gold in a number of significant respects. Platinum is much more sensitive to political developments in South Africa. In the summer of 1986, for example, labor difficulties and civil unrest in South Africa sparked a rally in gold prices above $400. Platinum exhibited considerably more strength and at one point achieved a $250 premium to gold. This premium was exceeded only during the historic 1980 bull market in precious metals. Similarly, platinum, which is a much smaller and less liquid market than gold, often exhibits more volatile changes in price. During periods of general price strength in metals, platinum often rises faster than gold. Similarly, platinum prices usually drop more rapidly during periods of bearish metals fundamentals.

Platinum has a proportionally larger industrial base than gold. As a result, platinum prices are more sensitive to the world economy and to developments in the jewelry and automobile industries. Also, rapid price changes exert a significant effect on platinum demand. In 1986, for example, Japanese jewelry imports of platinum dropped rapidly when prices rallied in response to South African unrest. Investors are less likely to sustain platinum prices against a fall in industrial demand because platinum is less well-established than gold as a hedge against political or economic adversity. In sharp contrast to gold, above-ground investment holdings of platinum are quite small.

PALLADIUM

Palladium is a platinum-group metal. However, the market for palladium is much smaller than that for platinum. Unlike platinum and

Figure 22-5. Free-world 1985 palladium demand by category.

Electrical	40%
Dental	32%
Autocatalyst	11%
Jewelry	8%
Others	9%
Total	100%

Source: Johnson Matthey, Ltd.

gold, it is almost entirely industrially based. The dominance of gold, silver, and to a lesser extent platinum, combined with palladium's industrial base, has limited the usefulness of the metal as a speculative vehicle. Nevertheless, a quick review of palladium fundamentals is warranted.

South Africa dominates free-world production of palladium, accounting for about 75% of output. The Soviet Union, however, is the world's largest producer of palladium and in recent years has outstripped free-world output. Therefore, one of the ongoing uncertainties in the palladium market revolves around Soviet sales intentions. Although recent discoveries in Canada, the Stillwater complex in Montana, and essential resources in Alaska, Australia, and Zimbabwe offer limited alternative sources of palladium, South African and Soviet domination of production remain unchallenged.

Palladium demand has grown domestically during the past 25 years. Much of the enhanced usage stems from Japanese efforts to overhaul its electromechanical telephone switching systems and from palladium's use as a dental alloy. Additionally, palladium is consumed by the jewelry industry as an alloy with platinum and is used by the chemical sector as a catalyst. The robust Japanese electrical industry and palladium's growing use in dentistry suggest that demand will continue to expand for the balance of the decade.

Currently, Japan and the United States are the world's largest users of palladium, together accounting for 78% of free-world demand. Japanese palladium demand has been supported by its usefulness in integrated circuits and by a government mandate limiting the amount of gold in dental alloys. In the United States, both the electronics and dental industries are active consumers of palladium. Use in the jewelry industry is limited. Figures 22-5 and 22-6 (see page 558) cover relevant palladium fundamentals.

Figure 22-6. Palladium supply and demand
(thousands of troy ounces).

Supply	1980	1981	1982	1983	1984	1985
South Africa	870	910	820	790	950	1,010
Canada	170	160	160	110	190	190
Others	60	70	70	80	90	90
U.S.S.R.	1,240	1,430	1,550	1,560	1,690	1,440
Total	2,340	2,570	2,670	2,540	2,920	2,730
Demand						
Japan	690	820	890	1,220	1,250	1,080
N. America	840	820	850	830	990	930
Total Free World*	2,030	2,090	2,270	2,700	2,960	2,740
Surplus	310	480	330	(160)	(40)	(10)

*Includes balance of free world
Source: Johnson Matthey, Ltd.

Although palladium, as a platinum-group metal, is heavily influenced by platinum prices and often responds in sympathy to movements in the precious metals complex, traders should remember that the market is almost totally dominated by industrial users. Additionally, the futures market for palladium is quite small and therefore of limited appeal to large traders.

SILVER

Mexico has become the free world's largest producer of silver, with annual output in excess of 60 million ounces. Production in Mexico is dominated by three large entities, two of which—Industrias Peñoles and Medimsa—are among the largest producers in the world. Most of Mexican silver output stems from primary operations that also produce smaller quantities of lead, zinc, and occasionally copper.

The rapid expansion of Mexican silver production during the 1980s stemmed from two factors. First is the nation's need for the foreign exchange provided by silver sales. Second is the opening of a number of resource-rich mines in the early 1980s. Although new silver finds have diminished in recent years, the nation's thirst for currency has not. The combination of Mexico's heavy debt burden and its ability to produce silver at relatively low cost is expected to accelerate output in the coming years.

Peru, the second-largest producer, reported total silver output of more than 58 million troy ounces in 1986. Peruvian output emanates from its large sulphide deposits that also contain lead, zinc, and quite often copper. Peru's need for hard currency to help reduce burdensome levels of foreign debt and its reliance on the mining industry as a large employer tend to sustain production.

Chile is another large Latin American producer of silver. The majority of Chilean silver comes from its active copper-mining industry. Smaller but still significant supplies are extracted from primary silver mines. Although a slump in Chilean copper production has limited silver output, the nation is expected to retain its position as the world's sixth-largest producer.

Canada is the third-largest producer of silver behind Mexico and Peru. Canadian silver production slumped in the early 1980s but has since reversed. Canadian silver output was about 44 million ounces in 1986. Canadian silver is recovered from mines as a primary product but also often as a by-product of lead, zinc, and copper. Canada's rich sulphide base-metal deposits imply sustained levels of silver production in years to come. However, Canadian silver output is often dependent on base-metal prices. In the 1980s, for example, weak zinc and copper prices have periodically limited Canada's production of silver.

In contrast to Canada, a surprisingly large amount of U.S. silver is recovered as a primary product. Two large primary operations—Hecla's Lucky Friday mine and Sunshine Mining's Sunshine mine—helped boost U.S. silver production to more than 44 million troy ounces in 1984. Both these mines, however, were subsequently closed, falling victim to low silver prices and the relatively high costs associated with deep pit mining.

Australia is another large producer of silver. Silver output in Australia has increased gradually in recent years and currently exceeds 30 million troy ounces. Most Australian silver emanates from mixed lead-zinc and silver-sulphide deposits. Although Australian silver output has been hindered in recent years by labor strikes, new mines continue to come on-line. Additionally, the Mount Ida Mines complex in Queens-

Figure 22-7. Free-world mine production of silver
(millions of troy ounces).

	1982	1983	1984	1985	1986
Mexico	59.1	63.6	63.9	59.8	62.4
Peru	53.6	55.9	56.5	57.7	58.5
Canada	42.2	35.5	37.6	38.0	35.4
United States	40.2	43.4	44.4	39.4	32.0
Australia	29.2	33.8	32.0	33.9	34.5
Other	80.6	82.5	83.0	84.0	82.5
Total	304.9	314.7	317.4	312.8	305.3

Source: Handy & Harman Statistics

land and Broken Hill in New South Wales, the largest Australian silver producers, have the potential to expand output well into the 1990s.

Secondary Production

Secondary production of silver is very important in the market's fundamental equation. Because new mine output of silver consistently falls far short of demand, secondary sources of silver determine whether the market is in a surplus or deficit situation. *Scrap* consists of silver that has been recovered from melted silverware, used photographic solutions, and discarded electrical contacts. Normally, silver that has been recovered from the photographic industry and electrical scrap dominates secondary production. During times of high prices, however, silverware and other items that contain silver are discarded by people not connected with the industry. Scrap recovery of silver is extremely price elastic. It has been estimated that a 10% change in silver prices impacts scrap recovery by 5%.

Indian Dishoarding

One of the interesting aspects of the silver market is that India, a nation that produces negligible amounts of silver, is a dominant source of secondary supplies. Through the years, Indian citizens have hoarded large amounts of silver in the form of jewelry, ornaments, coins, and ingots as insurance against poverty in old age and for dowries. During

Figure 22-8. Free-world silver supplies (millions of troy ounces).

	1982	1983	1984	1985	1986
Mine Production	304.9	314.7	317.4	312.8	305.3
Old Scrap	81.0	84.1	75.1	72.2	69.0
From Government Stocks	11.1	14.8	5.0	9.4	13.5
Indian Dishoarding	29.0	32.2	22.5	20.9	11.1
Demonetized Coin	13.0	8.0	4.0	3.0	1.0
Net Imports from					
Communist Nations	(21.0)	(19.3)	(19.3)	3.2	(14.0)
Total Secondary Supplies	113.1	119.8	87.3	108.7	76.6
Total	418.0	434.5	404.7	421.5	381.9

Source: Handy & Harman Statistics

periods of high domestic silver prices or economic distress in India, a substantial amount of this silver may be dishoarded. Dishoarding of India's ample silver supplies occasionally exceeds 40 million troy ounces annually and can represent close to 10% of free-world supplies. In recent years, the Indian government has limited silver exports and prevented the smuggling of bullion on the grounds of protecting a national treasure. As a result, Indian dishoarding has contracted dramatically since the 1979/1980 bull market.

Government Sales

Unlike gold, official government reserves of silver are limited. The U.S. and the Indian governments hold much of these stocks. Latin American governments, which retain small amounts of silver, have sold bullion in recent years as a way of alleviating their debt difficulties. Nevertheless, government sales of silver are not expected to exceed 5 to 7 million ounces annually in the near future.

Silver for Centrally Planned Economies

Although the Soviet Union is a large producer of silver, in recent years East bloc exports of silver have fallen dramatically and, occasionally, communist nations have been net importers of silver. Polish exports of silver appear to have remained relatively constant, but enhanced military and industrial demand for silver in the Soviet Union has made this nation an unreliable exporter. Thus, silver output from centrally planned nations is expected to exhibit volatility over the near future. Occasionally, this sector may even consume supplies of Western silver.

Consumption

Silver is used for a myriad of purposes in the Western world. The photographic industry is the single largest user. The metal is also actively consumed by the electrical industry, which values silver for its excellent conductivity, alloy characteristics, and ability to resist corrosion. Silver is also actively used by the jewelry industry and for other purposes such as battery manufacturing and for dental fillings. Photographic-industry consumption of silver has remained relatively steady during the 1980s at well over 120 million ounces annually. Despite sluggish film demand and declining usage of X-rays (which include high levels of silver), U.S. photographic demand for silver remains high. Japanese photographic demand for silver is the highest in the world and shows no signs of abating. In fact, the photographic industry is responsible for well over 50% of Japanese silver usage. The photographic industry is also a dominant user of silver in Western Europe. However, the outlook for photographic demand for silver remains questionable. The move to smaller negatives has been offset by the increased use of silver-intensive high-speed film. Nevertheless, increased efficiency in recycling discarded film for silver and the advent of electronic film mediums represent long-term threats to the market.

Electronics

Free-world electronics demand for silver has ranged between 60 and 80 million ounces in recent years. Silver is used in electromechanical switching systems and in the manufacture of integrated circuits. The growing industrialization of the Western world bodes well for electronics demand for silver. On the other hand, a trend toward miniaturization in electronic processes and the increased use of fiber optics in the telephone industry represent long-term threats.

Jewelry

In contrast to the electronics and photographic industries, jewelry demand for silver is very price elastic. For example, between 1979 and

Figure 22-9. Silver supply and demand (millions of troy ounces).

Demand	1982	1983	1984	1985	1986
United States	118.8	116.3	114.8	118.6	127.8
Japan	63.2	71.5	78.7	75.3	79.4
W. Germany	35.9	30.3	30.1	31.7	36.9
United Kingdom	20.0	18.0	19.0	19.0	20.5
Other	107.5	104.6	110.7	112.6	116.1
Total Industrial Demand	345.4	340.7	353.3	357.2	380.7
Coinage	12.8	19.6	8.7	12.7	22.8
Total Demand	358.2	360.3	360.3	369.9	403.5
Total Supply	418.0	434.5	404.7	421.5	381.9
Net Surplus	59.8	74.2	44.4	51.6	(21.6)

Source: Handy & Harman Statistics

1981, free-world jewelry demand fell amost 57% as silver prices soared. However, the growing use of gold, wood, and other diverse materials by Americans and Europeans and the sustained demand for platinum jewelry by the Japanese have retarded the silver industry's subsequent recovery. European jewelry makers, who use the most silver in their manufacturing, have also reduced output during the 1980s. As a result, free-world jewelry usage of silver declined from over 90 million ounces in 1978 to approximately 40 million in 1984.

Other Uses

Silver is used for a variety of other purposes, including the manufacturing of batteries, in dental applications, and as an alloy for brazing and soldering.

Figure 22-9 shows the major fundamental trends of the mid-1980s. During the 1970s, silver regularly showed a production deficit that averaged about 116 million ounces. During the next six years, however, the combinations of the sharp 1979/1980 price advance, sluggish demand, and enhanced mine production led to burdensome supplies.

COPPER

Copper, unlike the other metals discussed so far, is strictly an industrial metal. However, it occasionally reacts to broad price trends in the precious metals and, like gold and silver, often responds to general currency and interest rate movements. Similarly, broad developments in the industrial sector influence metals, such as copper, which boast relatively defined manufacturing uses. On the whole, however, copper remains most sensitive to its own specific fundamentals.

Production

The free world's six leading copper producers are: Chile, the United States, Canada, Zambia, Zaire, and Peru. Together, they account for about 70% of free-world output.

Chile, the world's largest copper producer, has seen annual output expand from about 1.0 million metric tons in 1980 to about 1.3 million metric tons in the mid-1980s. Although Chilean output has occasionally been hindered by mechanical difficulties and other problems, the state mining company, Codelco, enjoys low costs of production, rich ore grades, and the potential to expand copper production further.

The United States, which as late as 1980 was the world's largest copper producer, has seen output fall from over 1.4 million metric tons to less than 1.1 million metric tons in 1985. Low copper prices and the competitive disadvantage of high labor costs are two of the many problems that have beset the U.S. copper industry.

Canadian copper mines, which produce more than 600,000 metric tons annually, are also important suppliers. In Canada, copper is mined by a variety of base-metal producers. Although copper is the primary product of many of the nation's mines, it is also a by-product of gold, zinc, nickel and molybdenum producers.

Zaire and Zambia, two large African copper-producing nations, together boast output levels of more than one million metric tons annually. In both these nations, copper production remains hampered by debt difficulties and economic instability. As a result, mine expansion and modernization is difficult, skilled laborers are few and far between, and production is constantly obstructed by a dearth of spare parts and proper transportation facilities. Until these problems and the unsettled labor situation are addressed, Zaire and Zambia will encounter difficulties realizing their full potential as copper producers.

Other large producers such as Peru, Mexico, South Africa, and the Philippines have helped boost free-world copper production. Total Western world copper output has expanded from just over 6.0 million metric tons in 1980 to more than 6.6 million in 1984.

Secondary sources of copper include both old and new scrap. *Old scrap* consists of copper recovered from discarded manufacturing items. *New scrap* includes cuttings and other materials that are immediately re-covered and recycled during the manufacturing process. Because of the difficulties of estimating new scrap, this supply component is usually subtracted from copper's fundamental equation. On average, total secondary production of copper has remained relatively constant at just over 1.1 million metric tons annually.

Consumption

Consumption of refined copper has gradually expanded in recent years. The United States remains the free world's largest consumer of copper, with usage levels expanding to more than 2 million metric tons annually in the mid-1980s. West Germany, France, Great Britain, and Italy are the next largest free-world users. Others include South Korea, Brazil, Canada, and Australia. Overall, broad trends in copper demand are dependent on the strength of the industrial economy, particularly that of the United States, Japan, and Europe, who collectively account for some 80% of free-world usage.

By sector, the electronics industry is the largest consumer of cop-per, accounting for well over a third of total demand for the metal. Cop-per cables are often used for the underground transmission of high-voltage electricity. Although aluminum represents a competitive threat in above-ground transmissions, copper remains actively utilized. Similarly, copper has so far withstood a competitive challenge from aluminum in the production of generators and transformers. Copper is also actively used in the telecommunications industry. In recent years, however, fiber optics have launched a serious competitive challenge in an area that was once thought to be the sole preserve of the copper industry.

Copper is also actively utilized by the construction and machinery sectors, which together are responsible for almost 40% of free-world demand for the metal. Copper is normally used in electrical wiring for houses, radiators, plumbing, air conditioning, and as a roofing material. Copper's use as a roofing material shows particular signs of growth po-

Figure 22-10. Copper supply and demand
(thousands of metric tons).

	1980	1981	1982	1983	1984	1985	1986(f)
Mine Production	6,041	6,483	6,284	6,269	6,309	6,423	6,644
Primary Refined Production	5,835	6,245	6,036	6,167	6,207	6,163	6,300
Secondary Refined Production	1,201	1,105	1,122	1,159	1,007	1,130	1,150
Total Refined Production	7,036	7,350	7,158	7,326	7,214	7,293	7,450
Refined Consumption	7,101	7,252	6,776	6,822	7,579	7,345	7,200
Net Refined Imports from Socialist blocs	41	53	473	(400)	(130)	(256)	(90)
Implied Surplus (Deficit)	(24)	151	425	104	495	(308)	160

Note: f = forecast.
Source: Shearson Lehman Brothers, Inc.

tential. The metal is also actively used in the manufacture of industrial machinery. As a result, the copper market often responds to housing start numbers and to data regarding industrial-sector activity in general.

The copper market also exhibits a high degree of sensitivity to automobile sales. In the automobile industry, copper is heavily used in electrical wiring by both U.S. and Japanese manufacturers. Overall, the transportation industry accounts for about 12% of free-world copper demand.

■ Chapter 23

■ *Energy Futures*

- Crude Oil
- Heating Oil
- Gasoline

Energy futures are a relatively new development. A few sporadic but unsuccessful attempts were made to develop energy futures between the mid-1960s and the late 1970s, but not until 1978 and the New York Mercantile Exchange's (NYMEX) No. 2 heating oil futures contract did such a market succeed.

In many respects it is surprising that it took so long for energy futures to attract an active and sustained base of participation. Thousands of products, from gasoline to heating oil and from asphalt to aspirin are derived from crude oil. Worldwide demand for oil is enormous, averaging some 47 million barrels per day (bpd) at the end of 1986. Crude oil is unquestionably a dominant component on the industrial landscape. And the price volatility of recent years has underscored the need for the risk-mitigating uses of the NYMEX markets.

To fully appreciate the changes in the oil industry that contributed to the success of energy futures, it is important to understand the structure and evolution of the petroleum business. At the beginning of the twentieth century, the oil industry was dominated by a small number of multinational companies. These firms each established vertically integrated operational structures that produced crude, refined the oil, and marketed the products. This integrated structure was maintained through

World War II. After the war, however, a number of smaller companies rushed to take advantage of the perceived profits available in the oil industry. These new firms were responsible for oil production that flowed outside the traditional integrated product lines. Soviet oil exports also diluted the multinationals' control of oil. Of greater concern to the industry, however, was the growing glut of oil. This surplus of supply maintained pressure on prices through the 1950s and forced the major oil companies to offer discounts and, in 1959, to lower the posted prices. A second reduction of posted prices in August 1960 forced oil companies to lower the taxes and royalties that were being paid to oil-producing nations.

These developments were of great historical importance to the oil industry. The steady decline of oil prices led to meetings of producers in 1959 and 1960. Finally, a meeting in Baghdad of representatives of Iraq, Iran, Kuwait, Saudi Arabia, and Venezuela resulted in the formation of the Organization of Petroleum Exporting Countries (OPEC). Although OPEC boasted close to 70% of the world's oil reserves and was responsible for 90% of oil exports, the eight major oil companies (collectively referred to as the *majors*) controlled more than 90% of the cartel's production. As a result, OPEC was unable to exert a sustained influence on prices.

Gradually, however, the cartel gained importance within the industry. In 1962, OPEC forced the majors to increase royalty payments and marketing funds. Of greater importance was the entrance of Indonesia, Qatar, Libya, and the United Arab Emirates to OPEC in 1968. Algeria, Nigeria, Ecuador, and Gabon joined in two year intervals beginning in 1969.

These new members and a gradual firming of oil prices in the late 1960s and very early 1970s allowed OPEC to exert more influence over the industry. The growing industrialization of the world during this period increased the demand for OPEC oil by approximately 60%. It was Libya that most effectively urged OPEC to force the hand of the majors. The Libyans themselves were successful in forcing the majors to give up some control over production and pricing of Libyan crude, while the balance of OPEC nations moved more slowly in this regard. In late 1970, however, OPEC did demand an increase in posted prices. In a July 1971 meeting in Tehran, OPEC requested an additional 45 cent per barrel increase in oil prices. Finally, in Geneva in mid-1971 and 1972, OPEC moved to consolidate its control over the oil industry.

The growing oil production deficit allowed OPEC to engineer the first major oil price increase. In late 1973, OPEC instituted on oil embargo against the United States in response to U.S. support for Israel and raised crude prices by 70%. Later that year, OPEC doubled oil prices and consolidated control over the operation of the entire industry. A spate of nationalizations of oil facilities changed the role of the majors to one of purchasers of crude and paid consultants who assisted in various operational areas. The majors did, however, retain control over the marketing of oil. As the 1970s progressed, though, the oil companies gradually began to cede marketing responsibilities to OPEC, which arranged sales of crude to various governments and private sector companies. By the mid-1970s, OPEC dominated the world oil market.

Between the turn of the century and the mid-1970s it would have been difficult for an oil futures market to develop. The multinational corporations and OPEC were dominant players in the market and exerted almost total control over prices. During this period, the oil industry had a number of characteristics that retarded the development of free-market pricing and limited the need for hedging. These characteristics included: substantial industry integration, a production oligopoly, and price stability. Later, OPEC was able to control oil pricing in such a way that the climate for oil futures trading was similarly inhospitable.

These characteristics also limited the emergence of spot oil markets. Spot petroleum markets first developed in the 1950s, but their operation for a number of years thereafter was limited to residual amounts that eluded the control of the multinationals. As a result, the majors determined crude prices in the 1960s and the spot market simply mirrored their decisions. In the 1970s, however, as OPEC gained control over oil prices, the scope of the spot market increased. Oil-producing nations involved themselves in spot trading, and a number of refiners began to look toward the spot market for some of their supply requirements.

The spot market grew in importance after the oil price rise of 1973 and a second sharp increase in 1979. The high oil prices that resulted from these shocks triggered greater production of crude. At the same time, conservation measures limited demand for oil. The worldwide recession of 1980 that was at least partly caused by the oil-price shocks also contributed to the growing surplus of oil. During these years, OPEC began to lose market share as oil finds in the North Sea and in Alaska and the emergence of Mexico and the Soviet Union as major exporters contributed to the growing glut of oil.

Thus, a situation evolved in which first supply disruptions and later heightened competition prompted unprecedented levels of oil-price volatility. During these years, the spot market rapidly displaced contract market influence over oil pricing. By the mid-1980s, some 65% of all oil transactions were done in the spot market. In essence, supply disruptions in the 1970s taught crude- and refined-product purchasers to utilize the spot market to meet unfilled requirements. Similarly, the limited demand of the 1980s forced producers to learn about selling their excess supply onto the spot market. Finally, the uncertainty that surrounded the oil market following the 1973 price rise increased spot trading as participants engaged in speculative stockpiling and selling of oil and refined products.

The development of a spot oil market is not surprising given the forces that emerged after 1973 that contributed to unstable crude prices. These developments stand in sharp contrast to the stabilizing forces that existed in prior years. As both producers and consumers looked to the spot market, the number of participants in such transactions naturally grew. By the early 1980s, the spot market was the arena for more than half of all oil transactions. Volume ranged from 18 million to upwards of 20 million barrels per day (bpd). Only five years earlier, the spot market had handled less than 10% of such transactions. Nevertheless, the spot market has shortcomings. For example, it is unregulated and devoid of performance guarantees, making credit analysis a key concern. Because most spot market trades are for prompt delivery, forward pricing needs are often not particularly well serviced. On a more theoretical level, the spot market does not disseminate information particularly well. Unlike a futures exchange, which boasts an administrative staff and traders who conduct their transactions in a central location, the spot market is unfocused. The secrecy that cloaks most spot trading contributes to price inefficiency.

These considerations fostered the development of futures trading in oil when the advent of price instability in the oil industry established an environment conducive to futures trading in energy products. NYMEX heating oil was the first successful energy futures contract and led to the development of active contracts on crude oil and different types of gasoline. We now turn to the fundamentals of these markets, beginning with crude oil.

CRUDE OIL

Supply

Throughout the 1970s it appeared that free-world crude oil production would continue its established growth, but free-world output
peaked in 1980 at 50.4 million bpd as the oil-price shock of 1979 led to
conservation of usage and the development of non-OPEC supplies. The
growth of non-OPEC supplies and the declining levels of Western-
world oil usage forced OPEC to limit production in order to maintain oil
prices of around $30 per barrel.

To understand crude oil supply, one must understand OPEC. It
was OPEC that met free-world demand for oil by increasing production
from 8.7 million bpd in 1960, to 14.3 million bpd in 1965, and to 23.4
million bpd in 1970. OPEC oil production totaled 27.2 million bpd in
1975 and peaked at 31.3 million bpd in 1977. Thus, OPEC oil production grew by 169% during the 1960s and by an additional 34% between 1970 and 1977. Thereafter, OPEC was forced to reduce output
so as to offset the aforementioned decline in world oil demand and enhanced levels of supply from other nations.

From Figure 23-1 (see page 572), it is clear that the bulk of OPEC
output cutbacks was absorbed by its largest producer, Saudi Arabia.
Other large and moderate Gulf producers such as Kuwait and the UAE
also effected dramatic declines in output.

The mix of output reductions among members is an important
consideration. It constitutes an issue that lies at the core of OPEC's very
composition and its future prospects. Despite the travails of recent
years, OPEC remains a cartel whose basic objectives are to establish
and implement output goals and target prices that are designed to maximize the present value of long-term oil revenues. The disunity among
OPEC members starting in the mid-1980s has centered on the issue of
who should bear the burden of reducing output when this is the chosen
approach to raising prices. Whether OPEC remains a viable organization in the latter years of the twentieth century depends in large part on
its ability to deal with the quota issue.

Figure 23-3 on page 573 shows the sharp decline in OPEC revenues between 1980, when these revenues peaked at $279 billion, and

Figure 23-1. OPEC crude-oil production (millions of bpd).

	1960	1965	1970	1975	1977	1980	1984	1985	1986
Saudi Arabia	1.31	2.21	3.80	7.08	9.20	9.90	4.59	3.20	4.70
Iran	1.07	1.91	3.83	5.35	5.66	1.47	2.17	2.20	1.90
Kuwait	1.70	2.36	2.99	2.08	1.97	1.66	1.13	0.80	1.20
Iraq	.97	1.31	1.55	2.26	2.35	2.65	1.20	1.40	1.70
UAE	0	.28	.78	1.66	2.00	1.70	1.15	1.20	1.30
Libya	0	1.22	3.32	1.48	2.06	1.83	1.07	1.00	1.00
Rest of OPEC	3.67	5.04	7.14	7.24	8.02	7.67	6.09	6.10	6.00
Total OPEC	8.72	14.33	23.41	27.15	31.26	26.88	17.40	15.90	17.80

Source: Cambridge Energy Research Associates

Figure 23-2. OPEC crude and product exports (millions of bpd).

	1965	1970	1975	1980	1984	1985
Crude Exports	13.51	20.22	24.06	22.84	11.99	10.80
Product Exports	1.63	1.97	1.56	2.02	2.36	2.45
Total Exports	15.14	22.19	25.62	24.86	14.35	13.25

Source: Cambridge Energy Research Associates

Figure 23-3. OPEC oil revenues (billions of dollars).

	1965	1970	1975	1980	1984	1985
Saudi Arabia	$1.3	$2.3	$27.9	$102.3	$45.8	$31.1
Iran	1.1	2.4	19.6	13.3	14.4	14.4
Kuwait	0.8	1.6	8.4	17.7	10.8	9.0
Iraq	0.7	0.8	8.2	26.1	10.0	11.7
UAE	0.1	0.5	6.8	19.4	13.1	11.7
Balance	4.2	6.9	35.1	100.2	60.5	56.2
Total OPEC	$8.1	$14.4	$106.0	$278.9	$154.6	$134.1

Source: Cambridge Energy Research Associates

1985. OPEC endured a 52% decline in oil revenue during this period. Saudi Arabia sustained a particularly large 70% drop. Together, Saudi Arabia and other Gulf producers saw revenues fall well over 50%. In contrast, Iranian revenues remained relatively constant during the period. Libya, Algeria, and other nations also suffered less onerous declines in oil revenue.

Crude oil prices are sensitive to political developments in the key Middle East producing countries. The prolonged Iran/Iraq war, incidents of terrorism, and religious disagreements can have important effects on the crude oil market. In recent years North Sea oil producers such as Great Britain and Norway, and other nations such as the United States and Mexico, have all increased oil output and achieved a greater influence on crude oil fundamentals and prices. For example, North Sea production almost doubled between 1980 and 1986. As a result, North Sea production decisions and output flows have become an important component in the supply/demand equation. Figure 23-4 on page 574 shows recent trends in free-world crude supply.

Figure 23-4. Free-world oil supply (millions of bpd).

	1980	1981	1982	1983	1984	1985	1986
United States	10.8	10.7	10.8	10.8	11.1	11.4	11.1
North Sea	2.2	2.4	2.7	3.1	3.5	3.6	3.8
Mexico	2.1	2.6	3.0	3.0	3.0	3.0	2.7
Canada	1.8	1.6	1.6	1.5	1.7	1.7	1.7
Net Communist Exports	1.2	1.1	1.4	1.7	1.9	1.5	1.6
Other	4.7	5.1	5.6	6.1	6.5	6.9	7.1
Total Non-Opec	22.8	23.5	25.1	26.2	27.7	28.1	28.0
Opec	26.6	22.4	18.6	17.2	17.1	15.9	18.0
Opec Natural Gas Liquid	1.0	1.1	1.2	1.2	1.3	1.3	1.4
Total	50.4	47.0	44.9	44.6	46.1	45.3	46.4

Sources: US Department of Energy; International Energy Agency; Salomon Brothers, Inc.

Demand

Total free-world oil consumption, which peaked in 1979 and 1980 at around 50 million bpd, has declined through the 1980s. Declining oil demand was directly attributable to the energy price shocks of 1973 and 1979. High oil prices and uncertain supply sources in the late 1970s precipitated and entrenched conservation measures. As a result, the share of free-world oil consumption by industrialized nations fell from 75% in 1965 to 64% in 1984. This statistic suggests that oil consumption by the United States, Canada, Japan, and Western Europe will not return to the levels existing in 1978 through 1980 unless a consensus develops that crude prices will remain low for years. Developing nations have naturally concentrated on sustaining economic development rather than on conservation.

Figure 23-5 shows the percent changes in world oil consumption among industrialized nations between 1965 and 1985 and highlights changes in the first half of the 1980s.

As Figure 23-5 demonstrates, oil consumption in the United States, Western Europe, and Japan declined between 1980 and 1985. By contrast, demand levels remained steady among developing nations. Latin American oil consumption totaled 3.52 million bpd in 1975, 4.40 million bpd in 1980, and 4.54 million bpd in 1984. Similarly, African oil consumption grew from 1.49 million bpd in 1980 to 1.70 million bpd in 1984.

Figure 23-5. World crude-oil consumption (millions of bpd).

	1965	1975	1980	1985	Change 1980–1985
United States	11.30	15.88	16.46	16.00	−3%
Western Europe	7.84	13.51	13.40	11.60	−13%
Japan	1.75	5.02	5.00	4.20	−16%
Middle East	.69	1.32	2.70	NA	NA
Latin America	1.98	3.52	4.40	4.54	+3%
Africa	.58	1.95	1.49	1.70	+14%

Source: Cambridge Energy Research Associates

Free-world oil consumption by fuel type has remained relatively steady through the years (see Figure 23-6 on page 576). Between 1970 and 1984, demand for oil moderated among stationary markets such as electricity generation. Coal and nuclear power have grown to be effective substitutes for crude in these applications. Although conservation has moderated the growth of gasoline usage, consumption levels have fallen more dramatically among fuel oil and middle distillates.

As Figure 23-7 (see page 576) shows, free-world demand levels moderated after 1980. Although supply levels also fell, it became increasingly incumbent upon OPEC to restrict output in order to bolster prices. The marketplace thus became increasingly sensitive to OPEC's resolve in this regard. Any indication of OPEC discord, or of conflicting economic goals among members, raised concern that the cartel's commitment to restrained production would waver, suggesting that the overall supply surplus might increase.

Though OPEC dominates crude oil fundamentals, other considerations often affect prices. Such factors include world economic growth rates, the composition of energy demand, and the degree of consumer preference for oil over alternative fuels. A lull in the world economy will, all other things being equal, reduce oil demand from previous levels. Similarly, the needs of new consumers and the preference of consumers for oil also influence market prospects.

Other factors, such as interest rates, can affect oil prices. Theoretically, a rise in interest rates is likely to depress crude prices by raising the cost of carrying inventories and bringing more oil to market. Similarly, a stronger United States dollar would depress crude prices. This is because the oil trade is denominated in dollars, so a strong dollar raises the price of oil to consumers and, as a result, limits demand.

Figure 23-6. Crude consumption by type (millions of bpd).

	1970	1975	1980	1984	1985
United States					
Gasoline	6.33	7.06	7.09	7.06	7.07
Middle Distillates	3.53	3.93	4.30	4.16	4.22
Fuel Oil	2.11	2.38	2.45	1.40	1.22
Other	2.38	2.50	2.62	2.56	2.67
Total	14.35	15.88	16.46	15.18	15.17
Total Free World					
Gasoline	11.27	13.55	14.44	14.44	14.45
Middle Distillates	10.83	12.86	14.67	14.80	14.97
Fuel Oil	11.05	11.76	11.93	8.60	7.94
Other	5.89	6.45	7.21	7.50	7.74
Total	39.04	44.62	48.26	45.34	45.10

Source: Cambridge Energy Research Associates

Figure 23-7. Free-world oil supply/demand (millions of bpd).

Demand:	1980	1981	1982	1983	1984	1985	1986
United States	17.4	16.4	15.7	15.4	16.1	16.0	16.4
Western Europe	13.4	12.5	12.1	11.8	11.8	11.6	12.0
Japan	5.0	4.7	4.5	4.4	4.5	4.2	4.2
Other Industrialized Nations	2.9	2.9	2.5	2.3	2.0	2.3	2.3
OPEC	2.7	2.9	3.0	3.1	3.2	3.3	3.3
Non-OPEC LDCs	8.3	8.3	8.2	8.2	8.3	8.3	8.4
Total Demand	49.7	47.7	46.0	45.2	46.1	45.6	46.6
Supply	50.4	47.0	44.9	44.6	46.1	45.3	46.4
Surplus/(Deficit)	.7	(.7)	(1.1)	(.6)	—	(.3)	(.2)
OPEC Spot Price	$34.00	$33.13	$30.36	$27.92	$27.41	$26.52	NA

Conversely, a depreciating dollar and lower interest rates normally stimulate usage and bolster prices. Crude oil is important primarily because of the products that are derived from it. The process that produces oil products is called *refining*, or *refinery distillation*. Two of the most important oil products are heating oil and gasoline, both of which enjoy active futures markets. The fundamentals of these two products are discussed in the following sections.

HEATING OIL

Heating oil, along with other gas fuels, is a middle-range product of refinery distillation. This group of distillate fuel oils includes a range of diesel fuels and numbers 1 through 4 fuel oil. Number 4 fuel oil, the heaviest distillate fuel, boasts a few industrial applications, particularly in plant burners. Number 1 fuel oil, the lightest of this type of distillate, is also used in a few industrial processes. Technological changes have rendered Number 3 fuel oil obsolete. As a result, Number 2 fuel oil is by far the largest component of distillate fuel-oil production, accounting for almost 97% of United States refinery output of these *middle distillates*. Thus, for all intents and purposes, the market for Number 2 fuel oil (the heating oil underlying NYMEX's heating oil futures contract) *is* the market for such distillates. A number of government agencies, for example, do not even bother to distinguish between these different types of fuel oil in their supply/demand releases. This is among the first things to understand in the fundamental analysis of heating oil. Most statistics do not separate Number 2 heating oil figures from other fuel oils.

Additionally, unlike the crude oil futures market, heating oil is dominated by U.S. production and usage patterns. The NYMEX heating oil contract calls for delivery in New York harbor. Although heating oil is impacted by crude oil price trends and, therefore, indirectly by international developments, U.S. fundamentals often constitute the dominant influence on the market.

In fact, the international market for distillate fuel oil is very different from the U.S. market. In 1984, for example, gasoline constituted approximately 43% of the refined and product utilization of total U.S. crude oil demand of 15.7 million bpd. On the other hand, distillate fuel oil made up 26% of refined petroleum products. In the world market, however, gasoline comprised only 19% of end product utilization of 44.4 million bpd of crude. Middle distillate fuel oil dominated consumption of refined crude products with 34% of the market.

One should also note that the week-by-week domestic refining mix varies depending on the type of crude oil that is refined and the demand requirements of the market. For example, distillate fuel oil production generally increases in late autumn when refiners increase inventories ahead of the peak winter demand season for heating oil. Conversely, in the late spring, gasoline's share of the petroleum and product mix increases as refiners position themselves for peak driving demand during the summer. Similarly, production of fuel oil is generally higher in the Northeast and Midwest than in the Southern part of the nation. Generally, however, distillate fuel oil represents at least 20% of domestic crude oil utilization.

It is also important to understand certain structural issues relating to the heating oil market. The United States has been divided into refining districts or *PADs* (Petroleum Administration for Defense). PAD District 1 includes Eastern and Appalachian states. PAD District 2 includes the Midwestern states. PAD District 3 is comprised of the states of Texas, Louisana, Arkansas, and New Mexico. PAD District 4 includes the Rocky Mountain states. PAD District 5 is made up of the West Coast states, Nevada, Arizona, Alaska, and Hawaii. These PAD Districts are important because often heating oil supply and demand trends vary widely by location.

Supply

Fuel-oil supplies come from three sources: refinery production, imports, and destocking. Of these, refinery production is by far the most dominant, contributing more than 90% of heating oil supplies. Refinery production of middle distillates varies with the types of crude oil utilized. The specialized equipment and the properties of petroleum products are so different that many refiners have resorted to simply producing one type of distillate. Generally, however, refineries produce some type of middle distillate fuel oil. For example, in 1985 between 175 and 186 refineries (depending on the month), representing about 90% of operating capacity, produced fuel oil. The refining industry it-

Figure 23-8. Percent refinery yield of U.S. petroleum products (1986).

Product	Percent
Finished motor gasoline	45.9
Distillate fuel oil	21.5
Kerosene-type jet fuel	9.3
Residual fuel oil*	7.1
Still gas	4.5
Petroleum coke	4.0
Liquefied refinery gases	3.4
Other oil for petro-feed use	2.0
Asphalt and road oil	1.7
Others	0.6

Source: Petroleum Supply Monthly (1/87) DOE/EIA
*Residual Fuel Oil is composed of the heaviest grades of distillates such as Number 5 and Number 6. This type of fuel oil is heavily utilized by the military and has applications in the production of electrical power among other uses. It is not, however, relevant in our analysis of heating oil.

self has also changed dramatically in recent years. In the early 1980s, the aforementioned substitution of petroleum products encouraged a number of inefficient refineries to cease operations. The number of refineries declined from a peak of approximately 320 in 1981 to 216 in mid-1986. The result of this change in the structure of the refining industry has been a move away from lower-priced residual fuels and a move to gasoline and distillate fuel oil production. This trend to refinery centralization, therefore, contributed to the previously described dominance of gasoline and distillate fuel oil among petroleum products.

The ten largest U.S. refineries account for about a quarter of all petroleum product output. The dominance of these refineries is the same for distillate fuel oil output as it is for the product mix as a whole. This concentration, however, is even more pronounced among kerosene products. Similarly, the 20 largest refining companies in 1983 accounted for more than 75% of total domestic refinery capacity.

The production decisions of the dominant refineries and refiners are critically important to the supply side of the heating oil equation. Similarly, the posted prices of these companies, which during particularly volatile periods change almost daily, often constitute a dominant influence on short-term price movements in heating oil.

Figure 23-9. Largest U.S. refiners—Refinery capacities: November 1985 (thousands of bpd).

Company	Distillation	Cracking Capacity			Reforming
		Thermal	Catalytic	Hydro	
Chevron (inc. Gulf)	2,110	9	457	191	381
Exxon	1,200	—	496	68	268
Shell	1,020	160	371	87	228
Amoco	990	—	420	105	255
Texaco (inc. Getty)	1,059	8	374	81	255
Mobil	750	—	290	49	199
Atlantic Richfield	756	—	152	90	196
Amarada Hess	575	—	63	8	131
Marathon	588	—	170	22	148
Union	490	—	135	49	134
Ashland	462	3	99	—	70
BP/Sohio	423	—	128	70	123
Sun	443	—	151	39	98
Conoco	385	10	100	—	75
Phillips	295	—	152	—	62

Source: Petroguide Ltd. 1985

Figure 23-10. Refinery production of petroleum products by PAD in July 1986 (millions of bpd).

	PAD 1	PAD 2	PAD 3	PAD 4	PAD 5	Total
Gasoline	23.382	53.066	96.324	8.104	35.302	216.178
Distillate Fuel Oil	9.491	19.696	38.165	3.496	13.179	84.027
Total (All Products)	49.868	100.495	207.260	15.377	84.127	457.127

Source: Petroleum Supply Monthly (7/86) DOE/EIA

These dominant refineries and refiners tend to be concentrated along the Gulf Coast. This explains this region's dominance as a domestic market. Similarly, PAD 3 produced almost half of the refined products made in the United States in 1982. In fact, Texas alone was responsible for 28% of domestic production and the Gulf region for more than 40%. This dominance has continued in recent years.

This analysis of PAD supply and demand yields other interesting results. For example, all of the PAD Districts except the East Coast (PAD 1) produced at least 75% of the distillate fuel oil that was consumed daily within their own districts. In 1985, PAD 1 refineries produced 29% of the distillate fuel oil that was consumed daily and even less of other products. Therefore, demand in PAD 1 exerts a large influence on all the petroleum markets, particularly heating oil.

Similarly, PAD 3, which dominates production, shifts substantial petroleum output to the East (PAD 1) and Midwest (PAD 2). For example, in July 1986, PAD 3 moved distillate fuel oil that totaled 16.054 million barrels to PAD 1 and 5.075 million barrels to PAD 2. Total shipments in the remaining two PADS totaled only 343,000 barrels. Similarly, PAD 3 shipped 46.125 million barrels of motor gasoline to PAD 1 and 14.334 million to PAD 2. Remaining shipments to PAD 4 and PAD 5 were a very modest 729,000 barrels. Overall, PAD 3 shipped approximately 77 million barrels of petroleum products each to PAD 1 and PAD 2. Shipments to PAD 4 and PAD 5 were only 1.738 million barrels in July 1986.

No other PAD had shipments even nearing the movement of petroleum products out of PAD 3. For example, total shipments of distillate fuel oil by all PADs, excluding PAD 3, totaled only 3.89 million barrels in July 1986. On the other hand, PAD 3 shipments to other PADs totaled 21.47 million barrels. Similarly, shipments of motor gasoline by PADs 1,2,4, and 5 totaled only 11.68 million barrels, or 19% of PAD 3 shipments. Overall, all PADs except PAD 3 shipped 52.66 million barrels of petroleum products. Excluding the 16.3 million barrels of crude oil shipments out of PAD 5, which primarily represent Alaskan crude output, total production was only 36.36 million barrels. This is substantially less than total petroleum product shipments by PAD 3 of more than 155 million barrels. Thus, the production and shipping decisions of PAD 3 (primarily that of the Gulf Coast states) is especially important to the heating oil and gasoline markets.

About 90% of the nation's distillate fuel oil imports comes from Western Hemisphere nations such as Venezuela, Canada, and the Virgin Islands. Gasoline imports come from Brazil, the Netherlands, Syria, and Venezuela. Generally, the movement of refined products, including that of heating oil and gasoline, is accomplished by pipeline, tanker, or barge. For example, it has been estimated that 29% of the petroleum products shipped out of PAD 3 to PAD 1 traveled by tanker and barge. The balance is shipped via the Colonial Pipeline, which extends along the coast from Houston to Linden, New Jersey. After delivery into terminals, the petroleum product is pumped into "racks" and then loaded into trucks. The trucks transport the product to bulk storage facilities, where refiners or jobbers complete the shipment to the retailer. Difficulties at any point along this transportation network, such as severe weather or an industrial accident, have the potential to impact heating oil and gasoline prices.

As previously mentioned, net imports account for only a small amount of distillate supply. In 1985, for example, distillate imports totaled only 200,000 bpd, accounting for only 4% of total supply. In no product did net imports exceed 6%. Most distillate imports arrive in PAD 1, both because of this region's ports and its chronic supply shortage.

Figure 23-11 depicts the minimal nature of imports of petroleum products. Of total imports of 1,200 million barrels during the first seven months of 1986, actual product imports (excluding crude) totaled only approximately 110 million barrels. Similarly, 92% of distillate fuel imports and 83% of motor-gasoline imports entered the United States through PAD 1. Thus, the import needs and harbor facilities can potentially affect the product markets.

An equally small amount of supply emanates from inventories, but because production and imports of heating oil and gasoline cannot instantaneously clear prevailing demand levels, inventories act as a buffer. Primary inventories consist of stocks held by crude oil producers, refineries, large bulk terminals, and product pipelines. Secondary inventories include stocks of wholesale distributors and retailers. Finally, end users of petroleum products hold substantial stocks (estimated at 49% of distillates by the National Petroleum Council). Secondary holdings are thought to be much smaller.

A number of difficulties exist with petroleum inventory data. First, only primary inventories are known with any degree of confi-

Figure 23-11. Imports of crude oil and petroleum products—
January–July, 1986 (millions of barrels).

Product	PAD 1	PAD 2	PAD 3	PAD 4	PAD 5	Total
Crude Oil	217.298	154.875	381.435	9.661	37.553	800.822
Distillate Fuel Oil	39.295	1.203	.164	.577	1.686	42.925
Motor Gasoline	54.742	.946	1.898	.362	8.363	66.311
Total (All Products)	484.516	175.934	463.034	14.316	62.526	1,200.326

Source: Petroleum Supply Monthly (7/86) DOE/EIA

Figure 23-12. U.S. primary stocks of crude oil and
products—7/31/86 (millions of barrels).

Product	PAD 1	PAD 2	PAD 3	PAD 4	PAD 5	Total
Crude Oil	17.364	69.923	669.898	10.846	77.176	845.207
Motor Gasoline	63.607	51.741	47.996	4.787	22.331	190.522
Distillate Fuel Oil	46.357	29.999	32.268	3.123	11.091	122.838
Total	193.608	235.608	951.333	28.092	169.501	1,578.142

Source: Petroleum Supply Monthly (7/86) DOE/EIA

dence. It is the astute and, often, the successful trader who is able to estimate secondary and end-user holdings of petroleum products with reasonable accuracy. Also, it should be remembered that some inventory is
unavailable for use. For example, procedures require that pipelines and
refineries be at least partially filled with petroleum products. Additionally, some inventory must be maintained as protection against various
types of disruptions. These minimum operating inventories, which total
around 60 million barrels, represent slack in actual, available stock
levels.

Figure 23-12 demonstrates that wide variations among regions
characterize inventory levels as well as production. Clearly, PAD 3,
representing the Gulf States, dominates the inventory picture for crude
oil. At times, these inventories are important to that market. Similarly,
PAD 1 and PAD 2 hold substantial inventories of distillate and gaso-
lines. This is not surprising. PADs 1 and 2, encompassing the East and
the Midwest, are both populous regions and heavy users of petroleum
products. It is only natural that these regions should contain substantial

inventories of these products. PAD 3's considerable inventory holdings of distillate fuel and gasoline are not a function of either population or demand, but are due to the region's refineries, which hold substantial crude inventories and act as product suppliers to the rest of the nation. Substantial fluctuations in these stock levels can clearly influence crude-oil and product futures markets. Figure 23-13 gives a historical perspective on fuel oil stocks.

A number of other factors also influence heating oil prices. We mentioned earlier that international developments usually filter through crude oil prices and then influence heating oil prices. It is very unusual for heating oil prices to follow a totally independent course from the larger and all-encompassing crude oil futures market. Although heating oil fundamentals may enhance or retard a prevailing trend in crude prices, the two markets will generally exhibit similar price movements.

There is a strong seasonality to spot heating oil prices. This seasonality exists for two reasons. First, with the exception of fuel oil, demand for the other components of this group of middle distillates is very predictable. In the case of diesel fuel, for example, farm and industry driving demand can be predicted relatively accurately month by month. The industrial applications of other types of middle distillates are tied to the economic environment and present no special analytical difficulties. However, demand for the largest component of this group of middle distillates, Number 2 fuel oil, is a function of heating needs.

As a result, demand for heating purposes and for inventory replenishment exhibits a very defined seasonal trend. During the autumn of each year, storage facilities throughout the United States acquire a substantial amount of heating oil. This inventory restocking is most defined in the Northeast. Additionally, the general trend to reduced demand has moderated the need for extreme levels of inventory buildup. Nevertheless, heating oil prices tend to firm during the autumn period of inventory restocking and the high usage period of the winter months.

During the winter months, heating oil traders should carefully gauge the relative demand for the product. This is best accomplished by comparing *heating degree days (HDD)*. The number of degree days in a 24-hour period is the number of degrees that the average temperature during that period falls below 65° Fahrenheit. Demand for heating oil correlates strongly with the number of degree days. Department of Energy statistics and a number of other publications make available this

Figure 23-13. U.S. distillate fuel oil supply and disposition (thousands of bpd).

Year	Supply			Disposition		
	Total Production	Imports	Stock Withdrawal[2]	Exports	Products Supplied	Ending Stocks
1973	2,822	392	-115	9	3,092	196
1974	2,669	289	-9	2	2,948	200
1975	1,654	155	40	1	2,851	209
1976	2,924	146	62	1	3,133	186
1977	3,278	250	-176	1	3,352	250
1978	3,167	173	93	3	3,432	216
1979	3,153	193	-34	3	3,311	229
1980	2,662	142	64	3	2,866	205
1981	2,613	173	38	5	2,829	192
1982	2,606	93	35	74	2,671	179
1983	2,456	174	124	64	2,690	140
1984	2,681	272	-57	51	2,845	161
1985	2,687	200	48	67	2,868	119
1986	2,798	235	-30	100	2,904	128

Source: Petroleum Supply Monthly 1/87 DOE/EIA
[1] Numbers are monthly averages.
[2] A positive number denotes an inventory increase; a negative number represents a stock decline.

data that, of course, must be compared to historical demand levels and degree days for an accurate appraisal of potential price moves in heating oil. It is also important to monitor the overall levels of inventories going into the winter months. For example, abundant inventories going into the fall or winter months will blunt such normally bullish factors as inventory restocking or above normal degree day accumulation. The American Petroleum Institute (API) makes available weekly inventory statistics. These stocks numbers are published by most major financial newspapers.

GASOLINE

Many of the relevant statistics for gasoline have been included in the fundamental tables for heating oil. As a result, only a brief review of gasoline fundamentals is necessary.

The NYMEX has traded contracts on both leaded gasoline and unleaded gasoline. However, the once-active leaded contract ceased trading in November 1986 because of EPA regulations restricting the use of lead. Thus, the unleaded contract completes the currently active mix of successful U.S. energy futures contracts, joining crude oil and Number 2 heating oil.

The shift from leaded to unleaded futures by NYMEX was not surprising because it mirrored the trend already evident in the physical market. In 1977, for example, unleaded gasoline comprised only 27.5% of total U.S. gasoline sales. By 1980, unleaded sales, hastened by government regulations, grew to 46.6% of the market. Unleaded sales passed the 50% mark by 1982 and averaged approximately 60% of the gasoline market during 1984. By July 1986, unleaded sales, manifesting a sustained upward trend, had captured 70% of the total monthly market for gasoline.

Nevertheless, it should be noted that leaded gasoline has a disproportionate influence on the U.S. gasoline industry. A wide range of refiners possess the capacity to produce leaded gasoline. The unleaded market, in contrast, is dominated by a smaller number of large refining companies. This concentration of production has limited spot and futures transactions of unleaded gasoline. It remains to be seen whether the steady demise of physical in-terminal market trading of leaded gasoline will have a beneficial impact on the unleaded market.

Like heating oil, the gasoline market has demonstrated a very defined seasonal trend. For example, in the vast majority of years August, a period of vacations, is the month of the highest gasoline usage. July also is a month of sustained driving and, hence, high demand for gasoline. Generally, May through October tends to be the period of peak demand for gasoline. As a result, gasoline prices exhibit more strength during this period than during the times of slack demand in the winter months. Statistics relating to driving mileage are available from the Federal Highway Administration (FHA). These numbers, combined with a knowledge of gasoline inventories, refinery capacity, and other fundamental factors establish a base for a solid fundamental analysis of the market. Of course, this analysis must be conducted with a knowledge of the historical trends of these relevant statistics. Once again, the API makes available supply/demand tables and weekly data on inventories and refinery production.

Figure 23-14 on page 588 gives the most important statistics relating to U.S. gasoline supply and usage from 1973 through mid-1986.

Weekly movements in gasoline are influenced by short-term movements in crude oil, which dominates the petroleum complex and the weekly API numbers. These API numbers are a good barometer of short-term supply and demand trends and serve as a useful measure of whether prevailing inventory levels are sufficient to meet current and anticipated demands. Of course, gasoline, as a member of the petroleum complex, manifests a broad long-term sensitivity to developments that influence crude oil prices. Thus, the general trends of crude prices, broad economic developments, and political activity in the Middle East and other oil-producing regions also impact gasoline prices.

NETBACK PRICING

Netback pricing is a method of shifting crude oil price risk from refiners and other intermediaries back to producers. It gained relatively widespread acceptance during the 1980s and has become an important feature on the energy-complex landscape. The idea that underlies netback pricing is that nobody consumes crude oil as such. It has value only because of the products into which it can be refined. Therefore, one can reason that the value of crude oil should equal the combined

Figure 23-14. U.S. gasoline supply and disposition (millions of bpd).

Year	Supply			Disposition			
	Total Output	Imports	Stock Withdrawal	Total Gas Supplied	Unleaded	Percent Unleaded	Total Gasoline Stocks
1973	6,535	134	–09	6,674	—	—	209
1974	6,360	204	–24	6,537	—	—	218
1975	6,520	184	28	6,675	—	—	235
1976	6,841	131	10	6,978	—	—	231
1977	7,033	217	–72	7,177	1,776	27.5	258
1978	7,169	190	54	7,412	2,521	34.0	238
1979	6,852	181	02	7,034	2,798	39.8	237
1980	6,506	140	–66	6,579	3,067	46.6	261
1981	6,405	157	–28	6,588	3,264	49.5	253
1982	6,338	147	–25	6,539	3,409	52.1	235
1983	6,340	247	–45	6,622	3,647	55.1	222
1984	6,453	299	–54	6,693	3,987	59.6	239
1985	6,419	381	41	6,831	4,426	64.5	221
1986	6,755	296	–12	7,018	4,850	69.1	192

Source: Petroleum Supply Monthly (1/87) DOE/EIA

value of its products plus a reasonable refining cost. Netback pricing is a method of implementing this logic. Under this approach, a producer does not know the actual price he will receive for his crude oil until after it has been refined and the products are sold. At that point, the parties who are involved in a netback arrangement work backwards from product values and refining costs to calculate the value of the crude oil. This approach enables refiners and merchants to purchase crude oil on an unpriced basis, leaving price risk concentrated in the hands of crude oil producers and oil product consumers.

CRACK SPREADS

The concepts on which netback pricing is based can be applied to the futures markets. *Crack spreads* permit traders to take positions on refining profit margins and product mixes. They are important to energy complex hedgers and have become popular among sophisticated speculators.

Refiners actively use crack spreads to hedge the risks that are associated with rising crude prices, falling product values, and the consequent possibility of eroding profit margins. Energy futures traders should understand how commercial participants use crack spreads. Additionally, understanding crack spreads leads to a better understanding of the relationship between crude oil and its products.

The NYMEX has taken steps to facilitate the execution of crack spreads in futures. Before its introduction of a computer system that accommodates crack spread quotes, traders had to execute separate transactions in the crude oil ring and in each of the two product rings. This process complicated the execution of crack spreads and introduced often unacceptable timing and transaction risks into the process. The NYMEX has standardized the quotation of crack spreads in dollars per barrel. This involves converting the prices of heating oil and gasoline, both of which are customarily quoted in dollars per gallon.

The formula for converting the per gallon price of heating oil or gasoline into a per-barrel price is the following:

$$P_B = 42 \times P_G \tag{1}$$

where

P_B = price per barrel
P_G = price per gallon

This equation follows directly from the fact that there are 42 gallons per barrel of crude oil.

This price conversion is necessary to compare product prices with crude prices. For example, suppose you were interested in knowing the relative importance of heating oil and gasoline to the value of crude oil given the futures prices in the following example. We are using March product futures and February crude oil futures to allow for the time lag between the receipt of crude by a refinery and the delivery of end products to consumers:

Example: Assume that current futures prices are as follows:

February crude oil:	$15.32 per barrel
March heating oil:	44.87 cents per gallon
March gasoline:	43.00 cents per gallon

Multiplying the heating oil and gasoline prices by 42 in accordance with equation (1) gives the following prices per barrel:

March heating oil: (42 gallons per barrel) x (44.87 cents per gallon)
= $18.85 per barrel
March gasoline: (42 gallons per barrel) x (43.00 cents per gallon)
= $18.06 per barrel

These per-gallon product prices form the basis for two different comparisons with the customary per-gallon crude price. We consider these two approaches separately, using the data from the previous example:

Example: The difference in per gallon prices of crude oil and one or both of the products follows from a simple subtraction. Thus:

$$D_H = P_H - P_C = \$18.85 - \$15.32 = \underline{\$3.53 \text{ per barrel}}$$

where

D_H = difference between heating oil and crude oil prices
P_H = heating oil price per barrel
P_C = crude oil price per barrel

If a trader believed that the value of heating oil were too low relative to the value of crude oil, she could then buy heating oil and sell crude oil.

Example: If you know the quantities of both heating oil and gasoline that are produced from one barrel of crude oil, it is possible to compute the product value of crude oil and to use that as a measure of refining margins. Referring back to Figure 23-8, we see that gasoline accounts for about 46% of the refinery yield of crude, or 0.46 barrels per barrel of crude. Heating oil (distilled fuel), jet fuel, and residual fuel oil combined account for another 38% (0.38 barrels per barrel of crude). If we assume that these fuel oils can be treated as equivalent from the perspective of pricing, we can calculate the product value for 84% (46% + 38% = 84%) of a barrel of crude oil as follows:

$$V_P = V_G + V_H = (0.46)P_G + (0.38)P_H$$

where

V_P = total value of two main products
V_G = value of gasoline
V_H = value of fuel oils

Using the gasoline and heating oil prices of the previous examples gives the following:

$$V_P = (0.46) \times \$18.06 + (0.38) \times \$18.85 = \underline{\$14.91}$$

This product value can be compared with the value of the crude oil to get a proxy for the refining margin as follows:

$$M = V_C - V_P = \$14.91 - \$15.32 = \underline{-\$0.41}$$

where

M = proxy for processing margin
V_C = value of crude

The margin is negative because only 84% of the product value is included. If we make the simplifying assumption that the remaining 16% of product value fluctuates in price in line with the dominant 84%, we get another proxy for the total processing margin:

$$V'_P = \frac{V_P}{0.84} = \frac{\$15.09}{0.84} = \$17.96$$
$$M' = V'_P - V_C = \$17.96 - \$15.32 = \underline{\$2.64}$$

Traders often compare the refining margin proxy calculated in this way with historical norms to see whether margins appear to be high or low by past standards.

Crack spreads provide a way of hedging or speculating on crude oil refining margins in the same way that soybean crush spreads (see Chapter 16) make possible transactions relating to soybean processing margins.

Astute readers may already have noticed the similarity between crack spreads and netback pricing. Netback pricing arrangements may take specific account of the products other than gasoline and distillate oil, but otherwise the calculations of the product value of a barrel of crude is the same as described here. The only difference in the case of netback pricing is that the refining margin is agreed upon in advance and is used together with the total value of the products to calculate the value of the crude oil. As netback pricing becomes more prevalent, crack spreads could become an increasingly common trading approach.

■ *Chapter 24*

■ *Imported and Tropical Commodities*

- Cocoa
- Coffee
- Sugar
- Frozen Concentrate Orange Juice

COCOA

Cocoa is a truly international commodity. It is produced almost exclusively in Africa and South America and consumed primarily in the industrialized countries of Europe and North America. Cocoa trees are indigenous to the West Indies and were transplanted to West Africa in the latter half of the nineteenth century. Africa subsequently became the center of world cocoa production and retains that position despite the emergence of Brazil as a major force in the market. Ghana was the world's leading cocoa producer for much of the twentieth century but lost this title to the Ivory Coast in the late 1970s. The shift was the result of radically different agricultural policies in these two neighboring West African countries and is interesting enough to warrant brief mention.

Ghana had long had a government-run Cocoa Marketing Board that bought cocoa beans from farmers at a fixed legislated price in local currency and resold them on the world market. When both prices and production costs rose in the inflationary 1970s, Ghanaian farmers were forced to sell their output to the government at prices well below those prevailing in the world market and in some cases below production costs as well. This created a real disincentive to produce cocoa, and farmers responded by abandoning their trees and moving to the cities. The result was a decline in cocoa production from more than 400 thousand metric tons annually in the early 1970s to less than 200 thousand metric tons annually by the early 1980s. Meanwhile, the Ivory Coast followed a policy of permitting farmers to receive more market-related prices for their crops and saw annual output rise from less than 200 thousand metric tons to more than 500 thousand metric tons during the same period.

Partly as a result of the Ghanaian performance, government marketing boards have been losing influence in recent years. The thinking is that the agricultural sector should be more productive if farmers receive market-related incentives. Nigeria, one of the major African producers, abolished its cocoa-marketing board in mid-1986. The effects of its new philosophy will be watched closely by other producers.

The world cocoa crop year runs from October to September with most harvesting taking place during the first five months of the crop year. The single important exception is Brazil, where the bulk of the harvest occurs between March and June. The key producing area in Brazil is the state of Bahia, and the Brazilian crop is often called the *Bahian crop*. Figure 24-1 shows the production statistics for several recent seasons. The emergence of Malaysia as a significant producer is worth noting.

The fact that cocoa is produced almost exclusively in developing countries presents special challenges for fundamental analysts. Few of the major cocoa-producing countries have the necessary infrastructure to gather comprehensive and accurate production statistics. Therefore, data relating to output is often unreliable, especially during the early part of the crop year. The key sources of production information for the world as a whole are the USDA, the Food and Agricultural Organization of the United Nations, and Gill and Duffus, Ltd., a private British cocoa merchant. Several key producing countries, notably Ghana, release weekly figures showing how much cocoa has moved off farms and into marketing channels. Many traders use these statistics as a measure of production.

As with any agricultural commodity, weather can play an important role in cocoa production. The major threat is usually hot, dry weather during the summer growing season. Cocoa trees are also sus-

Figure 24-1. World production of raw cocoa (thousands of metric tons).

Nation	1980/ 1981	1981/ 1982	1982/ 1983	1983/ 1984	1984/ 1985	1985/ 1986	1986/1987 (Estimate)
Ivory Coast	405	465	360	411	565	565	525
Brazil	349	314	336	302	415	395	400
Ghana	258	225	178	159	175	215	240
Malaysia	43	60	65	80	100	130	150
Nigeria	156	183	156	115	170	135	125
Cameroon	120	122	106	108	120	117	120
Ecuador	81	88	46	48	100	100	100
Colombia	39	42	40	38	42	44	45
Mexico	30	41	42	35	42	41	43
Dominican Republic	32	40	40	39	39	37	43
Rest of World	150	158	167	182	195	185	186
Total	1,661	1,736	1,536	1,517	1,963	1,964	1,974

Source: Gill & Duffus, Ltd.

ceptible to excessive rains that can wash the cocoa-producing flowers off the tree before maturity. Available output can sometimes be restricted by labor or transportation difficulties in some of the African producing nations. Problems with the Brazilian crop can have a dramatic impact on prices even though this crop is less than 20% of the world total. This is because the Brazilian harvest comes after the African harvest has moved to market, so an unexpected shortfall can leave the market with smaller than expected supplies in the final months of the crop year.

The demand side of the cocoa supply/demand equation is usually less interesting than the supply side. This is because usage tends to be price inelastic, growing over the long term along with population in the industrialized consuming countries. As Figure 24-2 shows, the United States, the U.S.S.R., West Germany, the Netherlands, and Brazil are the top consuming nations. Cocoa consumption is measured by *grindings*, a term that refers to the process of converting raw cocoa beans into confectionery products.

Although cocoa demand has trended upward since World War II, two areas of potential concern have emerged in recent years. One is a trend away from chocolate products and toward other types of snack food in the United States and Europe. The second is a perception among some in the cocoa trade that the U.S.S.R. may attempt to curtail cocoa imports in the context of a broader initiative to conserve hard currency reserves.

On the potentially positive side, it is worth noting that many of the more populous areas of the world are still insignificant consumers of cocoa. India and the People's Republic of China are two countries that could add significantly to overall demand for cocoa. Though chocolate products are widely viewed as luxuries, cocoa itself is a relatively inexpensive food that could become increasingly popular in developing countries.

Figure 24-3 on page 594 shows the balance between world production and usage since 1970. Historically, bull markets in cocoa have been associated with closing stocks of 20% or less of annual consumption. In recent seasons, carryover has been rather burdensome by this standard. Futures price activity has generally reflected this ample supply situation.

Figure 24-2. World consumption of raw cocoa (thousands of metric tons).

Nation	1980	1981	1982	1983	1984	1985	1986 (Est.)
West Germany	158	167	175	180	194	207	200
Netherlands	133	141	148	157	161	175	175
United Kingdom	65	85	88	77	90	81	85
France	48	52	52	53	52	42	40
Total W. Europe	548	598	620	627	663	686	673
U.S.S.R.	130	120	130	145	150	160	160
Total U.S.S.R. and Europe (incl. E. Europe)	766	810	823	856	894	930	919
United States	142	190	199	194	209	205	205
Brazil	200	195	170	198	214	234	200
Africa	139	125	127	130	101	164	168
Asia	77	93	110	110	98	109	154
World Total	1,510	1,599	1,607	1,652	1,750	1,830	1,812

Source: Gill & Duffus, Ltd.
Note: Columns do not add to total because of exclusion of minor consumers.

Figure 24-3. Cocoa supply/demand (thousands of metric tons).

Season	Opening Stocks	Net World Crop	Total Supply	Grindings	Closing Stocks	Stock Change
1970/1971	500	1,484	1,984	1,399	585	+85
1971/1972	585	1,567	2,152	1,536	616	+31
1972/1973	616	1,383	1,999	1,583	416	−200
1973/1974	416	1,433	1,849	1,512	337	−79
1974/1975	337	1,534	1,871	1,452	419	+82
1975/1976	419	1,499	1,918	1,523	395	−24
1976/1977	395	1,330	1,725	1,438	287	−108
1977/1978	287	1,497	1,784	1,394	390	+103
1978/1979	390	1,478	1,868	1,457	411	+21
1979/1980	411	1,611	2,022	1,488	534	+123
1980/1981	534	1,644	2,178	1,592	586	+52
1981/1982	586	1,719	2,305	1,600	705	+119
1982/1983	705	1,521	2,226	1,620	606	−99
1983/1984	606	1,502	2,108	1,720	388	−218
1984/1985	388	1,931	2,319	1,795	524	+136
1985/1986	524	1,907	2,431	1,803	628	+104

Source: Gill & Duffus, Ltd.

International Cocoa Agreement

In November 1980, the International Cocoa Agreement (ICA) was negotiated despite decisions by the Ivory Coast (the largest producer) and the United States (the largest consumer) not to sign the agreement. The agreement essentially called for target prices of $1.00 to $1.60 per pound to be defended by a series of buffer stock operations. If cocoa prices rose above $1.60 per pound the buffer stock manager would sell cocoa, and if prices fell below $1.00 per pound the buffer stock manager would purchase sufficient quantities of cocoa to return prices to the target range. The buffer stock was limited to a maximum of 250,000 metric tons and financing for the ICA operations was arranged through a one-cent-per-pound fee on cocoa imports and exports.

The ICA was doomed by the refusal of the Ivory Coast and the United States to join and by a sustained erosion in prices. It failed in early 1982. At that point all buffer stock operations were suspended and the fee on imports and exports was increased to 2 cents per pound in order to increase finances. The intervention floor was also reduced by 4 cents to 96 cents per pound. After four years of negotiations the

Ivory Coast agreed to enter the agreement. Whether this agreement will prove more successful than its predecessor remains an open question. Nevertheless, the ICA may once again constitute at least a minor market influence.

COFFEE

Coffee, which is indigenous to Africa, became a major commercial commodity in the nineteenth century and is now one of the most important agricultural products in the world. The dollar value of the world's coffee crop usually approximates that of the major grains such as wheat, corn, and soybeans. There are several distinct and significant varieties, or *growths*, of coffee, and it is important for traders to understand the basic differences between the key growths.

Two types of coffee account for the overwhelming portion of world production—*arabicas* and *robustas*. Arabicas are grown primarily in cool climates and high altitudes in the Western Hemisphere. They are considered milder than robustas and are particularly important in analyses of the North American market. Robustas are produced principally in Africa and parts of Asia. Their more pungent flavor makes them suitable for use in instant coffees.

The futures contract that is traded on the New York Coffee, Sugar, and Cocoa Exchange is based on central American and Colombian mild arabicas; other varieties are deliverable at various premiums and discounts. The London Terminal Market trades a futures contract that is based on African robustas. Prices for these two different varieties generally follow similar long-term trends, but over the short term it is possible for differing fundamentals to produce weakness in one market and strength in the other.

Figure 24-4 on pages 600–601 gives the production statistics for key coffee-producing countries for several recent seasons. Notice the dominance of the Latin American producers, and especially that of Brazil and Colombia.

Though it is not evident from the numbers in Figure 24-4, Brazil's share of world coffee output has been in a long-term downtrend. From World War II until the late 1950s, Brazil often accounted for about 50% of total global coffee output. The percent is now usually in

Figure 24-4. World coffee production (thousands of 60 kilogram bags).

Nation	1981/1982	1982/1983	1983/1984	1984/1985	1985/1986	1986/1987
Brazil	33,000	17,790	30,000	27,000	33,000	13,800
Colombia	14,342	13,300	13,000	11,000	12,500	12,400
Ecuador	1,792	1,800	1,380	1,500	1,966	2,100
Peru	1,100	1,100		1,150	1,250	1,300
Venezuela	1,107	791	1,025	1,213	1,150	1,100
Total South America	51,731	35,188	47,122	44,058	49,803	31,212
El Salvador	2,886	2,800	2,400	2,840	2,300	2,375
Guatemala	2,653	2,530	2,340	2,703	2,530	2,950
Mexico	3,900	4,530	4,530	4,250	4,480	4,660
Costa Rica	1,782	2,300	2,070	2,516	2,013	2,200
Honduras	1,200	1,500	1,310	1,400	1,300	1,600
Nicaragua	950	1,257	710	800	775	NA
Dominican Republic	850	1,100	810	909	780	910
Total North America	15,495	17,449	15,591	16,870	15,307	16,925

Figure 24-4. (Cont.)

Nation	1981/1982	1982/1983	1983/1984	1984/1985	1985/1986	1986/1987
Ivory Coast	4,160	4,510	1,420	4,900	5,000	4,700
Uganda	2,885	3,000	2,700	3,300	3,300	3,000
Ethiopia	3,212	3,390	3,300	2,600	3,150	3,190
Zaire	1,425	1,354	1,350	1,503	1,540	1,620
Madagascar	1,305	1,000	1,100	1,200	1,300	1,250
Tanzania	959	1,033	843	877	950	810
Kenya	1,489	1,541	2,000	1,568	2,105	2,000
Total Africa	20,107	20,052	16,220	19,599	21,023	21,331
Indonesia	5,785	4,750	5,515	5,400	5,750	5,800
India	2,540	2,170	1,667	2,917	2,334	2,700
Philippines	1,067	1,225	973	1,111	1,150	1,250
Total Asia	9,982	8,795	8,841	10,778	9,724	10,588
World Total	98,240	82,138	88,717	90,357	98,647	80,962

Source: USDA Foreign Agriculture Circular —Coffee (1/87)
Note: Regional totals and world total do not add up because smaller producing nations are omitted.

the 30 to 35 range, except in 1982/1983, when the Brazilian crop was decimated by a severe frost. The declining Brazilian market share was paralleled by increasing usage of African robustas as instant coffee gained popularity worldwide. Nevertheless, Brazil dominates the coffee market as Mexico does silver and South Africa does gold and platinum.

The coffee market is quite responsive to weather in Brazil and especially to frosts, which are the major threat to coffee output. A frost in the winter months of Brazil (July and August), when the beans are being picked, is especially serious. A frost in September, after much of the crop has been harvested, is usually much less troublesome. An extended frost can kill all or part of the coffee plant. Because it takes two to three years to reproduce these plants, an extended frost can reduce Brazilian output during the next few seasons following the frost. This happened to some degree after the severe Brazilian frost in the South American winter of 1982.

Two other recent examples provide some useful perspective. In 1975, for example, a significant frost in Brazil doubled coffee prices from 45 cents per pound to 90 cents. Abundant levels of world stocks subsequently moderated the effect of the frost, but after these inventories were drawn down, diminished levels of Brazilian output had a more dramatic impact on price. Coffee prices exploded during 1977 to more than $3.30 per pound. Thus, over a two-year period, this disastrous Brazilian frost rallied coffee prices sevenfold.

Other weather problems can also affect coffee prices. The May-November 1985 drought in major coffee-growing regions of Brazil had a dramatic influence on coffee prices once it became known during the October flowering period that the plants were affected. Prices doubled between October 1985 and January 1986 to more than $2.75 per pound. The 1986/1987 Brazilian crop plunged from a forecast 30 million bags prior to the drought to less than 14 million bags. As this recent example highlights, Brazil remains key to the supply side of the coffee market.

Demand

Coffee demand has grown steadily through the years, with particularly dramatic growth during the 1950s and 1960s. Coffee demand did, however, decrease after the 1975 Brazilian frost and the subsequent price explosion. This was not surprising given the sustained advance in prices. Yet, because of the rapid expansion of African output in the mid-1970s, coffee prices might otherwise have languished below 50 cents per pound.

Although coffee demand exhibited signs of improvement during the early 1980s, a number of difficulties lingered on the demand side. For example, the United States, by far the world's largest consumer of coffee, has seen demand for the product moderate because of a discernible shift in consumer preference. Beer and soft drinks have apparently gained favor at the expense of coffee consumption. In 1960, for example, daily per-capita American coffee consumption was estimated at 3 1/2 cups versus just under 2 cups in 1981. Additionally, growth in Western European coffee consumption has apparently moderated, suggesting that much of the prevailing coffee market is reaching saturation. Thus, the third-world and Soviet-bloc nations may have to pick up the slack for coffee demand to hold steady or increase.

Coffee demand picks up seasonally during the winter, peaking around the Thanksgiving-Christmas holidays. Consumption weakens during the spring and summer, yet this trend is not strong enough to exert a substantive influence on prices. There is no important seasonal influence on coffee production. In fact, because of the diversity of growing seasons, coffee is produced around the year somewhere in the world. Also, coffee can be stored for two to three years, so stocks are usually available to offset any modest or temporary deficit.

Generally, the two largest factors in the coffee market are Brazilian production and the absolute levels of stocks. Abundant stock levels can occasionally offset production difficulties in Brazil and elsewhere, but we have already discussed the dramatic impact that Brazilian developments can have on coffee prices. Figure 24-5 on page 604 summarizes coffee supply and demand.

International Coffee Organization (ICO)

The ICO is designed to maintain coffee prices within a defined range. A majority of the world coffee consuming and producing nations have signed the International Coffee Agreement (ICA), which restricts exports. If prices move out of a predetermined $1.20-to-$1.40

Figure 24-5. *World coffee supply and demand (thousands of 60 kilogram bags).*

Season	Production	Imports	Beginning Stocks	Total Supply	Domestic Use	Exports	Ending Stocks
1980/1981	86,308	671	25,607	112,586	20,555	59,880	32,151
1981/1982	98,240	765	32,151	131,156	21,189	64,992	44,979
1982/1983	82,138	773	44,975	127,886	22,871	64,867	42,148
1983/1984	88,717	678	42,148	131,543	21,340	68,207	41,996
1984/1985	92,065	529	41,996	134,610	23,632	72,469	38,509
1985/1986	96,447	541	38,509	135,786	21,930	67,653	46,203
1986/1987(E)	82,935	523	46,203	130,224	21,998	71,079	37,147

Source: USDA
Note: (E) = Estimate

per-pound range (as measured by an ICA formula), individual export quotas are adjusted to bring prices back within the parameters of the agreement. In early 1986, for example, high coffee prices triggered a sustained release of exports.

Each year, negotiations over new ICA export quotas for individual nations affect the coffee market. Coffee market participants should remain aware of these negotiations. Additionally, it should be noted that "smuggling" (the export of coffee without ICA stamps) constitutes a threat to the agreement and a potential bearish influence on world prices. Finally, both American and Brazilian representatives to the ICA have occasionally threatened to resign participation in the agreement. This is a threat that occasionally occupies the attention of a market that is normally preoccupied with Brazilian production trends.

SUGAR

Sugar has a history as an internationally traded commodity that dates back to ancient times. There are two types of sugar-producing plants, but the sugars that they produce are identical. Sugarcane is grown above ground in grass that is indigenous to tropical and subtropical regions of the world. Sugarcane crops are harvested yearly with replanting only necessary every two to six years.

Unlike sugarcane, sugar beets are harvested every year and must be replanted annually. Sugar beets grow underground and because of an extensive root network are relatively impervious to droughts. However, the leaves of the beet, which photosynthesize sugar, are affected by extended periods of cloudy or inclement weather. Thus, while rainfall affects tropical sugarcane, cloudy weather influences the important European beet crop. Because of these two sharply different types of sugar and the myriad of nations that grow the product, the market does not have a seasonal trend to output. Harvesting occurs all year round.

Production

Sugar is produced around the world. Asia, led by India, the Philippines, Thailand, and China, is the largest regional producer. The 12 nations of the European Community (EC) are also large producers of

Figure 24-6. World sugar production by region
(millions of metric tons).

Region	1985/1986 Season Sugar Production			1986/1987 Season Sugar Production		
	Beet	*Cane*	*Total*	*Beet*	*Cane*	*Total*
Asia	1.49	20.94	22.43	1.47	21.89	23.36
EC	14.42	0.01	14.44	14.13	0.02	14.15
South America	0.38	12.83	13.22	0.46	13.73	14.18
North America	2.78	6.39	9.17	3.02	6.52	9.55
Caribbean	0.00	8.48	8.48	0.00	8.97	8.97
Soviet Union	8.25	0.00	8.25	7.70	0.00	7.70
Africa	0.51	7.32	7.83	0.51	7.40	7.91
E. Europe	5.54	0.00	5.54	5.36	0.00	5.36
World Total	36.26	61.72	98.08	35.74	64.39	100.13

Source: USDA Foreign Agriculture Circular: Sugar, Molasses, and Honey (11/86)
Note: World totals do not add up because smaller sugar producing regions are excluded.
Crop Year: September-August

sugar. North America, because of U.S. beet output, is also a key producer although, as we discuss later, U.S. sugar does not enter the world market on which the active futures contracts are based. Equally large is South American production, mainly because of the large Brazilian industry. The Soviet Union, and the Caribbean (because of Cuba), are also significant producers of sugar. Figure 24-6 breaks down recent sugar production by type and region.

The data in Figure 24-6 shows the relative dominance of sugarcane over beets. The importance of Asian, European, and American producers is also evident. Figure 24-7 lists total sugar output by country for the most important producers.

As Figure 24-7 shows, Brazil, Cuba, India, and the U.S.S.R. are the world's largest producers, together accounting for more than 30% of total global output. Although the Soviet Union is a large producer, its output is insufficient to supply domestic needs, so the nation remains a net importer. Most Soviet sugar is obtained from Cuba, but occasionally Soviet purchases in the open market ignite significant rallies. In recent years the largest percent gains in output have come from Brazil, Cuba, the European Community (EC), and Australia. The sugar market

Figure 24-7. World centrifugal sugar production—
Selected countries (millions of metric tons).

Country	1983/1984	1984/1985	1985/1986	1986/1987 (F)
United States	5,275	5,289	5,475	5,800
Mexico	3,242	8,847	3,630	3,670
Cuba	8,330	8,100	7,100	7,600
Brazil	9,400	7,300	8,200	9,100
Colombia	1,235	1,367	1,272	1,320
Argentina	1,621	1,535	1,160	1,120
France	4,153	4,301	4,323	3,575
West Germany	2,726	3,146	3,432	3,450
Poland	2,141	1,878	1,809	1,700
U.S.S.R.	8,700	8,587	8,250	7,700
South Africa	1,402	2,514	2,247	2,268
India	7,042	7,071	7,983	8,730
China	3,825	4,627	5,535	5,480
Australia	3,414	3,548	3,352	3,300
World Total	96,542	100,183	98,079	100,129

Source: USDA Foreign Agriculture Circular: Sugar, Molasses and Honey (11/86)
Note: (F) = Forecast

is sensitive to weather developments in these nations and to other information relating to their output.

Traders should also remain aware of the many government programs that influence sugar production. Among EC nations, for example, years of determined efforts contributed to substantial growth in production levels. The EC is currently a net exporter of sugar, in part because of subsidies to sugar producers. The United States has sustained its domestic industry by very high tariffs on imported sugar. These tariffs have held prices over 20 cents per pound despite a world price around 6 cents per pound or lower. The Cuban and Soviet governments, among centrally planned economies, have implemented long-range plans that are designed to encourage higher levels of sugar output. Additionally, these nations have utilized sugar as a method of distributing foreign aid. Finally, a number of Asian governments have controlled export levels in various ways.

Although much less successful and therefore only a minor market factor, the International Sugar Agreement (ISA) has attempted to maintain sugar prices within a specified range by using export quotas and stockpiling measures. By and large the ISA is ineffective, in part because the EC, a large producer, has declined membership and pursued sugar policies that are contrary to ISA objectives.

Also, because of Brazilian ethanol production, the sugar market has occasionally exhibited a mild sensitivity to oil prices. Brazil, in an attempt to reduce a dependence on foreign oil, has encouraged individuals to convert cars to run on various types of alcohol. As a result, during some years a significant percent of sugarcane output has been used to produce ethanol and not raw sugar. There is a particular incentive to accomplish this diversion when world sugar prices are low or oil prices are high.

Consumption

Sugar demand has consistently increased through the years. This is largely because of the steady growth in world population. Sugar demand was also aided by the high oil prices of the 1970s. A number of Middle Eastern and third-world oil-producing nations found themselves with unexpectedly high foreign exchange revenues. This resulted in increases in per-capita sugar consumption. Conversely, the subsequent decline in oil prices limited sugar consumption by these nations. The bearish influence of this development was heightened by a reduced incentive for Brazilian sugar producers to divert processing of cane to ethanol. India and China have attempted to limit domestic consumption in order to increase the availability of sugar for export.

The U.S. sugar industry is highly regulated, with prices supported by the government at levels well above those usually prevailing in the free-world market. The USDA restricts sugar imports by assigning quota levels to producing nations. These quotas often reflect U.S. foreign-policy initiatives in the Caribbean and other areas. The Coffee, Sugar and Cocoa Exchange lists two different sugar futures contracts. Sugar #11 is based on the free-world market and trades actively. Sugar #12 is based on the regulated U.S. market and seldom enjoys significant trading activity. U.S. quota restrictions and price-support programs for sugar have encouraged the development and consumption of substitutes, such as made-from-corn artificial sweeteners like high-fructose corn syrup. These substitutes have achieved almost total market penetration in areas such as certain types of soft drinks, and they continue to displace sugar in the United States and other industrialized

Figure 24-8. Centrifugal sugar consumption—Selected countries (thousands of metric tons).

Nation and Region	1982/1983	1983/1984	1984/1985	1985/1986 (E)
United States	8,090	7,782	7,346	7,121
Caribbean Total	11,924	1,364	1,444	1,453
Central American Total	769	872	940	938
Brazil	6,178	6,300	6,300	6,300
United Kingdom	2,500	2,450	2,440	2,350
W. Germany	2,272	2,191	2,296	2,250
France	2,107	2,085	2,067	2,067
Other E.C. Total	7,330	7,256	7,270	7,177
Other W. Europe Total	1,332	1,336	1,321	1,312
E. Europe Total	5,961	6,047	6,199	6,024
U.S.S.R.	13,778	13,300	13,300	13,300
N. Africa Total	3,664	3,667	3,707	3,825
Other African Total	4,228	4,290	4,287	4,430
Middle East Total	4,458	4,828	5,070	5,233
India	7,622	8,900	9,116	9,260
China	4,919	5,044	5,600	6,100
Japan	2,737	2,759	2,875	2,873
Indonesia	2,640	2,000	1,516	1,870
Oceania Total	1,031	1,006	1,010	1,035
World Total	93,848	95,773	96,721	97,729

Source: USDA Foreign Argiculture Circular: Sugar, Molasses and Honey (11/86)
Note: (E) = Estimate

nations. If this trend continues, the United States may need substantially less imported sugar. Reduced import quotas for sugar could have an adverse impact on many Latin American and Asian nations that rely on sugar as a source of foreign exchange earnings. The implications of this for banking stability and foreign policy goals may lead many Western nations to adopt other artificial price-maintenance programs. This could suggest either an increase in world sugar stocks or diminished U.S. demand. Either way, the demand side of sugar's fundamental equation is not without its share of difficulties.

In general, North and South America, Western Europe, Asia, and the Eastern-bloc nations are the largest consumers of sugar. Demand trends in these nations often have an influence on long-term sugar prices. As can be seen from the sugar production and demand tables, world sugar has been in surplus during the 1980s.

Figure 24-9. *World supply and demand (millions of metric tons).*

Season	Initial Stocks	Production	Total Supply	Consumption	Final Stocks	Stocks as Pct. of Demand
1972/1973	17.9	75.6	93.5	76.3	16.4	21.5
1973/1974	16.4	78.5	94.9	78.3	16.2	20.7
1974/1975	16.2	78.0	94.2	75.9	17.6	23.2
1975/1976	17.6	81.1	98.7	78.5	20.6	26.2
1976/1977	20.6	86.7	107.3	81.3	25.1	30.9
1977/1978	25.1	91.2	116.3	85.1	37.6	35.9
1978/1979	30.7	90.8	121.5	89.3	31.5	35.3
1979/1980	31.5	85.0	116.5	90.0	25.7	28.6
1980/1981	25.7	88.7	114.4	89.9	25.5	28.4
1981/1982	25.5	100.9	126.4	92.1	33.6	36.5
1982/1983	33.6	100.6	134.2	94.3	39.3	41.7
1983/1984	39.3	98.0	137.3	96.4	40.1	41.6
1984/1985	40.1	100.0	140.1	98.6	40.3	40.9
1985/1986	40.3	97.8	138.1	100.1	37.3	37.3
1986/1987	37.3	100.1	137.4	99.6	37.8	40.0

Sources: F.O. Licht & E.D.F. Mann

610

F.O. Licht is a West German sugar firm that publishes widely followed data on world sugar production and consumption. Their statistics deserve attention from serious sugar traders. Figure 24-9 gives Licht's world supply/demand data for recent seasons.

The far right-hand column deserves mention. Over the years, average world sugar prices have correlated relatively well with the projected level of ending stocks as a percent of total consumption. Low expected carryover often leads to higher prices; high expected carryover to lower prices. Many sugar traders use this statistic as a starting point for fundamental forecasts of sugar prices. The historic bull markets of the early 1970s were characterized by carryover ratios in the area of 25% or lower.

FROZEN CONCENTRATE ORANGE JUICE

Frozen concentrate orange juice (FCOJ) is a market that developed in the United States after World War II. Florida is the largest orange-producing state by a wide margin, usually accounting for 75% or more of total U.S. output. Florida's dominance is such that traders seldom pay attention to production data from any other state. California produces about one-fourth the quantity of oranges that Florida does, but a large percent of these are eaten as fruit rather than processed into juice. Until the late 1970s, imports were a negligible factor in the FCOJ market. However, since then, Brazil has emerged as an important supplier to the U.S. market. This followed a combination of high U.S. orange prices and a desire of Brazil to increase agricultural exports.

The important Florida orange crop is harvested between December and March. Valencia oranges, which are harvested toward the end of this period, receive particular attention from futures traders because they are the key ingredient in FCOJ.

FCOJ is the quintessential weather market. FCOJ futures are usually rather dull, but this dullness is punctuated by periodic bursts of spectacular activity when the Florida crop is hit with a winter freeze. Temperatures below about 28°F can damage the quality of oranges. Two to four hours below 25°F damage both the oranges and the trees themselves, reducing juice output for at least several seasons. Weather is also a threat, though a less severe one, during the summer and early autumn, when drought or hurricanes can impair production prospects.

Figure 24-10. *Florida FCOJ supply/demand balance (millions of gallons).*

Season (Dec./Nov.)	Beginning Stocks	Production	Imports	Total Supply[1]	Total Usage	Ending Stocks
1977/1978	27.7	175.0	42.6	245.3	211.7	33.5
1978/1979	33.5	187.9	31.2	268.6	228.0	40.6
1979/1980	40.6	251.1	17.9	319.0	259.4	59.6
1980/1981	59.6	187.5	59.1	319.1	250.2	68.9
1981/1982	68.9	133.3	70.3	283.6	230.2	53.4
1982/1983	53.4	169.5	48.7	281.7	238.9	42.8
1983/1984	42.8	121.2	101.2	282.7	228.3	54.4
1984/1985	54.4	118.4	77.5	263.8	215.5	48.3
1985/1986	48.3	132.4	76.1	263.6	226.7	36.9
1986/1987[2]	36.9					

1 Includes other supplies
2 Forecast
Source: Florida Citrus Processors' Association

The most important FCOJ supply statistics are those released weekly by the Florida Canners Association that cover the amount of FCOJ produced (the *pack*) and the amount shipped to retail outlets (the *movement*). The USDA Florida orange crop reports are also followed closely by traders. These reports are released monthly beginning in October (the start of the crop year).

Figure 24-10 shows the overall supply/usage balance for FCOJ in recent years. Notice particularly the growth in imports, which reflects the growing importance of Brazil in the U.S. market. Above all, though, traders should remember that FCOJ is a market that is dominated by Florida winter weather and is subject to price volatility that is unmatched in any other futures contract.

■ PART SIX

■ OPTIONS

■ Chapter 25

■ Introduction to Options

Options have been bought and sold in various forms for centuries, but they emerged as an important trading and risk-management vehicle only in the 1970s. The catalyst for this emergence was the formation of the Chicago Board Options Exchange (CBOE) in 1973. The CBOE introduced standardized options contracts, a physical location for trading to take place, and a clearing mechanism to ensure the financial integrity of its contracts. The fact that this sounds very much like our earlier discussion of futures markets should not be surprising, because the CBOE was conceived and developed by the Chicago Board of Trade (CBOT)— the nation's oldest and largest futures exchange. Despite its relationship to the commodity-based CBOT, the CBOE was formed as and remains a securities options exchange. There are two reasons for this. First, the CBOT recognized the enormous potential inherent in the huge U.S. equities markets. Second, there were more severe legal and regulatory obstacles to the introduction of commodity options than securities options—a subject to which we return later in this chapter.

The important point is that the founding of the CBOE transformed the options business from a small and highly fragmented principal-to-principal market into a centralized activity that quickly became vastly more liquid and efficient than its over-the-counter ancestors. Later on, we cover the history and development of options in more detail. But first, let us discuss the basics of options contracts themselves.

WHAT IS AN OPTION?

Following are two descriptions of an option. The first is a relatively standard definition. The second may make it easier to see what is really going on:

> *Definition:* An option is the *right*, but not the *obligation*, to buy (in the case of a call option) or to sell (in the case of a put option) a particular item at a predetermined price on or before a specific date.

> *Definition:* An option is a forward or futures contract that may be canceled prior to maturity if one of the two parties involved so chooses. The party who has the cancellation privilege is the buyer of the option.

Consider the following examples:

- If a farmer enters into a forward or futures contract to sell corn at $2.50 per bushel in December, he is obligated to perform on that contract even if corn prices should later rise to $3.50 or $4.00 per bushel.
- If a farmer purchases an option contract to sell corn at $2.50 per bushel in December, he retains the right to cancel the contract—as he would obviously want to do if corn prices rose to $3.50 or $4.00 per bushel.

Now clearly, whoever is on the opposite side of this contract would recognize that this cancellation privilege gives the farmer a much more advantageous position and would want the farmer to pay for this privilege. The price paid is known as the *option premium*. The price at which the farmer may, if he wishes, elect to sell his corn ($2.50 per bushel in this example) is known as the *exercise price*, the *strike price*, or the *striking price*. These frequently encountered terms are synonymous. The use of an option's privilege to buy or to sell at the exercise price is known as *exercising the option*. When an option is exercised, the option owner receives the item that underlies the option contract.

Before moving on to a few definitions and a discussion of how options can be useful, let us look at this example from a slightly different perspective. The farmer has paid a price (the premium) to put himself in a position that allows him to sell his corn at either the prevailing market price, or at $2.50 per bushel, whichever is higher. In other words, he has insured himself against corn prices falling below $2.50 per bushel. Expressed somewhat differently, he has purchased price insurance. The *option premium* paid for this insurance against possible misfortune in the form of falling prices is analogous to the *insurance premium* that might be paid to protect against misfortune in the form of fire or flood. The fact that options can be simply a form of insurance is intriguing because insurance is widely perceived as among the most conservative investments, while options are widely perceived as among the most speculative. This is another topic to which we will return. For the moment, though, several definitions are in order:

Definitions of Options-Related Terms

American option: An option that may be exercised at any time prior to its expiration (*see* European option).

At-the-money: An option whose exercise price exactly equals the current price of the underlying item.

Call option: An option that gives the owner the right to *buy* a particular item at a specified price during a fixed period of time (*see* Put option).

European option: An option that can be exercised only at its expiration, not before (*see* American option).

Exercise price: The price at which the holder of an option may buy the underlying item (in the case of a call option) or sell the underlying item (in the case of a put option).

Expiration time: The specific time (date and hour) at which an option contract becomes null and void. After this time, the option is worthless.

In-the-money: An option that has an intrinsic value that is greater than zero (*see* Intrinsic value).

Intrinsic value: The value that an option would have if it were to expire immediately. For a call option, intrinsic value equals the prevailing forward price of the underlying item minus the exercise price of the call option, if this difference is greater than zero. If this difference is equal to or less than zero, the intrinsic value is zero. For a put option, intrinsic value equals the exercise price of the put option minus the prevailing forward price of the underlying item, if this difference is greater than zero. If this difference is equal to or less than zero, the intrinsic value is zero. Neither a call nor a put can ever have a negative intrinsic value.

Out-of-the-money: An option that has zero intrinsic value (*see* Intrinsic value).

Premium: The price of an option; the premium equals the sum of the option's intrinsic value and its time value (*see* Intrinsic value, Time value).

Put option: An option that gives the owner the right to *sell* a particular item at a specified price during a fixed period of time (*see* Call option).

Strike price: Another term for *exercise price.*

Striking price: Synonymous with *exercise price* and *strike price.*

Time value: The amount by which the price of an option exceeds its intrinsic value.

Volatility: A measure of how much the price of an item fluctuates. There are many different approaches to defining and measuring volatility.

Write: To sell an option.

OPTION RISK CHARACTERISTICS

The most important difference between options and futures is the risk profile. Regardless of whether one buys or sells a futures contract, the risk and the reward are both limited only by the fact that prices will not fall below zero. Options, on the other hand, possess more limited risk for the buyer and more limited reward for the seller. The buyer cannot lose more than the total amount paid for the option (the premium). If he or she simply forfeits this premium, there is no further exposure or financial obligation. Regardless of how far the price of the underlying item may move against the buyer, the owner of an option can hold the position in the hope of a possible price turnaround without worry about losses in addition to the premium paid for the option in the first place.

The seller (or *writer*), on the other hand, is in a very different position. The premium he or she receives from the buyer is the maximum possible profit. This is logical because the premium represents the buyer's maximum risk, and there are no other potential profit sources for the seller. However, the seller's potential losses are unlimited.* The premium that is received at the outset of the transaction is compensation for shouldering unlimited risk and limited profit potential.

GENERAL CHARACTERISTICS OF OPTIONS PRICES

The price (premium) of an option depends on the likely value of the cancellation privilege that it purchases. Four factors contribute to this valuation:

- The relationship between the option's exercise price and current futures prices.
- The time that remains before the option expires.
- The prevailing level of interest rates.
- The expected volatility in the price of the item underlying the option.

Let us now discuss each of these factors in a little more detail. First though, we point out that both this chapter and the next deal with options on futures contracts rather than options on cash market items. There are subtle distinctions between the two that need not concern most

---

*Actually, risk is limited to the total price of the underlying item in the case of a put option because prices cannot fall below zero.

readers. Those interested in understanding the technicalities should consult specialized options literature.

Relationship Between Exercise Price and Current Futures Price

The opportunity to pay $5.00 for something worth $6.00 is obviously more valuable than the opportunity to pay the same $5.00 for something worth $5.50. It therefore stands to reason that the premium (i.e., the value) for a call option *increases* as the free-market price of the underlying item *increases*.

How rapidly the option value increases as the underlying price increases depends on the relationship between the exercise price of the option and the price of the underlying futures contract. When the exercise price of a call option is significantly below the price of the underlying futures contract, the option price will rise or fall almost dollar for dollar along with the futures price. For example, if December gold is trading at $350 per ounce, an option to buy December gold at $250 per ounce is obviously worth at least $100 per ounce ($350 per ounce minus $250 per ounce). However, it isn't likely to be worth much more than this $100-per-ounce *intrinsic value*. The reason is that any additional value is due to the option owner's right to choose *not* to buy the gold at $250 per ounce. This flexibility to cancel the contract would be worth something only if gold prices fell below $250 per ounce before December. Intuition tells us correctly that the chances of this happening don't change much either way if December gold rises to $351 per ounce or falls to $349 per ounce. This is why *deep-in-the-money* options fluctuate in value one-for-one with the forward price of the underlying item.

What if the forward price is much lower than the exercise price of the call option? For example, suppose that December gold is trading at $350 per ounce and the option's exercise price is $450 per ounce. Why would someone pay anything for the right to buy something for $450 per ounce that he can already buy for $350 per ounce? The only reason is because of the possibility that the price *might* rise above $450 per ounce. Once again, intuition tells us that the chances of this happening are about the same (quite small) whether December futures rise or fall a few dollars from their current $350 level. This means that the value of *deep-out-of-the-money* options changes much more slowly than the price of the underlying futures contract. The exact relationship depends on the other factors discussed later, but it is not unusual for deep-out-of-the-money options to change in value only one-tenth as much, or even less, than the related futures price.

When the underlying futures price is about the same as the option exercise price, the option value changes about half as fast as that of the underlying futures price. In this case, however, intuition does not help us understand why the relationship is so simple. The mathematics just happens to work out that way.

The ratio between the price change of an option and the price change of the underlying forward or futures contract is known as the *delta* of the option. Delta is always between zero and 1.0. As we have just seen, it is close to zero for deep-out-of-the-money options; about 0.5 for near-the-money options; and nearly 1.0 for deep-in-the-money options.

The delta of an option is an important concept for several reasons. First, as we have seen, it tells you how much the price of an option will rise or fall in relation to a price change in the underlying futures contract. Second, it enables you to calculate the *hedge ratio*, which is the number of option contracts needed to hedge an underlying futures (or cash) position. For example, if you are using at-the-money puts to hedge a long position, the hedge will require *two puts* for each *one underlying contract*. This, of course, is because the at-the-money delta of 0.5 means that the puts will change in value only half as much as the price of the underlying contract changes. The general rule is to divide 1.0 by the delta of the option in question to obtain the hedge ratio. Thus, if we are considering a deep-out-of-the-money option with a delta of 0.1, then ten options (1.0/0.1 = 10) would be needed to hedge each underlying future.

A third important function of delta is that it permits risk comparisons among different options on the same underlying item. For example, suppose you wondered whether, with both September and December T-bond prices at 98–16, there would be greater volatility in the September 102–00 call or the December 104–00 call. Knowing the delta of the two options would enable you to answer this question. Suppose, hypothetically, that the value of delta for the September 102–00 call is 0.4 and the delta for the December 104–00 call is 0.3. This would tell you to expect the September 102–00 to fluctuate about 1.33 (= 0.4/0.3) times more than the December 104–00 call.

One final point deserves mention before we part company from delta:

Delta does not remain constant for a given option. We have seen that deep-out-of-the-money options can have deltas of 0.1 or less; that at-the-money options have deltas of 0.5; and that deep-in-the-money options have deltas of 1.0. Naturally, this means that if the price of an underlying futures contract in soybeans rises from $5.00 per bushel to $7.00 per bushel, then an option with a $6.00 per bushel exercise price will evolve from being deep-out-of-the-money, to at-the-money, to deep-in-the-money. As it does so, its delta will change from, say, 0.1 to 1.0. But exactly how does it change? The answer is neither simple nor intuitively clear. Suffice it to say that traders should be aware that deltas can and do change, and that what was a perfectly good hedge ratio at yesterday's prices may be well off the mark at tomorrow's.

Mathematical formulas exist that calculate the rate at which delta changes in comparison with changes in the underlying price. We do not discuss the details here, but will merely point out that traders should bear in mind the fact that delta varies as prices fluctuate. The Greek letter that is used to represent the rate at which *delta* changes is *gamma*. Gamma can range between zero and infinity. A very small gamma would indicate that the number of option contracts that are needed to hedge a cash or a futures position will not change much as prices fluctuate; a large gamma would mean that the size of an options hedge might need to be adjusted frequently as prices change. As a rule, gamma is small for options that are deep-in- or deep-out-of-the-money. It is largest for options that are near-the-money and also near expiration.

Time to Expiration

An option contract, like a futures contract, has a specific maturity date. The more time that remains until the option matures (or *expires*), the more valuable it is. This certainly makes sense, because the longer the time until expiration of the option, the more opportunity there is for the underlying price to move in the direction the option's owner desires.

It turns out that, all else being equal, the value of an option changes at a rate about equal to the square root of the change in the option's lifetime. For example, if a three-month option has a value of $5.00, then a six-month option will be worth about $7.00 ($5.00 x $\sqrt{2}$ = $5.00 x 1.4 = $7.00); a twelve-month option is worth about $10.00 ($5.00 x $\sqrt{4}$ = $5.00 x 2 = $10.00). Once again, it is not obvious why things turn out this way, but they do.

All else being equal, the value of an option decreases somewhat with each passing day because there is always a decreasing amount of time until expiration. This change is known as the *time decay* in the option's price. The dollar amount of the one-day decrease in value is known as the option's *theta*. All else being equal, theta increases as time passes. This is because one day more or less counts for little when 100 or so days remain until expiration, but that same one day counts for a lot when only two or three days of price movement remain.

Interest Rates

This is usually the least important influence on options values, but it shouldn't be overlooked entirely. The reason why interest rates matter is simple. A person who is considering buying an option could always decide instead to put the money in the bank. As the interest rates on alternative investment rise, option premiums must decline in order to induce prospective buyers to forego earning the higher interest rate and instead purchase the option.

As the alert reader has no doubt guessed, there is a Greek letter that denotes the rate at which option values change relative to changes in interest rates. The letter is *rho*.

Anticipated Volatility

We've saved the most interesting for last. Volatility is really what options are all about. The reason is that volatility is the only factor contributing to an option's value that cannot be known with certainty. Consider the three factors that have been discussed already. There is no room for disagreement on what the exercise price of a given option is, on how much time remains until it expires, or on the prevailing level of interest rates. These are all facts. But what about volatility? To back up even further, what is volatility? Let's consider the second question first.

What is volatility? The answer is that nobody knows for sure. *Volatility* is a measure of how much a price fluctuates, but this can be measured in various ways. For example, which is more volatile, price *A*, which changes by 10% many times each year, but never by more than 25%, or price *B*, which changes by 10% only half as often as price *A*, but which sometimes moves 40% or 50%? To a certain extent, volatility is in the eye of the beholder, although the options industry has tended to adopt certain mathematical measures as standard. Only the most technically minded readers need worry about just how volatility is calculated. The important point to remember is that calculating volatility is partly art, so two different analysts can come up with different results when measuring the same thing.

Volatility is measured on a scale from zero to infinity, but in practice, volatilities that are greater than 40% to 50% are rarely encountered. The following table and the accompanying charts should help the reader get his bearings on what volatility numbers mean. Keep in mind, though, that these categories are subjective and that others could define them differently.

Volatility	Description
0	Price never fluctuates
0.0–0.10	Very low volatility
0.10–0.20	Low volatility
0.20–0.30	Moderate volatility
0.30–0.40	High volatility
0.40–Up	Very high volatility

Figures 25-1 through 25-3 are graphic examples of how different volatility levels might appear. The charts represent actual gold futures prices during three different 60-day periods. This facilitates comparison and also leads naturally into a discussion of the most crucial point relating to volatility.

Figure 25-1. Daily closing gold futures prices—10% volatility.

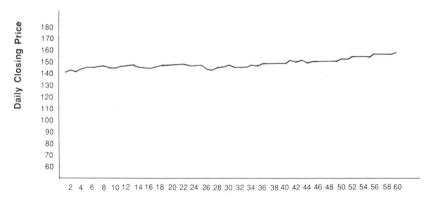

Figure 25-2. Daily closing gold futures prices—30% volatility.

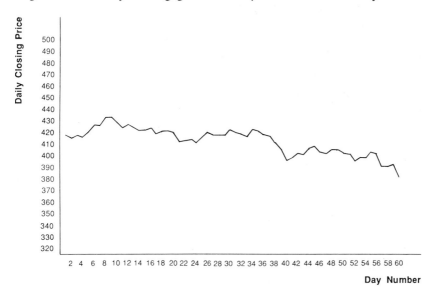

Figure 25-3. Daily closing gold futures prices—50% volatility.

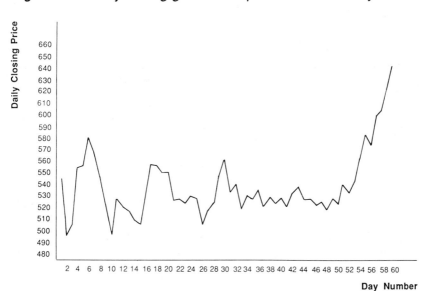

The point is this: An option's value depends on what volatility is going to be *during the lifetime of the option*. How are we supposed to know this? The answer is that we cannot know, which is part of what makes options so fascinating. Options traders and analysts always assume that *past* volatility provides the best measure of probable *future* volatility. This assumption is made partly because it seems logical and partly because nobody has figured out a better approach. But it leaves a great deal to individual judgment. Some analysts believe that the past three months' volatility is the best predictor of the next three months' volatility. Others prefer to look at only the most recent three or four weeks regardless of the time remaining to maturity. Still others use some type of weighted average, usually attaching the greatest importance to the most recent days.

This flexibility in deciding how to measure volatility gives options an added dimension compared to futures. To see this, consider two traders, A and B, who both believe that July soybeans are accurately priced at their current level of, say, $6.00 per bushel. Neither trader would then be inclined to buy or sell July soybeans. But what about options on July soybeans? Suppose that soybean prices had been relatively stable for many months but began to fluctuate more actively during the past few weeks. Suppose also that trader A believes that the average volatility of the past six months is the best predictor of future volatility, while trader B weights the most recent three weeks' activity more heavily. In such a case, trader A could be a seller of options (either calls or puts) and trader B could be a buyer of options (either calls or puts) at prevailing options prices *despite the fact that both are completely neutral on the outlook for July soybean prices.*

How can this be? The easiest way to understand is to think of *volatility* as the item that is being traded. Trader A thinks that the market is pricing volatility too high; trader B thinks it is pricing volatility too low. Put somewhat differently, both traders may think that soybean prices will be exactly $6.00 per bushel in July, but trader B expects them to fluctuate more in the meantime than does trader A.

As this example shows, a trader might buy or sell an option because of his views on either the likely *price direction* or the likely *price volatility* of the underlying item. This "trading of volatility" is the extra dimension that separates options not only from futures but from all other investment vehicles.

Figure 25-4. Option valuation characteristics.

Characteristic	Measure	Comments
Relationship between exercise price and underlying price	Delta	Always between zero and 1.0. Near zero for deep-out-of-the-money options; near 0.5 for near-the-money options; near 1.0 for deep-in-the-money options.
Rate at which delta changes	Gamma	Always between zero and infinity. Near zero for deep-in- or deep-out-of-the-money options.
Time Decay	Theta	A dollar amount that is always between zero and the total value of the option. Decreases as the square root of remaining lifetime of option.
Interest Rates	Rho	Can range from zero to infinity. Usually the least sensitive parameter in valuing options.
Volatility	Kappa	Can range from zero to infinity. Increases as time to maturity increases.

The relationship between volatility and option prices is complex. All else being equal, option prices always rise as volatility increases and always fall as volatility decreases. However, the precise effect of changing volatility on an option's price depends on the prevailing levels of the other three contributors to the option's price—the relationship between market price and exercise price, time to maturity, and interest rates. The Greek letter that denotes the relationship of volatility to option prices is *kappa*. Kappa can range from zero to infinity.

Readers who study options in greater detail often encounter references to the factors that influence options prices and the functions that measure option-price dependency on these various factors. Figure 25-4 briefly summarizes the relationships discussed in this chapter and should help readers keep track of which letters refer to which option characteristics.

OPTIONS VERSUS FUTURES

Having discussed the basics of options, let us now consider how they compare with futures and what might justify the use of one of these trading vehicles as opposed to the other.

The essential difference between options and futures is a trade-off between risk and immediate revenue. To have a more concrete sense of what this means, consider a comparison between a futures contract and a call option. In the case of a futures contract, the buyer has unlimited profit potential and a risk equal to the total dollar value that is represented by the contract. Furthermore, no money flows between buyer and seller when the futures positions are initiated. (Remember that initial margins are good-faith deposits that are held by FCMs and clearinghouses.)

In the case of a call option, several things change:

- The buyer's total risk is limited to the option premium rather than to the total value of the underlying item.
- The seller's profit potential is limited to the option premium.
- The seller receives this premium at the outset of the transaction.

The seller of a futures contract has a *potential profit* equal to the total value of the contract. The seller of an option on this contract effectively sells that portion of this profit below the exercise price for a *guaranteed initial profit* in the form of the option premium. He is trading a large possible profit for a small but guaranteed *initial* profit and keeping the risk side of his position unchanged. The buyer, on the other hand, is paying someone (the seller) to relieve him of that portion of the risk below the exercise price. To put it metaphorically, the option buyer and seller have very different views on the subject of whether a bird in the hand is worth several in the bush.

Clearly, buying options will tend to appeal to traders who are risk-averse, while selling options will strike a resonant chord with those who value guaranteed cash flow. In addition, the options-vs.-futures choice will be influenced by one's view of the relative probabilities that various types of price movement might occur. Let us discuss some of these.

- If you knew with absolute certainty how prices were going to change, you would always be a buyer or a seller of futures rather

Figure 25-5. Comparative risk profiles of futures and options.

	Futures Contract	*Call Option on Futures Contract*
Buyer's Profit Potential	Unlimited	Unlimited
Buyer's Risk	Limited by price of zero for long position.	Limited to option premium.
Seller's Profit Potential	Limited by price of zero for long position.	Limited to option premium.
Seller's Risk	Unlimited	Unlimited
Cash Flow	None initially; full value at maturity.	Option premium initially; full value at maturity if option is exercised.

than options. There would be no reason to pay the option premium as protection against an adverse price move that you knew with certainty would not occur.

- If you were reasonably sure that prices would rise but believed there was a small possibility that they could fall sharply, then buying a call option would usually be the best strategy. There is a strong analogy with conventional disaster insurance (fire, flood, and so forth) in this case. You are reasonably sure the disaster won't occur, but you are willing to pay for protection just in case you're wrong.

- If you believe that prices will change substantially but have no idea in which direction, you would want to buy an option (or better yet, both a call option *and* a put option). This is a pure volatility trade. Because you have no idea where prices are headed, trading that is based on *price* makes little sense. The fact that options enable you to trade *volatility* is what creates opportunity in this case.

- If you knew with absolute certainty that prices were not going to change at all, your best strategy would be to sell options. In fact, this is the *only* strategy that will generate profits in a market with no price fluctuation at all and is another manifestation of the new dimension that options add to trading strategy. As in the previous example, this is a pure volatility trade as opposed to a price trade.

One final point may help clarify the relationship between futures and options. A futures contract is really just an extreme example of an option; it is a call option with an exercise price of zero. To see this, consider the following:

- If you refer to Figure 25-5 and assume that the exercise price is zero, then the price of the option will equal the value of the futures contract. There would be no time value because prices cannot fall below the exercise price of zero. The only distinction between futures and options would be the timing of the cash flow. If the two parties agree to defer payment of the premium to maturity (and to post good faith margin in the interim) the futures contract and the option become identical.
- If the exercise price of an option is zero, it can never have any time value. This is because time value is the price paid to protect against prices falling beneath the exercise price, and this risk does not exist if the exercise price is zero.

Once you have an understanding of what determines the value of options, it is appropriate to consider how to trade options. Option trading strategies are covered in the next chapter. First, though, we digress briefly to cover the interesting and checkered history of options on commodities and futures in the United States.

A BRIEF HISTORY OF FUTURES OPTIONS

Nearly all traders today think of options on futures as a new financial instrument that was authorized by the CFTC in 1982. While it is true that exchange-listed trading in options on futures dates from 1982, options in other forms have played a role in the U.S. futures business almost since its inception.

Options became a fixture on the Chicago Board of Trade when the Civil War brought greater trading activity and volatility to the grain markets in the 1860s. These options were often referred to as *privileges* and differed from modern-day options in two respects. First, they were usually of very short maturity—often overnight. They were viewed as an alternative to liquidating a position by traders who did not want to carry overnight risk. Second, they were not officially authorized by the exchange. In fact, they were widely viewed as being illegal under Illinois state law, which put the CBOT in a rather awkward position.

A somewhat vague Illinois statute that prohibited options trading was passed in 1874 but was unsuccessful in stopping a practice that many traders had come to regard as an important weapon in their trading arsenal. The CBOT spent decades walking a fine line between the law and the wishes of its membership. The exchange regularly spoke out against options trading but took no forceful action to prevent it. Because options were traded member-to-member, rather than through a clearing entity, this *laissez-faire* stance permitted privilege trading to continue.

Trading in options ebbed and flowed for decades, centering on overnight puts and calls on grain futures on the Chicago Board of Trade. However, this option activity ended abruptly following a dramatic collapse in wheat futures on July 20, 1933. The plunge in prices, from $1.07 per bushel to 90 cents per bushel, was precipitated in part by the failure of E.A. Crawford & Co. This company was a trading enterprise whose principal, Edward A. Crawford, had risen from obscurity to become one of the largest grain market speculators in the country. Crawford was estimated to hold more than 20 million bushels of various grains when prices plunged, and E.A. Crawford & Co. was suspended from the CBOT for "inability to meet obligations."

Rightly or wrongly, options were blamed in part for both contributing to excessive volatility and for precipitating a sudden decline in farm prices. Option trading ceased following the July 1933 grain price collapse and did not resume until October 6, 1935, when limited trading in overnight "privileges" was resumed at the CBOT. The resumption was short-lived, though, because the Commodity Exchange Act of 1936 banned all trading in options or privileges on regulated commodities.

This ban on the trading of options on regulated commodities all but eliminated commodity options and futures options from the U.S. financial scene for nearly four decades. However, a small number of hedgers and sophisticated speculators traded options on such items as cocoa, coffee, and sugar in the London markets, where no prohibitions existed and where commodity options trading was only modestly active but nonetheless reputable.

When commodity price volatility began to increase in the early 1970s, a broader spectrum of traders became intrigued by the potential benefits of options. Several entrepreneurs noticed that the legal ban on commodity options did not extend to *unregulated* commodities, which meant that U.S. agricultural products such as grains and livestock were the only important market segments that were statutorily off limits to options trading. Cocoa, coffee, sugar, silver, and copper were among the products not affected by the legislation of the 1930s.

The most aggressive of the commodity options entrepreneurs was Harold Goldstein. His company, Goldstein, Samuelson Inc., started on a shoestring in 1971 and was selling options at a rate of about $50 million annually (premium value) by late 1972. Unfortunately, Goldstein, Samuelson was essentially writing naked calls. When prices rose, early buyers of these calls were able to be paid off only with the premiums paid by later investors. By early 1973, the Goldstein, Samuelson house of cards collapsed, leaving its customers with losses estimated at up to $30 million. Harold Goldstein was convicted of mail fraud in California and served a brief prison term.

The Goldstein, Samuelson affair was among the considerations that led to the formation of the CFTC in 1974. As we discussed in Chapter 6, the CFTC was given regulatory jurisdiction over all futures trading, and it broadened the long-standing ban on agricultural options to include all commodities and futures contracts in the United States.

However, the fledgling regulatory body soon found itself faced with another type of options scandal. Various firms began to buy legitimate London commodity options and to resell them at exorbitant markups to unsophisticated investors who had no idea what the options were really worth. A cottage industry of high-pressure telephone sales organizations sprang up in 1977 and 1978, and stories began to circulate of people's life savings disappearing into hugely overpriced (and often nonexistent) commodity options. The quintessential practitioner of this business was an escaped convict named Alan Abrahams. Using the alias James A. Carr, he established a Boston firm named Lloyd, Carr, & Co., which specialized in the marketing of London commodity options. Largely as a result of Lloyd, Carr's activities, the CFTC banned the sale of London commodity options in the United States as of June 1, 1978. Only a handful of established and legitimate metals dealers were specifically permitted to continue their commercial options activities.

The CFTC ban effectively halted the trading of options on commodities and futures in the United States. However, it did so at the cost of eliminating entirely the use of options for many legitimate and productive purposes. After extensive research and consultation with the futures industry and prospective commercial users, the CFTC concluded that the most effective way to both make the benefits of options available in the U.S. marketplace and to prevent the recurrence of abuses would be to permit trading in options on futures only on designated contract markets (futures exchanges) that are subject to CFTC regulation. This decision led to the pilot options program of 1982, which has since been expanded to include options on a wide variety of futures contracts. The success of this approach is evident in Figure 25-6 (see pages 636–638), which presents the growth in trading volume during the mid-1980s.

Figure 25-6. Options contracts traded 1983–1986.

Option	Contract Unit	1986	1985	1984	1983
Gold	100 oz	2,128	36,240	0	0
AMEX Commodities Corp		2,128	36,240	0	0
Corn	5,000 bu	575,634	363,549		
Soybeans	5,000 bu	775,139	840,786	72,969	
Wheat	5,000 bu	9,314			
Silver	1,000 oz	3,081	10,820		
T-Bonds	$100,000	17,314,349	11,901,116	6,636,209	1,664,921
T-Notes	$100,000	1,000,682	177,292		
Chicago Board of Trade		19,678,199	13,293,563	6,709,178	1,664,921
Live Hogs	30,000#	105,516	57,042		
Live Cattle	40,000#	718,099	326,724	20,722	
Pork Bellies	38,000 lbs	1,981			
Eurodollar	$1,000,000	1,757,426	743,080		
British Pound	25,000	496,591	329,071		
Deutsche Mark	125,000	2,205,579	1,562,438	727,634	
Swiss Franc	125,000	817,897	324,806		
Japanese Yen	12,500,000	864,586			
Canadian Dollar	100,000	26,465			
T-Bill	$1,000,000	63,768			
S&P 500	$500 x Index	1,886,445	1,090,068	672,884	281,090
Chicago Mercantile Exch		8,944,353	4,433,229	1,421,240	281,090

Figure 25-6. (Cont.)

Option	Contract Unit	1986	1985	1984	1983
Sugar	112,000 lbs	254,491	91,400	11,960	7,583
Coffee	37,500 lbs	5,319			
Cocoa	10 M tons	999			
Coffee, Sugar & Cocoa Exch		260,809	91,400	11,960	7,583
Gold	100 oz	1,646,791	1,395,896	1,432,514	386,501
Silver	5,000 oz	579,425	531,315	99,843	
Copper	25,000 lbs	127,501			
Commodity Exchange, Inc.		2,353,717	1,927,211	1,532,357	386,501
Wheat	5,000 bu	18,302	16,856	878	168
Value Line Index	$500 x Index				
Kansas City Board of Trade		18,302	16,856	878	168
Soybeans	1,000 bu	6,635	8,790		
Soft Red Winter Wheat	5,000 bu	7,492	6,076	2,149	
Gold	33.2 oz	91	678	318	
MidAmerica Commodity Exch		14,218	15,544	2,467	0

Figure 25-6. (Cont.)

Option	Contract Unit	1986	1985	1984	1983
Spring Wheat	5,000 bu	3,259	5,414	624	
Minneapolis Grain Exchange		3,259	5,414	624	0
Cotton	50,000 lbs	60,507	29,218	3,078	
FCOJ	15,000 lbs	3,354	435		
Dollar Index	$500 x Index	198			
New York Cotton Exchange		64,059	29,653	3,078	0
NYSE Composite Index	$500 x Index	296,303	195,634	246,359	306,602
New York Futures Exchange		296,303	195,634	246,359	306,602
Crude Oil	1,000 bbl	135,266			
New York Mercantile Exchange		135,266			
Total Options		31,770,613	20,044,744	9,928,141	2,646,865
Percent Change from Previous Year		58.50%	101.90%	275.09%	1392.45%

638

■ Chapter 26

■ Options Trading Strategies

The previous chapter introduced options on futures, discussed their general features, and examined the four basic factors that influence option prices. We now turn to the practical question of how to trade these fascinating and flexible instruments. Options are often traded in combinations or in conjunction with futures, which can make it difficult to see quickly how price changes in the underlying futures contract affect the overall position. For instance, if you buy a futures contract, write an out-of-the-money call, and buy an at-the-money put, are you likely to make or lose money if the futures price rises modestly? If the answer doesn't immediately leap to mind, don't worry. Even professional options traders would have to stop and think for a few moments.

Because options economics are not intuitive, it is very helpful to use *profit/loss graphs* to see the impact of price changes in the underlying futures contract on an option contract at maturity. These graphs plot the profit (or loss) on an options position against changes in the price of the underlying futures contract. First let us consider profit/loss graphs for simple long and short positions in futures themselves. The graphs show exactly what you would expect. Every one-dollar increase in the price of the futures contract itself creates a one-dollar profit on a long position and a one-dollar loss on a short position; every one-dollar decrease in the price of the futures contract has the opposite effect.

Now let's look at a long call option position (Figure 26-3, page 641). Above the exercise price, the profit line has the same slope as that for a long position, but it is shifted downward by the amount of the pre-

Figure 26-1. *Profit/loss graph: Long position.*

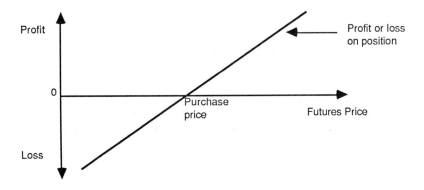

The profit/loss line has a 45° slope. This reflects the fact that the holder of a long position profits by $1 when the futures price rises $1, and loses $1 when the futures price falls $1.

Figure 26-2. *Profit/loss graph: Short position.*

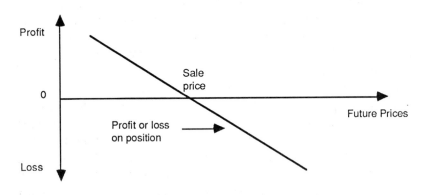

The profit/loss line has a 45° slope in the opposite direction from the graph of a long position in figure 26-1. This reflects the fact that the holder of a short position profits by $1 when futures prices fall $1 and loses $1 when futures prices rise $1.

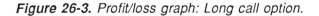

Figure 26-3. *Profit/loss graph: Long call option.*

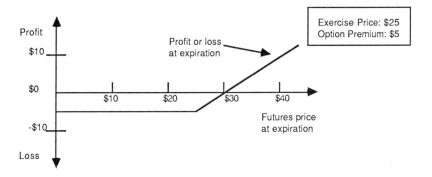

The owner of a call option profits dollar for dollar when the price rises above the exercise price plus the premium paid. Regardless of how low prices fall, he cannot lose more than the premium paid.

mium. Once the exercise price is reached, however, the profit/loss line shifts to the horizontal. This graphically represents the limited-risk feature of options. Regardless of how low prices fall, the holder of a long-call position cannot lose more than the initial premium.

How about a short-call position (Figure 26-4, page 642)? Not surprisingly, the graph is the mirror image of that for the long call. No matter how low prices fall, the profit cannot exceed the initial premium received by the seller; above the exercise price, the profit line has the same slope as for a short futures position (Figure 26-2), but shifted upward to reflect the premium received.

The graphs corresponding to long and short put option positions are shown in Figures 26-5 and 26-6 (see page 643). We leave it to the reader to make the appropriate comparisons with Figure 26-2 for a simple short position.

These six graphs can be combined to show the value at maturity of combinations of options and futures. How? Just add together the graphs that correspond to the components of the position. As an example, consider the hypothetical position mentioned in the first paragraph of this chapter: long futures, short out-of-the-money call, and long at-the-money put (see Figure 26-7, page 643).

The graphic representation makes it easy to see that a modest price increase will result in a small net loss because the premium paid for an at-the-money put (which expires worthless) will be more than the premi-

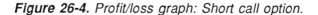
Figure 26-4. *Profit/loss graph: Short call option.*

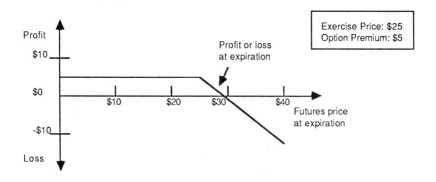

The seller of a call option loses dollar for dollar when the price rises above the expiration price plus the premium received. He cannot profit by more than the premium received.

um received for an out-of-the-money call (which also expires worthless).

We emphasize that these graphs show the value of an option position at *the maturity of the option*. This is because they reflect only intrinsic value. Graphs that include time value can also be constructed, but it is prohibitively difficult to calculate the precise values for any but the simplest positions. The intrinsic value graphs are useful despite the fact that they ignore time value. Their accurate representation of the net profit/loss distribution at maturity makes clear what the holder of the position would prefer to see happen as the options mature.

We have stressed the fact that options make possible trading strategies that could not be created using futures alone. In the next several sections, we will discuss how options can be used in trading approaches that are motivated primarily by each of four very different lines of reasoning: price expectations, volatility expectations, arbitrage opportunities, and cash flow considerations. First, though, let us discuss briefly what differentiates these various approaches from one another.

As a simple example, consider the question of whether to purchase a call option on June British pound futures with an exercise price of $1.50 or one with the same maturity and an exercise price of $1.60.

1. A decision to buy the June $1.50 call because you doubt that prices will reach $1.60 is based on price expectations.

Figure 26-5. *Profit/loss graph: Long put option.*

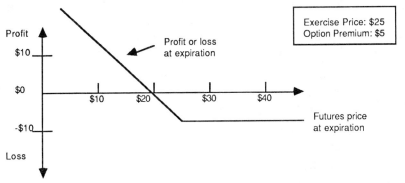

The owner of a put option profits dollar for dollar when the price falls below the exercise price minus the premium paid. He cannot lose more than the premium paid. He also cannot profit by more than the exercise price minus the premium paid since the price cannot fall below zero.

Figure 26-6. *Profit/loss graph: Short put option.*

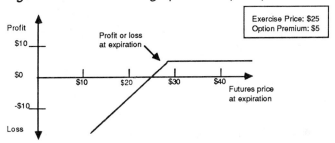

The seller of a put option loses dollar for dollar when the price falls below the exercise price minus the premium received. He cannot profit by more than the premium received.

Figure 26-7. *Profit/loss graph: Long futures + short call option + long put option.*

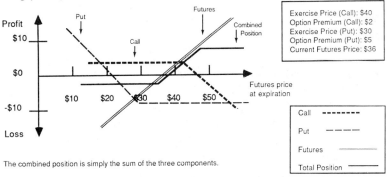

The combined position is simply the sum of the three components.

2. A decision to buy the June $1.60 call because an analysis of the two options shows that its premium (cost) reflects expectations of lower volatility is based on volatility expectations.

3. Buying the June $1.60 and simultaneously selling the June $1.50 because the former option reflects expectations of much lower volatility is an example of an opportunity that seeks to capitalize on relative inconsistencies in the markets.

4. Buying the June $1.60 because it costs less or selling the June $1.50 because it generates more initial cash are examples of strategies driven by cash flow considerations.

Most options trading decisions take into account several or all of these considerations, at least subjectively. Often, though, one predominates. In any event, examining these motives separately helps clarify the various ways in which options can be analyzed and traded. The question of whether any of these approaches are superior to any others is interesting and complex. We will return to it at the end of this chapter. First, though, let us discuss each of these basic approaches in more detail.

STRATEGIES BASED ON PRICE EXPECTATIONS

Most nonprofessional options traders focus primarily on price expectations rather than volatility expectations. Price expectation strategies analyze the profit/loss risk profile for different possible prices of the underlying futures contract at expiration. Volatility analysis is usually a secondary consideration and is sometimes not considered at all. The profit/loss graphs introduced earlier in this chapter are very useful in connection with these strategies. We will use them here as we consider a variety of bullish and bearish strategies.

Example 1: Buy call option (bullish). In January, a speculator who anticipated sharply higher gold prices buys an April $450 call when April gold futures are trading at $444 per ounce. The premium paid is $18 per ounce, or $1,800 per 100 ounce contract. If April gold futures rise to, say, $525 per ounce in March, the call option would have a value of about $7,500. On the other hand, if the trader's analysis is wrong and April gold futures fall beneath $400 per ounce, the option will expire worthless and the trader will lose the $1,800 spent on the premium.

Figure 26-8. Profit/loss graph: Long gold futures call option.

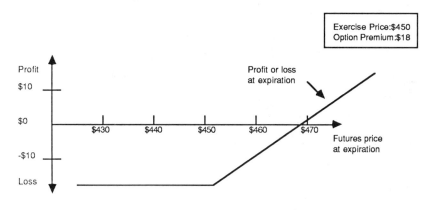

The long call option position loses $18 if the futures price is at or below $450 at expiration.
The position then gains dollar for dollar at higher prices. It breaks even at $468 and shows
a net profit at higher expiration prices.

A trader who wants to buy a call option because he is bullish can
use an analysis of the deltas of various options as an aid in deciding
which option to buy. As we discussed in the previous chapter, the delta
of an option is the ratio of the price change of the option to the price
change of the underlying futures. A trader who feels that a short-term,
moderate price rise is likely might buy a short-term, in-the-money call
(delta close to 1.0) that would rise roughly dollar-for-dollar along with
futures. Another trader who expects a much greater price advance might
prefer an out-of-the-money call (delta less than 1.0) that would rise in
value more slowly at first, but would cost less and therefore provide
greater leverage in the course of a major price advance.

Example 2: Sell put option (bullish/neutral). A trader who in April
feels that June gold at $450 per ounce is likely to rise modestly and
unlikely to decline by more than a few dollars could sell a June
$450 put for, say, $22 per ounce. If the option expires with June
futures above $450 per ounce, the trader will keep the entire pre-
mium. If the option expires with June gold above $428 per ounce,
he will retain some portion of the premium. However, once June
gold falls beneath $428 per ounce, the trader faces essentially un-
limited risk.

Figure 26-9. Profit/loss graph: Short gold futures put option.

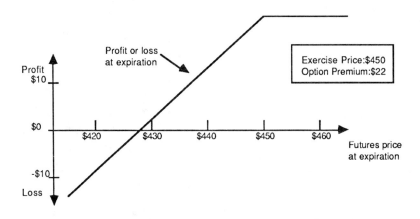

The short put option profits if prices are above $428 at expiration. The maximum profit equals the $22 premium received.

As the graph shows, this strategy yields a profit if prices advance by any amount or decline by less than $22 per ounce. This makes it a reasonable approach for someone who is neutral to slightly bullish, but not so bullish as to be unwilling to forego additional profits above the $450 per ounce level.

> *Example 3: Bullish call spread.* Spread trading is possible in options as well as in futures. The existence of different exercise prices as well as different maturities creates a wide array of spread possibilities. One of the more straightforward is often called a *debit spread.* It involves the simultaneous sale of a call with a higher exercise price (usually out-of-the-money) and purchase of a call with a lower exercise price (usually in-the-money). The term *debit spread* refers to the fact that the premium paid for the lower exercise price call will be greater than that received for the higher exercise price call. Consider the following example:

> > *July sugar futures = 8.00 cents per pound*
> > Buy July 8.00¢ call @ 0.80 cents per pound
> > Sell July 9.00¢ call @ 0.40 cents per pound

> The profit/loss graph is shown in Figure 26-10.

Figure 26-10. Profit/loss graph: Bullish sugar futures call spread.

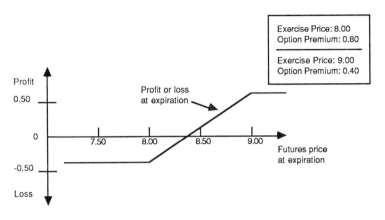

The maximum profit of 0.60 is earned if the price at expiration is 9.00 or higher. The maximum loss of 0.40 occurs at expiration prices of 8.00 or lower.

An advantage of a debit spread is that the premium received reduces the initial cash outlay that is needed to take advantage of a rising market. (Naturally, it limits the upside potential as well.) If the market rises, the in-the-money call (which the trader is long) will rise in value more quickly than the out-of-the-money call (which the trader is short). This is because in-the-money options have larger deltas than out-of-the-money options. Eventually, if prices rise high enough, both options will have deltas of 1.0 and the profit graph becomes horizontal. Similarly, if prices fall, the option that the trader is long will lose value more quickly (because of the greater delta) until prices have fallen to the point where both deltas are near zero and the graph again becomes horizontal.

Notice that in this type of spread, the maximum possible profit equals the difference between the two exercise prices minus the net premium paid. The maximum risk, of course, is the net premium paid.

Example 4: Bearish call spread. Call spreads can also be constructed to take advantage of bearish market expectations. One such spread would, not surprisingly, be the reverse of the bullish debit spread of the previous example. Let us stay with the same market data and look at the profit/loss picture at expiration:

Figure 26-11. Profit/loss graph: Bearish sugar futures call spread.

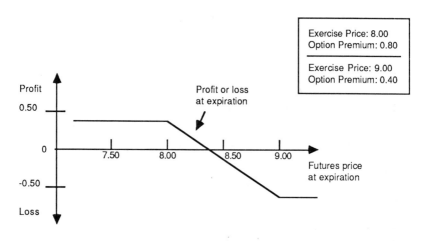

The maximum profit of 0.40 is earned if the price at expiration is 8.00 or lower. The maximum loss of 0.60 occurs at expiration prices of 9.00 or higher.

July sugar futures = 8.00 cents per pound
Sell July 8.00¢ call @ 0.80 cents per pound
Buy July 9.00¢ call @ 0.40 cents per pound

In this case, the premium received exceeds the premium paid, hence the term *credit spread.*

This strategy would make sense given a mildly bearish view on prices. The maximum possible profit equals the net premium received. The maximum possible loss equals the difference between the two exercise prices minus the net premium received. This is just the opposite of the previous example, which stands to reason because these two examples are the opposite sides of the same trade.

Example 5: Bullish put spread. Put options can also be used to construct either bullish or bearish spreads. A bullish put spread involves the simultaneous purchase of a low exercise-price put and sale of a higher exercise-price put. This is another example of a credit spread because the premium received for the put with the higher exercise price will be greater than that paid for the put with the lower exercise price. Consider the following example:

Figure 26-12. Profit/loss graph: Bullish T-bill futures put spread.

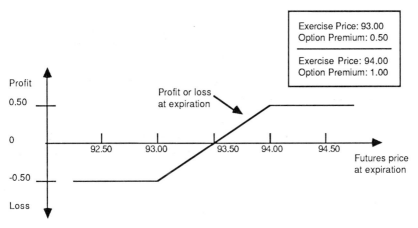

The maximum profit of 0.50 is earned if the price at expiration is 94.00 or higher. The maximum loss results if the price at expiration is 93.00 or lower.

June T-Bill futures = 94.00
Buy June 93.00 put @ 0.50
Sell June 94.00 put @ 1.00

The possible outcomes at maturity are shown in Figure 26-12.

Notice that in the cases of both bullish call and bullish put spreads, you buy the option with the lower exercise price.

Example 6: Bearish put spread. Figure 26-13 (page 650) presents the opposite side of the previous example, which is known as a bearish debit spread because there is a net outflow of premium.

Example 7: Buy futures/sell call (bearish). This position is called a *covered write* because the call option that has been sold (written) is covered by the long futures contract. If prices rise, the potentially unlimited loss on the short call option will be offset by a corresponding profit on the long futures position. However, if prices decline, the possible profit from the call is limited to the premium received, whereas the possible loss on the long futures position is virtually unlimited. Let us again consider an example from the gold market:

Figure 26-13. *Profit/loss graph: Bearish T-bill futures put spread.*

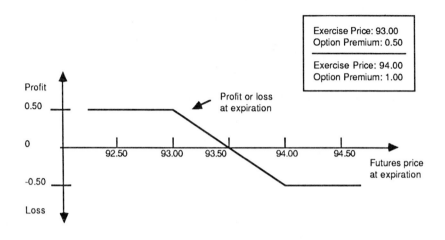

The maximum profit of 0.50 is earned if the price at expiration is 93.00 or below. The maximum loss results if the price at expiration is 94.00 or higher.

> Buy June gold futures @ $450 per ounce
> Sell June $450 call @ $22 per ounce

The profit/loss possibilities are shown in Figure 26-14.

Alert readers may be getting a sense of *deja vu* from this example. The graph is exactly the same as that for the sale of a put option in Figure 26-9. This is because the combination of a long futures position and a call option sale is equivalent to a short put position. Both have limited profit potential in a rising market and unlimited risk in a declining market. In fact, the short underlying futures/long call combination that is the opposite of this position is also known as a *synthetic put*. Similarly, the combination of a long underlying futures position and a put option purchase is termed a *synthetic call*.

The fact that the profit/loss profile of a covered write is exactly equivalent to that of a short put option leads to an interesting anomaly that readers who pursue options trading will discover sooner or later. A covered write is widely perceived to be a very conservative strategy. The call option sale is often viewed as enhancing the return on an asset through the premium inflow from the option. On the other hand, the naked sale of a put option is generally considered to be a very risky speculative strategy. What is the difference? In each case, there will be

Figure 26-14. Profit/loss graph: Covered write.

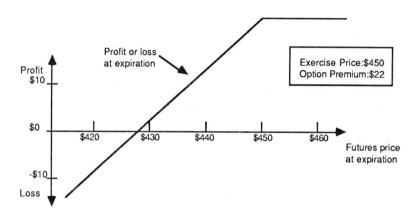

modest profits if prices rise and potentially large losses if prices fall. From an economic, risk-profile perspective there is no difference whatever. The only substantive distinction arises if you assume that the trader already owns the underlying asset and, for one reason or another, should not sell it. As an example, consider a corporation president who owns a block of his company's stock. He might prefer to retain both appearances and his voting rights by writing calls rather than selling his stock and writing puts. Likewise, a grain exporter might feel more comfortable holding a long futures position that he could hold for delivery if he needed inventory rather than simply being short puts, which might not generate actual supplies.

STRATEGIES BASED ON VOLATILITY EXPECTATIONS

As we discussed in the previous chapter, options provide a mechanism for "trading volatility." We now examine in a little more detail what this means and how it is done.

All options valuation models depend on volatility in the same general way. When volatility increases, the option value rises; when volatility decreases, the option value falls. This is true regardless of whether the option is in or out of the money and of how much time remains until expiration. If you are long any option and volatility increases (all else being equal), you will make money; if volatility decreases, you will lose money. In options terminology, being long a put or a call option means that you are *long volatility*; being short an option means that you are *short volatility*.

Two issues come to mind:

- What should you know about volatility and how do you learn it?
- How do you use this information to analyze specific market situations?

What Should You Know about Volatility?

When you look in a newspaper or on a price-quotation machine, you will have no problem finding the prices of various options and the underlying futures contracts. But how do you relate these to volatility? The answer is that it is not easy. You must take the option price and the other known information (exercise price, underlying futures price, time to expiration, interest rate), plug these numbers into your favorite option-valuation model, and solve the resulting equation to find the volatility level anticipated by the current price. This number is called the *implied volatility*, and it is important enough to warrant further discussion.

What is done to arrive at the implied volatility is the reverse of what might seem the more natural approach to the volatility/option price relationship. Rather than assuming some level of volatility, putting it into an option valuation model along with all the other known information and calculating the option price, the opposite approach is employed. You take the known price of the option and "back into" the volatility level implied by the price at which the option is trading. Hence the term *implied volatility*.

Implied volatility is a creature of convenience. Almost nobody, even full-time options professionals, forecasts absolute volatility levels. Because volatility is so difficult to define or measure, much less to forecast, most traders opt not to first predict a volatility of, say, 18.5% and then to search the market for opportunities to buy lower or sell higher volatilities. Instead, a more pragmatic approach suggests itself. Because the options prices are already known, why not just figure out what volatility assumptions are built into these prices? That way, the difficult task of predicting a specific volatility level is replaced by the more manageable task of deciding whether particular implied volatility levels seem too high, too low, or inconsistent with one another.

Figure 26-15. Hypothetical options data.

Futures Contract	Futures Price	Option Contract	Option Price	Implied Volatility
June Gold	$348.60	$360 call	$ 8.50	21.4%
June Gold	348.60	370 put	24.80	20.4%
Oct Gold	358.40	340 put	6.30	20.8%
Dec Gold	362.20	400 call	2.60	23.3%

So far, so good, but one problem remains: how do you calculate implied volatility? The answer is that you need a computer or, at the very least, a fairly sophisticated hand-held calculator. There are various formulas for valuing options and complexity is one feature shared by all. Anyone who is serious about incorporating volatility into a trading strategy will need either a personal computer or one of the very few account executives who track volatility for their option customers. This makes it possible to create tables such as the one shown in Figure 26-15, which is the first step toward incorporating volatility into trading strategies.

Volatility and Trading Decisions

There are two basic approaches to using volatility in trading decisions. One is to favor buying options with the lowest implied volatility if you expect volatility to rise, and to favor selling those with the highest implied volatility if you expect volatility to fall. This would suggest buying the June $370 put or selling the Dec $400 call among the alternatives in Figure 26-15. In practice, though, the decision may not be so simple. What if you expect volatility to increase but are bullish on gold prices? Would you want to buy a put, even if it does offer the "cheapest volatility"? Does the fact that the cash outlay for the June $370 put is about four times that required for the Oct $340 put justify buying the Oct $340 put since this would increase your leverage at only a slightly higher volatility?

These types of questions do not have obvious answers or even mathematical formulas that yield unobvious but "correct" answers. To a considerable extent, what matters is how much importance you attach to the various components of your trading decision. To continue with the first example above, if you were extremely bullish on gold prices, being outright long a put option would be a foolish strategy regardless of its

Figure 26-16. *Hypothetical options data.*

Futures Contract	Futures Price	Option Contract	Option Price	Implied Volatility	Kappa
June Gold	$348.60	$360 call	$11.30	26.6%	0.42
June Gold	348.60	370 put	32.20	25.8%	0.38
Oct Gold	358.40	340 put	8.10	26.4%	0.56
Dec Gold	362.20	400 call	5.30	29.6%	0.72

implied volatility. If cash flow is a major consideration, then buying a less expensive, higher exercise price call is worth a few extra tenths of a point in implied volatility. We will return to this topic later in this chapter in the section *Is There a Best Options Trading Strategy?*

The second volatility-based trading strategy focuses on the question of how much profit (and risk) there will be as implied volatility changes from prevailing levels. Suppose, for instance, that gold prices begin to fluctuate wildly and that two weeks after the table in Figure 26-15 was prepared, June gold futures are again trading at $348.60 after having risen as high as $400.00 and fallen as low as $300.00. These dramatic fluctuations might yield a table along the lines of Figure 26-16.

Comparing Figure 26-15 with Figure 26-16 shows that the greatest dollar gain would have come from the June $370 put. The greatest percent gain would have come from the Dec $400 call. From a return on investment perspective, the Dec $400 call is clearly the best performer. How might we have known this in advance? Part of the answer lies in the far right-hand column, which we added in Figure 26-16. As we mentioned in the preceding chapter, kappa measures how much the price of an option will change as volatility changes. Thus, the information in the table tells us that if volatility changes by 1.0%, the price of the June $360 call should change by $0.42, and that of the Dec $400 call by $0.72. These dollar figures can be converted into percent figures using the prevailing options prices. In this example, a 1.0% change in volatility would yield percentage changes in the options as shown in Figure 26-17.

Unfortunately for those who prefer simplicity, this is not all. A comparison between the implied volatilities in Figures 26-15 and 26-16 reveals that they did not all change by the same amounts. This is not uncommon. If, for example, the market perceives that a flurry of trading activity is due to a handful of large one-time buyers, then the implied volatilities could increase significantly more for short-term near-the-

Figure 26-17.

June 360 call—0.42/11.30 = <u>3.7%</u>
June 370 put—0.38/32.20 = <u>1.2%</u>
Oct 340 put—0.56/8.10 = <u>6.9%</u>
Dec 400 call—0.72/5.30 = <u>13.6%</u>

---

money options than for longer-term out-of-the-money options. Kappa only tells you how option prices will change in response to changes in implied volatility. It does not tell you how implied volatilities will change, and all implied volatilities will generally not change at the same rate.

Let us now consider volatility from the perspective of a trader who holds positions in more than one option. Suppose that you decide to employ one of the spreading strategies discussed in the preceding section by purchasing a June $360 call and selling a Dec $400 call. How will this position react to changes in volatility? It turns out that this one is easy. If you put a minus sign in front of the kappas relating to short options positions (because your volatility exposure is the opposite from that of long positions) you can find the aggregate volatility exposure of your options portfolio by simply adding the various kappas. Remember to multiply each kappa by the number of options of that type. Figure 26-18 gives an example.

Figure 26-18.

Long/Short	Quantity	Option Contract	Option Price	Implied Volatility	Kappa
L	2	June $360 call	$11.30	29.6%	0.42
L	5	June 340 put	8.10	29.4%	0.56
S	3	Dec 400 call	5.30	32.6%	0.72

Total kappa = (2 x 0.42) + (5 x 0.56) – (3 x 0.72) = <u>1.48</u>

Notice that the option prices and the implied volatilities do not enter into the computation. We have included them here for reference only.

Finally, a few comments on aggregate risk are in order. The owner of the portfolio in Figure 26-18 could reduce his total exposure to volatility by, for example, selling more Dec $400 calls. But this would affect the overall exposure to price changes—perhaps favorably, perhaps unfavorably from the trader's perspective. Calculating and balancing the various exposures—price, volatility, time decay, and interest rates—is a daunting proposition. For the most part, it is done regularly only by options professionals.

Commentary on Deep-Out-of-the-Money Options

In Figures 26-15 and 26-16, the implied volatility for the Dec $400 calls is significantly higher than for the other options. This is neither oversight on our part nor coincidence. Deep-out-of-the-money options frequently trade with much higher implied volatilities than do in- or near-the-money options. The reasons and consequences deserve a brief discussion. The following three reasons are largely responsible for the *volatility premium* often carried by deep-out-of-the-moneys:

- These options are speculative favorites because they are inexpensive and offer the prospect of large profits on small investments. This means added demand relative to other options, which tends to boost prices.
- From the option writer's perspective, deep-out-of-the-money options offer the rather unappealing prospect of small initial premiums and potentially unlimited losses. Even though these losses are unlikely, writers generally want a risk premium to compensate for the uncomfortable risk/reward scenario.
- Buying a deep-out-of-the-money option strongly suggests the expectation of higher volatility. If December crude oil is currently $14.00, it is unlikely (though not impossible) that it could rise to $20.00 without an accompanying increase in volatility. Buyers of deep-out-of-the-money options expect large price moves, and these price moves are likely to be accompanied by higher volatility. This means that purchasers of these options tend to be more willing to buy higher volatility than are purchasers of other options.

The fact that deep-out-of-the-money options tend to carry high implied volatilities has interesting implications for traders who focus on volatility. A trader who consistently buys options that have low implied volatility and sells options that have high implied volatility will soon find himself with a portfolio that consists of long positions in options that are in- or near-the-money and short positions that are deep-out-of-the-money. Let us consider for a moment what this means.

If the trader attempts to balance the quantities underlying his long positions and his short positions, he will pay out much more in premium cost than he will receive in premium income. This, of course, is because deep-out-of-the-moneys are much cheaper than in- or near-the moneys. He will also have an overall position with a very large delta because, as we saw in Chapter 25, deltas are much larger for in- or near-the-moneys than for deep-out-of-the-moneys. This combination of substantial premium cost and a large delta means that the overall position is more similar to a naked long options position than to a volatility arbitrage.

If, on the other hand, the trader wants to construct a portfolio with no current price exposure that is long low-priced volatility and short high-priced volatility, then he must sell deep-out-of-the-moneys on much greater quantities than those underlying his long near- and at-the-moneys. This creates a *delta-neutral* portfolio, meaning that small changes in the price of the underlying futures contract will have little effect on the portfolio's value. The problem arises if there are large, sudden changes in the price of the underlying contract in the direction that makes the value of the short deep-out-of-the-moneys rise in value. The deltas of these short positions will rise much faster than will the deltas of the long positions, leaving the trader with the equivalent of a large naked position with prices moving rapidly against him. The unpleasantness of this possibility is another illustration of why the market attaches a premium to deep-out-of-the-money options.

OPTIONS ARBITRAGE STRATEGIES

We described *arbitrage* in Chapter 12 in connection with cash and futures markets. Arbitrage principles can also be employed in the options markets. Let us return for a moment to the concept of a synthetic put that we discussed earlier in this chapter. The basic idea is that buying a futures contract and selling a call option on that future creates a position that is equivalent to being short a put option. The existence of both "real options" and "synthetic options" can give rise to a variety of arbitrage opportunities.

Consider a specific example assuming the price configuration shown in Figure 26-19 (see page 658).

Figure 26-19. *Dec Eurodollar futures: 93.50.*

Dec 93.50 call—0.42
Dec 93.50 put—0.40

Buying the futures at 93.50 and simultaneously selling the Dec 93.50 call creates a position equivalent to being short a Dec 93.50 put at 0.42. Doing this and also buying the "real" Dec 93.50 put at 0.40 would create a locked-in arbitrage profit of two points—long the "real put" at 0.40/short the "synthetic put" at 0.42. This general type of position—long the underlying/short the call/long the put—is known as a *conversion*. The opposite configuration—short underlying/long call/short put—is called a *reverse conversion*. These are among the most commonly followed option arbitrage opportunities.

Conversions and reverse conversions are arbitrages in the strictest sense of the term—the profit/loss profiles of the two different positions exactly mirror each other. Options can also be used to construct a wide variety of positions that involve different levels of risk, but still qualify as arbitrage under most definitions. Suppose, for example, that the prices shown in Figure 26-20 prevailed in T-bond options. It would be highly unusual to find such a large difference in implied volatilities for two similar options, but were it to occur there would be a *volatility arbitrage* opportunity. The trade would involve buying the June 102–00 call and selling the June 104–00 call, expecting that the 6.1% implied volatility difference would decrease. This would not be a pure arbitrage because the different exercise prices give the two positions differing risk profiles. For example, if the price of June T-bond futures at expiration were under 102–00, the trade would generate a net loss that was equal to the difference between the premium paid and that received ($4^{12}/_{32} - 2^{16}/_{32} = 1^{28}/_{32}$ loss). Still, the two calls are similar enough so that the expectation of a narrowing in the volatility spread prior to maturity warrants viewing this as an arbitrage.

For the most part, options arbitrage, like other forms of arbitrage, is the province of professional traders. There are two reasons for this: First, professionals are capable of monitoring the various price relationships on a second-to-second basis and will quickly notice and respond to any price anomalies. Second, professionals generally have lower transaction costs than do other customers, which better enables them to profit from the slim margins that characterize nearly all real-life arbitrage opportunities.

Figure 26-20.

Option Contract	Price	Implied Volatility
June 102-00 call	4^{12}/32	21.3%
June 104-00 call	2^{16}/32	27.4%

FINANCING STRATEGIES

In addition to making possible the various trading and risk management techniques that we have already discussed, listed options can also provide financing opportunities. To see how, let us describe a position known as a *box spread*. A box spread consists of simultaneously established debit and credit spreads in the same market for the same maturity.

Consider the example from the gold market shown in Figure 26-21. The key point to notice is that the trader who buys the credit spread and sells the debit spread will have funds credited to his account in an amount equal to the sum of the net credits of the two spreads. This amount will be available for use by the trader until the spreads mature. At that time, he will be obligated to pay $20.00.

Two points are important to notice:

- The trader who establishes this position will receive an immediate credit of $19.70 per ounce to his account.

Figure 26-21. Hypothetical box spread.

Assumptions:

April Gold Futures:	$370.00
April 360 Call:	17.80
April 380 Call:	8.00
April 360 Put:	7.80
April 380 Put:	17.70

Box Spread:	Buy April 380 Call:	($8.00)	Buy April 360 Put:	($7.80)
	Sell April 360 Call:	17.80	Sell April 380 Put:	17.70
		$9.80		$9.90

Total Premium Received: $19.70 (credit)

- Upon maturity of the position, the trader will owe $20.00, because this will be the debit value of this position regardless of the price of April futures at expiration. For example, an expiration price of $390 would lead to the following valuations:

Long April 380 Call:	$10.00	Long April 360 Put:	$0.00
Short April 360 Call:	(30.00)	Short April 380 Put:	0.00
	($20.00)		$0.00

Total Premium Owed: $20.00 (debit)

The reader can easily verify that the trader will have this same $20.00 per ounce obligation at expiration for any exercise price. This scenario can be described from a different perspective as follows:

The trader borrowed $19.70 on February 20 and repaid $20.00 two months later. The $0.30 difference is, in effect, interest paid on a two-month loan of $19.70. In percentage terms, the annual rate is

$$\$0.30/19.70 \times 365/60 = \underline{\underline{9.26\% \text{ per annum}}}$$

Similarly, if a single trader were on the opposite side of all segments of this transaction, he would effectively have lent two-month money at 9.26% per annum.

What is the point of this, since there are far easier ways to borrow and lend money than through four-sided options transactions? The answer is that both borrower and lender are taking advantage of the clearinghouse's role as financial intermediary and performance guarantor. A prospective borrower might find it easier or cheaper to borrow via a box spread than to access alternative sources of funding such as commercial banks. Conversely, a prospective lender might feel comfortable with the financial backing of a futures exchange clearinghouse (see Chapter 7), which is the effective guarantor of performance on the box spread. This is one of the less common uses of the listed options markets, but it is surely one of the best illustrations of the tremendous flexibility that options offer.

Figure 26-22.

Trader	Number of Profits	Number of Losses	Average Profit	Average Loss	Average Profit per Trade
A	420	80	$4,000	$20,000	$160
B	240	260	3,000	2,470	156

Is There A Best Options Trading Strategy?

The best trading strategies are always those with the highest mathematical profit expectations, but options offer so many different strategies with such complex and diverse risk/reward profiles that translating this elementary concept into practical trading approaches is difficult. Before we discuss the subject in some detail, let us consider an oversimplified example that illustrates some of the complications. Suppose that two traders, A and B, employed the following strategies. Trader A writes very deep-out-of-the-money T-bond calls whenever the implied volatility is more than 5.0 percentage points greater than the actual T-bond futures volatility of the past three months. Trader B establishes bullish call spreads whenever the implied volatility of the option being bought is 2.0 points less than that of the option being sold. Suppose also that we somehow knew that over a period of five years each trader would establish 500 positions and that the profit/loss results (net of all expenses) would be as shown in Figure 26-22.

From the perspective of cumulative results, strategy A is superior. It yields an extra $4 average profit per trade. But is this $4 enough extra compensation for the vastly greater uncertainties associated with trader A's strategy? If, for example, both traders begin with $40,000 in capital, could trader A prudently take the risk that three of his losses would occur within the first 15 or so trades, thereby putting him out of business? Would you take this risk for an extra $4 per trade?

This question has no "correct" answer. Trader A is following the best strategy from the perspective of maximizing expected profit. Trader B is following the best strategy when the desirability of avoiding catastrophic losses is taken into account. So the issue really boils down to one of whether avoiding catastrophic losses is worth $4 per trade, and the answer to this depends on whether we are talking about pure statistics or the real world. The question can be answered from two perspectives—risk preference and resource availability. If Trader *B* opts for the lesser expected profit simply because he does not like the idea of possibly losing more than $20,000 on a single trade, then he is making a decision that is emotionally correct but mathematically wrong. On the other hand, if he chooses strategy *B* because he has only $40,000 trading capital, he is making the mathematically correct choice. He may arrive at this conclusion intuitively or by calculating his probability of ruin, a concept discussed in detail in Chapter 15.

It turns out that, with $40,000 in initial capital, strategy *B* has a probability of ruin of about 20%, whereas strategy *A* has a probability of ruin of more than 85%. If the initial capital were $1 million instead of only $40,000, the probability of ruin for either strategy would be under 1%. What this means is that the optimum strategy depends very much on the amount of available trading capital.

However, all "optimum" strategies are not equal. The fact that strategy *B* is better given our assumed capital constraints does not alter the fact that its expected profit per trade is less than that for strategy *A*. This means that a trader who has enough capital to employ strategy *A* without concern about probability of ruin issues can be expected to fare better in time than will someone who has less capital, regardless of which strategy the less well-capitalized trader employs. The reason is the following: As more capital becomes available, the probability of ruin becomes smaller, and as this happens the optimum real-life strategy comes closer and closer to the "best" mathematical strategy. In other words, there is a mathematical basis for the saying that it is easier to make money if you have money.

A second important consideration in evaluating options strategies is the role played by price or volatility expectations. We mentioned in Chapter 25 that buying options would be bad strategy if you knew exactly how prices were going to fluctuate. This is because the time premium paid would have no value, because it would protect against price changes that you already knew would not occur. In this case (perfect knowledge of upcoming price changes) the best strategy would be either to establish a futures position in the direction of the known price move or to write options that you knew would expire worthless to earn premium income. The choice between these two approaches, given certainty about upcoming price changes, would be determined solely by return on invested capital calculations that, in turn, would depend on prevailing margin requirements for futures and options. In the real world, of course, nobody knows with certainty how prices will fluctuate. But as the foregoing suggests, the more confidence you have in your price forecasts, the more appropriate is options writing as opposed to options buying.

When you have a strong opinion about upcoming volatility changes the best strategy is straightforward. If, for example, you expect volatility to rise, find those options trading with the lowest implied volatility and select from this group those with a kappa/option-premium ratio that will give the highest return on capital. The discussion relating to Figures 26-15 and 26-16 in this chapter illustrates this type of analysis. Similarly, if you strongly believe that volatility will fall, the best strategy is to sell options that combine high implied volatility and a high kappa.

What if you have less fervent views on price or volatility, or are an "efficient market" advocate who believes it impossible to predict price or volatility changes? Is there a "best" options strategy under these circumstances? The answer is, yes. Buy those options that have the lowest implied volatility and sell those that have the highest implied volatility. If you believe that prices and volatility will fluctuate at random, this is the mathematically correct strategy. This is straightforward in theory, but complications often arise in practice. As we discussed earlier in this chapter, deep-out-of-the-money options tend to trade with the highest implied volatilities, so the strategy of buying low volatility and selling high volatility will usually lead to a portfolio that is highly vulnerable to large, sudden price movements.

This brings us back to the probability of ruin idea. Very often, the mathematically optimum strategy is appropriate only for well-capitalized traders who are philosophically willing and financially able to accept occasional very large losses. Remember, though, that this analysis assumes random, unpredictable fluctuations in both price level and price volatility. Most traders, whether speculators or hedgers, individual or institutional, participate in markets precisely because they at least occasionally have opinions regarding price, volatility, or both. When it comes to putting these opinions into practice, options offer a richer variety of approaches than any other investment vehicle.

COMMERCIAL USES OF OPTIONS

Both speculators and hedgers can take advantage of the risk-limitation and cash flow opportunities offered by options. In addition to this flexibility, options are inherently more suitable than futures for certain commercial situations. Generally, these situations involve some uncertainty as to whether the commercial hedger will actually complete the transaction being hedged. Let us consider two examples.

Example 1: Agricultural production hedge. Selling corn futures to hedge the value of a growing corn crop is a classic example of a futures hedge. However, there is a potential problem with this hedge. Suppose that a farmer anticipated harvesting 200,000 bushels and hedged by selling the same quantity of December futures at $2.50 per bushel. Suppose further that after this hedge is established, December futures skyrocket to $3.50 per bushel as a result of widespread and severe drought during the growing season. The $200,000 loss on the futures hedge should, in theory, be offset by a corresponding increase in the value of the crop. But what if this particular farmer is among those whose crop losses caused prices to advance from $2.50 to $3.50? In this case, his futures hedge could prove quite costly. Let us assume that the drought reduced his corn crop by 50%, from the expected 200,000 bushels to only 100,000 bushels.

The results are summarized in Figure 26-23. The 100,000 bushels actually produced were, in effect, sold at $2.50 per bushel when 100,000 bushels of the futures hedge is taken into account. The remaining 100,000 bushel futures position is effectively a naked short on which the farmer suffers a $1.00 per bushel loss. Subtracting this from the $250,000 net proceeds from the hedged crop leaves the farmer with revenues of only $150,000 rather than the $500,000 that he expected when placing his futures hedge. As if this were not enough, he is also likely to notice that the major bull market in corn would have brought him revenues of $350,000 ($3.50 per bushel x 100,000 bushels) despite his crop losses had he not bothered to hedge in the first place.

What happened, of course, is that the farmer was dealt an economically devastating double whammy:

Figure 26-23. Impact of drought on corn futures hedge.

Date	Cash Market Transactions	Futures Market Transactions
May 15:	Expect 200,000 bushel crop	Sell 200,000 bushels Dec. futures @$2.50 per bushel
July, August:	Lose 100,000 bushels to drought	
November 1:	Sell 100,000 bushels @$3.50 per bushel	Buy 200,000 bushels Dec. futures @$3.50 per bushel
Result:	+ $350,000 (income)	− $200,000 (loss)

Net Revenue: + $150,000

- Crop losses reduced to zero the revenue that was generated from a portion of his land.
- The futures hedge compounded matters by heaping an out-of-pocket loss on top of the absence of revenue from this portion of his land. This loss of a portion of the expected cash market position effectively converted the corresponding portion of the futures position from a hedge into a naked and costly short position.

Lest there be a temptation to think that the farmer could as easily have gotten lucky and reaped a $1.00 per bushel profit on his 100,000-bushel shortfall if corn prices had fallen rather than risen, let us emphasize the fundamental asymmetry here. When production problems create shortfalls, prices are obviously more likely to rise than to decline, so there is a positive correlation between the occurrence of losses on short futures hedges on the one hand and the inability to completely offset such losses as a result of production shortfalls on the other.

This problem, of course, is not unique to the agricultural sector. As other examples, consider a major gold producer whose mine collapses after he sells gold futures, or a corporate treasurer whose cash flow unexpectedly drops by 50% after he buys Eurodollar futures as an anticipatory hedge against falling interest rates. In each case, the basic difficulty is that the hedger has assumed full exposure on the futures side despite quantity uncertainties on the physical or cash side.

Figure 26-24. Impact of drought on corn options hedge.

Date	Cash Market Transactions	Options Market Transactions
May 15:	Expect 200,000 bushel crop	Buy 200,000 bushels Dec $2.50 puts @15 cents per bushel
July, August:	Lose 100,000 bushels to drought	
November 1:	Sell 100,000 bushels @$3.50 per bushel	Abandon worthless puts
Result:	+ $350,000 (income)	− $30,000 (cost of puts)

Net Revenue: + $320,000

Options can significantly alleviate such problems because the holder of an option has no exposure or performance obligation beyond payment of the initial premium. Let us revisit our drought-plagued corn farmer and see how he would have fared had he bought put options rather than sold futures to hedge his crop. If he had chosen puts on December futures with a $2.50 strike price at a premium of 15 cents per bushel, his results would have been as shown in Figure 26-24.

With prices at $3.50 per bushel, he would clearly allow the puts to expire unexercised, leaving revenues of $320,000 after subtracting the initial premium paid for the options. The benefits are twofold:

- The ability to benefit from the bull market in corn by not being locked into a fixed price of $2.50 per bushel on the 100,000 bushel crop.
- The loss of only the initial options premium of $30,000 (15 cents per bushel x 200,000 bushels), rather than the entire difference between hedge price and market price ($100,000 = $1.00 per bushel x 100,000 bushels) on the portion of the crop lost to drought.

Options made it possible for the farmer to manage the risk of *quantity uncertainty* as well as the risk of *price uncertainty*. Futures enable a hedger to protect against price risk, but not quantity risk. The ability to manage both types of risk is clearly important in businesses such as agriculture, where production uncertainties are unavoidable.

Example 2: Contingent exposure hedge. Consider a U.S. construction company that is bidding on a contract for a large project in West Germany. The company must submit a Deutsche mark (DM)-denominated bid, but many of its costs are dollar-based. If the company must wait, say, 30 days to learn whether it has won the contract, it is in a potentially uncomfortable situation:

- If the company does not hedge by selling DM futures, it is vulnerable to a decline in the value of this currency relative to the dollar. If it wins the contract, it would receive as compensation Deutsche marks worth less than expected when the bid was submitted. If the decline in the DM's value were sharp enough, the firm could win the contract, but find itself losing money as a result of the exchange rate change.

Figure 26-25. Possible outcomes: Hedge of contingent contract with put option.

Currency Movement	Contract Bid Accepted	Contract Bid Rejected
DM Declines	*Profits*	*Profits*
	• increase in value of put option	• increase in value of put option
	Losses	*Losses*
	• lower dollar value of DM revenue • premium paid for put option	• premium paid for put option
DM Advances	*Profits*	*Profits*
	• higher dollar value of DM revenue	• none
	Losses	*Losses*
	• premium paid for put option	• premium paid for put option

- If the company does hedge by selling DM futures, it is vulnerable to a rise in the value of the DM relative to the dollar. The risk comes about because the company could fail to win the construction contract. This would leave it with a loss on its futures position with no offsetting inflow of DM revenues.

The difficulty here is that a futures position is an *actual* contract, whereas a competitive bid represents a *contingent* contract. There is no way to hedge one type of contract against the other in a way that completely eliminates risk.

Options provide the solution. In this case, the company could buy a put option on DM or on DM futures of the appropriate maturity. The four possible outcomes are summarized in Figure 26-25.

Whether the option hedge provides total protection or only partial protection depends on the premium paid for the put, on whether it is in- or out-of-the-money, and on the value of the put at maturity or sale. The important point, though, is that the unlimited exposure that surfaces somewhere in any scenario not including options has been replaced by a worst-case result that involves only the loss of the option premium. The contingent nature of a long option position makes it possible to hedge a contingent cash-market obligation.

■ BIBLIOGRAPHY

Arthur, Henry B. *Commodity Futures as a Business Management Tool.* Cambridge, Mass: Harvard University Press, 1971.

Barron's. Dow Jones & Co., Inc., 200 Liberty St., New York, N.Y. 10281 (Weekly).

Belveal, L. D. *Commodity Speculation: With Profits in Mind.* Wilmette, Ill.: Commodities Press, 1968.

Besant, Lloyd, et al., eds. *Commodity Trading Manual.* Chicago: Chicago Board of Trade, 1980.

Chicago Board of Trade. *An Introduction to Financial Futures.* Chicago, 1981.

Chicago Board of Trade Annual Report, 1858 to date.

Chicago Board of Trade. *Commodity Trading Manual.* Chicago, 1981.

Chicago Board of Trade Statistical Annual.

Chicago Board of Trade. Symposium proceedings. 1948 to date.

Chicago Board of Trade Year Book. Chicago Board of Trade, 141 West Jackson Boulevard, Chicago, Ill.

Chicago Mercantile Exchange. *Opportunities in Interest Rates: Treasury Bill Futures.* Chicago, 1977.

Chicago Mercantile Exchange Year Book. Chicago Mercantile Exchange, 444 West Jackson Boulevard, Chicago, Ill. 1923 to date.

Cocoa Statistics. London: Gill and Duffus. Published annually.

Commodity Futures Trading Commission Regulatory Authority Review: Hearing, Feb. 12 and May 21, 1980, House Committee on Agriculture, 1981.

Commodity Futures Trading Commission Act; Hearings, 93d Cong., 2d Sess., on S. 2485, S. 2578, S. 2837, and H.R. 13113, Senate Committee on Agriculture and Forestry, 1974.

The Commodity Futures Trading Commission Act of 1974, 93d Cong., 2d Sess, H.R. 13113, Publ. L. 93-463, Senate Committee on Agriculture and Forestry, 1974.

Commodity Futures Trading Commission Annual Report. Washington, D.C.: U.S. Government Printing Office, published annually.

Commodity Research Bureau. *Understanding the Commodity Futures Markets,* New York, 1977.

Commodity Year Book. New York: Commodity Research Bureau, 1939 to date.

Consensus, 30 W. Pershing Rd., Kansas City, Mo. 64108 (Weekly).

Cootner, Paul H., ed. *The Random Character of Stock Market Prices.* Cambridge, Mass.: M.I.T., 1964.

Edwards, Robert D., and John Magee. *Technical Analysis of Stock Trends.* Springfield, Mass.: John Magee, 1961.

Feller, W. *An Introduction to Probability Theory and Its Applications,* Vol. 2, New York: Wiley, 1966.

Futures, 219 Parkade, Cedar Falls, Iowa 50613 (Monthly).

Futures Industry, 224 Joseph Square, Columbia, Md. 21044 (Biweekly).

Futures Trading Act of 1978, Senate Committee on Agriculture, Nutrition and Forestry, 1979.

Gastineau, Gary. *The Stock Options Manual.* New York: McGraw-Hill, 1979.

Gold, Gerald. *Modern Commodity Futures Trading.* New York: Commodity Research Bureau, 1975.

Hieronymus, Thomas. *Economics of Futures Trading for Commercial and Personal Profit.* New York: Commodity Research Bureau, 1977.

Horn, Frederick. *Trading in Commodity Futures.* New York: New York Institute of Finance, 1979.

Jiler, Harry, ed. *Forecasting Commodity Prices: How the Experts Analyze the Market.* New York: Commodity Research Bureau, 1975.

Jiler, William. *How Charts Can Help You in the Stock Market*. New York: Commodity Research Publishing Corporation, 1961.

——, ed. *Guide to Commodity Price Forecasting*. New York: Commodity Research Bureau, 1965.

Kaufman, Perry J. *Commodity Trading Systems and Methods*. New York: Wiley, 1978.

——. *Technical Analysis in Commodities*. New York: Wiley, 1980.

——. *Handbook of Futures Markets*. New York: Wiley, 1984.

Kroll, Stanley and Irwin Shisko. *The Commodity Futures Market Guide*. New York: Harper & Row, 1973.

Lefevre, Edwin. *Reminiscences of a Stock Operator*. New York: American Research Council, 1923.

Loosigian, Allan M. *Interest Rate Futures*. New York: Dow Jones Books, 1980.

——. *Foreign Exchange Futures*. Homewood, Ill.: Dow Jones–Irwin, 1981.

Lowell, Fred R. *The Wheat Market*. Kansas City, Mo.: Keltner Statistical Service, 1968.

MacKay, Charles. *Extraordinary Popular Delusions and the Madness of Crowds*. London: Page, 1932.

Mann, Jitendar S., and Richard G. Heifner. *The Distribution of Shortrun Commodity Price Movements,* USDA, Economic Research Service, Technical Bulletin 1536, March 1976.

McMillian, L. *Options as a Strategic Investment*. New York: New York Institute of Finance, 1980.

New York Mercantile Exchange Year Book.

Murphy, John J. Technical Analysis of the Futures Markets. New York: New York Institute of Finance, 1986.

Norris, Frank. *The Pit*. New York: Doubleday, Page, 1903.

Powers, Mark J. *Getting Started in Commodity Futures Trading,* 2d ed. Cedar Falls, Iowa: Investor Publications, 1977.

Powers, Mark J., and D. Vogel. *Inside the Financial Futures Markets*. New York: Wiley, 1981.

Russo, Thomas. *Regulations of the Commodities Futures and Options Markets*. New York: McGraw-Hill, 1984.

Sklarew, Arthur. *Techniques of a Professional Commodity Chart Analyst*. New York: Commodity Research Bureau, 1980.

Smith, Adam. *An Inquiry Into the Nature and Causes of the Wealth of Nations*. 1776.

Smith, Courtney. *Commodity Spread Analysis*. New York: Wiley, 1982.

Taylor, C. H. *History of the Board of Trade of the City of Chicago*. Chicago: Robert O. Law Co., 1917.

Teweles, Richard J., Charles V. Harlow, and Herbert L. Stone. *The Commodity Futures Trading Guide*. New York: McGraw-Hill, 1969.

—— and Frank J. Jones. *The Futures Game*. New York: McGraw-Hill, 1987.

Von Neumann, John, and Oskar Morgenstern. *The Theory of Games and Economic Behavior*. Princeton, N.J.: Princeton University Press, 1947.

The Wall Street Journal. Dow Jones & Co., Inc. 200 Liberty St., New York, N.Y. 10281.

■ INDEX

A

Abrahams, Alan, 634
Account executive (AE), 166
Accounting:
  delivery, 55–58
  disclosure requirements, 295
  hedging criteria and, 290–93
  income recognition and, 290–91
  margins and, 293–94
  off-balance sheet, 295
Acreage-reduction programs, 538–39
Actual obligations, 289
Administrative law judge (ALJ), 125
Agricultural commodities:
  domestic, 516–44
  government programs and, 534–44
  imported and tropical, 593–613
Agricultural market, 3
Agriculture, Department of:
  Cattle-on-Feed report, 532
  Cold Storage report, 531
  Commodity Credit Corp., 534–44
  farm programs of, 534–44
  Foreign Agricultural Service, 309
  Hogs and Pigs report, 531
  Preliminary Planting Intentions, 518
  Prospective Plantings, 518
  protein-consuming animal unit, 527
  statistics kept by, 309
  Stocks-in-all-Positions report, 518
Alternative order, 192
American option, 619
American system (currency quotes), 29
AMEX Commodities Corporation, 636
Analysis (*see* Fundamental analysis; Technical analysis)
Anticipated volatility, 625–29
Anticipatory hedging:
  accounting and, 292–93
  example of, 262–63
Arbitrage:
  basis and, 288
  conversions and, 658
  defined, 282
  interest rate futures and, 215–19
  options and, 657–58
  pseudo-, 288

opportunities for, 287
  stock index futures and, 513–14
Arbitration, 126
Associated person (AP):
  complaint against, 126
  defined, 107–8
  regulation of, 108
"A Study of the Effects on the Economy of Trading in Futures and Options," 13
At-the-market price, 188
At-the-money option, 619

B

Bahian crop, 594
Balance of payments, 484–88
Balance of trade, 485
Balance on capital account, 485
Balance on current account, 485
Bank for International Settlements (BIS), 481
Bank of England, 132
Bar chart:
  construction of, 371–72
  trends and trendlines in (*see* Trends and trendlines)
  uses of, 371–72
  volume and open interest and, 372
Barley, 518
Basis:
  arbitrage and, 288
  charts, 237–41
  carrying charges and, 204–10
  hedging and, 232, 235–37
  movement of, 201–4
  point, 446
  principles governing behavior of, 226
  risk (*see* Basis risk)
Basis risk:
  dealer management of, 271–72
  hedging and, 243
Beta, 508–9
Bid, 68
Bid/ask spread:
  defined, 12
  interbank dealers and, 484
  locals and, 68–69
  money management and, 339–40

671

4   377PT   BR   **5653**   GBC
IO/93   03-097-00